Volume 10 presents a wealth of documents, including important reports of the Federal Convention, revealing the quantity of work Madison undertook during this period. The chronicle begins on the eve of the Federal Convention in 1787 and closes with Madison's departure for Orange County, Virginia, after completing his last number of *The Federalist*, to stand for election to the state ratifying convention.

The editors have selected a substantial number of Madison's own speeches, including accounts of those speeches recorded by other delegates, from the entire Federal Convention Debates. Madison's Notes on Debates, a voluminous record of the proceedings, provide an indispensable source for the study of the creation of the Constitution. Both as a participant and observer in Philadelphia, Madison demonstrated his tremendous energy and leadership ability.

The twenty-nine numbers of *The Federalist* written by Madison as one of the trinity of founding fathers signing themselves "Publius" are included here. These essays, along with his extensive correspondence relating to the prospects of ratifying the Constitution, help us understand why Madison

has, in popular terms, come to be "the father of the Constitution."

This collection offers readers convenient access to Madison's most important speeches at the Federal Convention, all of his numbers of *The Federalist*, and all of the known correspondence and other papers that he produced or received during a prolific year of his life.

BACK of the STATE HOUSE, PHILADELPHIA.

Contemporary view of the State House, Philadelphia. (Courtesy of the University of Virginia Library.)

THE PAPERS OF

James Madison

VOLUME 10

27 MAY 1787—3 MARCH 1788

EDITED BY

ROBERT A. RUTLAND   CHARLES F. HOBSON
editor-in-chief

WILLIAM M. E. RACHAL   FREDRIKA J. TEUTE

JEANNE K. SISSON
editorial assistant

THE UNIVERSITY OF CHICAGO PRESS

CHICAGO AND LONDON

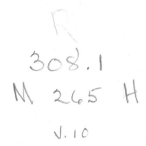
The Papers of James Madison have been edited with financial aid from the Ford and Rockefeller Foundations, the National Archives Trust Fund, and the Commonwealth of Virginia. The Virginia Historical Society has contributed aid-in-kind generously. From 1956 until 1970 the editorial staff was maintained jointly by the University of Chicago and the University of Virginia.

The University of Chicago Press, Chicago 60637
The University of Chicago Press, Ltd., London

International Standard Book Number: 0-226-50107-8
Library of Congress Catalog Card Number: 62-9114

To

COLGATE W. DARDEN, JR.

CONTENTS

1787

CONTENTS

CONTENTS

CONTENTS

CONTENTS

CONTENTS

1788

CONTENTS

ILLUSTRATIONS

PREFACE

Throughout his long career as a statesman James Madison was probably never busier than during the nine months covered in this volume. The record for this brief period reveals in depth his great energy and capacity for concentrated mental activity. The chronicle begins on the eve of the Federal Convention, which met in May 1787 to write the Constitution, and closes with Madison's departure for Orange County, Virginia, after completing his last number of *The Federalist*, to stand for election to the state ratifying convention. In the intervening nine months, Madison's labors had won the respect of those leaders who were determined to make the American experiment in self-government succeed.

At the outset of the Philadelphia meeting Madison, having thoroughly prepared himself for this critical occasion, assumed a role of leadership that he never relinquished. Applying his vast scholarly knowledge of confederacies to his practical political experience, he offered cogent observations on nearly every topic, great or small, that came before the convention. As a participant in the convention Madison contributed significantly to its outcome; as a witness he compiled a voluminous record of its debates, which he preserved for a grateful posterity. His Notes on Debates have become a national treasure, an indispensable source for our knowledge of how the Constitution came into being. If the Constitution did not fulfill all his expectations, he nevertheless overcame his disappointment and in no small measure was responsible for making the new plan of government a reality.

Nearly four months of constant debate and note-taking left Madison exhausted. Yet almost immediately after the convention adjourned, he returned to New York to resume his duties in Congress. By mid-November he had sufficiently recovered to accept Alexander Hamilton's invitation to contribute a series of essays defending the proposed Constitution. From then until the end of February Madison, as one of the trinity of "Publius," wrote twenty-nine numbers of *The Federalist*. He seemed almost chained to his writing desk, for in addition to *The Federalist* essays, a steady stream of private letters poured forth from his pen. Throughout the ratification campaign Madison was at the center of an extensive correspondence relating to the prospects for the Constitution. He broadened his circle of regular correspondents beyond Virginia to include leading supporters of the plan from other states, such as Tench Coxe of Pennsylvania and Rufus King of Massachusetts.

xix

Concerned as he was about the progress of the Constitution in the other states, Madison believed that the key contest would take place at the Virginia ratifying convention, which was to meet in June. Letters from fellow Virginians George Washington, Edmund Randolph, Archibald Stuart, Joseph Jones, and others contained varying assessments of the strength of the opposition, but all accounts agreed that the outcome would be close. Even in Orange County, feeling ran high against the Constitution. Troubled by this uncertainty, Madison allowed himself to become a candidate for the convention. After repeated urging from his family and friends, he prudently decided to return home early to make a personal appearance on election day.

Thomas Jefferson, still serving in France as the American minister, continued to be Madison's principal correspondent. The friendship between these two Virginians deepened, even though they did not always share the same political views. Jefferson did not hesitate to register his strong dissent to Madison's favorite reform proposal, a federal "negative," or veto, of state laws. This criticism drew forth a remarkable reply from Madison (24 October 1787) that went well beyond the conventional bounds of a letter to include a lengthy and careful exposition of his political ideas.

Instead of publishing the entire Federal Convention Debates at this time, the editors have selected a substantial number of Madison's own speeches, including accounts of those speeches recorded by other delegates. This selection makes it possible to bring together material that, if previously published, has appeared in scattered sources. Readers thus will have convenient access to Madison's most important speeches at the Federal Convention, all of his numbers of *The Federalist*, and all of the known correspondence and other papers that he produced or received during this period.

ACKNOWLEDGMENTS

In preparing this volume the editors acknowledge the aid and assistance of Julian Boyd, Robert Brugger, Donald Jackson, George Reese, Dorothy Twohig, and the staffs of the Alderman Library of the University of Virginia and the Manuscript Division of the Library of Congress. They extend a special thanks to Dumas Malone for his wise counsel and the use of his extensive personal library, which is housed so conveniently in the "presidential wing" of the Alderman Library.

EDITORIAL METHOD

The editorial guidelines set forth in *PJM*, I, xxxiii–xxxix, and VIII, xxiii, have been followed in this volume except that errors in coded passages are no longer enclosed within brackets. JM's own notes of speeches in the Federal Convention are used for selections from the debates except as noted in the annotation section, where other versions of the same remarks or of a speech JM failed to record himself are printed. Minor errors have been silently corrected, while substantial errors or discrepancies have been annotated. Notations and dockets made by various editors and collectors through the years have not been recognized in the provenance unless germane to an understanding of the document. The same rule has been applied to routine endorsements JM made on documents that he retrieved late in his lifetime. Unless otherwise indicated, words or parts of words within brackets are editorial additions made for the sake of clarity. Symbols from the National Union Catalog of the Library of Congress have been used to designate the libraries and other depositories holding the original copies of documents printed in this volume. When standing alone the symbol DLC is employed to cite the Madison Papers in the Library of Congress. Otherwise, a specific collection in the Library of Congress is designated. The location symbols for depositories most frequently used are set forth below.

DLC   Library of Congress, Washington, D.C.

DNA   National Archives, Washington, D.C.

Vi   Virginia State Library, Richmond

ViHi   Virginia Historical Society, Richmond

ViU   University of Virginia Library, Charlottesville

NN   New York Public Library, New York City

NHi   New-York Historical Society, New York City

CSmH   Henry E. Huntington Library, San Marino, California

PHi   Historical Society of Pennsylvania, Philadelphia

MA   Amherst College Library, Amherst, Massachusetts

MH   Harvard University Library, Cambridge, Massachusetts

ABBREVIATIONS

FC File copy. Any version of a letter or other document retained by the sender for his own files and differing little if at all from the completed version. A draft, on the other hand, is a preliminary sketch, often incomplete and varying frequently in expression from the finished version.

JM James Madison.

Ms Manuscript. A catchall term describing numerous reports and other papers written by Madison, as well as items sent to him which were not letters.

PCC Papers of the Continental Congress, a collection in the National Archives. An extensive index is in preparation.

RC Recipient's copy. The copy of a letter intended to be read by the addressee. If the handwriting is not that of the sender, this fact is mentioned.

Tr Transcript. A copy of a manuscript, or a copy of a copy, customarily handwritten, made considerably later than the date of the manuscript and ordinarily not by its author or by the person to whom the original was addressed.

SHORT TITLES FOR BOOKS AND OTHER FREQUENTLY CITED MATERIALS

In addition to these short titles, bibliographical entries are abbreviated if a work has been cited in the previous volumes.

AHR. American Historical Review.

Boyd, *Papers of Jefferson.* Julian P. Boyd et al., eds., *The Papers of Thomas Jefferson* (19 vols. to date; Princeton, 1950———).

Brant, *Madison.* Irving Brant, *James Madison* (6 vols.; Indianapolis and New York, 1941–61).

Burnett, *Letters.* Edmund C. Burnett, ed., *Letters of Members of the Continental Congress* (8 vols.; Washington, 1921–36).

CVSP. William P. Palmer et al., eds., *Calendar of Virginia State Papers and Other Manuscripts* (11 vols.; Richmond, 1875–93).

DAB. Dictionary of American Biography.

Evans. Charles Evans, ed., *American Bibliography ... 1639 ... 1820* (12 vols.; Chicago, 1903–34).

Executive Letter Book. Executive Letter Book, 1786–1788, manuscript in Virginia State Library.

Farrand, *Records.* Max Farrand, ed., *The Records of the Federal Convention of 1787* (4 vols.; New Haven, 1911–37).

Fitzpatrick, *Writings of Washington.* John C. Fitzpatrick, ed., *The Writings of George Washington, from the Original Sources, 1745–1799* (39 vols.; Washington, 1931–44).

Heitman, *Historical Register Continental.* F. B. Heitman, *Historical Register of Officers of the Continental Army during the War of the Revolution* (Washington, 1914).

Hening, *Statutes.* William Waller Hening, ed., *The Statutes at Large; Being a Collection of All the Laws of Virginia, from the First Session of the Legislature, in the Year 1619* (13 vols.; Richmond and Philadelphia, 1819–23).

JCC. Worthington C. Ford et al., eds., *Journals of the Continental Congress, 1774–1789* (34 vols.; Washington, 1904–37).

JCSV. H. R. McIlwaine et al., eds., *Journals of the Council of the State of Virginia* (4 vols. to date; Richmond, 1931———).

JHDV. Journal of the House of Delegates of the Commonwealth of Virginia; Begun and Held at the Capitol, in the City of Williamsburg. Beginning in 1780, the portion after the semicolon reads, *Begun and Held in the Town of Richmond, In the County of Henrico.* The journal for each session has its own title page and is individually paginated. The edition used is the one in which the journals for 1777–1790 are brought together in three volumes, with each journal published in Richmond in either 1827 or 1828 and often called the "Thomas W. White reprint."

Madison, *Letters* (Cong. ed.). [William C. Rives and Philip R. Fendall, eds.], *Letters and Other Writings of James Madison* (published by order of Congress; 4 vols.; Philadelphia, 1865).

Madison, *Papers* (Gilpin ed.). Henry D. Gilpin, ed., *The Papers of James Madison* (3 vols.; Washington, 1840).

Madison, *Writings* (Hunt ed.). Gaillard Hunt, ed., *The Writings of James Madison* (9 vols.; New York, 1900–1910).

PJM. William T. Hutchinson et al., eds., *The Papers of James Madison* (10 vols. to date; Chicago, 1962———).

Massachusetts Debates. Debates and Proceedings in the Convention of the Commonwealth of Massachusetts Held in the Year 1788 (Boston, 1856).

McLean. *The Federalist, A Collection of Essays, written in favour of the New Constitution, By a Citizen of New-York.* Printed by J. and A. McLean (New York, 1788).

Strayer, *Delegate from N.Y.* Joseph R. Strayer, ed., *The Delegate from New York or Proceedings of the Federal Convention . . . from the Notes of John Lansing, Jr.* (Princeton, 1939).

Swem and Williams, *Register.* Earl G. Swem and John W. Williams, eds., *A Register of the General Assembly of Virginia, 1776–1918, and of the Constitutional Conventions* (Richmond, 1918).

Syrett and Cooke, *Papers of Hamilton.* Harold C. Syrett and Jacob E. Cooke, eds., *The Papers of Alexander Hamilton* (21 vols. to date; New York, 1961———).

Tyler's Quarterly. Tyler's Quarterly Historical and Genealogical Magazine.

Va. Gazette, and General Advertiser. Virginia Gazette, and General Advertiser (Richmond: Augustine Davis, 1790–1809). Formerly *Virginia Independent Chronicle.*

Va. Gazette and Weekly Advertiser. Virginia Gazette and Weekly Advertiser (Richmond: Thomas Nicolson et al., 1781–97).

Va. Independent Chronicle. Virginia Independent Chronicle (Richmond: Augustine Davis, 1786–90). Beginning on 13 May 1789 entitled, *Virginia Independent Chronicle, and General Advertiser.*

VMHB. Virginia Magazine of History and Biography.

WMQ. William and Mary Quarterly.

MADISON CHRONOLOGY

1787

27 May– 17 September	JM attends Federal Convention at Philadelphia. Takes notes on the debates.
29 May	Virginia Plan presented.
6 June	JM makes first major speech, containing analysis of factions and theory of extended republic.
8 June	Defends "negative" (veto) on state laws.
19 June	Delivers critique of New Jersey Plan.
27 June–16 July	In debate on representation, JM advocates proportional representation for both branches of legislature.
16 July	Compromise on representation adopted.
26 July	Convention submits resolutions to Committee of Detail as basis for preparing draft constitution.
6 August	Report of Committee of Detail delivered.
7 August	JM advocates freehold suffrage.
7 August– 10 September	Convention debates, then amends, report of 6 August.
31 August	JM appointed to Committee on Postponed Matters.
8 September	Appointed to Committee of Style.
17 September	Signs engrossed Constitution. Convention adjourns.
ca. 21 September	Leaves Philadelphia for New York.
24 September	Arrives in New York to attend Congress.
26 September	Awarded Doctor of Laws degree in absentia by College of New Jersey.

26–28 September	Congress considers report of the Federal Convention; agrees to forward Constitution to the states.
ca. 10–16 November	JM visits Philadelphia.
17 November	Returns to New York.
22 November	Presents credentials to new Congress for federal year 1787–1788.
22 November– 1 March 1788	As "Publius," JM writes twenty-nine essays of *The Federalist* for New York newspapers.

1788

21 January	Session of Congress has quorum for first time.
ca. 3–4 March	JM leaves New York for Orange County to seek election to Virginia ratifying convention.

THE PAPERS OF

James Madison

Madison at the Federal Convention
27 May–17 September 1787

JM had already committed himself to work for a new constitution to replace the Articles of Confederation when he arrived in Philadelphia on 5 May 1787, nearly three weeks before the Federal Convention had a quorum. The government he hoped to see established would be "republican," deriving its authority from the great body of the people and administered by persons appointed directly or indirectly by the people. Beyond the republican principle, which enjoyed nearly universal acceptance among Americans and would not become a matter of serious debate at the convention, JM envisioned three fundamental reforms. First, he proposed to replace the existing "federal" government that acted through sovereign states with a "national" one that acted directly on individuals, exercising an authority superior to that of the state governments. Second, he hoped to substitute proportional representation in the national legislature for equal representation of the states. JM confidently predicted that the convention would accept this new mode of representation with little difficulty. "A majority of the States," he wrote Washington, "and those of greatest influence, will regard it as favorable to them. To the Northern States it will be recommended by their present populousness; to the Southern by their expected advantage in this respect. The lesser States must in every event yield to the predominant will. But the consideration which particularly urges a change in the representation is that it will obviate the principal objections of the larger States to the necessary concessions of power" (16 Apr. 1787, *PJM*, IX, 383). Third, he favored vesting the general government with a negative, or veto, "*in all cases whatsoever* on the legislative acts of the States" (ibid.). He regarded the negative as the indispensable anchor of the new system; it would both establish the supremacy of the national government and serve to protect individual and minority rights (*PJM*, IX, 347–48). These were the principal changes JM hoped the convention would adopt. He also expected as a matter of course that the new government would have additional positive powers—taxation and the regulation of trade, for example—and be organized into separate legislative, executive, and judiciary departments.

JM's reform proposals were largely embodied in the fifteen resolutions of the Virginia Plan, which Governor Edmund Randolph presented to the convention on 29 May. The Virginia resolutions became the basis of debate on 30 May, when the convention formed a Committee of the Whole. Reaping the benefits of initial strategy and organization, the Virginia delegation, supported by those of Pennsylvania and Massachusetts, secured the committee's acceptance of the plan within two weeks. Although the committee approved proportional representation for both branches of the legislature, the close vote to extend the principle to the second branch hinted at future difficulty. On 13 June the Committee of the Whole submitted its report, an expanded and revised version of the Virginia Plan. This report represented the high point of JM's influence at the Philadelphia convention, but even then he had not gained all he sought. He was dissatisfied with the decision to give the national legislature only a qualified veto power over state laws. On 8 June he had supported Charles Pinckney's unsuccessful motion to authorize

3

the national legislature to disallow any state law that it judged improper. JM's advocacy of an unlimited negative, which he called "the great pervading principle that must controul the centrifugal tendency of the States" (first speech of 8 June), revealed a doctrinaire cast to his mind that became even more apparent when he defended proportional representation. Any departure from that "doctrine," he warned, was "inadmissible, being evidently unjust" (first speech of 7 June). JM thus served notice that on certain matters of principle he would resist compromise. He proved notably unyielding on the subject of proportional representation, convinced that his views were grounded in right and justice.

During the first two weeks of the convention the Virginians and their large-state allies had perhaps been too successful, their proposals too easily and too quickly adopted. That the representatives of the small states, caught unprepared at the beginning, would eventually offer stiffer resistance was predictable. On 15 June their leader, William Paterson of New Jersey, presented an alternative plan, "one purely federal, and contradistinguished from the reported plan" (Farrand, *Records*, I, 240). JM regarded the New Jersey Plan, which was modeled on the existing Confederation, as a direct challenge to his own reform program. He accordingly devoted his longest speech at Philadelphia to a searching critique of this plan. Immediately following this speech (19 June) the committee again voted to report the expanded Virginia Plan in preference to that of New Jersey.

Despite rejection of the New Jersey Plan, the reported Virginia Plan still had to pass formal consideration by the convention. Opponents of the plan used this opportunity to reopen fundamental questions. The principle of bicameralism, for instance, which the Committee of the Whole had accepted without debate on 31 May, underwent a lengthy discussion on 20 and 21 June before the convention officially endorsed it. The "great difficulty," however, as JM noted on 19 June, was the matter of representation—if this problem could be solved, "all others would be surmountable." Debate on this thorniest of issues resumed on 27 June and reached a climax on 2 July, when the convention, having earlier approved proportional representation for the first branch of the legislature, deadlocked on a motion to establish equal representation of the states in the second branch. On that same day the delegates referred the entire question to a grand committee, and from that point on sentiment in favor of compromise grew steadily. On 16 June the convention adopted the "Great Compromise," providing for proportional representation in the first branch and equal representation in the second branch.

Throughout this debate JM tenaciously adhered to his position that the principle of proportional representation should apply to both branches of the legislature. Time and again he entreated the delegates from the small states to see the justice and expediency of his views. To their fears of a combination of the larger states against the smaller, he replied that the real political division was between the northern and southern states (first speech of 30 June; 9 July). When the grand committee on 5 July reported the compromise that the convention later adopted, JM only intensified his efforts to retain proportional representation in both branches. He even tried to intimidate his opponents by warning that the large states would not be deterred from founding a government on "just principles"; the small states, unable to stand alone, would have no choice but to join it (5 July). "The people of the large States," he added, "would in some way or other secure to themselves a weight proportioned to the importance accruing from their superior numbers" (14 July). These threats, however, had the opposite effect JM intended and only confirmed the worst fears of the small-state delegates. Indeed, as the debate wore on, JM's influence within his own faction diminished. The morning following the compromise vote of 16 July, he tried to persuade the members of this group, "comprising the principal States, and a majority of the people of America," to draw up their own separate plan to propose to the states (Farrand, *Records*, II, 19–20). This meeting ended without any agreement, and the members from the large states accordingly accepted the compromise.

After one major defeat on 16 July, JM suffered another the following day when the convention rejected the negative on state laws. At this point he might well have given up hope of obtaining a fundamental reform. Yet, rather than quit the meeting in disgust, JM reluctantly sacrificed "theoretical propriety to the force of extraneous considerations" (*The Federalist* No. 37). Within the limits imposed by the convention, he continued to participate fully in the work of building a national government on a broad republican foundation. Some reform was better than none, he must have concluded, and the present moment offered possibly the only chance to bring about even a modest change. If the compromise on representation and the rejection of the negative on state laws meant that the states would have too great an influence in the proposed government, especially in one branch of the legislature, JM hoped to curtail such influence by promoting a more equal distribution of power among the three departments of government. To ensure a proper balance he believed it was most important to check the legislative power, for the experience of the states "had evinced a powerful tendency in the Legislature to absorb all power into its vortex" (first speech of 21 July). Now that the states were to have equal representation in the Senate and the state legislatures were to elect senators, JM was even more inclined to restrict the power of the national legislature and enlarge that of the other two departments, particularly the executive.

During the latter half of the convention JM consistently sought to promote the power and independence of the executive as the best means of preserving the national principle. Soon after the 16 July compromise, for example, he changed his mind on the appointment of judges. Earlier he had opposed vesting this power in the executive and was "inclined to give it to the Senatorial branch" (first speech of 5 June); he now moved that the executive should nominate judges and that this nomination should become an appointment unless disagreed to by two-thirds of the Senate. He justified this change by referring to the altered constitution of the Senate. The "principle of compromise," he said on 21 July (third speech), required "a concurrence of two authorities, in one of which the people, in the other the States, should be represented. The Executive Magistrate wd. be considered as a national officer, acting for and equally sympathising with every part of the U. States." In order to transform the executive into a truly "national officer," JM now believed that the election of the executive should be by the people at large rather than by both branches of the legislature, as provided in the Virginia Plan. He also advocated a veto over acts of the national legislature, originally preferring to associate the judiciary with the executive in this "revisionary" power. Although opposed to an absolute veto, he later supported an amendment to require a three-fourths, rather than two-thirds, majority in each house of the legislature to over-rule the executive.

On 26 July the convention adjourned for ten days while the Committee of Detail prepared a draft constitution. After receiving the committee's report on 6 August, the delegates took the rest of that month to consider the twenty-two draft articles.

They then referred all postponed matters to a grand committee, which included JM as the representative of Virginia. On the recommendation of this committee, the convention adopted several substantial amendments to the 6 August draft. In place of election by the legislature, it substituted the electoral college system of choosing the president, as the executive was now styled. It vested the power to make treaties and to appoint ambassadors and judges of the Supreme Court, which in the 6 August draft belonged exclusively to the Senate, in the president and Senate jointly. On the other hand, the power of appointment to offices not provided for in the Constitution, formerly in the hands of the president alone, became conditional on the advice and consent of the Senate. The Senate also gained the power to try impeachments. JM opposed this last change, arguing that the trial of impeachments properly belonged to the Supreme Court. He apparently accepted the other changes as improvements over the report of 6 August. Although the president had gained power as a result of these amendments late in the convention, JM believed that the impeachment power left the president still "too dependent" on the legislature (14 Sept.).

Several times during August and September JM attempted unsuccessfully to revive the negative on state laws. Although the draft constitution contained specific prohibitions on the states, in his opinion these were insufficient. Nor did he place much confidence in the Supreme Court as the source of redress for wrongs committed by the states. JM clearly regarded the loss of the negative as a serious, perhaps fatal, omission from the Constitution. Writing to Jefferson on 6 September, he predicted that the proposed plan would "neither effectually answer its national object nor prevent the local mischiefs which every where excite disgusts agst the state governments" (partly in code).

JM was thus disappointed with the outcome of the lengthy proceedings at Philadelphia. No other delegate had so thoroughly diagnosed the ills of the American Confederation. The majority of his colleagues, while agreeing with his diagnosis, nevertheless rejected his most important proposals to remedy these defects. To replace the discredited Confederation government, the convention devised not a national government, but one "partly federal, and partly national," a mixed form that JM later celebrated in *The Federalist* No. 39. This change, mild as it was in his eyes, excited such intense opposition that the Constitution only narrowly escaped defeat. It seems clear that a plan embodying JM's favorite ideas would have stood little chance of success in the state ratifying conventions.

Although the Constitution fell short of his high hopes, JM accomplished more at the Federal Convention than he fully understood at the time. He was most effective in demonstrating the impotence of the Articles of Confederation, thereby convincing the delegates that a mere patching up of the existing system would be wholly inadequate. His emphasis on the need to protect private and minority rights, which the state governments so often violated, provided a persuasive rationale for strengthening the national government. Finally, JM contributed a novel, yet encouraging, vision of republican government capable of realizing its full potential when it operated over an extensive territory.

The Notes on Debates

Had JM not uttered a word at the Philadelphia convention, his name would still be inseparably linked with that epochal meeting because of the priceless manuscript he left to posterity, his Notes on Debates in the Federal Convention. Although Secretary William Jackson kept an official Journal, and other delegates left behind notes and memorandums, these materials are merely supplementary to JM's remarkably full and complete Debates, which constitute the heart of the surviving records of the convention. Less than a stenographic transcript of the speeches, which JM as an active participant could not have been expected to render, this work remains the closest thing we have to a daily account of the convention's deliberations.

In an unfinished memorandum prepared late in life and evidently intended as a preface to the first published edition of the Debates, JM recalled that he undertook the arduous labor of reporting the debates in order to satisfy the historical curiosity of future generations. Aware of the deficiency of the historical materials relating to confederacies, he resolved to preserve as far as he could "an exact account of what might pass in the Convention" (Farrand, *Records*, III, 550). JM had gained valuable experience for this assignment by keeping notes on the proceedings in the Continental Congress, most recently in the winter and spring of 1787, but his convention notes far exceeded in magnitude these earlier notes. For nearly four uninterrupted months he conscientiously carried out his self-imposed task, an ordeal that "almost killed him," he later told Edward Coles (Grigsby, *Virginia Convention of 1788*, I, 95 n. 107). In the same memorandum JM described his method of note-taking: "In pursuance of the task I had assumed I chose a seat in front of the presiding member with the other members, on my right & left hand. In this favorable position for hearing all that passed, I noted in terms legible & in abreviations & marks intelligible to myself what was read from the Chair or spoken by the members; and losing not a moment unnecessarily between the adjournment & reassembling of the Convention I was enabled to write out my daily notes during the session or within a few finishing days after its close in the extent and form preserved in my own hand on my files" (Farrand, *Records*, III, 550). The manuscript of the Debates is thus actually a transcript made from rough notes that JM presumably destroyed as he wrote out the speeches in full after the day's session adjourned. He kept this manuscript among his papers for the rest of his life, working on it from time to time in preparation for eventual publication. Although he expected the Debates to be published, JM resisted pressure to publish the manuscript during his lifetime (Jefferson to JM, 16 Jan. 1799, P. L. Ford, *Writings of Jefferson*, VII, 318; JM to Jefferson, 8 Feb. 1799, to Thomas Ritchie, 15 Sept. 1821, to J. G. Jackson, 27 Dec. 1821, to S. H. Smith, 2 Feb. 1827, to James Robertson, 27 Mar. 1831, Farrand, *Records*, III, 381, 447–48, 448, 475, 497). Until JM's death in 1836 the only persons besides family members and secretaries known to have looked at the Debates were Thomas Jefferson and John Wayles Eppes, Jefferson's nephew and son-in-law. Jefferson first saw the Debates in the early 1790s, when he and JM were together in Philadelphia. Eppes studied under Jefferson's tutelage in Philadelphia between 1791 and 1793, and one of his handwriting assignments, probably carried out in the summer of 1791, was to copy the Debates (Boyd, *Papers of Jefferson*, XIX, 544–51). Late in 1795, after Jefferson returned to Virginia, JM permitted his manuscript to be delivered to Monticello for Jefferson's inspection (JM to Jefferson, 8 Nov. 1795 and 4 Apr. 1796, Madison, *Letters* [Cong. ed.], II, 61, 90; Jefferson to JM, 17 Apr. 1796, P. L. Ford, *Writings of Jefferson*, VII, 70).

The manuscript as JM left it at his death in 1836 contains numerous deletions, interlineations, and insertions. These corrections are in JM's hand except for a few by John C. Payne made under JM's direction (Farrand, *Records*, II, 649). Many of the alterations are doubtless contemporary corrections of mistakes—for example, copying the wrong word or skipping a line—that occurred as JM wrote out the speeches and proceedings from his rough notes. Other changes are clearly of a later date, as indicated by differences in the fading of the ink (ibid., I, xviii). When Farrand first published his *Records* in 1911, he assumed that JM did not begin the extensive revision of his manuscript until after retiring from public life, an assumption suggested by the fact that the official *Journal, Acts and Proceedings of the Convention* . . . (Boston, 1819) was apparently not accessible to JM until it was published. We now know that in the fall of 1789 JM made his own copy of the Journal from the original that Secretary Jackson turned over to George Washington after the convention adjourned. That copy came to the Yale University Library in 1926 and was the subject of an article by Charles R. Keller and George W. Pierson published in 1930 ("A New Madison Manuscript Relating to the Federal Convention of 1787," *AHR*, XXXVI [1930–31], 17–30). Keller and Pierson offered convincing evidence that JM used his copy of the Journal to make a substantial number of additions and corrections to his manuscript of the Debates within a few years after the Federal Convention adjourned. They concluded, for example, that as many as twenty of the twenty-two slips of paper containing revisions that JM pasted into the manuscript were done before he obtained a copy of the printed *Journal*. Unaware of its location, Keller and Pierson predicted that if the Eppes copy of the Debates ever came to light, "it should be found to include many of these slips and corrections in its running text" (ibid., XXXVI, 29).

It is now possible to confirm this prediction, for large parts of the Eppes copy, both the original and a letterpress copy, survive. Eppes did not copy that section of the Debates from 21 June through 18 July, as JM himself noted (Farrand, *Records*, I, 354 n.). In 1836 John C. Payne used the Eppes copy, correcting it and filling in the omissions, to make a complete transcript of the Debates for translation into foreign languages (John C. Payne to Albert Gallatin, 30 Sept. 1836 [NHi: Albert Gallatin Papers]). This transcript, incorporating much of the original Eppes copy, is in the Edward Everett Papers at the Massachusetts Historical Society in Boston. The surviving fragment of the letterpress copy is at the New York Public Library.

Together the Eppes copy and JM's copy of the Journal prove that JM did indeed make numerous corrections and additions to his manuscript of the Debates before Eppes copied it (Boyd, *Papers of Jefferson*, XIX, 548–49). He was evidently in the midst of these revisions early in 1791, some months before Eppes arrived in Philadelphia, for he told Jefferson that he was busy "compleating the little task" he had allotted for himself (13 Mar. 1791, ibid., XIX, 552). Part of this task, as Keller and Pierson predicted, consisted of copying material from the Journal on separate slips of paper and pasting them into the manuscript. The Eppes copy incorporates fourteen of these pasted slips into its text. Of the remaining eight, one is obviously copied from the 1819 *Journal*, while seven fall into sections not copied by Eppes or on dates for which his copy is no longer extant. JM added not only the pasted slips, but a large number of other revisions from the Journal at this early date rather than after 1819 as Farrand believed (*Records*, I, xvi–xviii; IV, 12–13). He also used the 1819 *Journal*, for in the margin he occasionally referred to "the printed Journal." Whenever he inserted material containing a vote tally, JM most likely obtained his information from the 1819 *Journal*, for he had omitted the table of votes in transcribing the Journal in 1789 (Keller and Pierson, "A New Madison Manuscript," *AHR*, XXXVI [1930–31], 18, 28–29).

Most of the revisions JM made in his manuscript after 1787 resulted from collating the Journal, both his own copy and the 1819 printed edition, with the Debates in order to obtain the exact wording of motions, the record of votes, or the names of those who introduced and seconded motions. He made comparatively few changes in the reports of speeches. Among these were some fifty brief insertions from Robert Yates's *Secret Proceedings and Debates of the Convention Assembled, in the year 1787* . . . (Albany, 1821). This work is an important supplement to JM's Debates through 5 July, when the New York delegate stopped taking notes. Unsympathetic with the aims of the convention, Yates soon thereafter left Philadelphia. JM borrowed from the *Secret Proceedings* to fill in his account of some of his own speeches even though he regarded Yates as a prejudiced and inaccurate reporter (see first speech of 29 June, n. 2). Besides the additions from Yates, the reports of speeches also contain a number of deletions and interlineations, most of them stylistic alterations rather than substantive changes in meaning or emphasis. A close study of JM's own speeches, comparing the Debates text with the Eppes text, once again shows that many of these corrections, if not contemporary, occurred at an early date.

After taking all these revisions into account, the editors are compelled to state their conviction that the manuscript of the Federal Convention Debates remains essentially as JM wrote it in 1787 and that the changes he made after that date were motivated by an earnest desire for completeness and accuracy.

The editors believe that it is beyond the scope of the present chronological series to reproduce the whole manuscript of JM's Federal Convention Debates. This volume therefore includes only selected reports of JM's speeches, extracted from his own voluminous notes and those of Robert Yates, John Lansing, Rufus King, James McHenry, William Pierce, William Paterson, and Alexander Hamilton. A new edition of the entire Debates will no doubt be published at some future day, either as a separate set of volumes within *The Papers of James Madison* or as part of another editorial enterprise comprehending all the records of the convention. Of the many published editions of the Debates the most accurate are *Documentary History of the Constitution*, III; Farrand, *Records;* and *The Debates in the Federal Convention of 1787 which Framed the Constitution of the United States of America. Reported by James Madison*, ed. Gaillard Hunt and James Brown Scott (New York, 1920). The Hunt and Scott text has been reprinted in *Documents Illustrative of the Formation of the Union of the American States*, ed. Charles C. Tansill (Washington, 1927), and in *Notes of Debates in the Federal Convention of 1787 Reported by James Madison* (Athens, Ohio, 1966). Most scholars will probably prefer Farrand because it incorporates JM's Debates with the other delegates' notes and memorandums, except those kept by Lansing.

Because JM spoke more than two hundred different times at the convention, the editors have perforce exercised their discretion in omitting a number of shorter speeches, incidental remarks, and motions. Their selection of more than eighty speeches and briefer remarks illustrates the full range of ideas he expressed at the Philadelphia convention. The selected speeches include most of those JM made in June and July, when the convention debated broad general principles.

The editors have used the original manuscript of the Debates as the text for JM's speeches, except in those few instances JM did not record his own speech. In such instances they have chosen the fullest account of one of the other seven delegates who took notes. Where there is more than one version of a speech, the most complete (almost always JM's) becomes the text and the others are placed in a footnote in descending order of fullness. In printing the other versions of JM's speeches the editors have employed the following sources: Farrand, *Records*, for those of Yates, King, McHenry, and Pierce; Strayer, *Delegate from N.Y.*, for those of Lansing; Syrett and Cooke, *Papers of Hamilton*, IV, for those of Hamilton; and Papers of William Paterson (DLC), for those of Paterson. Preceding the speeches are headings supplied by the editors and, where deemed necessary, brief context notes. The heading is not repeated if JM made two or more consecutive speeches on the same subject. The purpose of the context notes is to give only enough information to make JM's speeches understandable, not to provide a running account of the convention.

In rendering the text of JM's reports of his speeches the editors have used his expansion of "Mr. M." to "Mr. Madison." The first word of a speech is capitalized if it begins a sentence. A comma following "Mr. Madison" has been omitted if "Mr. Madison" is part of the first sentence (example: "Mr. Madison, observed . . ." becomes "Mr. Madison observed . . ."). JM's brackets have been rendered as parentheses by the editors, who have resorted to textual notes sparingly, ignoring deletions and interlineations resulting from minor stylistic changes. When alterations have been noted, the editors where possible have indicated whether JM made the change before or after Eppes copied the Debates. For a printed text that attempts an exact reproduction of the Debates, showing all deletions and interlineations, see *Documentary History of the Constitution*, III.

To James Madison, Sr.

PHILADA. May 27th. 1787.

HON'D SIR

We have been here for some time suffering a daily disappointment from the failure of the deputies to assemble for the Convention. Seven States were not made up till the day before yesterday. Our intelligence from N. York promises an addition of three more by tomorrow. General Washington was unanimously called to the Chair & has accepted it. It is impossible as yet to form a judgment of the result of this experiment. Every reflecting man becomes daily more alarmed at our situation. The unwise and wicked proceedings of the Governments of some States, and the unruly temper of the people of others, must if persevered in soon produce some new scenes among us.

My inquiries concerning the iron do not promise any supply from the quarter you wished it.[1] Nor do I find the advantage which formerly existed in sending the other articles. The late regulations of Trade here & in Virginia, particularly the Act of the latter requiring the Cargoes destined to Fredg. &c. to be deposited in the first instance at ports below, are obstructions to the intercourse.[2] Tobacco however of the first quality may be sent hither to advantage. *Old* Tobo. of this description will command six dollars. Mine which has arrived safe being *new* will not I fear fetch me more than 32*l*. Virga. currency.[3]

Mr. William Strother who was lately here gave me the first information of the event of the election. I was not more concerned than surprised at the rejection of Majr. Moore.[4] I am unable utterly to account for so sudden & great a change in the disposition of the people towards him. False reports occur as the most probable cause.

I have enjoyed good health since I left Virginia and learnt with much pleasure from Mr. Strother that he had heard nothing otherwise with respect to my friends in general in Orange. Remember me affectionately to my mother & the rest of the family and accept of the dutiful regards of your Son

Js. Madison Jr.

RC (DLC).

[1] JM's father sought information concerning the Andover Iron Works in Sussex County, New Jersey. See *PJM*, IX, 358–59 and n. 1.

[2] JM was possibly referring to the Pennsylvania law of 15 Mar. 1787 "to amend and explain the Act, entitled 'An Act to encourage and protect the Manufactures of this State, by laying additional Duties on the Importation of certain Manufactures which interfere with them, and for the further Encouragement of the Navigation of this State'" (Mitchell and Flanders, *Pa. Statutes*, XII, 403–9). The Virginia law was "An act to amend the act, intituled An act to restrict foreign vessels to certain ports within this commonwealth" passed at the October 1786 session of the legislature (Hening, *Statutes*, XII, 320–23). The port of delivery for vessels entering the Rappahannock was Tappahannock, about forty miles below Fredericksburg.

[3] JM referred to the tobacco which Ambrose Madison had sent him (*PJM*, IX, 258–59). Since 1785 the price of tobacco in Virginia had been dropping sharply, and the Madison family had found it advantageous to sell in the Philadelphia market (*PJM*, VIII, 365–66; IX, 120–21 and n. 1). On the decline of tobacco prices in Virginia, see Schaffer, "Virginia's 'Critical Period,'" in *The Old Dominion*, ed. Rutman, p. 163; Myra L. Rich, "Speculations on the Significance of Debt: Virginia, 1781–1789," *VMHB*, LXXVI (1968), 308–9; Jacob M. Price, *France and the Chesapeake: A History of the French Tobacco Monopoly, 1674–1791, and of Its Relationship to the British and American Tobacco Trades* (2 vols.; Ann Arbor, 1973), II, 728–87.

[4] William Strother (1726–1808) of Culpeper County later moved to Kentucky (*Tyler's Quarterly*, XI [1929–30], 127). William Moore, a former delegate from Orange, apparently sought JM's vacated seat in the House of Delegates. Hardin Burnley and Thomas Barbour won the two seats (*PJM*, I, 148 n. 2; Swem and Williams, *Register*, p. 27).

To Edmund Pendleton

Philada. May 27. 1787.

Dear Sir

I have put off from day to day writing to my friends from this place in hopes of being able to say something of the Convention. Contrary to every previous calculation the bare quorum of seven States was not made up till the day before yesterday. The States composing it are N York, N. Jersey, Pena. Delaware, Virga. N. Carolina & S. Carolina. Individual members are here from Massts. Maryland & Georgia; and our intelligence promises a compleat addition of the first and last, as also of Connecticut by tomorrow. General Washington was called to the chair by a unanimous voice, and has accepted it. The Secretary is a Major Jackson. This is all that has yet been done except the appointment of a Committee for preparing the rules by which the Convention is to be governed in their proceedings. A few days will now furnish some data for calculating the probable result of the meeting. In general the members seem to accord in viewing our situation as peculiarly critical and in being averse to temporising expedients. I wish they may as readily agree when particulars are brought forward. Congress are reduced to five or six States, and are not likely to do any thing during the term of the Convention. A packet has lately arrived from France but brings no news.

I learnt with great pleasure by the Governour that you continued to enjoy a comfortable degree of health, and heartily wish this may find it still further confirmed, being with sincere affection & the highest esteem Your obedt. friend & servant

Js. Madison Jr.

RC (DLC). Addressed and franked by JM. Docketed by Pendleton.

To Joseph Jones

Letter not found.

27 May 1787, Philadelphia. Acknowledged in Jones to JM, 7 June 1787. Reports attendance at the Federal Convention and the prospect of more delegates arriving.

The Virginia Plan

EDITORIAL NOTE

The Federal Convention plunged into its momentous assignment without great delay chiefly because a prepared outline for a new government was ready for the delegates' consideration—the so-called Virginia Plan. JM never claimed to be the author of this plan, but his guiding influence in the Virginia caucus, which drafted the resolutions, is beyond dispute. Some weeks before the delegates assembled at

Philadelphia, JM had sketched the main features of the plan in letters to Jefferson, Randolph, and Washington (*PJM*, IX, 318–19, 369–71, 383–85). JM later recalled that the task of introducing the resolutions to the convention fell to Edmund Randolph, "being then the Governor of the State, of distinguished talents, and in the habit of public speaking. Genl. Washington, tho' at the head of the list was, for obvious reasons disinclined to take the lead. It was also foreseen that he would be immediately called to the presiding station" (JM to John Tyler, [March?] 1833, Farrand, *Records*, III, 525). Although Randolph submitted the fifteen resolutions "in writing," the original draft has not been found and may have been among "all the loose scraps of paper" Secretary William Jackson burned (ibid., I, 16 and n. 3; Jackson to Washington, 17 Sept. 1787, ibid., III, 82).

The text below is from the copy in JM's Notes on Debates, which the editors believe to be an accurate transcription of the original resolutions despite the doubts raised more than seventy years ago by J. Franklin Jameson. Jameson argued that none of the copies then existing was "the exact text of the original" and concluded that "the exact form of those resolutions can be recovered only by inference, and in one or two particulars remains uncertain" ("Studies in the History of the Federal Convention of 1787," *Annual Report of the American Historical Association for the Year 1902* [2 vols.; Washington, 1903], I, 103–11). This conclusion was supported by Homer C. Hockett (*The Critical Method in Historical Research and Writing* [New York, 1955], pp. 35–39) and disputed by Max Farrand, who maintained that JM's was "an accurate copy of the original" (*Records*, III, 593–94). In comparing manuscript copies of the Virginia Plan, Farrand noted that they were alike in all significant details. But he failed to give complete information concerning the number and location of the extant copies, and he did not distinguish between the working copies (actually used by the delegates in the convention) and fair copies possibly made at a later time. Jameson and Hockett, on the other hand, relied almost entirely on printed texts, and thus failed to avoid the pitfalls that occur when pertinent manuscript evidence is overlooked.

Of the fifteen resolutions in the Virginia Plan, Jameson cast doubt on the wording of only two clauses of the ninth resolution. JM's copy reads: "Resd. that a National Judiciary be established to consist of one or more supreme tribunals, and of inferior tribunals to be chosen by the National Legislature. . . . That the jurisdiction of the inferior tribunals shall be to hear & determine in the first instance, and of the supreme tribunal to hear and determine in the dernier resort, all Piracies & felonies on the high seas. . . ." According to Jameson, certain phrases of these clauses were not in the original resolution, but were added by the Committee of the Whole on 4 and 12 June. On 4 June, as recorded in the Journal, the committee agreed to a motion "to add these words to the first clause of the ninth resolution namely 'to consist of One supreme tribunal, and of one or more inferior tribunals[']" (ibid., I, 95). Although he noted that this wording is slightly different from the clause in JM's text (e.g., the transposition of "one or more"), Jameson assumed that JM's was a garbled version of the motion agreed to on 4 June. He thus denied that the original resolution included a distinction between supreme and inferior courts. That such a distinction existed in the original resolution, however, is indicated by William Paterson's notes for 29 May, a source evidently unknown to Jameson at the time (ibid., I, 28). Thus the motion of 4 June might well have been intended merely to change the wording of the original clause to make it consistent with the remainder of the resolution. As it reads in JM's text the ninth resolution is carelessly worded, referring to "one or more supreme tribunals" in the first clause, but to one supreme tribunal in the last.

Jameson also called attention to the motion of 12 June "to alter the resolution submitted by Mr Randolph, so as to read as follows namely. 'That the jurisdiction of the supreme Tribunal shall be to hear and determine in the dernier resort all piracies, felonies &ca.'" (ibid., I, 211). He cited this motion as proof that the first mention of the jurisdiction of the supreme tribunal did not occur until 12 June. He assumed that the motion of that day was the result of the action of 4 June, when, so he argued, the Committee of the Whole first divided the judiciary into supreme and inferior courts. Yet Jameson did not explain how the reference to the jurisdiction of the inferior courts had crept into JM's text. It obviously did not come from the motion of 12 June. A simpler explanation is that the intent of the latter motion was to delete that part of the original resolution defining the jurisdiction of the inferior courts. This action was necessary, for on 5 June the committee had eliminated the constitutional provision for inferior tribunals (ibid., I, 118).

Jameson's argument rests on what Farrand called "the somewhat doubtful authority of the Journal." Even if the Journal is correct, however, Jameson's is not the only plausible explanation of the motions of 4 and 12 June. Paterson's notes contain evidence supporting the accuracy of JM's version of the ninth resolution. More important evidence is to be found in the surviving manuscript copies of the Virginia Plan, each of which incorporates into the text the disputed phrases of the ninth resolution. The existence of several of these copies was doubtless unknown to Jameson at the time he wrote his article, but there is at least one he could have consulted. Instead he used two printed versions that led him astray.

The extant manuscript copies of the Virginia Plan may be divided into two groups: fair copies and working copies. We can assume that the fair copies were made at a later time (although some of them could well have been made at the time the resolutions were first submitted). The working copies, containing deletions, interlineations, and marginalia, were prepared and used by the delegates as the resolutions progressed through the Committee of the Whole. These copies have the greater authority because they are closer to the original. The copy in JM's Notes on Debates of course belongs to the first group, but from our knowledge of the Virginian's conscientious effort to preserve a full record of the convention, it is difficult to believe that he did not have an accurate text from which to make this copy. The other fair copies are those of George Washington (DLC: Washington Papers), James McHenry (DLC: McHenry Papers), Charles Cotesworth Pinckney (DLC: Pinckney Family Papers), and William Paterson (DLC: Paterson Papers, photostat). The working copies are those of William Paterson (DLC: William Samuel Johnson Papers), David Brearley (DNA: RG 360, Records of the Constitutional Convention of 1787, microfilm M866), and John Lansing (Strayer, *Delegate from N.Y.*, pp. 113–18). The copy of Jacob Broom, with a few interlineations in the hand of John Dickinson, does not clearly fall into either group (PPL: John Dickinson Papers).

By examining the working copies it is possible to distinguish the original text from the later alterations. In each of them there is no doubt that the disputed parts of the ninth resolution belong to the original text and are not later insertions. The Brearley and Lansing texts do embody a few phrases that were not added until after 29 May. The marginal insertions on the former, however, indicate that Brearley made his copy no later than 1 June. Lansing did not arrive until 2 June and presumably made his copy that day (Strayer, *Delegate from N.Y.*, p. 14). Their versions of the ninth resolution, which first came under discussion on 4 June, should therefore still be considered accurate texts of the original. Paterson's working copy needs no such qualification.

The only manuscript Jameson examined was Paterson's fair copy, which the New Jersey delegate included in a notebook containing copies of other documents of the convention. Because this text incorporates later changes, Jameson correctly rejected it as a copy representing the original. Evidently he was unaware of the existence of Paterson's earlier working copy. What is more difficult to explain is why he failed to look at the Brearley manuscript, which has been in the public archives since 1818. This manuscript was the source of two printed texts discussed by Jameson, one printed in the official *Journal* of 1819, pp. 67–70, the other in *Documentary History of the Constitution*, I, 329–32. In the former the text of the first clause of the ninth resolution omits not only what Brearley deleted, but also some of what remained. The result is confusing: the first clause does not mention supreme and inferior courts, but the last clause defines the jurisdiction of these hitherto unmentioned tribunals. Jameson noted this inconsistency and concluded not that something was missing from the first clause, but that the last clause contained too much. The latter text follows the Brearley manuscript as corrected by him, incorporating his later insertions and deletions. The important fact is that both printed versions seriously distort the original manuscript. Jameson correctly stated that Brearley's text of the Virginia Plan, as printed in *Documentary History of the Constitution*, "represents the original, plus most of the modifications made up to about June 11 or 12." If he had inspected the manuscript, Jameson could have easily distinguished the original from the later modifications. Thus he overlooked a valuable aid to the restoration of the original text of the Virginia Plan.

Resolutions proposed by Mr. Randolph in Convention
May 29, 1787

1. Resolved that the Articles of Confederation ought to be so corrected & enlarged as to accomplish the objects proposed by their institution; namely, "common defence, security of liberty and general welfare."

2. Resd. therefore that the rights of suffrage in the National Legislature ought to be proportioned to the Quotas of contribution, or to the number of free inhabitants, as the one or the other rule may seem best in different cases.

3. Resd. that the National Legislature ought to consist of two branches.

4. Resd. that the members of the first branch of the national Legislature ought to be elected by the people of the several States every   for the term of   ; to be of the age of   years at least, to receive liberal stipends by which they may be compensated for the devotion of their time to public service; to be ineligible to any office established by a particular State, or under the authority of the United States, except those beculiarly

[*sic*] belonging to the functions of the first branch, during the term of service, and for the space of   after its expiration; to be incapable of re-election for the space of   after the expiration of their term of service, and to be subject to recall.

5. Resold. that the members of the second branch of the National Legislature ought to be elected by those of the first, out of a proper number of persons nominated by the individual Legislatures, to be of the age of   years at least; to hold their offices for a term sufficient to ensure their independency; to receive liberal stipends, by which they may be compensated for the devotion of their time to public service; and to be ineligible to any office established by a particular State, or under the authority of the United States, except those peculiarly belonging to the functions of the second branch, during the term of service, and for the space of   after the expiration thereof.

6. Resolved that each branch ought to possess the right of originating Acts; that the national Legislature ought to be impowered to enjoy the Legislative Rights vested in Congress by the Confederation & moreover to legislate in all cases to which the separate States are incompetent, or in which the harmony of the United States may be interrupted by the exercise of individual Legislation; to negative all laws passed by the several States, contravening in the opinion of the National Legislature the articles of Union;[1] and to call forth the force of the Union agst. any member of the Union failing to fulfill its duty under the articles thereof.[2]

7. Resd. that a National Executive be instituted; to be chosen by the National Legislature for the term of   years, to receive punctually at stated times a fixed compensation for the services rendered, in which no increase or diminution shall be made so as to affect the Magistracy, existing at the time of increase or diminution, and to be ineligible a second time; and that besides a general authority to execute the National laws, it ought to enjoy the Executive rights vested in Congress by the Confederation.

8. Resd. that the Executive and a Convenient number of the National Judiciary, ought to compose a Council of revision with authority to examine every act of the National Legislature before it shall operate, & every act of a particular Legislature before a Negative thereon shall be final; and that the dissent of the said Council shall amount to a rejection, unless the Act of the National Legislature be again passed, or that of a particular Legislature be again negatived by   of the members of each branch.[3]

9. Resd. that a National Judiciary be established to consist of one or more supreme tribunals, and of[4] inferior tribunals to be chosen by the National Legislature,[5] to hold their offices during good behaviour; and to

receive punctually at stated times fixed compensation for their services, in which no increase or diminution shall be made so as to affect the persons actually in office at the time of such increase or diminution. That the jurisdiction of the inferior tribunals shall be to hear & determine in the first instance, and of the supreme tribunal[6] to hear and determine in the dernier resort, all Piracies & felonies on the high seas, captures from an enemy; cases in which foreigners or citizens of other States applying to such jurisdictions may be interested, or which respect the collection of the National revenue; impeachments of any national officers, and questions which may involve the national peace and harmony.[7]

10. Resolvd. that provision ought to be made for the admission of States lawfully arising within the limits of the United States, whether from a voluntary junction of Government & Territory or otherwise, with the consent of a number of voices in the National legislature less than the whole.

11. Resd. that a Republican Government & the territory of each State, except in the instance of a voluntary junction of Government & territory, ought to be guaranteed by the United States to each State.

12. Resd. that provision ought to be made for the continuance of Congress and their authorities and privileges, until a given day after the reform of the articles of Union shall be adopted, and for the completion of all their engagements.

13. Resd. that provision ought to be made for the amendment of the Articles of Union whensoever it shall seem necessary, and that the assent of the National Legislature ought not to be required thereto.

14. Resd. that the Legislative Executive & Judiciary powers within the several States ought to be bound by oath to support the articles of Union.

15. Resd. that the amendments which shall be offered to the Confederation, by the Convention ought at a proper time, or times, after the approbation of Congress to be submitted to an assembly or assemblies of Representatives, recommended by the several Legislatures to be expressly chosen by the people to consider & decide thereon.

Ms (DLC).

[1]JM preferred a negative "*in all cases whatsoever*" (*PJM*, IX, 318). On 8 June he supported Charles Pinckney's motion for an unlimited veto over state laws. The vote on this unsuccessful motion indicates that Randolph and Mason were responsible for the milder version of the veto provided for in the sixth resolution (Farrand, *Records*, I, 168).

[2]See fourth speech of 31 May 1787 and n. 1.

[3]The idea for a "Council of revision" was borrowed from the New York Constitution of 1777. A proposal to create such a council had been discussed in the Virginia legislature in 1782, and Jefferson included a provision for one in his 1783 draft of a constitution for Virginia (*PJM*, V, 218; Boyd, *Papers of Jefferson*, VI, 302–3). See also JM to Caleb Wallace, 23 Aug. 1785, *PJM*, VIII, 351–52.

[4]. A blank space appears at this point in Brearley's working copy and also in Paterson's fair copy.

[5] JM acceded to, rather than approved, this provision, as his remarks on 5 June (first speech) indicated. He preferred that judges be elected by the "Senatorial branch."

[6] McHenry's copy has "tribunals." All others have the singular form.

[7] For a discussion of the correct text of the ninth resolution, see the Editorial Note above.

Establishment of a National Government

[30 May 1787]

The delegates were considering in place of the first resolution of the Virginia Plan a substitute offered by Randolph: "that a *national* Government ⟨ought to be established⟩ consisting of a *supreme* Legislative, Executive & Judiciary" (Farrand, *Records*, I, 33).

Mr. Maddison—The motion does go to bring out the sense of the house—whether the States shall be governed by one power. If agreed to it will decide nothing. The meaning of the States that the confed. is defect. and ought to be amended. In agreeing to the . . .[1]

Farrand, *Records*, I, 44 (McHenry).

[1] Left incomplete by McHenry.

Proportional Representation in the Legislature

[30 May 1787]

The second resolution of the Virginia Plan was under consideration. JM's suggestion that the words "or to the number of free inhabitants" be struck out to avoid diversionary debates had led to a number of motions. JM finally moved "in order to get over the difficulties, the following resolution—'that the equality of suffrage established by the articles of Confederation ought not to prevail in the national Legislature, and that an equitable ratio of representation ought to be substituted'" (Ms [DLC]). Read then moved to postpone the whole clause because the Delaware delegates were restricted from approving any change in the rule of suffrage.

Mr. Madison observed that whatever reason might have existed for the equality of suffrage when the Union was a federal one among soverigen [*sic*] States, it must cease when a National Govermt. should be put into the place. In the former case, the acts of Congs. depended so much for their efficacy on the cooperation of the States, that these had a weight both within & without Congress, nearly in proportion to their extent and importance. In the latter case, as the acts of the Genl. Govt. would take effect without the intervention of the State legislatures, a vote from a small State wd. have the same efficacy & importance as a vote from a large one, and there was the same reason for different numbers of representatives from different States, as from Counties of different extents within particular States. He suggested as an expedient for at once taking the sense of the members on this point and saving the Delaware deputies from embarrassment, that the question should be taken in Committee, and the clause on report to the House be postponed without a question there.

Ms (DLC).

Popular Election of the First Branch of the Legislature

[31 May 1787]

Mr. Madison considered the popular election of one branch of the national Legislature as essential to every plan of free Government. He observed that in some of the States one branch of the Legislature was composed of men already removed from the people by an intervening body of electors. That if the first branch of the general legislature should be elected by the State Legislatures, the second branch elected by the first—the Executive by the second together with the first; and other appointments again made for subordinate purposes by the Executive, the people would be lost sight of altogether; and the necessary sympathy between them and their rulers and officers, too little felt. He was an advocate for the policy of refining the popular appointments by successive filtrations, but thought it might be pushed too far. He wished the expedient to be resorted to only in the appointment of the second branch of the Legislature, and in the Executive & judiciary branches of the Government. He thought too that the great fabric to be raised would be more stable and durable, if it should rest on the solid foundation of the people themselves, than if it should stand merely on the pillars of the Legislatures.[1]

Ms (DLC).

[1]King's version:
"Madison—agrees with Wilson—this mode immediately introduces the people, and naturally inspires that affection for the Genl. Govt. wh. takes place towards our own offspring—The alternative of a Legislative appt. removes the Genl. Govt. too far from the

People—in Maryland the Senate is two removes from the People, a Depy. appointed by them will be three, the first Br. having power to appt. the 2d. Br. they will be four, the Genl. Legis. appts. the Executive which will be five removes from the People—if the Election is made by the Peop. in large Districts there will be no Danger of Demagogues" (Farrand, *Records*, I, 56).

Pierce's version:

"Mr. Maddison was of the opinion that the appointment of the Members to the first branch of the national Legislature ought to be made by the people for two reasons,—one was that it would inspire confidence, and the other that it would induce the Government to sympathize with the people" (ibid., I, 57).

Election of the Senate

[31 May 1787]

Wilson had suggested that the Senate should be chosen from special political units created by a fusion of several districts formed for selecting members of the first branch.

Mr. Madison observed that such a mode would destroy the influence of the smaller States associated with larger ones in the same district; as the latter would chuse from within themselves, altho' better men might be found in the former. The election of Senators in Virga. where large & small counties were often formed into one district for the purpose, had illustrated this consequence. Local partiality, would often prefer a resident within the County or State, to a candidate of superior merit residing out of it. Less merit also in a resident would be more known throughout his own State.[1]

Ms (DLC).

[1]Pierce's version:

"Mr. Maddison thinks the mode pointed out in the original propositions the best" (Farrand, *Records*, I, 59).

Powers of the National Legislature

[31 May 1787]

The clause of the sixth resolution of the Virginia Plan giving the national legislature power "to legislate in all cases to which the separate States are incompetent" was under debate.

Mr. Madison said that he had brought with him into the Convention a strong bias in favor of an enemeration and definition of the powers necessary to be exercised by the national Legislature; but had also brought doubts concerning its practicability. His wishes remained unaltered; but his doubts had become stronger. What his opinion might ultimately be he could not yet tell. But he should shrink from nothing which should be found essential to such a form of Govt. as would provide for the safety, liberty and happiness of the Community. This being the end of all our deliberations, all the necessary means for attaining it must, however reluctantly, be submitted to.[1]

Ms (DLC).

[1] Pierce's version:

"Mr. Maddison said he had brought with him a strong prepossession for the defining of the limits and powers of the federal Legislature, but he brought with him some doubts about the practicability of doing it:—at present he was convinced it could not be done" (Farrand, *Records*, I, 60).

According to Pierce, during this debate JM had also commented prior to this speech: "it was necessary to adopt some general principles on which we should act,—that we were wandering from one thing to another without seeming to be settled in any one principle" (ibid., I, 60).

[31 May 1787]

The coercive-power clause of the sixth resolution, authorizing the use of force against a state "failing to fulfill its duty" to the Union, was under debate.

Mr. Madison, observed that the more he reflected on the use of force, the more he doubted, the practicability, the justice and the efficacy of it when applied to people collectively and not individually. A Union of the States containing such an ingredient seemed to provide for its own destruction. The use of force agst. a State, would look more like a declaration of war, than an infliction of punishment, and would probably be considered by the party attacked as a dissolution of all previous compacts by which it might be bound. He hoped that such a system would be framed as might render this recourse unnecessary, and moved that the clause be postponed.[1]

Ms (DLC).

[1] After "postponed," JM deleted "till the contrary should be found on trial to be the case," a change he made before Eppes copied the Debates. Many years later JM explained that the coercive-power clause was "suggested by the inefficiency of the Confederate system, from the want of such a sanction; none such being expressed in its Articles" (to John Tyler,

[March?] 1833, Farrand, *Records*, III, 528). JM himself in 1781 had drafted a proposed amendment to the Articles of Confederation authorizing the use of force to compel the states "to fulfill their federal engagements" (*PJM*, III, 17–19). As long as the U.S. remained a confederation of sovereign states, JM believed that the federal government needed this coercive power, although he admitted "the difficulty & awkwardness of operating by force on the collective will of a State" (JM to Washington, 16 Apr. 1787, *PJM*, IX, 385). Such a provision would be unnecessary, however, if the convention devised a national government operating directly over individuals. See JM to Jefferson, 24 Oct. 1787.

Powers of the Executive

[1 June 1787]

Mad: agrees wth. Wilson in his difinition of executive powers— executive powers ex vi termini, do not include the Rights of war & peace &c. but the powers shd. be confined and defined—if large we shall have the Evils of elective Monarchies—probably the best plan will be a single Executive of long duration wth. a Council, with liberty to depart from their Opinion at his peril—[1]

Farrand, *Records*, I, 70 (King).

[1]Hamilton's version:
> "1—The way to prevent a majority from having an interest to oppress the minority is to enlarge the sphere.

"Madison" "2—Elective Monarchies turbulent and unhappy—Men unwilling to admit so decided a superiority of merit in an individual as to accede to his appointment to so preeminent a station.

> "If several are admitted as there will be many competitors of equal merit they may be all included—contention prevented—& the republican genius consulted" (Syrett and Cooke, *Papers of Hamilton*, IV, 161).

Pierce's version:
"Mr. Maddison was of opinion that an Executive formed of one Man would answer the purpose when aided by a Council, who should have the right to advise and record their proceedings, but not to control his authority" (Farrand, *Records*, I, 74).

[1 June 1787]

The Committee of the Whole postponed a motion for a single executive.

Mr. Madison thought it would be proper, before a choice shd. be made between a unity and a plurality in the Executive, to fix the extent of the Executive authority; that as certain powers were in their nature Executive, and must be given to that departmt. whether administered by one or more persons, a definition of their extent would assist the judgment in determining how far they might be safely entrusted to a single officer. He accordingly moved that so much of the clause before the Committee as related to the powers of the Executive shd. be struck out & that after the words "that a national Executive ought to be instituted" there be inserted the words following viz. "with power to carry into effect, the national laws, to appoint to offices in cases not otherwise provided for, and to execute such other powers 'not Legislative nor Judiciary in their nature,' as may from time to time be delegated by the national Legislature."[1]

Ms (DLC).

[1]Charles Pinckney moved to strike out "'and to execute such other powers not Legislative nor Judiciary in their nature as may from time to time be delegated'" as unnecessary (Farrand, *Records*, I, 67). JM replied that he "did not know that the words were absolutely necessary, or even the preceding words, 'to appoint to offices &c.['] the whole being perhaps included in the first member of the proposition. He did not however see any inconveniency in retaining them, and cases might happen in which they might serve to prevent doubts and misconstructions" (Ms [DLC]).

Term of the Executive

[1 June 1787?]

Bedford favored a triennial election and ineligibility after nine years because the executive could be ousted for "misfeasance only, not incapacity" (Farrand, *Records*, I, 69).

Mr. Maddison observed that to prevent a Man from holding an Office longer than he ought, he may for malpractice be impeached and removed;—he is not for any ineligibility.[1]

Farrand, *Records*, I, 74 (Pierce).

[1]King also recorded JM speaking on the term of office: "Mad. 7 years and an exclusion for ever after—or during good behavior" (ibid., I, 71). King's version is contradicted by internal evidence as well as by Pierce's account. JM apparently favored reeligibility, not exclusion. However, King may be correct in placing JM's speech before Mason's and Bedford's, rather than after, as Pierce has it.

Removal of the Executive

[2 June 1787]

Dickinson had moved that the executive be subject to removal by the national legislature when such an action was requested by a majority of the state legislatures.

Mr Madison & Mr. Wilson observed that it would leave an equality of agency in the small with the great States; that it would enable a minority of the people to prevent the removal of an officer who had rendered himself justly criminal in the eyes of a majority; that it would open a door for intrigues agst. him in States where his administration tho' just might be unpopular, and might tempt him to pay court to particular States whose leading partizans,[1] he might fear, or wish to engage as his partizans. They both thought it bad policy to introduce such a mixture of the State authorities, where their agency could be otherwise supplied.[2]

Ms (DLC).

[1]JM deleted a word and interlined "leading partizans" some time after Eppes copied the Debates. The deleted word is illegible in the Debates, but in the Eppes copy it is clearly "demagogues."

[2]Pierce recorded: "Mr. Maddison said it was far from being his wish that every executive Officer should remain in Office, without being amenable to some Body for his conduct" (Farrand, *Records*, I, 92). Whether this remark is part of the speech printed above, or a separate comment made by JM later, is uncertain.

Power of the Executive to Veto Laws

[4 June 1787]

Wilson and Hamilton moved to give the executive an absolute veto on laws.

Mr. Madison supposed that if a proper proportion of each branch should be required to overrule the objections of the Executive, it would answer the same purpose as an absolute negative. It would rarely if ever happen that the Executive constituted as ours is proposed to be would have firmness eno' to resist the legislature, unless backed by a certain part of the body itself.[1] The King of G.B. with all his splendid attributes would not be able to withstand the unanimous and eager wishes of both houses of Parliament. To give such a prerogative would certainly be obnoxious to the temper of this Country;[2] its present temper at least.[3]

Ms (DLC).

[1]Before Eppes copied the Debates, JM here interlined and then deleted: "or actuated by some foreign support agst. his own Country."

[2]JM first wrote: ". . . be obnoxious in our present situation," but substituted the present wording before Eppes copied the Debates.

[3]Some time after Eppes copied the Debates, JM heavily deleted a sentence and interlined the concluding clause.

Yates's version:

"Mr. Madison against it—because of the difficulty of an executive venturing on the exercise of this negative, and is therefore of opinion that the revisional authority is better" (Farrand, *Records*, I, 106).

King's version:

"Mad: I am opposed to the complete negative, because no man will dare exercise it whn. the law was passed almost unanimously. I doubt whether the Kng of Eng. wd. have firmness sufficient to do it" (ibid., I, 107).

Pierce's version:

"Mr. Maddison was of opinion that no Man would be so daring as to place a veto on a Law that had passed with the assent of the Legislature" (ibid., I, 109).

Revisionary Power of the Executive and the Judiciary

[4 June 1787]

This speech preceded Wilson's motion, seconded by JM, to combine the judiciary with the executive in vetoing legislative acts.

Mad. The Judicial ought to be introduced in the business of Legislation—they will protect their Department, and uniting wh. the Executive render their Check or negative more respectable—there is weight in the objections agt. this measure—but a Check is necessary experience proves it, and teaches us that what we once thought the Calumny of the Enemies of Republican Govts. is undoubtedly true—There is diversity of Interest in every Country the Rich & poor, the Dr. & Cr. the followers of different Demagogues, the diversity of religious Sects—The Effects of these parties are obvious in the ant'. Govts.—the same causes will operate with us—

We must introduce the Checks, which will destroy the measures of an interested majority—in this view a negative in the Ex: is not only necessary for its own safety, but for the safety of a minority in Danger of oppression from an unjust and interested majority—The independent condition of the Ex. who has the Eyes of all Nations on him will render him a just Judge—add the Judiciary and you increase the respectability—[1]

Farrand, *Records*, I, 108 (King).

[1]Pierce's version:

"Mr. Maddison in a very able and ingenious Speech, ran through the whole Scheme of the Government,—pointed out all the beauties and defects of ancient Republics; compared their situation with ours wherever it appeared to bear any anology, and proved that the only way to make a Government answer all the end of its institution was to collect the wisdom of its several parts in aid of each other whenever it was necessary. Hence the propriety of incorporating the Judicial with the Executive in the revision of the Laws. He was of opinion that by joining the Judges with the Supreme Executive Magistrate would be strictly proper, and would by no means interfere with that indepence so much to be approved and distinguished in the several departments" (ibid., I, 110).

J. Franklin Jameson believed that Pierce here fused JM's two speeches of 6 June. However, the present editors concur with Farrand's opinion that Pierce was recording a second speech made by JM on 4 June (ibid., I, 110 n.).

Method of Choosing the Judiciary

[5 June 1787]

The clause of the ninth resolution of the Virginia Plan proposing that the judiciary be chosen by the national legislature was under consideration.

Mr. Madison disliked the election of the Judges by the Legislature or any numerous body. Besides the danger of intrigue and partiality, many of the members were not judges of the requisite qualifications. The Legislative talents which were very different from those of a Judge, commonly recommended men to the favor of Legislative Assemblies. It was known too that the accidental circumstances of presence and absence, of being a member or not a member, had a very undue influence on the appointment. On the other hand he was not satisfied with referring the appointment to the Executive. He rather inclined to give it to the Senatorial branch, as numerous eno' to be confided in—as not so numerous as to be governed by the motives of the other branch; and as being sufficiently stable and independent to follow their deliberate judgments. He hinted this only and moved that the *appointment by the Legislature* might be struck out, & a blank left to be hereafter filled on maturer reflection.[1]

Ms (DLC).

[1]Yates's version:

"Mr Madison opposed the motion, and inclined to think that the executive ought by no means to make the appointments, but rather that branch of the legislature called the senatorial; and moves that the words, *of the appointment of the legislature*, be expunged" (Farrand, *Records*, I, 126).

Lansing's version:

"Mr. Maddison opposed—the Judges ought to be appointed by the Senetorial Branch of the Legislature. Moves *that* the words *the national Legislature* be struck out" (Strayer, *Delegate from N.Y.*, p. 33).

King's version:

"Madison—I am for farther Diliberation perhaps it will be best that the appointment shd. be by the Senate" (Farrand, *Records*, I, 128).

Pierce's version:

"Mr. Madison was for appointing the Judges by the Senate" (ibid., I, 128).

Method of Ratifying the Constitution

[5 June 1787]

The Virginia Plan resolution (fifteen) providing for popularly elected ratifying conventions was under debate.

Mr. Madison thought this provision essential. The articles of Confedn. themselves were defective in this respect, resting in many of the States on the Legislative sanction only. Hence in conflicts between acts of the States, and of Congs. especially where the former are of posterior date, and the decision is to be made by State Tribunals, an uncertainty must necessarily prevail, or rather perhaps a certain decision in favor of the State authority. He suggested also that as far as the articles of Union were to be considered as a Treaty only of a particular sort, among the Governments of Independent States, the doctrine might be set up that a breach of any one article, by any of the parties, absolved the other parties from the whole obligation. For these reasons as well as others he thought it indispensable that the new Constitution should be ratified in the most unexceptionable form, and by the supreme authority of the people themselves.[1]

Ms (DLC).

[1] Yates's version:
"Mr. Madison endeavored to enforce the necessity of this resolve—because the new national constitution ought to have the highest source of authority, at least paramount to the powers of the respective constitutions of the states—points out the mischiefs that have arisen in the old confederation, which depends upon no higher authority than the confirmation of an ordinary act of a legislature—Instances the law operation of treaties, when contravened by any antecedent acts of a particular state" (Farrand, *Records*, I, 126–27).
Lansing's version:
"Mr. Maddison enforced the Necessity of this Resolve for that the new Constitution ought to have the highest Source of Authority—at least paramount to the several Constitutions—points out the Mischiefs arising from the present Confederation depending on ordinary State Authorities—Instance the Effect of Treaties when contrasted with antecedent Acts of Legislature" (Strayer, *Delegate from N.Y.*, p. 34).
Lansing was ill on this day and took his account of the proceedings from Yates (ibid., pp. 32–33).

Establishment of Inferior Courts

[5 June 1787]

Rutledge moved to strike out the clause of the ninth resolution providing for inferior national courts. He argued that the state courts "ought to be left in all cases to decide in the first instance" and that the right of appeal to the supreme national tribunal was sufficient to secure the national rights (Farrand, *Records*, I, 124).

Mr. Madison observed that unless inferior tribunals were dispersed throughout the Republic with *final* jurisdiction in *many* cases, appeals would be multiplied to a most oppressive degree; that besides, an appeal would not in many cases be a remedy. What was to be done after improper Verdicts in State tribunals obtained under the biassed directions of a dependent Judge, or the local prejudices of an undirected jury? To remand the cause for a new trial would answer no purpose. To order a new trial at the supreme bar would oblige the parties to bring up their witnesses, tho' ever so distant from the seat of the Court. An effective Judiciary establishment commensurate to the legislative authority, was essential. A Government without a proper Executive & Judiciary would be the mere trunk of a body, without arms or legs to act or move.[1]

Ms (DLC).

[1] King's version:

"Madison proposes to vest the Genl. Govt. with authority to erect an Independent Judicial, coextensive wt. the Nation" (Farrand, *Records*, I, 128).

After Rutledge's motion passed, Wilson and JM moved "to add to Resol: 9 the words following 'that the National Legislature be empowered to institute inferior tribunals.' They observed that there was a distinction between establishing such tribunals absolutely, and giving a discretion to the Legislature to establish or not establish them. They repeated the necessity of some such provision" (Ms [DLC]).

To Thomas Jefferson

PHILADA. June 6th. 1787.

DEAR SIR

The day fixed for the meeting of the Convention was the 14th. ult. On the 25th. and not before seven States were assembled. General Washington was placed unâ voce in the chair. The Secretaryship was given to Major Jackson. The members present are from Massachussetts Mr. Gherry, Mr. Ghorum, Mr. King, Mr. Strong. From Connecticut Mr. Sherman Docr. S. Johnson, Mr. Elseworth. From N. York Judge Yates, Mr. Lansing, Col. Hamilton. N. Jersey, Governour Livingston, Judge Brearly, Mr. Patterson, Attorney Genl. [Mr. Houston & Mr. Clarke are absent members.][1] From Pennsylvania Doctr. Franklyn, Mr. Morris, Mr. Wilson, Mr. Fitzimmons, Mr. G. Clymer, Genl. Mifflin, Mr. Governeur Morris, Mr. Ingersoll. From Delaware Mr. Jno. Dickenson, Mr. Reed, Mr. Bedford, Mr. Broom, Mr. Bassett. From Maryland Majr. Jenifer

only. Mr. McHenry, Mr. Danl. Carrol, Mr. Jno. Mercer, Mr. Luther
Martin are absent members. The three last have supplied the resignations
of Mr. Stone, Mr. Carrol of Carolton, and Mr. T. Johnson as I have
understood the case. From Virginia Genl. Washington, Governor Randolph, Mr. Blair, Col. Mason, Docr. McClurg, J Madison. Mr. Wythe
left us yesterday, being called home by the serious declension of his lady's
health.[2] From N. Carolina, Col. Martin late Governor, Docr. Williamson,
Mr. Spaight, Col. Davy. Col. Blount is another member but is detained
by indisposition at N. York. From S. Carolina Mr. John Rutlidge, General Pinkney, Mr. Charles Pinkney, Majr. Pierce Butler, Mr. Laurens is in
the Commission from that State, but will be kept away by the want of
health. From Georgia Col. Few, Majr. Pierce, formerly of Williamsbg. &
aid to Genl. Greene, Mr. Houston. Mr. Baldwin will be added to them in
a few days. Walton and Pendleton are also in the deputation. N. Hamshire has appointed Deputies but they are not expected; the State treasury
being empty it is said, and a substitution of private resources being inconvenient or impracticable. I mention this circumstance to take off the appearance of backwardness, which that State is not in the least chargeable
with, if we are rightly informed of her disposition. Rhode Island has not
yet acceded to the measure. As their Legislature meet very frequently,
and can at any time be got together in a week, it is possible that caprice
if no other motive may yet produce a unanimity of the States in this
experiment.

In furnishing you with this list of names, I have exhausted all the means
which I can make use of for gratifying your curiosity. It was thought
expedient in order to secure unbiassed discussion within doors, and to
prevent misconceptions & misconstructions without, to establish some
rules of caution which will for no short time restrain even a confidential
communication of our proceedings. The names of the members will
satisfy you that the States have been serious in this business. The attendance of Genl. Washington is a proof of the light in which he regards it.
The whole Community is big with expectation. And there can be no
doubt but that the result will in some way or other have a powerful effect
on our destiny.

Mr. Adams' Book which has been in your hands of course, has excited a
good deal of attention. An edition has come out here and another is in the
press at N. York. It will probably be much read, particularly in the
Eastern States, and contribute with other circumstances to revive the
predilections of this Country for the British Constitution. Men of learning
find nothing new in it. Men of taste many things to criticize. And men
without either not a few things, which they will not understand. It will

nevertheless be read, and praised, and become a powerful engine in forming the public opinion. The name & character of the Author, with the
critical situation of our affairs, naturally account for such an effect. The
book also has merit, and I wish many of the remarks in it, which are
unfriendly to republicanism, may not receive fresh weight from the operations of our Governments.[3]

I learn from Virga. that the appetite for paper money grows stronger
every day. Mr. H—n—y is an avowed patron of the scheme, and will not
fail I think to carry it through unless the County [Prince Edward][4] which
he is to represent shall bind him hand and foot by instructions. I am told
that this is in contemplation. He is also said to be unfriendly to an acceler-
ation of Justice.[5] There is good reason to beleive *too that* ⟨he is⟩ *hostile to*
the object of the convention and that *he wishes either a partition or total dissolution*
of the confederacy.

I sent you a few days ago by a Vessel going to France a box with peccan
Nuts planted in it. Mr Jno. Vaughn was so good as to make the arrangements with the Capt: both for their preservation during the voyage & the
conveyance of them afterwards. I had before sent you via Eangland a few
nuts sealed up in a letter.

Mr. Wythe gave me favorable accounts of your Nephew in Williamsburg. And from the Presidt. of Hampden Sidney who was here a few
days ago I recd. information equally pleasing as to the genius, progress,
and character of your younger Nephew.

I must beg you to communicate my affecte. respects to our friend
Mazzei, and to let him know that I have taken every step for securing his
claim on Dorhman, which I judged most likely to succeed. There is little
doubt that Congress will allow him more, than he owes Mr. Mazzei, and I
have got from him such a draught on the Treasury board as I think will
ensure him the chance of that fund.[6] Dorman is at present in Virga. where
he has also some claims & expectations, but they are not in a transferrable
situation. I intended to have written to Mazzei and must beg his pardon
for not doing it. It is really out of my power at this time. Adieu Yrs Affy

RC (DLC). Unsigned. Docketed by Jefferson. Italicized words are those encoded by JM
using the code Jefferson sent him on 11 May 1785. Words within angle brackets were added
by JM at a later time.

[1]Brackets inserted by JM.

[2]Mrs. Elizabeth Wythe died 18 Aug. 1787 (*Va. Gazette and Weekly Advertiser*, 23 Aug.
1787).

[3]The first volume of John Adams's *A Defence of the Constitutions of Government of the United
States of America* was originally published in London in 1787. The treatise eventually filled
three volumes, the last two published in 1788 (C. F. Adams, *Works of John Adams*, IV,
275–76). The *Defence* was largely a reply to Turgot's attack (contained in a letter of 1778 to

Richard Price that Price published in 1785) on the American state constitutions as absurd imitations of the British constitution. For a discussion of the "international argument" on the American state constitutions, see Palmer, *Age of the Democratic Revolution*, I, 263–82. See also the sharp attack on Adams's work in the Reverend James Madison's letter to JM of 11 June 1787.

[4]Brackets and "Prince Edward" inserted by JM, probably at some later time.

[5]JM meant that Patrick Henry was opposed to court reforms in Virginia. JM had struggled in vain for an overhauling of the judicial system during the 1784, 1785, and 1786 sessions of the General Assembly (*PJM*, VIII, 163–72, 475; IX, 185, 243, 245 n. 1).

[6]The Board of Treasury report of 19 Mar. 1787 recommended that Arnold Henry Dohrman be paid less than $6,000 to satisfy his claim of $25,084 40/90, but he also was to receive an annual salary of $1,300 in back pay for services rendered as the U.S. agent in Lisbon. A report on 1 Oct. 1787 increased the settlement to a sum of $5,806 72/90 with interest, plus $1,600 per annum for retroactive salary, and a title to one township in the Northwest Territory (*JCC*, XXXII, 119–21; XXXIII, 586–88; A. J. Morrison, "Arnold Henry Dohrman," *Ohio Archaeological and Historical Publications*, XXIII [1914], 227–31).

To William Short

PHILADA. June 6th. 1787.

DEAR SIR

I have been sensibly obliged by your favor of the 23. of March which arrived by the last Packet. I had previously received from Mr. Jefferson information concerning the dislocation of his wrist, and the remedial journey which he had projected. His friends are particularly interested and none more than myself in his recovering the entire use of a member, without which they must lose the pleasure of many of his valuable communications and reflections. I should not go too far in saying that it will be a loss to the world, if the use of his pen should be frustrated or even abridged, by the permanent effect of the accident. I write to him by this conveyance on the supposition that it will find him returned to Paris.

The Convention has been formed about 12 days. It contains in several instances the most respectable characters in the U.S. and in general may be said to be the best contribution of talents the States could make for the occasion. What the result of the experiment may be is among the arcana of futurity. Our affairs are considered on all hands as at a most serious crisis. No hope is entertained from the existing Confederacy. And the eyes and hopes of all are turned towards this new Assembly. The result therefore whatever it may be must have a material influence on our destiny, and on that of the cause of republican liberty. The personal characters of the members promise much. The spirit which they bring with them seems in general equally promising. But the labor is great indeed; whether we consider the real or imaginary difficulties, within doors or without doors.

I learn with much pleasure that the Marquis de la fayette is so actively engaged in the reforms aimed at in the Convention at Paris.[1] I sincerely wish his influence may be as great as it deserves to be. I beg you to make my most affectionate respects to him, and to let him know that I shall write to him as soon as I can make a letter interesting. I should not wait indeed for such materials, if the present opportunity did not happen to find me too much occupied, to trouble him with one of a contrary character. With the sincere esteem & regard I am dear Sir Yr. Affecte. hble. servt.

Js. Madison Jr.

RC (DLC: William Short Papers). Docketed by Short, "June. 6./July. 11." The latter date is probably when Short received the letter.

[1] JM was referring to the Assembly of Notables (see *PJM*, IX, 329, 330 n. 2).

Popular Election of the First Branch of the Legislature

[6 June 1787]

Charles Pinckney moved that the first branch of the legislature be elected by the state legislatures, not by the people.

Mr. Madison considered an election of one branch at least of the Legislature by the people immediately, as a clear principle of free Govt. and that this mode under proper regulations had the additional advantage of securing better representatives, as well as of avoiding too great an agency of the State Governments in the General one. He differed from the member from Connecticut (Mr. Sharman) in thinking the objects mentioned to be all the principal ones that required a National Govt. Those were certainly important and necessary objects; but he combined with them the necessity, of providing more effectually for the security of private rights, and the steady dispensation of Justice. Interferences with these were evils which had more perhaps than any thing else produced this convention. Was it to be supposed that republican liberty could long exist under the abuses of it practiced in some of the States. The gentleman (Mr. Sharman) had admitted that in a very small State, faction & oppression wd. prevail. It was to be inferred then that wherever these prevailed the State was too small. Had they not prevailed in the largest as well as the smallest tho' less than in the smallest; and were we not thence admonished to enlarge the sphere as far as the nature of the Govt. would admit. This was the only defence agst. the inconveniencies of democracy consistent with the democratic form of Govt. All civilized Societies would be divided into different Sects, Factions, & interests, as they happened to consist of rich & poor, debtors & creditors, the landed the manufacturing the commercial interests, the inhabitants of this district or that district, the followers of this political leader or that political leader, the disciples of this religious Sect or that religious Sect. In all cases where a majority are united by a common interest or passion, the rights of the minority are in danger. What motives are to restrain them? A prudent regard to the maxim that honesty is the best policy is found by experience to be as little regarded by bodies of men as by individuals. Respect for character is always diminished in proportion to the number among whom the blame or praise is to be divided. Conscience, the only remaining tie, is known to be inadequate in individuals: In large numbers little is to be expected from it. Besides, Religion itself may become a motive to persecution & oppression. These observations are verified by the Histories of every Country antient & modern. In Greece & Rome the rich & poor, the creditors & debtors, as well as the patricians & plebians alternately oppressed each other with equal unmercifulness. What a source of oppression was the relation between the parent Cities of Rome, Athens & Carthage, & their respective provinces: the former possessing the power, & the latter being sufficiently distinguished to be separate objects of it? Why was America so justly apprehensive of Parliamentary injustice? Because G. Britain had a separate interest real or supposed, & if her authority had been admitted, could have pursued that interest at our expence. We have seen the mere distinction of colour made in the most enlightened period of time, a ground of the most oppressive dominion ever exercised by man over man. What has been the source of those unjust laws complained of among ourselves? Has it not been the real or supposed interest of the major number? Debtors have defrauded their creditors. The landed interest has borne hard on the mercantile interest. The Holders of one species of property have thrown a disproportion of taxes on the holders of another species. The lesson we are to draw from the whole is that where a majority are united by a common sentiment and have an opportunity, the rights of the minor party become insecure. In a Republican Govt. the Majority if united have always an opportunity. The only remedy is to enlarge the sphere, & thereby divide the community into so great a number of interests & parties, that in the 1st. place a majority will not be likely at the same moment to have a common interest separate from that of the whole or of the minority; and in the 2d place, that in case they shd have such an interest, they may not be apt to unite in the pursuit of it.[1] It was incumbent on us then to try this remedy, and with that view to frame a republican

Revisionary Power of the Executive
and the Judiciary

[6 June 1787]

Wilson moved to reconsider the vote excluding the judiciary from a share in vetoing legislative acts.

Mr. Madison 2ded. the motion. He observed that the great difficulty in rendering the Executive competent to its own defence arose from the nature of Republican Govt. which could not give to an individual citizen that settled pre-eminence in the eyes of the rest, that weight of property, that personal interest agst. betraying the national interest, which appertain to an hereditary magistrate. In a Republic personal merit alone could be the ground of political exaltation, but it would rarely happen that this merit would be so pre-eminent as to produce universal acquiescence. The Executive Magistrate would be envied & assailed by disappointed competitors: His firmness therefore wd. need support. He would not possess those great emoluments from his station, nor that permanent stake in the public interest which wd. place him out of the reach of foreign corruption: He would stand in need therefore of being controuled as well as supported. An association of the Judges in his revisionary function wd both double the advantage and diminish the danger. It wd. also enable the Judiciary Department the better to defend itself agst. Legislative encroachments. Two objections had been made 1st. that the Judges ought not to be subject to the bias which a participation in the making of laws might give in the exposition of them. 2dly. that the Judiciary Departmt. ought to be separate & distinct from the other great Departments. The 1st. objection had some weight; but it was much diminished by reflecting that a small proportion of the laws coming in question before a Judge wd. be such wherein he had been consulted; that a small part of this proportion wd. be so ambiguous as to leave room for his prepossessions; and that but a few cases wd. probably arise in the life of a Judge under such ambiguous passages. How much good on the other hand wd. proceed from the perspicuity, the conciseness, and the systematic character wch. the Code of laws wd. receive from the Judiciary talents. As to the 2d. objection, it either had no weight, or it applied with equal weight to the Executive & to the Judiciary revision of the laws. The maxim on which the objection was founded required a separation of the Executive as well as of the Judiciary from the Legislature & from each other. There wd. in truth however be no improper mixture of these distinct powers in the present case. In England,

35

whence the maxim itself had been drawn, the Executive had an absolute negative on the laws; and the supreme tribunal of Justice (the House of Lords) formed one of the other branches of the Legislature. In short, whether the object of the revisionary power was to restrain the Legislature from encroaching on the other co-ordinate Departments, or on the rights of the people at large; or from passing laws unwise in their principle, or incorrect in their form, the utility of annexing the wisdom and weight of the Judiciary to the Executive seemed incontestable.[1]

Ms (DLC).

[1]King's version:
"Madison
"A check is devised for three purposes—to prevent encroachments by the Legislature on the Executive, the Judicial, or on private Rights. If on the executive, his negative will be corroberated by an union with the Judicial; and so in every other case—The Dificulty is this; the check will be too weak if in the Executive only—perhaps the British King wd not interpose his negative agt. the unanimous voice of both houses of Parliament" (Farrand, *Records*, I, 144).

From Joseph Jones

RICHMOND 7th. June 1787.

DR. SR.

Since my return to Richmond, which place I left soon after the Governor set out, I have yours of the 27th. from Philadelphia. Mr. Dorhman who has arrived here within a few days past informed us your information from New York of other Delegates coming forward was well founded as you had ten States represented when he came away. I entertain hopes from the disposition of the Members convened that harmony will prevail and such improvements of the fœderal system adopted as will afford us a prospect of peace and happiness. I am however strongly impressed with fears, that your labours in Convention, though wisely conducted and concluded, will in the end be frustrated by some of the States under the influence of interests operating for particular rather than general we[l]fare. Be this as it may I cannot doubt but the meeting in Philadelphia will (composed as it is of the best and wisest persons in the Union) establish some plan that will be generally approved.

The Lieutenant Governor tells me he does and shall continue to write to the Governor once a week at least. I shall do the same to you if I can furnish any sort of materials for a letter worth communicating.[1] At any rate I may support a correspondence by inclosing you the News papers if I can entertain you with nothing more interesting.

A letter from Mr. A. Lee which the Governor has sent us intimates the propriety of proceeding withot. delay (if the Executive have any money at their command) to purchase up continental securities, which are now low, but which he seems to think will, (if the Convention do any thing that will probably meet the approbation of the States, and the Sales of the lands by Congress take place,) rapidly rise in value. He says also that other States are doing this while it is to be effected on easy terms.[2] I wish for information as to the fact, and your Sentiments so far as you conjecture respecting the rise of the value of these papers. We have forbid any further advances of Specie to the Commr. of the U.S. untill we can be assured the proportion of indents will be admitted. Those on the requisition of the last year have been withheld consequently it is too late for the present collection to furnish a proportion of them, and we understand the construction of the Treasury board of the U.S. is that under the requisitions of 84 & 85, the indents issued under each requisition can be received in payment of each and none of the one be admitted in the other, and so of the last year, had they come forward; and of the year 85 none to be recd. but such as were in hands of the State Treasurer the 1st. Janry 87 and of 86 none but such as shod. be in his hands by the 1st. July 87. This was not I believe so understood here by the requisitions, and if they were so intended, wch. may Probably have been the case, a point so material for the States to be acquainted with shod. have been clearly, and not doubtfully expressed.[3] We have letters from several of the County Lieutenants of the Kentucke district of Indian incursions and depredations many persons killed and horses carried off, of the families many of them on the frontier coming in particularly in Jefferson. These letters are sent to the Delegates in Congress. We have authorised measures of defence only, well knowing an adherence to the Militia law our best Policy as a State but the measures of the U.S. should go further whenever there is reason for it. Our informations seem to call for such measures or I am persuaded very great distress will attend the Kentucke district.[4] We hear nothing of or from Mr. Butler or the Commander of the Troops of the U. St.[5] My Compliments to the Governor. I beg your excuse as I really had forgot your former request abt. the 2 books. It shall be attended to now but you will inform me where they are to be sent.

RC (DLC). Docketed by JM. Signature clipped.

[1] The lieutenant governor of Virginia was Beverley Randolph. Jones was a member of the Council of State and frequently reported its proceedings to JM.

[2] See Edmund Randolph to Beverley Randolph, 24 May 1787, enclosing Arthur Lee's letter of 20 May 1787 to Edmund Randolph (*CVSP*, IV, 288–89). The states had begun to assume public securities as early as 1784 in response to Congress's continuing default on its

obligations to public creditors (Ferguson, *Power of the Purse*, pp. 228–34). Acquiring these securities benefited the states by providing them with "gilt-edged assets against the day when Congress and the states would finally settle their accounts" (ibid., p. 232). Lee, who had inside information by virtue of his position on the Board of Treasury, urged his state to enter the securities market "speedily and secretly. If it must be deferred till the next General Assembly, the loss of the State will be inevitable." The Council of State declined acting on this advice, however, not having "the power and the means" to follow it (Jones to JM, 29 June 1787). As a result, Virginia did not begin to purchase public securities until after the creation of a sinking fund at the October 1787 session of the legislature (Hening, *Statutes*, XII, 452–54; *JCSV*, IV, 355–59).

[3]The Board of Treasury had refused to issue indents to Virginia on the requisition of 1786 because the state had failed to provide adequate funds to meet that requisition (*PJM*, IX, 300 and n. 1, 363, 364 n. 5). By the terms of the requisition of 1785 the indents collected for taxes under that requisition had to be in the hands of the state treasurer by 1 Jan. 1787; the indents issued under the 1786 requisition had to be collected by 1 July 1787. If the state did not collect its full quota of indents by those dates, the deficiency would have to be paid in specie (*JCC*, XXIX, 770; XXXI, 464). It was also the intention of Congress, though not expressly stated in the requisitions, that the indents issued on a given requisition could be collected and turned into the Continental treasury only in discharge of that requisition. State Treasurer Jacquelin Ambler had recently presented $187,000 in indents issued on the requisition of 1785 to John Hopkins, Continental loan office commissioner for Virginia, of which more than $56,000 had been collected after 1 Jan. 1787. Hopkins, on the advice of the Board of Treasury, informed Ambler that he would receive only those collected before 1 Jan. and accompanied by the proper proportion of specie in payment of the 1785 requisition. The Council of State, evidently expecting the surplus indents to be admitted on the requisition of 1786, for which no indents had yet been issued, ordered the treasurer to stop further payments of specie on the requisitions of 1785 and 1786 (Hopkins to Ambler, 29 May 1787, enclosed in Edmund Randolph to Speaker of the House of Delegates, 15 Oct. 1787 [Vi: Executive Communications]; *JCSV*, IV, 102). Despite the protests of Hopkins and the treasury commissioners, the council refused to rescind this order (Hopkins to Beverley Randolph, 11 June 1787, enclosing Board of Treasury to Hopkins, 29 May 1787 [Vi: Continental Congress Papers]). Rebuffed by the authorities in Richmond, the Board of Treasury turned to the Virginia delegation in Congress. In a statement of 16 June 1787 to the delegates, the commissioners explained how the state could advantageously use the indents it had collected under the requisition of 1785. For example, if the state did not have enough specie to accompany the indents collected on that requisition, it could make specie payments in installments until all the indents in the state treasury as of 1 Jan. 1787 had been turned over to the loan office commissioner. Moreover, having met the specie requirement of the 1784 requisition, the state by special resolution of Congress could present without an accompanying specie payment the indents collected after 1 Jan. 1787 in fulfillment of its quotas of 1782 and 1784. In short, the commissioners concluded, even though they could not permit the indents issued on the 1785 requisition to be paid on that of 1786, the state could easily dispose of the surplus indents in its treasury. The situation in Virginia with respect to indents was no worse than that of many of the other states, they added, and it appeared likely that a majority of them would support a proposal extending the time for receiving the indents on the 1785 requisition or making them receivable on the 1786 requisition. Persuaded by the reasonableness of this statement, the delegates enclosed it in their letter of 22 July 1787 to Beverley Randolph, and urged the state to resume specie payments to the Continental treasury (Burnett, *Letters*, VIII, 625–26; enclosure [Vi: Continental Congress Papers]). The Council of State relented only to the extent of allowing Hopkins to become a purchaser of public tobacco for a specified sum, which was to be applied to the specie portion of the quota of 1785. The restriction on specie payments for the requisition of 1786 remained in effect (Jones to JM, 6 July 1787 and n. 3; *JCSV*, IV, 132; Beverley Randolph to Virginia Delegates, 3 Aug. 1787, Executive Letter Book, pp. 142–44; Hopkins to Edmund Randolph, 1 Nov.

1787 [Vi: Continental Congress Papers]). Congress, as the treasury commissioners had foreseen, soon yielded to the wishes of the states by eliminating many of the requirements governing the requisition system (JM to Randolph, 7 Oct. 1787 and n. 5; Virginia Delegates to Randolph, 3 Nov. 1787).

[4]See the letters of Levi Todd, 30 Apr. 1787, Alexander Bullitt, 16 May 1787, and Benjamin Logan, 17 May 1787, to Edmund Randolph (*CVSP*, IV, 277, 284–85, 286–87). The attacks mentioned in these letters were committed by the Shawnee and Wabash tribes, who inhabited the region north of the Ohio River. The Virginia Council of State advised the Kentucky county lieutenants to organize a system of defense but not to "go without the limits of the State, except in the immediate pursuit of an invading Enemy" (*JCSV*, IV, 104–5). Lt. Gov. Beverley Randolph forwarded copies of the letters and council proceedings to the Virginia delegates on 6 June, requesting the aid of federal troops or permission for the Virginia militia to carry out an expedition at federal expense (PCC). These papers were laid before Congress on 6 July and referred to the secretary at war (William Grayson to Beverley Randolph, 7 July 1787, Burnett, *Letters*, VIII, 617). Secretary Knox submitted a gloomy report on 10 July stating that Congress was unable to provide additional troops along the western frontier owing to "the depressed state of the finances." He could only recommend that the troops already in service in that region be so distributed "as best to restrain the incursions of the savages" and that the commanding officer immediately undertake treaty negotiations with the hostile tribes. Congress agreed to these recommendations on 21 July (*JCC*, XXXII, 327–32, 370–75; XXXIII, 385–87).

[5]Richard Butler was the Indian superintendent for the northern district; Col. Josiah Harmar was the commander of U.S. forces along the Ohio.

Election of the Senate

[7 June 1787]

Dickinson moved that the members of the Senate be elected by the state legislatures.

Mr. Madison. If the motion (of Mr. Dickenson) should be agreed to, we must either depart from the doctrine of proportional representation; or admit into the Senate a very large number of members. The first is inadmissible, being evidently unjust. The second is inexpedient. The use of the Senate is to consist in its proceeding with more coolness, with more system, & with more wisdom, than the popular branch. Enlarge their number and you communicate to them the vices which they are meant to correct. He differed from Mr. D. who thought that the additional number would give additional weight to the body. On the contrary it appeared to him that their weight would be in an inverse ratio to their number. The example of the Roman Tribunes was applicable. They lost their influence and power, in proportion as their number was augmented. The reason seemed to be obvious: They were appointed to take care of the popular interests & pretensions at Rome, because the people by reason of their numbers could not act in concert; were liable to fall into factions among themselves, and to become a prey to their aristocratic adversaries. The more the representatives of the people therefore were multiplied, the more they partook of the infirmities of their constituents, the more liable they became to be divided among themselves either from their own indiscretions or the artifices of the opposite factions, and of course the less capable of fulfilling their trust. When the weight of a set of men depends merely on their personal characters; the greater the number the greater the weight. When it depends on the degree of political authority lodged in them the smaller the number the greater the weight. These considerations might perhaps be combined in the intended Senate; but the latter was the material one.[1]

Ms (DLC).

[1]King's version:

"*Madison*—We are about to form a national Govt. and therefore must abandon Ideas founded alone in the plan of confedn. the Senate ought to come from, & represent, the Wealth of the nation, and this being the Rule, the amendment cannot be adopted—besides the numbers will be too large—the Proofs of History establish this position, that delegated power will have the most weight & consequence in the hands of a few—when the Roman Tribunes were few, they checked the Senate; when multiplied, they divided, were weak, ceased to be that Guard to the people which was expected in their institution" (Farrand, *Records*, I, 158).

Lansing's version:

"Maddison—If each State retained its Sovereignty an Equality of Suffrage would be proper, but not so now" (Strayer, *Delegate from N.Y.*, p. 38).

[7 June 1787]

Mr. Madison could as little comprehend in what manner family weight, as desired by Mr. D. would be more certainly conveyed into the Senate through elections by the State Legislatures, than in some other modes. The true question was in what mode the best choice wd. be made? If an election by the people, or thro' any other channel than the State Legislatures promised as uncorrupt & impartial a preference of merit, there could surely be no necessity for an appointment by those Legislatures. Nor was it apparent that a more useful check would be derived thro' that channel than from the people thro' some other. The great evils complained of were that the State Legislatures run into schemes of paper money &c. whenever solicited by the people, & sometimes without even the sanction of the people. Their influence then, instead of checking a like propensity in the National Legislature, may be expected to promote it. Nothing can be more contradictory than to say that the Natl. Legislature witht. a proper check, will follow the example of the State Legislatures, & in the same breath, that the State Legislatures are the only proper check.

Ms (DLC).

Power of the Legislature to Negative State Laws

[8 June 1787]

Charles Pinckney moved "'that the National Legislature shd. have authority to negative all Laws which they shd. judge to be improper'" (Farrand, *Records*, I, 164). This motion was a substitute for the qualified negative contained in the sixth resolution of the Virginia Plan.

Mr. Madison seconded the motion. He could not but regard an indefinite power to negative legislative acts of the States as absolutely necessary to a perfect system. Experience had evinced a constant tendency in the States to encroach on the federal authority; to violate national Treaties; to infringe the rights & interests of each other; to oppress the weaker party within their respective jurisdictions. A negative was the mildest expedient that could be devised for preventing these mischeifs. The existence of such a check would prevent attempts to commit them. Should no such precaution be engrafted, the only remedy wd. lie in an appeal to coercion. Was such a remedy eligible? Was it practicable? Could the national resources, if exerted to the utmost enforce a national decree agst. Massts. abetted perhaps by several of her neighbours? It wd. not be possible. A small proportion of the Community, in a compact situation, acting on the defensive, and at one of its extremities might at any time bid defiance to the National authority. Any Govt. for the U. States formed on the supposed practicability of using force agst. the unconstitutional proceedings[1] of the States, wd. prove as visionary & fallacious as the Govt. of Congs. The negative wd. render the use of force unnecessary. The States cd. of themselves then pass no operative act, any more than one branch of a Legislature where there are two branches, can proceed without the other. But in order to give the negative this efficacy, it must extend to all cases. A discrimination wd. only be a fresh source of contention between the two authorities. In a word, to recur to the illustrations borrowed from the planetary system, This prerogative of the General Govt. is the great pervading principle that must controul the centrifugal tendency of the States; which without it, will continually fly out of their proper orbits and destroy the order & harmony of the political System.[2]

Ms (DLC).

[1]JM substituted "unconstitutional proceedings" for "misdeeds" before Eppes copied the Debates.

[2]Yates's version:

"Mr. Madison wished that the line of jurisprudence could be drawn—he would be for it—but upon reflection he finds it impossible, and therefore he is for the amendment. If the clause remains without the amendment it is inefficient—The judges of the state must give the state laws their operation, although the law abridges the rights of the national government—how is it to be repealed? By the power who made it? How shall you compel them? By force? To prevent this disagreeable expedient, the power of negativing is absolutely necessary—this is the only attractive principle which will retain its centrifugal force, and without this the planets will fly from their orbits" (Farrand, *Records*, I, 169).

King's version:

"*Madison*—The amendment or a reconsideration for discussion seems necessary—I am of opinion that the Genl. Govt. will not be able to compel the large and important State to rescind a popular law passed by their Legislature. If this power does not rest in the national Legisl: there will be wanting a check to the centrifugal Force which constantly operates in the several states to force them off from a common Centre, or a national point" (ibid., I, 171).

Lansing's version:

"*Madison*—wished the precise Line of Power could be ascertained—But totally impracticable—for if a Dispute arises the State Judiciaries are compelled to expound the Laws so as to give those of the individual State an Operation—National Government *centrifugal*" (Strayer, *Delegate from N.Y.*, p. 40).

[8 June 1787]

Bedford asserted that the negative would enable the large states to "crush the small ones" and that it would keep state laws suspended until reviewed by the national legislature, which would have to sit continuously (Farrand, *Records*, I, 167–68).

Mr. Madison observed that the difficulties which had been started were worthy of attention and ought to be answered before the question was put. The case of laws of urgent necessity must be provided for by some emanation of the power from the Natl. Govt. into each State so far as to give a temporary assent at least. This was the practice in Royal Colonies before the Revolution and would not have been inconvenient; if the supreme power of negativing had been faithful to the American interest, and had possessed the necessary information. He supposed that the negative might be very properly lodged in the senate alone, and that the more numerous & expensive branch therefore might not be obliged to sit constantly. He asked Mr. B. what would be the consequence to the small States of a dissolution of the Union wch. seemed likely to happen if no effectual substitute was made for the defective System existing, and he did not conceive any effectual system could be substituted on any other basis than that of a proportional suffrage? If the large States possessed the Avarice & ambition with which they were charged, would the small ones in their neighbourhood, be more secure when all controul of a Genl. Govt was withdrawn.[1]

Ms (DLC).

[1]Yates's version:

"Mr. Madison confesses it is not without its difficulties on many accounts—some may be removed, others modified, and some are unavoidable. May not this power be vested in the senatorial branch? they will probably be always sitting. Take the question on the other ground, who is to determine the line when drawn in doubtful cases? The state legislatures cannot, for they will be partial in support of their own powers—no tribunal can be found. It is impossible that the articles of confederation can be amended—they are too tottering to be invigorated—nothing but the present system, or something like it, can restore the peace and harmony of the country" (Farrand, *Records*, I, 170–71).

To James Monroe

PHILADA. June 10. 1787.

DEAR SIR

I have been discouraged from answering sooner your favor of   [1] by the bar which opposes such communications as I should incline not less to make than you must do to receive. One of the earliest rules established by the Convention restrained the members from any disclosure whatever of its proceedings, a restraint which will not probably be removed for some time. I think the rule was a prudent one not only as it will effectually secure the requisite freedom of discussion, but as it will save both the Convention and the Community from a thousand erroneous and perhaps mischievous reports. I feel notwithstanding great mortification in the disappointment it obliges me to throw on the curiosity of my friends. The Convention is now as full as we expect it to be unless a report should be true that Rh. Island has it in contemplation to make one of the party.[2] If her deputies should bring with them the complexion of the State, their company will not add much to our pleasure, or to the progress of the business. Eleven States are on the floor. All the deputies from Virga. remain except Mr. Wythe who was called away some days ago by information from Williamsburg concerning the increase of his lady's ill health. I had a letter by the last packet from Mr. Short, but not any from Mr. Jefferson. The latter had sett out on his tour to the South of France. Mr. Short did not expect his return for a considerable time. The last letter from him assigned as the principal motive to this ramble, the hope that some of mineral springs in that quarter might contribute to restore his injured wrist. Present me most respectfully to Mrs. Monroe. Yrs. Affecy.

JS. MADISON JR.

RC (DLC). Addressed and franked by JM.

[1]JM left the space blank. The letter was Monroe's to JM, 23 May 1787 (*PJM*, IX, 416–17).

[2]The Rhode Island House of Deputies had passed a resolution in May 1787 authorizing a delegation to the Federal Convention, but the measure died when the upper house disapproved. A few weeks later, the Assistants (upper chamber) reconsidered their vote and sent a bill back to the lower chamber providing for a delegation; but the deputies refused to consent (Polishook, *Rhode Island and the Union*, pp. 184–85).

From the Reverend James Madison

June 11th. 1787

Dear Col.

I am greatly indebted to you for the Books you were so good as to send me by Mr Griffin, particularly the Observations of Mr Adams; not however that he has made a Convert of me, any more than I trust, he has of you, to what appears to be the secret Design of his Work. Is it probable, my dear Friend, that all that Trouble was taken, & Shew of Learning displayed, merely to refute the Opinion of Mr. Turgot—an opinion suffly. innocent in itself, and which had no, or but very few Advocates in America, if we judge from the Govts. wch. have been established. Mr. Adams is greatly mortified that our Executives have not a Negative upon the Legislatures—and thinks the British System of Govt., beyond Comparison, the wisest & the best ever yet invented. He must wish then to introduce a similar Govt. into America. His Executive (wch. he also thinks shd be single) must be a King, the Senate—Lords, the House of Delegates—Plebeians or Commons. Thus under the Mask of attacking M. Turgot, he seems insidiously attempting, notwithstanding now & then a saving Clause, to overturn our present Constitutions, or at least to sow the Seeds of Discontent. I beleive, if this Supposition be just, it is the first Instance wherein a public Minister at a foreign Court, has been foremost in openly & avowedly plotting Revolutions in the Govt. he represents. I fear his Optics have been too weak to withstand the Glare of European Courts. Their Air may have corrupted the plain Republican, & lest he should be farther Mortified, I think Congress wd. do well, to give him as speedily as possible, the oppy. of breathing once more the purer American Air. Jefferson thanks his God, that the Days of Kings, Nobles & Priests are almost past. Adams must trust in his, that they will be seen to rise in America with new Splendor; which Sentiment is the most worthy of a Man of common Sense, I will not say political Knowledge, we need not determine. The Truth is I beleive—the Outlines of the American Govts. are as well drawn, in Order to promote public & private Happiness, & to secure that greatest possible Portion of Liberty which we have so successfully contended for, as human sagacity could possibly devise. These Outlines only require to be skilfully filled up—perhaps in some Cases to be somewhat extended; but as to a Renunciation of the original Plan, I hope in God, no honest, independant Man will hesitate. The least that ought to be done surely, is to make a fair Experi[men]t. This requires Time—particularly as we may reasonably expect that the rising Generation will be much better Actors upon the republican Theatre than their Predecessors.

Besides, Time is essentially necessary to give Force & Energy to any Govts. Nothing is more illusory on most Occasions, than the Use of metaphorical Language. I question whether, this Balance, wch. Adams talks so much about, has not served somewhat to mislead him. Governments must be properly balanced. But a Balance must be supported or held up, & there must also be something to be weighed in each Scale. Hence the Idea of a Monarch, King or Executive with negative Powers, holding in his all powerful Hand, the Beam—& Lords & Commons dancing up & down in each Scale, untill his Majesty takes as many of his good People out of one Scale, & throws them into the other, as will produce the desired Equipoise. Then arises a goodly Govt. admirably balanced.

There is another[1] Circumstance of much more Importance which these Admirers of British Govt. seem entirely to forget. There did exist in that Country, & indeed throughout both antient & modern Europe, from the earliest Periods, this spurious Race of Men called Nobles. They became so firmly established either thro Power or Prejudice, that to eradicate them was impossible; so that, in settling the British Govt.—the only Question could be, how shall we moderate this enormous Evil as much as possible. It could not be removed, & therefore it was wise to adopt a System, by wch. the least probable Injury should be sustained from it. Perhaps the British Govt. may be considered as having fortunely adopted that which would best temper an Evil inseperable from the Nation. But surely, notwithstanding what Adams may dream, & De Lome[2] think, it would be as rational for a healthy, robust Mountaineer to take a moderate Dose of Arsenic, or something else, in Order to reduce himself to the Temperament of a Lowlander, as for America, free & uncorrupted as she now is, to encourage a System by wch. a Race of Men might be gradually introduced, which must eventually prove a certain Poison both to public & private Happiness, tho' she might be assimilated to that Idol—Great B. Fortunate as we are in knowing no Distinction amongt Men, but such as Nature has established; singularly fortunate indeed, in being free from the most absurd & degrading Differences amongst Citizens—Differences which Ignorance & Poverty gave Birth to, & wch. Nothing but Folly & Pride would introduce or maintain—I trust the Patriots of America will ever evince to their Country & the World, not only the Resolution to maintain our present Forms of Govt.—pure as they originated—but that they will discover the Means of giving them that Energy wch. a Govt. of Law requires—& that Permanence which, if possible, may be everlasting.[3]

Thus have I said twice as much as I intended, or need have said to you. But the Subject is interesting & you see the Impressions wch. the first

From John Dawson

[12 June 1787]

DEAR SIR

After an absence of near three weeks I have just return'd to this place[1] and am favour'd with your letter of the 27 of May.[2] The prospect of a *general* convention of the States appears to me very faint, and I wish to be inform'd, whether the states assembled, or those that probably will meet, will proceed to any business. I apprehend that nothing decisive can be done, without the concurrence of the whole.

I have lately been on the south side of James River—the people, in general appear very much discontented, and I realy fear that a majority of that part of the state are in favour of paper money—neighbours to the Carolinians, (whose money had depreciated one hundred pr Cent—) they have contra[c]ted a similar way of thinking. And inattentive to the future honour and interest of the state they are friends to any measure, which will afford present relief. In Henry county the high Sheriff has not given security for the collection of the taxes, and I was told it wou'd be dangerous for any person to offer.[3] Of course no collection goes on, and they[4] people appear happy in this expedient of evading payment. In King William, the night before their May court, the court house with all the records of the county, was burnt down. Some circumstances prove that it was designedly done.[5]

You, I know, are oppos'd to the plan of incorporating towns, which in this state, has been so much in vogue, for some years past. The people in this county, convinc'd of the bad policy, intend to petition the next assembly for a repeal of the law incorporating this town.[6] I have promis'd to forward their wishes, and will thank you for any information you can give me on this subject, together with your reasons for being unfriendly to them. Are any towns in the Eastern states incorporated? Is Philadelphia? Was it before the war and how long?[7]

I had the pleasure of seeing your Father a few days since. He is very well.

RC (DLC). Addressed by Dawson. The lower portion of the last page is missing, which must have contained the signature and date. Docketed in an unknown hand: "Dawson Jno. June 12. 1787."

[1] Fredericksburg.

[2] Letter not found.

[3] Abraham Penn had been appointed sheriff of Henry County in 1783, but he apparently resigned in the spring of 1787 to run for the House of Delegates. Penn's successor, Henry Lyne, was issued a commission on 24 Dec. 1787 (*JCSV*, III, 313; IV, 154, 191; *JHDV*, Oct. 1787, pp. 15–16). Sheriffs were required to give security for the collection of taxes. If they

refused, or were unable to do so, the county court was to appoint one or more collectors who would provide the required bond (Hening, *Statutes*, XI, 66). The perennial problem of tax collection in Virginia during the 1780s is covered in *PJM*, VI, 500, 501 n. 8; VII, 32–33; and Louis Maganzin, "Economic Depression in Maryland and Virginia, 1783–1787" (Ph.D. diss., Georgetown University, 1967), pp. 203–27.

[4]Dawson obviously meant "the."

[5]The King William court met 28 May 1787, the fourth Monday of the month, as required by law (Hening, *Statutes*, XII, 407). Only the clerk's office with the records was burned, for the King William courthouse, built in 1725, is still standing. As a result of the burning of court records during the spring and summer of 1787, the General Assembly passed "An act for the relief of persons who have been or may be injured by the destruction of the records of county courts" (ibid., XII, 497–99). To implement this act the Council of State appointed commissioners on 21 June 1788 to investigate the loss of court records in New Kent and King William counties (*JCSV*, IV, 253). See also McClurg to JM, 22 Aug. 1787, n. 4.

[6]Fredericksburg had been incorporated in 1781 (Hening, *Statutes*, X, 439–43). Before the Revolution Williamsburg and Norfolk were the only "boroughs," or incorporated towns, in Virginia. Other towns that had been incorporated since the Revolution were Alexandria (1779), Winchester (1779), Richmond (1782), and Petersburg (1784). See *Hornbook of Virginia History*, pp. 31–38. The petition to repeal the Fredericksburg incorporation act, if submitted to the legislature at the October 1787 session, was unsuccessful.

[7]In 1775 there were some fifteen incorporated towns in the thirteen colonies. Boston retained the town meeting system of local government until it was incorporated in 1822. The corporation government of colonial Philadelphia came to an end in 1776. A new act of incorporation passed in March 1789 (Ernest S. Griffith, *The Modern Development of City Government in the United Kingdom and the United States* [2 vols.; London, 1927], I, 10–11; Gerard B. Warden, *Boston, 1689–1776* [Boston, 1970], pp. 73–79, 108–9, 272–73, 336–37; Edward P. Allinson and Boies Penrose, "The City Government of Philadelphia," *Johns Hopkins University Studies in Historical and Political Science*, 5th ser., I–II [1887], 31–35).

Term of the First Branch of the Legislature

[12 June 1787]

Jenifer proposed a three-year term for members of the first branch of Congress.

Mr. Madison seconded the motion for three years. Instability is one of the great vices of our republics, to be remedied. Three years will be necessary, in a Government so extensive, for members to form any knowledge of the various interests of the States to which they do not belong, and of which they can know but little from the situation and affairs of their own. One year will be almost consumed in preparing for and travelling to & from the seat of national business.[1]

Ms (DLC).

[1]Lansing's version:

"Madison—Instability of popular Government his Reason for wishing three Years.

"Distance of Extremities of Union renders it necessary. The Lessons the Representatives have to learn another Reason" (Strayer, *Delegate from N.Y.*, p. 48).

Yates's version:

"Mr. Madison was for the last amendment—observing that it will give it stability, and induce gentlemen of the first weight to engage in it" (Farrand, *Records*, I, 220).

[12 June 1787]

Gerry, replying to JM's first speech, warned that the people of New England would insist upon annual elections.

Mr. Madison observed that if the opinions of the people were to be our guide, it wd. be difficult to say what course we ought to take. No member of the Convention could say what the opinions of his Constituents were at this time; much less could he say what they would think if possessed of the information & lights possessed by the members here; & still less what would be their way of thinking 6 or 12 months hence. We ought to consider what was right & necessary in itself for the attainment of a proper Governmt. A plan adjusted to this idea will recommend itself. The respectability of this convention will give weight to their recommendation of it. Experience will be constantly urging the adoption of it, and All the most enlightened & respectable citizens will be its advocates. Should we fall short of the necessary & proper point, this influential class of Citizens will be turned against the plan, and little support[1] in opposition to them can be gained to it from the unreflecting multitude.[2]

Ms (DLC).

[1]JM heavily deleted nine or ten words following and completed the sentence as it stands.
[2]Yates's version:

"Mr. Madison. The people's opinions cannot be known, as to the particular modifications which may be necessary in the new government—In general they believe there is something wrong in the present system that requires amendment; and he could wish to make the republican system the basis of the change—because if our amendments should fail of securing their happiness, they will despair it can be done in this way, and incline to monarchy" (Farrand, *Records*, I, 220–21).

Lansing's version:

"Madison—Public Opinion fluctuating—it has no Standard—is changing Rapidly.

"Local Attachments and temporary Opinions ought to be laid aside" (Strayer, *Delegate from N.Y.*, p. 49).

Salaries for Members of the First Branch of the Legislature

[12 June 1787]

The clause of the fourth resolution providing for the members "to receive liberal stipends" was under consideration.

Mr. Madison moves to insert the words "*& fixt.*" He observed that it would be improper to leave the members of the Natl. legislature to be provided for by the State Legisls: because it would create an improper dependence; and to leave them to regulate their own wages, was an indecent thing, and might in time prove a dangerous one. He thought wheat or some other article of which the average price throughout a reasonable period precedn'g might be settled in some convenient mode, would form a proper standard.[1]

Ms (DLC).

[1] JM and Jefferson were convinced that wheat was the most suitable standard for fixing salaries. Jefferson had proposed the equivalent of two bushels as a proper daily wage for state legislators in 1783, and JM suggested a salary scale based on "the medium value of wheat" for the Kentucky constitution in 1785 (Boyd, *Papers of Jefferson*, VI, 297; *PJM*, VIII, 351).

Term of the Senate

[12 June 1787]

Mr. Madison considered 7 years as a term by no means too long. What we wished was to give to the Govt. that stability which was every where called for, and which the Enemies of the Republican form alledged to be inconsistent with its nature. He was not afraid of giving too much stability by the term of Seven years. His fear was that the popular branch would still be too great an overmatch for it. It was to be much lamented that we had so little direct experience to guide us. The Constitution of Maryland was the only one that bore any analogy to this part of the plan. In no instance had the Senate of Maryd. created just suspicions of danger from it. In some instances perhaps it may have erred by yielding to the H. of Delegates. In every instance of their opposition to the measures of the H. of D. they had had with them the suffrages of the most enlightened and impartial people of the other States as well as of their own. In the States where the Senates were chosen in the same manner as the other branches, of the Legislature, and held their seats for 4 years, the institution was found to be no check whatever agst. the[1] instabilities of the other branches. He conceived it to be of great importance that a stable & firm Govt. organized in the republican form should be held out to the people. If this be not done, and the people be left to judge of this species of Govt. by the operations of the defective Systems under which they now live, it is much to be feared the time is not distant when, in universal disgust, they will renounce the blessing which they have purchased at so dear a rate, and be ready for any change that may be proposed to them.[2]

Ms (DLC).

[1]JM heavily deleted several words and completed the sentence as it stands before Eppes copied the Debates.

[2]JM wrote here and then heavily crossed through, "He was a friend to Republican [*illegible*]," before Eppes copied the Debates.

Yates's version:

"Mr. Madison was for 7 years—Considers this branch as a check on the democracy—It cannot therefore be made too strong" (Farrand, *Records*, I, 222).

To Ambrose Madison

PHILADA. June 13th. 1787

DEAR BROTHER

Your favor of the 28th. of April, the first I have recd. from you, has but just come to hand. It gave me the first information of the indisposition of my Father. I hope he has since fully recovered, and flatter myself the more that this is the case, as you or some one else would not have left me so long unapprized of the Contrary.

I was disappointed at the arrival of 8 Hhds only.[1] Tobo. only of the best quality had sold as high as 45/. of this currency. *Old* Tobo. will still fetch that price. Mine is being now sold for 42/6. As this is considerably better than the Va. price, I wish you to lose no time in forwarding the 2 remaining Hhds. If you chuse to add others on your own account or that of any body else you may do it. Send none but of the best quality. All below that sells for 32/. only.

The event of the Election was contrary to my expectation as far as it related to Majr. Moore. Mr. Wm. Strother gave me the first acct. of it.

The Convention have been sitting several weeks. Eleven States are on the floor, including between 40 & 50 members. The rules adopted oblige me to disappoint the curiosity you will naturally feel to know something of their proceedings. I think the Session will be of considerable length. Remember me affly. to all friends. Adieu Yrs. &c.

Js. MADISON JR

RC (MH). Addressed and franked by JM. Sent "To the Care of Mr. F. Maury Fredericksbg."

[1]On 10 Feb. 1787 JM had requested his brother to send ten hogsheads of tobacco (*PJM*, IX, 259).

From Edward Carrington

Dear Sir,

I am favoured with yours of the 10th. Instant[1] and thank you for it. Be good enough to pay Major George Turner, if he is still in the City, £4.5.6 Pensylvania Currency, and, at your leisure, send me the balance of the 100 dollars by some freind who may be coming here.[2] It will, however, be unnecessary for you to put yourself to the least inconvenience to do so. Nothing yet of the remittance from South Carolina for our freind Monroe,[3] nor will the distribution of Mordicais effects take place until sometime in July. It is supposed that it will not exceed 5/. in the pound.[4]

Had the rules of the convention permitted communications from thence, you would have conferred an obligation by including me in the number of your correspondents upon the subjects of deliberation in that assembly. My curiosity is, however, perfectly suppressed by the propriety of the prohibition. Having matured your opinions and given them a collected form, they will be fairly presented to the public, and find their own advocates—but caught by detachments, and while indeed immature, they would be equally the victims of ignorance and misrepresentation. The public mind is now on the point of a favourable turn to the objects of your meeting, and, being fairly met with the result, will, I am persuaded, eventually, embrace it. Being calculated for the permanent fitness, and not the momentary habits of the country, it may at first be viewed with hesitation, but derived and patronised as it will be, its influence must extend into an adoption as the present fabric gives way. The work once well done will be done forever, but patched up in accommodation to the whim of the day, it will soon require the hand of the cobbler again, and in every unfortunate experiment, the materials are rendered the less fit for that Monument of Civil liberty which we wish to erect. Constitute a federal Government, invigorate & check it well—give it then independent powers over the Trade the Revenues, and forces of the Union, and all things that involve any relationship to foreign powers. Give it also the revisal of all State Acts. Unless it possesses a compleat controul over the State Governments, the constant effort will be to resume the delegated powers, nor do I see what inducement the federal Sovereignty can have to negative an innocent act of a State. Constitute it in such shape that, its first principles being preserved, it will be a good republic. I wish to see that system have a fair experiment—but let the liability to encroachments be rather from the federal, than the State, Governments. In the first case we shall insensibly glide into a Monarchy, in the latter nothing but Anarchy can be the consequence.

Some Gentlemen think of a total surrender of the State Sovereignties. I see not the necessity of that measure for giving us National Stability or consequence. The negative of the federal Sovereignty will effectually prevent the existence of any licentious or inconsiderate Act. And I beleive that even under a Monarchy it would be found necessary thus to continue the local administrations. General Laws would operate many particular oppressions and a general legislature would be found incompetent to the formation of local ones. The Interests of the United States may be well combined for the Common good—but the affairs of so extensive a Country are not to be thrown into one mass. An attempt to confederate upon terms materially opposed to the particular Interests would in all probability occasion a dismemberment, and in that event, within a long time yet to come, the prospects of America will be at an end as to any degree of National importance, let her fate be what it may as to freedom or Vassalage. Be good enough to present me to your honourable Collegues and beleive me to be with the Utmost sincerity Your affectionate Freind & Humble Servt.

ED. CARRINGTON

RC (DLC).

[1]Letter not found.

[2]Maj. George Turner was in Philadelphia to attend the meeting of the Society of the Cincinnati, which elected him assistant secretary-general. He had served as an officer in the Continental line from South Carolina and was captured at the fall of Charleston in 1780. Following his parole, he was appointed commissary of marine prisoners (Hume, *Washington's Correspondence Concerning . . . the Cincinnati*, pp. 308, 454–55). During the summer of 1787 Turner aspired to a position in the government of the Northwest Territory (Carrington to JM, 11 Aug. 1787; Grayson to JM, 31 Aug. 1787). Two years later he was appointed one of the three judges of the Northwest Territory (Bond, *Correspondence of John Cleves Symmes*, p. 119 n.).

[3]See JM to Monroe, 19 Apr. 1787, *PJM*, IX, 391 n. 2.

[4]See Monroe to JM, 6 Feb. 1787, and JM to Monroe, 25 Feb. 1787, *PJM*, IX, 256, 257 n. 2, 298.

Method of Choosing the Judiciary

[13 June 1787]

Charles Pinckney and Sherman moved that the judges of the supreme tribunal be appointed by the national legislature.

Mr. Madison objected to an appt. by the whole Legislature. Many of them were incompetent Judges of the requisite qualifications. They were too much influenced by their partialities. The candidate [*sic*] who was present, who had displayed a talent for business in the legislative field, who had perhaps assisted ignorant members in business of their own, or of their Constituents, or used other winning means, would without any of the essential qualifications for an expositor of the laws prevail over a competitor not having these recommendations, but possessed of every necessary accomplishment. He proposed that the appointment should be made by the Senate, which as a less numerous & more select body, would be more competent judges, and which was sufficiently numerous to justify such a confidence in them.[1]

Ms (DLC).

[1]Yates's version:
"Mr. Madison is of opinion that the second branch of the legislature ought to appoint the judiciary, which the convention agreed to" (Farrand, *Records*, I, 238).
Lansing's version:
"Madison moves second Branch to appoint" (Strayer, *Delegate from N.Y.*, p. 51).

Power of Originating Money Bills in the Legislature

[13 June 1787]

Gerry moved to prohibit the Senate from originating money bills.

Mr. Madison observed that the Commentators on the Brit: Const: had not yet agreed on the reason of the restriction on the H. of L. in money bills. Certain it was there could be no similar reason in the case before us. The Senate would be the representatives of the people as well as the 1st. branch. If they sd. have any dangerous influence over it, they would easily prevail on some member of the latter to originate the bill they wished to be passed. As the Senate would be generally a more capable sett of men, it wd. be wrong to disable them from any preparation of the business, especially of that which was most important, and in our republics, worse prepared than any other. The Gentleman in pursuance of his principle ought to carry the restraint to the *amendment*, as well as the originating of money bills, since, an addition of a given sum wd. be equivalent to a distinct proposition of it.

Ms (DLC).

Reply to the New Jersey Plan

[19 June 1787]

On 13 June the Committee of the Whole reported to the convention the amended Virginia Plan. Consideration of that report was postponed on 14 June at the request of Paterson in order that the small states might have time to prepare a plan "purely federal, and contradistinguished from the reported plan" (Farrand, *Records*, I, 240). Paterson introduced the New Jersey Plan the next day. Yates's notes leave the impression that JM was trying to block consideration of the small states' proposals by moving "for the report of the committee [the Virginia Plan], and the question may then come on whether the convention will postpone it in order to take into consideration the system now offered." However, according to the Journal and Lansing, JM only moved to commit Paterson's resolutions to the Committee of the Whole (ibid., I, 246, 241; Strayer, *Delegate from N.Y.*, p. 52). The convention agreed to consider the New Jersey Plan and the amended Virginia Plan in the Committee of the Whole "in order to place the two plans in due comparison" (Farrand, *Records*, I, 242). The next three days of debate were taken up with extensive discussion of the two proposals. After JM's speech, the New Jersey Plan was rejected in favor of the amended Virginia Plan.

Mr. Madison. Much stress had been laid by some gentlemen on the want of power in the Convention to propose any other than a *federal* plan. To what had been answered by others, he would only add, that neither of the characteristics attached to a *federal* plan would support this objection. One characteristic was that in a *federal* Government, the power was exercised not on the people individually; but on the people *collectively*, on the *States*. Yet in some instances as in piracies, captures &c. the existing Confederacy, and in many instances, the amendments to it proposed by Mr. Patterson, must operate immediately on individuals. The other characteristic was that a *federal* Govt. derived its appointments not immediately from the people, but from the States which they respectively composed. Here too were facts on the other side. In two of the States, Connect. and Rh. Island, the delegates to Congs. were chosen, not by the Legislatures, but by the people at large; and the plan of Mr. P. intended no change in this particular.[1]

It had been alledged (by Mr. Patterson), that the Confederation having been formed by unanimous consent, could be dissolved by unanimous Consent only. Does this doctrine result from the nature of compacts? Does it arise from any particular stipulation in the articles of Confederation? If we consider the federal union as analogous to the fundamental compact by which individuals compose one Society, and which must in its theoretic origin at least, have been the unanimous act of the component

55

members, it cannot be said that no dissolution of the compact can be effected without unanimous consent. A breach of the fundamental principles of the compact by a part of the Society would certainly absolve the other part from their obligations to it. If the breach of *any* article by *any* of the parties, does not set the others at liberty, it is because, the contrary is *implied* in the compact itself, and particularly by that law of it, which gives an indefinite authority to the majority to bind the whole in all cases. This latter circumstance shews that we are not to consider the federal Union as analogous to the social compact of individuals: for if it were so, a Majority would have a right to bind the rest, and even to form a new Constitution for the whole, which the Gentn: from N. Jersey would be among the last to admit. If we consider the federal Union as analogous not to the social compacts among individual men: but to the conventions among individual States, What is the doctrine resulting from these conventions? Clearly, according to the Expositors of the law of Nations, that a breach of any one article, by any one party, leaves all the other parties at liberty, to consider the whole convention as dissolved, unless they choose rather to compel the delinquent party to repair the breach. In some treaties indeed it is expressly stipulated that a violation of particular articles shall not have this consequence, and even that particular articles shall remain in force during war, which in general is understood to dissolve all subsisting Treaties. But are there any exceptions of this sort to the Articles of confederation? So far from it that there is not even an express stipulation that force shall be used to compel an offending member of the Union to discharge its duty. He observed that the violations of the federal articles had been numerous & notorious. Among the most notorious was an act of N. Jersey herself; by which she *expressly refused* to comply with a constitutional requisition of Congs.—and yielded no farther to the expostulations of their deputies, than barely to rescind her vote of refusal without passing any positive act of compliance.[2] He did not wish to draw any rigid inferences from these observations. He thought it proper however that the true nature of the existing confederacy should be investigated, and he was not anxious to strengthen the foundations on which it now stands.

Proceeding to the consideration of Mr. Patterson's plan, he stated the object of a proper plan to be twofold. 1. to preserve the Union. 2. to provide a Governmt. that will remedy the evils felt by the States both in their united and individual capacities. Examine Mr. P.s plan, & say whether it promises satisfaction in these respects.

1. Will it prevent those violations of the law of nations & of Treaties which if not prevented must involve us in the calamities of foreign wars?[3] The tendency of the States to these violations has been manifested in

sundry instances. The files of Congs. contain complaints already, from almost every nation with which treaties have been formed. Hitherto indulgence has been shewn to us. This cannot be the permanent disposition of foreign nations. A rupture with other powers is among the greatest of national calamities. It ought therefore to be effectually provided that no part of a nation shall have it in its power to bring them on the whole. The existing Confederacy does not sufficiently provide against this evil. The proposed amendment to it does not supply the omission. It leaves the will of the States as uncontrouled as ever.

2. Will it prevent encroachments on the federal authority? A tendency to such encroachments has been sufficiently exemplified among ourselves, as well in every other confederated republic antient and Modern. By the federal articles, transactions with the Indians appertain to Congs. Yet in several instances, the States[4] have entered into treaties & wars with them. In like manner no two or more States can form among themselves any treaties &[c]. without the consent of Congs. Yet Virga. & Maryd. in one instance—Pena. & N. Jersey in another, have entered into compacts, without previous application or subsequent apology. No State again can of right raise troops in time of peace without the like consent. Of all cases of the league, this seems to require the most scrupulous observance. Has not Massts, notwithstanding, the most powerful member of the Union, already raised a body of troops? Is she not now augmenting them, without having even deigned to apprize Congs. of Her intention? In fine have we not seen the public land dealt out to Cont. to bribe her acquiescence in the decree constitutionally awarded agst. her claim on the territory of Pena.? For no other possible motive can account for the policy of Congs. in that measure?[5] If we recur to the examples of other confederacies, we shall find in all of them the same tendency of the parts to encroach on the authority of the whole. He then reviewed the Amphyctionic & Achæan confederacies among the antients; and the Helvetic, Germanic & Belgic among the moderns, tracing their analogy to the U. States—in the constitution and intent[6] of their federal authorities—in the tendency of the particular members to usurp on these authorities; and to bring confusion & ruin on the whole.[7] He observed that the plan of Mr. Pat——son besides omitting a controul over the States as a general defence of the federal prerogatives[8] was particularly defective in two of its provisions. 1. Its ratification was not to be by the people at large, but by the *legislatures*. It could not therefore render the Acts of Congs. in pursuance of their powers, even legally *paramount* to the Acts of the States. 2. It gave to the federal Tribunal an appellate jurisdiction only—even in the criminal cases enumerated. The necessity of any such provision supposed a danger of

undue acquittals in the State tribunals. Of what avail cd. an appellate tribunal be, after an acquittal? Besides in most if not all of the States, the Executives have by their respective *Constitutions* the right of pardg. How could this be taken from them by a *legislative* ratification only?

3. Will it prevent trespasses of the States on each other? Of these enough has been already seen. He instanced Acts of Virga. & Maryland which give a preference to their own Citizens in cases where the Citizens of other States are entitled to equality of privileges by the Articles of Confederation. He considered the emissions of paper money & other kindred measures as also aggressions. The States relatively to one another being each of them either Debtors or Creditor; The Creditor States must suffer unjustly from every emission by the debtor States. We have seen retaliating acts on this subject which threatened danger not to the harmony only, but the tranquility of the Union. The plan of Mr. Patterson, not giving even a negative on the Acts of the States, left them as much at liberty as ever to execute their unrighteous projects agst. each other.

4. Will it secure the internal tranquility of the States themselves? The insurrections in Massts. admonished all the States of the danger to which they were exposed. Yet the plan of Mr. P. contained no provisions for supplying the defect of the Confederation on this point. According to the Republican theory indeed, Right & power being both vested in the majority, are held to be synonimous. According to fact & experience, a minority may in an appeal to force be an overmatch for the majority. 1. If the minority happen to include all such as possess the skill & habits of military life, with such as possess the great pecuniary resources, one third may conquer the remaining two thirds. 2. One third[9] of those who participate in the choice of rulers may be rendered a majority by the accession of those whose poverty disqualifies them from a suffrage, & who for obvious reasons may be more ready to join the standard of sedition than that of the established Government. 3. Where slavery exists, the Republican Theory becomes still more fallacious.

5. Will it secure a good internal legislation & administration to the particular States? In developing the evils which vitiate the political system of the U.S. it is proper to take into view those which prevail within the States individually as well as those which affect them collectively: Since the former indirectly affect the whole; and there is great reason to believe that the pressure of them had a full share in the motives which produced the present Convention. Under this head he enumerated and animadverted on 1. the multiplicity of the laws passed by the several States. 2. the mutability of their laws. 3. the injustice of them. 4. the impotence of them: observing that Mr. Patterson's plan contained no remedy for this

dreadful class of evils; and could not therefore be received as an adequate provision for the exigences of the Community.

6. Will it secure the Union agst. the influence of foreign powers over its members. He pretended not to say that any such influence had yet been tried: but it was naturally to be expected that occasions would produce it. As lessons which claimed particular attention, he cited the intrigues practised among the Amphyctionic Confederates first by the Kings of Persia, and afterwards fatally by Philip of Macedon: Among the Achæans, first by Macedon & afterwards no less fatally by Rome: Among the Swiss by Austria, France & the lesser neighbouring powers: among the members of the Germanic Body by France, England, Spain & Russia: And in the Belgic Republic, by all the great neighbouring powers. The plan of Mr. Patterson, not giving to the general Councils any negative on the will of the particular States, left the door open for the like pernicious machinations among ourselves.

7. He begged the smaller States which were most attached to Mr. Pattersons plan to consider the situation in which it would leave them. In the first place they would continue to bear the whole expence of maintaining their Delegates in Congress. It ought not to be said that if they were willing to bear this burden, no others had a right to complain. As far as it led the small States to forbear keeping up a representation, by which the public business was delayed, it was evidently a matter of common concern. An examination of the minutes of Congress would satisfy every one that the public business had been frequently delayed by this cause; and that the States most frequently unrepresented in Congs. were not the larger States. He reminded the convention of another consequence of leaving on a small State the burden of maintaining a Representation in Congs. During a considerable period of the War, one of the Representatives of Delaware, in whom alone before the signing of the Confederation the entire vote of that State and after that event one half of its vote, frequently resided, was a Citizen & Resident of Pena. and held an office in his own State incompatible with an appointment from it to Congs. During another period, the same State was represented by three delegates two of whom were citizens of Penna. and the third a Citizen of New Jersey.[10] These expedients must have been intended to avoid the burden of supporting delegates from their own State. But whatever might have been the cause, was not in effect the vote of one State doubled, and the influence of another increased by it? In the 2d. place the coercion, on which the efficacy of the plan depends, can never be exerted but on themselves. The larger States will be impregnable, the smaller only can feel the vengeance of it. He illustrated the position by the history of the Amphyctionic

Confederates: and the ban of the German Empire. It was the cobweb wch. could entangle the weak, but would be the sport of the strong.

8. He begged them to consider the situation in which they would remain in case their pertinacious adherence to an inadmissible plan, should prevent the adoption of any plan. The contemplation of such an event was painful; but it would be prudent to submit to the task of examining it at a distance, that the means of escaping it might be the more readily embraced. Let the Union of the States be dissolved, and one of two consequences must happen. Either the States must remain individually independent & sovereign; or two or more Confederacies must be formed among them. In the first event would the small States be more secure agst. the ambition & power of their larger neighbours, than they would be under a general Government pervading with equal energy every part of the Empire, and having an equal interest in protecting every part agst. every other part? In the second, can the smaller expect that their larger neighbours would confederate with them on the principle of the present confederacy, which gives to each member, an equal suffrage; or that they would exact less severe concessions from the smaller States, than are proposed in the scheme of Mr. Randolph?

The great difficulty lies in the affair of Representation; and if this could be adjusted, all others would be surmountable. It was admitted by both the gentlemen from N. Jersey, (Mr. Brearly and Mr. Patterson) that it would not be *just to allow Virga.* which was 16 times as large as Delaware an equal vote only. Their language was that it would not be *safe for Delaware* to allow Virga. 16 times as many votes. The expedient proposed by them was that all the States should be thrown into one mass and a new partition be made into 13 equal parts. Would such a scheme be practicable? The dissimilarities existing in the rules of property, as well as in the manners, habits and prejudices of the different States, amounted to a prohibition of the attempt. It had been found impossible for the power of one of the most absolute princes in Europe (K. of France), directed by the wisdom of one of the most enlightened and patriotic Ministers (Mr. Neckar) that any age has produced, to equalize in some points only the different usages & regulations of the different provinces. But admitting a general amalgamation and repartition of the States, to be practicable, and the danger apprehended by the smaller States from a proportional representation to be real; would not a particular and voluntary coalition of these with their neighbours, be less inconvenient to the whole community, and equally effectual for their own safety. If N. Jersey or Delaware conceived that an advantage would accrue to them from an equalization of the States, in which case they would necessaryly form a junction with their neighbours, why might not this end be attained by leaving them at liberty by the Constitution to form such a junction whenever they pleased? And why should they wish to obtrude a like arrangement on all the States, when it was, to say the least, extremely difficult, would be obnoxious to many of the States, and when neither the inconveniency, nor the benefit of the expedient to themselves, would be lessened, by confining it to themselves. The prospect of many new States to the Westward was another consideration of importance. If they should come into the Union at all, they would come when they contained but few inhabitants. If they shd. be entitled to vote according to their proportions of inhabitants, all would be right & safe. Let them have an equal vote, and a more objectionable minority than ever might give law to the whole.[11]

Ms (DLC).

[1]JM repeated this point in *The Federalist* No. 40, where he denied that the convention had exceeded its powers.

[2]See *PJM*, VIII, 506–7; IX, 25.

[3]Beginning here and continuing through the fifth point in his enumeration, JM drew extensively from his Vices of the Political System (*PJM*, IX, 348–57).

[4]JM originally wrote "in question Georgia"—then deleted it before Eppes copied the Debates. Yates's, Lansing's, and King's versions of JM's speech all contain this reference to Georgia.

[5]See *PJM*, IX, 61–62.

[6]JM may have meant to write "extent."

[7]See Notes on Ancient and Modern Confederacies, April–June? 1786, *PJM*, IX, 4–22.

[8]Some time after Eppes copied the Debates JM interlined "besides... prerogatives."

[9]JM originally wrote "or less," which he deleted before Eppes copied the Debates.

[10]Thomas McKean was chief justice of Pennsylvania from 1777 to 1799 and represented Delaware in Congress from 1774 to 1783. McKean, Samuel Wharton, also of Pennsylvania, and Philemon Dickinson of New Jersey were elected delegates to Congress from Delaware in 1782 (Madison, *Papers* [Gilpin ed.], Table of References, III, lx n. 215; John A. Munroe, "Nonresident Representation in the Continental Congress: The Delaware Delegation of 1782," *WMQ*, 3d ser., IX [1952], 166–90).

[11]Yates's version:

"Mr. Madison.—This is an important question—Many persons scruple the powers of the convention. If this remark had any weight, it is equally applicable to the adoption of either plan. The difference of drawing the powers in the one from the people and in the other from the states, does not affect the powers. There are two states in the union where the members of congress are chosen by the people. A new government must be made. Our all is depending on it; and if we have but a clause that the people will adopt, there is then a chance for our preservation. Although all the states have assented to the confederation, an infraction of any one article by one of the states is a dissolution of the whole. This is the doctrine of the civil law on treaties.

"Jersey pointedly refused complying with a requisition of congress, and was guilty of this infraction, although she afterwards rescinded her non-complying resolve. What is the object of a confederation? It is two-fold—1st, to maintain the union; 2dly, good government. Will the Jersey plan secure these points? No; it is still in the power of the confederated states to violate treaties—Has not Georgia, in direct violation of the confederation made war with the Indians, and concluded treaties? Have not Virginia and Maryland entered into a partial compact? Have not Pennsylvania and Jersey regulated the bounds of the Delaware? Has not the state of Massachusetts, at this time, a considerable body of troops in pay? Has not congress been obliged to pass a conciliatory act in support of a decision of their federal court, between Connecticut and Pennsylvania, instead of having the power of carrying into effect the judgment of their own court? Nor does the Jersey plan provide for a ratification by the respective states of the powers intended to be vested. It is also defective in the establishment of the judiciary, granting only an appellate jurisdiction, without providing for a second trial; and in case the executive of a state should pardon an offender, how will it effect the definitive judgment on appeal? It is evident, if we do not *radically* depart from a federal plan, we shall share the fate of ancient and modern confederacies. The amphyctionic council, like the American congress, had the power of judging in the *last resort* in war and peace—call out forces—send ambassadors. What was its fate or continuance? Philip of Macedon, with little difficulty, destroyed every appearance of it. The Athenian had nearly the same fate—The Helvetic confederacy is rather a league—In the German confederacy the parts are too strong for the whole—The Dutch are in a most wretched situation—weak in all its parts, and only supported by surrounding contending powers.

"The rights of individuals are infringed by many of the state laws—such as issuing paper money, and instituting a mode to discharge debts differing from the form of the contract. Has the Jersey plan any checks to prevent the mischief? Does it in any instance secure internal tranquility? Right and force, in a system like this, are synonymous terms. When force is employed to support the system, and men obtain military habits, is there no danger they may turn their arms against their employers? Will the Jersey plan prevent foreign influence? Did not Persia and Macedon distract the councils of Greece by acts of corruption? And is not Jersey and Holland at this day subject to the same distractions? Will not the plan be burthensome to the smaller states, if they have an equal representation? But how is military coercion to enforce government? True, a smaller state may be brought to obedience, or crushed; but what if one of the larger states should prove disobedient, are you sure you can by force effect a submission? Suppose we cannot agree on any plan, what will be the condition of the smaller states? Will Delaware and Jersey be safe against Pennsylvania, or Rhode-Island against Massachusetts? And how will the smaller states be situated in case of partial confederacies? Will they not be obliged to make larger concessions to the greater states? The point of representation is the great point of difference, and which the greater states cannot give up; and although there was an equalization of states, state distinctions would still exist. But this is totally impracticable; and what would be the effect of the Jersey plan if ten or twelve new states were added?" (Farrand, *Records*, I, 325–27).

Lansing's version:

"Madison—The Distinction between fœderal and national Representation—the one from the State collectively—the other from the People is not well taken—There are two States in the Union in which Delegates are chosen by the People.

"Probability of adopting Plan—We must adopt such an one as will ensure Safety—Let us have a Chance. Confederation on same ground as Compact made by a Number of Persons— If one violates it all are discharged—in Treaties it is agreed that a Breach of any is a Dissolution of all—Jersey has refused to comply with Requisitions—He is anxious to perpetuate Union—but will not consent to prolong it on its present Principles. How is Confederation observed?

"Georgia has entered into War and made Treaties in express Violation of Union.

"Virginia and Maryland entered into Compact in like Violation. Massachusetts has a regular Body of Forces without Approbation of Congress.

"The conciliatory Resolution of Congress resp[ectin]g Wioming Dicision evinces Weakness of general Government.

"The Power retained by the different States Executives of pardoning would alone defeat national Government. The Amphictionic Council had a Right of judging between Members, mulcting Aggressors—drawing out Force of States—and several other important Powers— The Confederacy was however of very short Duration. It will not be denied that the Convention has as much Power as Congress—They have exercised it in recommending a new Rule of Apportionment—11 States agreed to it" (Strayer, *Delegate from N.Y.*, pp. 68–69).

states was to act during their vacations. But the referring to this Committee all executive business as it should present itself, would require a more persevering self-denial than I supposed Congress to possess. It will be much better to make that separation by a federal act. The negative proposed to be given them on all the acts of the several legislatures is now for the first time suggested to my mind. Primâ facie I do not like it. It fails in an essential character, that the hole & the patch should be commensurate. But this proposes to mend a small hole by covering the whole garment. Not more than 1. out of 100. state-acts concern the confederacy. This proposition then, in order to give them 1. degree of power which they ought to have, gives them 99. more which they ought not to have, upon a presumption that they will not exercise the 99. But upon every act there will be a preliminary question[:] Does this act concern the confederacy? And was there ever a proposition so plain as to pass Congress without a debate? Their decisions are almost always wise; they are like pure metal. But you know of how much dross this is the result. Would not an appeal from the state judicatures to a federal court, in all cases where the act of Confederation controuled the question, be as effectual a remedy, & exactly commensurate to the defect. A British creditor, e.g. sues for his debt in Virginia; the defendant pleads an act of the state excluding him from their courts; the plaintiff urges the Confederation & the treaty made under that, as controuling the state law; the judges are weak enough to decide according to the views of their legislature. An appeal to a federal court sets all to rights. It will be said that this court may encroach on the jurisdiction of the state courts. It may. But there will be a power, to wit Congress, to watch & restrain them. But place the same authority in Congress itself, and there will be no power above them to perform the same office. They will restrain within due bounds a jurisdiction exercised by others much more rigorously than if exercised by themselves. I am uneasy at seeing that the sale of our Western lands is not yet commenced. That precious fund for the immediate extinction of our debt will I fear be suffered to slip thro' our fingers. Every delay exposes it to events which no human foresight can guard against. When we consider the temper of the people of that country, derived from the circumstances which surround them, we must suppose their *separation possible* at every moment. If they can be *retained til* their governments *become* settled & wise, they will *remain* with us always, and be a precious part of our strength & of our virtue. *But* this affair of *the Missisipi* by shewing that *Congress is capable* of hesitating on a question which proposes a *clear sacrifice* of the *western* to the *maritime states* will with difficulty be *obliterated*. The proposition of *my going to Madrid* to *try* to *recover* there the ground which has been *lost* at *New York* by the *concession* of the vote of *seven states* I should think desperate. With respect to *myself* weighing the pleasure of *the journey* & bare possibility of *success* in one scale, and the strong *probability* of *failure* and the public *disappointment directed* on *me* in the other, the latter preponderates. Add to this that *jealousy*[2] might be *excited* in the *breast* of a *person* who could find occasions of making *me uneasy.*

The late changes in the ministry here excite considerable hopes. I think we *gain in them all.* I am particularly happy at the *reentry* of *Malsherbes* into the *council.* His knolege, his integrity render his value inappreciable, and the greater *to me* because while he had no *views* of *office we* had established together the most unreserved *intimacy.* So far too *I am pleased* with *Montmorin. His* honesty proceeds from *the heart* as well as *the head* and therefore may be more surely *counted on. The king* loves *business oeconomy order* & *justice. He* wishes sincerely the good of *his people. He* is *irascible rude* & very *limited in his understanding*[,] *religious* bordering only on *bigotry. He* has no *mistress loves his queen* and is too much *governed by her. She is capricious* like *her brother and governed* by *him* devoted to *pleasure and expence not remarkable* for any other *vices or virtues. Unhappily the king* shews a propensity for the *pleasures* of the *table.* That for *drink* has *increased lately* or at least it is *become more known.* For European news in general I will refer you to my letter to Mr. Jay. Is it not possible that the occurrences in Holland may excite a desire in many of leaving that country & transferring their effects out of it? may make an opening for shifting into their hands the debts due to this country, to it's officers & farmers? It would be surely eligible. I believe Dumas,[3] if put on the watch, might alone suffice: but surely if mr. Adams should go when the moment offers. *Dumas* has been in the habit of sending his *letters open* to *me* to be *forwarded* to Mr. *Jay.* During my absence they passed through Mr. *Short's* hands who made *extracts* from them by which I see he has been recommending himself and *me* for the *money negociations in Holland.* It might be thought perhaps that *I have* encouraged *him in* this. Be assured, my dear Sir, that no such idea ever entered my head. On the contrary it is a *business* which would be the most *disagreeable to me* of all others, & for which *I am* the most *unfit person living. I do* not understand *bargaining* nor possess the *dexterity* requisite to *make* them. On the other hand Mr. *A.* whom I expressly and sincerely recommended, stands already on ground for that business which *I* could not gain in years. Pray set *me* to rights in the minds of those who may have supposed *me privy* to this proposition. En passant, I will observe with respect to Mr. *Dumas* that the death of the *C.* de *V.* places *Congress* more at *their* ease how to dispose of *him.* Our credit here has been ill treated here in public debate, and our *debt* deemed *apocriphal.* We should try to transfer this *debt* elsewhere, & leave nothing capable of exciting ill thoughts between us. I shall mention in my letter to mr. Jay a disagreeable affair in which *Mr. Barclay* has been thrown into at *Bordeaux.* [4] An honester man cannot be found, nor a *slower* nor more *indecisive one. His affairs* too are so *embarrassed and desperate* that the *public reputation* is every moment in danger of being *compromitted* with *him.* He is perfectly amiable & honest with all *this.*

By the next packet I shall be able to send you some books as also your watch & pedometer. The two last are not yet done. To search for books and forward them to Havre will require more time than I had between my return & the departure of this packet. You did perfectly right as to the paiment by the Mr. Fitzhughs. Having been a witness heretofore to the divisions in Congress on the subject of their foreign ministers, it would be a weakness in me to suppose none with respect to myself, or to count with any confidence on the renewal of my commission, which expires on the 10th day of March next: and the more so as, instead of requiring the disapprobation of 7. states as formerly, that of one suffices for a recall when Congress consists of only 7. states, 2 when of 8. &c which I suppose to be habitually their numbers at present. Whenever I leave this place, it will be necessary to begin my arrangements 6. months before my departure: and these, once fairly begun and under way, and my mind set homewards, a change of purpose could hardly take place. If it should be the desire of Congress that I should continue still longer, I could wish to know it at farthest by the packet which will sail from New York in September. Because were I to put off longer the quitting my house, selling my furniture &c I should not have time left to wind up my affairs: and having once quitted, and sold off my furniture, I could not think of establishing myself here again. I take the liberty of mentioning this matter to you not with a desire to change the purpose of Congress, but to know it in time. I have never fixed in my own mind the epoch of my return so far as shall depend on myself, but I never suppose it very distant. Probably I shall not risk a second vote on this subject. Such trifling things may draw on one the displeasure of one or two states, & thus submit one to the disgrace of a recall.

I thank you for the Paccan nuts which accompanied your letter of March. Could you procure me a copy of the bill for proportioning crimes & punishments in the form in which it was ultimately rejected by the house of delegates? Young Mr. Bannister desired me to send him regularly the Mercure de France. I will ask leave to do this thro' you, & that you will adopt such method of forwarding them to him as will save him from being submitted to postage, which they would not be worth. As a compensation for your trouble you will be free to keep them till you shall have read them. I am with sentiments of the most sincere esteem Dear Sir Your friend & servt

TH: JEFFERSON

RC (DLC); FC (DLC: Jefferson Papers). Italicized words are those encoded by Jefferson using the code he sent JM on 11 May 1785. Jefferson's FC is accompanied by a single sheet listing the coded words.

[1]JM had sent the 18 and 19 Mar. 1787 letters to Jefferson via John Adams in London.
[2]In code, "jelosey."
[3]Charles G. F. Dumas was the unofficial agent for the U.S. at The Hague.
[4]Coded phonetically, "Bordo." Jefferson omitted the place Barclay had been "thrown into." Jefferson explained the circumstances to John Jay in a letter written the next day: Barclay was imprisoned for debt for five days at Bordeaux (Boyd, *Papers of Jefferson*, XI, 491–92).

Relationship between Federal and State Governments

[21 June 1787]

Having rejected the New Jersey Plan, the convention now was considering the amended Virginia Plan as reported out of the Committee of the Whole on 13 June. The resolution calling for a legislature with two branches was under debate. Johnson argued the small states' view that it was necessary to give each state an equal vote in the legislature in order to preserve state sovereignty against the encroachment of the national government.

Mr. Madison was of opinion that there was 1. less danger of encroachment from the Genl. Govt. than from the State Govts. 2. that the mischeif from encroachments would be less fatal if made by the former, than if made by the latter.[1] 1. All the examples of other confederacies prove the greater tendency in such systems to anarchy than to tyranny; to a disobedience of the members than to usurpations of the federal head. Our own experience had fully illustrated this tendency. But it will be said that the proposed change in the principles & form of the Union will vary the tendency, that the genl. Govt. will have real & greater powers, and will be derived in one branch at least from the people, not from the Govts. of the States. To give full force to this objection, let it be supposed for a moment that indefinite power should be given to the Genl. Legislature, and the States reduced to corporations dependent on the Genl. Legislature; Why shd. it follow that the Genl. Govt. wd. take from the States any branch of their power as far as its operation was beneficial, and its continuance desireable to the people? In some of the States, particularly in Connecticut, all the Townships are incorporated, and have a certain limited juris-diction. Have the Representatives of the people of the Townships in the Legislature of the State ever endeavored to despoil the Townships of any part of their local authority? As far as this local authority is convenient to the people they are attached to it; and their representatives chosen by & amenable to them naturally respect their attachment to this, as much as their attachment to any other right or interest. The relation of a general Govt. to State Govts. is parallel. 2. Guards were more necessary agst. encroachments of the State Govts. on the Genl. Govt. than of the latter on the former. The great objection made agst. an abolition of the State Govts. was that the Genl. Govt. could not extend its care to all the minute objects which fall under the cognizance of the local jurisdictions. The objection as stated lay not agst. the probable abuse of the general power, but agst. the imperfect use that could be made of it throughout so great an extent of Country, and over so great a variety of objects. As far as its operation would be practicable it could not in this view be improper; as far as it would be impracticable, the conveniency of the Genl. Govt. itself would concur with that of the people in the maintenance of subordinate Gov-ernments. Were it practicable for the genl. Govt. to extend its care to every requisite object without the cooperation of the State Govts. the people would not be less free as members of one great Republic than as members of thirteen small ones. A Citizen of Delaware was not more free than a Citizen of Virginia: nor would either be more free than a Citizen of America: supposing therefore a tendency in the genl. Government to absorb the State Govts. no fatal consequence could result. Taking the reverse of the supposition, that a tendency should be left in the State Govts. towards an independence on the General Govt. and the gloomy consequences need not be pointed out. The imagination of them, must have suggested to the States the experiment we are now making to prevent the calamity, and must have formed the cheif motive with those present to undertake the arduous task.[2]

Ms (DLC).

[1]JM returned to this theme in his letter to Jefferson of 24 Oct. 1787 and in *The Federalist*, Nos. 45 and 46.

[2]Yates's version:

"Mr. Madison. I could have wished that the gentleman from Connecticut had more accurately marked his objections to the Virginia plan. I apprehended the greatest danger is from the encroachment of the states on the national government—This apprehension is justly founded on the experience of ancient confederacies, and our own is a proof of it.

"The right of negativing in certain instances the state laws, affords one security to the national government. But is the danger well founded? Have any state governments ever encroached on the corporate rights of cities? And if it was the case that the national govern-ment usurped the state government, if such usurpation was for the good of the whole, no mischief could arise.—To draw the line between the two, is a difficult task. I believe it cannot be done, and therefore I am inclined for a general government.

"If we cannot form a general government, and the states become totally independent of each other, it would afford a melancholy prospect" (Farrand, *Records*, I, 363–64).

King's version:

"Madison—The history of antient Confedys. proves that there never has existed a danger of the destruction of the State Govts. by encroachments of the Genl. Govts the converse of the proposition is true—I have therefore been assiduous to guard the Genl. from the power of the State Governments—the State Govts. regulate the conduct of their Citizens, they punish offenders—they cause Justice to be administered and do those arts wh endear the Govt. to its Citizens. The Citizens will not therefore suffer the Genl. Govt. to injure the State Govts" (ibid., I, 367).

Lansing's version:

"Madison—Legislature of States have not shewn Disposition to deprive Corporations of Priviledges—Why should they here" (Strayer, *Delegate from N.Y.*, p. 76).

Election of the First Branch of the Legislature

[21 June 1787]

Charles Cotesworth Pinckney moved that the members of the first branch of the legislature "'instead of being elected by the people, shd. be elected in such manner as the Legislature of each State should direct'" (Farrand, *Records*, I, 358).

Wilson & Madison

Agt. the Election by the Legislatures and in favor of one by the People—the Election by the States will introduce a State Influence, their interest will oppose that of the Genl. Govt: the Legislators will be not only Electors of the members of the House—but they will manage the affairs of the States—The mode of Election may be essential to the Election, this may be different in the several States—if the Legislatures appt. they will instruct, and thereby embarrass the Delegate—not so if the Election is by the people—there will be no difficulty in their Election. The Returns may be made to the Legislatures of the several States—They may judge of contested Elections.[1]

Farrand, *Records*, I, 367 (King).

[1]Yates's version:

"Mr. Madison. I oppose the motion—there are difficulties, but they may be obviated in the details connected with the subject" (ibid., I, 364).

Term of the First Branch of the Legislature

[21 June 1787]

Ellsworth moved to substitute annual for triennial elections in the first branch of the legislature.

Mr. Madison was persuaded that annual elections would be extremely inconvenient and apprehensive that biennial would be too much so: he did not mean inconvenient to the electors; but to the representatives. They would have to travel seven or eight hundred miles from the distant parts of the Union; and would probably not be allowed even a reimbursement of their expences. Besides, none of those who wished to be re-elected would remain at the seat of Governmt.; confiding that their absence would not affect them. The members of Congs. had done this with few instances of disappointment. But as the choice was here to be made by the people themselves who would be much less complaisant to individuals, and much more susceptible of impressions from the presence of a Rival candidate,[1] it must be supposed that the members from the most distant States would travel backwards & forwards at least as often as the elections should be repeated. Much was to be said also on the time requisite for new Members who would always form a large proportion, to acquire that knowledge of the affairs of the States in general without which their trust could not be usefully discharged.

Ms (DLC).

[1] JM interlined here "than the Legislatures had been," but he evidently tried to erase it.

From Philip Mazzei

PARIGI, 22. Giugno 1787.

CARO E STIMATO AMICO,

Alquanto infermo di corpo, e più di spirito, vi scrivo in fretta pochi versi, per ringraziarvi delle tante prove d'amicizia che mi avete dato finora, per pregarvi di continovarmele in riguardo al mio bisogno più che al mio merito, e per includervi quella porzione del mio libro che è già stampata. Ò ricevuto, a poca distanza l'una dall'altra, le 3 lettere che mi avete favorito da New-York, delle quali mi ricordo il contenuto, sebbene non l'abbia presenti onde trascriverne le date.[1] Sul particolare di Dohrman, sarà per me un gran sollievo il sollecito saldo de suoi conti col Congresso,

WILLIAM PATERSON
Portrait by Mrs. B. S. Church.
(Courtesy of the Art Museum,
Princeton University.)

ALEXANDER HAMILTON
Portrait by John Trumbull.
(Courtesy of Yale University Art
Gallery.)

GOUVERNEUR AND ROBERT MORRIS
Portrait by Charles Willson Peale. (Courtesy of the Pennsylvania
Academy of the Fine Arts.)

RUFUS KING, U.S. Sen. 1792.

RUFUS KING
Portrait by John Trumbull.
(Courtesy of Yale University A
Gallery.)

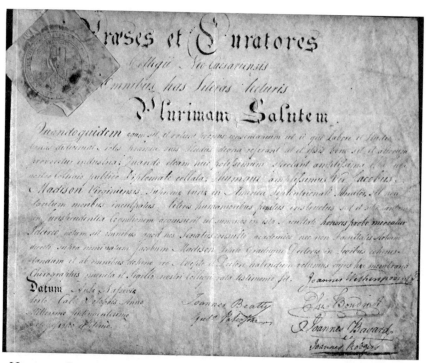

Honorary Degree of Doctor of Laws awarded to Madison. Latin diploma conferred in absentia by the College of New Jersey on 26 September 1787. (Courtesy of Princeton University Archives.)

The first page of Madison's Notes on Debates at the Federal Convention. (Courtesy of the Library of Congress.)

purchè mi ceda immediatamente (al prezzo della piazza) un fondo bastante a bilanciare il mio credito, il quale sarà dai Fratelli Van Staphorst accettato in pagamento del mio debito con essi, voltandolo in testa loro, conforme vi notificai nella mia precedente. Vi prego dunque di procurare al mio spirito questo sollievo il più presto possibile.

L'infermità del mio corpo è una conseguenza dell'abbattimento di spirito, procedente da varie cause, la principale delle quali è la continovata serie di lugubri notizie dalla nostra cara Patria, che le vostre lettere pur troppo mi confermano. Di grazia non mi ritardate neppure un giorno la notizia del primo raggio di futuro bene. Se i miei compatriotti non vogliono adattarsi alle circostanze, preferendo una prudente e saggia economia alla meschina disprezzabil soddisfazione di soddisfare l'indiscrete voglie giornaliere; se non vogliono darsi l'incomodo di riflettere alla nobile, durevole, incomparabil soddisfazione di sacrificare i frivoli appetiti al dover d'uomo giusto e di buon cittadino; se il frutto di un'acquisto fatto col sangue di tanti eroi dev'essere il disonor della Patria, non vi aspettate, Amico, di ricevere molte più lettere scritte di mia mano. Addio, il soggetto è troppo triste, e la mia mente non resiste. Tutto vostro,

FILIPPO MAZZEI.

P.S. Avevo negletto di parlarvi di ciò che riguarda il mio libro. La rimostranza è giunta in tempo, e ve ne ringrazio di vero cuore. Non giudicate della carta, nè dell'impressione dai foglj che vi mando, perchè son prove. Ò fatto cucire quei che contengono la prima parte, ai quali unisco i primi 4 della seconda, che è tutto ciò che ci è di stampato finora. Vi mando l'introduzione manoscritta. La seconda parte conterrà la confutazione dei due Abati, Mably e Raynal. Saranno 3. parti in vece di 4. La terza conterrà la descrizione del presente e il prospetto dell'avvenire, tratterà delle finanze, delle cause 𝄐 cui sono in sì cattivo stato, del denaro di carta, dei selvaggj, dei cincinnati &c.[2] Potrei io sperare che fosse tradotto in Inglese, sotto la vostra inspezione, arricchito da qualche vostra aggiunta, purgato d'errori, e stampato costà in modo che potessi io ricavarne qualche vantaggio? Volevo mandarvi l'originale italiano, ma non ò potuto copiarlo. Procurerò di mandarvelo quanto più presto potrò. Vi prego di dirmi quanti esemplari potrò mandare del francese, per esser venduti per mio conto. Di nuovo, addio.

CONDENSED TRANSLATION

Mazzei is indisposed but sends the introductory part of his book, which has recently been printed. He has received three letters from JM addressed from New York. The settlement of the Dohrman claims will relieve some of Mazzei's distress if enough money is remitted to the Van Staphorst brothers to cover his debt to them. His poor health is owing to a spiritual despondency caused by a variety of problems, including reports of distress in the United States. Mazzei hopes that Americans will forego frivolous whims and follow the course of virtuous men. He hints that further news of dishonorable conduct in America will cause unbearable personal suffering. In the postscript, Mazzei mentions receipt of JM's Memorial and Remonstrance. His book is only in the first stages of printing. The second part will have a confutation of Mably and Raynal. A third section will describe the United States at present and give a prospectus of the future, including remarks on paper money, Indians, and the Society of the Cincinnati. Mazzei hopes JM will supervise an English translation, enriching the text with some additions of his own. Mazzei intended to send the text in the original Italian but cannot. JM is asked to speculate upon the number of copies of the French text Americans will buy.

RC (DLC).

[1] None of JM's letters has been found.

[2] Mazzei's *Recherches historiques et politiques sur les États-Unis* was published in four volumes, the first of which was a history of the U.S., the second a rebuttal of Mably, the third a refutation of Raynal, and the fourth a description of the current situation of the U.S. See Mazzei to JM, 14 Aug. 1786, *PJM*, IX, 100–101, 103 n. 1.

Salaries for Members of the First Branch of the Legislature

[22 June 1787]

The clause in the report of 13 June providing that the members of the first branch of the legislature "receive fixed stipends... to be paid out of the National-Treasury" was under debate (Farrand, *Records*, I, 228).

Mr. Madison concurred in the necessity of preserving the compensations for the Natl. Govt. independent on the State Govts. but at the same time approved of *fixing* them by the Constitution, which might be done by taking a standard which wd. not vary with circumstances. He disliked particularly the policy suggested by Mr. Wiliamson of leaving the members from the poor States beyond the Mountains, to the precarious & parsimonious support of their constituents. If the Western States hereafter arising should be admitted into the Union, they ought to be considered as equals & as brethren. If their representatives were to be associated in the Common Councils, it was of common concern that such provisions should be made as would invite the most capable and respectable characters into the service.[1]

Ms (DLC).

[1]Yates's version:

"Mr. Madison. Our attention is too much confined to the present moment, when our regulations are intended to be perpetual. Our national government must operate for the good of the whole, and the people must have a general interest in its support; but if you make its legislators subject to and at the mercy of the state governments, you ruin the fabric—and whatever new states may be added to the general government the expence will be equally borne" (Farrand, *Records*, I, 378).

[22 June 1787]

Wilson moved that in place of fixed stipends the salaries be determined by the national legislature.

Mr. Madison. I oppose this motion. Members are too much interested in the question. Besides, it is indecent that the legislature should put their hands in the public purse to convey it into their own.[1]

Farrand, *Records*, I, 378 (Yates).

[1]JM did not originally report this speech. Paraphrasing Yates, he inserted it later: "Mr. Madison thought the members of the Legisl: too much interested to ascertain their own compensation. It wd. be indecent to put their hands into the public purse for the sake of their own pockets" (Ms [DLC]).

Members of the First Branch of the Legislature Barred from Federal Offices

[22 June 1787]

Gorham moved to strike out that part of the third resolution of the report of 13 June making a member ineligible to hold any office "under the national government for the space of one year after" the member's term of service expired (Farrand, *Records*, I, 228).

Mr. Madison. Some gentlemen give too much weight and others too little to this subject. If you have no exclusive clause, there may be danger of creating offices or augmenting the stipends of those already created, in order to gratify some members if they were not excluded. Such an instance has fallen within my own observation. I am therefore of opinion, that no office ought to be open to a member, which may be created or augmented while he is in the legislature.

Farrand, *Records*, I, 380 (Yates).

[23 June 1787]

Mr. Madison renewed his motion yesterday made[1] & waved to render the members of the 1st. branch "ineligible during their term of service, & for one year after—to such offices only as should be established, or the emoluments thereof, augmented by the Legislature of the U. States during the time of their being members." He supposed that the unnecessary creation of offices, and increase of salaries, were the evils most experienced, & that if the door was shut agst. them, it might properly be left open for the appointt. of members to other offices as an encouragemt. to the Legislative service.[2]

Ms (DLC).

[1]Although there is no record of such a formal motion by JM on 22 June, see his brief remarks on the subject recorded by Yates for that day. JM himself noted the absence of a recorded motion in an undated memorandum (ibid.; Farrand, *Records*, I, 390).

[2]Lansing's version:

"Madison moves after *established* insert *or Emoluments whereof shall have been augmented by the Legislature of the United States during the Time they have been Members or within one Year thereafter*—He wishes Executive to have Appt of Officers—He thinks it necessary to hold out Inducements to Men of first Fortune to become Members" (Strayer, *Delegate from N.Y.*, p. 79).

Yates's version:

"Mr. Madison then moved, that after the word *established*, be added, *or the emoluments whereof shall have been augmented by the legislature of the United States, during the time they were members thereof, and for one year thereafter*" (Farrand, *Records*, I, 391).

[23 June 1787]

Mr. Madison had been led to this motion as a middle ground between an eligibility in all cases, and an absolute disqualification. He admitted the probable abuses of an eligibility of the members, to offices, particularly within the gift of the Legislature. He had witnessed the partiality of such bodies to their own members, as had been remarked of the Virginia assembly by his colleague (Col. Mason). He appealed however to him, in turn to vouch another fact not less notorious in Virginia, that the backwardness of the best citizens to engage in the Legislative service gave but too great success to unfit characters. The question was not to be viewed on one side only. The advantages & disadvantages on both ought to be fairly compared. The objects to be aimed at were to fill all offices with the fittest characters, & to draw the wisest & most worthy citizens into the Legislative service. If on one hand, public bodies were partial to their own members; on the other they were as apt to be misled by taking characters on report, or the authority of patrons and dependents. All who had been concerned in the appointment of strangers on those recommedations must be sensible of this truth. Nor wd. the partialities of such Bodies be obviated by disqualifying their own members. Candidates for office would hover round the seat of Govt. or be found among the residents there, and practise all the means of courting the favor of the members. A great proportion of the appointments made by the States were evidently brought about in this way. In the general Govt. the evil must be still greater, the characters of distant states, being much less known throughout the U. States than those of the distant parts of the same State. The elections by Congress had generally turned on men living at the seat of the fedl Govt. or in its neighbourhood. As to the next object, the impulse to the Legislative service, was evinced by experience to be in general too feeble with those best qualified for it. This inconveniency wd. also be more felt in the Natl. Govt. than in the State Govts. as the sacrifices reqd. from the distant members, wd. be much greater, and the pecuniary provisions, probably, more disproportiate. It wd. therefore be impolitic to add fresh objections to the Legislative service by an absolute disqualification of its members. The point in question was whether this would be an objection with the most capable citizens. Arguing from experience he concluded that it would. The Legislature of Virga. would probably have been without many of its best members, if in that situation, they had been ineligible to Congs. to the Govt. & other honorable offices of the State.[1]

Ms (DLC).

[1]JM's version may be a blend of two separate speeches. Yates has him speaking twice. Yates's version (first speech):

"Mr. Madison. My wish is that the national legislature be as uncorrupt as possible. I believe all public bodies are inclined, from various motives, to support its members; but it is not always done from the base motives of venality. Friendship, and a knowledge of the abilities of those with whom they associate, may produce it. If you bar the door against such attachments, you deprive the government of its greatest strength and support. Can you always rely on the patriotism of the members? If this be the only inducement, you will find a great indifference in filling your legislative body. If we expect to call forth useful characters, we must hold out allurements; nor can any great inconveniency arise from such inducements. The legislative body must be the road to public honor; and the advantage will be greater to adopt my motion, than any possible inconveniency" (Farrand, *Records,* I, 392).

Yates's version (second speech):

"Mr. Madison. This question is certainly of much moment. There are great advantages in appointing such persons as are known. The choice otherwise will be chance. How will it operate on the members themselves? Will it not be an objection to become members when they are to be excluded from office? For these reasons I am for the amendment" (ibid., I, 393).

Lansing's version:

"Madison—Men of Ability are not found [?] in Virginia to step forward in Public. Persons of other Descriptions press for Admission" (Strayer, *Delegate from N.Y.,* pp. 79–80).

Term of the Senate

[26 June 1787]

Read moved that the term be nine years.

Mr. Madison. In order to judge of the form to be given to this institution, it will be proper to take a view of the ends to be served by it. These were first to protect the people agst. their rulers: secondly to protect the people agst. the transient impressions into which they themselves might be led. A people deliberating in a temperate moment, and with the experience of other nations before them, on the plan of Govt. most likely to secure their happiness, would first be aware, that those chargd. with the public happiness, might betray their trust. An obvious precaution agst. this danger wd. be to divide the trust between different bodies of men, who might watch & check each other. In this they wd. be governed by the same prudence which has prevailed in organizing the subordinate departments of Govt., where all business liable to abuses is made to pass thro' separate hands, the one being a check on the other. It wd. next occur to such a people, that they themselves were liable to temporary errors, thro' want of information as to their true interest, and that men chosen for a short term, & employed but a small portion of that in public affairs, might err from the same cause. This reflection wd. naturally suggest that the Govt. be so constituted, as that one of its branches might have an oppy. of acquiring a competent knowledge of the public interests. Another reflection equally becoming a people on such an occasion, wd. be that they themselves, as well as a numerous body of Representatives, were liable to err also, from fickleness and passion. A necessary fence agst. this danger would be to select a portion of enlightened citizens, whose limited number, and firmness might seasonably interpose agst. impetuous counsels. It ought finally to occur to a people deliberating on a Govt. for themselves, that as different interests necessarily result from the liberty meant to be secured, the major interest might under sudden impulses be tempted to commit injustice on the minority. In all civilized Countries the people fall into different classes havg. a real or supposed difference of interests. There will be creditors & debtors, farmers, merchts. & manufacturers. There will be particularly the distinction of rich & poor. It was true as had been observd. (by Mr. Pinkney) we had not among us those hereditary distinctions, of rank which were a great source of the contests in the ancient Govts. as well as the modern States of Europe, nor those extremes of wealth or poverty which characterize the latter. We cannot however be regarded even at this time, as one homogeneous mass, in which every thing that affects a part will affect in the same manner the whole. In framing a system which we wish to last for ages, we shd. not lose sight of the changes which ages will produce. An increase of population will of necessity increase the proportion of those who will labour under all the hardships of life, & secretly sigh for a more equal distribution of its blessings. These may in time outnumber those who are placed above the feelings of indigence. According to the equal laws of suffrage, the power will slide into the hands of the former. No agrarian attempts have yet been made in this Country, but symtoms, of a leveling spirit, as we have understood, have sufficiently appeared in a certain quarters to give notice of the future danger. How is this danger to be guarded agst. on republican principles? How is the danger in all cases of interested coalitions to oppress the minority to be guarded agst.? Among other means by the establishment of a body in the Govt. sufficiently respectable for its wisdom & virtue, to aid on such emergences, the preponderance of justice by throwing its weight into that scale. Such being the objects of the second branch in the proposed Govt. he thought a considerable duration ought to be given to it. He did not conceive that the term of nine years could threaten any real danger; but in pursuing his particular ideas on the subject, he should require that the long term allowed to the 2d. branch should not commence till such a period of life, as would render a perpetual disqualification to be re-elected little inconvenient either in a public or private view. He observed that as it was more than probable we were now digesting a plan which in its operation wd. decide for ever the fate of Republican Govt. we ought not only to provide every guard to liberty that its preservation cd. require, but be equally careful to supply the defects which our own experience had particularly pointed out.[1]

Ms (DLC).

[1]Yates's version:

"Mr Madison. We are now to determine whether the republican form shall be the basis of our government—I admit there is weight in the objection of the gentleman from South Carolina; but no plan can steer clear of objections. That great powers are to be given, there is no doubt; and that those powers may be abused is equally true. It is also probable that members may lose their attachments to the states which sent them—Yet the first branch will control them in many of their abuses. But we are now forming a body on whose wisdom we mean to rely, and their permanency in office secures a proper field in which they may exert their firmness and knowledge. Democratic communities may be unsteady, and be led to action by the impulse of the moment. Like individuals they may be sensible of their own weakness, and may desire the counsels and checks of friends to guard them against the turbulency and weakness of unruly passions. Such are the various pursuits of this life, that in all civilized countries, the interest of a community will be divided. There will be debtors and creditors, and an unequal possession of property, and hence arises different views and different objects in government. This indeed is the ground-work of aristocracy; and we find it blended in every government, both ancient and modern. Even where titles have survived property, we discover the noble beggar haughty and assuming.

"The man who is possessed of wealth, who lolls on his sofa or rolls in his carriage, cannot judge of the wants or feelings of the day laborer. The government we mean to erect is intended to last for ages. The landed interest, at present, is prevalent; but in process of time, when we approximate to the states and kingdoms of Europe; when the number of landholders shall be comparatively small, through the various means of trade and manufactures, will not the landed interest be overbalanced in future elections, and unless wisely provided against, what will become of your government? In England, at this day, if elections were open to all classes of people, the property of the landed proprietors would be insecure. An agrarian law would soon take place. If these observations be just, our government ought to secure the permanent interests of the country against innovation. Landholders ought to have a share in the government, to support these invaluable interests and to balance and check the other. They ought to be so constituted as to protect the minority of the opulent against the majority. The senate, therefore, ought to be this body; and to answer these purposes, they ought to have permanency and stability. Various have been the propositions; but my opinion is, the longer they continue in office, the better will these views be answered" (Farrand, *Records*, I, 430–31).

Lansing's version:

"Madison—The Advantages of Government cannot be extended equally to all—Those remote from Seat of Government cannot be placed in a Situation equally advantageous with such as near it—Distinctions will always exist—that of Debtor and Creditor—Property had made Distinctions in Europe before a Nobility was created—Inequality of Property will produce the same Distinctions here—The Man in affluent Circumstances has different Feelings from the man who daily toils for a Subsistence. The landed Interest has now the Supreme Power—a Century hence the commercial may prevail—The Government ought to be so organized as to give a Ballance to it and protect one Order of Men from the predominating Influence of the other. The Senate ought to represent the opulent Minority—If this is not done the System cannot be durable" (Strayer, *Delegate from N.Y.*, p. 84).

Salaries for Members of the Senate

[26 June 1787]

Ellsworth moved that the members of the Senate be paid by their respective states instead of by the national treasury.

Mr. Madison considered this a departure from a fundamental principle, and subverting the end intended by allowing the Senate a duration of 6 years. They would if this motion should be agreed to, hold their places during pleasure; during the pleasure of the State Legislatures. One great end of the institution was, that being a firm, wise and impartial body, it might not only give stability to the Genl. Govt. in its operations on individuals, but hold an even balance among different States. The motion would make the Senate like Congress, the mere Agents & Advocates of State interests & views, instead of being the impartial umpires & Guardians of justice and general Good. Congs. had lately by the establishment of

Europe, they would not hesitate to treat as equals, and to make the regulations perfectly reciprocal. Wd. the case be the same, if a Council were to be formed of deputies from each with authority and discretion, to raise money, levy troops, determine the value of coin &c? Would 30 or 40. million of people submit their fortunes into the hands, of a few thousands? If they did it would only prove that they expected more from the terror of their superior force, than they feared from the selfishness of their feeble associates. Why are Counties of the same states represented in proportion to their numbers? Is it because the representatives are chosen by the people themselves? So will be the representatives in the Nationl. Legislature. Is it because, the larger have more at stake than the smaller? The case will be the same with the larger & smaller States. Is it because the laws are to operate immediately on their persons & properties? The same is the case in some degree as the articles of confederation stand; the same will be the case in a far greater degree under the plan proposed to be substituted. In the cases of captures, of piracies, and of offences in a federal army, the property & persons of individuals depend on the laws of Congs. By the plan proposed a compleat power of taxation, the highest prerogative of supremacy is proposed to be vested in the national Govt. Many other powers are added which assimilate it to the Govt. of individual States. The negative proposed on the State laws, will make it an essential branch of the State Legislatures & of course will require that it should be exercised by a body established on like principles with the other branches of those Legislatures. That it is not necessay. to secure the small States agst. the large ones he conceived to be equally obvious: Was a combination of the large ones dreaded? This must arise either from some interest common to Va. Masts. & Pa. & distinguishing them from the other States or from the mere circumstance of similarity of size. Did any such common interest exist? In point of situation they could not have been more effectually separated from each other by the most jealous citizen of the most jealous State. In point of manners, Religion, and the other circumstances which sometimes beget affection between different communities, they were not more assimilated than the other States. In point of the staple productions they were as dissimilar as any three other States in the Union. The Staple of Masts. was *fish*, of Pa. *flower*, of Va. *Tobo.* Was a Combination to be apprehended from the mere circumstance of equality of size? Experience suggested no such danger. The journals of Congs. did not present any peculiar association of these States in the votes recorded. It had never been seen that different Counties in the same State, conformable in extent, but disagreeing in other circumstances, betrayed a propensity to such combinations. Experience rather taught a contrary lesson. Among individuals of superior eminence & weight in Society, rivalships were much more frequent than coalitions. Among independent nations, pre-eminent over their neighbours, the same remark was verified. Carthage & Rome tore one another to pieces instead of uniting their forces to devour the weaker nations of the Earth. The Houses of Austria & France were hostile as long as they remained the greatest powers of Europe. England & France have succeeded to the pre-eminence & to the enmity. To this principle we owe perhaps our liberty. A coalition between those powers would have been fatal to us. Among the principal members of antient & modern confederacies, we find the same effect from the same cause. The contentions, not the Coalitions of Sparta, Athens & Thebes, proved fatal to the smaller members of the Amphyctionic Confederacy. The contentions, not the combinations of Prussia & Austria, have distracted & oppressed the Germanic empire. Were the large States formidable *singly* to their smaller neighbours? On this supposition the latter ought to wish for such a general Govt. as will operate with equal energy on the former as on themselves. The more lax the band, the more liberty the larger will have to avail themselves of their superior force. Here again Experience was an instructive monitor. What is the situation of the weak compared with the strong in those stages of Civilization in which the violence of individuals is least controuled by an efficient Government? The Heroic period of antient Greece the feudal licentiousness of the middle ages of Europe, the existing condition of the American Savages, answer this question. What is the situation of the minor sovereigns in the great society of independent nations, in which the more powerful are under no controul but the nominal authority of the law of Nations? Is not the danger to the former exactly in proportion to their weakness. But there are cases still more in point. What was the condition of the weaker members of the Amphyctionic Confederacy. Plutarch (life of Themistocles) will inform us that it happened but too often that the strongest cities corrupted & awed the weaker, and that Judgment went in favor of the more powerful party. What is the condition of the lesser states in the German Confederacy? We all know that they are exceedingly trampled upon; and that they owe their safety as far as they enjoy it, partly to their enlisting themselves, under the rival banners of the pre-eminent members, partly to alliances with neighbouring Princes which the Constitution of the Empire does not prohibit. What is the state of things in the lax system of the Dutch Confederacy? Holland contains about ½ the People, supplies about ½ of the money, and by her influence, silently & indirectly governs the whole republic. In a word; the two extremes before us are a perfect separation & a perfect incorporation, of the 13 States. In the first case they would be independent nations subject

not sufficiently analyze the subject. Their remarks, in general, are vague and inconclusive" (Farrand, *Records*, I, 455–56).

Yates's version (second speech):

"Mr. Madison. There is danger in the idea of the gentleman from Connecticut. Unjust representation will ever produce it. In the United Netherlands, Holland governs the whole, although she has only one vote. The counties in Virginia are exceedingly disproportionate, and yet the smaller has an equal vote with the greater, and no inconvenience arises" (ibid., I, 457).

King's version:

"Madison—The Gentlemen who oppose the plan of a representation founded on Numbers, do not distinguish accurately—they use general terms—speake of Tyranny—of the small states being swallowed up by large ones. of combinations between Mass. Penn. & Virgin. no circumstance of Religion, Habits, manners, mode of thinking, course of Business, manufactures, commerce, or natural productions establishes a common interest between them exclusive of all the other States—If this was the case, there is no Fact in the History of man or nations that authorities the Jealousy. Engld. & France might have divid America—The great States, of Athens & Sparta members of the Amphictionic Council never combined to oppress the other Cities—they were Rivals and fought each other—The larger members of the Helvetic Union never combined agt. the small states—Those of the Netherlands never entered into such a combination—In Germany the large Members have been at war wh. each other, but never combined agt. the inferior members—

"These Facts are founded in an inherent principle in the Nature of man & Nations who are but an aggregate of men—When Men or Nations are large, strong, and also nearly equal, they immediately become Rivals—The Jealousy of each other prevents their Union" (ibid., I, 458).

Lansing's version (first speech):

"Madison—Fallacy of Argument owing to a Connection of Legislative Ideas with Right of making Treaties.

"Are the larger States congenial to each other by Proximity common Interests or Similarity of Pursuits? They are not—they are so situated as to perpetuate Diversity of Interests.

"The Staple of Massachusetts is *Fish* and she has carrying Trade—that of Pennsylvania *Wheat* and Virginia Tobacco.

"Equality will uniformly excite Jealousy—Did Rome and Carthage combine to destroy their Neighbours?

"This Question will determine whether we shall confederate at all or partial Confederations shall be formed" (Strayer, *Delegate from N.Y.*, pp. 90–91).

Lansing's version (second speech):

"Madison—Efficient Government can only be formed by apportioning Representation.

"The States may be equalized by general Government" (ibid., p. 91).

Paterson's version (first speech):

"Mr. Madison

"Have we seen the Great Powers of Europe combining to oppress the small—

"They talk in vague Terms of the great States combining &c" (Ms [DLC: Paterson Papers]).

Immediately following the first sentence appears the phrase, apparently in Paterson's hand: "Yes—the division of Poland."

Paterson's version (second speech):

"Mr. Madison

"If you form the present Government, the States will be satisfied—and they will divide and sub-divide so as to become nearly equal" (ibid.).

From Joseph Jones

Richmond 29th. June 1787.

Dr. Sr.

We are not to know the result of your deliberations for five or six weeks to come, as from all accounts your Session will continue untill some time in August. Some of your uxorious members will become impatient from so long absence from home. How does the Dr. stand it—enjoy himself as usual in the society of his friends, or cast longing looks towards Richmond. Mrs. McClurg is, and looks well, and will I dare say on his return prove at least a full match for him. Mrs. Randolph & the children have I hope got up Safe. Present her if you please my compliments. Tell the Governor we shall not venture to speculate in indents or any other cont. securities. Had we the power and the means to follow a certain Gentlemans advise the adoption of his plan wod., with me at le[as]t, have required other authority to support it.[1] We have directed the sale of the Tobacco on hand in the manner as you will see by the inclosed paper and have some hopes the price will be advanced nearly to the State price by the receipt of the interest warrants. These will soon answer the purposes of specie. I am told it has had the effect to appreciate the warrants 2 [½] Pct.[2] The sudden demand at Petersburg the last week for Tobacco in consequence of many arrivals started The price there to 24/6 wch. had for some time stood at 22/6. Here it rose from 23 to 24/. I am told at Fredericksburg the price has got to 22/6—it has been 20/ only. Somehow it is kept down here and will I fear be checked in Petersburg.

We last evening had a letter from the Searcher at Alexandria[3] complaining of a rescue from his possession of a Schooner he had seized. She is from St. Kitts[,] had entered in Maryland but was detected in landing in Alexandria some rum [(]the number of Hhds. not mentioned) which occasioned her seizure by the Searcher. The communication we have received shews that the people of the Town were more disposed to act in opposition to law than support the Officer in the execution of his duty. We have directed one of the armed Boats to endeavour to recover the Vessell wch. we hear moved towards G. Town. We have also called for the names of those who assisted the Capt of [the] Vessell to escape and directed the Searcher to move for the penalty agt. those who refused to assist him, when summoned by him to afford their aid.[4] The last post I heard, late in the evening, that Mr. Harrison was to set out in the Stage in the morning, I sent Anty. to him with the two books, requesting he wod. convey them to you. Yr. friend & Servt

Jos: Jones

Will you send me the 7th. essay on Finance.[5] Adams's book is here and I can get the reading of it.

RC (DLC). Docketed by JM. Enclosure not found. Brackets enclose letters and numbers illegible in the Ms.

[1] See Jones to JM, 7 June 1787 and n. 2.

[2] The revenue appropriation law of 1786 authorized the council "to direct the treasurer in the mode of selling the tobacco paid for taxes" (Hening, *Statutes*, XII, 329). See also the "act to enable the citizens of this commonwealth to discharge certain taxes, by the payment of tobacco" (ibid., XII, 258–60). The sale was to take place on 12 July, "one fourth of the purchase to be paid in specie and three fourths in military interest Warrants" (*JCSV*, IV, 115). Jones doubtless sent JM the *Va. Independent Chronicle* of 27 June 1787, which announced the sale. The "State price" of tobacco was that set by the legislature at the October 1786 session as the rate at which tobacco would be receivable in taxes. The price ranged from eighteen to twenty-eight shillings per hundredweight, depending on the location of the warehouse (Hening, *Statutes*, XII, 258–59). Military interest warrants were issued by the state auditors for interest due on "military certificates" that had been paid to the officers and soldiers of the state and Continental lines (ibid., X, 462).

[3] James Mease McRea (1765–1809), who was appointed 7 June 1786 (*JCSV*, III, 557). His letter to Governor Randolph of 26 June 1787 is in *CVSP*, IV, 301.

[4] See *JCSV*, IV, 119–20, 122. McRea's letter describing the rescue of the schooner *Dart*, commanded by a Captain Dodds, was followed on 29 June by a lengthy report from Charles Lee, naval officer of the South Potomac district. The searcher's first attempt to seize the vessel was resisted by the captain and crew, "who were on deck armed with handspikes, &c." McRea then summoned help from "sundry persons . . . who all refused." The searcher and naval officer were later permitted to board, but after the two officials left the schooner Captain Dodds and his men, assisted by several persons on shore, overpowered their guards and set sail for Georgetown on the Maryland side of the river. Lee attempted to have the captain arrested at Georgetown, but the Maryland authorities were uncooperative (*CVSP*, IV, 308–9). Shortly thereafter the *Dart* sailed down the river and slipped by Alexandria at night. The state boat *Patriot*, which had been dispatched to intercept the *Dart*, was forced to return to Hampton for repairs after losing her main mast "in a gale of Wind." The delay enabled the *Dart* to make a clean escape (McRea to Beverley Randolph, 2 and 11 July 1787, ibid., IV, 311, 314; Beverley Randolph to McRea, 16 July 1787, and Beverley Randolph to Capt. Michael James, 27 July 1787, Executive Letter Book, pp. 131, 140). To prevent similar incidents in the future the Council of State ordered the other state boat, the *Liberty*, to cruise the Potomac constantly between Georgetown and Quantico, "and chiefly near the Town of Alexandria." The *Liberty* was not ready for duty until August, however, after undergoing repairs for a "bottom much eat with the worm" (*JCSV*, IV, 137; Michael James to Beverley Randolph, 22 July and 1 Aug. 1787, *CVSP*, IV, 323, 325).

Smuggling was a chronic problem in Virginia, the inevitable result of restrictive trade laws and the lack of an effective means of enforcement. In the case of the *Dart* the searcher's attempts to carry out the law were forcibly resisted by a hostile populace thirsty for cheap rum. At least one prominent Alexandria merchant, Robert Townsend Hooe (1743–1809), openly encouraged the resistance to the seizure of the *Dart*. When McRea attempted to board the vessel, Hooe shouted, "*Knock the Damn'd Imperious Raskal down and don't suffer him to make Seizure, &c.*" McRea noted that Hooe's behavior would have great influence "among the lower class of people, who wou'd think they wou'd thereby be justified in commiting every outrage" (McRea to Beverley Randolph, 11 July and 24 Aug. 1787, ibid., IV, 314, 335).

[5] A Citizen of Philadelphia [Pelatiah Webster], *Seventh Essay on Free Trade and Finance*.

Rule of Representation in the First Branch of the Legislature

[29 June 1787]

Mr. Madison agreed with Docr. Johnson, that the mixed nature of the Govt. ought to be kept in view; but thought too much stress was laid on the rank of the States as political societies. There was a gradation, he observed from the smallest corporation, with the most limited powers, to the largest empire with the most perfect sovereignty. He pointed out the limitations on the sovereignty of the States, as now confederated their laws in relation to the paramount law of the Confederacy were analogous to that of bye laws to the supreme law, within a State.[1] Under the proposed Govt. the Powers of the States will be much farther reduced. According to the views of every member, the Genl. Govt will have powers far beyond those exercised by the British Parliament, when the states were part of the British Empire.[2] It will in particular have the power, without the consent of the state Legislatures, to levy money directly on the people themselves; and therefore not to divest such *unequal* portions of the people as composed the several States, of an *equal* voice, would subject the sy[s]tem to the reproaches & evils which have resulted from the vicious representation in G.B.

He entreated the gentlemen representing the small States to renounce a principle wch. was confessedly unjust, which cd. never be admitted, & if admitted must infuse mortality into a Constitution which we wished to last for ever. He prayed them to ponder well the consequences of suffering the Confederacy to go to pieces. It had been sd. that the want of energy in the large states wd. be a security to the small. It was forgotten that this want of energy proceeded from the supposed security of the States agst. all external danger. Let each state depend on itself for its security, & let apprehensions arise of danger, from distant powers or from neighbouring states, & the languishing condition of all the states, large as well as small, wd. soon be transformed into vigorous & high toned Govts. His great fear was that their Govts. wd. then have too much energy, that these might not only be formidable in the large to the small States, but fatal to the internal liberty of all. The same causes which have rendered the old world the Theatre of incessant wars, & have banished liberty from the face of it, wd. soon produce the same effects here. The weakness & jealousy of the small States wd. quickly introduce some regular military force agst. sudden danger from their powerful neighbours. The example wd. be followed by others, and wd. soon become universal. In time of actual war, great discretionary powers are constantly given to the Executive Magistrate. Constant apprehension of war, has the same tendency to render the head too large for the body. A standing military force, with an overgrown Executive will not long be safe companions to liberty. The means of defence agst. foreign danger, have been always the instruments of tyranny at home. Among the Romans it was a standing m[a]xim to excite a war, whenever a revolt was apprehended. Throughout all Europe, the armies kept up under the pretext of defending, have enslaved the people. It is perhaps questionable, whether the best concerted system of Absolute power in Europe cd. maintain itself, in a situation, where no alarms of external danger cd. tame the people to the domestic yoke. The insular situation of G. Britain was the principal cause of her being an exception to the general fate of Europe. It has rendered less defence necessary, and admitted a kind of defence wch. cd. not be used for the purpose of oppression. These consequences he conceived ought to be apprehended whether the States should run into a total separation from each other, or shd. enter into partial confederacies. Either event wd. be truly deplorable; & those who might be accessary to either, could never be forgiven by their Country, nor by themselves.[3]

Ms (DLC).

[1]JM interlined "their laws . . . State" at a later time. He evidently derived the substance of this insertion from Yates.

[2]When Yates's notes were first published in full in 1821, JM took strong exception to the New Yorker's account of JM's speeches. He particularly objected to Yates's version of this first section of his 29 June speech. See, for example, JM to Joseph Gales, 26 Aug. 1821; JM to Nicholas P. Trist, December 1831; JM to William C. Rives, 21 Oct. 1833 (Farrand, *Records*, III, 446–47, 516–18, 521–24). See also the discussion in Brant, *Madison*, III, 21–22, 85–87, and Arnold A. Rogow, "The Federal Convention: Madison and Yates," *AHR*, LX (1954–55), 327–29.

[3]Yates's version:

"Mr. Madison. Some gentlemen are afraid that the plan is not sufficiently national, while others apprehend that it is too much so. If this point of representation was once well fixed, we would come nearer to one another in sentiment. The necessity would then be discovered of circumscribing more effectually the state governments and enlarging the bounds of the general government. Some contend that states are sovereign, when in fact they are only political societies. There is a gradation of power in all societies, from the lowest corporation to the highest sovereign. The states never possessed the essential rights of sovereignty. These were always vested in congress. Their voting, as states, in congress, is no evidence of sovereignty. The state of Maryland voted by counties—did this make the counties sovereign? The states, at present, are only great corporations, having the power of making by-laws, and these are effectual only if they are not contradictory to the general confederation. The states ought to be placed under the control of the general government—at least as much so as they formerly were under the king and British parliament. The arguments, I observe, have taken a different turn, and I hope may tend to convince all of the necessity of a strong energetic government, which would equally tend to give energy to, and protect the state governments. What was the origin of the military establishments of Europe? It was the jealousy which one state or kingdom entertained of another. This jealousy was ever productive of evil. In Rome the patricians were often obliged to excite a foreign war to divert the attention of the plebeians from encroaching on the senatorial rights. In England and France, perhaps, this jealousy may give energy to their governments, and contribute to their existence. But a state of danger is like a state of war, and it unites the various parts of the government to exertion. May not our distractions, however, invite danger from abroad? If the power is not immediately derived from the people, in proportion to their numbers, we may make a paper confederacy, but that will be all. We know the effects of the old confederation, and without a general government this will be like the former" (Farrand, *Records*, I, 471–72).

King's version:

"Madison—We are vague in our Expressions—we speak of the sovereignty of the States—they are not sovereign—there is a regular gradation from the lowest Corporation, such as the incorporation of mechanicks to the most perft. Sovereignty—The last is the true and only Sovereignty—the states are not in that high degree Sovereign—they are Corporations with power of Bye Laws" (ibid., I, 477).

Paterson's version:

"Mr. Madison

"Will have the States considered as so many great Corporations, and not otherwise" (Ms [DLC: Paterson Papers]).

Rule of Representation in the Senate

[29 June 1787]

Ellsworth, arguing the advantages of making "the general government *partly federal and partly national*," moved that each state have an equal vote in the Senate (Farrand, *Records*, I, 474).

Mr. Madison. I would always exclude inconsistent principles in framing a system of government. The difficulty of getting its defects amended are great and sometimes insurmountable. The Virginia state government was the first which was made, and though its defects are evident to every person, we cannot get it amended. The Dutch have made four several attempts to amend their system without success. The few alterations made in it were by tumult and faction, and for the worse. If there was real danger, I would give the smaller states the defensive weapons—But there is none from that quarter. The great danger to our general government *is the great southern and northern interests of the continent, being opposed to each other. Look to the votes in congress, and most of them stand divided by the geography of the country, not according to the size of the states.*

Suppose the first branch granted money, may not the second branch, from state views, counteract the first? In congress, the single state of Delaware prevented an embargo, at the time that all the other states thought it absolutely necessary for the support of the army. Other powers, and those very essential, besides the legislative, will be given to the second branch—such as the negativing all state laws. I would compromise on this question, if I could do it on correct principles, but otherwise not—if the old fabric of the confederation must be the ground-work of the new, we must fail.[1]

Farrand, *Records*, I, 475–76 (Yates).

[1]King's version:

"Madison—The Gentleman from Connecticut has proposed doing as much at this Time as is prudent, and leavg. future amendments to posterity—this a dangerous Doctrine—the Defects of the Amphictionick League were acknowledged, but they never cd. be reformed, the U Netherlands have attempted four several Times to amend their Confederation, but have failed in each Attempt—The fear of Innovation, and the Hue & Cry in favor of the Liberty of the people will prevent the necessary Reforms—If the States have equal, influence, and votes in the Senate, we are in the utmost Danger—Delaware during the War opposed and defeated an Embargo agreed to by 12. States; and continued to supply the Enemy with provisions during the war" (ibid., I, 478).

Lansing's version:

"Madison—Examine Journals of Congress—see whether States have been influenced by Magnitude. Small States have embarrassed us—Embargo agreed to by twelve States during the War—Deleware declined it. . . .

"Madison—If there was any Difference of Interests would agree to equal Representation.

"Let Gentleman recollect the Experiments that have been made to amend Con-federation—they always miscarried. The Dutch Republics made four several Experiments all ineffectual" (Strayer, *Delegate from N.Y.*, pp. 94–95).

Lansing divided JM's second speech in two (see ibid., pp. 94–95 nn. 135, 141).

[30 June 1787]

Ellsworth spoke in favor of equal representation of the states in the Senate.

Mr. Madison did justice to the able & close reasoning of Mr. E. but must observe that it did not always accord with itself.[1] On another occasion, the large States were described by him as the Aristocratic States, ready to oppress the small. Now the small are the House of Lords requiring a negative to defend them agst. the more numerous Commons. Mr. E. had also erred in saying that no instance had existed in which confederated States had not retained to themselves a perfect equality of suffrage. Passing over the German system in which the K. of Prussia has nine voices, he reminded Mr. E. of the Lycian confederacy, in which the component members had votes proportioned to their importance, and which Montesquieu recommends as the fittest model for that form of Government. Had the fact been as stated by Mr. E. it would have been of little avail to him, or rather would have strengthened the arguments agst. him; The History & fate of the several Confederacies modern as well as Antient, demonstrating some radical vice in their structure. In reply to the appeal of Mr. E. to the faith plighted in the existing federal compact, he remarked that the party claiming from others an adherence to a common engagement ought at least to be guiltless itself of a violation. Of all the States however Connecticut was perhaps least able to urge this plea. Besides the various omissions to perform the stipulated acts from which no State was free, the Legislature of that State had by a pretty recent vote, *positively refused* to pass a law for complying with the Requisitions of Congs. and had transmitted a copy of the vote to Congs. It was urged, he said, continually that an equality of votes in the 2d. branch was not only necessary to secure the small, but would be perfectly safe to the large ones whose majority in the 1st. branch was an effectual bulwark. But notwithstanding this apparent defence, the Majority of States might still injure the majority of people. 1. they could *obstruct* the wishes and interests of the majority. 2. they could *extort* measures repugnant to the wishes & interest of the Majority. 3. they could *impose* measures adverse thereto; as the 2d. branch will probly. exercise some great powers, in which the 1st. will not participate. He admitted that every peculiar interest whether in any class of Citizens, or any description of States, ought to be secured as far as possible. Wherever there is danger of attack there ought be given a constitutional power of defence. But he contended that the States were divided into different interests not by their difference of size, but by other circumstances; the most material of which resulted partly from climate, but principally from the effects of their having or not having slaves. These two causes concurred in forming the great division of interests in the U. States. It did not lie between the large & small States: It lay between the Northern & Southern. And if any defensive power were necessary, it ought to be mutually given to these two interests.[2] He was so strongly impressed with this important truth that he had been casting about in his mind for some expedient that would answer the purpose. The one which had occurred was that instead of proportioning the votes of the States in both branches, to their respective numbers of inhabitants computing the slaves in the ratio of 5 to 3, they should be represented in one branch according to the number of free inhabitants only, and in the other according to the whole no. counting the slaves as free. By this arrangement the southern Scale would have the advantage in one House, and the Northern in the other. He had been restrained from proposing this expedient by two considerations; one was his unwillingness to urge any diversity of interests on an occasion where it is but too apt to arise of itself—the other was the inequality of powers that must be vested in the two branches, and which wd. destroy the equilibrium of interests.[3]

Ms (DLC).

[1]JM interlined "did justice . . . itself" at a later time. He originally wrote "observed that the

reasoning of Mr. E. at different times did not well [*illegible*]." The first part of the insertion is a paraphrase of Yates.

²JM later crossed through the concluding clause: "as a security agst. the encroachments of each other."

³Yates's version:

"Mr. Madison. Notwithstanding the admirable and close reasoning of the gentleman who spoke last, I am not yet convinced that my former remarks are not well founded. I apprehend he is mistaken as to the fact on which he builds one of his arguments. He supposes that equality of votes is the principle on which all confederacies are formed—that of Lycia, so justly applauded by the celebrated Montesquieu, was different. He also appeals to our good faith for the observance of the confederacy. We know we have found one inadequate to the purposes for which it was made—Why then adhere to a system which is proved to be so remarkably defective? I have impeached a number of states for the infraction of the confederation, and I have not even spared my own state, nor can I justly spare his. Did not Connecticut refuse her compliance to a federal requisition? Has she paid, for the two last years, any money into the continental treasury? And does this look like government, or the observance of a solemn compact? Experience shows that the confederation is radically defective, and we must in a new national government, guard against those defects. Although the large states in the first branch have a weight proportionate to their population, yet as the smaller states have an equal vote in the second branch, they will be able to controul and leave the larger without any essential benefit. As peculiar powers are intended to be granted to the second branch, such as the negativing state laws, &c. unless the larger states have a proportionate weight in the representation, they cannot be more secure" (Farrand, *Records*, I, 496–97).

Paterson's version:

"Mr. Maddison.	The Confedn. inadequate to its Purposes. Resoln. of Cont. refusing
"*Lycia*.	to comply with a federal Reqn.
Germanick	"Repeated Violations in every State. The Rule of Confdn. obtained
Body."	by the Necessity of the Times.

"The large States will not be secure by the lower Branch.

"2d. Branch may possess a Negative over the Laws of the State-Lgs."
(Ms [DLC: Paterson Papers]).

Paterson recapitulated part of JM's speech in notes made for a speech apparently never delivered. See Farrand, *Records*, I, 506.

Lansing's version:

"Madison—Equality of Representation was dictated by the Necessity of the Times. The larger States cannot be safe unless they have a greater Share in Government. Connecticut has shewn a Disregard to her fœderal Compact—She has declined complying with Requisition" (Strayer, *Delegate from N.Y.*, p. 97).

[30 June 1787]

Wilson proposed that there be a senator for every 100,000 people, and that states having less than that population be allowed one senator.

Mr. Madison would acquiesce in the concession hinted by Mr. Wilson, on condition that a due independence should be given to the Senate. The plan in its present shape makes the Senate absolutely dependent on the States. The Senate therefore is only another edition of Congs.¹ He knew the faults of that Body & had used a bold language agst. it. Still he wd. preserve the State rights, as carefully as the trials by jury.²

Ms (DLC).

[1]JM deleted the concluding phrase of this sentence: "with very few amendments."

[2]JM interlined the two preceding sentences, paraphrasing Yates, and heavily crossed through his original concluding sentence.

Yates's version:

"Mr. Madison. I will not answer for supporting chimerical objects—but has experience evinced any good in the old confederation? I know it never can answer, and I have therefore made use of bold language against it. I do assert, that a national senate, elected and paid by the people, will have no more efficiency than congress; for the states will usurp the general government. I mean, however to preserve the state rights with the same care, as I would trials by jury; and I am willing to go as far as my honorable colleague" (Farrand, *Records*, I, 499–500).

Paterson's version:

"Mr. Maddison.   The Amt. is Congress in a new Form; servile to the States.
              "No Disposn. in [Cy.?] Rep. or Corporations to swallow up the Rest" (Ms [DLC: Paterson Papers]).

Rule of Representation in the Legislature

[5 July 1787]

A grand committee (one delegate from each state) was appointed on 2 July to resolve the differences concerning representation in the two branches of the legislature and to submit a compromise plan. Its 5 July report proposed proportional representation in the first branch, which would have exclusive control over money bills, and equal representation of the states in the Senate.

Mr. Madison could not regard the exclusive privilege of originating money bills as any concession on the side of the small States. Experience proved that it had no effect. If seven States in the upper branch wished a bill to be originated, they might surely find some member from some of the same States in the lower branch who would originate it. The restriction as to amendments was of as little consequence. Amendments could be handed privately by the Senate to members in the other house. Bills could be negatived that they might be sent up in the desired shape. If the Senate should yield to the obstinacy of the 1st. branch the use of that body as a check would be lost. If the 1st. branch should yield to that of the Senate, the privilege would be nugatory. Experience had also shewn both in G.B. and the States having a similar regulation that it was a source of frequent & obstinate altercations. These considerations had produced a rejection of a like motion on a former occasion when judged by its own merits. It could not therefore be deemed any concession on the present, and left in force all the objections which had prevailed agst. allowing each State an equal voice. He conceived that the Convention was reduced to the alternative of either departing from justice in order to conciliate the smaller States, and the minority of the people of the U.S. or of displeasing these by justly gratifying the larger States and the majority of the people. He could not himself hesitate as to the option he ought to make. The Convention with justice & the majority of the people on their side, had nothing to fear. With injustice and the minority on their side they had every thing to fear. It was in vain to purchase concord in the Convention on terms which would perpetuate discord among their Constituents. The Convention ought to pursue a plan which would bear the test of examination, which would be espoused & supported by the enlightened and impartial part of America, & which they could themselves vindicate and urge. It should be considered that altho' at first many may judge of the system recommended, by their opinion of the Convention, yet finally all will judge of the Convention by the System. The merits of the System alone can finally & effectually obtain the public suffrage. He was not apprehensive that the people of the small States would obstinately refuse to accede to a Govt. founded on just principles, and promising them substantial protection. He could not suspect that Delaware would brave the consequences of seeking her fortunes apart from the other States, rather than submit to such a Govt.: much less could he suspect that she would pursue the rash policy of courting foreign support, which the warmth of one of her representatives (Mr. Bedford) had suggested, or if she shd. that any foreign nation wd. be so rash as to hearken to the overture. As little could he suspect that the people of N. Jersey notwithstanding the decided tone of the gentlemen from that State, would choose rather to stand on their own legs, and bid defiance to events, than to acquiesce under an establishment founded on principles the justice of which they could not dispute, and absolutely necessary to redeem them from the exactions levied on them by the Commerce of the neighbouring States. A review of other States would prove that there was as little reason to apprehend an inflexible opposition elsewhere. Harmony in the Convention was no doubt much to be desired. Satisfaction to all the States, in the first instance still more so. But if the principal States comprehending a majority of the people of the U.S. should concur in a just & judicious Plan, he had the firmest hopes, that all the other States would by degrees accede to it.[1]

Ms (DLC).

[1]JM deleted the concluding sentence of his speech: "These observations wd. show that he was not only fixed in his opposition to the Report of the Comme. but was prepared for any [risk?] that might follow a negative of it."
Yates's version:
"Mr. Madison. I restrain myself from animadverting on the report, from the respect I bear

to the members of the committee. But I must confess I see nothing of concession in it.

"The originating money bills is no concession on the part of the smaller states, for if seven states in the second branch should want such a bill, their interest in the first branch will prevail to bring it forward—it is nothing more than a nominal privilege.

"The second branch, small in number, and well connected, will ever prevail. The power of regulating trade, imposts, treaties, &c. are more essential to the community than raising money, and no provision is made for those in the report—We are driven to an unhappy dilemma. Two thirds of the inhabitants of the union are to please the remaining one third by sacrificing their essential rights.

"When we satisfy the majority of the people in securing their rights, we have *nothing* to fear; in any other way, *every thing*. The smaller states, I hope will at last see their true and real interest. And I hope that the warmth of the gentleman from Delaware will never induce him to yield to his own suggestion of seeking for foreign aid" (Farrand, *Records*, I, 535).

Lansing's version:

"Madison—Altho' the House was equally divided on the *2nd* Branch—on the first there was a considerable Majority for departing from Equality—All the Concessions are on one Side—We are reduced to the Alternative of displeasing *Minority* or *Majority*—by deciding for the latter we have Nothing to fear—the former every Thing. He would rather have a System received by three or four States than none" (Strayer, *Delegate from N.Y.*, p. 103).

Paterson's version:

"Maddison.

"The Interest of the smaller States to come into the Measure—

"Delaware—foreign Power—

"New-Jersey. Single and unconnected" (Ms [DLC: Paterson Papers]).

From Joseph Jones

RICHMOND 6th. July 1787

DR. SR.

I have your letter of the 26th. ult. The Post preceding the arrival of yours brought a letter from the Governor, inclosing Mr. Wythes resignation, when the filling the vacancy made by that Gentlemans departure from Convention was considered, and determined by the Executive to be unnecessary. The length of time the Convention had been seting, and the representation of the State then attending, being within one of the number at first appointed, and these Gentlemen of established Character and approved abilities—were considerations that I believe had weight and governed the determination. Had the supplying Mr. Wythes place been thought necessary, I have no doubt Mr. Corbins well known abilities, and his being on the Spot, wod. have pointed him out to the Executive as a proper person.[1] It is supposed by some Doctr. M.Clurg will soon retire. Should that be the case and the other Gentlemen remain I am inclined to think from what formerly passed at the Board, they will be deemed a representation competent to the great objects for which they were appointed.

If the Mass: Assembly should pursue such measures as from the specimens you mention there is reason to fear they will, the example may probably prove contagious and spread into New Hampshire, whereby the eastern politics will become formidable, and from the principles which appear to govern them and the number of adherents, pernicious consequences are to be apprehended.[2]

Tobacco still rises. The price now current will nearly bring us what the State allowed and it is probable by next Thursday the day we have fixed for the Sale we shall find purchasers giving a price for all the upland Tobacco at least equal to if not higher than the State price. Although the Treasury board refused to take the Tobacco at the State price, we have been applied to this day by Hopkins to postpone the Sale untill he can apply to and be directed by them what to do, or allow him to bid for the Tobacco to the amount of the Bills on him wch. he says is about 25000 dols. All circumstances considered we have agreed he may purchase to the amount of 4000£. to be considered as Specie, and to be accompanied with the proper proportion of indents under the requisition of 85.[3] Yr. friend

J JONES

RC (DLC). Docketed by JM.

[1] See *JCSV*, IV, 120. George Mason had suggested Francis Corbin, who was then in Philadelphia, as a replacement for Wythe (Mason to Beverley Randolph, 30 June 1787, Rutland, *Papers of George Mason*, III, 918–19).

[2] The spring elections in Massachusetts had returned a legislature more sympathetic toward the participants in the recent Shays uprising (Starkey, *A Little Rebellion*, pp. 184–86). In June the General Court repealed the act disqualifying the insurgents from voting and holding office. The House of Representatives also passed a resolution for removing the seat of government from Boston, but rejected a motion granting a general pardon to the insurgents (James Sullivan to Rufus King, 14 June 1787; Theodore Sedgwick to King, 18 June 1787, C. R. King, *Life and Correspondence of Rufus King*, I, 222–23, 223–24; *Pa. Gazette*, 27 June 1787).

[3] On the sale of public tobacco (tobacco collected in payment of taxes), see Jones to JM, 29 June 1787 and n. 2. In refusing to accept tobacco at the "State price" the Board of Treasury indicated that the money commanded by the market price of the tobacco could be paid toward the state's requisition quota (Board of Treasury to John Hopkins, May 1787 [extract], enclosed in Edmund Randolph to Speaker of the House of Delegates, 15 Oct. 1787 [Vi: Executive Communications]). Following the announcement that the tobacco would be sold to the highest bidder, Hopkins informed the council that the Board of Treasury would probably "agree to the receipt of it specifically on Account of the Quota of Virginia to the United States." He requested a postponement of the sale until he received specific instructions, however, because at the time he had "no authority to receive any thing but Specie in discharge of the Specie proportion of the Requisitions of Congress" (Hopkins to Beverley Randolph, 6 July 1787 [Vi: Continental Congress Papers]). As Jones indicated, the council denied this request, but did allow Hopkins to become a purchaser of the public tobacco (*JCSV*, IV, 124).

Rule of Representation in the Legislature

[7 July 1787]

Gerry wished to enumerate and define the powers to be vested in the general government before deciding on the rule of representation in the Senate.

Mr. Madison observed that it wd. be impossible to say what powers could be safely & properly vested in the Govt. before it was known, in what manner the States were to be represented in it. He was apprehensive that if a just representation were not the basis of the Govt. it would happen, as it did when the Articles of Confederation were depending, that every effectual prerogative would be withdrawn or withheld, and the New Govt. wd. be rendered as impotent and as short lived as the old.[1]

Ms (DLC).

[1]King and Paterson may have recorded a speech given by JM earlier in the day, which he did not note.

King's version:

"*Madison* An Equality of votes in the Senate will enable *a minority* to hold the Majority— they will compel the majority to submit to their particular Interest or they will withhold their Assent to essential & necessary measures—I have known one man where his State was represented by only two & were divided oppose Six States in Cong. on an import. occasion for 3 days, and finally compelled them to gratify his Caprice in order to obtain his suffrage— the Senate will possess certain exclusive powers, such as the appointment to Offices &c—If the States have equal votes—a minority of the people or an Aristocracy will appt. the Gt. Officers. Besides the small States will be near the Seat of Govt. a Quorum of the first Br. may be easily assembled they may carry a measure in that Br. agt. the sense of the Majority if present, & the Senate may confirm it—Virgin. has objected to every addition of powers to those of Congress, because they made but 1/13 of the Legislature when they ought to have 1/6" (Farrand, *Records*, I, 554).

Paterson's version:

"Madison.

"1. The Upper Branch may put a Veto upon the Acts of the lower Branch.

"2. may extort a Concurrence. The smaller States near the Centre; they may compose a Majority of the Quorum" (Ms [DLC: Paterson Papers]).

[9 July 1787]

Paterson objected to counting slaves in apportioning representation, noting that "if Negroes are not represented in the States to which they belong, why should they be represented in the Genl. Govt." He defined representation as "an expedient by which an assembly of certain individls. chosen by the people is substituted in place of the inconvenient meeting of the people themselves" (Farrand, *Records*, I, 561).

Mr. Madison reminded Mr. Patterson that his doctrine of Representation which was in its principle the genuine one, must for ever silence the pretensions of the small States to an equality of votes with the large ones. They ought to vote in the same proportion in which their citizens would do, if the people of all the States were collectively met. He suggested as a proper ground of compromise, that in the first branch the States should be represented according to their number of free inhabitants; and in the 2d. which had for one of its primary objects the guardianship of property, according to the whole number, including slaves.

Ms (DLC).

From James Madison, Sr.

Letter not found.

9 July 1787. Mentioned in JM to James Madison, Sr., 28 July 1787. Concerned activities of slaves, weather conditions, and poor crops.

Apportionment of Representatives in the First Branch of the Legislature

[10 July 1787]

A grand committee proposed that the first branch should initially consist of sixty-five members.

Mr. Madison moved that the number allowed to each State be doubled. A *majority* of a *Quorum* of *65* members, was too small a number to represent the whole inhabitants of the U. States; They would not possess enough of the confidence of the people, and wd. be too sparsely taken from the people, to bring with them all the local information which would be frequently wanted. Double the number will not be too great, even with the future additions from New States. The additional expence was too inconsiderable to be regarded in so important a case. And as far as the augmentation might be unpopular on that score, the objection was overbalanced by its effect on the hopes of a greater number of the popular Candidates.

Ms (DLC).

From Ambrose Madison

Letter not found.

10 July 1787. Mentioned in JM to Ambrose Madison, 18 July 1787. Contained information regarding the health of James Madison, Sr., and requested JM's advice on a proposed sale of land.

Apportionment of Representatives in the Legislature

[11 July 1787]

Williamson proposed that apportionment of representatives be based on a periodic census. Gouverneur Morris preferred to entrust the legislature with adjusting its representation.

Mr. Madison was not a little surprised to hear this implicit confidence urged by a member who on all occasions, had inculcated so strongly, the political depravity of men, and the necessity of checking one vice and interest by opposing to them another vice & interest. If the Representatives of the people would be bound by the ties he had mentioned, what need was there of a Senate? What of a Revisionary power? But his reasoning was not only inconsistent with his former reasoning, but with itself. At the same time that he recommended this implicit confidence to the Southern States in the Northern Majority, he was still more zealous in exhorting all to a jealousy of the Western Majority. To reconcile the gentln. with himself, it must be imagined that he determined the human character by the points of the compass. The truth was that all men having power ought to be[1] distrusted to a certain degree. The case of Pena. had been mentioned where it was admitted that those who were possessed of the power in the original settlement, never admitted the new settlemts. to a due share of it. England was a still more striking example. The power there had long been in the hands of the boroughs, of the minority; who had opposed & defeated every reform which had been attempted. Virga. was in a lesser degree another example. With regard to the Western States, he was clear & firm in opinion, that no unfavorable distinctions were admissible either in point of justice or policy. He thought also that the hope of contributions to the Treasy from them had been much underrated. Future contributions it seemed to be understood on all hands would be principally levied on imports & exports. The extent and fertility of the Western Soil would for a long time give to agriculture a preference over manufactures. Trials would be repeated till some articles could be raised from it that would bear a transportation to places where they could be exchanged for imported manufactures. Whenever the Mississpi. should be opened to them, which would of necessity be the case, as soon as their population would subject them to any considerable share of the Public burdin, imposts on their trade could be collected with less expence & greater certainty, than on that of the Atlantic States. In the mean time, as their supplies must pass thro' the *Atlantic States,* their contributions would be levied in the same manner with those of the Atlantic States. He could not agree that any substantial objection lay agst. fixing numbers for the perpetual standard of Representation. It was said that Representation & taxation were to go together; that taxation and wealth ought to go together, that population & wealth were not measures of each other. He admitted that in different climates, under different forms of Govt. and in different stages of civilization the inference was perfectly just. He would admit that in no situation, numbers of inhabitants were an accurate measure of wealth. He contended however that in the U. States it was sufficiently so for the object in contemplation. Altho' their climate varied considerably, yet as the Govts. the laws, and the manners of all were nearly the same, and the intercourse between different parts perfectly free, population, industry, arts, and the value of labour, would constantly tend to equalize themselves. The value of labour, might be considered as the principal criterion of wealth and ability to support taxes; and this would find its level in different places where the intercourse should be easy & free, with as much certainty as the value of money or any other thing. Wherever labour would yield most, people would resort, till the competition should destroy the inequality. Hence it is that the people are constantly swarming from the more to the less populous places—from Europe to Ama. from the Northn. & Middle parts of the U.S. to the Southern & Western. They go where land is cheaper, because there labour is dearer. If it be true that the same quantity of produce raised on the banks of the Ohio is of less value, than on the Delaware, it is also true that the same labor will raise twice or thrice, the quantity in the former, that it will raise in the latter situation.

Ms (DLC).

[1]JM crossed through the following words: "both distrusted & confided in to a certain degree, that if there was any difference in men it did not depend in different situations it must and that if any real difference lay between them in the different situations mentioned."

From John Dawson

July 14. 1787.

DEAR SIR

It is now some time since I was honourd with a letter from you. Either your engagements in public business, or the want of something new, I presume has been the cause of it.

Nothing has taken place in this state worth communicating. The people in general appear much discontented. To make property receivable in payment of debts appears to be the most favour'd plan at present. The people of this and several of the neighbouring counties are now signing petitions to that purpose.[1]

Early tomorrow morning I set out for the springs.[2] The remote situation of that place, and the difficulty of procuring any information from Pha. or New York, will render any communications from you doubly acceptable. If you will enclose and direct to Majr. Charles Magill,[3] at Winchester I shall receive your letters in a direct line. I am with much respect & esteem Your sin: Friend & Very hm: Sert

J DAWSON

RC (DLC).

[1]Dawson was a resident of Spotsylvania County. In November 1787 citizens of Albemarle County petitioned the legislature to pass an act "for an emission of paper money, or for making property, by valuation, a tender in payment of debts." The House of Delegates rejected the petition in a series of resolutions, one of which declared "that the making paper currency, or any thing but gold and silver coin, a tender in discharge of debts contracted in money, is contrary to every principle of sound policy, as well as justice" (*JHDV*, Oct. 1787, pp. 28, 29).

[2]"The springs" were located at the town of Bath, in what was then Berkeley County. The town is now called Berkeley Springs and falls within the limits of Morgan County, West Virginia.

[3]*PJM*, II, 68 n. 1. See also J. R. Graham, *Sketches, Biographical and Genealogical, of the Magill Family of Winchester, Virginia* (Winchester, 1908), pp. 12–17.

Rule of Representation in the Senate

[14 July 1787]

Mr Madison expressed his apprehensions that if the proper foundation of Governmt. was destroyed, by substituting an equal in place of a proportional Representation, no proper superstructure would be raised.[1] If the small States really wish for a Government armed with the powers necessary to secure their liberties, and to enforce obedience on the larger

100

members as well as on themselves he could not help thinking them extremely mistaken in their means. He reminded them of the consequences of laying the existing confederation on improper principles. All the principal parties to its compilation, joined immediately in mutilating & fettering the Governmt. in such a manner that it has disappointed every hope placed on it. He appealed to the doctrine & arguments used by themselves on a former occasion. It had been very properly observed by (Mr. Patterson)[2] that Representation was an expedient by which the meeting of the people themselves was rendered unnecessary; and that the representatives ought therefore to bear a proportion to the votes which their constituents if convened, would respectively have. Was not this remark as applicable to one branch of the Representation as to the other? But it had been said that the Governt. would in its operation be partly federal, partly national; that altho' in the latter respect the Representatives of the people ought to be in proportion to the people: yet in the former it ought to be according to the number of States. If there was any solidity in this distinction he was ready to abide by it, if there was none it ought to be abandoned. In all cases where the Genl. Governmt. is to act on the people, let the people be represented and the votes be proportional. In all cases where the Governt. is to act on the States as such, in like manner as Congs. now act on them, let the States be represented & the votes be equal. This was the true ground of compromise if there was any ground at all. But he denied that there was any ground.[3] He called for a single instance in which the Genl. Govt. was not to operate on the people individually. The practicability of making laws, with coercive sanctions, for the States as Political bodies, had been exploded on all hands. He observed that the people of the large States would in some way or other secure to themselves a weight proportioned to the importance accruing from their superior numbers. If they could not effect it by a proportional representation in the Govt. they would probably accede to no Govt. which did not in great measure depend for its efficacy on their voluntary cooperation, in which case they would indirectly secure their object. The existing confederacy proved that where the Acts of the Genl. Govt. were to be executed by the particular Govts. the latter had a weight in proportion to their importance. No one would say that either in Congs. or out of Congs. Delaware had equal weight with Pensylva. If the latter was to supply ten times as much money as the former, and no compulsion could be used, it was of ten times more importance, that she should voluntarily furnish the supply. In the Dutch confederacy the votes of the Provinces were equal. But Holland, which supplies about half the money, governs the whole republic. He enumerated the objections agst. an equality of votes in the 2d. branch, not-

ture. In R. Island the Judges who refused to execute an unconstitutional law were displaced, and others substituted, by the Legislature who would be willing instruments of the wicked & arbitrary plans of their masters. A power of negativing the improper laws of the States is at once the most mild & certain means of preserving the harmony of the System. Its utility is sufficiently displayed in the British System. Nothing could maintain the harmony & subordination of the various parts of the empire, but the prerogative by which the Crown, stifles in the birth every Act of every part tending to discord or encroachment. It is true the prerogative is sometimes misapplied thro' ignorance or a partiality to one particular part of the empire: but we have not the same reason to fear such misapplications in our System.[1] As to the sending all laws up to the Natl. Legisl: that might be rendered unnecessary by some emanation of the power into the States, so far at least, as to give a temporary effect to laws of immediate necessity.

Ms (DLC).

[1]JM heavily deleted a sentence here and added his concluding sentence.

Term of the Executive

[17 July 1787]

McClurg moved to strike out seven years and insert "'during good behavior'" (Farrand, *Records*, II, 33). He believed that since the executive had been made reeligible he would be dependent on the legislature and that the independence of the executive was essential.

Mr. Madison. If it be essential to the preservation of liberty that the Legisl: Execut: & Judiciary powers be separate, it is essential to a maintenance of the separation, that they should be independent of each other. The Executive could not be independent of the Legislure., if dependent on the pleasure of that branch for a re-appointment. Why was it determined that the Judges should not hold their places by such a tenure? Because they might be tempted to cultivate the Legislature, by an undue complaisance, and thus render the Legislature the virtual expositor, as well the maker of the laws. In like manner a dependence of the Executive on the Legislature, would render it the Executor as well as the maker of laws; & then according to the observation of Montesquieu, tyrannical laws may be made that they may be executed in a tyrannical manner. There was an analogy between the Executive & Judiciary departments in several respects. The latter executed the laws in certain cases as the former did in others. The former expounded & applied them for certain purposes, as the latter did for others. The difference between them seemed to consist chiefly in two circumstances—1. the collective interests & security were much more in the power belonging to the Executive than to the Judiciary department. 2. in the administration of the former much greater latitude is left to opinion and discretion than in the administration of the latter. But if the 2d. consideration proves that it will be more difficult to establish a rule sufficiently precise for trying the Execut: than the Judges, & forms an objection to the same tenure of office, both considerations prove that it might be more dangerous to suffer a Union between the Executive & Legisl: powers, than between the Judiciary & Legislative powers. He conceived it to be absolutely necessary to a well constituted Republic that the two first shd. be kept distinct & independent of each other. Whether the plan proposed by the motion was a proper one was another question, as it depended on the practicability of instituting a tribunal for impeachmts. as certain & as adequate in the one case as in the other. On the other hand, respect for the mover entitled his proposition to a fair hearing & discussion, until a less objectionable expedient should be applied for guarding agst. a dangerous union of the Legislative & Executive departments.[1]

Ms (DLC).

[1]JM later wrote a note to McClurg's motion: "The probable object of this motion was merely to enforce the argument against the re-eligibility of the Executive Magistrate, by holding out a tenure during good behaviour as the alternative for keeping him independent of the Legislature" (ibid.). JM also later noted that "the view here taken of the subject was meant to aid in parrying the animadversions likely to fall on the motion of Dr. McClurg, for whom J. M. had a particular regard, [and whose appointment to the Convention he had actively promoted (crossed out by JM)]. The Docr. though possessing talents of the highest order, was modest & unaccustomed to exert them in public debate" (ibid.).

[17 July 1787]

Mason spoke against executive tenure during good behavior, insisting that it would be the first step towards monarchy.

Mr. Madison was not apprehensive of being thought to favor any step towards monarchy. The real object with him was to prevent its introduction. Experience had proved a tendency in our governments to throw all power into the Legislative vortex. The Executives of the States are in general little more than Cyphers; the legislatures omnipotent. If no effectual check be devised for restraining the instability & encroachments of the latter, a revolution of some kind or other would be inevitable. The preservation of Republican Govt. therefore required some expedient for the purpose, but required evidently at the same time that in devising it, the genuine principles of that form should be kept in view.

Ms (DLC).

To Thomas Jefferson

PHILADA. July 18. 1787.

DEAR SIR

I lately received & forwarded to Mr. Jno. Banister Jr. a packet which came from you under cover to me. I had an opportunity which avoided the charge of postage.

The Convention continue to sit, and have been closely employed since the Commence[me]nt of the Session. I am still under the mortification of being restrained from disclosing any part of their proceedings. As soon as I am at liberty I will endeavor to make amends for my silence, and if I ever have the pleasure of seeing you shall be able to give you pretty full gratification. I have taken lengthy notes of every thing that has yet passed, and mean to go on with the drudgery, if no indisposition obliges me to discontinue it. It is not possible to form any judgment of the future duration of the Session. I am led by sundry circumstances to guess that the residue of the work will not be very quickly dispatched. The public mind is very impatient for the event, and various reports are circulating which tend to inflame curiosity. I do not learn however that any discontent is expressed at the concealment; and have little doubt that the people will be as ready to receive as we shall be able to propose, a Government that will secure their liberties & happiness.

I am not able to give you any account of what is doing at N. York. Your correspondents there will no doubt supply the omission. The paper money here ceased to circulate very suddenly a few days ago. It had been for some time vibrating between a depreciation of 12. & of 20 PerCt. Its entire stagnation is said to have proceeded from a combination of a few people with whom the Country people deal on market days, agst. receiving it. The consequence was that it was refused in the market, and great distress brought on the poorer Citizens. Some of the latter began in turn to form Combinations of a more serious nature in order to take revenge on the supposed authors of the stagnation. The timely interposition of some influencial characters prevented a riot, and prevailed on the persons who were opposed to the paper, to publish their willingness to receive it. This has stifled the popular rage, and got the paper into circulation again. It is however still considerably below par, and must have recd. a wound which will not easily be healed.[1] Nothing but evil springs from this imaginary money wherever it is tried, and yet the appetite for it where it has not been tried, continues to be felt.[2] There is great reason to fear that the bitterness of the evil must be tasted in Virga. before the appetite there will be at an end.

The Wheat harvest throughout the Continent has been uncommonly fine both in point of quantity & quality. The crops of Corn & Tobo. on the ground in Virginia are very different in different places. I rather fear that in general they are both bad; particularly the former. I have just recd. a letter from Orange which complains much of appearances in that neighbourhood; but says nothing of them in the parts adjacent. Present my best respects to Mr. Short & Mr. Mazzei. Nothing has been done since my last to the latter with regard to his affair with Dorhman. Wishing you all happiness. I am Dr Sir Yr. Affee. friend & servt.

Js. Madison Jr.

RC (DLC). For the delivery of this letter to Jefferson, see Carrington to JM, 25 July 1787 and n. 1.

[1]"The city has been much alarmed within a few days, by the paper currency of the state, having in great measure stopped circulating," wrote "A Mechanic" in the Philadelphia *Independent Gazetteer* of 20 July 1787. He blamed the depreciation of the paper money on the writings of Pelatiah and Noah Webster and on the consumption of foreign goods. "Columbiadis" believed a conspiracy of brokers had caused paper money to cease circulating: "Reports are spread about town, that 'a great number of you *Brokers*, went among the country people on Saturday-last, and persuaded them not to take any of our *paper currency*, as it would no longer pass in the stores,' hoping by this means, to buy it up at a great discount; and then, when you have sufficient, to sell it to the mechanics and traders to pay their taxes" (ibid., 21 July 1787). Others blamed the "stagnation" on the negligence and irresponsibility of the state government (ibid., 23 July and 4 Aug. 1787). For other reactions to this incident, see ibid., 27, 28, 30 July, and 1 Aug. 1787.

[2]For a favorable view of Pennsylvania's paper currency, written before the incident described by JM, see the article by "S. T." from the *Pa. Packet*, reprinted in the *Pa. Gazette* of 18 July 1787.

To Ambrose Madison

Philada. July 18th. 1787.

Dear Brothr.

I have this moment your favor of the 10th. instant. I am extremely sorry to learn that My father's health is not yet fully reestablished. I hope it soon may. His letter to me which you refer to has never come to hand. I write in a hurry in order to answer your enquiry by the first mail relative to the land purchased of Jones. If you can rely on the punctuality of the purchaser, and on his taking no advantage of paper money, my advice is that you sell it. As a safeguard you may insert an option between cash & Tobo. at a moderate rate. The Convention is still sitting. The rule heretofore mentioned still imposes a silence with regard to their proceedings. I think it will be some time before they are brought to a conclusion. Remember me affecly. to the family & other friends. Adieu

Js. M. Jr.

RC (NN). Addressed and franked by JM. Sent "Care of Mr Maury Fredericksburg."

To Edward Carrington

Letter not found.

ca. 18 July 1787. Acknowledged in Edward Carrington to JM, 25 July 1787. Requests Carrington to forward by John Paul Jones JM's letter of 18 July to Jefferson. Has settled Carrington's account with Major Turner.

Method of Appointing the Executive

[19 July 1787]

Mr. Madison If it be a fundamental principle of free Govt. that the Legislative, Executive & Judiciary powers should be *separately* exercised, it is equally so that they be *independently* exercised. There is the same & perhaps greater reason why the Executive shd. be independent of the Legislature, than why the Judiciary should: A coalition of the two former powers would be more immediately & certainly dangerous to public liberty. It is essential then that the appointment of the Executive should either be drawn from some source, or held by some tenure, that will give him a free agency with regard to the Legislature. This could not be if he was to be appointable from time to time by the Legislature. It was not clear that an appointment in the 1st. instance even with an ineligibility afterwards would not establish an improper connection between the two departments. Certain it was that the appointment would be attended with intrigues and contentions that ought not to be unnecessarily admitted. He was disposed for these reasons to refer the appointment to some other source. The people at large was in his opinion the fittest in itself.[1] It would be as likely as any that could be devised to produce an Executive Magistrate of distinguished Character. The people generally could only know & vote for some Citizen whose merits had rendered him an object of general attention & esteem. There was one difficulty however of a serious nature attending an immediate choice by the people. The right of suffrage was much more diffusive in the Northern than the Southern States; and the latter could have no influence in the election on the score of the Negroes. The substitution of electors obviated this difficulty and seemed on the whole to be liable to fewest objections.

Ms (DLC).

[1]Here JM crossed through "It was the source from which the Legislature He was persuaded."

Impeachment of the Executive

[20 July 1787]

Mr. Madison thought it indispensable that some provision should be made for defending the Community agst the incapacity, negligence or perfidy of the chief Magistrate. The limitation of the period of his service, was not a sufficient security. He might lose his capacity after his appointment. He might pervert his administration into a scheme of peculation or oppression. He might betray his trust to foreign powers. The case of the Executive Magistracy was very distinguishable, from that of the Legislature or of any other public body, holding offices of limited duration. It could not be presumed that all or even a majority of the members of an Assembly would either lose their capacity for discharging, or be bribed to betray, their trust. Besides the restraints of their personal integrity & honor, the difficulty of acting in concert for purposes of corruption was a security to the public. And if one or a few members only should be seduced, the soundness of the remaining members, would maintain the integrity and fidelity of the body. In the case of the Executive Magistracy which was to be administered by a single man, loss of capacity or corruption was more within the compass of probable events, and either of them might be fatal to the Republic.

Ms (DLC).

Revisionary Power of the Executive
and the Judiciary

[21 July 1787]

Wilson revived a proposal to associate the judiciary with the executive in the veto of legislative acts. JM seconded Wilson's motion.

Mr. Madison considered the object of the motion as of great importance to the meditated Constitution. It would be useful to the Judiciary departmt. by giving it an additional opportunity of defending itself agst. Legislative encroachments; It would be useful to the Executive, by inspiring additional confidence & firmness in exerting the revisionary power: It would be useful to the Legislature by the valuable assistance it would give in preserving a consistency, conciseness, perspicuity & technical propriety in the laws, qualities peculiarly necessary; & yet shamefully wanting in our republican Codes. It would moreover be useful to the Community at large as an additional check agst. a pursuit of those unwise & unjust measures which constituted so great a portion of our calamities. If any solid objection could be urged agst. the motion, it must be on the supposition that it tended to give too much strength either to the Executive or Judiciary. He did not think there was the least ground for this apprehension. It was much more to be apprehended that notwithstanding this co-operation of the two departments, the Legislature would still be an overmatch for them. Experience in all the States had evinced a powerful tendency in the Legislature to absorb all power into its vortex. This was the real source of danger to the American Constitutions; & suggested the necessity of giving every defensive authority to the other departments that was consistent with republican principles.

Ms (DLC).

[21 July 1787]

Gerry objected to a joint revisionary power as "establishing an improper coalition between the Executive & Judiciary departments" (Farrand, Records, II, 75).

Mr. Madison could not discover in the proposed association of the Judges with the Executive in the Revisionary check on the Legislature any violation of the maxim which requires the great departments of power to be kept separate & distinct. On the contrary he thought it an auxiliary precaution in favor of the maxim. If a Constitutional discrimination of the departments on paper were a sufficient security to each agst. encroachments of the others, all further provisions would indeed be superfluous. But experience had taught us a distrust of that security; and that it is necessary to introduce such a balance of powers and interests, as will guarantee the provisions on paper. Instead therefore of contenting ourselves with laying down the Theory in the Constitution that each department ought to be separate & distinct, it was proposed to add a defensive power to each which should maintain the Theory in practice. In so doing we did not blend the departments together. We erected effectual barriers for keeping them separate. The most regular example of this theory was in the British Constitution. Yet it was not only the practice there to admit the Judges to a seat in the legislature, and in the Executive Councils, and to submit to their previous examination all laws of a certain description, but it was a part of their Constitution that the Executive might negative any law whatever; a part of *their* Constitution which had been universally regarded as calculated for the preservation of the whole. The objection agst. a union of the Judiciary & Executive branches in the revision of the laws, had either no foundation or was not carried far enough. If such a Union was an improper mixture of powers, or such a Judiciary check on the laws, was inconsistent with the Theory of a free Constitution, it was equally so to admit the Executive to any participation in the making of laws; and the revisionary plan ought to be discarded altogether.

Ms (DLC).

Method of Choosing the Judiciary

[21 July 1787]

JM had moved on 18 July that the national judiciary should be nominated by the executive and "such nomination should become an appointment if not disagreed to . . . by ⅔ of the 2d. branch" (Ms [DLC]). After being postponed, debate on this motion was now resumed.

Mr. Madison stated as his reasons for the motion. 1 that it secured the responsibility of the Executive who would in general be more capable & likely to select fit characters than the Legislature, or even the 2d. b. of it, who might hide their selfish motives under the number concerned in the appointment. 2 that in case of any flagrant partiality or error, in the nomination it might be fairly presumed that ⅔ of the 2d. branch would join in putting a negative on it. 3. that as the 2d. b. was very differently constituted when the appointment of the Judges was formerly referred to it, and was now to be composed of equal votes from all the States, the principle of compromise which had prevailed in other instances required in this that there shd. be a concurrence of two authorities, in one of which the people, in the other the States, should be represented. The Executive Magistrate wd. be considered as a national officer, acting for and equally sympathising with every part of the U. States. If the 2d. branch alone should have this power, the Judges might be appointed by a minority of the people, tho' by a majority of the States, which could not be justified on any principle as their proceedings were to relate to the people, rather than to the States; and as it would moreover throw the appointments entirely into the hands of the Northern States, a perpetual ground of jealousy & discontent would be furnished to the Southern States.[1]

Ms (DLC).

[1] After Gerry objected to the two-thirds requirement, JM said "that he was not anxious that ⅔ should be necessary to disagree to a nomination. He had given this form to his motion cheifly to vary it the more clearly from one which had just been rejected. He was content to obviate the objection last made, and accordingly so varied the motion as to let a majority reject" (ibid.).

From Joseph Jones

RICHMOND 23. July 1787.

DR. SR.

Since my last to you I have been very much indisposed and untill a few days past unable to write or attend to any business. At this time I am barely strong enough to take exercise. Are we likely to have a happy issue of your meeting, or will it pass over withot. effect. Finding you still continue together our hopes are not lost. My fears, however, I must confess are rather increased, than diminished by the protraction of yr. Session taking it for granted many and great difficulties have been encountered, as there were many and great to remove before a good system could be established. We have been amused with your either soon separating or continuing to set untill September. I have nothing to tell you of but that I have been disappointed in my expectations we shod. get for our Tobacco the State price. The James Appomattox & York have been sold here the two former at near the State price the latter some shillings below it. A few lotts of Rap: & Pot: were offered. They sold at a loss of 5 or 6/℔ hundd. Seeing no prospect of a better price here for those Tobaccos the Com: of

Council who attended the Sale to assist the Treasurer with their advice postponed the Sale and the Rap: Tobaccos are to be sold at Fredericksburg the 1st. next month and the Poto: at Alexa. the 6th. being the monday after. Col. Meriweather is appointed to do the business under the direction of two of the Council Col. Mathews & Genl. Wood who are to attend. It is hoped a better price will be obtained by selling in the manner proposed.[1] I am Dr Sr. Yr. friend & Sert

JOS: JONES

P.S. I shall leave this place abt. the 3d. of next month and keep on towards the Mountains for the sake of healt[h]. Your future letters therefore please to direct to Fredericksburg.[2]

RC (DLC). Docketed by JM. Brackets enclose letter obscured in right margin of Ms.

[1] See *JCSV*, IV, 126, 127. Col. Thomas Meriwether was a clerk of the Council of State. The committee of Meriwether, Sampson Mathews, and James Wood was authorized to sell the tobacco "at private sale if they shall find it more advantageous for the public" (ibid., IV, 129).

[2] An earlier printed version of the RC has what appears to be an additional paragraph (W. C. Ford, *Letters of Joseph Jones*, p. 157). However, this paragraph is obviously the editor's explanatory note, which was inadvertently set in the same size of type.

Method of Ratifying the Constitution

[23 July 1787]

The delegates had previously voted to send the Constitution to state conventions for ratification, but Ellsworth now moved that final approval should come from the state legislatures.

Mr. Madison thought it clear that the Legislatures were incompetent to the proposed changes. These changes would make essential inroads on the State Constitutions, and it would be a novel & dangerous doctrine that a Legislature could change the constitution under which it held its existence. There might indeed be some Constitutions within the Union, which had given a power to the Legislature to concur in alterations of the federal Compact. But there were certainly some which had not; and in the case of these, a ratification must of necessity be obtained from the people. He considered the difference between a system founded on the Legislatures only, and one founded on the people, to be the true difference between a *league* or *treaty*, and a *Constitution*. The former in point of *moral obligation* might be as inviolable as the latter. In point of *political operation*, there were two important distinctions in favor of the latter. 1. A law violating a treaty ratified by a pre-existing law, might be respected by the Judges as a law, though an unwise or perfidious one. A law violating a constitution established by the people themselves, would be considered by the Judges as null & void. 2. The doctrine laid down by the law of Nations in the case of treaties is that a breach of any one article by any of the parties, frees the other parties from their engagements. In the case of a union of people under one Constitution, the nature of the pact has always been understood to exclude such an interpretation. Comparing the two modes in point of expediency he thought all the considerations which recommended this Convention in preference to Congress for proposing the reform were in favor of State Conventions in preference to the Legislatures for examining and adopting it.

Ms (DLC).

From Edward Carrington

New York July 25. 1787

DEAR SIR,

I was favoured with yours inclosing a letter for Mr. Jefferson, which I delivered, agreably to your request, to Chevalier Jones—his business with Congress is not finished, and therefore he has not gone with the packet, which sailed this morning. No passenger was going whose personal delivery of the letter could be relied upon, and it seems the Capt. could not take it, otherwise than in the Mail. Not knowing it to be matter of indifference with you, whether it should be exposed to inspection or not, it has been determined, in a conference between the Chevalier & myself, that he should keep it until his own departure, which he expects will be in a short time.[1]

I recd. by Colo. R H Lee Ninety dollars which, with the sum you was good enough to pay Major Turner for me, sets us even. Your acknowledgement for the 100 dollars is inclosed.

We are trying to do something with our Western Territory to make it useful to the purposes for which the United States were vested with it. You have seen in the papers the scheme for the temporary as well as perpetual Government of it. A practicable measure for the sale of it, or rather, by means of it to redeem the domestic debt, remains still to be agreed upon, and I fear the difficulties which have always stood in the way of this great object, are not yet to be surmounted. Colo Lee joins Grayson

& myself with great zeal, but what will be the issue of our efforts I know not.[2]

Indian affairs wear an hostile aspect, and money must, in all probability, be expended in Treaties with them. A general confederacy is formed of all the Nations & Tribes from the Six Nations inclusive, to the Mississippi under the immediate influence of Brandt. A general Council has been held in form, near detroit, as long ago as last december, in which have been considered as greivances, our Surveying over the Ohio, the Cessions being made by only parts of the Tribes having rights in the ceded Tracts. Of these injuries or greivances they have sent an United representation to Congress requesting that a general Treaty may be held—perhaps this business may be directed by an authority higher than that of Brandt, and should our titles to the Land be compleat it will still be better to spend a little money in Treating, rather than expend a great deal in War, which from the generality of the confederacy is seriously to be apprehended. This subject is now under consideration.[3]

As to the hostilities upon Kentucky the superintendant of Indian affairs, or in case of his inability to go, Colo. Josiah Harmar, is ordered to proceed immediately to some convenient place for holding a Treaty with the hostile tribes, and by that means restore peace between them and our people if practicable. In the mean time Colo. Harmar is so to post the Federal Troops as to provide the best defence for the Country, and to call for such aids of Militia as he shall find necessary. Should the Treaty not succeed report is to be made to Congress for their further orders as to offensive operations.[4] The state of the general confederacy requires some care in the direction of this business. The desperate state of things in the United Netherlands you see in the papers. Be good enough to present me respectfully to your Collegues and beleive me to be with great regard Your Affe. Hl serv

ED CARRINGTON

RC (DLC). Enclosure not found.

[1]John Paul Jones's departure was delayed until 11 Nov. He arrived in Paris five weeks later and delivered JM's letter of 18 July 1787 to Jefferson (John Paul Jones to Jefferson, ca. 19 Dec. 1787, Boyd, *Papers of Jefferson*, XII, 438). His "business with Congress" concerned prize money due to the officers and crew of the *Bonhomme Richard* and *Alliance* (Morison, *John Paul Jones*, pp. 350–55).

[2]For the differences between New Englanders and Southerners over the proper method of selling the western territory—by townships or by "indiscriminate locations"—see *PJM*, IX, 401–2 n. 1.

[3]Indian tribes northwest of the Ohio, discontented since the signing of the peace between Great Britain and the U.S., met at Detroit in December 1786 under the leadership of Joseph Brant, chief of the Mohawk (Downes, *Council Fires*, pp. 299–301). Their representation of 18 Dec. 1786 requesting a treaty was not received by Congress until 18 July 1787 (*JCC*,

tary, interested all Europe, and was much influenced by foreign interference. In the latter, altho' the elective Magistrate has very little real power, his election has at all times produced the most eager interference of for[e]ign princes, and has in fact at length slid entirely into foreign hands. The existing authorities in the States are the Legislative, Executive & Judiciary. The appointment of the Natl. Executive by the first, was objectionable in many points of view, some of which had been already mentioned. He would mention one which of itself would decide his opinion. The Legislatures of the States had betrayed a strong propensity to a variety of pernicious measures. One object of the Natl. Legislre. was to controul this propensity. One object of the Natl. Executive, so far as it would have a negative on the laws, was to controul the Natl. Legislature, so far as it might be infected with a similar propensity. Refer the appointmt of the Natl. Executive to the State Legislatures, and this controuling purpose may be defeated. The Legislatures can & will act with some kind of regular plan, and will promote the appointmt. of a man who will not oppose himself to a favorite object. Should a majority of the Legislatures at the time of election have the same object, or different objects of the same kind, The Natl. Executive would be rendered subservient to them. An appointment by the State Executives, was liable among other objections to this insuperable one, that being standing bodies, they could & would be courted, and intrigued with by the Candidates, by their partizans, and by the Ministers of foreign powers. The State Judiciarys had not & he presumed wd. not be proposed as a proper source of appointment. The option before us then lay between an appointment by Electors chosen by the people—and an immediate appointment by the people. He thought the former mode free from many of the objections which had been urged agst. it, and greatly preferable to an appointment by the Natl. Legislature. As the electors would be chosen for the occasion, would meet at once, & proceed immediately to an appointment, there would be very little opportunity for cabal, or corruption. As a further precaution, it might be required that they should meet at some place, distinct from the seat of Govt. and even that no person within a certain distance of the place at the time shd. be eligible. This Mode however had been rejected, so recently & by so great a majority that it probably would not be proposed anew. The remaining mode was an election by the people or rather by the qualified part of them, at large. With all its imperfections he liked this best. He would not repeat either the general argumts. for or the objections agst. this mode. He would only take notice of two difficulties which he admitted to have weight. The first arose from the disposition in the people to prefer a Citizen of their own State, and the disadvantage this wd. throw on the smaller States. Great as this objection might be he did not think it equal to such as lay agst. every other mode which had been proposed. He thought too that some expedient might be hit upon that would obviate it. The second difficulty arose from the disproportion of qualified voters in the N. & S. States, and the disadvantages which this mode would throw on the latter. The answer to this objection was 1. that this disproportion would be continually decreasing under the influence of the Republican laws introduced in the S. States, and the more rapid increase of their population. 2. That local considerations must give way to the general interest. As an individual from the S. States he was willing to make the sacrifice.

Ms (DLC).

Qualifications for Holding National Office

[26 July 1787]

Mr. Madison moved to strike out the word *landed*, before the word "qualifications." If the proposition sd. be agreed to he wished the Committee to be at liberty to report the best criterion they could devise. Landed possessions were no certain evidence of real wealth. Many enjoyed them to a great extent who were more in debt than they were worth. The unjust laws of the States had proceeded more from this class of men, than any others. It had often happened that men who had acquired landed property on credit, got into the Legislatures with a view of promoting an unjust protection agst. their Creditors. In the next place, if a small quantity of land should be made the standard, it would be no security; if a large one, it would exclude the proper representatives of those classes of Citizens who were not landholders. It was politic as well as just that the interests & rights of every class should be duly represented & understood in the public Councils. It was a provision every where established that the Country should be divided into districts & representatives taken from each, in order that the Legislative Assembly might equally understand & sympathise, with the rights of the people in every part of the Community. It was not less proper that every class of Citizens should have an opportunity of making their rights be felt & understood in the public Councils. The three principal classes into which our citizens were divisible, were the landed the commercial, & the manufacturing. The 2d. & 3d. class, bear as yet a small proportion to the first. The proportion however will daily increase.

We see in the populous Countries in Europe now, what we shall be hereafter. These classes understand much less of each others interests & affairs, than men of the same class inhabiting different districts. It is particularly requisite therefore that the interests of one or two of them should not be left entirely to the care, or the impartiality of the third. This must be the case if landed qualifications should be required; few of the mercantile, & scarcely any of the manufacturing class, chusing whilst they continue in business to turn any part of their Stock into landed property. For these reasons he wished if it were possible that some other criterion than the mere possession of land should be devised. He concurred with Mr. Govr. Morris in thinking that qualifications in the Electors would be much more effectual than in the elected. The former would discriminate between real & ostensible property in the latter; But he was aware of the difficulty of forming any uniform standard that would suit the different circumstances & opinions prevailing in the different States.

Ms (DLC).

To James Madison, Sr.

PHILADA. July 28. 1787.

HOND. SIR

Since my letter to my brother Ambrose, I have received yours of the 9th. instant. The enquiries which I have at different times made of Billey concerning Anthony satisfy me that he either knows, or will tell nothing of the matter. It does not appear to me probable that all the circumstances mentioned by Anthony with regard to his rambles can be true. Besides other objections which occur, there seems to have been scarcely time for all the trips which he pretends to have made.[1] I have not communicated to John the suspicions entertained of him. Whilst he remains in my service it will be well for him to suppose that he has my confidence, and that he has a character staked on his good behaviour. He has been very attentive & faithful to me as yet, particularly since I left Virginia. His misbehaviour in Fredericksbg. was followed by some serious reprehensions, & threats from me, which have never lost their effect.

I am sorry that I cannot gratify your wish to be informed of the proceedings of the Convention. An order of secresy leaves me at liberty merely to tell you that nothing definitive is yet done, that the Session will probably continue for some time yet, that an Adjournment took place on thursday last until Monday week, and that a Committee is to be at work in the mean time. Late information from Europe presents a sad picture of things in Holland. Civil blood has been already spilt, and various circumstances threaten a torrent of it.[2] Many it is said are flying with their property to England. How much is it [to] be lamented that America does not present a more inviting Asylum!

Congress have been occupied for some time past on Western affairs. They have provided for the Governmt. of the Country by an ordinance of which a copy is herewith inclosed.[3] They have on the anvil at present, some projects for the most advantageous sale of the lands. Col. Carrington informs me that Indian Affairs wear a very hostile appearance; that money must in all probability be expended in further Treaties; that a General Confederacy has been formed of all the Nations & tribes from the six nations inclusive to the Mississippi under the auspices of Brandt; that a Genl. Council was held in Decr. last in form, near detroit, in which was considered as a greivance, the Surveying of lands on the N.W. side of the Ohio, the pretext being, as usual that the Treaties which preceded that measure were made by parts only of the Nations whose consent was necessary; and that a united representation of this grievance has been recd. by Congress. That as to the hostilities on Kentucky the Superintendant of Indian Affairs, or in case of his inability to go, Col. Harmar, is ordered to proceed immediately to some convenient place for holding a Treaty with the Hostile tribes, and by that means restore if possible peace in that quarter. In the mean time Col. Harmar is so to post the federal troops as to provide the best defence for the Country, and to call for such aids of Militia as he shall find necessary.

The Crops of wheat in this & the neighbouring States, and indeed throughout the Continent as far as I can learn have been remarkably fine. I am sorry to hear that your crops of Corn are likely to be so much shortened by the dry weather. The weather has been dry in spots in this quarter. At present it is extremely seasonable just here, and I do not know that is otherwise, elsewhere. I hope Virginia partakes of the blessing.[4]

A letter from my brother gave me the first notice of your indisposition. It is my most fervent wish that this may find your health thoroughly re-established, and that of my mother & the rest of the family, unimpaired: Being with entire affection Yr. dutifully Son.

Js. MADISON JR.

RC (DLC). Enclosure not found.

[1] Billey was JM's former slave, whom JM had left in Philadelphia at the close of his first period of service in Congress in 1783 (*PJM*, VII, 304, 304–5 n. 4). Anthony, a family slave, had run away in June 1786 (*PJM*, IX, 155 n. 1).

[2] Civil war broke out in the United Provinces in the spring of 1787, the culmination of the

Dutch Patriot movement of the 1780s (Palmer, *Age of the Democratic Revolution*, I, 324–40). The *Pa. Gazette* of 25 July 1787 carried news of clashes between "free corps" (Patriot) troops of Utrecht and The Hague and forces loyal to the Prince of Orange.

[3] JM could have clipped a copy of the Northwest Ordinance from the *Pa. Gazette* of 25 July 1787. More likely he enclosed one of the official copies of the ordinance printed on two folio pages (*JCC*, XXXIII, 757).

[4] According to Madison family weather records, the summer at Montpelier was cool and dry. The temperature ranged in the seventies and eighties throughout June, July, and August and climbed to ninety degrees on just two occasions. The only precipitation was an occasional drizzle or thundershower (Madison Meteorological Journal [PPAmP]).

To James McClurg

Letter not found.

ca. 28 July 1787. Acknowledged in McClurg to JM, 5 Aug. 1787. Reports proceedings of the Federal Convention since McClurg's departure and requests his return to Philadelphia.

To Jacquelin Ambler

PHILADA. July 30. 1787.

SIR

Please to pay ⟨to Messrs. Francis and John West of Philadelphia or order⟩ five hundred and fifty two dollars for value received, as an advance for one quarters attendance on ⟨Congress⟩,[1] to   Yr. Obedt. & hble servt.

Js. MADISON JR.

RC (Vi). Endorsed at bottom of the page: "Philadelphia August 2. 1787. This bill will certainly be paid on sight. Edm: Randolph." Endorsed on verso: "Pay the within Contents to Messrs: Henry & Joyce or Order for our Accot. Fran: & Jno: West." Docketed in the hand of auditor John Pendleton: "10th Augt. 1787. The Hon. Jas Madison £165.12.0." Words within angle brackets supplied by Randolph.

[1] JM had written here "the Convention," which Randolph deleted.

From the Reverend James Madison

Aug. 1. 1787. WILLIAMSB.

DEAR COL.

We are here, & I beleive every where, all Impatience to know Something of your conventional Deliberations. If you cannot tell us what you are doing, you might at least give us some Information of what you are not doing. This wd. afford a Clue for political Conjecture, and perhaps be sufficient to satisfy present Impatience. I hope you have already discoverd the Means of preserving the American Empire united—& that the Scheme of a Disunion has been found pregnant with the greatest Evils. But we are not at this Distance able to judge with any Accuracy upon subjects so truely important & interesting as those wch. must engage you at present. We can only hope, that you will all resemble Cæsar, at least in one particular, "nil actum reputans si quid superesset agendum";[1] & that your Exertions will be commensurate to the great Expectations wch. have been formed. It is probable my Observations upon Mr. A's Book must have appeared to you to be hasty & undigested. I wish to know what you think of it. Congress, I find, by a late Ordinance establishing temporary Govts. in the new States, have adopted the Adamic Idea.[2] Would not the other States be wise to wait for the Issue of the Experiment wch. will there be made. We shall then have two important Expts. going on at the same Time—The Results of wch. may be the best Guide.

If you be not better or too much engaged I beg you wh. is the principal Object of this Letter to favour me with a few Lines & to beleive me to be most sincerely Dr Col. Yr. Friend

J MADISON

Pray remember me to Mr Blair The Govr. & M'Clurg.

RC (DLC). Docketed by JM.

[1]"Thinking nothing done while anything remained to do." The quotation, "nil actum credens, cum quid superesset agendum," is from Marcus Annaeus Lucanus, *Pharsalia*, bk. II, line 657 (Lucan, *The Civil War*, bks. I–X, Loeb Classical Library [London, 1928], pp. 105–6).

[2]The Northwest Ordinance provided for a governor with substantial powers, including an absolute veto over acts of the legislature; an elected house of representatives; and a "legislative council" of five members, appointed by Congress on the recommendation of the house of representatives (*JCC*, XXXII, 335–39). The Williamsburg clergyman believed this plan corresponded to John Adams's scheme of balanced government under the direction of a strong executive, discussed in his *Defence of the Constitutions of Government* (Reverend James Madison to JM, 11 June 1787 and nn. 2, 3). In the conclusion to this work Adams himself remarked that the Northwest Ordinance, along with the Constitution, was an acknowledgment of the principles he had "attempted to defend" (C. F. Adams, *Works of John Adams*, VI, 219).

From William Short

PARIS Aug. 1. 1787

DEAR SIR

Since I had last the honor of writing to you I have recieved your two favors of May 16. & June 6. The first brought me a letter from my friend

Mr. Nelson, & at the same time recommended to my care an affair which a letter from one of the parties (Mr. Hollingsworth) explained. I beg you to be persuaded Sir, of the pleasure it will at all times give me to render every service in my power to my countrymen who may have business on this side of the Atlantic. In this instance particularly it can give no trouble, as a mercantile gentleman is joined with me in the commission, who will dictate the proper measures, when the powers to act shall arrive.

Mr. Jefferson has returned from his journey, & recieved the letter you wrote him by the last packet. I leave to him therefore Sir, to give you an account of the effects of the waters on a wrist which you appreciate so properly. I mentioned to the Marquis de la fayette what you desired in your letter of the 6th. He expects to hear from you as soon as your time will permit you to write to your friends here, & regrets much your late silence. He sets out in a few days to the Province of Auvergne where he is a member of the assembly under the new regulations that are taking place in this kingdom. His friends had once expected that he would have been made the president of that assembly: but the crime of having only thirty years of age though with more experience than others have at sixty, has prevented his nomination to that place. In this instance the presidents are chosen by the court; in future they will be chosen by the assembly themselves, & then I think the Marquis's popular talents, without counting his merit, will insure him the preference.

From the public papers, & from Mr. Jefferson you will recieve a much better idea of the present critical situation of affairs in Europe than I can give you. Yet I may add that every circumstance seems to threaten war, except the impossibility in which the two principal champions are to raise money sufficient for the purpose. The treaty of commerce they have lately made, & the advantages which both nations may expect to derive from it would not be sufficient to restrain the two sovereigns if they were free of pecuniary embarassments. You may form some idea of the situation of the finances of this country when you are told that the deficit, after four years peace, is found to be 140. millions annually—that in order to cover this deficit, supposing a peace to continue, it is necessary first to make a loan of 50. millions—secondly, that the King should submit to an oeconomy of 40. millions—& thirdly that new taxes should be imposed to the amount of 50. millions. The loan has been effected—the oeconomies have been promised by the crown—& the new taxes have been absolutely & repeatedly refused by the Parliament of Paris notwithstanding positive orders to enregister the edict creating them. The Princes & Peers have been assembled with the Parliament. This from long desuetude is regarded as a phaenomenon; as yet however they have been able to get nothing from the

Parliament but remonstrances. They were assembled yesterday, after a committee of the Parliament had been summoned to Versailles. The event of yesterday's session is not known with precision. The freedom & the firmness with which these remonstrances have been expressed do great honor to the authors of them, & still more to the influence of philosophy which begins to teach subjects the proper bounds of the authority of sovereigns.

We are happy Sir, in being of a country where the rights of man are considered the gift of heaven and not the grant of [a crow]ned head—but we should be still more happy if our countrymen knew how to estimate such a situation. The result of the deliberations of the convention, & the spirit with which they may be recieved in the different states, will show whether we know how to make small sacrifices where necessary to secure general happiness. I confess to you Sir, that past experience makes me fear to look forward to the event of the trial now making. A want of certainty of its doing good, & a certainty of its doing much harm if it does not, makes me regard with anxiety the dubious event. The representation however is such an one as must effect whatever can be effected by such a convention. You may be sure Sir, I am happy to see that Virginia has furnished her full quota of virtue & talents on this occasion. I am sorry that the Socrates of our State should have been obliged to withdraw his aid on account of the indisposition of a part of his family.[1]

Mr. Nelson's letter informed me that the plan of paper money had been rejected in Maryland, & that the ardor for it in Virginia was disappearing. If so the symptom may be considered as favorable, but I fear that Mr. Nelson could speak of only a small part of the State, & that not in a quarter most to be feared. I hope, & intreat you Sir, to return to the next Assembly in Virginia. I know nobody but yourself who can oppose with success the dangerous influence of Mr. Henry. Accept, my dear Sir the sincerest wishes for your success in all your enterprizes & particularly in this, from Your friend & servant

W SHORT

RC (DLC). Addressed by Short. Docketed by JM. Brackets enclose blotted letters.

[1] "The Socrates of our State"—George Wythe—left the convention to attend his ailing wife (JM to Jefferson, 6 June 1787 and n. 2).

To John Pendleton

PHILADA. Augst. 2. 1787.

SIR

Inclosed is the account on which my claim is founded for another quarters advance; for which I have drawn a bill on the Treasurer in favor of Messrs. Wests Merchts. of this City.[1] I was so unlucky as to make out & dispose of the bill before I adverted to the surplus of £14. advanced for the last quarter by mistake of your Clerk.[2] I could not therefore correct the error at this time. In my next account, it shall certainly be attended to. I am Sir with great respect Yr. Obdt. & hble servt.

Js. MADISON JR.

[Enclosure]

1787. The Commonwealth of Virginia to James Madison Jr. Dr.
To Attendance as a member of Congress from July 20.
to Octr. 20. being 92 days at 6 dollars per day.   £165..12-

$$\begin{array}{r} 6 \\ \hline 552 \\ 3 \\ \hline 165.12^3 \\ \hline \end{array}$$

E. E. Js. MADISON JR.

RC and enclosure (Vi). Docketed by Pendleton: "Warrant issd 9. Augt. 87 Entd. 27. Nov. 1787."

[1]JM to Ambler, 30 July 1787.
[2]See *PJM*, IX, 403.
[3]On the conversion of Virginia dollars into pounds, see *PJM*, IX, 393.

From Thomas Jefferson

PARIS Aug. 2. 1787.

DEAR SIR

My last was of June 20. Your's received since that date are May 15. and June 6. In mine I acknoleged the receipt of the Paccan nuts which came sealed up. I have reason to believe those in the box are arrived at Lorient. By the Mary capt Howland lately sailed from Havre to N. York I shipped three boxes of books one marked I.M. for yourself, one marked B.F. for Doctr. Franklin, & one marked W.H. for William Hay in Richmond. I have taken the liberty of addressing them all to you as you will see by the inclosed bill of lading, in hopes you would be so good as to forward the other two. You will have opportunities of calling on the gentlemen for the freight &c. In yours you will find the books noted in the account inclosed herewith. You have now Mably's works complete except that on Poland, which I have never been able to get, but shall not cease to search for. Some other volumes to compleat your collection of Chronologies. The 4th. vol. of D'Albon was lost by the bookbinder, & I have not yet been able to get one to replace it. I shall continue to try. The Memoires sur les droits et impositions en Europe (cited by Smith) was a scarce & excessively dear book. They are now reprinting it. I think it will be in three or four quartos of from 9. to 12 a volume. When it is finished I shall take a copy for you. Amelot's travels into China I can learn nothing of. I put among the books sent you, two somewhat voluminous, & the object of which will need explanation; these are the Tableau de Paris & L'espion Anglois. The former is truly a picture of private manners in Paris, but presented on the dark side & a little darkened moreover. But there is so much truth in it's ground work that it will be well worth your reading. You will then know Paris (& probably the other large cities of Europe) as well as if you had been here years. L'Espion Anglois is no Caricature. It will give you a just idea of the wheels by which the machine of government is worked here. There are in it also many interesting details of the last war, which in general may be relied on. It may be considered as the small history of great events. I am in hopes when you shall have read them you will not think I have mis-spent your money for them. My method for making out this assortment was to revise the list of my own purchases since the invoice of 1785. and to select such as I had found worth your having. Besides this I have casually met with & purchased some few curious & cheap things. I have made out the Dr. side of the account, taking for my ground work yours of March 18. 1786. correcting two errors of computation in that which were to your prejudice. The account of the Mr. Fitzhughs stood thus. 1785. Sep. 1. cash 600 lt. Nov. 10. pd. their bill of exchange in favor of Limozin 480 lt. making 1080 lt. The money they paid you was worth 1050 lt. according to our mode of settling at 18 lt. for 20/ Virginia money. The difference of 30 lt. will never be worth notice unless you were to meet with them by chance, & hardly then. I must trouble you on behalf of a Mr. Thos. Burke at Loughburke near Loughrea in Ireland, whose brother James Burke is supposed to have died in 1785. on his passage from Jamaica, or St. Eustatius to New York. His property on board the vessel is understood to have come to the hands of Alderman Groom at New York. The inclosed copy of a letter to him will more fully explain it. A particular friend of mine here applies to me for information, which I must ask the favor of you to procure and forward to me.[1]

[Enclosure]

pa. 1.

State of account between James Madison esq. & Th: Jefferson copied
from J. M's letter of Mar. 18. 1786.

	J: M. to Th: J.	Dr.	
			lt
1785. Sep. 1.	To amount of books		1164- 3

Cr.

		lt	
By balance stated by Th: J. 77 ⅔ Dollars.		407-15	
By advance to Le Maire 10. Guineas		234-	
By 6. copies of revisal @ 2½ dollars.		81-	
By 25£ Virga. currcy. remitted to mrs. Carr		441- 8	1164- 3

pa.2.

James Madison esq. to Th: Jefferson Dr.

		lt		
	To 58£ -6s-8 Virga. currency received from the Fitzhughs	1050- 0- 0		
1785. Nov. 4.	To repaid mr. Short for a Spy-glass bought in England	50-		
Nov. 21.	To Limozin at Havre transportation of 2. trunks of books Sep. 1785.	34- 8- 9		
1786. Aug. 2.	To paid for an Umbrella cane	30-		
	a copying press & apparatus, paper & ink	144-		
Oct. 13.	a chemical box	69-		
1787. July 4.	To paid Cabaret for binding books[3]	46-14		
	To paid for books, to wit.			

	lt	s	d
Guerre de 1775–83. 4to[4]	10-	0-	0
Voyage en Suisse par Mayer. 2. v. 8vo.	7-	4	
Ordonnance de marine 8vo.	4-	4	
Voiage aux Alpes par Saussure. 4. v. 8vo.	18-		

Experiences d'Ingenhousz. 8vo.	4-10	
Chymie de Fourcroy. 4. v. 8vo.	24- 0	
Peines infamantes par La Cretelle. 8vo.	3-12	
Savary sur l'Egypte 3. v. 8vo.	15- 0	
Voiages de Volney. 2. v. 8vo.	10- 4	
la France et les etats Unis par Warville. 8vo	4-10	
Loix criminelles par Warville 2. v. 8vo.	7- 4	
Vie de Turgot par Condorcet. 8vo.	4-10	
L'Espion Anglois. 10. v. 12mo.	25- 0	
Annales Romaines par Macquer. 12mo.	5-	
	─────	─────
	142-18	1424- 2- 9
		pa. 3.

	lt s	lt s d
Brought forward	142-18	1424- 2- 9
Troubles de l'Amerique par Soulés. 4. v. 8vo.	16- 0-	
Bibliotheque physico-oeco-nomique (1786) 2. v. 12mo.	5- 4	
Mably. Principes de legisla-tion. 12mo.	3-	
_____ de la Grece. 12mo.	2-	
De Juvigny sur la decadence des lettres. 8vo.	6-	
Abregé chronologique d'Angleterre de Salmon. 2. v. 8vo.	12-	
Abregé chronol. de l'his-toire ecclesiastique	18-	
Abregé chronol. de l'Alle-magne par Pfeffel. 2. v. 12mo.	12-	

		lt s	lt s d
	Histoire ancienne de Milot.		
	4. v. 12mo.	12-	
	Moderne 5. v. 12mo.	15	
	de France 3. v. 12mo.	7-10	
	De Thou. 11. v. 4to	55-	
	Bibliotheque Physico-oeco-		
	nomique. (1787.) 2. v.		
	12mo.	5- 4	
	Pieces interessantes. 4. v.		
	12mo.	12-	
	Tableau de Paris 4. v. 12mo.	13-	
(given)	Demarcation entre l'Espagne		
	et le Portugal en Amerique.		
	Histoire de Kentuckey. 8vo.	4- 5	
	Smith's history of New York.		
	8vo.	6-	
	Voiages de Chastellux. 2. v.		
	8vo.	11-	
	Memoires de Brandenburgh.		
	8vo.	6-	
	Examen de Chastellux par		
	Warville. 8vo.	2- 8	
	Hennepin. 12mo.	2-	
	Vie de Voltaire par l'Abbé		
	Duvernet. 8vo.	7- 5	
		375-14	1424- 2- 9

pa. 4.

		lt s	lt s d
	Brought forward	375-14	1424- 2- 9
	Histoire de la Nouvelle		
	France par Lescarbot 8vo.	2-10	
	Gibson's Saxon chronicle.		
	4to. 6/ sterl.	7- 4	
	Avantages et desavantages de		
	la decouverte de l'Amerique	1- 4	
	Encyclopedie. 16th. 18th.		
	19th. 20th. 22d. livraisons		
	@ 24 lt. each. 120		
	15th. 23 lt-10—17th.		
	& 21st. 36 lt-10		
	each 96-10	216-10	

	*5th. Oiseaux to. 1.		
	part 2.	7- 0	610- 2
1787. Aug. 4.	To paid Limozin carriage of	———	
	books to Havre (exclus. of		
	Dr. F's & Hay's)		27-14- 9
			2061-19- 6

Graecorum respublicae Ub-
   bonis Emmii (qu. if
   sent?)   9 lt.
*when your duplicate vol.
shall be returned they will
give you credit for it.

Cr.

By error in computing the value of 10
   Guineas in former account
      s lt   s lt s   lt
      (20:18::28:25-4)   18
         £   lt
By do. 25=441-8 remitted to mrs. Carr
      £   lt
      (25=450)   8-12

NB.   Having been very desirous of collecting the original
             Spanish writers on American history, I commissioned
             mr. Carmichael to purchase some for me. They came
             very dear, & moreover he was obliged to take duplicates
             in two instances. I have packed one copy of these in
             mr. Madison's box, & will beg the favor of him to sell
             them for me if he can. I state below the exact prices they
             cost me in Spain, adding nothing for transportation to
             France, which was high.

             La Florida de Garcilasso de
                la Vega. fol.
             Historia General de la Florida   200. reals= 10. Dollars
                por De Cadenasz Caro. fol.
             Herrera Historia General
                4. v. fol.   500. reals=25. Dollars.
                                                 TH: JEFFERSON
                                                 Aug. 3. 1787

1784. Cr.

livres sous den.

	Doll.	lt s	
By balance brought forward 77⅔ @ 5-5			407-15-0
By[5] advance to le Maire 10 Guineas			234-
By do. for 6 Revisals at 2½ drs.			81-

722-15-

By £25 Va. Currency remitted to Mrs.
Carr for use of Peter & Dabney equal
to the Balance 441- 8

1164- 3

RC and enclosures (DLC); FC (DLC: Jefferson Papers). Italicized words are those encoded by Jefferson using the code he sent JM on 11 May 1785. The enclosed bill of lading has not been found.

[1] Thomas Burke's deceased brother was John, not James. "Alderman Groom" was the New York merchant John Broome (*New-York Directory, 1786*, pp. 22, 61). The enclosed letter-copy was from Thomas Burke to John Broome, 30 Sept. 1786. See Boyd, *Papers of Jefferson*, XI, 668 n.; XII, 138 n.

[2] See John Adams to Jefferson, 10 July 1787, ibid., XI, 575.

[3] Jefferson may have enclosed a bill from Cabaret for bookbinding, dated 4 July 1787 (DLC), and an invoice from Frouillé, a Parisian bookseller, dated 27 June 1787 (DLC).

[4] In the left margin of the RC, JM wrote: "From hence to the end, the books are to pay duty. The preceding articles were recd. in Virga." Someone also placed an "X" in front of the titles of most of the books listed under 4 July 1787.

[5] The remainder of the account is in JM's hand.

From John Dawson

BATH Augt. 5. 1787.

DEAR SIR

Two days before I left Frdksburg I did myself the pleasure of addressing a letter to you, and have not receivd one since my arrival at this place. By directing to the care of Majr. Magill, Winchester, there would be a certainty of my receiving any communications you will honour me with.

Yesterday I visited "a flowing spring" abt. thirteen miles from this place, in the state of Pennsylvania and in my estimation it is the greatest *curiosety* I have ever seen. About twenty years ago a Farmer, who is now the proprietor; as he went out in the morning to his labour, observing a very bold stream, in the woods, stopt, and drank some of the water. As he found it exceedingly cold, on his return he determin'd to repeat his draught; but was much astonish'd when he came to the place to find no water. *He* informd me that since that period he has observd that it flows generally every six hours, altho sometimes he has known it five time in the day—that it always rises to the same height, whether in winter or summer; in wet or dry weather—that after heavy rains, when the water from the other springs is unfit for use, this is clear—That he has not discoverd any quality in it, which is not possessd by the other springs in his farm, except its coldness.

I arrived at *it* about eleven oCk at which time it did not contain more than two gallons of water, settled at the bottom. On being informd by the old Farmer that it woud not run untill about *two*, I immediately had the bed much enlarg'd; and after digging about two feet down discoverd a firm rock.

We then waited untill about half past one with much anxiety, and realy I began to doubt the information receivd from the Farmer. About this time I discoverd some water boiling up from the bottom of the bed, through the rock. It continud untill the hole was nearly full. It then fell—then rose again—and this it repeated six different times, but never rose high enough to discharge any water from the hole. However—about 2 oCk, it rushd up in a dozen places through the rock, and in three minutes the discharge of water was sufficient to have turnd a mill. This continu'd near half an hour, when it began to fall, and in five minutes entirely ceas'd to flow.

I then left it, much astonishd—and unable even to hazard a conjecture of the cause. To you, Who I know are fond of these things, I leave the investigation, and shoud you wish for information on any points I will with pleasure procure it.[1]

The spring is situated at the bottom of a small hill, about five miles from the Patowmac and from tide-water about one hundred. The country is montainous. There are several other springs within thirty years[2] all of which continue to flow constantly. The water is remarkably cold, and strongly empregnated with the lime stone, as are all the neighbouring springs.

About the last of the month I shall leave this place, and intend to take Phia. in my way to Frdksburg. I flatter myself with the pleasure of seeing you. With much respect I am Yr. Friend & hm: Sert

J Dawson

RC (DLC).

[1] If JM was fond of investigating artesian wells and springs the evidence for such interest is lacking. Possibly Dawson confused JM with the Reverend James Madison at Williamsburg.

See "*A Letter from* J. Madison, *Esq. to* D. Rittenhouse, *Esq. containing Experiments and Observations upon what are commonly called the Sweet Springs*," (*Transactions of the American Philosophical Society*, II [1786], 197–99).

[2] Dawson evidently meant to write "yards."

From Lafayette

Paris August the 5th 1787

My dear friend

Your Correspondents in france, Besides me, are So Well informed that You Have only to Be affraid of tedious Repetitions. They Will tell You that the dutch are divided into Several Parties, Which are Ranged in two opposite Armies. Three provinces and a Half, among Whom is that of Holland, and the Volunteer Corps are on the Side of freedom. The Remainder of the provinces, the Regulars, and a part of the Mobs Want to Make the State Holder a Kind of King—for the Rage for Kings, altho' it is Wearing off, is Still Subsisting in the old World. France Has Her interest Connected With the Republican Party—England and Prussia With the other. Preparations are Making for War But Will End, I think, into a Mediation.

The People in the Austrian flanders Have Made a Clever Stand Against Arbitrary Authority—and altho' the Cause of the Revolt is Stained With Superstition—We are to Admire the Execution of it. It is Still Uncertain Wether the Emperor Will Make Up the difference With the deputies Sent to Him, or Undertake the Long and Expensive March of an Army to that Remote Part of His dominions.[1] The first division of the opinions of the Notables Has Been Sent to You. I Will forward the other When it is Ready. You Will find in the Begining Some principles Which are in themselves, and to a Republican Ear ought to Appear Very foolish. But all Cannot Be done at once, and Great deal it is to Have in Each province A full Representation, Half of Which Commoners, and the Whole Choosen By the people at large. You Will see By the New Constitutions that We Could not get it fixed in that Manner for the present. But it Will Begin With the fourth Year. Those Assemblies are good Seeds of a proper Governement.

Now the Parliaments, Warmed By the debates of the Notables, ask for the States generals of the Kingdom. It Will not Be granted for the present, But the political Notions Widen a Great deal. Our Present Administration is Excellent—and there is No abler and Honester Man in the World than the Arch Bishop of toulouse.[2]

I am Very Anxious to Hear of the Convention. The fame of the United

States Requires that Some thing Be immediately done. It is Still More Important to their Happiness. Our Notions on that Subject are So Much alike that I Have only to tell you that Such immediate Measures are Necessary to the Consequence of America in Europe. I Know We Have Every thing to Expect from the Liberality, Wisdom, and Patriotism of our fellow Citizens. Should they Be deficient in that Glory and Happiness Which I Expect for them, I feel that the tranquillity of My Life Will Be poisoned. But I See a More pleasant prospect Before me and I do Assure You, My dear friend, that My Best Wishes Have Attended Your Exertions. I don't write to Clel. Hamilton, not Because He is Lazy, But Because I Will Let Him Hear from me after the Meeting of our first Assembly in a fortnight. Pray Communicate to Him those intelligences as Well as to Gnl. Knox and Clel Lee to Whom I will write also in a few days.

M. de Beaumarchais Waited on me With His Complaints against Congress and the State of Virginia, and Said Congress Had Not Answered His Letters. I told Him that His Wish to obtain an Answer Appeared to me Very proper—that I Would go *that Length* in My Recommendations— and that the Answer Being obtained He Might See What He Had to do. At the Same time I Advised Him to Wait on Mr. jefferson, and promised I would give a Letter for You to His Envoy M. chevalier. I observed to M. Beaumarchais that His affairs Could Be Settled either By a Resolve of Congress or instructions to their Ambassadors, or in Case it Was *doubted* Wether the Envoices Were on account of the *Court* or M. de Beau Marchais, By an Application to this Governement to *Know the truth.* Adieu, My dear Sir, Most affectionately Yours

LAFAYETTE

RC (PHi). Docketed by JM, "Recd. April 6. 1788."

[1]To protest certain edicts of Joseph II, the Estates of Brabant refused to pay him the ordinary subsidy in 1787. Lafayette speculated further on Joseph's reaction in a letter to Washington: "I rather think he will negociate, but would not be surprised if he acted the contrary way" (Lafayette to Washington, 3 Aug. 1787, Gottschalk, *Letters of Lafayette to Washington*, p. 325 and n.).

[2]Étienne-Charles Loménie de Brienne (1727–1794), who succeeded Calonne as the French minister of finance in May 1787.

From James McClurg

RICHMOND Augt. 5. 87.

DEAR SIR,

I am much obliged to you for your communication of the proceedings of the Convention, since I left them;[1] for I feel that anxiety about the result, which it's Importance must give to every honest citizen. If I thought that my return could contribute in the smallest degree to it's Improvement, nothing should keep me away. But as I know that the talents, knowledge, & well-establish'd character, of our present delegates, have justly inspired this country with the most entire confidence in their determinations; & that my vote could only *operate* to produce a division, & so destroy the vote of the State, I think that my attendance now would certainly be useless, perhaps injurious.[2]

I am credibly inform'd that Mr. Henry has openly express'd his disapprobation of the circular letter of Congress, respecting the payment of British debts; & that he has declared his opinion that the Interests of this state cannot safely be trusted with that body.[3] The doctrine of three Confederacies, or great Republics, has it's advocates here. I have heard Hervie support it, along with the extinction of State Legislatures within each great department.[4] The necessity of some independent power to controul the Assembly by a negative, seems now to be admitted by the most Zealous Republicans—they only differ about the mode of constituting such a power. B. Randolph seems to think that a Magistrate annually elected by the people might exercise such a controul as independently as the King of G.B. I hope that our representative, Marshall, will be a powerful aid to Mason in the next Assembly. He has observ'd the continual depravation of Mens manners, under the corrupting Influence of our Legislature; & is convinc'd that nothing but the adoption of some efficient plan from the Convention can prevent Anarchy first, & civil Convulsions afterwards. Mr. H——y has certainly converted a Majority of Prince Edward, formerly the most averse to paper-money, to the patronage of it. The opposers of this Scheme are generally favourers of Installments, together with a total prohibition of foreign Luxuries; that people having no temptation to spend their money, may devote it to Justice. The Importance of the next Assembly, with respect to so many objects of great public Interest, makes me wish most sincerely that Congress was deprived of you, at least for this Session.

Mr. Jones has left town, on a pilgrimage to the Temple of health, somewhere about the Mountains. He had been very sick, but seem'd well enough recover'd before he left us.

You will please to present my Compts. to your Colleagues, & my Acquaintance in your house, & believe me, with perfect esteem & regard, Dear Sir, Your friend, & humble Servt.

JAMES MCCLURG

RC (DLC). Addressed by McClurg and franked. Docketed by JM.

[1] McClurg left Philadelphia sometime after 20 July. By the end of the month he had resumed his seat on the Council of State (Farrand, *Records*, III, 589; *JCSV*, IV, 134).

[2] McClurg meant that if he returned the delegation might be split evenly on controversial

issues: JM, Washington, and McClurg on one side; Mason, Randolph, and Blair on the other (Brant, *Madison*, III, 122). A division in the Virginia ranks appeared during the debate over the executive in late July, about the time JM wrote to McClurg. On 26 July Mason moved to reinstate the clause appointing the executive for seven years and making him ineligible for a second term. This motion passed, the Virginians voting in the affirmative. When the whole resolution came to a vote, however, the Virginia delegation was split and JM recorded the breakdown: Mason and Blair for, JM and Washington against. Randolph "happened to be out of the House," but he was known to be against the reeligibility of the executive (Farrand, *Records*, II, 118–21, 54–55).

³McClurg was referring to the resolutions of 21 Mar. 1787 urging the states to repeal all laws contrary to the peace treaty between Great Britain and the U.S. The resolutions were embodied in the circular letter approved by Congress on 13 Apr. (*JCC*, XXXII, 124–25, 177–84). The circular letter was printed in the *Va. Independent Chronicle* of 16 May 1787.

⁴The advocate of three confederacies was probably John Harvie, register of the Virginia Land Office and justice of the peace for Henrico County (*PJM*, I, 188–89 nn. 1, 2; *JCSV*, IV, 1).

From Philip Mazzei

PARIGI 6 Agosto 1787.

CARMO: AMICO,

Siccome non ò tempo da prender copia delle mie lettere, non so se nella precedente di circa 6. 7mane. sono vi notificai d'aver ricevuto la gratissima vostra dei 24. Aprile.¹ Mi prevalsi dell'occasione di due francesi, ⅌ i quali Mr. Jefferson mandò i suoi dispaccj, per mandarvi colla da. mia precedente, la prima parte del mio libro e i primi 4. foglj della seconda. Pochi giorni sono consegnai al Dr. Gibbons di Filadelfia il resto della seconda e i primi 4. foglj della terza. Ora gli mando a Havre con questa i due foglj seguenti. Con altra occasione vi manderò il resto della terza, e forse la quarta, cioè il tutto. Parmi d'avervi già scritto che questi che vi mando son foglj di prove. Non credo che potrò mandarvi gli esemplari bene stampati e legati prima della fin d'8bre. o del principio di 9bre. Spero che avrò prima d'allora ricevuto la vostra risposta alla mia precedente, nella quale mi direte la vostra opinione riguardo al numero che dovrei mandarne in America. Il figlio di Mr. Rutlidge è di parere che potrassene vendere 70, o 80. in Charlestoun, dove dice che la lingua francese è molto in voga.²

Riguardo all'affare di Dohrman, vi reitero le mie premure per la sbrigazione, giacchè per mia buona sorte avete avuto la bontà d'incaricarvene. Riposo interiamente sulla vostra amicizia. Il tutto si riduce a fargli cedere in pagamento di quel che mi dovrà una porzione del suo credito col Congresso, bastante a saldarmi al prezzo che i detti fondi si venderanno sulla piazza nel tempo della cessione. Voltato poi il mio credito col Congresso in testa dei Fratelli Van-Staphorst, essi non solo mi accorderanno tempo, ma di più mi assisteranno per sollevarmi almeno in parte dalle mie angustie. Di grazia, procuratene la sbrigazione, e soprattutto è necessario di badare che Dohrman non ci faccia qualche brutto scherzo. Non vi sarebbe modo di prender passi tali che impedissero a lui di fare alcun'uso del suo credito col Congresso prima d'avermi sodisfatto? Di avere in somma una preferenza assicurata? Amico, io temo, e non senza ragione. Il mio timore dipende dalla mia trista situazione, dall'esperienza che ò degli uomini in generale, e di Mr. Dohrman in particolare. Ei mi scrisse, in data dei 15. Agosto 1786., che aveva convenuto con Monroe, di accordarmi l'interesse col cambio e ricambio principiando dal primo Gennaio 1786. Io gli sborsai il denaro nel Marzo precedente, la cambiale è dell'istessa data, onde non vedo una sola ragione per cui debba io perdere il cambio di 10. mesi contro l'uso e contro le leggi. Mi pare che i gravi danni già sofferti e da soffrirsi a motivo del disappunto, per il che Dohrman non è certamente scusabile, non richiedano da me nè in giustizia, nè in equità, ulteriori sacrifizj. Giacchè avete la bontà d'assistermi, vi prego di provveder che non mi sia fatto maggior torto, e di avvertirmi se in ciò che mi scrisse Dohrman vi è sbaglio, o almeno farmi sapere il motivo che indusse Monroe ad accordare una tal cosa.

Il Marchese de la F. vi egli comunicato ciò che noi pensiamo riguardo al Mediterraneo? Vi par'egli che io potessi esser'utile. Non posso scrivere di più: amico, addio. Tutto vostro,

FILIPPO MAZZEI.

Sigillate le lettere di Edmond e del Bellini, dopo lette, se ne avete il tempo e la pazienza.

18. 7bre.

Dall'inclusa, diretta a Edmond R; o piuttosto da quella che scrivo a de Rieux inclusa ad E; vedrete la causa del ritardo di questa, delle due dette e di quella del Bellini, coi due foglj E, F.

Spero che il Dr. Gibbons vi avrà recapitato il compimento della seconda parte del mio libro e i primi 4. foglj della terza. Ora vi aggiungo il compimento della terza, e una lettera per il vostro cugino non sigillata. Ve ne includo una per Mr. Oster il quale non so se ora stia a Norfolk o in Williamsburgo.[3] La lettera diretta al Minghini mi è fortemente raccomandata dall'Agente di Toscana. Se poteste farla recapitar sicuramente e farmi pervenir la risposta, mi fareste favore.

Riguardo ai miei affari non potrei che ripetervi quanto contiene la precedente. Aspetto con grande ansietà la vostra risposta, con una consolante notizia del resultato nelle Convenzione di Filadelfia. Addio.

Mazzei is uncertain whether he wrote that he had received JM's letter of 24 April. Mazzei has sent JM the first portion of his book and the first four sheets of the second section. He has since consigned the rest of the second part and the first four sheets of the third to Dr. Gibbons of Philadelphia. Mazzei is anxious for JM's opinion on how many copies of the book could be sold in America. Mr. Rutledge's son thinks seventy or eighty might be sold in Charleston, where the French language is much in vogue. Mazzei is depending entirely on JM to square his account with Dohrman, for Mazzei's finances are in an embarrassing state, and the Van Staphorst brothers would assist him if Dohrman's account with Congress allowed a remittance to Mazzei. He cautions JM to be vigilant lest Dohrman resort to some vulgar trick. Dohrman wrote Mazzei in August 1785 that he had agreed with Monroe to grant Mazzei the interest from the first day of 1786, but the money was paid to him in March 1785, so why should Mazzei lose the interest for those ten months? Mazzei cannot understand why Monroe agreed to such an arrangement. Has JM heard from Lafayette regarding their thoughts on the Mediterranean? Letters to Edmund Randolph and Bellini are enclosed for JM to forward— JM is free to read them if he has the time and patience. In the postscript Mazzei explains that he is sending the rest of the third part of his book, along with a letter to Mr. Oster, who is either in Norfolk or Williamsburg. Another enclosed letter, addressed to Minghini, was entrusted to Mazzei by the Tuscan agent. Mazzei hopes JM can have it delivered, and also see that the reply is sent to Mazzei. He is anxious for news of the convention being held in Philadelphia.

RC (DLC). Enclosures not found.

[1]JM's 24 Apr. letter to Mazzei has not been found. The bulk of Mazzei's correspondence was destroyed in World War II during the battle for Pisa, Italy (*VMHB*, LXIII [1955], 306 n. 2).

[2]John Rutledge, Jr. (1766–1819), the son of John Rutledge and nephew of Edward Rutledge, was in Europe taking the "grand tour" and found, as had Mazzei, that his expenses in Paris exceeded his income (*Biographical Directory of Congress* [1971 ed.], p. 1646; Boyd, *Papers of Jefferson*, XII, 340–41).

A year later JM wrote to Jefferson that he feared Mazzei's "calculations will not be fulfilled by the demand for them here in the French language" (ibid., XIII, 499).

[3]Martin Oster was the French consul in Norfolk (*PJM*, VIII, 233 n. 8).

Suffrage Qualifications for Electing the House of Representatives

[7 August 1787]

The Committee of Detail report provided that the qualifications for voting in the election of the House of Representatives should be the same as for the largest branch of a state legislature.

Mr. Madison. The right of suffrage is certainly one of the fundamental articles of republican Government, and ought not to be left to be regulated by the Legislature. A gradual abridgment of this right has been the mode in which Aristocracies have been built on the ruins of popular forms. Whether the Constitutional qualification ought to be a freehold, would with him depend much on the probable reception such a change would meet with in States where the right was now exercised by every description of people. In several of the States a freehold was now the qualification. Viewing the subject in its merits alone, the freeholders of the Country would be the safest depositories of Republican liberty. In future times a great majority of the people will not only be without landed, but any other sort of, property. These will either combine under the influence of their common situation: in which case, the rights of property & the public liberty, will not be secure in their hands: or which is more probable, they will become the tools of opulence & ambition, in which case there will be equal danger on another side. The example of England had been misconceived (by Col Mason). A very small proportion of the Representatives are there chosen by freeholders.[1] The greatest part are chosen by the Cities & boroughs, in many of which the qualification of suffrage is as low as it is in any one of the U.S. and it was in the boroughs & Cities rather than the Counties, that bribery most prevailed, & the influence of the Crown on elections was most dangerously exerted.[2]

Ms (DLC).

[1]Gouverneur Morris had moved to limit the suffrage for congressional elections to freeholders. Mason had implied that the limitation of voting rights to freeholders was a holdover from the prevailing English practice, which he thought too narrow. In fact, since 1430 the minimum voting qualification for a rural Englishman was a freehold of real estate yielding forty shillings in annual income, but in boroughs eligibility ranged widely. Sometimes a voting male who had paid his taxes through "scot and lot" (church and poor rates) was eligible, and at other times and places every male resident voted "if he had control of a separate doorway to his dwelling, if he could provide his own sustenance, and if he had a fireplace at which to cook his meals" (George S. Veitch, *The Genesis of Parliamentary Reform* [Hamden, Conn., 1965], pp. 4–5). A 1780 report to the Westminster Association estimated that 92 county members were elected by 130,000 voters, compared to 421 members chosen from cities, towns, and universities by 84,000 voters (ibid., p. 2).

[2]King's version:

"Madison—I am in favr. of the rigt. of Election being confind. to Freeholders—we are not governed by British Attachments—because the Knights of Shires are elected by Freeholders, but the Members from the Cities & Boroughs are elected by persons qualified by as small property as in any country and wholly without Freeholds—where is the Corruption in England: where is the Crown Influence seen—in the Cities & Boroughs & not in the Counties" (Farrand, *Records*, II, 208).

Note on Suffrage

[7 August 1787?]

note to speech of J. M. in convention
of 1787, Augus[t] 7th.

As appointments for the General Government here contemplated will, in part, be made by the State Govts: all the Citizens in States where the right of suffrage is not limited to the holders of property, will have an indirect share of representation in the General Government. But this does not satisfy the fundamental principle that men can not be justly bound by laws in making which they have no part. Persons & property being both essential objects of Government, the most that either can claim, is such a structure of it, as will leave a reasonable security for the other. And the most obvious provision, of this double character, seems to be that of confining to the holders of property the object deemed least secure in popular Govts., the right of suffrage for one of the two Legislative branches. This is not without example among us, as well as other constitutional modifications, favoring the influence of property in the Government. But the U.S. have not reached the Stage of Society in which conflicting feelings of the Class with, and the Class without property, have the operation natural to them in Countries fully peopled. The most difficult of all political arrangements is that of so adjusting the claims of the two Classes as to give security to each and to promote the welfare of all. The federal principle, which enlarges the sphere of Power without departing from the elective basis of [it] and controuls in various ways the propensity in small republics to rash measures & the facility of forming & executing them, will be found the best expedient yet tried for solving the problem.

Ms (DLC); Tr (DLC) in an unidentified hand. The Ms is one of a series of memorandums and notes JM appended to his Notes on Debates. Although the precise date of the Ms cannot be determined, it is placed here because of its relation to JM's speech on suffrage of 7 Aug. 1787 at the Federal Convention. It is possible that JM wrote the note shortly after that speech, for he speaks of "appointments for the General Government here contemplated," as if the Constitution had not yet become a reality. The note is one of three notes on suffrage that are placed together in JM's appendix to his Debates. From internal evidence (an allusion to the New York Constitution of 1821) the second note, which is by far the longest of the three, could not have been written before 1821. The third note was written during the Virginia Convention of 1829–1830. All three notes were printed in the appendix to the first edition of JM's writings (Madison, *Papers* [Gilpin ed.], III, viii–xvi). Rives included them in a section entitled, "Notes on Suffrage, written at different periods after [JM's] retirement from public life" (Madison, *Letters* [Cong. ed.], IV, 21–30). Hunt printed the first two as a footnote to JM's speech of 7 Aug. 1787 and the third as a footnote to a speech by JM at the convention of 1829–1830 (Madison, *Writings* [Hunt ed.], IV, 121–27 n.; IX, 358–60 n.). Farrand printed the first as a footnote to JM's speech of 7 Aug. 1787 and the second as one of the documents in his appendix volume (*Records*, II, 204 n. 17; III, 450–55).

Citizenship Qualifications for Senators

[9 August 1787]

Gouverneur Morris moved to make the qualification fourteen years, rather than four.

Mr. Madison was not averse to some restrictions on this subject; but could never agree to the proposed amendment. He thought any restriction however in the *Constitution* unnecessary, and improper. Unnecessary; because the Natl. Legislre. is to have the right of regulating naturalization, and can by virtue thereof fix different periods of residence as conditions of enjoying different privileges of Citizenship: Improper; because it will give a tincture[1] of illiberality to the Constitution: because it will put it out of the power of the Natl. Legislature even by special acts of naturalization to confer the full rank of Citizens on meritorious strangers & because it will discourage the most desireable class of people from emigrating to the U.S. Should the proposed Constitution have the intended effect of giving stability & reputation to our Govts. great numbers of respectable Europeans: men who love liberty and wish to partake its blessings, will be ready to transfer their fortunes hither. All such would feel the mortification of being marked with suspicious incapacitations though they sd. not covet the public honors. He was not apprehensive that any dangerous number of strangers would be appointed by the State Legislatures, if they were left at liberty to do so: nor that foreign powers would make use of strangers as instruments for their purposes. Their bribes would be expended on men whose circumstances would rather stifle than excite jealousy & watchfulness in the public.[2]

Ms (DLC).

[1] JM appears to have first written "a tincture," then interlined "dishonourable," and later erased the adjective.

[2] McHenry's version:

"Mr. Maddison was against such an invidious distinction. The matter might be safely intrusted to the respective legislatures" (Farrand, *Records*, II, 243).

Power to Regulate Elections to the Legislature

[9 August 1787]

Charles Pinckney and Rutledge sought to give the states exclusive control of the time, place, and manner for holding elections.

Mr Madison. The necessity of a Genl. Govt. supposes that the State Legislatures will sometimes fail or refuse to consult the common interest at the expence of their local conveniency or prejudices. The policy of referring the appointment of the House of Representatives to the people and not to the Legislatures of the States, supposes that the result will be somewhat influenced by the mode. This view of the question seems to decide that the Legislatures of the States ought not to have the uncontrouled right of regulating the times places & manner of holding elections. These were words of great latitude. It was impossible to foresee all the abuses that might be made of the discretionary power. Whether the electors should vote by ballot or viva voce, should assemble at this place or that place; should be divided into districts or all meet at one place, shd. all vote for all the representatives; or all in a district vote for a number allotted to the district; these & many other points would depend on the Legislatures, and might materially affect the appointments. Whenever the State Legislatures had a favorite measure to carry, they would take care so to mould their regulations as to favor the candidates they wished to succeed. Besides, the inequality of the Representation in the Legislatures of particular States, would produce a like inequality in their representation in the Natl. Legislature, as it was presumable that the Counties having the power in the former case would secure it to themselves in the latter. What danger could there be in giving a controuling power to the Natl. Legislature? Of whom was it to consist? 1. of a Senate to be chosen by the State Legislatures. If the latter therefore could be trusted, their representatives could not be dangerous. 2. of Representatives elected by the same people who elect the State Legislatures; surely then if confidence is due to the latter, it must be due to the former. It seemed as improper in principle, though it might be less inconvenient in practice, to give to the State Legislatures this great authority over the election of Representatives of the people in the Genl. Legislature, as it would be to give to the latter a like power over the election of their Representatives in the State Legislatures.

Ms (DLC).

will mention to our Colleagues your suggestion of giving the names and wishes of those Gentlemen to Mr. Jay.[2] I return you Mr. Fitch's letter with a note of the Secretary upon it, which furnishes a satisfactory answer.[3]

I received a letter from Major Turner upon the subject of the Secretariship, previous to which I had turned my views for that appointment, upon a Worthy Man, Major Sergeant. Of this I informed the said Turner. He has again written me that he will not stand in competition with his freind Sergeant, & will take a chance for a Seat on the Bench. My ideas of his fitness for such an office are favorable, and it will give me pleasure to be instrumental in placing him there. When these appointments, or any other business will be done, I know not.[4] The departure of No Carolina & Georgia left us only 7 States, and the day before yesterday we lost another in the decampment of Doctor Holton, whose declining State of health obliged him to retrograde. The doctor is tolerably free from localities, and I am sorry to lose him: but on account of the breaking up of Congress, we have but little to regret, unless there had been an early prospect of raising the number of States above 7, for with that number, I think, there will never be a good act passed. All the indian affairs still remain to be acted upon, and many other things of great consequence. The President has been requested to write to the States unrepresented, pressing upon them the objects which require the attendance of their delegations, & urging them to come forward, amongst those Objects is that of the report of the Convention, which, it is supposed, is now in the State of parturition. This bantling must receive the blessing of Congress this session, or, I fear, it will expire before the new one *will* assemble; every experiment has its critical stages which must be taken as they occur, or the whole will fail. The peoples expectations are rising with the progress of this work, but will desert it, should it remain long with Congress. Permit me to Suggest one idea as to the mode of obtaining the accession of the States to the new plan of government. Let the convention appoint *one* day, say the 1st. of May, upon which a convention appointed by the people shall be held in each State, for the purpose of accepting or rejecting in toto, the project. Supposing an act of the ordinary legislatures to be equally authentic, which would not be true, yet many reasons present themselves in favor of special conventions. Many men would be admitted, who are excluded from the legislatures. The business would be taken up unclogged with any other—and it would effectually call the attention of all the people to the object as seriously affecting them. All the States being in convention at the same time, opportunities of speculating upon the views of each other would be cut off. The project should be decided upon without an attempt to alter it. You have doubtless found it difficult to reconcile the different opinions in your body. Will it not be impossible then, to reconcile those which will arise amongst numerous assemblies in the different States? It is possible there never may be a general consent to the project as it goes out; but it is absolutely certain there will never be an agrement in amendments. It is the lot of but few to be able to descern the remote principles upon which their happiness & prosperity essentially depend. The many must be asked to consent to, but not[5]

RC (DLC). The remaining page or pages of this letter have not been found.

[1] Letters not found.

[2] According to Burnett, "those Gentlemen" were probably Richard Anderson and Fontaine Maury (*Letters*, VIII, 635 n. 2). However, the latter was more likely Fontaine Maury's older brother James, who was seeking the appointment as consul at Liverpool (*PJM*, VIII, 262 n. 2; James Maury to Jefferson, 17 Sept. 1786, Boyd, *Papers of Jefferson*, X, 387–89; Anne Fontaine Maury, ed., *Intimate Virginiana: A Century of Maury Travels by Land and Sea* [Richmond, 1941], p. 318). No letters of this period from Anderson or Maury to JM or to other members of the Virginia delegation in Congress have been found.

[3] Letter not found. "Mr. Fitch" was almost certainly John Fitch, inventor of an early model of the steamboat. At the October 1785 meeting of the Virginia General Assembly JM had been chairman of a committee to consider a petition from Fitch for financial support (*JHDV*, Oct. 1785, pp. 33, 39). Fitch was in Philadelphia during the summer of 1787 and on 22 Aug. successfully demonstrated his invention on the Delaware River before an audience that included most of the convention delegates (Thompson Westcott, *Life of John Fitch, the Inventor of the Steamboat* [Philadelphia, 1857], p. 192).

[4] See Carrington to JM, 13 June 1787, n. 2. The first appointments to the government of the Northwest Territory were made on 5 Oct., when Arthur St. Clair was elected governor and Winthrop Sargent secretary. The three judges elected on 16 Oct. were Samuel Holden Parsons, John Armstrong, Jr., and James Mitchell Varnum (*JCC*, XXXIII, 610, 686). Maj. George Turner replaced Varnum on the bench in 1789.

[5] The last page of the extant Ms ends here.

Location of the National Government

[11 August 1787]

The report of the Committee of Detail provided that Congress could adjourn to a new location. King, supported by JM, proposed that a law be required to authorize such removal. Spaight objected that this would permanently locate the capital at New York.

Mr. Madison supposed that a central place for the seat of Govt. was so just and wd. be so must [*sic*] insisted on by the H. of Representatives, that though a law should be made requisite for the purpose, it could & would be obtained. The necessity of a central residence of the Govt. wd. be much greater under the new than old Govt. The members of the new

Govt. wd. be more numerous. They would be taken more from the interior parts of the States; they wd. not like members of the present Congs. come so often from the distant States by water. As the powers & objects of the new Govt. would be far greater than heretofore, more private individuals wd. have business calling them to the seat of it, and it was more necessary that the Govt. should be in that position from which it could contemplate with the most equal eye, and sympathize most equally with, every part of the nation. These considerations he supposed would extort a removal even if a law were made necessary. But in order to quiet suspicions both within & without doors, it might not be amiss to authorize the 2 Houses by a concurrent vote to adjourn at their first meeting to the most proper place, and to require thereafter, the sanction of a law to their removal.

Ms (DLC).

To James Madison, Sr.

PHILADA. Augst. 12. 1787.

HOND. SIR

I wrote to you lately inclosing a few Newspapers. I now send a few more, not because they are interesting but because they may supply the want of intelligence that might be more so. The Convention reassembled at the time my last mentioned that they had adjourned to. It is not possible yet to determine the period to which the Session will be spun out. It must be some weeks from this date at least, and possibly may be computed by months. Eleven States are on the ground, and have generally been so, since the second or third week of the Session. Rhode Island is one of the absent States. She has never yet appointed deputies. N.H. till of late was the other. That State is now represented. But just before the arrival of her deputies, those of N. York left us. We have till within a few days had very cool weather. It is now pleasant, after a fine rain. Our accts. from Virga. give us but an imperfect idea of the prospects with you. In particular places the drouth we hear has been dreadful. Genl. Washington's neighbourhood is among the most suffering of them. I wish to know how your Neighbourhood is off.[1] But my cheif anxiety is to hear that your health is re-established. The hope that this may procure me that information is the principal motive for writing it, having as you will readily see, not been led to it by any thing worth commun[i]cating. With my love to my mother & the rest of the family I remain Dear Sir Yr. Affe. Son

Js. MADISON JR

RC (DLC). Addressed and franked by JM. Enclosures not found.

[1] In late August General Washington received the welcome news that a steady rain had ended the drought at Mount Vernon (Washington to George Augustine Washington, 26 Aug. and 2 Sept. 1787, Fitzpatrick, *Writings of Washington*, XXIX, 265, 267). For the weather at Montpelier, see JM to James Madison, Sr., 28 July 1787, n. 4.

From Edmund Pendleton

Letter not found.

12 August 1787, Edmundsbury. The list probably kept by Peter Force (DLC: Madison Miscellany) notes that Pendleton wrote a one-page letter to JM from Edmundsbury on this day. The summary reads: "Expectations about the Convention. Secresy beneficial. Threatened riots in opposition to the payment of debts and taxes. Money scarce."

Citizenship Qualifications for Representatives

[13 August 1787]

Hamilton moved that the term of citizenship for members of the House of Representatives should not be fixed in the Constitution, but should be left to the discretion of Congress.

Mr Madison seconded the motion. He wished to maintain the character of liberality which had been professed in all the Constitutions & publications of America. He wished to invite foreigners of merit & republican principles among us. America was indebted to emigrations for her settlement & Prosperity. That part of America which had encouraged them most had advanced most rapidly in population, agriculture & the arts. There was a possible danger he admitted that men with foreign predilections might obtain appointments but it was by no means probable that it would happen in any dangerous degree. For the same reason that they would be attached to their native Country, our own people wd. prefer natives of this Country to them. Experience proved this to be the case. Instances were rare of a foreigner being elected by the people within any short space after his coming among us. If bribery was to be practised by foreign powers, it would not be attempted among the electors but among the elected; and among natives having full Confidence of the people not among strangers who would be regarded with a jealous eye.

Ms (DLC).

[13 August 1787]

Morris moved that the requirement of seven years' citizenship should not apply to those who were already citizens. Sherman objected, pointing out that pledges to foreigners of equal privileges with native citizens had only been made by the individual states, and thus the national government was at liberty to make discriminations.

Mr. Madison animadverted on the peculiarity of the doctrine of Mr. Sharman. It was a subtilty by which every national engagement might be evaded. By parity of reason, wherever our Public debts, or foreign treaties become inconvenient nothing more would be necessary to relieve us from them, than to new model the Constitution. It was said that the *U.S.* as such have not pledged their faith to the naturalized foreigners, & therefore are not bound. Be it so, & that the States alone are bound. Who are to form the New Constitution by which the condition of that class of citizens is to be made worse than the other class? Are not the States the Agents? Will they not be the members of it? Did they not appoint this Convention? Are not they to ratify its proceedings? Will not the new Constitution be their Act? If the new Constitution then violates the faith pledged to any description of people will not the makers of it, will not the States, be the violators. To justify the doctrine it must be said that the States can get rid of their obligation by revising the Constitution, though they could not do it by repealing the law under which foreigners held their privileges. He considered this a matter of real importance. It woud expose us to the reproaches of all those who should be affected by it, reproaches which wd. soon be ecchoed from the other side of the Atlantic; and would unnecessarily enlist among the Adversaries of the reform a very considerable body of Citizens: We should moreover reduce every State to the dilemma of rejecting it or of violating the faith pledged to a part of its Citizens.

Ms (DLC).

Power to Originate Money Bills in the Legislature

[13 August 1787]

The report of the Committee of Detail proposed that all money bills should originate in the House of Representatives and not be altered or amended in the Senate. The convention struck out this section on 8 August, but Randolph then offered the following substitute: "'all bills for raising money for the purposes of revenue, or for appropriating the same, shall originate in the House of representatives; and shall not be so altered or amended by the Senate, as to encrease or diminish the sum to be raised, or change the mode of raising or the objects of it's appropriation'" (Farrand, *Records*, II, 266).

Mr Madison thought If the substitute offered by Mr. Randolph for the original section is to be adopted it would be proper to allow the Senate at least so to amend as to *diminish* the sum to be raised. Why should they be restrained from checking the extravagance of the other House? One of the greatest evils incident to Republican Govt. was the spirit of contention & faction. The proposed substitute, which in some respects lessened the objections agst. the section, had a contrary effect with respect to this particular. It laid a foundation for new difficulties and disputes between the two houses. The word *revenue*, was ambiguous. In many acts, particularly in the regulations of Trade, the object would be twofold. The raising of revenue would be one of them. How could it be determined which was the primary or predominant one; or whether it was necessary that revenue shd. be the sole object, in exclusion even of other incidental effects. When the Contest was first opened with G.B. their power to regulate Trade was admitted. Their power to raise revenue rejected. An accurate investigation of the subject afterward proved that no line could be drawn between the two cases. The words *amend or alter*, form an equal source of doubt & altercation. When an obnoxious paragraph shall be sent down from the Senate to the House of Reps. it will be called an origination under the name of an amendment. The Senate may actually couch extraneous matter under that name. In these cases, the question will turn on the *degree* of connection between the matter & object of the bill and the alteration or amendment offered to it. Can there be a more fruitful source of dispute, or a kind of dispute more difficult to be settled? His apprehensions on this point were not conjectural. Disputes had actually flowed from this source in Virga. where the Senate can originate no bill.[1] The words "so as to *increase or diminish* the sum to be raised," were liable to the same objections. In levying indirect taxes, which it seemed to be understood were to form the principal revenue of the new Govt. the sum to be raised, would be increased or diminished by a variety of collateral circumstances influencing the consumption, in general, the consumption of foreign or of domestic articles—of this or that particluar species of articles, and even by the mode of collection which may be closely connected with the productiveness of a tax. The friends of the section had argued its necessity from the permanency of the Senate. He could not see how this argumt. applied. The Senate was not more permanent now than in the form it bore in the original propositions of Mr. Randolph and at the time when no objection whatever was hinted agst. its originating money bills. Or if in consequence of a loss of the present question, a proportional vote in the Senate should be reinstated as has been urged as the indemnification the permanency of the senate will remain the same. If the right to originate be vested exclusively in the House of Reps. either the Senate must yield agst. its judgment to that House, in which case the Utility of the check will be lost—or the Senate will be inflexible & the H. of Reps. must adapt its money bill to the views of the Senate, in which case, the exclusive right will be of no avail. As to the Compromise of which so much had been said, he would make a single observation. There were 5 States which had opposed the equality of votes in the Senate, viz. Masts. Penna. Virga. N. Carolina & S Carola. As a compensation for the sacrifice extorted from them on this head, the exclusive origination of money bills in the other House had been tendered. Of the five States a majority viz. Penna. Virga. & S. Carola. have uniformly voted agst. the proposed compensation, on its own merits, as rendering the plan of Govt. still more objectionable. Massts. has been divided, N. Carolina alone has set a value on the compensation, and voted on that principle. What obligation then can the small States be under to concur agst. their judgments in reinstating the section?

Ms (DLC).

[1] JM interlined the two preceding sentences at a later time.

From Thomas Jefferson

Paris Aug. 15. 1787.

Dear Sir

A gentleman going from hence by Lorient to Boston[1] furnishes me an opportunity of recommending to your care the inclosed letters which I could not get ready for the last packet. Pray inform me in your next whether letters directed to your foreign ministers or franked by them are free of postage. That they ought to be so, is acknoleged substantially by the resolution of Congress allowing us to charge postages. I have sometimes suspected that my letters stagnate in the post-offices.

My letters by the last packet brought down the domestic news of this country to the day in which the bed of justice was held. The day before yesterday the parliament house was surrounded by ten thousand people, who received them, on their adjournment, with acclamations of joy, took out the horses of the principal speakers & drew their chariots themselves to their hotels. The parliament not having taken the desperate step (as far as is known yet) of forbidding the execution of the new tax laws by an Arret de defense sur peine de mort, we presume it is the fear of a popular commotion which has occasioned the king to exile them to Troyes. This is known only this morning. The ministry here have certain information that the English squadron has sailed, & took it's course Westwardly. This is another move towards war. No other important fact has taken place since my letters by the packet. Adieu yours affectionately

TH: JEFFERSON

RC (DLC); FC (DLC: Jefferson Papers).

[1] Boyd identifies the homeward-bound gentleman as probably Elias Hasket Derby, the son of a Salem, Massachusetts, merchant (*Papers of Jefferson*, XI, 192; XII, 41 n.).

To William Grayson

Letter not found.

ca. 15 August 1787. Acknowledged in Grayson to JM, 31 Aug. 1787. Requests Grayson to promote the appointment of Major George Turner to a position in the government of the Northwest Territory.

Power of Congress to Tax Exports

[16 August 1787]

Mason moved to prohibit Congress from taxing exports.

Mr Madison 1. the power of taxing exports is proper in itself, and as the States can not with propriety exercise it separately, it ought to be vested in them collectively. 2. it might with particular advantage be exercised with regard to articles in which America was not rivalled in foreign markets, as Tobo. &c. The contract between the French Farmers Genl. and Mr. Morris stipulating that if taxes sd. be laid in America on the export of Tobo. they sd. be paid by the Farmers, shewed that it was understood by them, that the price would be thereby raised in America, and consequently the taxes be paid by the European Consumer. 3. it would be unjust to the States whose produce was exported by their neighbours, to leave it subject to be taxed by the latter. This was a grievance which had already filled N.H. Cont. N. Jery. Del: and N. Carolina with loud complaints, as it related to imports, and they would be equally authorised by taxes by the States on exports. 4. The Southn. States being most in danger and most needing naval protection, could the less complain if the burden should be somewhat heaviest on them. 5. we are not providing for the present moment only, and time will equalize the situation of the States in this matter. He was for these reasons agst. the motion.

Ms (DLC).

From Tench Coxe

Augt. 18th. 1787.

DEAR SIR

Some matters of a good deal of consequence to myself render it necessary for me to be known to Mr. Jefferson—just so far as to take the liberty of addressing two or three letters to him. You will oblige me very much by favoring me with two copies of a short letter of introduction to go by different opportunities. It will be much more agreeable to me to receive them from you *sealed* than open. My situation in point of property is not essential, in the present Case, but principally my general estimation as a gentleman. A letter adapted to a personal introduction would answer every purpose, but I do not expect to make any use of those I may receive from you further than to enclose them in my first letter.[1]

I have no better Apology to make for this liberty than the sincere esteem for you with which I really am, Sir, Yr. mo. respectf. h. Servt

TENCH COXE

RC (DLC: Rives Collection, Madison Papers). Docketed by JM.

[1]Coxe wrote to Jefferson on 3 Sept. 1787, presumably enclosing JM's letter of 19 Aug. 1787 to Jefferson. Neither letter has been found (Boyd, *Papers of Jefferson*, XII, 47, 93).

Power to Regulate the State Militia

[18 August 1787]

Mr. Madison thought the regulation of the Militia naturally appertaining to the authority charged with the public defence. It did not seem in its nature to be divisible between two distinct authorities. If the States would trust the Genl Govt. with a power over the public treasure, they would from the same consideration of necessity grant it the direction of the public force. Those who had a full view of the public situation wd. from a sense of the danger, guard agst. it: the States would not be separately impressed with the general situation, nor have the due confidence in the concurrent exertions of each other.[1]

Ms (DLC).

[1]JM interlined this sentence before Eppes copied the Debates.

To Thomas Jefferson

Letter not found.

19 August 1787. Introduces Tench Coxe as requested in Coxe's letter to JM of 18 Aug. Recorded in list of letters from "J. M. to Ths. Jefferson" (DLC: Rives Collection, Madison Papers). Noted in Jefferson's "Summary Journal of Letters" as received 13 Dec. 1787 (Boyd, *Papers of Jefferson*, XII, 47).

Defining the Crime of Treason against the United States

[20 August 1787]

The Committee of Detail report had defined treason as a crime limited to "levying war against the United States, or any of them; and in adhering to the enemies of the United States, or any of them" (Farrand, *Records*, II, 182).

Mr. Madison thought the definition too narrow. It did not appear to go as far as the Stat. of Edwd. III.[1] He did not see why more latitude might not be left to the Legislature. It wd. be as safe as in the hands of State legislatures; and it was inconvenient to bar a discretion which experience might enlighten, and which might be applied to good purposes as well as be abused.

Ms (DLC).

[1]This 1350 law defined treason as a crime committed "if a Man do levy War against our Lord the King in his Realm, or be adherent to the King's Enemies . . . giving to them Aid and Comfort, in the Realm, or elsewhere" (25 Edw. 3, chap. 2, "A Declaration which Offences shall be adjudged Treason," *The Statutes at Large* [1769 ed.], I, 261).

Power of Congress to Tax Exports

[21 August 1787]

The Committee of Detail report provided that "No tax or duty shall be laid by the Legislature on articles exported from any State" (Farrand, *Records*, II, 183).

Mr Madison As we ought to be governed by national and permanent views, it is a sufficient argument for giving the power over exports that a tax, tho' it may not be expedient at present, may be so hereafter. A proper regulation of exports may & probably will be necessary hereafter, and for the same purposes as the regulation of imports; viz, for revenue—domestic manufactures—and procuring equitable regulations from other nations. An Embargo may be of absolute necessity, and can alone be effectuated by the Genl. authority. The regulation of trade between State and State can not effect more than indirectly to hinder a State from taxing its own exports; by authorizing its Citizens to carry their commodities freely into a neighbouring State which might decline taxing exports in order to draw into its channel the trade of its neighbours. As to the fear of disproportionate burdens on the more exporting States, it might be remarked that it was agreed on all hands that the revenue wd. principally be drawn from trade, and as only a given revenue would be needed, it was not material whether all should be drawn wholly from imports—or half from those, and half from exports. The imports and exports must be pretty nearly equal in every State—and relatively the same among the different States.

Ms (DLC).

From James McClurg

Richmond Augt. 22. 87.

Dear Sir,

I have so much pleasure from your communications, that I shall be careful to acknowledge the reciept of them, with a view to secure their continuance.

I have still some hope that I shall hear from you of the reinstatement of the *Negative*—as it is certainly the only mean by which the several Legislatures can be restrain'd from disturbing the order & harmony of the whole; & the Governmt. render'd properly *national*, & *one*. I should suppose that some of its former opponents must by this time have seen the necessity of advocating it, if they wish to support their own principles.

We have been inform'd from Green-bryar that a number of Men in that county, to the amount, it is said, of 300, have sign'd an Association, to oppose the payment of the certificate Tax, & in genl. of all debts; & it is apprehended there, that they will attempt forcibly to stop the proceedings of the next court. The Ringleader of this riot, I apprehend from the Length & sound of his christian name, Adonijah Matthews, must have come from New-England.[1]

A News-paper writter, from Prince-Edward, has promised to investigate, & expose, the dangerous tendency, as well as unsoundness of John Adam's doctrines—supposed by some to be Mr. H——y.[2] This book is squibb'd at in almost every paper—but I have not heard that any body speaks of it with more acrimony than your namesake at Wmsburg.[3]

We have got the burner of one prison & a Mr. Posey of N. Kent, deposited in the goal of this city.[4] I have told you all our domestic anecdotes that I can think of, & am with the most sincere regard, Dear Sir, Your most obedt. friend & Servt.

JAS. MCCLURG

RC (DLC). Docketed by JM.

[1] On 20 Aug. 1787 the Council of State received a letter dated 11 Aug. from George Clendenin, county lieutenant of Greenbrier, and an affidavit from Robert Renick setting forth the details of the so-called riot in that county. Clendenin hesitated to use force against Matthews and his followers, for "they Seemed the Strongest party." Moreover, "some il[l-]minded person or persons had previou[s]ly burned the Jail." The county lieutenant was fearful that if Matthews returned to Greenbrier and was placed in the new jail, it would "Immediately Experience the Same fate of the former" (enclosed in Edmund Randolph to Speaker of the House of Delegates, 15 Oct. 1787 [Vi: Executive Communications]; *JCSV*, IV, 144). The riot was short-lived, however, and by 1 Sept. the commotion had "totally subsided." As proof that law and order had returned to Greenbrier, the governor was informed that Matthews was "now in Custody for Debt" (Henry Banks to Randolph, 1 Sept. 1787, *CVSP*, IV, 336–37; *Va. Gazette and Weekly Advertiser*, 20 Sept. 1787).

The "certificate tax" was levied on lands and lots, free males, slaves, horses, cattle, carriages, billiard tables, and ordinary licenses. The fund arising from the tax was appropriated to the redemption of military certificates and certificates issued for impressed property (Hening, *Statutes*, XI, 93–95, 417–19).

[2] McClurg referred to the piece by "Senex" in the *Va. Independent Chronicle* of 15 Aug. 1787. "Senex" denounced Adams's *Defence of the Constitutions of Government* as "one of the most deep wrought systems of political deception, that ever was penn'd by the ingenuity of man" and added this warning: ".Americans, beware!—for if you imbibe a particle of his political poison, you are undone for ever." Patrick Henry's authorship cannot be established.

[3] See the Reverend James Madison to JM, 11 June 1787.

[4] See the *Va. Independent Chronicle* of 22 Aug. 1787. John Price Posey, a former justice of the peace and delegate to the General Assembly from New Kent County, had long had a reputation as "a most consummate villain" (George Washington to Bartholomew Dandridge, 18 Dec. 1782, Fitzpatrick, *Writings of Washington*, XXV, 443). In 1783 he was accused of "diverse gross misdemeanors," apparently in connection with his management of the estate of the late John Parke Custis, son of Mrs. George Washington by her first marriage. The same year the General Court found Posey guilty of a misdemeanor and the Council of State accordingly stripped him of his commission as a justice of the peace. In 1786 Posey was

convicted of another misdemeanor in defrauding Bartholomew Dandridge, brother of Mrs. Washington. The following year Posey, imprisoned for assaulting the sheriff, escaped from the New Kent jail. On the night of 15 July he persuaded one Thomas Green, a laborer, to help him "burn the Damn'd Prison down." This mission accomplished, the arsonists proceeded to the clerk's office, which apparently contained incriminating records, and Posey declared this "Damn'd object . . . must be destroyed, too, and Damn'd himself if that should not go." The two men were arrested the same night and Green later turned state's evidence. Posey was found guilty at the October 1787 session of the General Court, a verdict sustained by the Supreme Court of Appeals in December. On hearing the sentence of death, Posey, choked with tears, confessed his crime "and said he hoped through the merits of his Saviour, to obtain a pardon for the sins of his past life." He died on the gallows on 25 Jan. 1788 (*PJM*, VI, 347–48 n. 5; *CVSP*, IV, 321, 329–30; *Va. Gazette and Weekly Advertiser*, 20 Dec. 1787 and 31 Jan. 1788; *JCSV*, IV, 201; Cullen, "St. George Tucker and Law in Virginia, 1772–1804" [Ph.D. diss., ViU, 1971], pp. 86–87).

Power to Regulate the State Militia

[23 August 1787]

A grand committee had reported a militia plan delineating national and state militia responsibilities.

Mr. Madison. The primary object is to secure an effectual discipline of the Militia. This will no more be done if left to the States separately than the requisitions have been hitherto paid by them. The States neglect their Militia now, and the more they are consolidated into one nation, the less each will rely on its own interior provisions for its safety & the less prepare its Militia for that purpose; in like manner as the militia of a State would have been still more neglected than it has been if each County had been independently charged with the care of its Militia. The Discipline of the Militia is evidently a *National* concern, and ought to be provided for in the *National* Constitution.[1]

Ms (DLC).

[1]During the debate over the control of the militia, JM also said: "As the greatest danger is that of disunion of the States, it is necessary to guard agst. it by sufficient powers to the Common Govt. and as the greatest danger to liberty is from large standing armies, it is best to prevent them, by an effectual provision for a good Militia" (ibid.).

Power of Congress to Prohibit the Slave Trade

[25 August 1787]

A grand committee report of 24 August proposed that Congress be prohibited from banning the slave trade before 1800. Charles Cotesworth Pinckney moved to extend the time limit to 1808 and was seconded by Gorham.

Mr. Madison. Twenty years will produce all the mischeif that can be apprehended from the liberty to import slaves. So long a term will be more dishonorable to the National character than to say nothing about it in the Constitution.

Ms (DLC).

[25 August 1787]

The second part of the report of 24 August granted Congress the power to tax imported slaves at a rate not exceeding the average of duties on other imports.

Mr. Madison thought it wrong to admit in the Constitution the idea that there could be property in men. The reason of duties did not hold, as slaves are not like merchandize, consumed, &c.

Ms (DLC).

To James McClurg

Letter not found.

ca. 25 August 1787. Alluded to in McClurg to JM, 5 Sept. 1787. JM is indisposed but continues to attend the convention.

Jurisdiction of the Supreme Court

[27 August 1787]

Johnson moved to extend the jurisdiction of the Supreme Court to cases arising under the Constitution.

Mr. Madison doubted whether it was not going too far to extend the jurisdiction of the Court generally to cases arising under the Constitution

& whether it ought not to be limited to cases of a Judiciary Nature. The right of expounding the Constitution in cases not of this nature ought not to be given to that Department.[1]

Ms (DLC).

[1] JM added that Johnson's motion "was agreed to nem: con: it being generally supposed that the jurisdiction given was constructively limited to cases of a Judiciary nature" (ibid.).

Power of Congress to Regulate Commerce

[29 August 1787]

Charles Pinckney moved to require the approval of two-thirds of each house to pass an act regulating foreign and interstate commerce, insisting that any regulatory power over trade was a concession made by the South.

Mr. Madison went into a pretty full view of the subject. He observed that the disadvantage to the S. States from a navigation act, lay cheifly in a temporary rise of freight, attended however with an increase of Southn. as well as Northern Shipping—with the emigration of Northern Seamen & merchants to the Southern States—& with a removal of the existing & injurious retaliations among the States on each other.[1] The power of foreign nations to obstruct our retaliating measures on them by a corrupt influence would also be less if a majority shd. be made competent than if ⅔ of each House shd. be required to Legislative acts in this case. An abuse of the power would be qualified with all these good effects. But he thought an abuse was rendered improbable by the provision of 2 branches—by the independence of the Senate, by the negative of the Executive, by the interest of Connecticut & N: Jersey which were agricultural, not commercial States; by the interior interest which was also agricultural in the most commercial States—by the accession of Western States which wd. be altogether agricultural. He added that the Southern States would derive an essential advantage in the general security afforded by the increase of our maritime strength. He stated the vulnerable situation of them all, and of Virginia in particular. The increase of the coasting trade, and of seamen, would also be favorable to the S. States, by increasing the consumption of their produce. If the Wealth of the Eastern should in a still greater proportion be augmented, that wealth wd. contribute the more to the public wants, and be otherwise a national benefit.

Ms (DLC).

[1]JM here deleted "and with successful retaliation on the injurious restrictions of foreign powers" and interlined the next sentence before Eppes copied the Debates.

From William Grayson

N York Augt. 31st. 1787.

Dr Sir

Inclosed is a Stragling letter which has found it's way to this place. I have recieved your favor & shall pay every attention to the case of Majr. Turner: his chance with respect to the Secretaryship is absolutely desperate; he must therefore be nominated for a Judges seat. This he has agreed to himself as appears by a letter to Mr. Carrington.

Judge Symms of Jersey yesterday made an application for All that tract of country lying between the Great & little Miami the East & West line & the Ohio supposed about two millions of acres, on the same terms with the Eastern Ohio Compy. His application has met with the intire approbation of the Members present: & there is no doubt but as soon [as] there is a Congress that this contract will be closed.[1]

A Commee. is appointed to draught an Ordnance for indiscriminate locations, but a difficulty has occurred which I fear will destroy the whole affair: the Commee don't know what the deficiency is on the Cumberland river & have figured to their timorous & suspicious imaginations that the Virginia officers & soldiers mean to take eight or ten million of acres, between the Scioto & Miami. The Commee. also contend that the State of Virga. should make proof of the *deficiency* of *good lands* on the Cumberland; should ascertain the quantity they want or have a right to on the Northern side of the Ohio; & should then take that quantity in *one Body*. I wish you would speak to our Governor on the subject. Perhaps it may be in his power shortly to obtain information of the quantity claimed by the Officers & Soldiers on the other side of the Ohio. If this fact was known other difficulties might perhaps be got over as I apprehend it is not very considerable.[2] Mrs. Grayson has been very ill since her lying in, but is now much better. From yr. Affect. frd. & Most Obed Sert.

Willm. Grayson

NB. The Missisippi is in a State of absolute dormification.

RC (DLC). Docketed by JM.

[1]John Cleves Symmes's petition for the "Miami Purchase," dated 29 Aug. 1787, was read in Congress on 21 Sept. and referred to a committee the next day. On 2 Oct. the committee

recommended acceptance of the offer (*JCC*, XXXIII, 509 n., 512, 593–94; R. Pierce Beaver, "The Miami Purchase of John Cleves Symmes," *Ohio Archaeological and Historical Quarterly*, XL [1931], 284–342). Congress had previously accepted the offer of the Reverend Manasseh Cutler of the Ohio Company for the purchase of between five and six million acres east of the Scioto. The terms included a price of one dollar per acre payable in public securities, allowing a deduction of up to one-third of a dollar per acre for bad land and incidental charges (*JCC*, XXXIII, 399–401, 427–30; Grayson to James Monroe, 8 Aug. 1787, Burnett, *Letters*, VIII, 632).

[2]The committee to draft an ordinance for the sale of lands between the Scioto and the Great Miami rivers was appointed on 30 July (*JCC*, XXXIII, 438 n.). By an act of 1779 the Virginia legislature had reserved a large tract of land in the Kentucky district, including lands along the Cumberland River, for the benefit of the state's troops serving in the war (Hening, *Statutes*, X, 55–56). Moreover, as a condition of Virginia's cession of the Northwest Territory in 1783, the legislature had reserved the territory between the Scioto and Little Miami to satisfy military bounties in case the lands southeast of the Ohio were found insufficient for that purpose (ibid., XI, 328). The committee evidently made no report on this subject and no further action was taken in 1787. However, on 17 July 1788, Congress adopted a resolution declaring invalid "all locations and surveys" made by Virginia between the Scioto and Little Miami on behalf of its soldiers before the deficiency of the lands, "if any, on the south east side of the Ohio shall be ascertained and stated to Congress" (*JCC*, XXXIV, 332–34).

Method of Ratifying the Constitution

[31 August 1787]

Mr. Madison considered it best to require Conventions; Among other reasons, for this, that the powers given to the Genl. Govt. being taken from the State Govts. the Legislatures would be more disinclined than conventions composed in part at least of other men; and if disinclined, they could devise modes apparently promoting, but really, thwarting the ratification. The difficulty in Maryland was no greater than in other States, where no mode of change was pointed out by the Constitution, and all officers were under oath to support it.[1] The people were in fact, the fountain of all power, and by resorting to them, all difficulties were got over. They could alter constitutions as they pleased. It was a principle in the Bills of rights, that first principles might be resorted to.

Ms (DLC).

[1]Carroll pointed out that the proposed Constitution would, in effect, alter the Maryland Constitution and that any amendments to the state constitution required the approval of the state legislature.

To James McClurg

Letter not found.

ca. 1 September 1787. Alluded to in McClurg to JM, 10 Sept. 1787. Commission to John Beckley. Inquires about reports of insurrection in Virginia.

To James Madison, Sr.

PHILADA. Sepr. 4. 1787.

[. . .] SIR

Your last favor was dated the 9th. of July. I have been long anxious to learn the re-establishment of your health, as well as to receive information concerning the family in general. The Convention has not yet broken up but its Session will probably continue but a short time longer. Its proceedings are still under the injunction of secresy. We hear that a spirit of insurrection has shewn itself in the County of Green Briar. Some other Counties have been added by Report as infected with the same spirit; but the silence of the letters from Richmond on this latter fact, gives us hopes that the Report is not well founded.[1] We understand also that the upper parts of the Country have suffered extremely from the drought, and that the crops will not suffice for the subsistence of the inhabitants. I hope the account is exaggerated, and wait with some impatience for a confirmation of this hope. The crops of wheat in this quarter have been uncommonly fine, and the latter rains have been so seasonable for the corn that the prospect of that crop is tolerably good. The price of good Tobo. here at present is 40/. Virga. money. As soon as the tie of secresy shall be dissolved I will forward the proceedings of the Convention. In the mean time with my affectionate regards for all the family, I remain yr. dutiful Son

Js. MADISON JR

RC (DLC). Addressed by JM and franked. Sent "to the care of F. Maury Esqr. Fredericksburg Virginia." Brackets indicate missing word owing to a tear in the Ms.

[1] JM's colleague, Gov. Edmund Randolph, had learned from a private correspondent that "commotions" were taking place in other counties besides Greenbrier and wrote to Lt. Gov. Beverley Randolph on 2 Sept. urgently requesting details (*CVSP*, IV, 338). The lieutenant governor replied on 8 Sept. that he had heard of no such disturbances, though "some irregularities" had occurred in Amelia County, where several "disorderly people of desperate circumstances" had threatened to prevent the court from sitting. They were immediately thrown into jail, but were rescued by friends the same evening. All was now quiet, however, and the great majority of the people "friendly to the regular administration of Government" (Executive Letter Book, pp. 156–59). Beverley Randolph's calm view of the situation in the commonwealth differed from that of another Virginian, who grumbled that the government

was not doing enough to quell the insurrectionary spirit: "You have heard, no doubt, that another Court House (New Kent) with the Clerk's office and all the Records has been burnt down. Where is the Executive? Ought not a Proclamation to have been issued by them to apprehend the offenders when King William Court House was burnt? And would not this probably have prevented the destruction of the New Kent one? But they are all Honorable men, and wise as they are Honorable—by Courtesy. Happy State with such an Executive! But oh! Happier Executive with such a State!" (Francis Corbin to Arthur Lee, 8 Aug. 1787 [ViU: Lee Family Papers, microfilm]). On the burning of the clerks' offices and records—the courthouses in fact were not burned—see Dawson to JM, 12 June 1787 and n. 5, and McClurg to JM, 22 Aug. 1787, n. 4.

From James McClurg

RICHMOND Septr. 5. 87.

DEAR SIR,

I am not surprized to hear that you have been indisposed, at this season, with such a weight of business upon you. I am more surprized that you have been able to persevere in the application, which that business required. I hope you will never take a moment either from that, or from the relaxation which it renders necessary, on account of such a correspondent as myself; who would readily give up the satisfaction he takes in your letters, for the pleasure of hearing that you are in health.

We have just reciev'd here a hand-bill from Norfolk, containing Intelligence from the British resident at Brussells, that a considerable body of french had march'd, from their Flanders frontier, into the United provinces—2 Letters from England accompanying it say, that freights of American bottoms had risen there considerably upon this news.[1] A general European War is expected, by which it is supposed, if we can keep clear of it, we shall be very much benefited. But I imagine that before this reaches you you will have more certain & accurate Accts. of this matter. I regret exceedingly that we have not such a government establish'd, as might inspire the Dutch-merchants with a well founded confidence, & induce them to seek here a retreat from the threaten'd storm.

Adonijah Matthews, of whose turbulent attempts I inform'd you, is said to be peaceably lodg'd in the Jail of Green-bryar. This neighbourhood, as well as that of Petersburg, is uncommonly healthy—& there is no account of the usual baneful effects of this season anywhere but at Norfolk. I am, with sincere regard, Dear Sir, Your most obedt. friend & Servt.

JAS. MCCLURG

RC (DLC). Docketed by JM.

[1] The handbill was an extract from the London *Gazette Extraordinary* of 22 June 1787. It was printed, without the two accompanying letters, in the *Va. Independent Chronicle* of 5 Sept.

1787. The next issue (12 Sept.) printed a letter from a London gentleman denouncing the report of a French invasion of Holland as "a spurious publication, forged by some designing person to effect the price of Stocks for sinister purposes." See McClurg to JM, 10 Sept. 1787.

To Thomas Jefferson

PHILADA. Sepr. 6. 1787.

DEAR SIR

My last was intended for the Augst. Packet and put into the hands of Commodore Paul Jones. Some disappointments prevented his going, and as he did not know but its contents might be unfit for the ordinary conveyance, he retained it. The precaution was unnecessary. For the same reason the delay has been of little consequence. The rule of secresy in the Convention rendered that as it will this letter barren of those communications which might otherwise be made. As the Convention will shortly rise I should feel little scruple in disclosing what will be public here, before it could reach you, were it practicable for me to guard by Cypher against an intermediate discovery. But I am deprived of this resource by the shortness of the interval between the receipt of your letter of June 20. and the date of this. This is the first day which has been free from Committee service both before & after the hours of the House, and the last that is allowed me by the time advertised for the sailing of the Packet.

The Convention consists now as it has generally done of Eleven States. There has been no intermission of its Sessions since a house was formed; except an interval of about ten days allowed a Committee appointed to detail the general propositions agreed on in the House. The term of its dissolution cannot be more than one or two weeks distant. A Govermt. will probably be submitted to the *people of* the *states* consisting of a [President][1] *cloathed* with *executive power:* a *Senate chosen* by the *Legislatures:*[2] and another *house chosen* by the *people of* the *states* jointly *possessing* the *legislative power* and a regular *judiciary* establishment. The mode of constituting the *executive* is among the few points not yet finally settled. The *Senate* will consist of two *members* from each *state* and *appointed sexennially:* The other, of *members appointed biennially* by the *people of* the *states* in proportion to their number. The Legislative power will *extend to taxation trade* and sundry other general matters. The powers of Congress will be *distributed* according to their *nature among the several departments.* The States will be *restricted from paper money* and in a *few other instances.* These are *the outlines.* The extent of them may perhaps surprize you. I hazard an opinion nevertheless that the *plan should* it *be adopted* will neither effectually *answer* its *national object* nor prevent the local *mischiefs* which every where

163

excite disgusts agst the *state governments*. The grounds of this opinion will be the subject of a future letter.

I have written to a friend in Congs. intimating in a covert manner the necessity of deciding & notifying the intentions of Congs. with regard to their foreign Ministers after May next, and have dropped a hint on the communications of Dumas.[3]

Congress have taken some measures for disposing of their public land, and have actually sold a considerable tract. Another bargain I learn is on foot for a further sale.

Nothing can exceed the universal anxiety for the event of the Meeting here. Reports and conjectures abound concerning the nature of the plan which is to be proposed. The public however is certainly in the dark with regard to it. The Convention is equally in the dark as to the reception wch. may be given to it on its publication. All the prepossessions are on the right side, but it may well be expected that certain characters will wage war against any reform whatever. My own idea is that the public mind will now or in a very little time receive any thing that promises stability to the public Councils & security to private rights, and that no regard ought to be had to local prejudices or temporary considerations. If the present moment be lost it is hard to say what may be our fate.

Our information from Virginia is far from being agreeable. In many parts of the Country the drouth has been extremely injurious to the Corn. I fear, tho' I have no certain information, that Orange & Albemarle share in the distress. The people also are said to be generally discontented. A paper emission is again a topic among them. So is an instalment of all debts in some places and the making property a tender in others. The taxes are another source of discontent. The weight of them is complained of, and the abuses in collecting them still more so. In several Counties the prisons & Court Houses & Clerks offices have been wilfully burnt. In Green Briar the course of Justice has been mutinously stopped, and associations entered into agst. the payment of taxes.[4] No other County has yet followed the example. The approaching meeting of the Assembly will probably allay the discontents on one side by measures which will excite them on another.

Mr. Wythe has never returned to us. His lady whose illness carryed him away, died some time after he got home. The other deaths in Virga. are Col. A. Cary, and a few days ago, Mrs Harrison, wife of Benjn. Harrison Junr. & sister of J. F. Mercer. Wishing you all happiness I remain Dear Sir Yrs. Affectly.

                                                                    Js. MADISON JR.

Give my best wishes to Mazzei. I have recd. his letter & book & will write by next packet to him. Dorhman is still in Va. Congs. have done nothing further in his affair. I am not sure that 9 Sts have been assembled of late. At present it is doubtful whether there are seven.

RC (DLC). Docketed by Jefferson. Italicized words, unless otherwise noted, are those encoded by JM using the code Jefferson sent him on 11 May 1785. Years later JM interlined the decoding in the Ms.

[1] JM failed to encode "President," but interlined it in brackets at the time he decoded the letter.
[2] Not encoded in Ms. Underlined by JM.
[3] No letter from JM to a fellow delegate in Congress has been found.
[4] See McClurg to JM, 22 Aug. 1787 and n. 1.

Impeachment of the President

[8 September 1787]

Mr. Madison objected to a trial of the President by the Senate, especially as he was to be impeached by the other branch of the Legislature, and for any act which might be called a misdemesnor. The President under these circumstances was made improperly dependent. He would prefer the supreme Court for the trial of impeachments, or rather a tribunal of which that should form a part.

Ms (DLC).

From James McClurg

RICHMOND Septr. 10. 87

DEAR SIR,

I have not yet been able to execute your commission to Mr. Beckley; but shall take care to forward the act as soon as it can be obtain'd. The report of a tendency to Insurrection in several quarters of the State is not without some foundation; tho' the friends of Order have hitherto mantain'd the Superiority, so as to prevent any very outrageous doings. An expectation of a remedy for their discontents, well or ill founded, from the next Assembly assists in keeping them quiet.

There is said to be a disposition generally prevalent thro' this state to comply with the plan of the Convention without much Scrutiny. Hervey, wh[o] has been in Albemarle lately, says that Nicholas is determin'd to support it however contrary it may be to his own Opinions. I am persuaded that those who sacrifice solid & permanent Advantages in this plan, to their Idea of the transitory disposition of the people, will condemn themselves hereafter. I find that I sent you some very crude Dutch Intelligence in my las[t] with which we were gull'd here for a day or two. I am Dear Sir Your most obt freind &ca

Jas. McClurg

RC (DLC). Docketed by JM. Brackets enclose letters obscured by the mounting of the Ms.

Power of Congress to Overrule the Executive Veto

[12 September 1787]

Williamson moved to insert a two-thirds vote of each house in place of a three-fourths majority as necessary to overrule an executive veto.

Mr. Madison. When ¾ was agreed to, the President was to be elected by the Legislature and for seven years. He is now to be elected by the people and for four years. The object of the revisionary power is twofold. 1. to defend the Executive Rights 2. to prevent popular or factious injustice. It was an important principle in this & in the State Constitutions to check legislative injustice and incroachments. The Experience of the States had demonstrated that their checks are insufficient. We must compare the danger from the weakness of ⅔ with the danger from the strength of ¾. He thought on the whole the former was the greater. As to the difficulty of repeals, it was probable that in doubtful cases the policy would soon take place of limiting the duration of laws so as to require renewal instead of repeal.

Ms (DLC).

From Joseph Jones

[ca. 13 September 1787]

Dr: Sr:

Although I wanted materials for a letter, I should have droped you a few lines had I not been absent sometime from Fredericksburg and had I not also been informed that convention wod. certainly rise the first week of this month.

The continuance of your Session and some Stories I have heard since my return and on my visit to Alexandria make me apprehensive there is not that unanimity in your Councils I hoped for and had been taught to believe. From whence it originated I know not, but it is *whispered* here, there is great disagreemt. among the Gent. of our Delegation—that the General and yourself on a very important question were together, Mr. M——n alone and singulir in his opinion and the Other two Gent. holding different sentiments. I asked what was the question in dispute and was answered that it respected either the defect in constituting the convention, as not proceeding immediately from the people, or the refering the proceedings of the Body, to the people for ultimate decision and confirmation. My informt. also assured me the fact might be relied on as it came, as he expressed it, from the fountainhead. I took the liberty to express my disbelief of the fact, And that from the circumstances related it was very improbable and unworthy attention. I mention this matter for want of some thing else to write to you and more especially as it respects our Delegation in particular. I shall towards the last of the month, if not sooner, visit the lower part of Potomack & Rappahannock—a rout the reverse of what I some time ago intended but I am desired by the Executive to visit the Naval Offices and Searchers in that quarter.[1] I hope this business will in future be placed under the direction of another power, I mean the regulation of our Trade. Adieu health & happiness attend you

Jos: Jones.

RC (DLC). Addressed by Jones and franked. Postmarked, "FREDS BURG, SEPT 13." Docketed by JM.

[1] See *JCSV*, IV, 135. The naval office act authorized members of the Council of State to inspect the offices, books, and public papers of the naval (customs) officers and searchers and empowered them to suspend those officers for a period of one month (Hening, *Statutes*, XII, 313).

Suspension of Impeached Officials

[14 September 1787]

Rutledge and Morris proposed that officials under impeachment should be suspended from office until tried and acquitted.

Mr. Madison. The President is made too dependent already on the Legislature by the power of one branch to try him in consequence of an impeachment by the other. This intermediate suspension, will put him in the power of one branch only. They can at any moment, in order to make way for the functions of another who will be more favorable to their views, vote a temporary removal of the existing Magistrate.

Ms (DLC).

To John Blair

PHILADA. Sepr. 15. 1787.

Recd. of the Honble John Blair one hundred dollars for which I promise to account to the Auditor of public Accounts of Virgina.

Js. MADISON JR

Ms (Vi). Docketed in the hand of auditor John Pendleton: "3d Octo. 1787. The Hon. Js. Madison £30.0.0 Upon Accot."

Power of Congress to Regulate Commerce

[15 September 1787]

McHenry and Carroll moved to allow the states to levy tonnage duties for the purpose of clearing harbors and erecting lighthouses. Gouverneur Morris objected, observing that the states were not restrained by the Constitution from laying tonnage duties.

Mr. Madison. Whether the States are now restrained from laying tonnage duties depends on the extent of the power "to regulate commerce." These terms are vague, but seem to exclude this power of the States. They may certainly be restrained by Treaty. He observed that there were other objects for tonnage Duties as the support of Seamen &c. He was more & more convinced that the regulation of Commerce was in its nature indivisible and ought to be wholly under one authority.

Ms (DLC).

From Thomas Jefferson

PARIS Sep. 17. 1787.

DEAR SIR

My last to you were of Aug. 2. & 15. Since that I have sent to Havre to be forwarded to you by the present packet 3. boxes marked I.M. G.W. and A.D. The two last are for mr. Wythe in Williamsburgh, and mr. Alexr. Donald merchant in Richmond. The first contains the books for yourself which shall be noted at the close of my letter, together with the following for mr. Rittenhouse; viz. la Chymie de Fourcroi 4. vols. 8vo. Connoissance des tems 1788–1789. and Dissertation de la Sauvagere. I have put into the same box 9. copies of the Notes on Virginia. That of the English edition, and one of the others are for yourself. The 7. remaining are for mr. Jay, mr. Thomson, mr. Hopkinson, mr. Mercer (late of Congress) mr. Rittenhouse, mr. Izard & mr. Ed. Rutledge, which I will pray of you to have delivered in my name to those gentlemen. I have also put into the box 100 copies of the map of Virginia Pennsylvania &c.[1] which be so good as to put into the hands of any booksellers you please in New York & Philadelphia to be sold at such price as you think proper, ready money only. I have sent some to Virginia to be sold at $5/6$ of a dollar. If it should appear that a greater number might be sold, I would have the plate retouched, and any number struck off which might be desired. It may serve to refund a part of the expences of printing the book & engraving the map.

In my letter of Aug. 2. I troubled you on the case of John Burke. I now inclose you a letter lately received, by which it will appear that mr. Broom (not Groom) of New York paid into the hands of a capt. William S. Browne of Providence in Rhode island a balance of £56. the property of John Burke deceased, brother to Thos. Burke who writes the letter: that possibly there may be more of his property in Brown's hands: and that it is Brown for whom your enquiries must be directed, and of whom the money must be demanded. If he will pay it on this letter of Thomas Burke, (in real money) it might be placed in the bank of Philadelphia till called for by T. B. If he requires more regular authority, be so good as to inform me what may be necessary and I will give notice to mrs. Burke the wife of Thomas who lives in France & to whom he has confided the pursuit of this object.[2]

I have received the box you were so kind as to send me with paccans. There were 13. nuts in it, which I mention, because I suspect it had been pillaged. Your situation at New York, & the packets coming from thence to Havre, where Mr. Limozin, agent for the U.S. will take care of any thing for me, may enable you to send me a few barrels of Newtown pippins & cranberries. If you could send me also 50. or 100 grafts of the Newtown pippin they would be very desireable. They should be packed between layers of moss, a layer of moss & a layer of plants alternately, in a box, & the box nailed close, with directions to Limozin to forward them by the Diligence. Red birds for the ladies, & Opossums for the naturalists would be great presents, if any passenger would take charge of them. I must either refer you to my public letter for news, or write you a letter of news if my time will permit. I am with sincere esteem, dear Sir, your friend & servant

TH: JEFFERSON

J. Madison esq. to Th: Jefferson Dr.	lt
To paid Frouille for the box marked J.M. No. 1. & packing	20- 0
Memoires sur les impositions de l'Europe 4. v. 4to.	36-
Loisirs d'Argenson. 2. v. 8vo.	8-10
Charlevoix histoire de la nouvelle France. 3. v. 4to.	27-
American traveller 4to.	3-
Pollucis onomasticon. 4to.	5.
Buffon Mineraux. 5th. 6th. 7th. 8th. volumes	12
Pieces interessantes. 5th. vol.	3.
Dissertation de la Sauvagere 8vo.	4-12
	119- 2

Your watch is done, & is in my possession. She costs 3. guineas more than I had told you she would. Two were owing to a mistake of mine in the price of my own, and the other to that of the workman who put that much gold into the case more than he had into mine. Yours costs therefore 600 lt. I have worn it a month during which, tho new, it is impossible for a watch to go better. I shall send her by the French minister, Monsieur le comte de Moustier. I wish the step-counter may be done in time to go by the same conveiance. I have been almost tempted to buy for you one of the little clocks made here mounted on marble columns. They strike, go with a pendulum, a spring instead of a weight, are extremely elegant & can be had for 10. guineas. But I shall wait your orders.

TH: J.

P.S. Will you be so good as to pay mr. C. Thomson 86.35. dollars for me, and to apologize to him for my not writing, the bearer going off a day sooner than he had told me. The letter to N. Lewis is of great consequence.[3]

RC and enclosure (DLC); FC (DLC: Jefferson Papers). RC endorsed on verso of last page: "New York. Decr. 27. 1787. Recd. from James Madison Jr the within mentioned Eighty six and 35/90. Dollars. Chas Thomson." For enclosure, see n. 2.

[1] The map engraved by Samuel J. Neele of London that was included in the French and English editions of Jefferson's work (*Notes on Virginia* [Peden ed.], p. xviii n. 24).

[2] Jefferson enclosed a copy of a letter from Thomas Burke to his wife, 4 Aug. 1787, incorporating the contents of a letter from John Broome to Thomas Burke, 16 May 1787.

[3] Jefferson to Nicholas Lewis, 17 Sept. 1787 (Boyd, *Papers of Jefferson*, XII, 134–36). JM in turn requested Randolph to deliver the letter (JM to Randolph, 18 Nov. 1787).

To Edmund Pendleton

PHILADA. Sepr. 20. 1787

DEAR SIR

The privilege of franking having ceased with the Convention, I have waited for this opportunity of inclosing you a copy of the proposed Constitution for the U. States. I forbear to make any observations on it; either on the side of its merits or its faults. The best Judges of both will be those who can combine with a knowledge of the collective & permanent interest of America, a freedom from the bias resulting from a participation in the work. If the plan proposed be worthy of adoption, the degree of unanimity attained in the Convention is a circumstance as fortunate, as the very respectable dissent on the part of Virginia is a subject of regret. The double object of blending a proper stability & energy in the Government with the essential characters of the republican Form, and of tracing a proper line of demarkation between the national and State authorities, was necessarily found to be as difficult as it was desireable, and to admit of an infinite diversity concerning the means among those who were unanimously agreed concerning the end.

I find by a letter from my father[1] that he & my unkle Erasmus[2] have lately paid their respects to Edmundsbury. I infer from his silence as to your health that no unfavorable change had happened in it. That this may find it perfectly re-established is the sincere and affecte. wish of Dr. Sir, Yr. friend & humble servt.

Js. MADISON JR.

RC (DLC). Enclosure not found. Docketed by Pendleton, "Ansd. Octr. 8th. 1787."

[1] Letter not found.
[2] Erasmus Taylor (1715–1794). See *VMHB*, XXXIV (1926), 270–71.

From Edward Carrington

NEW YORK Sept. 23. 1787

MY DEAR SIR,

The Gentlemen who have arrived from the Convention inform us that you are on the way to join us—least, however, you may, under a supposition that the State of the delegation is such as to admit of your absence, indulge yourself in leisurely movements, after the fatiguing time you have had, I take this precaution to apprise you that the same schism which unfortunately happened in our State in Philadelphia, threatens us here also. One of our Colleagues Mr. R. H. Lee is forming propositions for essential alterations in the Constitution, which will, in effect, be to oppose it.[1] Another, Mr. Grayson, dislikes it, and is, at best for giving it only a Silent passage to the States. Mr. H. Lee joins me in opinion that it ought to be warmly recommended to ensure its adoption. A lukewarmness in Congress will be made a ground of opposition by the unfreindly in the States. Those who have hitherto wished to bring the conduct of Congress into contempt, will in this case be ready to declare it truly respectable.

Next wednesday is fixed for taking under consideration this business, and I ardently wish you could be with us.[2]

The New York faction is rather active in spreading the seeds of opposition—this, however, has been expected, and will not make an impression so injurious as the same circumstance would in some other States. Colo. Hamilton has boldly taken his ground in the public papers and, having truth and propriety on his side, it is to be hoped he will stem the torrent of folly and inequity.[3]

I do not implicitly accede, in sentiment, to every article of the scheme proposed by the convention, but I see not how my utmost wishes are to be gratified until I can withdraw from society. So long as I find it necessary to combine my strength and interests with others, I must be satisfied to make some sacrifices to the general accommodation. I am my dear Sir with great sincerity Your Freind & Humble Servt.

ED. CARRINGTON

RC (DLC). Addressed and franked by Carrington. Docketed by JM. The letter was sent to JM in Philadelphia and forwarded to him in New York.

[1]Lee's proposed amendments are printed in Burnett, *Letters*, VIII, 648–49.

[2]JM arrived in New York on Monday, 24 Sept., and was present in Congress during the consideration of the report of the Federal Convention on 26, 27, and 28 Sept. The report had been delivered to Congress on 20 Sept. and read the same day (JM to James Madison, Sr., 30 Sept. 1787; *JCC*, XXXIII, 488–503).

[3]The reference is apparently to Alexander Hamilton's letter of 15 Sept. 1787 in the N.Y. *Daily Advertiser* (Syrett and Cooke, *Papers of Hamilton*, IV, 248–53). In that letter Hamilton

acknowledged and defended his earlier attack on Governor Clinton that had appeared in the N.Y. *Daily Advertiser* of 21 July 1787 (ibid., IV, 229–32).

From Ambrose Madison

Letter not found.

24 September 1787. Acknowledged in JM to Ambrose Madison, 11 Oct. 1787. Reports the state of the crops in Orange County. Informs JM that his brother William wishes to enter public life.

From John Dawson

FREDERICKSBURG Sepr. 25. 1787

DEAR SIR

On my arrival in this town, on the last evening, I was much disappointed in receiving no letter from you.

The proceedings of the Convention have been forwarded by Mr. Randolph to Messrs. Mercer and Monroe, and are at this moment the subject of general conversation in every part of the town, and will soon be in every quarter of the state. Opinions have already been deliver'd, and that work, which was the production of much labour & time, has been in a few hours either damn'd or applauded, according to the wish, sentiments, or interest of the politician. Altho there are many warm friends to the plan, be assurd that the opposition will be powerful. Our old friend, the Colo from Frederick,[1] will, I think, be much alarm'd, and will not fail to paint his fears in strong colours. I also think the powerful member from P.E. will be unfriendly.[2] A report is circulated, that some few days since the people of that county (P.E) were assembled, and harangued by Mr H. in favour of a paper currency—that a Mr Smith,[3] of the Academy, opposd the scheme—that on a decision a large majority conceded with Mr. Smith— That Mr. Smith then recommended to them the adoption of whatever shoud be done in convention; to which they agreed—That Mr H. informd them, that they shoud no longer consider him as their representative.

The improbabality of this report is sufficient to destroy its authenticity, altho it comes well supported, & I think we may receive it in part.

You are intimate with Mr. G. Mason—will you be kind enough to enclose me a letter of introduction to him, as an intimacy may be of consequence in the assembly?

Our correspondence will be more regular, I hope, from this time. I shall be on the Theater of Virginia politicks, & shall not fail to communicate to you whatever is transacted, worthy notice. Your engagements in public business, I am aware take up much of our[4] time. I however flatter myself you will find leisure of[5] express your sentiments on some political points, [whic]h will be agitated in our Legislatu[re] as I shall deem it as a matter of the first consequence to me. With much esteem & respect I am Yr. Freind & hm: Sert

J Dawson

RC (DLC). Addressed by Dawson. Parts of words obscured by the seal are restored within brackets.

[1]Probably Charles Mynn Thruston.
[2]Patrick Henry, recently elected to the House of Delegates from Prince Edward County.
[3]John Blair Smith, president of Hampden-Sydney Academy.
[4]Dawson meant "your."
[5]Dawson meant "to."

Samuel McDowell to Virginia Delegates

Danville, Septemr. 25. 1787.

Gentlemen,

I have the honour to inclose you two Resolutions of a Convention of the Representatives for the District of Kentucky, by which you will be certified of their determinations respecting its separation from the State of Virginia.[1]

As you are instructed by Government, to use your endeavours to obtain the assent of Congress to the Measure; we rely on your exertions for success, and are happy that we shall have your Influence in our favour.[2]

The Convention, however, to manifest their anxiety for the Event; and at the same time, to manifest their unfeigned respect for Congress, as well as their attachment to the American Union, have judged it proper to address them on the momentous occasion; and have directed me to solicit your favour in having it preferred to that august Body.[3] I have the honour to be, with every sentiment of respect, Gentlemen, Your most obt. Servant

Saml McDowell—president

RC and enclosure (PCC). Addressed by McDowell.

[1]The enclosed document containing the two resolutions was headed, "Extracts from the Journals of a Convention of the Representatives of the District of Kentucky in the state of Virginia, begun and held at Danville on Monday the 17th day of September 1787" (PCC). The resolutions, calling for the establishment of Kentucky as an independent state by 31

Dec. 1788, are printed in William Littell, *Political Transactions in and concerning Kentucky, from the First Settlement Thereof, Until It Became an Independent State, in June, 1792* (1806; Louisville, 1926 reprint), p. 85.

[2]The Virginia act providing for Kentucky statehood instructed the delegates in Congress to obtain congressional approval of the proposed measure by 4 July 1788 (*PJM*, IX, 208).

[3]See the address of "the Representatives of the good people of Kentucky," signed by Samuel McDowell and attested by Thomas Todd (PCC; printed in Littell, *Political Transactions*, pp. 85–87). The address and resolutions were read in Congress on 29 Feb. 1788, followed by a motion of the Virginia delegates providing for the assent of Congress to the proposed separation of Kentucky from Virginia. A grand committee was appointed on 3 June to prepare "an act for acceding to the independence of. . . Kentucky," but the committee was discharged a month later on notification that Virginia had ratified the federal Constitution. Congress thereupon suspended further proceedings on the matter, declaring that it should be taken up by the new federal government (*JCC*, XXXIV, 72–73, 194, 198, 287, 287–94; Littell, *Political Transactions*, pp. 88–93).

From Tench Coxe

PHILADA. 27th. Sept. 1787.

DEAR SIR

My anxiety in favor of the new federal Constitution has induced me to attempt some comments on it, that might render it more clear and agreeable to the people at large, than the concise manner, in which it was necessarily drawn up, would admit of. A friend, with whom I ventured to converse on the Subject, has pressed me to pass them thro the papers of Virginia and New York. This will apologize to you for the trouble I give you in enclosing to you copies of the first & second Numbers. I beg the favor of your perusing them with Col. Hamilton, to whom make my apology also for the liberty, and, if you and he think they will be of any Service be pleased to have them reprinted in the papers of those States. I would beg leave to suggest, that if they appear worthy of this, it would be most useful to have them inserted in such Virginia paper, as circulates most in your western Counties. By the next post I will forward the third Number, which treats of the house of Representatives. The good Effects of the government I have not spoken of, my Object has been to remove apprehensions & to obviate popular reasonings drawn from the public feelings. In doing this in a public Newspaper more attention to those feelings, in the language I have used, was necessary, than if I had addressed a philosophic mind.[1]

I will not give you pain by expressing the high sense I entertain of your partiality in your letter to Mr. J. but I trust it will appear excusable when I assure you that the Sentiments you there express will ever operate as an incentive to aim at the Qualities you have enumerated. With my respectful compliments to Col. Hamilton, and with sentiments of the highest Esteem, I am, Sir, yr. mo. obedt. hum. Servt.

TENCH COXE

RC (DLC). Addressed by Coxe. Docketed by JM. Enclosures not found.

[1] The first three numbers of Coxe's letters of "An American Citizen" were printed in the Philadelphia *Independent Gazetteer* on 26, 28, and 29 Sept. 1787. Coxe sent the fourth and last number to JM on 21 Oct., and it appeared in the *Gazetteer* on 24 Oct. The *Pa. Gazette* for 24 Oct. 1787 printed all four letters, which were subsequently published as a pamphlet, *An Examination of the Constitution for the United States of America . . .* (Philadelphia, 1788), reprinted in Paul L. Ford, ed., *Pamphlets on the Constitution of the United States, Published during its Discussion by the People, 1787–1788* (Brooklyn, 1888), pp. 133–54. JM arranged to have the letters printed in Virginia through the agency of Joseph Jones (Jones to JM, 29 Oct. and 22 Nov. 1787). The first three numbers appeared in the *Va. Independent Chronicle* on 7 Nov. 1787 and the fourth on 21 Nov. 1787.

From Tench Coxe

PHILADELPHIA Sept. 28th. 1787.

DEAR SIR

I troubled you with a few lines by Mr Moore, in which I promised myself the pleasure of sending you the third Number of the American Citizen, which I have now the pleasure to enclose. Our house is at this Moment on the Adoption of the plan. A Motion to postpone was made by our Western Members, but on the Question only 12 were for the postponement. The house are now proceeding, and the Resolution before them is to this Effect "that the house *recommend* to the people of Pennsylvania the calling a Convention agreeably to the plan proposed by the late federal Convention for the purposing of considering the new Constitution &ca."

A second Resolution is to follow fixing the times of Election & Meeting.[1] There is *very* little doubt that it will be carried. I have none indeed. Mr. Findley stated his ideas on the subject fully, and went so far as to say that he thought a Convention ought to be called and expected it would be called. He made no observation unfavorable to the new Constitution. With much Respect, I am, dear Sir yr. obedt. hum. Servt.

TENCH COXE

The *only* ground of Opposition was not having the Constitution before the house from Congress.

29th. Our assembly on a Division on the first Question were 43 for it, & 19 against, Mr Morris was not in the house. There were 34 Republicans &

9 Constitutionalists in the 43.[2] The *principal* Germans were among the nine. The Western Members chiefly composed the 19. This took place about two O'Clock when the house adjourned till after dinner. On the call of the Roll there appeared but 45 Members, 46 is a quorum. This appearing designed to prevent the second Resolution fixing the time, manner &ca. of electing and convening the State Convention[,] the Sarjeant at Arms was sent for the 17 Absentees who were found together at the House [of] a great constitutional partizan a Major Boyd, with two constitutional Members of the Council from the Western Counties Messrs. J. McClene & Smilie. They recd. the speakers Message from the Sarjeant, but refused to go to the House. The house adjourned till this Morning at ½ past nine.

It appears probable to me from the information I have been able to collect that Judge Bryan was with the 17 prior to the Sarjeants finding them, but not at the time. A Mr. Whitehill, one of the constitutional leaders, certainly was at his house at dinner.

It appears from these facts, that the Western people have a good deal of Jealousy about the new constitution, and it is very clear that the men, who have been used to lead the Constitutional are against it decidedly. I am sorry for any thing that appears irregular, or looks like an interruption of peace, but I have no doubt of a large Majority of the Convention adopting the new frame of gouvernment in toto. One thing will certainly follow the rending the constitutional party to pieces, when the animosities among them will be more bitter from their former cordiality.

The enclosed paper has also the resolution of the house at large.[3]

The arrival of the recommendation of Congress before ten O'Clock to day would be a most happy circumstance.[4]

RC (DLC). Addressed by Coxe. Carried by "Major Giles." Docketed by JM. Enclosures not found.

[1] The debates and proceedings on these resolutions in the Pennsylvania Assembly are printed in John Bach McMaster and Frederick D. Stone, eds., *Pennsylvania and the Federal Constitution* (1888; 2 vols.; New York, 1970 reprint), I, 27–72.

[2] The "Republicans" and "Constitutionalists" were rival factions that had dominated Pennsylvania politics since the Revolution. The Constitutionalists were so called because of their support of the "radical" state constitution, featuring a unicameral legislature annually elected by taxpayers. They drew their strength mainly from the western counties and, in general, were hostile to the proposed federal Constitution. The Republicans, concentrated in Philadelphia, sought to replace the state constitution and tended to be warm supporters of the federal Constitution (Jackson T. Main, *The Antifederalists: Critics of the Constitution, 1787–1788* [Chapel Hill, 1961], pp. 42–47, 189–93).

[3] Probably the 29 Sept. 1787 issue of the Philadelphia *Independent Gazetteer*, which printed the first of the resolutions mentioned above.

[4] When the roll was called at the opening of the morning session of 29 Sept., the number present was still two short of a quorum. At the same time the resolution of Congress

submitting the Constitution to the states, agreed to the day before and sent by express to Philadelphia, was read before the House. Shortly thereafter two of the missing members were forcibly brought back to the House and kept there against their will. Having made a quorum, the legislature passed resolutions providing for a convention to meet at Philadelphia the third Tuesday in November (McMaster and Stone, *Pennsylvania and the Federal Constitution*, I, 63–72).

To Edmund Randolph

Letter not found.

ca. 28 September 1787. Mentioned in JM to Randolph, 7 Oct. 1787. Relates proceedings of Congress on the report of the Federal Convention.

To James Madison, Sr.

New York Sepr. 30. 1787

HOND. SIR

By Mr. Blair who left Philada. immediately after the rising of the Convention, I sent to the care of Mr. F. Maury a copy of the New Constitution proposed for the U.S. Mr. Blair set out in such haste that I had no time to write by him, and I thought the omission of the less consequence as your last letter led me to suppose that you must about that time be absent on your trip to Frederick. I arrived here on monday last.[1] The Act of the Convention was then before Congress. It has been since taken up, & by a unanimous vote, forwarded to the States to be proceeded on as recommended by the Convention. What reception this new System will generally meet with cannot yet be pronounced. For obvious reasons opposition is as likely to arise in Virginia as any where. The City of Philada. has warmly espoused it. Both parties there, it is said, have united on the occasion. It may happen nevertheless that a Country party may spring up and give a preponderancy to the opposite scale. In this City, the general voice coincides with that of Philada. but there is less apparent unanimity, and it is pretty certain that the party in power will be active in defeating the new system. In Boston the reception given to it is extremely favorable we are told; but more will depend on the Country than the Town. The eccho from Connecticut & New Jersey, as far as it has reached us denotes a favorable disposition in those States.

I inclose a few plumb Stones from an excellent Tree. I am aware that this is not the true mode of propagating the fruit, but it sometimes suc-

less urgent than the present state of our affairs, if any faith were due to the representations made by Congress themselves, ecchoed by 12 States in the Union, and confirmed by the general voice of the People. An attempt was made in the next place by R. H. L. to amend the Act of the Convention before it should go forth from Congress. He proposed a bill of Rights—provision for juries in civil cases & several other things corresponding with the ideas of Col. M.[2] He was supported by Mr. Me——[3] Smith of this State. It was contended that Congress had an undoubted right to insert amendments, and that it was their duty to make use of it in a case where the essential guards of liberty had been omitted.[4] On the other side the right of Congress was not denied, but the inexpediency of exerting it was urged on the following grounds. 1. that every circumstance indicated that the introduction of Congress as a party to the reform, was intended by the States merely as a matter of form and respect. 2. that it was evident from the contradictory objections which had been expressed by the different members who had animadverted on the plan, that a discussion of its merits would consume much time, without producing agreement even among its adversaries. 3. that it was clearly the intention of the States that the plan to be proposed should be the act of the Convention with the assent of Congress, which could not be the case, if alterations were made, the Convention being no longer in existence to adopt them. 4. that as the Act of the Convention, when altered would instantly become the mere act of Congress, and must be proposed by them as such, and of course be addressed to the Legislatures, not conventions of the States, and require the ratification of thirteen instead of nine States, and as the unaltered act would go forth to the States directly from the Convention under the auspices of that Body—Some States might ratify one & some the other of the plans, and confusion & disappointment be the least evils that could ensue. These difficulties which at one time threatened a serious division in Congs. and popular alterations with the yeas & nays on the journals, were at length fortunately terminated by the following Resolution—"Congress having recd. the Report of the Convention lately assembled in Philada., Resold. *unanimously* that the said Report, with the Resolutions & letter accompanying the same, be transmitted to the several Legislatures, in order to be submitted to a Convention of Delegates chosen in each State by the people thereof, in conformity to the Resolves of the Convention made & provided in that case." Eleven States were present, the absent ones R.I. & Maryland. A more direct approbation would have been of advantage in this & some other States, where stress will be laid on the agency of Congress in the matter, and a handle taken by adversaries of any ambiguity on the subject. With regard to Virginia & some other States, reserve on the part of Congress will do no injury. The circumstance of unaninimity must be favorable every where.[5]

The general voice of this City seems to espouse the new Constitution. It is supposed nevertheless that the party in power is strongly opposed to it. The Country must finally decide, the sense of which is as yet wholly unknown. As far as Boston & Connecticut has been heard from, the first impression seems to be auspicious. I am waiting with anxiety for the eccho from Virginia but with very faint hopes of its corresponding with my wishes. With every sentiment of respect & esteem, & every wish for your health & happiness, I am Dear Sir, Your Obedient, humble servt.

Js. Madison Jr.

P.S. A small packet of the size of 2 Vol. 80. addressed to you, lately came to my hands with books of my own from France. Genl. Pinkney has been so good as to take charge of them. He set out yesterday for S. Carolina & means to call at Mount Vernon.

RC (DLC: Washington Papers). Docketed by Washington.

[1] See *JCC*, XXXIII, 540–44.
[2] JM interlined "Mason" here.
[3] JM interlined here the rest of Smith's given name, Melancton.
[4] See Burnett, *Letters*, VIII, 648–49.
[5] "The people do not scrutinize terms; the unanimity of Congress in recommending a measure to their consideration, naturally implies approbation" (Edward Carrington to Thomas Jefferson, 23 Oct. 1787, Burnett, *Letters*, VIII, 660). But see Richard Henry Lee's comment on the compromise resolution: "This compromise was settled and they took the opportunity of inserting the word unanimously, which applies only to simple transmission, hoping to have it mistaken for an unanimous approbation of the thing. . . . It is certain that no approbation was given" (Richard Henry Lee to George Mason, 1 Oct. 1787, ibid., VIII, 653).

From Edmund Randolph

Bowling green Sepr. 30. 1787.

My dear friend

We arrived here last night, with as little inconvenience as possible. Betsey has recovered by travelling.

Baltimore resounds with friendship for the new constitution, and Mr. Chase's election depends, as it is said, upon his opinion concerning it. He waited on me, with an expectation, I suspect, of learning something to foster his opposition. I was prepared, because I had heard of his harangue to the people of Fell's point the night before I saw him. It was represented to me, that after he had finished his speech, Colo Sam: Smith and Mr.

Zebulon Hollingsworth asked him, whether he espoused the constitution or not? He replied to this effect: "Here gentleme[n] is a form of government, (pulling out the Maryland Act) under which we have lived happily for more than ten years. Shall we make a new experiment precipitately? Are we to pay taxes indefinitely, have our Militia led from one End of the continent to the other, and be dragooned by a standing army, if we fail in the smallest article of duty? But—I have not made up my mind." However in the discourse between us, altho' he discovered a tendency to reject the constitution, unless amended, he declared he would labour to Establish a fœderal government.[1]

In Bladensburg the constitution is approved. In Alexandria the inhabitants are enthusiasts, and instructions to force my dissenting colleague[2] to assent to a convention are on the anvil.[3] I wrote to him yesterday, suggesting to him this expedient: to urge the calling of a convention as the first act of the assembly; if they shd. wish amendments, let them be stated and forwarded to the states: before the meeting of the convention an answer may be obtained: if the proposed amendments be rejected, let the constitution immediately operate: if approved, by nine states, let the assent of our convention be given under the exception of the points amended. This will, I believe, blunt the opposition, which will be formidable, if they must take altogether or reject. The reeligibility of the president and senate has excited Mr. Jas. Mercer's resentment, and he positively objects to the constitution without an alteration. I learn nothing of Mr. H——y nor of Mr. Pendleton except that he is almost perfectly recovered. Adieu: and believe me My dear sir, always & inviolably to be yr. affectionate friend

E. R.

RC (DLC). Docketed by JM. Brackets enclose letter obscured by frayed margin.

[1] At the time of his "harangue" Samuel Chase was seeking election to the Maryland House of Delegates. Once safely elected, he took a more open stand against the Constitution (Philip A. Crowl, "Anti-Federalism in Maryland, 1787–1788," *WMQ*, 3d ser., IV [1947], 457).

[2] George Mason.

[3] At a meeting of freeholders of Fairfax County on 2 Oct. 1787, George Mason and David Stuart, delegates to the General Assembly from that county, were instructed "to declare the Opinion of your Constituents... to be for the immediate Convocation of a Convention" to ratify the Constitution (Rutland, *Papers of George Mason*, III, 1000–1001).

they will consider themselves as justly represented. This was a great Point gained, & I think may promise a Durability to the Union, wch. it's warmest Friends scarce hoped for. I doubt not also, but under the new Constitution, national Faith, a great & important Object certainly, will be effectually restored. I doubt not but it will be the Means of giving Stability & Vigour to the State Govts., & prevent those frequent Vacillations from one iniquitous or absurd Scheme to another, wch. has destroyed all Confidence amongst Individuals. It will create the Habit of Obedience to the Laws, & give them that Energy wch. is unquestionably essential to a free Govt. These & many other happy Effects, may reasonably be expected from a Govt. so wisely conceived in it's general Plan, & wch. must possess Vigour & Energy sufft. to execute the Measures adopted under it. With all these Advantages, then, ought any one to raise Objections against 'it? Should we not, under the Consciousness, that it is impossible to form a Constitution agreable to the Minds of all, rest satisfied with this, wch. promises so many Advantages? I confess, under these Considerations, I feel myself as a Citizen, strongly inclined to add my Voice of Approbation to that of the many who so highly extol the Labours of the Convention. But, I must also declare that it appears to me to possess a Defect, wch. perhaps threatens Ruin to Republicanism itself. Is it not my Friend, received by all, as a political Axiom—that it is essential to every free Govt., that the Legislative & executive Departments should be entirely distinct & independent? Upon what Principle was it, that this fundamental Axiom in Politics has been disregarded—since, it appears almost a Certainty, that where those Powers are united, Govt. must soon degenerate into a Tyranny. A sole Executive, who may be for Life, with almost a Negative upon the Legislature; the Senate, a principal Part of the Legislature, wch. may also be for Life, occasionally a Part of the Executive—these appear to me to be most unfortunate Features in the new Constn. I may be deceived, but they present to my Mind so strong a Stamp of Monarchy or Aristocracy, that, I think, many Generations would not pass before one or other wd. spring from the new Constn. provided, it were to continue in it's present Form. It is true it may be amended—the only Danger is in permitting that to be received, wch. may never be amended. It is not the Quantum of Power proposed to be given to the new Congress, of wch. I complain. I am persuaded, if it be wisely exercised, it must be most happy for the States both individually & collectively, to have a Power equally restrictive & energetic lodged in the supreme Council. I only complain & lament that that Power was not distributed in such a Manner as might preserve, instead of, threaten Destruction to the Liberties of Ama.

Yet, after all, so greatly do I respect the Framers of that Constitution, so beneficial must it's Effects be in many important Instances—that, I shd. rejoice to see it adopted—*provided*, it's Continuance was limited to a certain fixed Period, revivable or not, as the States might determine. We shd. then feel it's good Effects, without running the Risque of the Dangers it seems to threaten. But I fear I shall only tire you with my Observations—So Adieu. Frondeur as I am, beleive me to be Most sincerely Yrs. Affe.

J. MADISON

RC (DLC). Docketed by JM. The Williamsburg clergyman wrote another letter criticizing the Constitution on 1 Oct. 1787 to his brother, Thomas Madison of Botetourt County. Thomas P. Abernethy saw this second letter in the Draper Collection (WHi) and mistakenly cited it as having been written by JM (*Western Lands and the American Revolution*, p. 361 n. 1).

[1] Letter not found.

To Edmund Randolph

New York Octr. 7th. 1787.

MR.[1] DEAR FRIEND

I was yesterday favored with yours of the 30th. Ult: and heard with particular pleasure the favorable influence of your journey on Mrs. Randolph's health.

I wrote to you shortly after my arrival here, and rehearsed the proceedings of Congress on the subject of the new federal Constitution. I have since forwarded by Mr. Hopkins[2] a large foreign letter for you with some others for the friends of Mr. Jefferson which you will be kind enough to dispose of. I have also delivered to Mr. Constable[3] of this City to be forwarded by water to your care, several volumes in sheets addressed to the University of W. & Mary. They came in a box of books which I received by the last packet, but without a single memorandum on the subject from any quarter. They were addressed to the two Universities of Virga. & Penna. & duplicate sheets being contained in each packet.[4] I know not how the duty in Virga. will be settled. The difficulty was avoided here, by the precaution of entering them for re-exportation. As they are a free gift, are of little value, and are destined for a public institution, I should suppose that no facility consistent with law will be witheld.

Congs. are at present deliberating on the requisition. The Treasury Board have reported one in Specie alone, alledging the mischiefs produced by "Indents." It is proposed by a Committee that indents be recd. from the States, but that the conditions tying down the States to a particular

185

mode of procuring them, be abolished, and that the indents for one year be receivable in the quotas of any year.[5]

Sinclair is appointed Govr. of the Western Territory, & a Majr. Sergeant of Masts. the Secretary of that Establishment. A Treaty with the Indians is on the anvil as a supplemental provision for the W. Country.[6] It is not certain however that any thing will be done, as it involves money, and we shall have on the floors nine States one day more only.

We hear nothing decisive as yet concerning the general reception given to the Act of the Convention. The Advocates for it come forward more promptly than the Adversaries. The Sea Coast seems every where fond of it. The party in Boston which was thought most likely to make opposition, are warm in espousing it. It is said that Mr. S. Adams, objects to one point only, viz. the prohibition of a Religious test. Mr. Bowdoin's objections are said to lie agst. the great number of members composing the Legislature, and the intricate election of the President. You will no doubt have heard of the fermentation in the Assembly of Penna.

Mr. Adams is permitted to return home after Feby. next, with thanks for the zeal, & fidelity of his services. As the commission of Smith[7] expires at that time and no provision is made for Continuing him, or appointing a Successor, the representation of the U.S. at the Court of London will cease at that period. With every wish for your happiness, and with the sincerest affection I remain My dear Sir, Your Friend,

Js. MADISON JR.

RC (DLC). Addressed and franked by JM. Docketed by Randolph.

[1]JM meant "My."

[2]Probably John Hopkins, Continental loan office commissioner for Virginia.

[3]Probably William Constable, a New York merchant and speculator (*New-York Directory, 1786*, pp. 24, 26; Syrett and Cooke, *Papers of Hamilton*, V, 242 n. 3; Ferguson, *Power of the Purse*, p. 258).

[4]In his letter of 2 Aug. 1787 to JM, Jefferson indicated that he had sent the books to JM's care. JM apparently had not yet received this letter.

[5]The Board of Treasury's report on the requisition, dated 28 Sept. 1787 and read in Congress the next day, described in detail the failure of the indent system of servicing the public debt. According to the board's estimate, nearly five million dollars in indents remained in circulation, unredeemed by state taxes. This estimate did not include the indents on the requisition of 1786, which the treasury refused to issue because no state had yet provided adequate funds to meet its quota (*JCC*, XXXIII, 569–78). This report was referred to a committee, which included JM, on 5 Oct. The committee rejected the Board of Treasury's recommendation of a requisition in specie alone, declaring "that the domestic Creditors will not be benefited so much by the change as the other parts of the community will be distressed." It proposed instead to allow the states to service the public debt *"in such manner as they judge most expedient."* To make the collection of indents easier the committee recommended repeal of the requirements in the previous requisitions. These changes were approved by Congress on 11 Oct. (*JCC*, XXXIII, 616 n. 1, 632–36, 649–58; Ferguson, *Power of the Purse*, pp. 226–28). Under the new rules, indent payments to the Continental treasury did

not have to be accompanied by a proportion of specie, and the indents issued for a given year could be received "indiscriminately" in payment of a state's quota for any year. For example, indents issued on the requisition of 1785 could be submitted in fulfillment of a state's quota for 1786. Moreover, the states were now free to obtain indents by direct purchase rather than by laying taxes payable in this paper medium.

[6]See Carrington to JM, 25 July 1787 and n. 3.
[7]William Stephens Smith, secretary to the legation at London.

To Joseph Jones

Letter not found.

7 October 1787. Acknowledged in Jones to JM, 29 Oct. 1787. Sends newspapers containing pieces by "An American Citizen" (Tench Coxe).

From Thomas Jefferson

Paris Oct. 8. 1787.

Dear Sir

The bearer hereof the count de Moustier, successor to Monsr. de la Luzerne, would from his office need no letter of introduction to you or to any body. Yet I take the liberty of recommending him to you to shorten those formal approaches which the same office would otherwise expose him to in making your acquaintance. He is a great enemy to formality, etiquette, ostentation & luxury. He goes with the best dispositions to cultivate society without poisoning it by ill example. He is sensible, disposed to view things favorably, & being well acquainted with the constitution of England, it's manners & language, is the better prepared for his station with us. But I should have performed only the lesser, & least pleasing half of my task, were I not to add my recommendations of Madame de Brehan. She is goodness itself. You must be well acquainted with her. You will find her well disposed to meet your acquaintance & well worthy of it. The way to please her is to receive her as an acquaintance of a thousand years standing. She speaks little English. You must teach her more, and learn French from her. She hopes by accompanying M. de Moustier to improve her health which is very feeble, & still more to improve her son in his education & to remove him to a distance from the seductions of this country. You will wonder to be told that there are no schools in this country to be compared to ours, in the sciences. The husband of Madame de Brehan is an officer, & obliged by the times to remain with the army.[1] Monsieur de Moustier brings your watch. I have

187

worn her two months, and really find her a most incomparable one. She will not want the little re-dressing which new watches generally do, after going about a year. She costs 600 livres. To open her in all her parts, press the little pin on the edge, with the point of your nail. That opens the chrystal. Then open the dial plate in the usual way. Then press the stem, at the end within the loop, & it opens the back for winding up or regulating. *De Moustier is remarkably communicative. With adroitness he may be pumped of anything. His openness is from character not from affectation. An intimacy with him will on this account be politically valuable.* I am Dear Sir your affectionate friend & servant

Th: Jefferson

RC (DLC); FC (DLC: Jefferson Papers). Italicized words are those encoded by Jefferson using the code he sent JM on 11 May 1785. Decoding interlined in the RC, probably by one of JM's earlier editors. FC accompanied by a separate sheet with the coded passage written out in Jefferson's hand.

[1] JM was one of the few Americans Madame de Bréhan found to her liking. In New York circles the majority soon believed "her connection with her brother-in-law [Moustier] was improper" (Malone, *Jefferson and the Rights of Man*, pp. 197–98).

From Edmund Pendleton

[Edmundsbury, 8 October 1787]

... A Republic was inevitably the American form, and its Natural danger Pop. Tumults & Convulsions. With these in view I read over the Constitution accurately; do not find a Trait of any Violation of the great Principles of the form, all Power being derived mediately or immediately from the People. No Title or Powers that are either hereditary or of long duration so as to become Inveterate; and the Laws & not the arbitrary will of any man, or body of men made the rule of Government. The People, the Origin of Power, cannot act personally, & can only exercise their Power by representation. The great bodies of both Federal & State Legislatures are to consist of their immediate choice, and from that choice all other Powers are derived; the secretions required in the choice of the Federal Senate and President, seem admirably contrived to prevent Popular Tumults, as well as to preserve that Equilibrium to be expected from the Ballancing Power of the three branches. In the President's Power of Negation to the laws, the modification strikes out a happy medium between an Absolute Negative in a single person, & having no stop, or cheque upon laws too harshly, or the Offspring of Party or Faction such as upon a re-consideration, are approved by ⅔rds of Each House, ought to pass independent of any other power.

The President is indeed to be a great man, but it is only in shew to represent the Federal dignity & Power, having no latent Prerogatives, nor any Powers but such as are defined and given him by law. He is to be Commander-in-Chief of the Army & Navy, but Congress are to raise & provide for them, & that not for above two years at a time. He is to nominate all officers, but Congress must first creat[e] the offices & fix the Emoluments, and may discontinue them at pleasure & he must have the consent of ⅔rds of the Senate to his nomination. Above all his tenure of Office is short, & the Danger of Impeachment a powerful restraint against abuse of Office. A Political Head and that adorned with powder'd hair, seems as necessary & useful in Governments as that member so adorned in the natural body, and I have observed in the history of the United Netherlands, that their affairs always succeeded best, when they allowed their Stadtholder to exercise his Constitutional powers. . . .

Printed extract (Stan. V. Henkels Catalogue No. 694 [1892]). Following the last sentence of the quoted excerpt, the catalogue notes that Pendleton "continues on, commenting on all the important points in that great masterwork of the founders of this great republic." The letter also contained a "criticism on the clause exempting vessels bound to or from a State from being obliged to enter &c in another" (JM to Pendelton, 28 Oct. 1787). The list probably kept by Peter Force (DLC: Madison Miscellany) notes that this letter consisted of four pages and calendars it as follows: "The results of the Philadelphia Convention. The two Virginia dissenters to the plan adopted. Pendleton's review of the proposed Constitution."

From George Washington

MOUNT VERNON Octr.. 10th. 1787

MY DEAR SIR,

I thank you for your letter of the 30th. Ult. It came by the last Post. I am better pleased that the proceedings of the Convention is handed from Congress by a unanimous vote (feeble as it is) than if it had appeared under stronger marks of approbation without it. This apparent unanimity will have its effect. Not every one has opportunities to peep behind the curtain; and as the multitude often judge from externals, the appearance of unanimity in that body, on this occasn, will be of great importance.

The political tenets of Colo M.[1] & Colo R. H. L. are always in unison. It may be asked which of them gives the tone? Without hesitation, I answer the latter; because the latter, I believe, will receive it from no one.[2] He has, I am informed, rendered himself obnoxious in Philadelphia by the pains he took to dissiminate his objections amongst some [of] the leaders of

189

the seceding members of the legislature of that State.[3] His conduct is not less reprobated in this County. How it will be relished, *generally*, is yet to be learnt, by me. As far as accts. have been received from the Southern & Western Counties, the Sentiment with respect to the proceedings of the Convention is favourable. Whether the knowledge of this, or conviction of the impropriety of withholding the Constitution from State Conventions has worked most in the breast of Col M I will not decide; but the fact is, he has declared unequivocally (in a letter to me) for its going to the people.[4] Had his sentiments however been opposed to the measure, Instructions, which are given by the freeholders of this County to their representatives, would have secured his vote for it.[5] Yet, I have no doubt but that this assent will be accompanied by the most tremendous apprehensions, and highest colourings to his objections. To alarm the people, seems to be the ground work of his plan. The want of a qualified Navigation Act, is already declared to be a mean by which the produce of the Southern States will be reduced to nothing, & will become a monopoly of the Northern & Eastern States. To enumerate all his objections, is unnecessary; because they are detailed in the address of the seceding members of the Assembly of Pensylvania; which, no doubt you have seen.[6]

I scarcely think that any powerful opposition will be made to the Constitution's being submitted to a Convention of the people of this State. If it is given, it will be at that meeting—In which I hope you will make it convenient to attend;[7] explanations will be wanting—none can give them with more precision and accuracy than yourself.

The Sentiments of Mr. Henry with respect to the Constitution which is submitted, are not known in these parts. Mr. Josh. Jones (who it seems was in Alexandr. a few days before my return home) was of opinion that they would not be inemical to it—others however conceive, that as the advocate of a paper emission, he cannot be friendly to a Constn. wch. is an effectual bar.

From circumstances which have been related, it is conjectured that the Governor wishes he had been among the subscribing members, but time will disclose more than we know at present with respect to the whole of this business; and when I hear more, I will write to you again. In the mean while I pray you to be assured of the sincere regard and affection with which I am, My dear Sir Yr. Most Obedt. & Very Hble Serv

GO: WASHINGTON

PS. Having received (in a letter) from Colo. Mason, a detail of his objections to the proposed Constitution I enclose you a copy of them.[8]

RC (MA); FC (DLC: Washington Papers). RC docketed by JM. FC in a clerk's hand. Minor variations between the FC and the RC have not been noted. For enclosure, see n. 8.

[1] Here JM added "ason."

[2] Washington's comments in the remainder of this paragraph indicate that he was referring to George Mason rather than to Richard Henry Lee. Thus he should have written "former" instead of "latter." JM evidently recognized Washington's error, as suggested by a note in his hand at the bottom of the first page of the RC. The note is heavily crossed through, however, and only a few words are legible.

[3] See Coxe to JM, 28 Sept. 1787. Washington may have seen a satirical piece in the *Pa. Gazette* of 3 Oct. 1787 listing eight reasons for "The Protest of the Minority, who objected to calling a Convention, for the purpose of adopting the fœderal Constitution," the seventh of which read: "Because a disaffected member of the fœderal convention, from Virginia, in a closet conversation with R. Whitehill, disapproved of the fœderal government, and we hold it to be our duty rather to follow his advice, than the inclinations of our constituents."

[4] See Mason to Washington, 7 Oct. 1787, Rutland, *Papers of George Mason*, III, 1001–2.

[5] In the FC this sentence reads: "Had his sentiments however been opposed to the measure, his instructions (for the delegates of this Country are so instructed) would have compelled him to vote for it." The instructions from the freeholders of Fairfax County to their representatives, George Mason and David Stuart, directed them to work for "the immediate Convocation of a Convention of Delegates" to ratify the Constitution (ibid., III, 1000–1001).

[6] Shortly after the Pennsylvania legislature voted to call an early convention to consider the Constitution, the dissenting minority issued "An Address . . . to their Constituents," which appeared in the *Pa. Packet* of 4 Oct. 1787 (McMaster and Stone, *Pennsylvania and the Federal Constitution*, I, 73–79). JM may have seen the address in the Pennsylvania paper or in the *N.Y. Journal, and Weekly Register* of 11 Oct. 1787.

[7] In the FC this sentence reads: "if it is given it will be there at which I hope you will make it convet. to be present."

[8] Mason composed the first draft of his "Objections To This Constitution of Government" just before the convention adjourned. He revised it before sending copies to Washington on 7 Oct. and to Elbridge Gerry on 20 Oct. (Rutland, *Papers of George Mason*, III, 991–94, 1001–2, 1006). Washington's copy of Mason's "Objections" is in the Washington Papers (DLC) and is printed in *Documentary History of the Constitution*, IV, 316–20. Another copy, in an unknown hand, is in the Mason Papers (DLC). Below the title on the first page of this copy appears the attribution in JM's hand: "By Col. Mason." An endorsement in an unknown hand, possibly that of John Jay, appears on the verso. Evidently this is the copy Washington sent JM.

To Ambrose Madison

N. YORK OCT. 11. —87.

DEAR BROTHER

Your favor of the 24. of Sepr. did not come to hand till the day before yesterday. I am glad to find the State of Crops in your quarter not worse. From the general information I had feared that very little Tobo. would be made, and scarce any corn. I am at a loss what to say as to brother Wms. adventurig. into public life. The prospect of service to His Country does not appear to me to call for much personal sacrifice. Nor can the honor, the profit or the pleasure of the undertaking, be any object. At the same time if his inclination is on that side, and his private affairs will admit, I would not be understood to discountenance the measure. I recommend it to him however not to make an attempt without a tolerable certainty of success, and by no means to run into the error of courting it by the usual practices. If he wishes to establish himself in the good will of the County, the only durable as well as honorable plan will be to establish a character that merits it.[1]

Congs. have just passed the annual requisition on the States. The interest on the domestic debt is called for in indents which the States are at liberty to procure in any way they please. I presume all of them, excepting such as have or mean to adopt a paper emis[sion] will buy up their quotas, instead of laying taxes payable in paper.[2]

We have no public news. The Act of the Convention has in general been pretty well recd. as yet in the Middle & Northn. States. Opposition however begins to shew itself. It is not possible to say now on which side the Majority will finally lie. The present appearance is in favor of the new Constitution. The adversaries differ as much in their objections as they do from the thing itself.

Let me know in your next whether my brother Willm. has sold Forrester, and whether Fancy & Lemon are with foal, & what horse the latter was put to. Remember me affecely to my sister & all others of the family. Yrs.

Js. Madison Jr.

RC (NN). Addressed and franked by JM. Sent "To the care of F. Maury Esqr. Fredericksburg Virginia." Letters missing, owing to a tear in the Ms, have been restored within brackets.

[1]JM's less than enthusiastic encouragement of his younger brother's political aspirations may have persuaded William, then twenty-five, to postpone his entry into public life. He represented first Culpeper County, 1791–1792, and then Madison County, 1794, 1804–1811, in the House of Delegates (Swem and Williams, *Register*, p. 403).

[2]The Virginia delegates in Congress recommended this mode of obtaining indents, i.e., by direct purchase, in their letter to Governor Randolph of 3 Nov. 1787.

From James Monroe

Richmond Octr. 13. 1787.

Dear Sir

I was favor'd with yours by Mr. Blair, and a late one covering one from Mr Jefferson a few days since.[1] I shod. have answer'd the former sooner but defer'd it untill my arrival here whither I was at that time on the point of siting out. Mrs. M. accompanied me & will remain untill my return wh. will not be untill the adjournmt. of the Assembly.

The report from Phila. hath presented an interesting subject to their consideration. It will perhaps agitate the minds of the people of this State, more than any subject they have had in contemplation since the commenc'mt. of the late revolution, for there will be a greater division among the people of character than then took place, provided we are well inform'd as to the sentiments of many of them. It is said that Mr. Henry, Genl. Nelson, Harrison & others are against it. This ensures it a powerful opposition more especially when associated with that of the 2. dissenting deputies.[2]

There are in my opinion some strong objections agnst. the project; wh. I will not weary you with a detail of. But under the predicament in wh. the Union, now stands, & this State in particular with respect to this business, they are overbalanc'd by the arguments in its favor. The assembly will meet to morrow, & we have reason to believe we shall have an house the first or 2d. day. We shall soon find how its pulse beats, & what direction this business will take. I believe there will be no opposition to a convention, however of this I shall be able to give you better information in a few days.

I am happy to hear you have recd. 100. dolrs. from Genl. for his brother Govr. Pinckney.[3] I have been much concern'd that I have not been able to remit you the sums that have been necessary to replace yr. advances as well as fulfil our ingagment with Taylor, but as yet I am unable to do it.[4] I had calculated on considerable sums that were due me, some contracted in a way that seem'd to ensure a payment soon after demanded. In the latter instance I have been entirely disappointed. This induc'd me to have recourse to other means with those on whom I had not that claim. But the administration of justice here did not promise an early decision in my favor. Fortunately I have lately obtain'd a judgmt. against a man of property for near 400£. It is however under such circumstances that it is possible for him to throw it into chy., altho the event of the business wod. infallibly be as it now stands. Provided I will wait a few weeks he now promises, as at first he did, to pay it. But he hath & may still disappoint me, & if I serve an executn. on him he may take the course suggested above. I give you this detail merely to inform you of my prospects, and at the same time to suggest the propriety of disingaging myself from the contract (if Taylor conceives himself injur'd & cannot wait the result) & of requesting you to do it for me upon the most advantageous terms. I shod. not suggest this to you if I did not know that it were equally difficult for you to raise the money as for myself. Perhaps from this cause both yours & my credit are at this time suffering—which must not be.

RC (DLC). Addressed by Monroe and franked. Postmarked on 15 Oct. The missing complimentary close and signature have been clipped.

[1]Letters not found. JM doubtless forwarded Jefferson's letter to Monroe of 5 Aug. 1787 (Boyd, *Papers of Jefferson*, XI, 687–88).
[2]George Mason and Edmund Randolph.
[3]See *PJM*, IX, 391 and n. 2.
[4]On JM's advances and the "ingagment with Taylor," see *PJM*, IX, 416–17 and n. 1.

To George Washington

NEW YORK Octr. 14. 1787.

DEAR SIR

The letter herewith inclosed was put into my hands yesterday by Mr. de Crœvecœr who belongs to the Consular establishment of France in this Country. I add to it a pamphlet which Mr. Pinkney has submitted to the public, or rather as he professes, to the perusal of his friends;[1] and a printed sheet containing his ideas on a very delicate subject; too delicate in my opinion to have been properly confided to the press. He conceives that his precautions against any farther circulation of the piece than he himself authorises, are so effectual as to justify the step. I wish he may not be disappointed. In communicating a copy to you I fulfil his wishes only.[2]

No decisive indications of the public mind in the Northn. & Middle States can yet be collected. The Reports continue to be rather favorable to the Act of the Convention from every quarter; but its adversaries will naturally be latest in shewing themselves. Boston is certainly friendly. An opposition is known to be in petto in Connecticut; but it is said not to be much dreaded by the other side. Rhode Island will be divided on this subject in the same manner as it has been on the question of paper money. The Newspapers here have contained sundry publications animadverting on the proposed Constitution & it is known that the Government party are hostile to it. There are on the other side so many able & weighty advocates, and the conduct of the Eastern States if favorable, will add so much force to their arguments, that there is at least as much ground for hope as for apprehension. I do not learn that any opposition is likely to be made in N. Jersey. The temper of Pennsylvania will be best known to you from the direct information which you cannot fail to receive through the Newspapers & other channels.

Congress have been of late employed cheifly in settling the requisition, and in making some arrangements for the Western Country. The latter consist of the appointment of a Govr. & Secretary, and the allotment of a sum of money for Indian Treaties if they should be found necessary. The Requisition so far as it varies our fiscal system, makes the proportion of indents receivable independently of specie, & those of different years indiscriminately receivable for any year, and does not as heretofore tie down the States to a particular mode of obtaining them. Mr. Adams has been permitted to return home after Feby. next, & Mr. Jeffersons appointment continued for three years longer. With the most perfect esteem & most affectionate regard, I remain Dr. Sir, Your Obedt. friend & servant

Js. Madison Jr.

RC (DLC: Washington Papers); Tr (DLC). Docketed by Washington. For the enclosures, see nn. 1, 2.

[1] The pamphlet was Charles Pinckney's *Observations on the Plan of Government Submitted to the Federal Convention, on the 28th of May, 1787* . . . (New York, [1787]), which is reprinted in Farrand, *Records*, III, 106–23. Washington's copy is listed in *A Catalogue of the Washington Collection in the Boston Athenæum* (Boston, 1897), p. 535. Many years later JM made extensive use of this pamphlet in questioning the authenticity of a document sent by Pinckney to John Quincy Adams in 1818, which the South Carolinian claimed to be the draft of the plan he had submitted to the Federal Convention. On the controversy over the Pinckney Plan, see Farrand, *Records*, III, 501–15, 531, 534–37, 595–609. See also Jameson, "Studies in the History of the Federal Convention of 1787," *Annual Report of the American Historical Association for the Year 1902*, I, 111–32; [Andrew C. McLaughlin], "Sketch of Pinckney's Plan for a Constitution," *AHR*, IX (1903–4), 735–47.

[2] The "printed sheet" was a broadside of *Mr. Charles Pinckney's Speech, in Answer to Mr. Jay . . . on the* Question of a Treaty with Spain. Delivered in Congress, August 16, 1786 (New York, n.d.; Evans 19926). JM also sent a copy of the speech to Jefferson on 24 Oct. 1787. A copy of the broadside, endorsed by JM, is in the Rare Book Division, Library of Congress, and is evidently the one used by Worthington C. Ford in his 1905 publication of the speech (*AHR*, X [1904–5], 817–27). See also the bibliographical discussion in Burnett, *Letters*, VIII, 427 n. 2. The South Carolinian's speech was an attempt to persuade Congress not to change Secretary Jay's instructions so as to permit him to cede the right of the U.S. to the free navigation of the Mississippi River. Pinckney later recalled that copies of his remarks were "desired by many of the southern members," and he accordingly "had a few printed which were confidentially delivered to some of my friends" (Pinckney to Washington, 14 Dec. 1789; Pinckney to Charles Lester, 8 July 1801, ibid., VIII, 427–28 n. 2). Although Pinckney implied that he had had his speech printed shortly after delivering it, JM's comments in this letter and in a subsequent one to Washington seem to indicate that it was not published until the following year. According to JM the South Carolinian's motives in publishing the speech were entirely self-serving: "His printing the secret paper at this time could have no motive but the appetite for expected praise: for the subject to which it relates has been dormant a considerable time, and seems likely to remain so" (JM to Washington, 28 Oct. 1787). Washington commented sarcastically that Pinckney was unwilling "to loose any fame that can be acquired by the publication of his sentiments" (Washington to JM, 22 Oct. 1787).

To George Washington

N. York Octr. 18. 1787.

Dear Sir

I have been this day honoured with your favor of the 10th. instant, under the same cover with which is a copy of Col. Mason's objections to the Work of the Convention. As he persists in the temper which produced his dissent it is no small satisfaction to find him reduced to such distress for a proper gloss on it; for no other consideration surely could have led him to dwell on an objection which he acknowledged to have been in some degree removed by the Convention themselves—on the paltry right of the Senate to propose alterations in money bills—on the appointment of the vice President, President of the Senate instead of making the President of the Senate the vice President, which seemed to be the alternative—and on the *possibility*, that the Congress may misconstrue their powers & betray their trust so far as to grant monopolies in trade &c. If I do not forget too some of his other reasons were either not at all or very faintly urged at the time when alone they ought to have been urged; such as the power of the Senate in the case of treaties[1] & of impeachments; and their duration in office. With respect to the latter point I recollect well that he more than once disclaimed opposition to it. My memory fails me also if he did not acquiesce in if not vote for, the term allowed for the further importation of slaves;[2] and the prohibition of duties on exports by the States.[3] What he means by the dangerous tendency of the Judiciary I am at some loss to comprehend. It never was intended, nor can it be supposed that in ordinary cases the inferior tribunals will not have final jurisdiction in order to prevent the evils of which he complains. The great mass of suits in every State lie between Citizen & Citizen, and relate to matters not of federal cognizance. Notwithstanding the stress laid on the necessity of a Council to the President I strongly suspect, tho I was a friend to the thing, that if such an one as Col. Mason proposed, had been established, and the power of the Senate in appointments to offices transferred to it, that as great a clamour would have been heard from some quarters which in general eccho his Objections. What can he mean by saying that the Common law is not secured by the new constitution, though it has been adopted by the State Constitutions. The common law is nothing more than the unwritten law, and is left by all the constitutions equally liable to legislative alterations. I am not sure that any notice is particularly taken of it in the Constitutions of the States. If there is, nothing more is provided than a general declaration that it shall continue along with other branches of law to be in force till legally changed. The Constitution of Virga. drawn up by Col Mason himself, is absolutely silent on the subject. An *ordinance* passed during the same Session, declared the Common law as heretofore & all Statutes of prior date to the 4 of James I. to be still the law of the land,[4] merely to obviate pretexts that the separation from G. Britain threw us into a State of nature, and abolished all civil rights and Obligations. Since the Revolution every State has made great inroads & with great propriety in many instances on this *monarchical* code. The "revisal of the laws" by a Committe[e] of wch. Col. Mason was a member, though not an acting one, abounds with such innovations. The abolition of the *right of primogeniture*, which I am sure Col. Mason does not disapprove, falls under this head. What could the Convention have done? If they had in general terms declared the Common law to be in force, they would have broken in upon the legal Code of every State in the most material points: they wd. have done more, they would have brought over from G.B. a thousand heterogeneous & antirepublican doctrines, and even the *ecclesiastical Hierarchy itself*, for that is a part of the Common law. If they had undertaken a discrimination, they must have formed a digest of laws, instead of a Constitution. This objection surely was not brought forward in the Convention, or it wd. have been placed in such a light that a repetition of it out of doors would scarcely have been hazarded. Were it allowed the weight which Col. M. may suppose it deserves, it would remain to be decided whether it be candid to arraign the Convention for omissions which were never suggested to them—or prudent to vindicate the dissent by reasons which either were not previously thought of, or must have been wilfully concealed. But I am running into a comment as prolix, as it is out of place.

I find by a letter from the Chancellor (Mr. Pendleton) that he views the act of the Convention in its true light, and gives it his unequivocal approbation. His support will have great effect. The accounts we have here of some other respectable characters vary considerably. Much will depend on Mr. Henry, and I am glad to find by your letter that his favorable decision on the subject may yet be hoped for. The Newspapers here begin to teem with vehement & virulent calumniations of the proposed Govt. As they are cheifly borrowed from the Pensylvania papers, you see them of course. The reports however from different quarters continue to be rather flattering. With the highest respect & sincerest attachment I remain Dear Sir Yr. Obedt. & Affecte. Servant

Js. Madison Jr.

RC (DLC: Washington Papers). Docketed by Washington.

[1]On 15 Aug. Mason had noted that the Senate could "sell the whole Country by means of Treaties," but he had not specifically opposed the power of the Senate in making treaties (Farrand, *Records*, II, 297–98).

[2] However, JM must have recalled Mason's powerful speech of 22 Aug. denouncing the "infernal trafic" in slaves (ibid., II, 370).
[3] Mason most likely voted against the motion of 28 Aug. to add export duties to the list of prohibitions on the states. He later successfully moved to ease the restriction by permitting the states to lay such duties to meet inspection costs (ibid., II, 442, 588, 607).
[4] See Hening, *Statutes*, IX, 127.

From John Dawson

RICHMOND. Oct. 19. 1787.

DEAR SIR

Your favour of the 2d. Int.[1] I receivd in due time. Before this I presume you have heard that one hundred and five members attended at the statehouse on the first day. Whether this is to be attributed to the *ten* pounds, or to a proper sense of duty I leave with you to determine—perhaps to both.[2] On motion of Colo Mathews, seconded by Mr. B. Harrison, Mr. Prentis was call'd to the chair, without any opposition. On the wednesday the Senate elected Mr. Jones[3] their Speaker. A number of papers had been laid before the house by the Executive. Among them are the proceedings of the convention, as forwarded by Congress.

On Thursday next we are to go into a committee of the whole house on this business. Altho the constitution offer'd has some able opponents, yet there is a decided majority in favour of it. There will be no opposition, I think, to a state convention, for it appears to be the general opinion that the legislature ought to send the Constitution to the people with out any mark either of censure or approbation. I enclose you a paper in which you will find a piece said, with truth I believe, to be written by Colo Mason.[4] He is not yet arriv'd, but is hourly expected.

The System of Politicks this year will I apprehend be too much like that of the last. Mr. Nicholas has already declared in favour of scaling the provision certificates by permiting the people to pay their certificate tax by a fourth of the sum in specie.[5] On tuesday the appointment of delegates to congress will take place. I suspect Mr. Harrison, Colo Bland & Mr. Corben will be brought forward.[6]

The freeholders of Fairfax have, in the most pointed terms directed Colo Mason to vote for a convention, and have as pointedly assur'd him he shall not be in it. With much respect & esteem I am dear Sir Yr. Friend & Very hm Sert

J DAWSON.

—This moment I receiv'd your favour of the 11 Int.[7]

J D

RC (DLC). Enclosure not found.

[1]Letter not found.
[2]By an act passed at the October 1785 session of the General Assembly, to take effect on 1 Jan. 1787, every delegate or senator who was absent from the assembly without sufficient cause was to "forfeit and pay to the use of this commonwealth ten pounds" (Hening, *Statutes*, XII, 128).
[3]John Jones of Brunswick County.
[4]Dawson may have enclosed a copy of the *Va. Independent Chronicle* for 17 Oct. 1787, which contained a piece by "Cato Uticensis" criticizing the Constitution. Mason's authorship cannot be established.
[5]On opposition to the certificate tax, see McClurg to JM, 22 Aug. 1787 and n. 1.
[6]On 23 Oct. the assembly elected JM, Edward Carrington, Henry Lee, John Brown, and Cyrus Griffin delegates to represent Virginia in Congress (*JHDV*, Oct. 1787, p. 12).
[7]The postscript was written on the verso of the last page of the letter. JM's letter of 11 Oct. has not been found.

To Edmund Randolph

New York Ocr. 21. 1787.

My dear friend

I mentioned in a late letter that I had addressed to your care a small box of books for the University.[1] I now inclose the Bill of lading. Inclosed also is a bill of lading for another Box destined for Mr. W. Hay. Will you be so good as to have it handed to him. I paid two dollars for its freight from France to this port, which he may repay to you. The money you remitted by me to Col. Carrington having somewhat exceeded the amount of his demand, the two dollars may the more properly pass into your hands.

I have recd. no letter from you since your halt at the Bolling-Green. We hear that opinions are various in Virginia on the plan of the Convention. I have recd. within a few days a letter from the Chancellor[2] by which I find that he gives it his approbation; and another from the President of Willm. & Mary[3] which, though it does not absolutely reject the Constitution, criticizes it pretty freely. The Newspapers in the middle & Northern States begin to teem with controversial publications. The attacks seem to be principally levelled agst. the organization of the Government, and the omission of the provisions contended for in favor of the Press, & Juries &c. A new Combatant however with considerable address & plausibility, strikes at the foundation. He represents the situation of the U.S. to be such as to render any Govt. improper & impracticable which forms the States into one nation & is to operate directly on the people.[4] Judging from the News papers one wd. suppose that the adversaries were the most numerous & the most in earnest. But there is no other evidence that it is the fact. On the contrary we learn that the Assembly of N. Hamshire which recd. the constitution on the point of their adjournment, were extremely pleased with it. All the information from Massts. denotes a favorable impression there. The Legislature of Connecticut have unanimously recommended the choice of a Convention in that State. And Mr. Baldwin who is just from the spot tells me that from present appearances the opposition will be inconsiderable; that the Assembly if it depended on them would adopt the System almost unanimously; and that the Clergy and all the literary men are exerting themselves in its favor. Rho. Island is divided; The majority being violently agst. it. The temper of this State cannot yet be fully discerned. A strong party is in favor of it. But they will probably be outnumbered if those whose sentiments are not yet known, should take the opposite side. N. Jersey appears to be zealous. Meetings of the people in different counties are declaring their approbation & instructing their representatives. There will probably be a strong opposition in Penna. The other side however continue to be sanguine. Docr. Carroll[5] who came hither lately from Maryland tells me, that the public voice there appears at present to be decidedly in favor of the Constitution. Notwithstanding all these circumstances, I am far from considering the public mind as fully known or finally settled on the subject. They amount only to a strong presumption that the general sentiment in the Eastern & middle States is friendly to the proposed System at this time. Present me respectfully to Mrs. R. and accept the most fervent wishes for your happiness from your Affece. friend

Js. Madison Jr.

RC (DLC). Addressed, franked, and marked "private" by JM. Docketed by Randolph. Enclosures not found.

[1] The College of William and Mary.
[2] Edmund Pendleton to JM, 8 Oct. 1787.
[3] The Reverend James Madison to JM, ca. 1 Oct. 1787.
[4] JM's brief description seems to fit the first number of the essays of "Brutus," which appeared in the *N.Y. Journal, and Weekly Register* of 18 Oct. 1787. Paul Leicester Ford assigned the authorship of these essays to Robert Yates, an identification accepted by Cecelia Kenyon (Paul L. Ford, ed., *Essays on the Constitution of the United States* [Brooklyn, 1892], p. 417; Cecelia Kenyon, ed., *The Antifederalists* [New York, 1966], p. 323). Morton Borden, however, expresses some doubt about this attribution (*The Antifederalist Papers* [East Lansing, Mich., 1965], p. 42). William Jeffrey, Jr., says that "Brutus" cannot be positively identified, but his candidate is Melancton Smith ("The Letters of 'Brutus'—A Neglected Element in the Ratification Campaign of 1787–1788," *University of Cincinnati Law Review*, XL [1971], 644–46). Jeffrey reprinted all sixteen of the "Brutus" letters (ibid., XL, 665–777). The first letter is also reprinted in *Debates and Proceedings in the Convention of the Commonwealth of Massachusetts Held in the Year 1788* (Boston, 1856), pp. 366–78.
[5] The Reverend John Carroll, who later became the first Roman Catholic bishop in the U.S. He was the brother of Daniel Carroll.

From Tench Coxe

PHILADA. Oct. 21. 1787.

DEAR SIR

I recd. your letter acknowleging the rect. of the three papers in the Gazetteer. At the request of Mr. Wilson, Dr. Rush and another friend or two I added a 4th. paper, calculated to shew the general advantages & obviate some of the Objections to the System. It was desired by these Gentlemen for the purpose of inserting in one of several handbills, which it was proposed to circulate thro our Western Counties. I beg leave to enclose you three of them with the same Views as in the former Case, and wish that you and Col. H. may make any use of them, which you think will serve the cause. I also send each of you a pamphlet of Pelatiah Websters.[1] Tho calculated principally for this State, it has other merit.

The opposition here has become more open. It is by those *leaders* of the constitutional interest, who have acted in concert with the Western interest. *The people* of the party in the city are chiefly federal, tho not so I fear in the Counties. However there is no doubt but that a Majority, and a very respectable one in our Convention will adopt the Constitution *in toto*. The matter seems likely to be attended with a good deal of warmth in the conversations & publications, perhaps some abuse; but these things will arise on such great occasions. The city Members of Convention as proposed are Mr. J Wilson & Dr. Rush—a Mr. Hilary Baker, a German, a Mr. Latimer formerly of the constl. party, & of great influence among their people here & in some of the Counties, and Chief J. McKean. The latter tho of the constl. party has always approved of two branches, and on this occasion has been called on by some of the republicans among the fedoralists, and has in the most explicit terms approved and engaged to support the plan. A good many people however are averse to him, but as he has a western influence, as he will shew them that one of their Men proposed for the federal convention has been run by the city, and as he will be a proof that the federalists do not go upon party distinctions I think he ought to be & hope he will be elected. I feel great hopes from appearances in Virginia. Col. Mason's conduct appears to be resented, & Mr. Randolph's is viewed with pain & regret. He is a very amiable, valuable man, but I fear will suffer from the circumstance. It seems as if his declining to sign has occasioned a powerful interest to seize the opportunity of overthrowing him by giving Countenance to the measures he has declined. The Country in this Case will be served, but at his expense. If his Views were pure, it is to be regretted that he should suffer—if otherwise we must rejoice that it produces, or tends to produce, public benefits.

I remember observing to him that I thought his not signing might lessen the Violence of Opposition, tho I did not think then nor do I now, that he was right in refusing.

You will oblige me exceedingly by having the inclosed pacquet for Mr. Jefferson put into the french Mail, which will be closed the 25th. inst. I am, Sir, with the most sincere esteem your respectful humble Servt.

TENCH COXE

RC (DLC). Docketed by JM. Enclosures not found.

[1]*Remarks on the Address of Sixteen Members of the Assembly of Pennsylvania, to their Constituents, dated September 29, 1787. With Some Strictures on their Objections to the Constitution Recommended by the late Federal Convention* (Philadelphia, 1787), reprinted in McMaster and Stone, *Pennsylvania and the Federal Constitution*, I, 89–106.

From Archibald Stuart

RICHMOND Octr 21st. 1787.

DR SIR

Contrary to custom we had a house of Delegates on the 15th. inst: & proceeded to read the Govrs. letter with its inclosures. We have resolved to discontinue the additional tax of 6/ P HH.D. on Tobo. Exported;[1] to amend the militia Law by furnishing the Militia with publick Arms & by annexing to each battalion of infantry a small troop of horses to be raised by voluntary enlistment & Accoutred at their own expence.[2]

The Language from every quarter of the house is the Necessity of alleviateing the publick burthens & at the same time supporting the publick credit, & the Certificate tax our Only sinking fund I fear will cease & those in the hands of the holders be added to the mass of our funded debt.[3]

Next thursday is set apart for adopting the necessary measures for calling a Convention on the subject of the fœderal constitution. From the disposition of some of the members I fear it will be difficult to execute that Business without entering into the merits of the Constitution itself.

Mr Henry has upon all Occasions however foreign his subject attempted to give the Constitution a side blow. Its friends are equally warm in its support & never fail to pursue him through all his Windings. From what I can learn the body of the people approve the proposed plan of Government, it has however no contemptible opposition[:] Our two dissenting members in the Genl Convention P: Hy:, the family of Cabells, St Geo: Tucker, J Taylor, W Nelson: Genl. Nelson W Ronald I fear, the Judges I am told except P Carrington & Others to tedious & at the same time too insignificant to mention.

The Doctrine of Installments is once more to be the subject of Debate & a clog to the District Bill an incunbrince which I fear will again damn that Important Measure.[4]

We have had Notice that a Commutation of Tobo. for specie in payment of taxes will be proposed & the Result of which you shall shortly hear.[5]

Would it be proper that the ensuing Convention should also reform Our State constitution. The Objection to these innovations is that in the mean time the minds of men are Agitated & Government unhinged & as we are about to encounter this & every Other Objection would not the present be the most favorable crisis for this important Business.[6] I am Dr Sir with respect & esteem yr most Obt H servant

ARCHD STUART

RC (DLC). Docketed by JM.

[1] The additional duty on exported tobacco had been levied at the 1786 session of the legislature in response to the special requisition of Congress of 21 Oct. 1786. Repeal of this act was unnecessary because it was to be in force only until the end of 1787 (Hening, *Statutes*, XII, 288–89).

[2] Ibid., XII, 432–33.

[3] The revenue act adopted on 1 Jan. 1788 repealed the certificate tax, substituting an additional duty on imported goods for redeeming the military certificates and certificates issued for impressed property (ibid., XII, 412–16).

[4] George Nicholas was the chief proponent of the "Doctrine of Installments" for paying private debts (*PJM*, IX, 365 and n. 7). A bill establishing district courts had failed to pass the previous year (*PJM*, IX, 185, 187 n. 2, 190, 192 n. 5).

[5] See Jones to JM, 22 Nov. 1787 and n. 4; Stuart to JM, 2 Dec. 1787.

[6] At the May 1784 session of the General Assembly, Stuart had unsuccessfully proposed a convention to reform the 1776 state constitution (*PJM*, VIII, 93).

From George Washington

MOUNT VERNON Octr. 22d. 1787.

MY DEAR SIR,

When I last wrote to you, I was uninformed of the Sentiments of this State beyond the circle of Alexandria, with respect to the New Constitution. Since, a letter which I received by the last Post, dated the 16th., from a Member of the Assembly, contains the following paragraphs.[1]

"I believe such an instance has not happened before, since the Revolution, that there should be a house on the first day of the Session, and business immediately taken up. This was not only the case on Monday, but there was a full house; when Mr. Prentice was called up to the Chair as Speaker, there being no opposition. Thus, the Session has commenced peaceably."

"It gives me much pleasure to inform you that the sentiments of the members are infinitely more favourable to the Constitution than the most zealous advocates for it could have expected. I have not met with one in all my enquiries (and I have made them with great diligence) opposed to it, except Mr. Henry who I have heard is so, but could only conjecture it, from a conversation with him on the Subject. Other members who have also been active in their enquiries tell me, that they have met with *none* opposed to it. It is said however that old Mr. Cabell of Amherst disapproves of it. Mr. Nicholas has declared himself a warm friend to it."

"The transmissory note of Congress was before us to day, when Mr. Henry declared that it transcended our powers to decide on the Constitution; that it must go before a Convention. As it was insinuated he would aim at preventing this, much pleasure was discovered at the declaration. Thursday week (the 25th.) is fixed upon for taking up the question of calling the Convention, and fixing the time of its meeting: In the meantime, five thousand copies are ordered to be printed, to be dispersed by the members in their respective Counties for the information of the People. I cannot forbear mentioning that the Chancellor, Pendleton, espouses the Constitution so warmly as to declare he will give it his aid in the Convention, if his health will permit. As their are few better judges of such subjects, this must be deemed a fortunate circumstance."

As the above quotations is the sum of my information, I shall add nothing more on the subject of the proposed government, at this time.

Mr. C. Pinkney is unwilling (I perceive by the enclosures contained in your letter of the 13th.)[2] to loose any fame that can be acquired by the publication of his sentiments. If the discussion of the navigation of the Mississipi *could* have remained as silent, & glided as gently down the Stream of time for a few years, as the waters do, that are contained within the banks of that River, it would, I confess, have comported more with my ideas of sound policy than any decision the case can obtain at this juncture. With sentiments the most Affecte. and friendly I am, Dear Sir Yr. Most Obedt Serv

RC (DLC); FC (DLC: Washington Papers). RC in Washington's hand, but not signed. Docketed by JM. FC in a clerk's hand. Minor variations between the RC and the FC have not been noted.

[1]In 1939, John C. Fitzpatrick erroneously stated that this letter was from Benjamin Harrison and that it was in the Washington Papers (DLC) (*Writings of Washington*, XXIX, 292 n. 33). No such letter has been found, and other circumstances point to David Stuart as Washington's correspondent. Stuart's letter of 16 Oct. to Washington, acknowledged by Washington on 5 Nov., has also not been found (ibid., XXIX, 302). In a conversation with Daniel Carroll, however, Washington discussed the contents of his letter from Stuart, and Carroll passed on the information to JM in his letter of 28 Oct.

[2]Washington should have written "14th."

To Thomas Jefferson

EDITORIAL NOTE

Shortly before the Philadelphia convention adjourned, JM confided to Jefferson his opinion that the proposed Constitution would "neither effectually answer its national object nor prevent the local mischiefs which every where excite disgusts agst the state governments" (6 Sept. 1787 [partly in code]). The letter printed below, running to seventeen manuscript pages, contains JM's detailed explanation of that opinion and reveals that the man who later became an indefatigable publicist in support of the new Constitution was in fact profoundly disappointed with the results of the convention. JM doubted the workability of the plan agreed upon at Philadelphia because it lacked the one ingredient that in his view was essential for establishing the supremacy of the central government and for protecting the private rights of individuals: a power vested in the national legislature to negative, or veto, state laws.

Unable to convince his colleagues at Philadelphia of the necessity of this veto power, JM knew that Jefferson was likewise not favorably disposed to lodge such a power in the hands of the central government. "Primâ facie I do not like it," Jefferson had remarked of the negative in his letter to JM of 20 June 1787. "It fails in an essential character, that the hole & the patch should be commensurate. But this proposes to mend a small hole by covering the whole garment." Because of the central importance of this prerogative in his scheme for a well-ordered confederacy, JM must have read these harsh comments with some displeasure. His response to Jefferson's criticism was a carefully reasoned defense of the negative, in effect a separate essay (an "immoderate digression," JM called it) within the letter, that drew upon his research into the history of confederations and restated his theory of the extended federal republic. This theory JM later embodied in *The Federalist*, Nos. 10 and 51, but "Publius," not being required to defend a general veto power over state legislation, did not refer to the negative.

Indeed, because "Publius" did not need to discuss the negative, JM's essays in *The Federalist* are an incomplete statement of his political thought. One must turn to this letter to Jefferson to observe the full scope of his ideas. Here for the first time he made clear the complementary role of the negative in his republican theory. JM had introduced the idea of a negative power in letters to Jefferson, Randolph, and Washington before the Federal Convention met, but he did not at that time explain why the central government, armed with this veto power over state laws, would act as a "disinterested & dispassionate umpire in disputes between different passions & interests in the State" without becoming an engine of tyranny (*PJM*, IX, 384). He provided that explanation in this letter to Jefferson, in which he undertook to prove that "private rights will be more secure under the Guardianship of the General Government than under the State Governments." JM developed this argument by means of a full exposition of his theory of the extended republic. A government of extended jurisdiction, composed of representatives of a multitude of diverse interests that would constantly check each other, would not likely fall into the hands of a majority "united by a common interest or passion." It followed that such a government, immune from the virus of tyranny by the majority, could safely be entrusted with the negative and thereby control that virus at the state level where it was most rampant.

To JM the Constitution, without the negative, was only a partial reform and thus probably doomed to failure. It was only a slight improvement over the Articles of Confederation—"a feudal system of republics" rather than "a Confederacy of independent States." It was not enough that the Constitution embodied his theory of the extended republic, which could only help to prevent injustice at the federal level. The real source of injustice, as JM repeatedly emphasized, was to be found at the state level, and the only effective barrier to the policies of oppressive majorities there was a federal veto on state laws. A constitution that did not vest the central government with this prerogative could not effectively provide justice, which JM believed to be the true end of republican government.

JM made his own copy of that part of the letter dealing with the negative, an indication that he considered it to be an important statement of his political thought. It is not known when JM made this extract, but the firm handwriting suggests that he might well have made the copy contemporaneously, perhaps during the week between the writing and sending of the letter. Although it is now among the Jefferson Papers (DLC), the recipient's copy of this letter, along with JM's other letters to Jefferson, was returned to JM after Jefferson's death. The letter was at Montpelier in the fall of 1834 when Nicholas P. Trist made a long extract from it, covering everything relating to the Constitution. Trist, whose wife was Jefferson's granddaughter, was at that time searching through Jefferson's papers "for materials to put the measures of '98–'99 in their true light, and thus to vindicate his memory & that of his co-laborers from the deep reproach of having given birth to the doctrine of Nullification as now understood." Trist requested and was given permission to consult JM's papers at Montpelier for the same purpose (Trist to JM, 20 and 29 Aug. 1834 [ViHi]; JM to Trist, 25 Aug. 1834, Madison, *Letters* [Cong. ed.], IV, 354).

NEW YORK Octr. 24. 1787.

DEAR SIR

My two last, though written for the two last Packets, have unluckily been delayed till this conveyance. The first of them was sent from Philada. to Commodore Jones in consequence of information that he was certainly to go by the Packet then about to sail. Being detained here by his business with Congress, and being unwilling to put the letter into the mail without my approbation which could not be obtained in time, he detained the letter also. The second was sent from Philada. to Col. Carrington, with a view that it might go by the last packet at all events in case Commodore Jones should meet with further detention here. By ill luck he was out of Town, and did not return till it was too late to make use of the opportunity. Neither of the letters were indeed of much consequence at the time, and are still less so now. I let them go forward nevertheless as they may mention some circumstances not at present in my recollection, and as they will prevent a chasm in my part of [*illegible*] correspondence which I have so many motives to cherish by an exact punctuality.

Your favor of June 20. has been already acknowledged. The last Packet

from France brought me that of August 2d. I have recd. also by the Mary
Capt. Howland the three Boxes for W.H. B.F. and myself.[1] The two first
have been duly forwarded. The contents of the last are a valuable addition
to former literary remittances and lay me under additional obligations,
which I shall always feel more strongly than I express. The articles included for Congress have been delivered & those for the two Universities
and for General Washington have been forwarded, as have been the various letters for your friends in Virginia and elsewhere. The parcel of rice
referred to in your letter to the Delegates of S. Carolina has met with some
accident. No account whatever can be gathered concerning it. It probably
was not shipped from France. Ubbo's book I find was not omitted as you
seem to have apprehended.[2] The charge for it however is, which I must
beg you to supply. The duplicate vol. of the Encyclopedie, I left in
Virginia, and it is uncertain when I shall have an opportunity of returning
it. Your Spanish duplicates will I fear be hardly vendible. I shall make a
trial wherever a chance presents itself. A few days ago I recd. your favor
of the 15 of Augst. via L'Orient & Boston. The letters inclosed along with
it were immediately sent on to Virga.

You will herewith receive the result of the Convention, which continued
its Session till the 17th. of September.[3] I take the liberty of making some
observations on the subject which will help to make up a letter, if they
should answer no other purpose.

It appeared to be the sincere and unanimous wish of the Convention to
cherish and preserve the Union of the States. No proposition was made,
no suggestion was thrown out, in favor of a partition of the Empire into
two or more Confederacies.

It was generally agreed that the objects of the Union could not be
secured by any system founded on the principle of a confederation of
sovereign States. A *voluntary*[4] observance of the federal law by all the
members, could never be hoped for. A *compulsive*[5] one could evidently
never be reduced to practice, and if it could, involved equal calamities to
the innocent & the guilty, the necessity of a military force both obnoxious
& dangerous, and in general, a scene resembling much more a civil war,
than the administration of a regular Government.

Hence was embraced the alternative of a Government which instead of
operating, on the States, should operate without their intervention on the
individuals composing them: and hence the change in the principle and
proportion of representation.

This ground-work being laid, the great objects which presented themselves were 1. to unite a proper energy in the Executive and a proper
stability in the Legislative departments, with the essential characters of

Republican Government. 2. to draw a line of demarkation which would give to the General Government every power requisite for general purposes, and leave to the States every power which might be most beneficially administered by them. 3. to provide for the different interests of different parts of the Union. 4. to adjust the clashing pretensions of the large and small States.[6] Each of these objects was pregnant with difficulties. The whole of them together formed a task more difficult than can be well concieved by those who were not concerned in the execution of it. Adding to these considerations the natural diversity of human opinions on all new and complicated subjects, it is impossible to consider the degree of concord which ultimately prevailed as less than a miracle.

The first of these objects as it respects the Executive, was peculiarly embarrassing. On the question whether it should consist of a single person, or a plurality of co-ordinate members, on the mode of appointment, on the duration in office, on the degree of power, on the re-eligibility, tedious and reiterated discussions took place. The plurality of co-ordinate members had finally but few advocates. Governour Randolph was at the head of them. The modes of appointment proposed were various, as by the people at large—by electors chosen by the people—by the Executives of the States—by the Congress, some preferring a joint ballot of the two Houses—some a separate concurrent ballot allowing to each a negative on the other house—some a nomination of several canditates [*sic*] by one House, out of whom a choice should be made by the other. Several other modifications were started. The expedient at length adopted seemed to give pretty general satisfaction to the members. As to the duration in office, a few would have preferred a tenure during good behaviour—a considerable number would have done so, in case an easy & effectual removal by impeachment could be settled. It was much agitated whether a long term, seven years for example, with a subsequent & perpetual ineligibility, or a short term with a capacity to be re-elected, should be fixed. In favor of the first opinion were urged the danger of a gradual degeneracy of re-elections from time to time, into first a life and then a heriditary tenure, and the favorable effect of an incapacity to be reappointed, on the independent exercise of the Executive authority. On the other side it was contended that the prospect of necessary degradation, would discourage the most dignified characters from aspiring to the office, would take away the principal motive to the faithful discharge of its duties—the hope of being rewarded with a reappointment, would stimulate ambition to violent efforts for holding over the constitutional term—and instead of producing an independent administration, and a firmer defence of the constitutional rights of the department, would render the officer more indifferent to the

from encroachments on each other. If the supremacy of the British Parliament is not necessary as has been contended, for the harmony of that Empire; it is evident I think that without the royal negative or some equivalent controul, the unity of the system would be destroyed. The want of some such provision seems to have been mortal to the antient Confederacies, and to be the disease of the modern. Of the Lycian Confederacy little is known. That of the Amphyctions is well known to have been rendered of little use whilst it lasted, and in the end to have been destroyed by the predominance of the local over the federal authority. The same observation may be made, on the authority of Polybius, with regard to the Achæan League. The Helvetic System scarcely amounts to a Confederacy, and is distinguished by too many peculiarities, to be a ground of comparison. The case of the United Netherlands is in point. The authority of a Statholder, the influence of a Standing army, the common interest in the conquered possessions, the pressure of surrounding danger, the guarantee of foreign powers, are not sufficient to secure the authority and interests of the generality, agst. the antifederal tendency of the provincial sovereignties. The German Empire is another example. A Hereditary chief with vast independent resources of wealth and power, a federal Diet, with ample parchment authority, a regular Judiciary establishment, the influence of the neighbourhood of great & formidable Nations, have been found unable either to maintain the subordination of the members, or to prevent their mutual contests & encroachments.[9] Still more to the purpose is our own experience both during the war and since the peace. Encroachments of the States on the general authority, sacrifices of national to local interests, interferences of the measures of different States, form a great part of the history of our political system.[10] It may be said that the new Constitution is founded on different principles, and will have a different operation. I admit the difference to be material. It presents the aspect rather of a feudal system of republics, if such a phrase may be used, than of a Confederacy of independent States. And what has been the progress and event of the feudal Constitutions? In all of them a continual struggle between the head and the inferior members, until a final victory has been gained in some instances by one, in others, by the other of them. In one respect indeed there is a remarkable variance between the two cases. In the feudal system the sovereign, though limited, was independent; and having no particular sympathy of interests with the great Barons, his ambition had as full play as theirs in the mutual projects of usurpation. In the American Constitution The general authority will be derived entirely from the subordinate authorities. The Senate will represent the States in their political capacity; the other House will represent the people of the States in their individual capac[it]y. The former will be accountable to their constituents at moderate, the latter at short periods. The President also derives his appointment from the States, and is periodically accountable to them. This dependence of the General, on the local authorities, seems effectually to guard the latter against any dangerous encroachments of the former: Whilst the latter, within their respective limits, will be continually sensible of the abridgment of their power, and be stimulated by ambition to resume the surrendered portion of it. We find the representatives of Counties and corporations in the Legislatures of the States, much more disposed to sacrifice the aggregate interest, and even authority, to the local views of their Constituents: than the latter to the former. I mean not by these remarks to insinuate that an esprit de corps will not exist in the national Government or that opportunities may not occur, of extending its jurisdiction in some points. I mean only that the danger of encroachments is much greater from the other side, and that the impossibility of dividing powers of legislation, in such a manner, as to be free from different constructions by different interests, or even from ambiguity in the judgment of the impartial, requires some such expedient as I contend for. Many illustrations might be given of this impossibility. How long has it taken to fix, and how imperfectly is yet fixed the legislative power of corporations, though that power is subordinate in the most compleat manner? The line of distinction between the power of regulating trade and that of drawing revenue from it, which was once considered as the barrier of our liberties, was found on fair discussion, to be absolutely undefinable. No distinction seems to be more obvious than that between spiritual and temporal matters. Yet wherever they have been made objects of Legislation, they have clashed and contended with each other, till one or the other has gained the supremacy. Even the boundaries between the Executive, Legislative & Judiciary powers, though in general so strongly marked in themselves, consist in many instances of mere shades of difference. It may be said that the Judicial authority under our new system will keep the States within their proper limits, and supply the place of a negative on their laws. The answer is, that it is more convenient to prevent the passage of a law, than to declare it void after it is passed; that this will be particularly the case, where the law aggrieves individuals, who may be unable to support an appeal agst. a State to the supreme Judiciary; that a State which would violate the Legislative rights of the Union, would not be very ready to obey a Judicial decree in support of them, and that a recurrence to force, which in the event of disobedience would be necessary, is an evil which the new Constitution meant to exclude as far as possible.

2. A constitutional negative on the laws of the States seems equally necessary to secure individuals agst. encroachments on their rights.[11] The mutability of the laws of the States is found to be a serious evil. The injustice of them has been so frequent and so flagrant as to alarm the most stedfast friends of Republicanism. I am persuaded I do not err in saying that the evils issuing from these sources contributed more to that uneasiness which produced the Convention, and prepared the public mind for a general reform, than those which accrued to our national character and interest from the inadequacy of the Confederation to its immediate objects. A reform therefore which does not make provision for private rights, must be materially defective. The restraints agst. paper emissions, and violations of contracts are not sufficient. Supposing them to be effectual as far as they go, they are short of the mark. Injustice may be effected by such an infinitude of legislative expedients, that where the disposition exists it can only be controuled by some provision which reaches all cases whatsoever. The partial provision made, supposes the disposition which will evade it. It may be asked how private rights will be more secure under the Guardianship of the General Government than under the State Governments, since they are both founded on the republican principle which refers the ultimate decision to the will of the majority, and are distinguished rather by the extent within which they will operate, than by any material difference in their structure. A full discussion of this question would, if I mistake not, unfold the true principles of Republican Government, and prove in contradiction to the concurrent opinions of theoretical writers, that this form of Goverment, in order to effect its purposes, must operate not within a small but an extensive sphere. I will state some of the ideas which have occurred to me on this subject. Those who contend for a simple Democracy, or a pure republic, actuated by the sense of the majority, and operating within narrow limits, assume or suppose a case which is altogether fictitious. They found their reasoning on the idea, that the people composing the Society, enjoy not only an equality of political rights; but that they have all precisely the same interests, and the same feelings in every respect. Were this in reality the case, their reasoning would be conclusive. The interest of the majority would be that of the minority also; the decisions could only turn on mere opinion concerning the good of the whole, of which the major voice would be the safest criterion; and within a small sphere, this voice could be most easily collected, and the public affairs most accurately managed. We know however that no Society ever did or can consist of so homogeneous a mass of Citizens. In the savage State indeed, an approach is made towards it; but in that State little or no Government is necessary. In all civilized Societies,

distinctions are various and unavoidable. A distinction of property results from that very protection which a free Government gives to unequal faculties of acquiring it. There will be rich and poor; creditors and debtors; a landed interest, a monied interest, a mercantile interest, a manufacturing interest. These classes may again be subdivided according to the different productions of different situations & soils, & according to different branches of commerce, and of manufactures. In addition to these natural distinctions, artificial ones will be founded, on accidental differences in political, religious or other opinions, or an attachment to the persons of leading individuals. However erroneous or ridiculous these grounds of dissention and faction, may appear to the enlightened Statesman, or the benevolent philosopher, the bulk of mankind who are neither Statesmen nor Philosophers, will continue to view them in a different light. It remains then to be enquired whether a majority having any common interest, or feeling any common passion, will find sufficient motives to restrain them from oppressing the minority. An individual is never allowed to be a judge or even a witness in his own cause. If two individuals are under the biass of interest or enmity agst. a third, the rights of the latter could never be safely referred to the majority of the three. Will two thousand individuals be less apt to oppress one thousand, or two hundred thousand, one hundred thousand? Three motives only can restrain in such cases. 1. a prudent regard to private or partial good, as essentially involved in the general and permanent good of the whole. This ought no doubt to be sufficient of itself. Experience however shews that it has little effect on individuals, and perhaps still less on a collection of individuals, and least of all on a majority with the public authority in their hands. If the former are ready to forget that honesty is the best policy; the last do more. They often proceed on the converse of the maxim: that whatever is politic is honest. 2. respect for character. This motive is not found sufficient to restrain individuals from injustice, and loses its efficacy in proportion to the number which is to divide the praise or the blame. Besides as it has reference to public opinion, which is that of the majority, the Standard is fixed by those whose conduct is to be measured by it. 3. Religion. The inefficacy of this restraint on individuals is well known. The conduct of every popular Assembly, acting on oath, the strongest of religious ties, shews that individuals join without remorse in acts agst. which their consciences would revolt, if proposed to them separately in their closets. When Indeed Religion is kindled into enthusiasm, its force like that of other passions is increased by the sympathy of a multitude. But enthusiasm is only a temporary state of Religion, and whilst it lasts will hardly be seen with pleasure at the helm. Even in its coolest state, it has been much oftener a motive to oppression than a restraint from it. If then there must be different interests and parties in Society; and a majority when united by a common interest or passion can not be restrained from oppressing the minority, what remedy can be found in a republican Government, where the majority must ultimately decide, but that of giving such an extent to its sphere, that no common interest or passion will be likely to unite a majority of the whole number in an unjust pursuit. In a large Society, the people are broken into so many interests and parties, that a common sentiment is less likely to be felt, and the requisite concert less likely to be formed, by a majority of the whole. The same security seems requisite for the civil as for the religious rights of individuals. If the same sect form a majority and have the power, other sects will be sure to be depressed. Divide et impera, the reprobated axiom of tyranny, is under certain qualifications, the only policy, by which a republic can be administered on just principles. It must be observed however that this doctrine can only hold within a sphere of a mean extent. As in too small a sphere oppressive combinations may be too easily formed agst. the weaker party; so in too extensive a one, a defensive concert may be rendered too difficult against the oppression of those entrusted with the administration. The great desideratum in Government is, so to modify the sovereignty as that it may be sufficiently neutral between different parts of the Society to controul one part from invading the rights of another, and at the same time sufficiently controuled itself, from setting up an interest adverse to that of the entire Society. In absolute monarchies, the Prince may be tolerably neutral towards different classes of his subjects, but may sacrifice the happiness of all to his personal ambition or avarice. In small republics, the sovereign will is controuled from such a sacrifice of the entire Society, but is not sufficiently neutral towards the parts composing it. In the extended Republic of the United States, The General Government would hold a pretty even balance between the parties of particular States, and be at the same time sufficiently restrained by its dependence on the community, from betraying its general interests.[12]

Begging pardon for this immoderate digression I return to the third object abovementioned, the adjustment of the different interests of different parts of the Continent. Some contended for an unlimited power over trade including exports as well as imports, and over slaves as well as other imports; some for such a power, provided the concurrence of two thirds of both House were required; Some for such a qualification of the power, with an exemption of exports and slaves, others for an exemption of exports only. The result is seen in the Constitution. S. Carolina & Georgia were inflexible on the point of the slaves.

The remaining object created more embarrassment, and a greater alarm for the issue of the Convention than all the rest put together. The little States insisted on retaining their equality in both branches, unless a compleat abolition of the State Governments should take place; and made an equality in the Senate a sine qua non. The large States on the other hand urged that as the new Government was to be drawn principally from the people immediately and was to operate directly on them, not on the States; and consequently as the States wd. lose that importance which is now proportioned to the importance of their voluntary compliances with the requisitions of Congress, it was necessary that the representation in both Houses should be in proportion to their size. It ended in the compromise which you will see, but very much to the dissatisfaction of several members from the large States.

It will not escape you that three names only from Virginia are subscribed to the Act. Mr. Wythe did not return after the death of his lady. Docr. MClurg left the Convention some time before the adjournment. The Governour and Col. Mason refused to be parties to it. Mr. Gerry was the only other member who refused. The objections of the Govr. turn principally on the latitude of the general powers, and on the connection established between the President and the Senate. He wished that the plan should be proposed to the States with liberty to them to suggest alterations which should all be referred to another general Convention, to be incorporated into the plan as far as might be judged expedient. He was not inveterate in his opposition, and grounded his refusal to subscribe pretty much on his unwillingness to commit himself, so as not to be at liberty to be governed by further lights on the subject. Col. Mason left Philada. in an exceeding ill humour indeed. A number of little circumstances arising in part from the impatience which prevailed towards the close of the business, conspired to whet his acrimony. He returned to Virginia with a fixed disposition to prevent the adoption of the plan if possible. He considers the want of a Bill of Rights as a fatal objection. His other objections are to the substitution of the Senate in place of an Executive Council & to the powers vested in that body—to the powers of the Judiciary—to the vice President being made President of the Senate—to the smallness of the number of Representatives—to the restriction on the States with regard to ex post facto laws—and most of all probably to the power of regulating trade, by a majority only of each House. He has some other lesser objections. Being now under the necessity of justifying his refusal to sign, he will of course muster every possible one. His conduct has given great umbrage to the County of Fairfax, and particularly to the Town of Alexandria. He is already instructed to promote in the Assembly the calling a Convention, and will probably be either not deputed to the Convention, or be tied up by express instructions. He did not object in general to the powers vested in the National Government, so much as to the modification. In some respects he admitted that some further powers would have improved the system. He acknowledged in particular that a negative on the State laws, and the appointment of the State Executives ought to be ingredients; but supposed that the public mind would not now bear them, and that experience would hereafter produce these amendments.

The final reception which will be given by the people at large to the proposed System can not yet be decided. The Legislature of N. Hampshire was sitting when it reached that State and was well pleased with it. As far as the sense of the people there has been expressed, it is equally favorable. Boston is warm and almost unanimous in embracing it. The impression on the Country is not yet known. No symptoms of disapprobation have appeared. The Legislature of that State is now sitting, through which the sense of the people at large will soon be promulged with tolerable certainty. The paper money faction in Rh. Island is hostile. The other party zealously attached to it. Its passage through Connecticut is likely to be very smooth and easy. There seems to be less agitation in this[13] State than any where. The discussion of the subject seems confined to the newspapers. The principal characters are known to be friendly. The Governour's party which has hitherto been the popular & most numerous one, is supposed to be on the opposite side; but considerable reserve is practised, of which he sets the example. N. Jersey takes the affirmative side of course. Meetings of the people are declaring their approbation, and instructing their representatives. Penna. will be divided. The City of Philada., the Republican party, the Quakers, and most of the Germans espouse the Constitution. Some of the Constitutional leaders, backed by the western Country will oppose. An unlucky ferment on the subject in their Assembly just before its late adjournment has irritated both sides, particularly the opposition, and by redoubling the exertions of that party may render the event doubtful. The voice of Maryland I understand from pretty good authority, is, as far as it has been declared, strongly in favor of the Constitution. Mr. Chase is an enemy, but the Town of Baltimore which he now represents, is warmly attached to it, and will shackle him as far as they can. Mr. Paca will probably be, as usual, in the politics of Chase. My information from Virginia is as yet extremely imperfect. I have a letter from Genl. Washington which speaks favorably of the impression within a circle of some extent; and another from Chancellor Pendleton which expresses his full acceptance of the plan, and the popularity of it in his district. I am told also that Innis and Marshall are patrons of it. In the opposite scale are Mr. James Mercer, Mr. R. H. Lee, Docr. Lee and their connections of course, Mr. M. Page according to Report, and most of the Judges & Bar of the general Court. The part which Mr. Henry will take is unknown here. Much will depend on it. I had taken it for granted from a variety of circumstances that he wd. be in the opposition, and still think that will be the case. There are reports however which favor a contrary supposition. From the States South of Virginia nothing has been heard. As the deputation from S. Carolina consisted of some of its weightiest characters, who have returned unanimously zealous in favor of the Constitution, it is probable that State will readily embrace it. It is not less probable, that N. Carolina will follow the example unless that of Virginia should counterbalance it. Upon the whole, although, the public mind will not be fully known, nor finally settled for a considerable time, appearances at present augur a more prompt, and general adoption of the Plan than could have been well expected.[14]

When the plan came before Congs. for their sanction, a very serious effort was made by R. H. Lee & Mr. Dane from Masts. to embarrass it. It was first contended that Congress could not properly give any positive countenance to a measure which had for its object the subversion of the Constitution under which they acted. This ground of attack failing, the former gentleman urged the expediency of sending out the plan with amendments, & proposed a number of them corresponding with the objections of Col. Mason. This experiment had still less effect. In order however to obtain unanimity it was necessary to couch the resolution in very moderate terms.

Mr. Adams has recd. permission to return, with thanks for his Services. No provision is made for supplying his place, or keeping up any represention there. Your reappointment for three years will be notified from the Office of F. Affrs.[15] It was *made without a negative eight states* being *present. Connecticut however*[16] *put in a blank ticket* the *sense of* that *state having been declared against embassies. Massachusets betrayed some scruple* on *like ground.* Every *personal consideration* was *avowed* & *I beleive with sincerity* to have *militated against these scruples.* It seems to be understood that letters to & from the foreign Ministers of the U.S. are not free of Postage: but that the charge is to be allowed in their accounts.

The exchange of our French for Dutch Creditors has not been countenanced either by Congress or the Treasury Board. The paragraph in your last letter to Mr. Jay, on the subject of applying a loan in Holland to the discharge of the pay due to the foreign Officers has been referred to the Board since my arrival here. No report has yet been made. But I have little idea that the proposition will be adopted. Such is the state & prospect of our fiscal department that any new loan however small, that should now be made, would probably subject us to the reproach of premeditated deception. The balance of Mr. Adams' last loan will be wanted for the interest due in Holland, and with all the income here, will, it is feared, not save our credit in Europe from further wounds. It may well be doubted whether the present Govt. can be kept alive thro' the ensuing year, or untill the new one may take its place.

Upwards of 100,000 Acres of the surveyed lands of the U.S. have been disposed of in open market. Five million of unsurveyed have been sold by private contract to a N. England Company, at ⅔ of a dollar per acre, payment to be made in the principal of the public securities. A negociation is nearly closed with a N. Jersey Company for two million more on like terms, and another commenced with a Company of this City for four million. Col. Carrington writes more fully on this subject.[17]

You will receive herewith the desired information from Alderman Broome in the case of Mr. Burke. Also the Virga. Bill on crimes & punishments. Sundry alterations having been made in conformity to the sense of the House in its latter stages, it is less accurate & methodical than it ought to have been.[18] To these papers I add a Speech of Mr. C. P. on the Missippi. business. It is printed under precautions of secrecy, but surely could not have been properly exposed to so much risk of publication. You will find also among the Pamplets & papers I send by Commodore Jones, another printed speech of the same Gentleman.[19] The Musæum, Magazine,[20] & Philada. Gazettes, will give you a tolerable idea of the objects of present attention.

The summer crops in the Eastern & Middle States have been extremely plentiful. Southward of Virga. They differ in different places. On the whole I do not know that they are bad in that region. In Virginia the drought has been unprecedented, particularly between the falls of the Rivers & the Mountains. The Crops of Corn are in general alarmingly short. In Orange I find there will be scarcely subsistence for the inhabitants. I have not heard from Albemarle. The crops of Tobo. are every where said to be pretty good in point of quantity; & the quality unusually fine. The crops of wheat were also in general excellent in quality & tolerable in quantity.

Novr. 1. Commodore[21] Jones having preferred another vessel to the packet, has remained here till this time. The interval has produced little necessary to be added to the above. The Legislature of Massts. has it seems taken up the Act of the Convention, and have appointed or probably will appoint an early day for its State Convention. There are letters also from Georgia which denote a favorable disposition. I am informed from Richmond that the New Election-law from the Revised Code produced a pretty full House of Delegates, as well as a Senate, on the first day. It had previously had equal effect in producing full meetings of the freeholders for the County elections. A very decided majority of the Assembly is said to be zealous in favor of the New Constitution. The same is said of the Country at large. It appears however that individuals of great weight both within & without the Legislature are opposed to it. A letter I just have from Mr. A. Stuart, names Mr. Henry, Genl. Nelson, W. Nelson, the family of Cabels, St. George Tucker, John Taylor and the Judges of the Genl. Court except P. Carrington. The other opponents he describes as of too little note to be mentioned, which gives a negative information of the Characters on the other side. All are agreed that the plan must be submitted to a Convention.

We hear from Georgia that that State is threatened with a dangerous war with the Creek Indians. The alarm is of so serious a nature, that law-martial has been proclaimed, and they are proceeding to fortify even the Town of Savannah. The idea there, is that the Indians derive their motives as well as their means from their Spanish neighbours. Individuals complain also that their fugitive slaves are encouraged by East Florida. The policy of this is explained by supposing that it is considered as a discouragement to the Georgians to form settlements near the Spanish boundaries.

There are but few States on the spot here which will survive the expiration of the federal year; and it is extremely uncertain when a Congress will again be formed. We have not yet heard who are to be in the appointment of Virginia for the next year. With the most affectionate attachment I remain Dear Sr. Your Obed friend & servant

Js. Madison Jr.

RC (DLC: Jefferson Papers); partial FC (DLC); partial Tr (ViU). There are numerous corrections and deletions on the seventeen-page RC, most of which appear to have been made contemporaneously, except for two clearly added later (see nn. 13 and 21, below). The RC was docketed by Jefferson. Some forty alterations on the RC, which are mainly stylistic, have been noted in Boyd, *Papers of Jefferson*, XII, 284–86. The FC, in JM's hand, is an abbreviated portion of the letter headed "Extract of a letter to Mr. J——son—dated Ocr 24. 1787." The Tr is endorsed by Nicholas P. Trist: "(This Extract comprises the whole of what relates to the Constitution.)." Trist also explained: "Copied from the original at Montpellier, (V[ir-ginia] J[efferson] T[rist] & C[ornelia] J[efferson] R[andolph] & M[artha] J[efferson] R[an-dolph] assisting) by N. P. T. Oct. 1. '34." Italicized words, unless otherwise noted, are those encoded by JM using the code Jefferson sent him on 11 May 1785. RC decoded interlinearly by Jefferson. Enclosures not found.

[1] "W.H." was William Hay; "B.F." was Benjamin Franklin.
[2] Ubbo Emmius, *Græcorum Respublicæ*. See *PJM*, IX, 23 n. 4.

[3]The final report of the Federal Convention. No copy known definitely to have belonged to Jefferson has been found (Boyd, *Papers of Jefferson*, XII, 149–50 n.).

[4]Underlined by JM.

[5]Underlined by JM.

[6]As "Publius," JM would also discuss these four "great objects" of the convention (*The Federalist* No. 37).

[7]Underlined by JM.

[8]JM began his extract with a slight rewording of the preceding sentence: "A negative in the Genl. Govt. on laws of States necessary 1. to prevent encroachts. on Genl. Govt. 2. instability & injustice in State legislation." See JM to Jefferson, 19 Mar. 1787 (*PJM*, IX, 318), for JM's earlier "opinion in favor of this ingredient."

[9]JM's discussion of ancient and modern confederacies in his speech of 19 June 1787 at the Philadelphia convention went largely unreported. JM presented a full treatment of this subject, based on his Notes on Ancient and Modern Confederacies (*PJM*, IX, 4–22), in *The Federalist*, Nos. 18, 19, and 20.

[10]JM incorporated the following observations on the greater danger of encroachments by the states on the general government into *The Federalist*, Nos. 45 and 46. See also JM's first speech of 21 June 1787.

[11]JM took the following observations on the necessity of a negative on state laws from the concluding section of his memorandum, Vices of the Political System (*PJM*, IX, 354–57). The same source also supplied much of the text for JM's first speech of 6 June 1787. After being removed from the context of defending the power to negative state laws, these observations were recast and incorporated into *The Federalist*, Nos. 10 and 51.

[12]JM's extract ends here.

[13]At a later time JM placed an asterisk here and wrote "*N. York" at the bottom of the page.

[14]The Trist extract, which begins with the third paragraph of the letter, ends here.

[15]Jefferson had been reappointed minister to France on 12 Oct. (*JCC*, XXXIII, 665).

[16]JM wrote "74," the code for "however," but Jefferson decoded it as "73"—"notw[i]thst[an]d[in]g."

[17]See Edward Carrington to Jefferson, 23 Oct. 1787, Boyd, *Papers of Jefferson*, XII, 256–57.

[18]See Boyd, *Papers of Jefferson*, II, 492–504, 505–6 n.; XII, 284 n.

[19]For Charles Pinckney's publications, see JM to Washington, 14 Oct. 1787 and nn. 1, 2.

[20]The *American Museum* and the *Columbian Magazine*, both of Philadelphia.

[21]At a later time JM placed an asterisk here and wrote "*Paul" in the margin.

To William Short

NEW YORK Octr. 24. 1787.

DEAR SIR

I offer you my sincere acknowledgments for your two favors of May 7th. and Augst: 1. The latter has been rendered particularly valuable by the acquaintance it has afforded me with Monsr. Crevecoeur who has already verified the character under which you present him.[1]

The paper which I inclose for Mr. Jefferson will shew you the result of the Convention.[2] The nature of the subject, the diversity of human opinion, and the collision of local interests, and of the pretensions of the large & small States, will not only account for the length of time consumed in the work, but for the irregularities which may be discovered in its structure and form. I shall learn with much solicitude the comments of the philosophical Statesmen of Europe, on this new fabric of American policy. Unless however their future criticisms should evince a more thorough knowledge of our situation as well as of the true genius of Republican Government, than many of their past, my curiosity will not be rewarded with much instruction.

The Constitution has not been yet long enough before the public here to warrant any decided opinion concerning its fate. The general impression seems to be favorable as far as it is known. The presumptive evidence of it is pretty strong with regard to the New-England States; Rho. Island excepted whose folly and fraud have not yet finished their career. Even there however a considerable party embrace the act of the Convention. It is difficult to say what is the prevailing sentiment in this State. The newspapers abound with anonimous publications on both sides, but there is a reserve in the general conversation which is scar[c]ely seen elsewhere. The men of abilities are generally on the side of the Constitution. The Governour whose party is at least a very strong one is considered notwithstanding his reserve to be a decided adversary to it. N. Jersey will pretty certainly accede. Pena. is divided. The advocates of the Constitution at present are certainly the more numerous party. Delaware will fall in of Course. Maryland gives evidence of being well disposed. Mr. Chase & Mr. Paca will as far as they may be at liberty, disappoint those who best know them, if they do not make opposition. Virga. I fear will be divided and extremely agitated. The Govr. & Col. Mason refused to subscribe the instrument. Their influence alone would produce difficulty. The Govr. was temperate in his opposition and may perhaps be neutral. Col. Mason will exert his influence as far as he can. His County is agst. him, and have given peremptory instructions on the subject. On the same side are known to be the Lees, and supposed to be Mr. Henry, Mr. Harrison, and Genl. Nelson. On the other will be the weight of Genl. Washingtons name, and some exertion of his influence, the Chancellor [Mr. Pendleton],[3] probably Mr. Wythe, Innis, Marshal & Monroe. I am not informed of other leading characters. The general impression as far as it has come to my knowledge, is rather on the favorable side. We know nothing of the States South of Virginia. The conjectures run on the same side.

Commodore Jones who was to have sailed in this packet having changed his plan, I make use of another hand for the conveyance of this which would otherwise have been committed to him. The apprehension of a war which might expose him & his papers in the French packet to inconveniences, has led him to prefer another Vessel. He proposes to sail in a few days, and to make the best of his way to Paris. My letter to Mr. Jefferson being very full and (having been prepared for a conveyance perfectly safe) not in cypher I have determined to submit to a short delay for the sake of the caution pursued by the Commodore, & to let him still be the bearer of it. Had I known the change in the Commodore's plan a little sooner I would have written to Mr. Jefferson by this conveyance also. But it is now impossible. I shall send him nevertheless a number of printed papers. You will be kind enough to communicate these circumstances to him, with my most affecte. respects, and be assured at the same time of the sincerity with which I am Dr. Sir your friend & servt.

Js. Madison Jr

RC (DLC: William Short Papers). Docketed by Short, "Madison Dec. 13." The date evidently refers to the day Short received the letter.

[1] Short introduced Crèvecoeur in his letter of 7 May 1787 (*PJM*, IX, 411–12). Thus JM should have written "former" instead of "latter."

[2] See JM to Jefferson, 24 Oct. 1787 and n. 3.

[3] JM's brackets.

From Ambrose Madison

Letter not found.

ca. 25 October 1787. Acknowledged in JM to Ambrose Madison, 8 Nov. 1787. Requests information concerning Mr. House's rule for calculating the weight of tobacco. Asks JM if he will be a candidate for the Orange County delegation to the state ratifying convention.

To Tench Coxe

New York Octr. 26. 1787.

Dear Sir

I have recd. your favor of the 21st. instant, and have disposed of the papers under the same cover according to direction. Col. Hamilton had returned to the City which gave me the opportunity of immediately putting into his hands such of them as were destined for him. I have no doubt that he will make the best use of them. I have recd. no answer yet from my correspondent[1] to whom I forwarded the three first numbers of the American Citizen. The 4th. is a valuable continuation, and I shall be equally desirous of seeing it in the Virginia Gazettes; and indeed in those of every State.

I have not yet recd. any certain information of the reception given in

Virginia to the Act of the Convention. I know only that within certain districts, and by respectable individuals, it is well relished, and that by some other individuals of influence it is likely to be opposed. The Legislature being now assembled, a few days will probably enable me to form a tolerable estimate of opinions there. With great respect & regard I remain Dr. Sir, Your Obedient & very respectful servt

Js. Madison Jr

RC (PHi). Addressed by JM.

[1] Joseph Jones, who replied on 29 Oct.

To Joseph Jones

Letter not found.

26 October 1787. Acknowledged in Jones to JM, 22 Nov. 1787. Requests copy of the survey of the upper James River. Wishes to know where he can obtain some wild crab trees.

To Edmund Pendleton

New York Octr. 28. 1787.

Dear Sir

I have recd. and acknowledge with great pleasure your favor of the 8th. instt. The remarks which you make on the Act of the Convention appear to me to be in general extremely well founded. Your criticism on the clause exempting vessels bound to or from a State from being obliged to enter &c in another is particularly so. This provision was dictated by the jealousy of some particular States, and was inserted pretty late in the Session.[1] The object of it was what you conjecture. The expression is certainly not accurate. Is not a religious test as far as it is necessary, or would operate, involved in the oath itself? If the person swearing believes in the supreme Being who is invoked, and in the penal consequences of offending him, either in this or a future world or both, he will be under the same restraint from perjury as if he had previously subscribed a test requiring this belief. If the person in question be an unbeliever in these points and would notwithstanding take the oath, a previous test could have no effect. He would subscribe it as he would take the oath, without any principle that could be affected by either.

I find by a letter from Mr. Dawson that the proposed Constitution is

223

receivd by the Assembly with a more prompt & general approbation than could well have been expected. The example of Virginia will have great weight, and the more so, as the disagreement of the deputation, will give it more the appearance of being the unbi[a]ssed expression of the Public mind. It would be truly mortifying if any thing should occur to prevent or retard the concurrence of a State which has generally taken the lead on great occasions. And it would be the more so in this case as it is generally believed that nine of the States at least will embrace the plan, and consequently that the tardy remainder must be reduced to the dilemma of either shifting for themselves, or coming in without any credit for it. There is great reason to believe that the Eastern States, R. Island excepted, will be among the foremost in adopting the system. No particular information is yet received from N. Hampshire. The presumptive evidence of its good disposition however is satisfactory. The Legislature of Massts. is now sitting, and letters from good authority, say that every thing goes well. Connecticut has unanimously called a Convention, and left no room to doubt her favorable disposition. This State has long had the character of being antifederal. Whether she will purge herself of it on this occasion, or not, is yet to be ascertained. Most of the respectable characters are zealous on the right side. The party in power is suspected on good grounds to be on the wrong one. N. Jersey adopts eagerly the Constitution. Penna. is considerably divided; but the majority are as yet clearly with the Convention. I have no very late information from Maryland. The reports are that the opposition will make no great figure. Not a word has been heard from the States South of Virginia, except from the lower parts of N. Carola. where the Constitution was well received. There can be little doubt I think that the three Southern States will go right unless the conduct of Virginia were to mislead them.

I inclose two of the last Newspapers of this place, to which I add one of Philadelphia, containing the report of a late important decision of the supreme Court there. If the report be faithful, I suspect it will not give you a high idea of the Chancery knowledge of the Cheif Justice.[2] I am Dear Sir with sincere affection Yr. Obedt. friend & servt.

Js. MADISON JR.

RC (DLC). Addressed by JM. Docketed by Pendleton, "Answd. Jan. 29—88." Enclosures not found.

[1] The reference is to Art. I, Sec. 9, clause 6. It originated in a motion submitted by Daniel Carroll and Luther Martin on 25 Aug. See William M. Meigs, *The Growth of the Constitution in the Federal Convention of 1787* (Philadelphia, 1900), pp. 173–75, and Farrand, *Records*, II, 417–18, 437, 480–81, 618.

[2] JM was perhaps referring to the case of *Pollard* v. *Shaffer*, decided at the September 1787

term of the Pennsylvania Supreme Court (A. J. Dallas, *Reports of Cases Ruled and Adjudged in the Courts of the United States, and of Pennsylvania* [4 vols.; Philadelphia, 1830–35], I, 230–35). The case concerned a suit over the rent and repair of property damaged by British troops during the war. The chief justice was Thomas McKean.

To George Washington

NEW YORK Octr. 28. 1787.

DEAR SIR

The mail of yesterday brought me your favor of the 22d. instant. The communications from Richmond give me as much pleasure, as they exceed my expectations. As I find by a letter from a Member of the Assembly,[1] however, that Col. Mason had not got down, and it appears that Mr. Henry is not at bottom a friend, I am not without fears that their combined influence and management may yet create difficulties. There is one consideration which I think ought to have some weight in the case over and above the intrinsic inducements to embrace the Constitution, and which I have suggested to some of my correspondents. There is at present a very strong probability that nine States at least will pretty speedily concur in establishing it. What will become of the tardy remainder? They must be either left as outcasts from the Society to shift for themselves, or be compelled to come in, or must come in of themselves when they will be allowed no credit for it. Can either of these situations be as eligible as a prompt and manly determination to support the Union, and share its common fortunes?

My last stated pretty fully the information which had arrived here from different quarters, concerning the proposed Constitution. I recollect nothing that is now to be added farther than that the Assembly of Massachussetts now sitting certainly gives it a friendly reception. I inclose a Boston paper by which it appears that Governour Hancock has ushered it to them in as propitious a manner as could have been required.[2]

Mr. P.   's character is as you observe well marked by the publications which I inclosed.[3] His printing the secret paper at this time could have no motive but the appetite for expected praise: for the subject to which it relates has been dormant a considerable time, and seems likely to remain so.

A foreign gentleman of merit, and who besides this general title, brings me a letter which gives him a particular claim, to my civilities, is very anxious to obtain a sketch of the Potowmac and the route from the highest navigable part of it, to the western waters which are to be connected with the potowmac by the portage; together with a sketch of the works which are going on, and a memorandum of the progress made in them. Knowing of no other channel through which I could enable myself to gratify this gentleman, I am seduced into the liberty of resorting to your kindness; and of requesting that if you have such a draught by you, your amanuensis may be permitted to take a *very rough copy* of it for me. In making this request I beseech you Sir to understand that I do it with not more confidence in your goodness than with the sincerest desire that it may be disregarded if it cannot be fulfilled with the most perfect conveniency. With sentiments of the most perfect esteem & the most Affecte. regard I remain Dear Sir, Your Obedt. friend & hble servt.

Js. Madison Jr.

The British Packet has arrived but I do not learn that any news comes by her. Her passage has been a tedious one.

RC (DLC: Washington Papers). Docketed by Washington. Enclosure not found.

[1]John Dawson to JM, 19 Oct. 1787.

[2]Governor Hancock's speech to the General Court, dated 17 Oct. 1787, was printed in the *Boston Gazette* of 22 Oct. 1787 and in the Boston *Independent Chronicle* of 25 Oct. 1787.

[3]See JM to Washington, 14 Oct. 1787 and nn. 1, 2.

From Daniel Carroll

Near Geo:Town Oct 28th. 1787

Dear sr.,

Yr. favor of the 17th Instant came to hand Yesterday.[1] Since my return I have been so engag'd, particularly by attending on an aged sick parent, that I have not been in the way of obtaining any intelligence to be depended on, untill last monday when I saw General Washington at a meeting of the Potomack Compy. The information from him was pleasing; Docr. Stuart, Representative for Fairfax, writes to him from Richmond, that their was a full House the 1st day; & that he did not find a Member, but what appeard to be in favor of the New Govt., except Patrick Henry, who was reserv'd, but express'd sentiments in favor of recommending a Convention. I shall not add on this subject, as you will certainly have information directly from that quarter.

If the information I have receivd relating to this State can be depended on, every thing I hope will be right. Mr Carroll who waited for me, soon after saw Mr. Johnson, & sends me word that he is a warm friend. That Gentleman Mess Lee & Potts were chosen the following week representatives with a view principally of preventing Mischief and forwarding this great object. Mr Chace has I hear publishd a pr. under the Signature of *Caution* which indicates an adverse disposn.[2] He has bound himself to propose a Convention; & if chosen of that Body will be bound to ratifye the proposed fœderal Govert; the impression in Baltimore being strong & general in favor of it.

The General informd me that Mr. Houston had call'd on him in his way to Georgia, & told him that Mr Yates (of the Co[n]vention) had declar'd himself a warm friend. Is this so?

Col. Mason had not sett off for the Assembly when I heard last: I overtook him & the Majr. on the road: By the time they had reachd within 9 Miles of Baltimore, they had exhausted all the stories of their youth &ca. and had enterd into a discusn. of the rights to the Western World. You know they are champions on opposite sides of this question. The Majr. having pushd the Col. hard on the Charters of Virginia the latter had just wax'd warm, when his Char[i]oteer put an end to the dispute, by jumbling their Honors together by an oversett. I came up soon after. They were both hurt—the Col. most so—he lost blood at Baltimore, & is well.[3] Present my Comps. to Col. Hamilton & his Lady. I am, My dear Sir, with great esteem Yr. very Affte hble Servt.

Danl. Carroll

RC (DLC). Addressed by Carroll. Docketed by JM.

[1] Letter not found.

[2] The letter signed "Caution," attributed to Samuel Chase, appeared in the *Md. Journal* of 12 Oct. 1787. It is reprinted in P. L. Ford, *Essays on the Constitution*, pp. 325–28.

[3] Mason's accident occurred on his homeward journey from the Philadelphia convention. "The Majr." was James McHenry. On 7 Oct. Mason wrote to Washington: "I got very much hurt in my Neck & Head, by the unlucky Accident on the road; it is now wearing off; tho' at times still uneasy to me" (Rutland, *Papers of George Mason*, III, 1001, 1002 n.).

From Joseph Jones

Richmond 29th. Octr. 1787.

Dr. Sr.

On my arrival in Richmond the other day I found your favor of the 7th. from New york with some news papers inclosed. Mr. Thomas Pleasants who called on me the next day inquired whether I had lately heard from you which being acknowledged brot. forward a conversation on the new constitution and finding him a strenuous advocate for it, I asked if he had seen or read some peices in favor of it under the signature of an American Citizen, he said he had not. I then informed him I had received some papers from you, which contained three numbers on the subject and did not doubt he wod. be pleased with the perusal of them; whereupon he signified his desire to possess them. When I delivered them to him I told him it wod. not I thought be amiss they were put into the Printers hands, that he might, if he thought proper, print them in the News paper here. He said he wod. think of it, and I have not seen him since. I shall speak to him again on the subject so soon as I meet with him but have no doubt he will endeavour to have them printed.[1]

I must confess I see many objections to the Constitution submitted to the Conventions of the States. That which has the greatest weight with me lies agt. the constitution of the Senate, which being both legislative and Executive and in some respects judiciary is I think radically bad. The President and the Senate too may in some instances legislate for the Union, withot. the concurrence of the popular branch as they may make treaties and alliances which when made are to be paramount the law of the land. The State Spirit will also be preserved in the Senate as they are to have equal numbers and equal votes. It is to be feared this Body united with the President as on most occasions it is to be presumed they will act in concert will be an overmatch for the popular branch. Had the Senate been merely legislative even proportioned as they are to the States, it wod. have been less exceptionable; and the President with a member from each State as a privy Council to have composed the Executive. There is also a strong objection agt. the appelate jurisdiction over law and fact, independent of a variety of other objections which are and may be raised agt. the Judiciary arrangement and the undefined powers of that department. I own I should have been pleased to see a declaration of rights accompany this constitution as there is so much in the execution of the Government to be provided for by the legislature and that Body possessing too great a portion of Aristocracy. The legislature may and will probably make proper and wise regulations in the Judiciary as in the execution of that branch of power the Citizens of all the States will generally be equally affected. But the reflection that there exists in the constitution a power that may oppress makes the mind uneasy and that oppression may and will result from the appelate power of unsetling facts does to me appear beyond a doubt. To rehearse the Doubts and difficulties that arise in my mind when I reflect on this part of the Judiciary power wod. I am sure to you be unnecessary. It wod. be more troublesome than usefull to recite the variety of objections that some raise some of them of more others of inconsiderable weight. Could I see a change in the Constitution of the Senate and the right of unsetling facts removed from the Court of Appeals I could with much less reluctance yeild my assent to the System. I could wish I own to see some other alterations take place but for the accomplishment of them, I wod. trust to time, and the wisdom and moderation of the legislature rather than impede the puting the new plan in motion, was it in my power, because I well know our desperate situation under the present form of Government. It is at this time very difficult to inform you what is the prevalent opinion among the people. If we are to judge of them at large from their representatives here they must be very much divided and I think the advocates for the new plan rather diminish than increase in number. You will have from the Executive an accot. of the proceedings of the Houses on the report of the Convention. I think they have taken a wise course in delivering it over to the People withot. conveying sentiments of approbation or Disapprobation. As yet nothing of consequence excepting the referring to the People the new Constitution, has been done in the assembly. Tomorow they are to discuss the recommendation of Congress respecting British debts. I think there will be a majority in the Delegates for the repeal of the laws.[2] How it will go down in the Senate I am unable to calculate. You shall be occasionally informed how we go on. With real affection and esteem, I am, Yr. friend & Servt

                                                                    JOS: JONES.

RC (DLC). Docketed by JM.

[1]See Coxe to JM, 27 Sept. 1787 and n. 1.

[2]See Hening, *Statutes*, XI, 75–76, 136–38, 176–80, 349, for examples of laws considered to be in violation of the fourth article of the 1783 peace treaty. See also Harrell, *Loyalism in Virginia*, pp. 123–52.

From Edmund Randolph

RICHMOND Oct: 23 [ca. 29]. 1787.

MY DEAR FRIEND

I have omitted to write to you since my return home, from an inability to obtain so accurate a grasp of the Opinions prevailing here, as to justify me in communicating the politics of our legislature.

The first raptures in favor of the constitution were excessive. Every town resounded with applause. The conjectures of my reasons for refusing to sign were extraordinary, and so far malicious, as to suppose, that I was chagrined at not carrying every point in my own way, or that I sought for popularity. These were the effluviæ until the assembly met.

A diversity of opinion appeared immediately on the convening of that body; which gave an evidence of the good fruit from one of the revised laws, by being punctual to the day. Among the heroes of opposition were

Mr. Henry, Mr. Wm. Cabell Colo. Bland and Mr. French Strother. A great ferment was kept up, until thursday last, when, contrary to my expectations the debate for calling the convention was conducted with temper, and a vote passed Unanimously for that purpose, *freely to discuss and deliberate on the constitution.* [1] This is a happy and politick resolution; for I am thoroughly persuaded, that if it had been propounded by the legislature to the people, as *we* propounded it, the constitution would have been rejected and the spirit of union extinguished.

At present the final event seems uncertain. There are many warm friends for taking the constitution altogether without the alteration of a letter; among these are Colo. Nicholas and Mr. F. Corbin. But I suspect, that the tide is turning. New objections are daily started, and the opinions of Mr. H——y gain ground. He and I have had several animated discourses; but he recedes so far from me, that we must diverge after a progress of half a degree further. An incidental question is allotted for tomorrow; by which it will be known, how the party *positively* against the constitution stand as to number. A motion was postponed until that day, for repealing the laws against the recovery of *british debts.* [2] Much of the repugnance to this motion will be founded on the danger of every defendant being hurried sooner or later to the seat of the fœderal government. This is the most vulnerable and odious part of the constitution. I shall therefore conclude, if the acts be repealed, that the majority of the legislature may be said to have overcome the most exceptionable points.

As to the *recusants*, we have been spoken of illiberally at least. Mr. Mason has declared in assembly that altho' he is for amendments, he will not quit the union, even if they should not be made. I have thought proper to postpone any explanation of myself, except in private, until Every thing is determined, which may relate to the constitution. I have prepared a letter, and shall send you a copy in a few days. [3] I see the Penna. papers abounding with eulogiums on some, and execrations on others, whose opinions they know not substantially.

Mr. Pendleton, who is here, has expressed himself to this effect: that the constitution is very full of radical faults, & that he would adopt it with a protest as to its imperfections, in order that they may be corrected at a future day.

The bar are generally against it. So are the judges of the general court. So is Wiley Jones of North Carolina.

In short I am persuaded, that there must be strong exertions made to carry it through, and my letter will not be the least conducive among the other supports to its adoption in the end.

Why would you not give me your opinion as to the scheme I proposed in my letter from the Bowling Green.[4] I am now convinced of the impropriety of the Idea, but I wish to open to you without reserve the innermost thoughts of my soul, and was desirous of hearing something from you on this head.

Colo. Mason has said nothing quoad te and you may rest yourself in safety in my hands: for I will certainly repel the smallest insinuation. You were elected by 126 out of 140. & for the second year by 137 out of 140. So that you see, circumsicision and uncircumcision avail nothing.[5] I sent your appointments on the other day.[6]

The people of this town are still in rage for the constitution and Harvie among the most strenuous. I have inquired about the reports concerning myself, and if popularity had been my object, as some supposed, I should have overshot my mark. Pardon this medley, written in a croud, and be assured of my most affectionate friendship—

E. R.

RC (DLC). Evidently misdated by Randolph, as explained below (nn. 1, 2, and 6).

[1] This vote took place Thursday, 25 Oct.; hence Randolph must have written this letter at least two days after that date. At the opening of the debate Francis Corbin moved that a convention be called according to the recommendation of the Philadelphia convention, that is, for the purpose of giving its assent and ratification to the Constitution. Henry objected to this motion on the grounds that it did not leave open the possibility of proposing amendments. At length John Marshall came up with a formula giving the convention "full latitude in their deliberations" without leaving the impression that the House disapproved of the Constitution. See the summary of the debate in the *Pa. Packet* of 10 Nov. 1787 and the N.Y. *Daily Advertiser* of 17 Nov. 1787. As passed by the House on 25 Oct. and agreed to by the Senate on 31 Oct., the resolutions called for submitting the Constitution "to a Convention of the people for their full and free investigation, discussion, and decision." The convention was to meet at Richmond the first Monday in June (*JHDV*, Oct. 1787, pp. 15, 25). The resolutions are printed in *Documentary History of the Constitution*, IV, 366–68.

[2] Joseph Jones wrote to JM on 29 Oct. that the House would discuss the British debt question the next day. Thus Randolph most likely wrote this letter on 29 Oct.

[3] This was Randolph's letter to the Speaker of the House of Delegates, dated 10 Oct. 1787. Randolph delayed submitting the letter for publication until December, when it appeared as a pamphlet (*A Letter of His Excellency Edmund Randolph, Esquire, on the Federal Constitution, Richmond, October 10, 1787* [Richmond, 1787; Evans 20669]). The letter was also widely circulated in the newspapers. A reprint in P. L. Ford, *Pamphlets on the Constitution*, pp. 259–76, omits the important concluding paragraph.

[4] Randolph to JM, 30 Sept. 1787.

[5] "For in Christ Jesus neither circumcision availeth any thing, nor uncircumcision, but a new creature" (Gal. 6:15).

[6] JM was elected to another term as a delegate to Congress on 23 Oct. 1787 (Dawson to JM, 19 Oct. 1787, n. 6). Randolph sent JM's credentials on 25 Oct. 1787 (PCC); he therefore could not have written this letter on 23 Oct.

To Archibald Stuart

DEAR SIR

I have been this day favored with yours of the 21st. instant & beg you to accept my acknowledgments for it. I am truly sorry to find so many respectable names on your list of adversaries to the federal Constitution. The diversity of opinions on so interesting a subject, among men of equal integrity & discernment, is at once a melancholy proof of the fallibility of the human judgment, and of the imperfect progress yet made in the science of Government. Nothing is more common here, and I presume the case must be the same with you, than to see companies of intelligent people equally divided, and equally earnest, in maintaining on one side that the General Government will overwhelm the State Governments, and on the other that it will be a prey to their encroachments; on the one side that the structure of the Government is too firm and too strong, and on the other that it partakes too much of the weakness & instability of the Governments of the particular States. What is the proper conclusion from all this? That unanimity is not to be expected in any great political question: that the danger is probably exaggerated on each side, when an opposite danger is conceived on the opposite side—that if any Constitution is to be established by deliberation & choice, it must be examined with many allowances, and must be compared not with the theory, which each individual may frame in his own mind, but with the system which it is meant to take the place of, and with any other which there might be a probability of obtaining.

I cannot judge so well as yourself of the propriety of mixing with the adoption of the federal Constitution a Revision of that of the State. If the latter point could be effected without risk or inconveniency to the former, it is no doubt desireable. The practicability of this will depend on the degree of unanimity with which it could be undertaken. I should doubt extremely whether the experiment could safely be made. Might not the blending those two things together unite those who are unfriendly to either, and thus strengthen the opposition you have to contend with? In case the Genl. Government should be established it will perhaps be easy to follow it with an amendment of our own Constitution. The example will have some influence by proving the practicability & safety of such experiments. And if the Convention think fit, they may lay a proper train of themselves for bringing the matter about.

The public mind in this quarter seems not finally settled as yet with regard to the proposed Constitution. The first impression has been every where favorable except in Rh. Island. Nor is there any reason to suspect that the generality of States will not embrace the measure. The character of this State has long been antifederal, & is known that a very powerful party continue so. Penna. is also divided into parties, but it is supposed that a majority will pretty certainly on the right side. With great respect & regard I am Dr Sir Yr. Obdt. & hble. servt.

Js. Madison Jr

RC (ViHi). Addressed and franked by JM.

From James McClurg

Richmond Octr. 31. 87.

Dear Sir,

I am to thank you for the favor you did me in inclosing a copy of the new constitution; which has ever since been the principal topic of political conversation in every company. It was at first reciev'd with a prepossession in it's favor almost enthusiastic, in our towns especially. The circumstances, however, which in this state partic[ularl]y tended to excite Suspicion & jealousy, have caus'd this disposition to subside sooner than it might otherwise have done; & every man's mind is turn'd to a subtle investigation of the plan. Various indeed are the objections made to it; but those which strike only the most moderate, & most federal, are confin'd chiefly to the Senate. Nor do they object to the equal representation of the States in the Senate, so much as to the additional weight thrown into that branch of the Legislature, by combining it with the Presidt. in the high executive offices of Government. It is supposed that the obligation of a common Interest may connect them in a dangerous Junto; & on this account, they imagine the Senate to be the worst court that could have been contriv'd for the Impeachment of the President. They concieve too that the Senators, in their executive business, may become liable to Impeachment, tho' they cannot see by what court they can be tried.

I see, in a pamphlet publish'd at Philada. in defence of the Constitution, a serious Objection made to the clause which empowers Congress to regulate the manner, time, & place, of chusing the representatives of the people in the several States.[1] This has been reecchoed here; & it has not been easy to find a sufficient reason for it's Insertion. Some have objected also to the Influence of the Presidt. in the house of representatives as capable of producing his reelection, even when the majority of the constitutional electors are against him.

233

These are Objections made by Men heartily dispos'd towards an energetic federal government, & concieving that defects in its frame must be equally obnoxious to the people of all the States, they hope to see them amended. For my part, I am so fearful of it's Loss, that I should be willing to trust the remedy of it's defects to the reason moderation & experience of the future Congress. By the by, what is to become of the State debts, when all the Sources of revenue in the states are seiz'd by Congress?[2] I am with the most sincere regard, Dear Sir, Your friend & Servt.

JAS. MCCLURG

RC (DLC). Docketed by JM.

[1] The reference is to Noah Webster's *An Examination into the leading principles of the Federal Constitution proposed by the late Convention held at Philadelphia . . .* (Philadelphia, 1787), reprinted in P. L. Ford, *Pamphlets on the Constitution*, pp. 25–65; see especially p. 61.

[2] The Constitution contained no provision for the federal assumption of state debts, though the subject was considered briefly at the convention. McClurg was evidently present when Rufus King first suggested such a proposal on 14 July, but he had long since returned to Virginia when the next discussion of the matter took place on 18 Aug. On that day the convention agreed to John Rutledge's motion that a grand committee "consider the necessity and expediency of the U- States assuming all the State debts." The committee reported an assumption provision on 21 Aug., but it was silently dropped the next day (Farrand, *Records*, II, 6, 327–28, 355–56, 377).

To the Reverend James Madison

Letter not found.

November–December 1787? Acknowledged in the Reverend James Madison to JM, 9 Feb. 1788. Replies to objections to the Constitution made by the Reverend James Madison in his letter to JM of ca. 1 Oct. 1787.

From Archibald Stuart

RICHMOND Novr 2d. 1787

DR SIR

Inclosed are the Resolutions of Virginia on the subject of the fœderal Government. It is generally considered necessary that you should be of the convention, not only that the Constitution may be adopted but with as much unanimity as possible.

For gods sake do not disappoint the Anxious expectations of yr friends & let me add of yr Country. The Govr. on his return here was coolly received, upon which it is said he discovd much anxiety, since the Opposition to the Constitution has been heard of from Difft parts of the State he speaks with more confidence against what he calls the Objectionable parts. He is a candidate for the Convention, Wilkinson & Southall having cleared the Coast for him the former of Whom is inimical to the Govt. propos'd (tutis auribus Deposui).[1]

The house went into committee yesterday on a petition to repeal the port Bill when Mason began to thunder, to the Great terror of all its friends & during the space of fiften Minutes I conceived its destruction inevitable. Henry however with the Aid of Ronald, Monroe, & al: who steped forth after the first pannick was removed Gave him a total over-throw. The Numbers were as 4 to 1. The Majority were fully convinced that an additional land tax would necessarily result from the Destruction of the port Bill.[2]

Masons Arguments in the Reply were vague & inconclusive in short altho he is sometimes much admired for great strength of Mind Original-ity of Expression & for the Comprehensive view which he takes of his subjects yet upon that Occasion he fell far short of the general Expecta-tion, & I fear the Effects of Age have sometimes been discoverable in him.

Some of Our young Countrymen have done themselves much credit On Dift subjects. We have hitherto dealt so much in Genl Conversations as they are called on the Business of the Session & have made so few Deci-sions that I cannot give you Any satisfactory Account of What Will be done. From yr most obt Servt

ARCHD STUART

RC (DLC). Addressed by Stuart and franked. Docketed by JM. Enclosure not found.

[1] Nathaniel Wilkinson represented Henrico County in the House of Delegates and Turner Southall represented the Henrico district in the Senate. Presumably Stuart meant that these two gentlemen "cleared the Coast" for Randolph by agreeing not to become candidates for the convention themselves. Randolph and John Marshall, Wilkinson's colleague in the House, were eventually elected to represent the county at the Richmond convention (Swem and Williams, *Register*, pp. 26, 27, 244).

A free translation of the Latin phrase is "confided to a trusted ear." This is from Horace's *Odes*, bk. I, ode XVII, lines 17–18: "quicquid habes, age, depone tutis auribus"—"Whatever 'tis, come, confide it to my trusty ear!" (*Horace: The Odes and Epodes*, Loeb Classical Library [Cambridge, Mass., 1914], pp. 74–75).

[2] Debate on the petition of freeholders of Spotsylvania County for the repeal of the act "to restrict foreign vessels to certain ports within this Commonwealth" took place in the Com-mittee of the Whole on 1 and 2 Nov. (*JHDV*, Oct. 1787, pp. 17, 26, 27). JM was the author of this act, which had passed at the May 1784 session of the General Assembly (*PJM*, VIII, 64–66). The original act restricted the entering, clearing, loading, and unloading of "foreign" (non-Virginian) vessels to five ports. An amending act of 1786 added to the number of ports permitted to receive foreign commerce and distinguished between ports of entry and ports of delivery. This act also permitted vessels made in the U.S. and owned by U.S. citizens to land at any port to pick up articles for exportation (Hening, *Statutes*, XI, 402–3; XII, 320–23). George Mason was the leading spokesman for repeal of the port act and as a private citizen had published a protest against it in 1786 (Rutland, *Papers of George Mason*, II, 859–64).

Although rejecting outright repeal, the legislature further amended the act in 1787 by adding more ports of delivery for foreign vessels and by creating separate ports of delivery for U.S. vessels (Alexander Donald to Jefferson, 12 Nov. 1787, Boyd, *Papers of Jefferson*, XII, 346; Dawson to JM, ca. 10 Nov. 1787; Stuart to JM, 14 Jan. 1788; Hening, *Statutes*, XII, 434–38). The result was that nearly every river town claiming "port" status received a measure of satisfaction.

Virginia Delegates to Edmund Randolph

NEW YORK November 3d. 1787

SIR,

The Requisition for the present year has already been transmitted to the States by the Secretary of Congress; we, however, now do ourselves the honor to inclose it to your Excellency, together with a Report of the Treasury Board, and a Return of payments by the Several States to the 30th of June, all which we beg the favor of you to lay before the General Assembly, for their more full information upon the Federal Resources.[1]

The report of the Treasury Board was proposed for the adoption of Congress as a Requisition, and the Statements contained in it, form the foundation of the Act which has been agreed to; but it was thought best to reverse the appropriations Suggested by the Board, and by that means call for the amount required upon the new Requisition, in facilities instead of Specie, conceiving that the ability of the States to comply with the demand, would be encreased by the extension of the Latitude of Accommodation. Upon the same Consideration the restrictions which were imposed upon the issues and payment of Indents, in the former Requisitions, are, by a Clause in this, Repealed. The way is now open for evidences of Interest to be issued up to the end of 1786, and it is left to the States to obtain, and pay the balances now due upon their Respective quota's in such ways as to them Shall seem expedient.

Virginia is greatly in arrear in the Indents which have been called for upon the Several Requisitions from September 1782 inclusive. For discharging these balances we beg leave to submit to the consideration of the Legislature, a mode different from that which has hitherto been pursued. Any observations upon the impolocy of the Systems by which Indents have been made Receiveable upon an equal footing with Specie, in Taxes, we conceive to be Unnecessary, as they must be evident to every one who has in any manner been connected with their Operation; they procure little or no Satisfaction to the public Creditor, while they enormously oppress the Laborious Taxpayer, and are productive of undue emolument to intermediate hands, who are not the objects of public provision, and who would be employed in more useful Occupations did not the public create this Scene of Speculation for them. This being the case, a change of System is necessarily called for, and it only remains to be decided what that change shall be. The first object that presents itself in considering this Subject is, justice to the public Creditors, who have a right to expect their interest in full Specie Value; and could Taxes be collected in specie, commensurate to this demand, it would in our Opinions, be the duty of the Public to collect the money and pay it to the Claimants; this measure is however impracticable, nor is it Material to a decision what other to adopt, to determine whether this impractibility arises from the poverty of the people, the situation of our Commerce, or any other Cause. It is reduced to a Certainty, that in any Operation the Creditor must find the public provision inadequate to his demand, and he must be satisfied to Negotiate his claim at a considerable Loss, or let it lay useless by him—it then behoves the public to make the best provision which the circumstances of the people will admit, and to open the best possible ground of Negotiation, which may be embraced or Neglected by the Creditor at his own option, but should he determine to Negotiate at a loss, it is highly proper that the loss he sustains, should rather be turned to the common relief, than the emolument of the Collectors and a few other Individuals. Upon these Considerations we beg leave to submit to the wisdom of the General Assembly, whether it would not be best to discard the mode of Collecting Indents in Taxes as has hitherto been done, and to lay as great a Tax as the people can reasonably pay in Specie, to be applied in the purchase of the Indents—upon the ground of Such a Tax the great Speculators would be ready to enter into Contracts for Supplying them at Certain prices. In addition to the prospect of Success in this Measure, which must now be evident, we have to observe that the Repeal of the restrictions upon the Issues of Indents will soon throw into the Market great sums of them, and as it is to be presumed that most of the States will Neglect to make proper provision for their Redemption, there must be a considerable fall in their Value.[2]

You will observe Sir, that for discharging our foreign demands, as well as the domestic expences of the Current year, Congress Rely upon a Surplusage in the former Requisitions, Occasioned by many of the Objects for which these Requisitions were made, being turned into the liquidated debt, and other Circumstances which appear in the Report of the Treasury Board; but as this surplusage exists altogether in the balances now remaining due from the States, and the purposes for which it is appropriated are indispensible, it becomes absolutely Necessary that these balances be fully paid. Our last payments in Europe have been effected by a New Loan of one Million of Guilders Negotiated by Mr Adams in Holland, but Congress from motives of Honor and Justice which must present themselves without further explanation have ordered that no farther Loans be Negotiated.[3] It remains therefore with the States to determine whether the Credit and administration of the Union, are to be Supported for another year, or abandoned. The 109,391 64/90ths Dollars appropriated in the hands of the Commissioners of Loans in Holland, is the balance now remaining of the late Negotiation, but it amounts to but a Triffling part of the sum Necessary for foreign purposes.

We also have the Honor to enclose to your Excellency the Ordinance for establishing a Temporary Government in the Western Territory, and providing for its passage into State Governments.[4] A part of this plan depends upon the Accession of Virginia, to which we beg leave to call the attention of the Legislature. The proposed arrangement of the Territory into three States we conceive to be much better than that which was formerly made in Conformity to the Act of Cession. A Division of the Country into many Small States would effectually disappoint the design of Virginia, that the inhabitants be admitted into the Federal Government, upon their becoming so numerous as to have reasonable pretentions to such admission, because it might, upon the whole, be very populous, and yet in no one of the described States, contain as many inhabitants as the smallest of the Original States; in this Situation it could not be expected, they would remain long contented, and the federal Government would be under the Necessity of suffering them to enter into other Alliances, or departing from the Stipulated terms of Admission. The proposed arrangement of the Territory into three States will avoid these difficulties, without any eventual inconvenience, from the Reduction of the Number—indeed, if it is thought Material to the interest of the Southern States, that their Scale be Strengthened by an Accession in this quarter, that object will be better secured by the New, than the old plan, because upon the former there may be an early admission of a State, but upon the latter such an event must be long, or perhaps forever, postponed.[5]

We are happy in being able to present to the View of your Excellency and the Legislature a prospect of an early and considerable reduction of the domestic debt by Sales of Western Territory. Seven Ranges of Townships have been surveyed agreeably to the Ordinance of the 20th of May 1785, containing upwards of one Million of Acres, about one hundred and Twenty thousand Whereof have been sold for some what more than the Average price of one dollar Pr. Acre in public securities. These Ranges extend west from the place of beginning directed in the

Ordinance nearly down to Muskingum. But a mode of Sale has lately presented itself which promises a more Rapid progress, while it will exempt the United States from the greatest part of the expence that would attend a strict pursuance of the Ordinance, without Materially departing from it. Companies of Adventurers have come forward with propositions for large Tracts, and a Contract is actually made with Messrs. Sargent and Cutler, in behalf of a considerable Company from the Eastern States, for all the Country between the Seventh Range of Townships, and Sciota, from the Ohio North, as far as a due West line to be extended from the Northern boundary of the Tenth Township—the whole of this tract is supposed to contain about five Millions of Acres. The terms are, that the United States, shall at the public expence, Survey & mark the external boundaries, and ascertain the Contents of the Tract—the Company to lay it out, at their own expence, into Townships and Sections, agreeably to the Ordinance, subject to the reserves therein described, except that one of the Sections for future Sale shall be granted forever for the purposes of Religion, and that two Complete Townships shall be granted for ever for the purposes of an University. All other Lands within the Tract, to be paid for, without any abatement whatever for bad Land, at the price of two thirds of a dollar per Acre in public Securities, excluding interest— half a million of dollars to be paid upon closing the Contract, and possession taken so far as that payment will cover; and afterwards payment and Occupancy to go on, pari passu, at certain periods, under Certain Stipulations of reciprocal assureance. Army Rights for Military bounties are made Receivable in payment of the purchase money, in the proportion of one Seventh part, but as Lands are Set apart and to be Surveyed, for Satisfying these Bounties, more to the advantage of the Claimants, it is not likely that many of these Rights will be rendered in discharge of this debt.

Another offer is made by Judge Symmes and his Associates from New-Jersey, for about two and an half Millions between the little and great Miami's, upon the same term[s]. Congress have Authorised the Treasury Board to close with this proposition, but it is not yet compleated; upon these two Contracts being carried into full effect they will take up, as may be seen by the Statement inclosed, upwards of three Millions and an half of dollars, even upon a supposition that the full proportion receiveable in Bounty Rights, be actually rendered.[6] Two other propositions have been made, whereupon Congress have given the Treasury Board a general Authority to sell by Contract; provided that no tract so disposed of shall contain less than one Million of Acres, making the Terms of Sargent and Cutlers purchase the ground, with deviations as to the grants for Religion, and an University, unless the Contract be for an equal quantity. This

would doubtless be disposed to sell; we, however have no principles on which to hazard an Opinion upon the demands that would be made, by the holders, for it.[11]

In pursuance of the enclosed Resolution of the 21st. of April last a Contract has been made for a Coinage of Copper, from which some aid will result to the resources of the United States—and we beg leave to call the attention of the Legislature to the Necessity of passing Laws for prevention of Counterfeits.[12] We have the honor to be, with the greatest re[gard?] for your Excellency & the Legislature Your Excellencies Most Obt. Ser[vts.]

> WILLM. GRAYSON
> JS. MADISON JUNR.
> ED. CARRINGTON
> HENRY LEE

RC and enclosures (Vi). In a clerk's hand, except for the signatures, with corrections and interlineations in several hands, and the address and complimentary close in Carrington's hand. For enclosures, see nn. 1, 4, 6, 10, and 12. Brackets enclose letters missing from the right margin of the Ms.

[1] On the requisition of 11 Oct. 1787 and report of the Board of Treasury of 28 Sept. 1787, see JM to Randolph, 7 Oct. 1787 and n. 5. The third enclosure in this group was a "Schedule of Requisitions on the several States by the United States in Congress assembled," dated 25 Sept. 1787 and signed by Joseph Nourse, register of the treasury. It listed the requisitions on each state from 10 Sept. 1782 through 2 Aug. 1786, the amount paid by each state on these requisitions, and the balances due.

[2] See JM to Ambrose Madison, 11 Oct. 1787. The assembly followed this advice in its revenue act of 1787, appropriating money to "be applied by the executive to procure indents for discharging the... requisition" (Hening, *Statutes*, XII, 426).

[3] See *JCC*, XXXIII, 649; Rufus King to John Adams, 27 Oct. 1787, Burnett, *Letters*, VIII, 688 and n. 3.

[4] The Northwest Ordinance of 13 July 1787, printed in *JCC*, XXXII, 334–43.

[5] The Virginia act ceding the Northwest Territory had stipulated that the territory should be formed into states of "not less than one hundred, nor more than one hundred and fifty miles square" (Hening, *Statutes*, XI, 327, 572). The ordinance of 23 Apr. 1784 provided for boundaries of two degrees latitude and meridians of longitude passing through the falls of the Ohio and the mouth of the Great Kanawha (Boyd, *Papers of Jefferson*, VI, 613). In July 1786 Congress recommended that Virginia alter its act of cession so as to empower Congress to divide the territory into "not more than five nor less than three" states, but the legislature had not acted on the recommendation by the time the new ordinance was enacted a year later (*JCC*, XXX, 390–91). The General Assembly finally ratified the Northwest Ordinance, repealing the contrary conditions of its act of cession, in December 1788 (Hening, *Statutes*, XII, 780–81). For a discussion of the political benefits the South expected from this ordinance, see Staughton Lynd, "The Compromise of 1787," *Political Science Quarterly*, LXXXI (1966), 225–50.

[6] The statement of the financial benefits expected from the two contracts, in Carrington's hand, is printed in Burnett, *Letters*, VIII, 674 n. 7.

[7] See *JCC*, XXXIII, 466–67, 467–74, 475–77.

[8] See *JCC*, XXXIII, 692–93; Secretary of Congress to Governors of North Carolina and Georgia, 25 Oct. 1787, Burnett, *Letters*, VIII, 664–65.

[9]William Grayson had offered a motion favoring such a confederacy on 27 July, which was referred to the secretary for foreign affairs. Citing the inadequacy of the public revenue, Secretary Jay in his report of 2 Aug. observed that the motion was "rendered unseasonable by the present State of our Affairs" (*JCC*, XXXIII, 420–21, 451–52).

[10]Printed in *JCC*, XXXII, 262–66.

[11]By an act of 5 Jan. 1788 the Virginia legislature repealed earlier laws permitting the payment of a part of the land tax in paper money funded according to the resolutions of Congress of 18 Mar. 1780. The new act required the treasurer to place one-tenth of the specie arising from the land tax under the direction of the General Assembly "in such manner as will conduce most to the public interest, and a compliance with the public engagements for the redemption of the said money" (Hening, *Statutes*, XII, 569).

[12]The resolution is printed in *JCC*, XXXII, 225. See *PJM*, IX, 396 and n. 4.

From George Washington

MOUNT VERNON Novr. 5th: 1787.

MY DEAR SIR,

Your favor of the 18th. Ulto. came duly to hand. As no subject is more interesting, and seems so much to engross the attention of every one as the proposed Constitution, I shall, (tho' it is probable your communications from Richmond are regular and full with respect to this, and other matters, which employ the consideration of the Assembly) give you the extract of a letter from Doctr Stuart, which follows—

"Yesterday (the 26th. of Octr.) according to appointment, the calling of a Convention of the people was discussed.[1] Though no one doubted a pretty general unanimity on this question ultimately, yet, it was feared from the avowed opposition of Mr. Henry and Mr. Harrison, that an attempt would be made, to do it in a manner that would convey to the people an unfavourable impression of the opinion of the House, with respect to the Constitution: And this was accordingly attempted. It was however soon baffled. The motion was to this effect; that a Convention should be called to adopt—reject—or amend—the proposed Constitution. As this conveyed an idea that the House conceived an amendment necessary, it was rejected as improper. It now stands recommended to them, on (I think) unexceptionable ground, for 'their full and free consideration.' My collegue[2] arrived here on the evening before this question was taken up: I am apt to think that the opponants to the Constitution were much disappointed in their expectations of support from him, as he not only declared himself in the fullest manner for a Convention, but also, that notwithstanding his objections, so federal was he, that he would adopt it, if nothing better could be obtained. The time at which the Convention is to meet, is fixed to the first of June next. The variety of sentiments on this subject was almost infinite; neither friends or foes agreeing in any one period. There is to be no exclusion of persons on acct. of their Offices.["]

Notwithstanding this decision the accounts of the prevailing sentiments without, especially on James River and Westwardly, are various; nothing decisive, I believe, can be drawn. As far as I can form an opinion however, from different persons, it should seem as if Men judged of others, by their own affection, or disaffection to the proposed government. In the Northern Neck the sentiment I believe, is very generally for it. I think it will be found such thro the State.

The Doctor further adds—"The subject of British debts was taken up the other day when Mr. Henry, reflected in a very warm declamatory manner, on the circular letter of Congress, on that subject. It is a great and important matter and I hope will be determined as it should be notwithstanding his opposition."

So far as the sentiments of Maryland, with respect to the proposed Constitution, have come to my knowledge, they are strongly in favor of it; but as this is the day on which the Assembly of that state *ought* to meet, I will say nothing in anticipation of the opinion of it. Mr. Carroll of Carrolton, and Mr. Thos. Johnson, are declared friends to it. With sincere regard and Affecte I am, My dear Sir Yr. sincere frd. & Obedt Ser

Go: WASHINGTON

RC (NN: Emmet Collection).

[1]Washington may have erroneously transcribed the date, for the action described in this paragraph took place on 25 Oct. David Stuart's letter to Washington, dated 26 Oct., has not been found, but Washington acknowledged its receipt in his reply to Stuart of 5 Nov. (Fitzpatrick, *Writings of Washington*, XXIX, 302).

[2]JM placed an asterisk here and at the bottom of the page wrote "*Col: Mason.*"

To Philip Mazzei

Letter not found.

5 November 1787. Acknowledged in Mazzei to JM, 21 Dec. 1787. Reports on the Dohrman affair and comments on Mazzei's book.

To Ambrose Madison

NEW YORK Novr. 8th. 1787.

DEAR BROTHER

Having mislaid your last favor, I can not acknowledge it by reference to its date. It contained two requests, the one relating to Mr. House's rule of calculating the weight of the Tobacco; the other to my being a candidate in Orange for the Convention. In answer to the first point I inclose the rule exemplified.[1] If this should not suffice, I will send you a calculation in detail for the whole account. In answer to the second point, I am to observe that it was not my wish to have followed the Act of the General Convention into the Convention of the State; supposing that it would be as well that the final decision thereon should proceed from men who had no hand in preparing and proposing it. As I find however that in all the States the members of the Genl. Convention are becoming members of the State Conventions, as I have been applied to on the subject by sundry very respectable friends, as I have reason to believe that many objections in Virginia proceed from a misconception of the plan, or of the causes which produced the objectionable parts of it; and as my attendance at Philadelphia, may enable me to contribute some explanations and informations which may be of use, I shall not decline the representation of the County if I should be honoured with its appointment. You may let this be known in such way as my father & yourself may judge best. I shall be glad to hear from [you] on the subject, and to know what competition there will probably be and by whom.

As far as present appearances denote, the N. England States R. Island excepted, will all adopt the new Constitution. N. Jersey certainly will. So will Penna. according to the best opinions, by a very decided majority. I have favorable information also from Maryland; though it is not improbable that the opposition likely to be made in Virginia will have some effect on that side, as well as on the side of N. Carolina, which in general has been said to be well disposed. Like information has been recd. from the two more Southern States; but it is too early to pronounce on their disposition. This State (N. York) is much divided. The party in power, are unwilling to surrender any portion of it. The other party is composed of the more respectable citizens, and is warmly attached to the proposed Constitution. Whatever may be the sense of the Majority the State will scarcely have a will of its own, if New England on one side and N. Jersey & Pena. on the other come heartily into the measure.

A French packet arrived a few days ago; but brings no decisive information concerning the Dutch. It continues to be uncertain what their fate is to be. A war between Russia & Turkey is said to have been declared by the latter. A great change has taken place in the French Ministry. The Parliament lately banished, has got back to Paris, and it is expected that the new taxes against which they remonstrated, will not be enforced. Provincial assemblies are at length established throughout the Kingdom. The Marquis de la Fayette is a leading member of one of them. The Count de Moustier is appointed Minister to the U. States in the place of the Chevalier de la Luzerne, and may soon be expected here.

I have now given you all the news foreign & domestic, and have only to add my dutiful regards to my father & Mother, and to request that I may be properly remembered to all others. Yrs. affectly.

Js. Madison Jr.

N.B. The Almanack & other papers herewith enclosed are for my father.

RC (NN). Addressed by JM. Enclosures not found.
[1] See *PJM*, IX, 296, 297 n. 2.

From Archibald Stuart

Richmond Novr. 9th. 1787

Dr Sir

Yrs of the 30th. Octr. came to hand yesterday & has afforded me infinite satisfaction to hear that the probability is that most of the Northern States will adopt the fœderal Govt. I have been for some time uncommonly Anxious on this subject lest the weakness & inefficacy of the State Governments should become so notorious & so disgusting to the people as to drive them into concessions of liberty much beyond that point which is actually necessary for Good Government. Should it however fail in the first instance I hope it will prove a Rock of Salvation on which we may rest in our career to that fatal extreme.

The Paper inclosed contained a piece signed *Publius* with which I am extremely pleased, from his introduction I have the highest expectations from him.[1] If it would not impose too great a task upon you I would request that his subsequent papers may be sent to me, the Nos. written by an American Citizen have had good effects & with some Other pieces of Merit have been printed in a small pamphlet for the information of the people.[2]

Inclosed are some Resolutions which were Occasioned by three or four petitions for paper money from the southern Counties, they were drawn by Mason & supported in a Masterly Manner, Upon many Other Occasions however Our friend is not what he has been.[3]

Yesterday the Doctrine of installments Came on were said to be the Child of Necessity & a price for a Speedy & uniform administration of Justice. Henry, Nichs. Ronald & Thruston *Pro* Mason, Corbin, Bushd: Washington Turberville & yr. H Sevt Con. Henry movd the Committee should rise as time did not allow him to reply & some other Gent. who he said would favor us with their sentiments. We accordingly adjourned the debate for two Days, what will be the Result, God knows.[4] Henry is loud on the distresses of the People & makes us tremble with the Apprehensions of a Rebellion if they are driven to dispair. He has also in a Decided tone opposed the payment of British Debts charged the Congress with neglecting the Interests of this State & Asserts that their Circular letter is sophistical & ought not to be regarded.[5] He sais if we do our best to comply we or some other State shall fail in some tittle & that will be a pretext for the british to continue their Open Violation of it that if we comply at all we must fulfill Lord Carmarthens requisitions on that subject, Stated in a conversation with Mr Adams.[6] He ask why we should go before the british in this Business, is it because they are more honest? or wear a Royal diadem &c.

Some of our young Country men who have come forward have done them selves & their country much honor. They speak & think for them selves but cannot give impulse to the Mass of our body.

On the subject of Installments I feel like a man Whose Character cannot be worsted, it will the sooner fill up the Measure of inequity & convince the people of the Necessity of a Change of Govt & Perhaps bring some good out of the Evil.

We have done nothing finally of any consequence, you shall hear of it when it happens. From yr Most Obt H Sevt

ARCHD STUART.

RC (DLC). Addressed by Stuart and franked. Postmarked, "Richmond Nov 12." Docketed by JM. Enclosure not found.

[1] The first number of *The Federalist* originally appeared in the N.Y. *Independent Journal*, 27 Oct. 1787.

[2] The first three numbers of "An American Citizen" (Tench Coxe) were printed in the *Va. Independent Chronicle* of 7 Nov. 1787. See Coxe to JM, 27 Sept. 1787 and n. 1. These pieces were included in *Various Extracts on the Fœderal Government, Proposed by the Convention Held at Philadelphia* (Richmond, 1787; Evans 20824). This pamphlet was apparently set as the various items included became available. The "small pamphlet" was probably an early issue of the first part of the whole, which was published in early December (Burnley to JM, 15 Dec. 1787 and n. 2).

[3] Petitions for an emission of paper money from the counties of Albemarle, Pittsylvania, and Washington were read before the House of Delegates on 3 Nov. The same day the House adopted Mason's resolutions condemning the use of paper money as "ruinous to Trade and Commerce" and "contrary to every Principle of sound Policy as well as Justice" (*JHDV*, Oct. 1787, pp. 28, 29–30; Rutland, *Papers of George Mason*, III, 1008–9, 1011).

[4] After more than a month of debate the installment plan for the payment of private debts was dropped in favor of a bill to amend the execution laws. Its passage was made dependent on the passage of the district court bill, "a kind of barter between the Creditor & Debtor" (Burnley to JM, 15 Dec. 1787 and n. 1). See also George Mason to Washington, 27 Nov. 1787, Rutland, *Papers of George Mason*, III, 1019–22.

⁵The circular letter of 13 Apr. 1787 urging the states to repeal all laws contrary to the peace treaty of 1783 (*JCC*, XXXII, 177–84).
⁶The reference is to Lord Carmarthen's letter of 28 Feb. 1786 to John Adams, enclosed in Adams to John Jay, 4 Mar. 1786 (*Diplomatic Correspondence of the U.S.*, II, 580–82). Copies of the letter were forwarded to the states in John Jay's circular letter of 6 July 1786 (Vi: Continental Congress Papers; Burnett, *Letters*, VIII, 402 n. 2). See also *PJM*, IX, 271, 273 n. 2.

From John Dawson

[ca. 10 November 1787]

Accept my thanks, my dear Sir, for your two favours of the 21st. and 28th. of the last month, which, with the enclosures, came to hand in due time.¹

On the receipt of a letter from you, some time since, I calld the attention of the Legislature to the Act of the last session, which is the subject of Mr. Vanburkels complaint.² That it is *a violation*, tho not an intended one, appears to be the general opinion. A committee was appointed, to prepare and bring in "a Bill to amend and reduce into one Act, the several Acts imposing duties on imported articles." Whether the indulgence will be extended to the Dutch, or withdrawn from the French is uncertain. I rather, however, apprehend that it will be extended.³ The committee have not yet reported the bill, but will in a day or two. The business of reducing all the acts into one was more difficult, and took up more time than was apprehended.

The subject of installments has been very warmly agitated—from what appeard in the house a day or two ago, when the business was brought forward, I am convinced that all internal debts will be install'd by three annual payments, provided the Circuit Courts can be establishd. To carry the latter many will agree to the former and vice versa. What will be the fate of British debts is very uncertain—if the assembly agree to pay them it will not be in less time than seven years, nor untill the posts to the West are evacuated.

On a petition from Frdksburg for the repeal of the Port-bill we went into a Committee of the whole—and after a full discussion on the subject, after Mr. Mason had supported the petition and reprobated the authors of this establishment, in his satiric turn; after Mr. Henry had opposd the petition, and in a very able manner supported the principles of the bill, the committee divided, when only about 15 appeard in favour of the petition.

A variety of petitions have been presended complaining of that impolitic and unjust Law "imposing new Taxes["]—whether it will be repeald or no is uncertain; if not repeald it will be amended.[4] Mr. Henry has introduced some resolutions, which have been agreed to in committee, to prohibit *entirely* the importation of rum, brandy, cordage, and many other articles.[5]

You have heard I presume that Colo Mathews and Mr. Selden were voted out of, and Colo Heth and Majr. Eggleston into the council.[6]

From the information we have receivd here, there is very little doubt, but the States South of this will adopt the new constitution. What will be done here is very uncertain. The opponents to it are many, able, and busy. Converts are daily made. Enclosd you will receive the resolutions of the assembly, and will, with me agree, I think, that they are exceedingly proper. By opening the door wide, it is probable all the eminent characters among us will be in convention. By fixing the meeting of the *convention* to so late a day we shall be able to act on the determinations of the other states, and to determine ourselves as circumstances may point out. Had the convention met at an early day, and the question have been, will you take this constitution, as offerd? I am persuaded a majority woud have said No. I also am of opinion there can be no time so unfavourable for this state to offer amendments as the present. The other states are adopting the Constitution with avidity, and woud pay little attention to any proposd amendment. But if the Goverment is a bad one it will press hard upon other states, and make them less ave[r]se to amend it. With much respect and esteem I am dear sir, Yr. Sin: Friend & hm: Sert

J DAWSON

RC (DLC). Enclosure not found. The approximate date of the letter has been determined from Dawson's reference to the installment plan debate of "a day or two ago." Archibald Stuart reported to JM on 9 Nov. that this debate had occurred "yesterday."

[1] Letters not found.

[2] Dawson evidently referred to one of JM's missing letters of 2 and 11 Oct. 1787, acknowledged by Dawson on 19 Oct. Dutch minister plenipotentiary Van Berckel had lodged a formal protest against "An act to impose certain duties," passed by the legislature the year before. He claimed that the act violated the Dutch treaty with the U.S. by discriminating against Dutch ships importing French brandy. See *PJM*, IX, 272–73, 273–74 nn. 5, 6, 333, 333–34 n. 2.

[3] By an amending act that passed 8 Jan. 1788 Dutch vessels were extended the same privilege enjoyed by French bottoms of importing French brandy duty-free (Hening, *Statutes*, XII, 514–15).

[4] The 1786 "act imposing new Taxes" included an additional tax on carriages and taxes on clerks of courts, attorneys, physicians, and retail merchants (ibid., XII, 283–87). Petitions for repeal of the act were presented in late October and early November. On 10 Dec. the Committee of the Whole agreed to amend the act, but an amending bill presented by Dawson was rejected on 28 Dec. (*JHDV*, Oct. 1787, pp. 17, 20–21, 29, 90, 113, 117, 120, 121, 122).

[5] These resolutions were presented on 5 Nov. and agreed to the next day (ibid., pp. 31, 32). Bills "prohibiting the importation of foreign distilled spirits" and for "imposing duties on sundry articles of importation" were debated at some length before being dropped from

further consideration on 27 Dec. (ibid., p. 120; Monroe to JM, 6 Dec. 1787; Randolph to JM, 27 Dec. 1787).

[6]The assembly voted to remove Sampson Mathews and Miles Selden from the Council of State on 31 Oct. William Heth and Joseph Eggleston were elected to replace them on 7 Nov. (*JHDV*, Oct. 1787, pp. 24, 35). Eggleston, a delegate to the General Assembly from Amelia County since 1785, resigned before taking his seat on the council (Swem and Williams, *Register*, p. 371; *JHDV*, Oct. 1787, p. 150).

From Caleb Wallace

FAYETTE COUNTY, Novemr. 12. 1787.

DEAR SIR,

For want of a safe conveyance, I omitted acknowledging your favour of the 5th. of January last[1] until the Delegates from this Country should go to Richmond; but when the time came a bilious complaint prevented my improving the opportunity. Hearing you are expected home this Fall, I shall now employ a leisure hour in preparing an answer to forward by the first trusty hand I can meet with.

I expect you have been informed that Committees of correspondence have been elected by all the considerable settlements on the Western Waters to counteract by petitions, remonstran[ces, &c] the occlusion of the Mississipi that was lately in contemplation.[2] I [hav]e not been present at any of the meetings of the Committee for this District; but I understand that, after the resolutions of our Assembly against the project, they judged any interference of the District would be unnecessary; at least, until it should be known whether the question is likely to be further agitated. Some of us are of opinion that the navigation of the Mississippi will be of little advantage to the present generation; but the prevailing sentiment is otherwise: So that I suppose a pretty general disgust would be the consequence of a cession to Spain of what is accounted an important privilege, which of right ought to be enjoyed. Indeed, I fear, if Congress cannot addjust this affair to the satisfaction of the western people, that their attachment to the American Union will be weakened. I can only say for myself that I entertain the opinions on which the resolutions alluded to are founded; but I shou'd be more happy if our people were less anxious for this priviledge and more affected with the importance of manufacturing for themselves.

Indian affairs, in this quarter, still wear a very serious aspect. About 50 of our inhabitants have been killed in the course of the present year, and the probability is that the number will be increased before the end. The number of horses that have been taken cannot be so easily ascertained, but it must be very considerable as this kind of plunder seems to be the principal object. Notwithstanding these difficultes people are emigrating to the District by thousands. It is feared that the few continental troops stationed in this quarter, Will be an object of contempt and not of terror to the inimicable Tribes, with which we are surrounded. It is also apprehended that we suffer much from the agency of British and Spanish partizans, who it is believed can no otherwise be counteracted, than by furnishing the Savages with the Trade which is now ingrossed by these incendiaries. If the Navigation of the Mississipi was justly regulated, and Detroit and the other western posts were in the hands of the Americans, this would be more practacable. In the mean time I am decided in opinion that the Indians can only be restrained by fear; for their Interest, and of consequence their friendship, is on the other side.

Before this reaches you, you will hear that our Convention has decided in favour of a Seperation. Only one member was absent; he it is said professes himself a strong advocate for the measure. The yeas and nays were not taken, because no one voted in the negative: afterwards however two members thought proper to enter a protest, and it is said that a few more were silent because they were not decided in opinion. A degree of coolness and order w[as obs]erved in the course of the deliberations equal to any thing I have seen [in othe]r popular Assemblies. It was also remarked that the abilities and [char]acters of a great majority of the members were no discredit to the District. The same spirit of moderation at present seems to prevail amongst the people at large, though there are a few instances of the reverse. In a very short time after the decision our Delegates to the Assembly were to set off for Richmond; and the Convention wishing to improve the favourable opportunity of giving the necessary notifications, directed their President to inclose their resolves to the Executive and also to our Delegates in Congress. It was also judged to be respectful to address Congress on the occasion, which from the same circumstance was a hasty performance. As the want of health prevented me from giving much attention, I can say little on its merits; only I think it contains one clause which needs explanation. I mean that where the Convention express a doubt what may be the conduct of their constituents if Congress shou'd not give sanction to the proposed separation. From the manner of expression, what was intended to be an argument has the appearance of a threat.[3] Repeated attempts had been made to introduce anarchy into the district, which proved abortive more through want of talents in the promoters than opportunity. Much of our most valuable Lands have been marked since my acquaintance with the District by those who avowed their expectation that a more equal distribution would shortly take place; and an apprehension that the defence of the District has been neglected by Virginia and by Congress has increased the number of mall-contents. Supposing that a constitutional separation would be the best preservative against the confusion that threatned us, I espoused the measure though contrary to my interest. This Sentiment had great influence in all our Conventions; and it is certain that the motions that have been made towards a Separation have had the good effect to keep the minds of the discontented in a state of suspence for two or three years past whilst the District has been filling with more orderly inhabitants, and the Courts of Justice gaining an ascendency over the licentious. But the danger in this way which has long been apprehended is not effectually removed. The deranged condition of Indian affairs, and the magnitude of the public debts are now generally understood. So that if Congress should discountenance an orderly separation, a train of arguments peculiarly adapted ad hominem would present themselves in favour of absolute independence. A Freedom from State and Federal obligations would enable us to govern and defend ourselves to advantage. We should no longer be in subjection to those who have an interest different from us. If we had the power in our own hands the Lands of non-residen[ts a]nd monopolisers would be subjected to a just partition, &c. &c. This was the evil which the Convention wished to suggest to Cong[re]ss on supposition that by granting our request the best remedy will be provided against it.

I have had an opportunity of conversing only with a few intelligent acquaintances on the merits of the American Constitution recommended by the late Federal Convention who seem to be well pleased therewith; and I wish it may be cordially embraced by every member of the Union. With every sentiment of friendship and res[pect] I am, Dear Sir, your most obt. Servt.

CALEB WALLACE

RC (DLC). Addressed by Wallace. Docketed by JM. Words and letters missing owing to torn portions of the Ms are supplied from conjecture by the editors and appear within brackets. The letter was sent to Orange and forwarded by JM's father on 30 Jan. 1788.

[1] Letter not found.

[2] See the circular letter to "the inhabitants on the western waters" of 29 Mar. 1787, signed by George Muter, Harry Innes, John Brown, and Benjamin Sebastian (Littell, *Political Transactions*, pp. 78–79). See also George Muter to JM, 20 Feb. 1787, *PJM*, IX, 280, 283 n. 8.

[3] See Samuel McDowell to Virginia Delegates, 25 Sept. 1787 and nn. 1, 3. The clause referred to by Wallace is contained in the following sentence of the address: "This separation we anxiously desire to effect in the regular constitutional mode, prescribed in the law under which we act, but so great are our present strivings, which must grow with our growth and increase with our population, that should we be unsuccessful in this application, we shall not consider ourselves in any manner answerable for the future conduct of our constituents" (Littell, *Political Transactions*, pp. 85–86).

To Edmund Randolph

N. York Novr. 18. 1787.

My dear friend

I returned hither yesterday from Philada. to which place I had proceeded under arrangements for either going on to Virginia, or coming back as I might there decide. Your very affectionate favor of the 23d. Ult:[1] found me in Philada. after travelling to N. York, and I should have answered it before my return, had any matters for communication occurred worth the expence of postage. I did not make any observations on the scheme mentioned in your letter from the Bolling-Green,[2] because it had an object which I thought it unadvisable to pursue; because I conceived that my opinion had been fully made known on the subject, and I wished not unnecessarily to repeat or dwell on points, on which our ideas do not accord; and because I considered that part of your letter merely as a friendly communication, and a pleasing pledge of your confidence, and not as a subject on which my ideas were wished. So much indeed was this the case, that at the time of answering that letter, I had not considered the expedient, with sufficient accuracy, as a means of attaining the end proposed, to justify any opinion or remarks touching its fitness. The difficulty which struck me on a subsequent attention to it, and which seemed insuperable was that several Legislatures would necessarily have provided for a Convention, and even adjourned before amendatory propositions from Virginia could be transmitted.

I have not since my arrival collected any additional information concerning the progress of the federal Constitution. I discovered no evidence on my journey through N. Jersey, that any opposition whatever would be made in that State. The Convention of Pennsylvania is to meet on tuesday next. The members returned I was told by several persons, reduced the adoption of the plan in that State to absolute certainty and by a greater majority than the most sanguine advocates had calculated. One of the Counties which had been set down by all on the list of opposition had elected deputies of known attachment to the Constitution.

I inclose herewith sundry letters which came by the French packet just arrived. The letter for Col. N. Lewis, Mr. Jefferson tells me is of great consequence.[3] You will have frequent opportunities during the Assembly, of giving it a safe conveyance. I have myself no public information by the packet, and have not yet learnt that any of moment has been received at the office of Foreign Affairs. The intelligence passing in conversation is that the Porte has declared war agst. Russia, that notwithstanding the advance of the Prussian troops into Holland, it is not certain that an accomodation may not prevent actual hostilities, and that in general it remains doubtful whether war or peace in the Western parts of Europe is to result from the present crisis of Affairs. A great change has taken place again in the French Ministry. The Count de la Luzerne, brother of the Chevalier, succeeds the Marshal de Castries in the department of Marine. The provincial Assemblies throughout are established, and some of them have already met. The Marquis[4] is a leading member in that of Auvergne. The Parliament is returned to Paris, and it is supposed that the Court will not enforce either the Stamp duty or the territorial impost. The Count de Moutier is appointed Minister to the U. States and may shortly be expected.

I do not find that a single State is represented except Virginia, and it seems very uncertain when a Congress will be made. There are individual members present from several States; and the attendance of this & the neighbouring States, may I suppose be obtained when it will produce a quorum. With the most sincere & invariable affection I remain my dear friend Yrs.

Js MADISON JR

RC (DLC). Addressed and marked *"private"* by JM. Docketed by Randolph.

[1]Randolph's letter of ca. 29 Oct. 1787 was misdated 23 Oct. 1787.
[2]Randolph to JM, 30 Sept. 1787.
[3]Jefferson to Nicholas Lewis, 17 Sept. 1787, Boyd, *Papers of Jefferson*, XII, 134–36.
[4]JM added "[de lafayette]" at a later time.

To George Washington

NEW YORK Novr. 18. 1787.

DEAR SIR

Your favor of the 5th. instant found me in Philada. whither I had proceeded, under arrangements for proceeding to Virginia or returning to this place, as I might there decide. I did not acknowledge it in Philada. because I had nothing to communicate, which you would not receive more fully and correctly from the Mr. Morris's who were setting out for Virginia.[1]

All my informations from Richmond concur in representing the enthusiasm in favor of the new Constitution as subsiding, and giving place to a spirit of criticism. I was fearful of such an event from the influence and co-operation of some of the adversaries. I do not learn however that the cause has lost its majority in the Legislature, and still less among the people at large.

I have nothing to add to the information heretofore given concerning the progress of the Constitution in other States. Mr. Gerry has presented his objections to the Legislature in a letter addressed to them, and signified his readiness if desired to give the particular reasons on which they were founded. The Legislature it seems decline the explanation, either from a supposition that they have nothing further to do in the business, having handed it over to the Convention; or from an unwillingness to countenance Mr. Gerry's conduct; or from both these considerations. It is supposed that the promulgation of this letter will shake the confidence of some, and embolden the opposition of others in that State; but I cannot discover any ground for distrusting the prompt & decided concurrence of a large majority.[2]

I inclose herewith the 7 first numbers of the federalist, a paper addressed to the people of this State. They relate entirely to the importance of the Union. If the whole plan should be executed, it will present to the public a full discussion of the merits of the proposed Constitution in all its relations. From the opinion I have formed of the views of a party in Virginia I am inclined to think that the observations on the first branch of the subject may not be superfluous antidotes in that State, any more than in this. If you concur with me, perhaps the papers may be put into the hand of some of your confidential correspondents at Richmond who would have them reprinted there. I will not conceal *from you* that I am likely to have such *a degree* of connection with the publication here, as to afford a restraint of delicacy from interesting myself directly in the republication elsewhere. You will recognize one of the pens concerned in the task. There are three in the whole. A fourth may possibly bear a part.[3]

The intelligence by the packet as far as I have collected it, is contained in the gazette of yesterday.

Virginia is the only State represented as yet. When a Congress will be formed is altogether uncertain. It is not very improbable I think that the interregnum may continue throughout the winter. With every sentiment of respect & attachment I remain dear Sir Yr. Affect. & hble servant

Js. MADISON JR.

RC (DLC: Washington Papers); Tr (DLC). RC docketed by Washington. Enclosures not found, but see n. 3 below.

[1]Robert and Gouverneur Morris stopped at Mount Vernon on 19 and 20 Nov. before going on to Richmond. The two mercantile partners came to Virginia on business and remained there seven months (Fitzpatrick, *Washington Diaries*, III, 269–70; Max Mintz, *Gouverneur Morris and the American Revolution* [Norman, Okla., 1970], p. 205).

[2]See Elbridge Gerry to the President of the Senate and Speaker of the House of Representatives of Massachusetts, 18 Oct. 1787, reprinted in Farrand, *Records*, III, 128–29.

[3]Washington asked David Stuart on 30 Nov. to put these numbers of *The Federalist* in the

hands of a Richmond printer "who is really well disposed to support the New Constitution," adding: "Altho' I am acquainted with some of the writers who are concerned in this work, I am not at liberty to disclose their names, nor would I have it known that they are sent by *me* to *you* for promulgation" (Fitzpatrick, *Writings of Washington*, XXIX, 323–24). The first number appeared in the *Va. Independent Chronicle* of 12 Dec. 1787. The three authors were Alexander Hamilton, JM, and John Jay. The "fourth," who wrote two or more papers that were not printed, was William Duer (*The Federalist* [Cooke ed.], p. xii).

To Lawrence Taliaferro

Letter not found.

ca. 18 November 1787, New York. Acknowledged in Taliaferro to JM, 16 Dec. 1787. Reports news of Taliaferro's nephew, John Taliaferro, whom JM saw at Princeton.

From Joseph Jones

RICHMOND 22d. Novr. 1787.

DR. SR.

I have your letter of the 26th. of October and have this day obtained from Mr. Thompson the survey of the upper part of James River, and shall Tomorow morning have an answer from Mr. Lambert to whom I was advised as a proper person to copy it whether he will undertake to do it.[1] If he does, the work will perhaps be well executed. Should he decline doing it my endeavours shall not be wanting to engage some other person to undertake the execution of it, and forward it to you as early as I am able. There are no wild crab trees that I can hear of near this place, except at Col. R. Goodes,[2] who I am told has a few Trees standing in one of his inclosures, where probably some Sprouts may be got if not injured by the Cattle. I will send there for the purpose, and if they can be obtained contrive them to you as safely as I can.

The Assembly have not yet passed any act of consequence. British debts—installments and the circuit or district plan of jurisprudence, are under consideration. There is great diversity of Opinion on these subjects. One party presses forward the removing impediments to the fullfillmt. of the Treaty—another for removing the legal impediments by one bill and introducing installmts. by another. A third class think the recommendation of Congress respecting the Treaty had better lye unmoved untill the convention shall have decided on the new constitution of Government. The introducer of the British debt proposition suspending the law if it shall pass untill the other States pass similar laws is the introducer of the plan of installments for these and all other private debts; and from the manner in which the business is managed will probably loose the whole.[3] This day a Com: of the whole are upon allowing Tobacco to be received as a commutable in Taxes. The price at these Warehouses & Manchester &c. 30/ those at the heads of the other Rivers 28/. and so on with all the other Warehouses in the same ratio of increase on the prices of last year as fixed by law, and from the spirit of accommodation which seemed to govern to day from what prevailed a few days past when the subject was first debated I think the measure will succeed.[4]

The New plan of Government is still very much the subject of conversation. I mix little in the croud and am unable as yet to form any estimate whether it gains or looses ground with the Members of the legislature. Wherever I hear the subject agitated I find Gentlemen pretty much divided, each party appear to maintain their opinions with apparent zeal. After a while more temper will prevail and the excellencies or defects of the System be treated with less prejudice and more moderation. I much doubt whether the people in this State whatever may be the situation of mens minds in other States are yet ripe for the great change which the new plan will ultimately effect. There would have been less repugnance to it here had the judiciary been less exceptionable and the Executive and legislative had been separate. The true line could it have been hit was to have yeilded full management of all exterior matters to Congress, leaving interior matters to the States, so far as the power of regulating trade as well between other nations as the States wod. have admitted of—with a Court of Appeals properly constituted for administering justice ultimately to all alike, and with some means of coercion, not violent or military. Some such improvements our State from all I can learn would have not hesitated in yeilding their assent to. The great change proposed will I think meet with strong opposition though it may be adopted. Cou[ld] the constitution of the Senate be varied and the Judiciary be better established than it now stands on the paper I could more willingly give the Constitution my assent. As it stands I shall receive it with reluctance. The 4th. Number of the American Citizen has been printed here in Davis's paper. The three numbers you sent me were printed and in the same paper.[5] I am Yr. friend

JOS: JONES

RC (DLC). Docketed by JM, "Novr. 27. 1787." Brackets enclose letters obscured in right margin.

[1]George Thompson was one of three commissioners appointed by the Council of State in the spring of 1785 to survey the James River northwest from Lynch's Ferry (Lynchburg) (*JCSV*, III, 438). "Mr. Lambert" was possibly William Lambert, a clerk who assisted

in preparing a statement of Virginia's accounts with the Confederation (*CVSP*, IV, 362, 466).

[2] Col. Robert Goode (1743–1809), whose plantation was in Chesterfield County. Goode represented that county in the House of Delegates in 1783 and 1788; in the latter year he was elected to the Council of State (Swem and Williams, *Register*, pp. 17, 28, 29 n.; *JCSV*, IV, 261).

[3] The "introducer" of these proposals was George Nicholas. On 17 Nov. the House had adopted by a majority of thirty a resolution calling for the repeal of all acts repugnant to the peace treaty. The resolution contained a clause suspending the repeal until all the other states had passed similar laws of repeal (*JHDV*, Oct. 1787, pp. 51–52). See also Stuart to JM, 2 Dec. 1787 and n. 3; Monroe to JM, 6 Dec. 1787.

[4] An act declaring tobacco receivable in taxes passed 1 Dec. 1787 (Hening, *Statutes*, XII, 455–57). The price of tobacco established in this act was two shillings per hundredweight more than that fixed in the 1786 act (ibid., XII, 258–60). See also George Mason to Washington, 27 Nov. 1787, Rutland, *Papers of George Mason*, III, 1020–21.

[5] See Coxe to JM, 27 Sept. 1787 and n. 1.

Virginia Delegates to Edmund Randolph

NEW YORK Nov. 22. 1787

SIR,

We do ourselves the honor to communicate to your Excellency the European intelligence which we have received to the 22d. of September by the last French packe[t.]

The Affairs of Holland were at that time in a gloomy state as they respected the Patriots, and it is to be apprehended that before this, they must have been brought to a serious issue: it appears hardly possible that the event can be any thing short of a perfect disappointment of the views of that party. The King of Prussia, urged by England, and incensed by the indignity alledged to have been offered to his Sister, has sent 30,000 Troops into these provinces. This formidable Army, Commanded by the Duke of Brunswic, made its invasion on the 15th. of September, and by the 22d. had obtained possession, against little or no opposition, of Utrecht and all the other places which had made an appearance of opposing the Stadtholder, except Amsterdam. This City is saved, for the present, by the inundation of the Country between it and the Enemy. The Patriots have no foreign Aid to expect but from France; she is by no means in a situation to engage two such powers as England & Prussia in their behalf, and a late event still adds to her embarrassments. This is a declaration of War by the Porte against Russia. As the powers now stand arranged, with a view to this War, the Parties are Turkey & France (perhaps Spain also) against Russia, the Emperor of Germany, Prussia & England: the inequality is so striking, that it would seem madness in France to proceed in it. She might plunge herself into Ruin in an attempt to support the Turks, and must still, eventually, leave them to their fate; in this State of things it might not be difficult for her to determine what conduct to observe were she left to decide intirely with a view to her own present circumstances, but it is not unlikely that the great ascendency which, one of the parties in the War, are about to possess, will excite such apprehensions in this Court, that she will not be content with barely withdrawing from it. The balance of powers, so essential to the tranquillity and safety of Europe, will be destroyed, and this she will not suffer to take place if she can by any means prevent it. Her only resort must be to such negotiations as may eventually place her in alliance with some, against others, of the powers at present concerned on the other side; the probability is, that in such event, she will be connected with the two Empires, and, consequently, be placed in the scale opposite to the Porte; in short, it must lead to an entire change of the System of Europe. In any event it appears that an extensive and bloody Continental War is inevitable, which will press hard upon the Turks, and may, eventually, drive them out of Europe.

Should the changes here suggested take place by an early period, the Patriotic Party in holland may possibly derive advantages from them. France will in every situation continue their Freind, and will not fail to exhibit proof of it whenever she can with effect.

It appears that the Emperor will carry into effect his new arrangements in Brabant; He has contrived to amuse his discontented subjects with pretended negotiations until he has established amongst them a sufficient force to compel them to compliance.

France is again in a State of tranquillity. The Parliaments have made such firm opposition against the Stamp-Act and territorial impost, that the King has suspended his efforts to carry them into effect, which is understood as an entire relinquishment. The Parliament of Paris, which was banished to Troyes, is recalled. The Provincial Assemblies are established as recommended by the Notables. Our Freind, the Marquis de la Fayette, is in Auvergne, and a principal Member in the Assembly of that province. This Nobleman is high in the estimation of his Country, and appears to be inspiring all orders of it, with those principles of liberty and equality which, though the growth of his own mind, have been confirmed in the American School. The Revenues of this Kingdom will be greatly increased by a more equal administration of the old systems than was formerly made. The property of the Nobles and Clergy, which were nearly exempted, will now be brought to Contribute to the support of the public burthens. This reform with reductions in the expenditures of the public money, it is hoped, will provide for the relief of our good Ally from the difficulties which now press her. It is much to be regretted that in this hour of her distress the American debt can not be paid.

The French Cabinet has undergone nearly an entire change. The Archbishop of Toulouse being made prime-Minister the Marechals of Castries & Segur, Ministers of the Marine & War departments have resigned. To the first the Count de la Lucerne (Brother of the late Minister in America), and to the latter Monsr. de Brienne have succeeded. The department of Controul has had a very rapid succession of Tenants. From Mr. Calonne it passed to Mr. de Fourqueux, from him to Villedeuil, & from him to Lambert who holds it at present. Great changes have also taken place in the foreign appointments. The Count de Moustier is to come to America, and the Chevalier de la lucerne, it is supposed, will go to London—& Mr. de St. Preist is sent to holland in pl[ace] of Mr. de Verac. We have the honor to be with the highest respect Your Excellencies Most Obedt. Servts.

Js. MADISON JR
ED. CARRINGTON

RC (Vi). In Carrington's hand, except for JM's signature. Letters in brackets indicate damaged portions of the Ms.

Madison's Authorship of *The Federalist*
22 November 1787–1 March 1788

EDITORIAL NOTE

After the adjournment of the Federal Convention and his return to Congress in New York, JM did not expect to participate actively in the campaign to ratify the proposed Constitution. Privately disappointed with the outcome of the convention, he nevertheless wished the new plan well and was an interested observer of its reception in the various states. Although the initial reaction was almost universally favorable, during October various newspapers, particularly those in the city of New York, began publishing pieces sharply critical of the Constitution. These attacks evidently provoked Alexander Hamilton, who had been even less enthusiastic about the Constitution than JM, to launch his own series of newspaper articles defending the new plan of government. In the first number of *The Federalist*, published in the N.Y. *Independent Journal* on 27 October, Hamilton as "Publius" promised his readers a comprehensive exposition of the Constitution. To carry out this ambitious scheme he enlisted the collaboration of John Jay, who wrote the next four essays, and William Duer, who wrote several essays that were not included in the final compilation. Gouverneur Morris was also "'warmly pressed'" to contribute his talents, but he refused the invitation (Douglass Adair, "The Authorship of the Disputed Federalist Papers," *WMQ*, 3d ser., I [1944], 242–45; *The Federalist* [Cooke ed.], pp. xi–xii). Hamilton apparently did not ask JM to join the enterprise until the middle of November, perhaps as late as the seventeenth, the day the Virginian returned from a trip to Philadelphia. The following day he confided to Washington his probable involvement in the publication, and shortly thereafter (22 Nov.) his first contribution to *The Federalist* appeared. Many years later JM recalled that at the time he agreed to Hamilton's request, he recommended Rufus King as "a proper auxiliary," but noted that Hamilton did not consider King's talents "as altogether of the sort required for the task in view" (Detached Memoranda [DLC: Rives Collection, Madison Papers], printed in Elizabeth Fleet, ed., "Madison's 'Detached Memoranda,'" *WMQ*, 3d ser., III [1946], 564–65).

JM must have agreed to contribute to *The Federalist* because he was deeply disturbed by both the quantity and nature of the Antifederalist denunciations of the Constitution. "The Newspapers here begin to teem with vehement & virulent calumniations of the proposed Govt.," he wrote Washington on 18 October. To Edmund Randolph he complained: "Judging from the News papers one wd. suppose that the adversaries were the most numerous & the most in earnest" (21 Oct. 1787). JM realized that the Constitution, whatever its faults, was preferable to anything proposed by its critics, who differed "as much in their objections" as they did "from the thing itself" (JM to Ambrose Madison, 11 Oct. 1787). Even before he was approached by Hamilton, JM had shown his willingness to become actively involved in the public debate by agreeing to stand for election to the Virginia ratifying convention. He justified this decision by noting that "many objections in Virginia proceed from a misconception of the plan, or of the causes which produced the objectionable parts of it" and that his attendance at the Philadelphia convention would enable him "to contribute some explanations and informations which may be of use" (JM to Ambrose Madison, 8 Nov. 1787). These remarks serve equally well to explain his decision to don the mask of "Publius."

JM soon became a virtually indispensable partner in the enterprise, especially after illness forced Jay to retire in November. Apart from his keen analytical powers and finely developed literary style, the Virginian brought with him valuable assets that facilitated a rapid production of papers of consistently high quality (Louis C. Schaedler, "James Madison, Literary Craftsman," *WMQ*, 3d ser., III [1946], 515–33). The most important of these was his unsurpassed knowledge of the Constitution from the earliest proposals to the final draft. JM alone had a comprehensive record of the convention debates, a storehouse of information that gave him an enormous advantage in his defense of the Constitution. He could also draw on the research memorandums he had prepared for his own use at the convention. Thus in composing his first essay, the celebrated No. 10, he relied heavily on one section of Vices of the Political System (*PJM*, IX, 354–57). And for three more of his early numbers (18, 19, and 20) he lifted whole passages from his Notes on Ancient and Modern Confederacies (*PJM*, IX, 4–22). So great was the pressure to produce copy, JM recalled that without the aid of these materials, "the performance must have borne a very different aspect" (Fleet, "Madison's 'Detached Memoranda,'" *WMQ*, 3d ser., III [1946], 565). Time was another precious asset at JM's disposal. Unlike Hamilton, busy with his law practice, the Virginian was relatively free of other duties throughout most of the period he was writing *The Federalist*. Attendance at Congress was seldom required, for that body had no regular quorum from November 1787 until the middle of February 1788.

According to JM's later recollection, the writers of *The Federalist* had no prearranged plan for dividing up the work (ibid.). Nevertheless, a more or less logical division of labor emerged. At the time the Virginian agreed to share the role of

"Publius," the two New Yorkers were in the midst of discussing the "utility of the Union," the first of the topics Hamilton had listed in his introductory essay (*The Federalist* [Cooke ed.], p. 6). When Jay fell ill, JM, having pertinent materials close at hand, contributed two papers (Nos. 10 and 14) to this section and three more (Nos. 18, 19, and 20) to the next, which focused upon the "insufficiency of the present Confederation to preserve that Union." After Hamilton considered the "necessity of a government at least equally energetic with the one proposed," JM took up the analysis of the Constitution proper, particularly its "conformity . . . to the true principles of republican government" (ibid., pp. 6–7). This was the core of the work, the part he was uniquely qualified to undertake. JM wrote twenty-four numbers (37 through 58, 62, and 63) under this heading before he was forced to leave for Orange County to secure his election to the Virginia ratifying convention (Adair, "The Authorship of the Disputed Federalist Papers," *WMQ*, 3d ser., I [1944], 248–54).

Although the original manuscripts have never been found and were most likely destroyed at the time of printing (except for the drafts of Jay's essays), the present editors believe that JM wrote twenty-nine of the eighty-five essays of "Publius," the number he claimed in a list first made public in 1818. According to that list Jay wrote Nos. 2, 3, 4, 5, and 64; JM wrote Nos. 10, 14, 18, 19, 20, 37 through 58, 62, and 63; and Hamilton wrote the remainder. This designation of authors differed significantly from one attributed to Hamilton, which had appeared ten years earlier in *The Port Folio*, a Philadelphia magazine. The 14 November 1807 issue of that magazine reproduced a memorandum, said to be in Hamilton's handwriting, that distributed the authorship as follows: Nos. 2, 3, 4, 5, and 54 to Jay; Nos. 10, 14, and 37 through 48 to JM; Nos. 18, 19, and 20 to Hamilton and JM jointly; and all the rest to Hamilton (*The Federalist*, ed. Henry B. Dawson [New York, 1864], p. xxviii). The discrepancy between these two lists gave rise to a famous literary dispute over the authorship of certain numbers of the *The Federalist* that continued well into this century. In recent years, however, the authorship question has evoked little controversy, for insofar as the known evidence can do it, the issue has been settled.

That JM's list of authors is the correct one is a conclusion previously reached by Edward G. Bourne, Douglass Adair, Jacob E. Cooke, and Frederick Mosteller and David L. Wallace (Bourne, "The Authorship of *The Federalist*," in *Essays in Historical Criticism* [1901; Freeport, N.Y., 1967 reprint], pp. 115–45 [earlier version in *AHR*, II (1896–97), 443–60]; Adair, "The Authorship of the Disputed Federalist Papers," *WMQ*, 3d ser., I [1944], 97–122, 235–64; *The Federalist* [Cooke ed.], pp. xix–xxx; Mosteller and Wallace, *Inference and Disputed Authorship: The Federalist* [Reading, Mass., 1964], p. vii and passim). Together their studies presented all the internal and external evidence available to resolve the question. Bourne was the first to compile the internal evidence, which he did with exemplary thoroughness. Using parallel columns, he showed similarities and identities between selected passages of the disputed essays and earlier writings or speeches by JM. In 1944 Adair extended Bourne's findings by reconstructing in detail the circumstances of the writing of *The Federalist* and by analyzing the political philosophies of JM and Hamilton. At the same time he effectively exposed the dubious reasoning of Henry Cabot Lodge and Paul Leicester Ford, the major spokesmen for Hamilton's claim to the disputed essays. Moreover, in a telling footnote Adair pointed out the difficulty of accepting the hypothesis that JM's contributions ended with No. 48, which was published on 1 February 1788: despite great pressure to return home for the Virginia ratifying convention election, JM nevertheless remained in New York for another month until after the publication of No. 63 ("The Authorship of the Disputed Federalist Papers," *WMQ*, 3d ser., I [1944], 252–53 and n. 47). The conclusions reached by Bourne and Adair using traditional methods have recently been upheld by the work of Mosteller and Wallace, mathematicians whose primary interest was to test the application of a certain mathematical theorem rather than to settle the authorship problem. Noting the frequency of certain "discriminator" words used by JM and Hamilton, they found high odds in favor of JM's authorship of the disputed papers. The lowest (for No. 55) were 90 to 1, but the next lowest (for No. 56) were 800 to 1 (*Inference and Disputed Authorship*, p. 263).

Skeptical of arguments based on internal evidence, Cooke relied instead on external evidence, chiefly the various lists of authors that have survived. Cooke conceded the superiority of JM's claim on the basis of the greater authenticity of the Virginian's list, although he was reluctant to dismiss the evidence in support of Hamilton's claim as completely untrustworthy. Because there is no extant list in Hamilton's hand, Cooke noted, one cannot be certain which papers the New Yorker believed to be his own. Moreover, the list attributed to him contains at least one error: Jay wrote No. 64, not No. 54, as a draft in Jay's hand found among his papers proved. A more reliable guide to Hamilton's distribution of authorship, Cooke argued, is a memorandum in the hand of Chancellor James Kent, which Kent showed to Hamilton. This memorandum differs from the one attributed to Hamilton by assigning No. 64 (written over "54") to Jay and Nos. 49 (written over "48") and 53 to JM. Significantly, however, Kent later accepted as correct a list nearly identical to the one drawn up by JM (*The Federalist* [Cooke ed.], pp. xxi–xxvi). There remains the intriguing possibility that Hamilton, who seems not to have shown much interest in the authorship question and who evidently did not refer back to the essays themselves when assigning authorship, made a few careless errors in reading the Roman numerals that were used in the older editions of *The Federalist* (Irving Brant, "Settling the Authorship of *The Federalist*," *AHR*, LXVII [1961–62], 71–75).

The external evidence on JM's side is free of such ambiguity. There are two extant lists of authors in JM's hand, drawn up at different times and with an identical distribution of authorship. The one most often cited is in a copy of *The Federalist*, now in the Rare Book Division, Library of Congress, in which JM made corrections and wrote the name of the author before each essay. This copy is the 1799 edition by John Tiebout (actually a reissue of the 1788 McLean edition) and is evidently the one JM sent to Jacob Gideon in 1818. Gideon used this information to prepare his own edition of *The Federalist* (Washington, 1818), which names the authors of the individual essays. JM later endorsed the Gideon edition as containing "a true distribution of the numbers of the Federalist among the three writers" (Fleet, "Madison's 'Detached Memoranda,' " *WMQ*, 3d ser., III [1946], 567).

The other list is in a copy of *The Federalist* that once belonged to Richard Rush, who served as both attorney general and secretary of state under JM. For many years the existence of this list was known only through a description of it in a letter from Benjamin Rush, son of Richard Rush, to Henry B. Dawson, 29 August 1863, printed in *The Federalist* (Dawson ed.), pp. xxxix–xlv. Cooke mentioned this list, but not having seen the Rush copy, he cautiously refused to accept it as authoritative. The present editors have examined this copy, now in the Special Collections,

Boston University Library, and can affirm that the marginal notes are in JM's hand. Rush's copy of *The Federalist* consists of the second and third volumes of *The Works of Alexander Hamilton* (3 vols.; New York, 1810). This edition was the first to name the authors of the individual essays, which was done according to the list attributed to Hamilton. Evidently at the owner's request, JM went through the two volumes and wrote the initials of the author before each number, crossing out Hamilton's name wherever it appeared before an essay the Virginian claimed. At No. 18 he wrote a long note explaining why Hamilton should not be considered coauthor of Nos. 18, 19, and 20 (see *The Federalist* No. 18, 7 Dec. 1787, n.). According to Richard Rush's memorandum on the flyleaf of the first volume, JM performed this task at least as early as 1816.

Although no list of authors of an earlier date than 1816 has been found, JM indicated on several occasions that he had drawn up such lists long before the authorship dispute arose, apparently near the time of the original publication of *The Federalist*. To Gideon, who had received JM's personally inscribed copy of the work, JM noted that he "had a considerable time ago, at the request of particular friends, given the same advantage to their copies" (20 Aug. 1818, Madison, *Writings* [Hunt ed.], VIII, 411 n.). And to Robert Walsh, after acknowledging the discrepancy between his claim and Hamilton's, JM stated that he had communicated a list of the authors "at a time & under circumstances depriving me of a plea for so great a mistake in a slip of the memory or attention" (2 Mar. 1819, ibid., VIII, 433). If his list was erroneous, JM wrote James K. Paulding, it "could not be ascribed to a lapse of memory," but must "be an impeachment of my veracity" (April 1831, ibid., IX, 454).

Although JM's numbers of *The Federalist* were first published in New York newspapers, the text of the essays below is from the original letterpress edition of 1788 printed by John and Archibald McLean. Both volumes of this edition were published after JM left New York, but he could have corrected the newspaper versions of all his numbers before departing. His last essay appeared on 1 March, several days before he left the city. The differences between the newspaper and McLean texts are slight, however, consisting of stylistic changes and typographical corrections. For the newspaper text, collated with the McLean, George Hopkins (1802), and Gideon editions, see *The Federalist* (Cooke ed.).

In reprinting JM's essays the editors have silently corrected typographical and other obvious errors in McLean. The titles at the head of each essay in the McLean edition have been omitted. The date in brackets indicates when the essay first appeared in the newspaper. Certain numbering changes in the McLean edition resulted from a rearrangement of the newpaper essays Nos. 29–35 (none by JM), so that in the McLean edition Nos. 36–78 bear one number higher than in the first printed version (ibid., p. xviii).

The Federalist Number 10

[22 November 1787]

Among the numerous advantages promised by a well constructed union, none deserves to be more accurately developed than its tendency to break and control the violence of faction.[1] The friend of popular governments, never finds himself so much alarmed for their character and fate, as when he contemplates their propensity to this dangerous vice. He will not fail therefore to set a due value on any plan which, without violating the principles to which he is attached, provides a proper cure for it. The instability, injustice and confusion introduced into the public councils, have in truth been the mortal diseases under which popular governments have every where perished; as they continue to be the favorite and fruitful topics from which the adversaries to liberty derive their most specious declamations. The valuable improvements made by the American constitutions on the popular models, both antient and modern, cannot certainly be too much admired; but it would be an unwarrantable partiality, to contend that they have as effectually obviated the danger on this side as was wished and expected. Complaints are every where heard from our most considerate and virtuous citizens, equally the friends of public and private faith, and of public and personal liberty; that our governments are too unstable; that the public good is disregarded in the conflicts of rival parties; and that measures are too often decided, not according to the rules of justice, and the rights of the minor party; but by the superior force of an interested and over-bearing majority. However anxiously we may wish that these complaints had no foundation, the evidence of known facts will not permit us to deny that they are in some degree true. It will be found indeed, on a candid review of our situation, that some of the distresses under which we labour, have been erroneously charged on the operation of our governments; but it will be found at the same time, that other causes will not alone account for many of our heaviest misfortunes; and particularly, for that prevailing and increasing distrust of public engagements, and alarm for private rights, which are echoed from one end of the continent to the other. These must be chiefly, if not wholly, effects of the unsteadiness and injustice, with which a factious spirit has tainted our public administration.

By a faction I understand a number of citizens, whether amounting to a majority or minority of the whole, who are united and actuated by some common impulse of passion, or of interest, adverse to the rights of other citizens, or to the permanent and aggregate interests of the community.

There are two methods of curing the mischiefs of faction: The one, by removing its causes; the other, by controlling its effects.

There are again two methods of removing the causes of faction: The one by destroying the liberty which is essential to its existence; the other, by giving to every citizen the same opinions, the same passions, and the same interests.

It could never be more truly said than of the first remedy, that it is worse than the disease. Liberty is to faction, what air is to fire, an aliment without which it instantly expires. But it could not be a less folly to abolish liberty, which is essential to political life, because it nourishes faction, than it would be to wish the annihilation of air, which is essential to animal life because it imparts to fire its destructive agency.

The second expedient is as impracticable, as the first would be unwise. As long as the reason of man continues fallible, and he is at liberty to exercise it, different opinions will be formed. As long as the connection subsists between his reason and his self-love, his opinions and his passions will have a reciprocal influence on each other; and the former will be objects to which the latter will attach themselves. The diversity in the faculties of men from which the rights of property originate, is not less an insuperable obstacle to an uniformity of interests. The protection of these faculties is the first object of government. From the protection of different and unequal faculties of acquiring property, the possession of different degrees and kinds of property immediately results: And from the influence of these on the sentiments and views of the respective proprietors, ensues a division of the society into different interests and parties.

The latent causes of faction are thus sown in the nature of man; and we see them every where brought into different degrees of activity, according to the different circumstances of civil society. A zeal for different opinions concerning religion, concerning government, and many other points, as well of speculation as of practice; an attachment to different leaders ambitiously contending for pre-eminence and power; or to persons of other descriptions whose fortunes have been interesting to the human passions, have in turn divided mankind into parties, inflamed them with mutual animosity, and rendered them much more disposed to vex and oppress each other, than to co-operate for their common good. So strong is this propensity of mankind to fall into mutual animosities, that where no substantial occasion presents itself, the most frivolous and fanciful distinctions have been sufficient to kindle their unfriendly passions, and excite their most violent conflicts. But the most common and durable source of factions, has been the various and unequal distribution of property. Those who hold, and those who are without property, have ever formed distinct interests in society. Those who are creditors, and those who are debtors, fall under a like discrimination. A landed interest, a manufacturing interest, a mercantile interest, a monied interest, with many lesser interests, grow up of necessity in civilized nations, and divide them into different classes, actuated by different sentiments and views. The regulation of these various and interfering interests forms the principal task of modern legislation, and involves the spirit of party and faction in the necessary and ordinary operations of government.

No man is allowed to be a judge in his own cause; because his interest would certainly bias his judgment, and, not improbably, corrupt his integrity. With equal, nay with greater reason, a body of men, are unfit to be both judges and parties, at the same time; yet, what are many of the most important acts of legislation, but so many judicial determinations, not indeed concerning the rights of single persons, but concerning the rights of large bodies of citizens; and what are the different classes of legislators, but advocates and parties to the causes which they determine? Is a law proposed concerning private debts? It is a question to which the creditors are parties on one side, and the debtors on the other. Justice ought to hold the balance between them. Yet the parties are and must be themselves the judges; and the most numerous party, or, in other words, the most powerful faction must be expected to prevail. Shall domestic manufactures be encouraged, and in what degree, by restrictions on foreign manufactures? are questions which would be differently decided by the landed and the manufacturing classes; and probably by neither, with a sole regard to justice and the public good. The apportionment of taxes on the various descriptions of property, is an act which seems to require the most exact impartiality, yet there is perhaps no legislative act in which greater opportunity and temptation are given to a predominant party, to trample on the rules of justice. Every shilling with which they over-burden the inferior number, is a shilling saved to their own pockets.

It is in vain to say, that enlightened statesmen will be able to adjust these clashing interests, and render them all subservient to the public good. Enlightened statesmen will not always be at the helm: Nor, in many cases, can such an adjustment be made at all, without taking into view indirect and remote considerations, which will rarely prevail over the immediate interest which one party may find in disregarding the rights of another, or the good of the whole.

The inference to which we are brought, is, that the *causes* of faction cannot be removed; and that relief is only to be sought in the means of controlling its *effects*.

If a faction consists of less than a majority, relief is supplied by the republican principle, which enables the majority to defeat its sinister views by regular vote: It may clog the administration, it may convulse the society; but it will be unable to execute and mask its violence under the forms of the constitution. When a majority is included in a faction, the form of popular government on the other hand enables it to sacrifice to its ruling passion or interest, both the public good and the rights of other citizens. To secure the public good, and private rights against the danger of such a faction, and at the same time to preserve the spirit and the form of popular government, is then the great object to which our enquiries are directed. Let me add that it is the great desideratum, by which alone this form of government can be rescued from the opprobrium under which it has so long labored, and be recommended to the esteem and adoption of mankind.

By what means is this object attainable? Evidently by one of two only. Either the existence of the same passion or interest in a majority at the same time, must be prevented; or the majority, having such co-existent passion or interest, must be rendered, by their number and local situation, unable to concert and carry into effect schemes of oppression. If the impulse and the opportunity be suffered to coincide, we well know that neither moral nor religious motives can be relied on as an adequate control. They are not found to be such on the injustice and violence of individuals, and lose their efficacy in proportion to the number combined together; that is, in proportion as their efficacy becomes needful.[2]

From this view of the subject, it may be concluded that a pure democracy, by which I mean a society, consisting of a small number of citizens, who assemble and administer the government in person, can admit of no cure for the mischiefs of faction. A common passion or interest will, in almost every case, be felt by a majority of the whole; a communication and concert results from the form of government itself; and there is nothing to check the inducements to sacrifice the weaker party, or an obnoxious individual. Hence it is, that such democracies have ever been spectacles of turbulence and contention; have ever been found incompatible with personal security, or the rights of property; and have in general been as short in their lives, as they have been violent in their deaths. Theoretic politicians, who have patronized this species of government, have erroneously supposed, that by reducing mankind to a perfect equality in their political rights, they would, at the same time, be perfectly equalized, and assimilated in their possessions, their opinions, and their passions.

A republic, by which I mean a government in which the scheme of representation takes place, opens a different prospect, and promises the cure for which we are seeking. Let us examine the points in which it varies from pure democracy, and we shall comprehend both the nature of the cure, and the efficacy which it must derive from the union.

The two great points of difference between a democracy and a republic, are first, the delegation of the government, in the latter, to a small number of citizens elected by the rest; secondly, the greater number of citizens, and greater sphere of country, over which the latter may be extended.

The effect of the first difference is, on the one hand, to refine and enlarge the public views, by passing them through the medium of a chosen body of citizens, whose wisdom may best discern the true interest of their country, and whose patriotism and love of justice, will be least likely to sacrifice it to temporary or partial considerations. Under such a regulation, it may well happen that the public voice pronounced by the representatives of the people, will be more consonant to the public good, than if pronounced by the people themselves convened for the purpose. On the other hand, the effect may be inverted. Men of factious tempers, of local prejudices, or of sinister designs, may by intrigue, by corruption, or by other means, first obtain the suffrages, and then betray the interests of the people. The question resulting is, whether small or extensive republics are most favourable to the election of proper guardians of the public weal; and it is clearly decided in favour of the latter by two obvious considerations.

In the first place it is to be remarked, that however small the republic may be, the representatives must be raised to a certain number, in order to guard against the cabals of a few; and that however large it may be, they must be limited to a certain number, in order to guard against the confusion of a multitude. Hence the number of representatives in the two cases not being in proportion to that of the constituents, and being proportionally greatest in the small republic, it follows, that if the proportion of fit characters be not less in the large than in the small republic, the former will present a greater option, and consequently a greater probability of a fit choice.

In the next place, as each representative will be chosen by a greater number of citizens in the large than in the small republic, it will be more difficult for unworthy candidates to practise with success the vicious arts, by which elections are too often carried; and the suffrages of the people being more free, will be more likely to centre on men who possess the most attractive merit, and the most diffusive and established characters.

It must be confessed, that in this, as in most other cases, there is a mean, on both sides of which inconveniencies will be found to lie. By enlarging too much the number of electors, you render the representative too little acquainted with all their local circumstances and lesser interests; as by reducing it too much, you render him unduly attached to these, and too little fit to comprehend and pursue great and national objects. The federal constitution forms a happy combination in this respect; the great and aggregate interests being referred to the national, the local and particular to the state legislatures.

The other point of difference is, the greater number of citizens and extent of territory which may be brought within the compass of republican, than of democratic government; and it is this circumstance principally which renders factious combinations less to be dreaded in the former, than in the latter. The smaller the society, the fewer probably will be the distinct parties and interests composing it; the fewer the distinct parties and interests, the more frequently will a majority be found of the same party; and the smaller the number of individuals composing a majority, and the smaller the compass within which they are placed, the more easily will they concert and execute their plans of oppression. Extend the sphere, and you take in a greater variety of parties and interests; you make it less probable that a majority of the whole will have a common motive to invade the rights of other citizens; or if such a common motive exists, it will be more difficult for all who feel it to discover their own strength, and to act in unison with each other. Besides other impediments, it may be remarked, that where there is a consciousness of unjust or dishonourable purposes, communication is always checked by distrust, in proportion to the number whose concurrence is necessary.

Hence it clearly appears, that the same advantage, which a republic has over a democracy, in controlling the effects of faction, is enjoyed by a large over a small republic—is enjoyed by the union over the states composing it. Does this advantage consist in the substitution of representatives, whose enlightened views and virtuous sentiments render them superior to local prejudices, and to schemes of injustice? It will not be denied, that the representation of the union will be most likely to possess these requisite endowments. Does it consist in the greater security afforded by a greater variety of parties, against the event of any one party being able to outnumber and oppress the rest? In an equal degree does the increased variety of parties, comprised within the union, encrease this security. Does it, in fine, consist in the greater obstacles opposed to the concert and accomplishment of the secret wishes of an unjust and interested majority? Here, again, the extent of the union gives it the most palpable advantage.

The influence of factious leaders may kindle a flame within their particular states, but will be unable to spread a general conflagration through the other states: A religious sect, may degenerate into a political faction in a part of the confederacy; but the variety of sects dispersed over the entire face of it, must secure the national councils against any danger from that source: A rage for paper money, for an abolition of debts, for an equal division of property, or for any other improper or wicked project, will be less apt to pervade the whole body of the union, than a particular member of it; in the same proportion as such a malady is more likely to taint a particular county or district, than an entire state.[3]

In the extent and proper structure of the union, therefore, we behold a republican remedy for the diseases most incident to republican government. And according to the degree of pleasure and pride, we feel in being republicans, ought to be our zeal in cherishing the spirit, and supporting the character of federalists.

PUBLIUS.

McLean, I, 52–61.

[1]Douglass Adair showed that in preparing this essay, especially that part containing the analysis of factions and the theory of the extended republic, JM creatively adapted the ideas of David Hume ("'That Politics May Be Reduced to a Science': David Hume, James Madison, and the Tenth *Federalist*," *Huntington Library Quarterly*, XX [1956–57], 343–60). The forerunner of *The Federalist* No. 10 may be found in JM's Vices of the Political System (*PJM*, IX, 348–57). See also JM's first speech of 6 June and his first speech of 26 June 1787 at the Federal Convention, and his letter to Jefferson of 24 Oct. 1787.

[2]In Vices of the Political System JM listed three motives, each of which he believed was insufficient to prevent individuals or factions from oppressing each other: (1) "a prudent regard to their own good as involved in the general and permanent good of the Community"; (2) "respect for character"; and (3) religion. As to "respect for character," JM remarked that "in a multitude its efficacy is diminished in proportion to the number which is to share the praise or the blame" (*PJM*, IX, 355–56). For this observation JM again drew upon David Hume. Adair suggests that JM deliberately omitted his list of motives from *The Federalist*. "There was a certain disadvantage in making derogatory remarks to a majority that must be persuaded to adopt your arguments" ("'That Politics May Be Reduced to a Science,'" *Huntington Library Quarterly*, XX [1956–57], 354). JM repeated these motives in his first speech of 6 June 1787, in his letter to Jefferson of 24 Oct. 1787, and alluded to them in *The Federalist* No. 51.

[3]The negative on state laws, which JM had unsuccessfully advocated at the Federal Convention, was designed to prevent the enactment of "improper or wicked" measures by the states. The Constitution did include specific prohibitions on the state legislatures, but JM dismissed these as "short of the mark." He also doubted that the judicial system would effectively "keep the States within their proper limits" (JM to Jefferson, 24 Oct. 1787).

Edmund Randolph to Virginia Delegates

Letter not found.

24 November 1787. Acknowledged in Virginia Delegates to Randolph, 11 Dec. 1787. Requests delegates to obtain the appointment of a separate superintendent of Indian affairs for Virginia and North Carolina. Recommends Major Dromgoole for this position.

To Archibald Stuart

N. YORK. NOVr. 25. 87.

DEAR SIR

I have recd. your favor of the 9th. instant and thank you for its Communications. I am sorry that I have none to make in return, no occurrences of moment having arrived since my last. The Pennsylvania Convention was to meet on Tuesday last, but I have heard nothing from that quarter. The election in Connecticut is over and the Returns it is said by those who[1] the members & their characters, reduce the adoption of the Constitution in that State, to certainty. We have no Congress yet. Col. Carringt[on] tells me he has sent you the papers you request up to the date of his letter. I add those which have since appeared. With much esteem & regd. I remain Yr. Obedt. Servt.

Js. Madison Jr

RC (Owned by Sol Feinstone, Washington Crossing, Pa., 1973). Addressed by JM and franked. Enclosures not found. Letters in brackets missing owing to a tear in the Ms.

[1] JM omitted "know" here.

From Adam Stephen

Martinburg Berkely County Novr 25h. 1787

Sir,

It appears that the Wild men of Franklin State have an intention to drive the Cherokees out of their Country.

They are a well behaved people. I carryd on an Expedition against them in —61 made a treaty with them at the long Island in Holston, kept the principals of the Nation with me untill such reputable person among them as I named carryd the Treaty to Charleston & Confirmed it There. This Treaty they faithfully Observed untill our People broke it, by wantonly killing Some their Hunters. Should these ill advisd people force them into a War, we shall have all the Southern Indians against us—and among other Evills they will infect the Navigation of the Mississippi, which would greatly distress our people settled on the Waters of the Ohio. If Mr Sevier has not authority to reclaim these intruders, which by the by he should be Strictly enjoind to do—perhaps it would be Adviseable to Post a hundred Rangers under a discreet Officer of insinuating Manners and Address, at some Convenient place between the Inhabitants and Indians—to see that the people of Franklin behaved According to treaty.[1] When treaties are made and promises given without seeing them fullfilld—It naturally gives the Savages an unfavourable Opinion of us and our Government.

The Cherokee Nation have conceived a good Opinion of Major Drumgoole,[2] and I am confident he will not deceive them, but as there is little or no government in Franklin I question if he can alone withstand the Torrent. The Banditti will probably get him knockd in the head.

The Western Territory belonging to N Carolina is extensive and Valuable, and well disposed of, may help the U States to discharge their debts. It merits attention as well as the Country N W of Ohio—from the head Wate[r] of Holston to their lower Settlements on Cumberland is at least 300 miles; and I do not imagine that there are abo[ve] 3500 Gunmen in that great distance.

The General Convention exceeded my Expectation. I hope the plan will be adopted as it is. When the defecets appear they can be mended. When America is so happy as to have it established, Congress Will have as many Ambassadors, as Augustus Cæsar had, when he first came to the imperial throne—and if we are happy to have men of Abilities and patriotism at the head of Affairs for one twenty years—Few States in Europe will command equall Respect. I have the honour to be sr your most hule. Sr.

ADAM STEPHEN[3]

RC (DLC). Docketed by JM. Brackets enclose letters obscured by mounting.

[1] The Treaty of Hopewell of 1785, which established a boundary between Cherokee hunting grounds and the area open to white settlement, had been repeatedly violated by the frontier inhabitants of North Carolina. Although Secretary at War Knox favored sending troops to expel white intruders on Indian lands, Congress during the Confederation period took little action to enforce the treaty (Horsman, *Expansion and American Indian Policy*, pp. 24–30, 50–52).

[2] Alexander Dromgoole. See Gates to JM, 26 Nov. 1787 and n. 2.

[3] A veteran of the French and Indian War, Adam Stephen (ca. 1730–1791) rose to the rank of major general in the Continental army during the Revolution. He served with Washington at the battles of Trenton, Princeton, and the Brandywine, but was dismissed on charges of drunkenness following Washington's defeat at Germantown. Stephen nevertheless made a successful transition to civilian life, representing Berkeley County in the Virginia House of Delegates from 1780 to 1785. As one of that county's delegates to the convention of 1788 he supported the new Constitution (F. Vernon Aler, *Aler's History of Martinsburg and Berkeley County, West Virginia* [Hagerstown, Md., 1888], pp. 149–58; *VMHB*, XVI [1908], 136–37 n. 7; Swem and Williams, *Register*, p. 432; Grigsby, *Virginia Convention of 1788*, I, 300–302, 301 n. 227, 336–37; II, 368).

From Horatio Gates

TRAVELLERS REST[1] 26th: Novem. 1787.

DEAR SIR

I take the Liberty to request your attention to an application to be made by Major Drumgole to Congress in behalf of the Cherokee Nation. Perhaps the Major may not be considered as the Official Character from whom in due course this application should come, but, as he is clearly the person the Cherokees confide in, I think so insubstantial a Fo[r]m may be dispersed with.[2] Every thing I hear, every thing I know, convinces me, that unless we have as Speedily as possible a Firm, Efficient, Federal Constitution establishd, all must go to Ruin, and Anarchy and Misrule, blast every Hope that so Glorious a Revolution entitled us to Expect. I am dear Sir with The Greatest Respect Your most Obedient Humble Servant

HORATIO GATES.

RC (DLC). Docketed by JM.

[1] Gates's estate in Berkeley County, now Jefferson County, West Virginia.

[2] Maj. Alexander Dromgoole had served in the Virginia militia during the Revolution (Gwathmey, *Historical Register of Virginians*, p. 237). After the war he traded with the Cherokee at their village of Echota, on the Little Tennessee River, and in that capacity acted as an emissary to the tribe on the part of Virginia and Congress. Seeking permanent employment from Congress, Dromgoole traveled to New York in December 1787, carrying this letter and another from the Cherokee to the president of Congress, dated 8 Sept. 1787, requesting that Dromgoole be appointed superintendent for their tribe. The letter from the Cherokee was referred to the secretary at war, who reported on 25 Feb. 1788 that he could not make the appointment. In denying the request Secretary Knox cited the ordinance regulating Indian affairs, which specifically prohibited superintendents and their deputies from trading with the Indians (Dromgoole to Edmund Randolph, 15 Sept. and 18 Dec. 1787, *CVSP*, IV, 341, 368; *JCC*, XXXII, 353–54; XXXIV, 10 n., 14, 59–60). See also Virginia Delegates to Randolph, 11 Dec. 1787; Charles Pettit to William Irvine, 29 Dec. 1787, Burnett, *Letters*, VIII, 692.

Additional Memorandums on Ancient and Modern Confederacies

EDITORIAL NOTE

In his advocacy of the Constitution, JM had frequent recourse to his knowledge of history. He used his Notes on Ancient and Modern Confederacies (*PJM*, IX, 4–22) extensively in writing *The Federalist* and apparently sometime during the winter of 1787–1788 decided to supplement those notes with additional memorandums on the constitutions and governments of a number of countries. The structure of the Memorandums is far more random and less cohesive than the Notes on Ancient and Modern Confederacies. Rather than making a systematic study and analysis of confederacies as in the earlier document, JM appears to have jotted down for his own reference fragmentary notes on various, and not necessarily related, aspects of the political composition of unions, constitutional monarchies, and republics: "examples shewing defects of mere confederacies"; the seat of power and character of representation in various European countries; "Examples of hostile consequences of rival communities not united by one Government"; dangers of invasions, if disunited; and the nature of representation and sources of authority in Sparta, Carthage, and Rome.

The specific purpose JM had in mind in drawing up the Memorandums is uncertain. He used them in writing *The Federalist*, Nos. 14 and 63, particularly the latter, in which he explained and defended the proposed Senate (see Bourne, "The Authorship of *The Federalist*," in *Essays in Historical Criticism* [1967 reprint], pp. 142–44). The title he added indicates that JM also used the Memorandums during the ratifying convention in Richmond. The extent to which he referred to them during the debates of that convention cannot be precisely ascertained because the recorder, David Robertson, often noted that he could not hear JM and apparently did not always take down sections of speeches containing specific historical illustrations. But during the first part of the convention both Federalists and Antifederalists ranged the entire field of history in search of examples that would buttress their arguments. JM drew on his vast knowledge of past confederacies and governments to counter the Antifederalists' attacks on the augmented powers of the new central government and their warnings against the dangers of consolidation (see Bourne, "Madison's Studies in the History of Federal Government," in ibid., pp. 168–69). The Memorandums, and especially his Notes on Ancient and Modern Confederacies, must have informed his arguments and enabled him to assert convincingly the necessity of adopting the Constitution.

[ante 30 November 1787][1]

Memorandums for the Convention of Virginia in 1788 on the federal Constitution—[2]

[1]
Examples shewing defect of mere confederacies

Amphyctionic League. See

Lycian do.

Achæan do.

German do.—note Germany has more than 150 sovereignties

Swiss do.

Belgic do.

United Colonies—see

Albany project—see Albany papers.[3]

Articles of Confederation

Hanseatic do.

Union of Calmar. See p. 4.

Engd. & Scotland—formed in 1706. by 32 Commssrs. appd. for each Kgdom: they sat from April 18th. to middle of July—they were appd. by crwn by acts of two Parlts—restrained from treating of Religion

The Scotch had got the notion of a *fœderal* Union like Holld. & Switzd—Engd. opposed decidedly amg. other reasons, because if differt. Parlts—eithr. cd. break it when pleased.

Many had despaired of Union as Burnet himself.[4]

In Scotland opposed violently, particularly by those who were for a new revolution, as Union fatal bar to it—carried in Parliamt. by inconsidble. majority—The presbyterians bro't into opposition by persuasion that religious rights wd. be in danger—this argt. used most by those known to be most adverse to that Religion—especially Dutchess of Hamilton & son, who as next in succession hoped for Crown if separate Kingdom.

Genl. argts. vs Union in Scotd.

1. antiquity & dignity of Kingdom to be given up & sold.
2. departing from Independt. State & to be swallowd by Engd.
3. wd. be outvoted in all questions by Engds: superiority in Parlt.
4. Scotland no more be regded. by foregin [*sic*] Nations.
5. danger to the Kirk.

Finally, Scotch parlt. prevailed on to annex conditions which advisers tho't wd. never be agd. to & thus the plan be defeated.

Opposers of Union findg. majority vs them—endeavd. to raise storm out of doors—petitions, addresses & Remonstrances came up from all quarters, instigated by Minority—Even riots excited abt Parlt. House.

In Engld. alarm also for Religion, & act passed to secure it—H. of Commons unan[im]ous—Lords 50 & 20.

[2]
Sweeden

2 remarkable circumstances—1. *Citizens*—elect by votes the multiples of their property—some rich merchts. have several hundred votes. 2. Country gentlemen between nobles & peasants—have no votes in electing the latter order—are not represented nor eligible at all.

Constitn. Prior to 1772. alternately monarchical & aristocratic. Foreign powers had chief agency in producing the Revolution of 1772. King had at the time only 2 Companies of Guards. [Power of King reduced to its lowest ebb at time of Revolution—Sheridan][5] [the power of peasants predominant originally—hence alternate anarchy & tyranny. Id][6]—on death of Ch: XII. all prerogatives of Ex. abolished—hence, legisl: soon exercised Ex. & Judicl. power both—any 3 out of 4. houses competent to legislation.

The Revol: of 72. owing to unpopularity of Diet owing to Abuse of power from union of Ex & Judl. with Legisl:—factions venality & foreign influence—The *people* favored the enterprize of the King.[7]

Denmark.

The change in 1660. produced by the aversion to the Nobility—who as feudal lords had almost all power, the peasants being slaves to them—the two other orders being the Clergy—and Commons or represent[ative]s of Tuns. The *Clergy* were the great agents in the revolution & the *King* rather passive—Ld. Molesworth[8] saith, Denmark differed little from an aristocracy when it became an absolute monarchy.

France—

The 3d. estate was composed accordg. to Robertson[9] of Reps. of Cities &c within *King's demesne only*—and the tillers of the earth the greatest body in all countries nothing or represented by the Nobles.

Spain—

Peasants never represented in Cortes—quere—

Poland

153 Senators—about 200 Nuncios—

[3]
Examples of hostile consequences of rival communities
not united by one Government.

All the antient & modern Confederacies.
Saxon Heptarchy (a)—England and Scotland (b) G.B. & Ireland Engd: & Wales—
Antient Republics of Italy—before Roman Empire
    do—after dissolution of do.

(a) [anno 827][10] "Thus were united all the Kingdoms of the Heptarchy in on[e] Great State near four hundd. years after 1st arrival of Saxons in Britain [& 250 after establisht.];[11] and the fortunate arms &c. of Egbert [King of Wessex] at last effectd. what had been so often attempted in vain by so many princes" Hume Vol. 1. p. 59.[12]

"Kent, Northumberland and Mercia had successively aspired to general dominion" Id. p. 60.

(b) question in 1713 in H. of Lords for dissolving Union as not answering & ruinous to Scotland, carried in negative by 4 voices only. Deb. Peers II. 313—Burg. 3. 360.[13]

Harrington (pol. aphorisms 49. 50. 51—page 517.[)][14] pronounced the Union destructive to both Engd. & Scotland.

Heptarchy reduced to two, after some ages—Mercia & W. Saxons—& then one (Egbert)
See Kennet. vol. 1. p. 37.[15] for an apt & short quotation as to Heptarchy

England & Wales prior to union under Edwd. 1—& more fully under H. VIII

[4]

Union at Calmar in 1397 of Sweeden—Denmark—& Norway— formed by Margaret Queen of the 2 last & elected Queen also of the former.† She convoked the deputies of the 3. Stas. Genl. at Calmar—40 from each attended & formed the Union or Treaty—main argumt used by Queen—the contentions & wars when disunited.

Union consisted of 3 principal articles:

1. that the 3 Kgdoms which were each elective—sd. have same King to be elected by turns out of each, with an exception however in favor of offspring whom the 3 Ks might elect.

2. The King to divide his residence by turns amg. each, & to spend in each the revenues of each Crown

3. The most important that each sd. keep its particular Senate— Customs—privileges. Govrs. Magistrs—Genls. Bishops & even troops & garrisons to be taken from respective Kigdoms. so that King sd. never be allowed to employ subjects of one in another; being mutually regarded as strangers.

This Union, thus *imperfect*, increased the mutual enmity & laid founda- tion for fresh & more bitter animosities & miseries.

[5]

Danger, if disunited,—1 of foreign Invasion by sea—2. of Eastern inva- sion, on S. Sts.[16]

Examples of invasions of defenseless Coasts†[17]

Such more formidable than by land, because more sudden & easily sup- ported by supplies.[18]

Romans invade England

(a) Saxons invade England
    Danes—do
    Normans do

(b) Danes do France   Egyptians & Phonicians invade Greece
    English—Ireland   Greece do. Italy
    Europeans America   Carthaginians do. Italy & Spain
    do. East-Indies   Visigoths from Spain—Barbary
    do. Africa

(a) See Hume Hist: Vol. 1.
(b) do. vol. 1. p 69–70.

—Countries without navy conquerable in proportion to extent of Coast— England more frequently & thoroughly conquered than France or Spain.[19]

[6]

Sparta.

2 Kings— } the two jointly forming a Council with power of life & 28 Senators } death.

Senate—1 for life
    2 vacancies filled by popular election, out of
      Candidates 60 years old
    3 had right of convoking & proposing to
      Assemblies—as had Kings*
    4 decrees of no force till ratified by people—

Kings—were for life—in other respects like 2 Consuls Generals during war—presided in assemblies & public sacrifices in peace—cd. propose to Assemblies—dissolve them when convoked by Kings—but cd do nothing with consent of nation—the 2 Kings alway's jealous & on ill terms with each other were watched by *field deputies* in war.

People
Assemblies general & particular—former of all Citizens—latter of Citizens of Sparta alone had power of peace & war—treaties—great affairs—& election of Magistrates.

Ephori—chosen annually by people, and concurred in their behalf with Kings & Senate over both when they had authority—They had more authority than Tribunes—presided at elections of Magistrates demanded acct. of their administration—could imprison Kings—had the adm[in]istration of Money—superintended Religion—in fine directed every thing.

lands divided in 39,000 shares—

[7]

Carthage—

500 years, says Ari[s]totle[20] without any considerable sedition—or tyrant—
        3 different authorities—Suffetes—Senate—people
Suffetes—like Consuls—and annual does not appear by whom chosen—assembled Senate presiding—proposing & collecting the votes— presided also in Judgmts. of most important affairs—sometimes commanded armies—at going out were made Pretors

*Usurped this right—[21]

Senate—composed of persons qualified by age—experience—birth—riches—were the Council of State—& the Soul of all public deliberation no. not known—must have been great since the 100 drawn out of it. Senate treated of great affrs—read letters of generals—recd. plaints of provinces—gave auds: to ambassrs—and decided peace and War† When Senate unanimous decided finally—in case of division people decided—Whilst Senate retained its authority says Polybius[22]—wisdom & success marked every thing.

People—at first gave way to Senate—at length intoxicated by wealth & conquests, they assumed all power—then cabals & factions prevailed & were one of the principal causes of the ruin of the State.

Tribunal of 100—composed of 104. persons—were in place of Ephori at Sparta, according to Aristotle—& instituted to balance the Great & the Senate—with this differe[n]ce that here the Council was perpetual—Generals accounted to them.

Tribunal of 5—taken out of 100 above—duration of office unknown—like the Council of 10 at Venice—filled vacancies—even in Senate—had great power—but no salaries—became tyranical.

[8]
Rome

power of Senate (exclusive of people). 1. care of Religion. 2. to regulate the provinces. 3.* over public treasury and expences of Govt. with appt. of stipends to Generals—no. of troops, & provisions & cloathing for armies—4** appd with such instructions—& recd. ambassrs—& gave such answrs as they thought fit. 5 decreed thanksgivings—& conferred honor of triumphs 6 inquire into crimes & treasons at Rome & in Italy—& decide disputes among dependent cities 7 interpreting dispensing with, & even abrogating laws—8 arm Consuls with absolute power—darent operam &c—9. prorogue & postpone assemblies of people—pardon & reward—declared any one enemy—Middleton on R. Sen.[23]

power of Senate—to propose to people who cd. not originate laws—this taken away by the Tribunes—& Senate not only obliged to allow assemblies at all times to be called, but to agree before hand to whatever acts of the people—Idem.

power of Senate unlimited almost at first—except legisl: power—choice of Magtres. and peace & war—all power in Senate—& a second

---

*Gracchiis transferred their criml. jurisdiction to equestrian order[24]
**ambassors. taken from their own body—Code d Humanitè[25]

Senatus consultum necessary—to ratify, act of people in consequence of proposition from Senate—Cod. d'Hum.

Senate consisted originally of 100—usually abt. 300—finally by Jul. Cæsar 1000—not agreed how appd. (whether by Consuls & Censors—or people &)²⁶—on extraordy. occasions by Dictator—censors—on ordinary (Middleton)—by people out of annual magistrates till these became a regular supply of course—Middleton

Censors could expel—but other Censors reinstate—& Senators had an appeal from them to people—Id.

Vertot²⁷ thinks people had nothing to do in appointg Senators—power being first in Kings—then Consuls—then Censors—& on extra. occasions in Dictator—age required but not ascertained by antiquaries—so estate between £6 & 7000 Stng. Senate assembled by Kings—Consuls—Dicta[t]ors—Tribunes.

[9]

power of Consuls 1. Heads of Repub. 2. command of armies—levy troops in consequence of author[it]y from Commitia—3. authy over Italy & provs—who cd. appeal to their tribunal—and could cite subjects to Rome & punish with death 4. convene Senate propose business—count votes— & draw up decrees—nor cd. any resol. pass if *one* of the Consuls *opposed*—5 addressed letters to Kings &c—Gave audience to Ambasrs— introdd: them to Senate—& carried into execution decrees touchg all these matters—6 convoked Commitia—presided therein 7. applied money.—Had all the power of the Kings—Must be 42 years

Tribunes—uncertain whether at first—2—3—or 5. estabd. in 260. increased to 10. in 297. confind to City & one mile. At first had no power but *to defend* people, their persons being sacred for that purpose—but soon arrogated right to call Senate & assembly of people—& propose to them.

They were—(1). protectors of people—under wch. title they interfered in all affairs—released malefactors—& imprisoned principal magistrates of Repub: as Consuls & after a time exerted their authority over dictators & censors—(2) had the *veto*, to stop the functions of all other Magistrs. & to negative all laws & decrees of Senate—to dissolve Comitia so that Repub: often in anarchy & once 5 years without other Magistrs: than Tribunes—by this veto particularly as opposed to levies of men by order of Senate, they extorted every thing they wanted. (3). sacredness of persons of wch. they availed themselves much—pretending that it was violated in the persons of their officers—(4) to convoke Senate—&

people—at first sat at door of Senate waiting to be informed of result of its deliberations† and had no right to assemble people—but Junius Brutus caught at incautious acknowledgt. of consul—got comit: tribut. estabd. in place of Centuries where votes unequal—& of curiata where as in Centuries, auspices necessary—& in both concurrence of Senate to the calling them & coming to Resolns† to these They soon brought trial of principal Citizens by appeal—& all sorts of affairs—got plebiscite made laws by Coma. trib: which they ma[na]ged & directed as they pleased†—(5) disposed of Govts. & command of armies—finances—& lands of the public—Sylla as dictator humbled the Tribunes but they were restored & Jul: Cæsar caused himself to be perpetual Tribune. The shadow continued down to Constantine the Great.
†

It appears that it was the design of Clodius to extend the suffrage to all the freedmen in the several tribes of the City, that the Tribunes might by corruption the more easily foment seditions.[28] Cicero's Milo with the note[29]

Above 30,000. voters in some Counties of Engd. 3,000. only in all Scotland—Dalrymple F.P.[30]

Writ of Error lies from B.R.[31] in Ireld. to B.R. in Engd—Blackst.[32]
   do. do.   from Wales to B.R. Jenkins' Cent:[33] & 1 W & M. c. 27.[34]
               as to Scotland into Parliament—see 6. Ann. c. 26. sect. 12.[35]

---

difficulty of drawing line between laws apparent in Act of Union between Engd. & Scotland—1. Art: 18.[36] The laws concerning regulation of trade, Customs &c. see Abridgt. by Cay—Vol. 2. 384. under "Scotland."[37] For line between Courts—see art: 19.[38]

Roman Empire more than 2000 M. from N-to-S. more than 3000 from W-to-E. Gibbon[39]
population of do. abt. 120 Million including slaves who abt. ½. this more than in Europe. Id.

Spain	700 by 500 Miles	Engd.	360 by 300
France	600 by 500	Scotd.	300 by 150
Italy—	600 by 400	Denmark	240 by 180
Germany	600 by 500	Norway	1000 by 900.
Poland	700 by 680		
Sweeden	800 by 500		

Ms, Tr (DLC). Ms in JM's hand. Tr in William C. Rives's hand and entitled by him "Additional Memoranda." In the left margin of the first page Rives wrote, "In this copy, there are a few transpositions here & there, of the contents of the original manuscript, in order to make the mutual dependance & connections of the parts more apparent to the reader." The order of the pages printed here follows the order in the Ms except for the notes on the verso of the first, half-size page. They relate to various sections of the following pages; JM apparently wrote them down as afterthoughts. Consequently, the editors have placed these notes at the end of the document.

The Ms pages were numbered (1–4) and lettered (A–I) in pencil, most probably by Rives. By transposing segments of the notes, Rives imposed a sequence which JM may not have intended. The document was printed in Madison, *Letters* (Cong. ed.), I, 389–98; here also the notes were rearranged, although not in accordance with the Rives Tr. The editors have found no reason to believe that JM conceived of the notes as a coherent whole. He probably added to the notes at different times, as a series of memorandums, and left portions of pages blank (perhaps leaving room for later additions). The editors have placed page numbers within brackets to indicate the beginning of each Ms page. The bracketed page numbers, which do not appear in the Ms, are meant to aid in distinguishing the various topics of these notes.

At various places throughout the Ms, JM made "x" marks as if he intended to add footnotes to the text, which in most instances he failed to do. There is no apparent correlation among these marks. The editors have inserted a dagger (†) where JM placed an "x," except for the few times when JM made a corresponding marginal note.

[1] The dating of the Ms is an approximation based on the first use JM apparently made of it: *The Federalist* No. 14, 30 Nov. 1787.

[2] This title, which appears on the front of the first, half-size leaf, was written by JM at some later time.

[3] Several of Benjamin Franklin's writings pertaining to the Albany Congress of 1754, and to the "Plan of Union" which it endorsed, were published in his *Political, Miscellaneous, and Philosophical Pieces* (London, 1779), under the heading "Albany Papers" (pp. 85–143).

[4] Gilbert Burnet, *Bishop Burnet's History of His Own Time* . . . , ed. Thomas Burnet (3d ed.; 4 vols.; London, 1766).

[5] Charles Francis Sheridan, *A History of the late Revolution in Sweden* . . . (2d ed.; London, 1783).

[6] Both sets of brackets are JM's.

[7] JM wrote this paragraph along the left margin.

[8] Robert Molesworth, *An Account of Denmark as It was in the Year 1692* . . . (London, 1694).

[9] William Robertson, *The History of the Reign of the Emperor Charles V* . . . (3d ed.; 4 vols.; London, 1777).

[10] JM's brackets. JM interlined the date above the beginning of the quotation, but failed to indicate a point of insertion. The editors have interpolated it here.

[11] This and the following set of brackets are JM's. JM interlined "[& 250 after establisht.]" above "Britain" but did not indicate a point of insertion. The editors have interpolated it here.

[12] David Hume, *The History of England, from the Invasion of Julius Caesar to the Revolution in 1688* (new ed.; 8 vols.; London, 1782).

[13] James Burgh, *Political Disquisitions: or, An Enquiry into public Errors, Defects, and Abuses* . . . (3 vols.; London, 1774–75). Burgh (III, 360) cited "Deb. Peers" (*The History and Proceedings of the House of Lords, from the Restoration in 1660, to the Present Time* . . . [8 vols.; London, 1742–43]), incorrectly placing the debate on dissolution at page 313 of volume II, instead of in its proper location at page 398.

[14] James Harrington, *The Oceana and Other Works of James Harrington* (4th ed.; London, 1771). "Political Aphorisms" 49, 50, and 51 are on page 485 of this edition.

[15] White Kennett, *A Complete History of England* . . . *to the Death of His Late Majesty King William III* . . . (2d ed.; 3 vols.; London, 1719).

[16]From "Danger" to here appears to have been interlined by JM above the title of the page, "Examples of invasions of defenseless Coasts." JM originally headed the page, "Examples of the Representative principle in Antiquity," which he later crossed through.

[17]JM placed an "x" here, perhaps to indicate that he was inserting "Danger . . . on S. Sts."

[18]This phrase appears as a marginal note in the Ms.

[19]JM wrote "Countries . . . or Spain" at the bottom of the page, leaving the middle of the page blank. The succeeding four Ms pages of the document are blank.

[20]Aristotle, *A Treatise on Government*, trans. William Ellis (London, 1776).

[21]JM's note appears near the bottom of the page in the middle of the section on "Ephori." He may have written part of his notes about the Ephori at a later time.

[22]*The General History of Polybius*, trans. James Hampton (3d ed.; 4 vols.; London, 1772–73).

[23]Conyers Middleton, *A Treatise on the Roman Senate . . .*, in *The Miscellaneous Works of . . . Conyers Middleton D.D.* (2d ed.; 5 vols.; London, 1755), IV, 177–303.

[24]JM wrote this note in the left margin.

[25]JM wrote this note in the left margin. Fortuné Barthélemy de Felice, ed., *Code de l'Humanité, ou la Législation universelle, naturelle, civile et politique . . .* (13 vols.; Yverdon, 1778).

[26]This parenthetical phrase was interlined by JM above the preceding four words. Since JM failed to indicate a point of insertion, the editors have interpolated it here.

[27]René Aubert de Vertot, *The History of the Revolutions That happened in the Government of the Roman Republic*, trans. John Ozell (6th ed.; 2 vols.; London, 1770).

[28]This note and the remainder of the memorandum were written on the verso of the first, half-size leaf.

[29]JM was referring to William Guthrie's translation and notes for the *Milo (The Orations of Marcus Tullius Cicero . . .*, trans. and ed. William Guthrie [4th ed. rev.; 3 vols.; London, 1778], I, 114–15 n.).

[30]John Dalrymple, *An Essay towards a general history of Feudal Property in Great Britain . . .* (4th ed.; London, 1759).

[31]"Bancus Regis"—"the king's bench," which was the "supreme tribunal of the king after parliament" (*Black's Law Dictionary* [4th ed. rev.], p. 183).

[32]William Blackstone, *Commentaries on the Laws of England* (4th ed.; 4 vols.; London, 1770).

[33]David Jenkins, *Eight Centuries of Reports: or, eight hundred cases solemnly adjudged in the Exchequer-Chamber, or, upon writs of error*, trans. Theodore Barlow (3d ed.; London, 1771).

[34]"An Act for taking away the Court holden before the President and Council of the Marches of *Wales*," *The Statutes at Large* (1770 ed.), III, 435.

[35]"An Act for settling and establishing a Court of *Exchequer* in the North Part of *Great Britain* called *Scotland*," ibid. (1769 ed.), IV, 319.

[36]5 Ann., chap. 8, "An Act for an Union of the two Kingdoms of *England* and *Scotland*," ibid., IV, 227–28.

[37]John Cay, *An Abridgement of the publick statutes in Force and of general Use from Magna Charta . . .* (2d ed.; 2 vols.; London, 1762).

[38]"An Act for an Union . . . ," *The Statutes at Large*, IV, 228.

[39]Edward Gibbon, *The History of the Decline and Fall of the Roman Empire* (6 vols.; London, 1776–88).

To George Washington

N. YORK Novr. 20. [30] 1787.[1]

DEAR SIR

My last inclosed the seven first numbers of the paper of which I gave you some account. I now add the seven following numbers, which close the first branch of the subject, the importance of the Union. The succeeding papers shall be forwarded from time to time as they come out.

The latest authentic information from Europe, places the Dutch in a wretched situation. The patriots will probably depend in the event on external politics for the degree of security and power that may be left them. The Turks & Russians have begun a war in that quarter. And a general one is not improbable.

I have heard nothing of consequence lately concerning the progress of the New Constitution. The Pennsylvania Convention has probably by this time come to a decision; but it is not known here.

Not more than two or three States are yet convened. The prospect of a quorum during the winter continues precarious. With every sentiment of respect & attachment I remain Dear Sir Yr. Affect. humble servt.

Js. MADISON JR

RC (DLC: Washington Papers); Tr (DLC). RC docketed by Washington. Enclosures not found.

[1] Although JM wrote "Novr. 20," this is clearly a mistake, and several circumstances point to 30 Nov. as the correct date of the letter. JM enclosed with this letter copies of *The Federalist*, Nos. 8–14, but the last of these was not printed until 30 Nov. In the letter he says that the Pennsylvania convention had "probably by this time come to a decision," but that convention did not begin until 21 Nov. On 7 Dec. Washington acknowledged JM's letters of 28 Oct. and 18 Nov., but not the one dated 20 Nov., which he should have received by that time.

The Federalist Number 14

[30 November 1787]

We have seen the necessity of the union as our bulwark against foreign danger, as the conservator of peace among ourselves, as the guardian of our commerce and other common interests, as the only substitute for those military establishments which have subverted the liberties of the old world, and as the proper antidote for the diseases of faction, which have proved fatal to other popular governments, and of which alarming symptoms have been betrayed by our own. All that remains, within this branch of our enquiries, is to take notice of an objection, that may be drawn from the great extent of country which the union embraces. A few observations on this subject will be the more proper, as it is perceived that the adversaries of the new constitution are availing themselves of a prevailing prejudice, with regard to the practicable sphere of republican administration, in order to supply by imaginary difficulties, the want of those solid objections, which they endeavour in vain to find.[1]

The error which limits republican government to a narrow district, has been unfolded and refuted in preceding papers. I remark here only, that it seems to owe its rise and prevalence chiefly to the confounding of a republic with a democracy: And applying to the former reasonings drawn from the nature of the latter. The true distinction between these forms was also adverted to on a former occasion. It is, that in a democracy, the people meet and exercise the government in person; in a republic they assemble and administer it by their representatives and agents. A democracy consequently must be confined to a small spot. A republic may be extended over a large region.

To this accidental source of the error may be added, the artifice of some celebrated authors, whose writings have had a great share in forming the modern standard of political opinions. Being subjects either of an absolute, or limited monarchy, they have endeavoured to heighten the advantages or palliate the evils of those forms; by placing in comparison with them, the vices and defects of the republican, and by citing as specimens of the latter, the turbulent democracies of ancient Greece, and modern Italy. Under the confusion of names, it has been an easy task to transfer to a republic, observations applicable to a democracy only, and among others, the observation that it can never be established but among a small number of people, living within a small compass of territory.

Such a fallacy may have been the less perceived, as most of the popular governments of antiquity were of the democratic species; and even in modern Europe, to which we owe the great principle of representation, no example is seen of a government wholly popular, and founded at the same time wholly on that principle. If Europe has the merit of discovering this great mechanical power in government, by the simple agency of which, the will of the largest political body may be concentred, and its force directed to any object, which the public good requires: America can claim the merit of making the discovery the basis of unmixed and extensive republics. It is only to be lamented, that any of her citizens should wish to deprive her of the additional merit of displaying its full efficacy in the establishment of the comprehensive system now under her consideration.

As the natural limit of a democracy is that distance from the central point, which will just permit the most remote citizens to assemble as often as their public functions demand; and will include no greater number than can join in those functions; so the natural limit of a republic is that distance from the centre, which will barely allow the representatives of the people to meet as often as may be necessary for the administration of public affairs. Can it be said, that the limits of the United States exceed this distance? It will not be said by those who recollect that the Atlantic coast is the longest side of the union; that during the term of thirteen years, the representatives of the states have been almost continually assembled; and that the members from the most distant states are not chargeable with greater intermissions of attendance, than those from the states in the neighbourhood of Congress.

That we may form a juster estimate with regard to this interesting subject, let us resort to the actual dimensions of the union. The limits, as fixed by the treaty of peace are on the East the Atlantic, on the South the latitude of thirty one degrees, on the West the Mississippi, and on the North an irregular line running in some instances beyond the forty-fifth degree, in others falling as low as the forty-second. The Southern shore of lake Erie lies below that latitude. Computing the distance between the thirty-first and forty-fifth degrees, it amounts to nine hundred and seventy three common miles; computing it from thirty one to forty two degrees to seven hundred, sixty four miles and an half. Taking the mean for the distance, the amount will be eight hundred, sixty eight miles and three fourths. The mean distance from the Atlantic to the Mississippi, does not probably exceed seven hundred and fifty miles. On a comparison of this extent, with that of several countries in Europe, the practicability of rendering our system commensurate to it, appears to be demonstrable. It is not a great deal larger than Germany, where a diet, representing the whole empire is continually assembled; or than Poland before the late dismemberment, where another national diet was the depositary of the supreme power. Passing by France and Spain, we find that in Great Britain, inferior as it may be in size, the representatives of the Northern extremity of the island, have as far to travel to the national council, as will be required of those of the most remote parts of the union.[2]

Favourable as this view of the subject may be, some observations remain which will place it in a light still more satisfactory.

In the first place it is to be remembered, that the general government is not to be charged with the whole power of making and administering laws. Its jurisdiction is limited to certain enumerated objects, which concern all the members of the republic, but which are not to be attained by the separate provisions of any. The subordinate governments which can extend their care to all those other objects, which can be separately provided for, will retain their due authority and activity. Were it proposed by the plan of the convention to abolish the governments of the particular states, its adversaries would have some ground for their objection, though it would not be difficult to show that if they were abolished, the general government would be compelled by the principle of self preservation, to reinstate them in their proper jurisdiction.

A second observation to be made is, that the immediate object of the federal constitution is to secure the union of the Thirteen primitive States, which we know to be practicable; and to add to them such other states, as may arise in their own bosoms, or in their neighbourhoods, which we cannot doubt to be equally practicable. The arrangements that may be necessary for those angles and fractions of our territory, which lie on our north-western frontier, must be left to those whom further discoveries and experience will render more equal to the task.

Let it be remarked in the third place, that the intercourse throughout the union will be daily facilitated by new improvements. Roads will every where be shortened, and kept in better order; accommodations for travellers will be multiplied and meliorated; an interior navigation on our eastern side will be opened throughout, or nearly throughout the whole extent of the Thirteen States. The communication between the Western and Atlantic districts, and between different parts of each, will be rendered more and more easy by those numerous canals with which the beneficence of nature has intersected our country, and which art finds it so little difficult to connect and complete.

A fourth and still more important consideration is, that as almost every state will on one side or other be a frontier, and will thus find in a regard to its safety, an inducement to make some sacrifices for the sake of the general protection; so the states which lie at the greatest distance from the heart of the union, and which of course may partake least of the ordinary circulation of its benefits, will be at the same time immediately contiguous to foreign nations, and will consequently stand on particular occasions, in greatest need of its strength and resources. It may be inconvenient for Georgia or the states forming our Western or North-Eastern borders, to send their representatives to the seat of government, but they would find it more so to struggle alone against an invading enemy, or even to support alone the whole expence of those precautions, which may be dictated by the neighbourhood of continual danger. If they should derive less benefit therefore from the union in some respects, than the less distant states, they will derive greater benefit from it in other respects, and thus the proper equilibrium will be maintained throughout.

I submit to you my fellow citizens, these considerations, in full confidence that the good sense which has so often marked your decisions, will allow them their due weight and effect; and that you will never suffer difficulties, however formidable in appearance or however fashionable the error on which they may be founded, to drive you into the gloomy and perilous scenes into which the advocates for disunion would conduct you. Hearken not to the unnatural voice which tells you that the people of America, knit together as they are by so many cords of affection, can no longer live together as members of the same family; can no longer continue the mutual guardians of their mutual happiness; can no longer be fellow citizens of one great respectable and flourishing empire. Hearken not to the voice which petulantly tells you that the form of government recommended for your adoption is a novelty in the political world; that it has never yet had a place in the theories of the wildest projectors; that it rashly attempts what it is impossible to accomplish. No my countrymen, shut your ears against this unhallowed language. Shut your hearts against the poison which it conveys; the kindred blood which flows in the veins of American citizens, the mingled blood which they have shed in defence of their sacred rights, consecrate their union, and excite horror at the idea of their becoming aliens, rivals, enemies. And if novelties are to be shunned, believe me the most alarming of all novelties, the most wild of all projects, the most rash of all attempts, is that of rending us in pieces, in order to preserve our liberties and promote our happiness. But why is the experiment of an extended republic to be rejected merely because it may comprise what is new? Is it not the glory of the people of America, that whilst they have paid a decent regard to the opinions of former times and other nations, they have not suffered a blind veneration for antiquity, for custom, or for names, to overrule the suggestions of their own good sense, the knowledge of their own situation, and the lessons of their own experience? To this manly spirit, posterity will be indebted for the possession, and the world for the example of the numerous innovations displayed on the American theatre, in favour of private rights and public happiness. Had no important step been taken by the leaders of the revolution for which a precedent could not be discovered, no government established of which an exact model did not present itself, the people of the United States might, at this moment, have been numbered among the melancholy victims of misguided councils, must at best have been labouring under the weight of some of those forms which have crushed the liberties of the rest of mankind. Happily for America, happily we trust for the whole human race, they pursued a new and more noble course. They accomplished a revolution which has no parallel in the annals of human society: They reared the fabrics of governments which have no model on the face of the globe. They formed the design of a great confederacy, which it is incumbent on their successors to improve and perpetuate. If their works betray imperfections, we wonder at the fewness of them. If they erred most in the structure of the union, this was the work most difficult to be executed, this is the work which has been new modelled by the act of your convention, and it is that act on which you are now to deliberate and to decide.

PUBLIUS.

McLean, I, 79–86.

[1] A common theme in Antifederalist arguments against the Constitution was that a republican government must be confined to a small geographical area and operate over a homogeneous population (Kenyon, *The Antifederalist*, pp. xxxix–xlviii). Perhaps the fullest development of this theme is to be found in the first letter of "Brutus," which appeared in the *N.Y. Journal, and Weekly Register* of 18 Oct. 1787. JM evidently referred to this essay in his letter to Randolph of 21 Oct. 1787.

[2] See JM's Additional Memorandums on Ancient and Modern Confederacies, ante 30 Nov. 1787, in which he listed the geographic dimensions of these European countries.

To Edmund Randolph

New York Decr. 2d. 1787.

My dear friend

The period since my last has been so unfruitful of occurrences that I have not thought it worth while to trouble you with a letter and I do it now more to prevent too long a chasm, than for the sake of any interesting communication. Our public letter gave you the latest authentic information from Europe. A general war seems not improbable; a war between the Turks & Russians has actually commenced. The enterprising movements of the Prussian troops have disconcerted the patriotic party & their supporters, and it seems as if the Stadtholder would gain a compleat triumph. What effect this may have on the Government of that Country I cannot undertake to foretell. I have never been inclined to think that compleat success to the views of either party would be favorable to the people. If the Stadtholdership were abolished, the Government unless further changes concurred, would be a simple aristocracy. Should the patriots as they call themselves be excluded from the Govt. the Stadtholder would be an absolute Monarch. Whilst both continue they check each other, which is absolutely necessary as the people have no check on either. The consequence of the people arises from the competitions of the two for their favor. In general the lower order have been partizans of the Stadtholder. They are so it is said in the present contest.

A British packet arrived here a few days ago but does not bring later information than the last one from France. She has had a long voyage and called in at Halifax, a circumstance which some connect with the probability of a war.

We have not more than two or three States as yet attending. It is altogether conjectural when the deficiency of a quorum will be made up.

No recent indications of the views of the States as to the Constitution have come to my knowledge. The elections in Connecticut are over and as

far as the returns are known, a large majority are friendly to it. Docr.
Johnson says, it will be pretty certainly adopted; but there will be opposition. The power of taxing any thing but imports appears to be the most
popular topic among the adversaries. The Convention of Pennsylvania is
sitting. The result there will not reach you first through my hands. The
divisions on preparatory questions, as they are published in the Newspapers, shew that the party in favor of the Constitution have 44 or 45. vs. 22
or 24. or thereabouts.[1]

The inclosed paper contains two numbers of the Federalist. This paper
was begun about three weeks ago, and proposes to go through the subject.
I have not been able to collect all the numbers, since my return from
Philada. or I would have sent them to you. I have been the less anxious as I
understand the Printer means to make a pamphlet of them, when I can
give them to you in a more convenient form. You will probably discover
marks of different *pens*. I *am not at liberty* to *give you any* other *key* than that
I *am in myself for a few numbers* & that *one besides myself* was a *member* of *the
convention*. I wish you all happiness and remain my dear Sir Yr. affecte.
friend

Js. Madison Jr.

RC (DLC). Addressed, franked, and marked "*private*" by JM. Italicized words are those
encoded by JM using the code Randolph sent him 22 Nov. 1782. Many years later JM
decoded this letter interlinearly. Enclosures not found.

[1] JM probably referred to the vote of 26 Nov. on Thomas McKean's motion that the
convention "now proceed to consider the proposed constitution by articles." A substitute
motion offered by Antifederalist Robert Whitehill for going into a Committee of the Whole
was defeated (McMaster and Stone, *Pennsylvania and the Federal Constitution*, I, 234–37).

From Archibald Stuart

Richmond Decr. 2d. 1787

Dr Sir

I find by yrs. of the 18th. Novr.[1] that one of my letters prior in date to
the One of the 2d. Novr. has miscaried.[2] This Gives me some uneasiness
on account of its contents which possibly may transpire. An Absence of
ten days prevented my writing last week. The legislature have taken up
the subject of British debts and after four days debate on the subject
passed a Vote for the payment of them by a Majority of thirty.[3] In this
business P H: took a Very Active part. His anxiety was too great to be
concealed & had such an effect upon his whole frame as to make him sweat
at every pore & appear to a greater disadvantage—in short when the
question was decided disappointment was painted in strikeing colours in

the Countenances of the Minority. A proposition for installing the Debts similar to the One made in 84 was also rejected by the same Majority.[4]

P: H: Brought forward some time ago resolutions prohibiting the farther importation of All distilled Spirits & Carried the Same by a very large majority. We have passed An Act for the Receipt of Tobo. in the taxes of the present yr. at 30/ P[er] H for the first quality &c notwithstanding there is a loss of £2:700 in what is already sold of the Last years collection.

We counted the money in the Treasury yesterday & found there £30.136:6.5. & Tobo. to the Amount of £9.692:7:4.½. Of this we have appropriated six thousand pounds Cash & the Whole of the Tobo. to the purchase of Government securities to be laid out under the Direction of the Executive. It is true the Bill for this purpose is not actually passed but it is ordered to be read the third time & its friends are as 3 to 1.[5]

It is my Opinion from conversing with the Members that we shall comply with the Requisitions of Congress so far as to pass an Act on the subject but I believe the funds will be doubtfull, it being the General wish to possess ourselves of a large proportion of the Publick securities before an Appreciation takes place under the New Government.[6]

A Resolution was brought forward the day before yesterday for paying the members to Convention in June their Wages & securing to them Certain priviledges &c seconded by P: H: & Mason which after making Provision for the purposes aforesaid goes farther & sais that should the Convention think proper to propose Amendments to the Constitution this state will make provision for carrying the same into effect & that Money shall be advanced for the Support of Deputies to the Neighbouring States &c. This Many of us opposed as improper & proposed that the same provision should be made in General terms which should not discover the sense of the house on the Subject but after a Long Debate the point was carried against us by a Majority of sixteen.[7] In the Course of the Debate P: Hy: Observed that if this Idea was not held forth our southern neighbours might be driven to despair seeing no door open to safety should they disapprove the new Constitution. Mason on the subject was less candid than ever I knew him to be. From the above mentioned Vote there appears to be a Majority vs the Govt. as it now Stands & I fear since they have discovered their Strength they will adopt other Measures tending to its prejudice. From this circumstance I am happy to find Most of the States will have decided on the Question before Virginia for I now have my doubts whether She would afford them as usual a good Example. Installments are yet in Statu quo. The form of the Courts is despaired of except some amendments to the County Court Bill.

Yesterday a Boat with sixteen men was brought down the Canall from

West Ham, to its termination which is within one mile & an half of Richmond.

Mathews & Selden are removed from Council & Wm Heth & Jos. Egglestone reign in their stead.

I do not Wish you to forget that yr friends are all anxious that you should come into the Convention.

Colo. T Mathews will Write to you his intentions of having you elected for the Borough of Norfolk should you think it proper.[8] I am Dr Sir yr most obt H Servant

ARCHD STUART

RC (DLC). Docketed by JM.

[1] Letter not found.

[2] The only extant letter from Stuart to JM before 2 Nov. 1787 is that of 21 Oct. 1787. Stuart evidently referred to another letter, however, for JM acknowledged receipt of the 21 Oct. letter on 30 Oct. JM eventually received the letter Stuart believed had miscarried (JM to Stuart, 14 Dec. 1787).

[3] At a later time, JM placed an asterisk here and wrote the following note in the left margin: "*A letter from another Gentleman dated 2 days later mentions that notwithstanding this majority of 30 for paying the debts, a Resolution had just passed by a majority of 50 on the other side suspending payment till G.B. sd. first comply with the Treaty." The letter from "another Gentleman," evidently dated 4 Dec. 1787, has not been found. The resolution of 17 Nov. 1787 calling for repeal of all acts contrary to the peace treaty, to take effect when all the other states passed similar repealing acts, had passed by a vote of 72 to 42. When the bill pursuant to this resolution was debated on 3 Dec., however, an amendment was offered suspending the act of repeal until Great Britain evacuated the western posts and compensated Virginians for the loss of slaves taken during the war. This amendment was adopted by a vote of 80 to 31 (*JHDV*, Oct. 1787, pp. 51–52, 79–80; Hening, *Statutes*, XII, 528). Monroe attributed this sudden reversal to George Nicholas, who "chang'd his former ground in every instance" under the sway of Henry's arguments (Monroe to JM, 6 Dec. 1787).

[4] JM had introduced a plan at the May 1784 session for the installment of debts owed to British citizens. This plan was defeated, as was JM's subsequent bill for that purpose in the fall of 1785 (*PJM*, VIII, 58–63, 229–31, 445–50; Evans, "Private Indebtedness and the Revolution in Virginia, 1776 to 1796," *WMQ*, 3d ser., XXVIII [1971], 363–65). The House journal does not record any vote on a plan to install British debts in 1787. The proposal most likely came up while the British debt bill was under consideration in the Committee of the Whole on 30 Nov. and 1 Dec. (*JHDV*, Oct. 1787, pp. 77, 78–79).

[5] The "Bill for this purpose" was that "providing a sinking fund for the gradual redemption of the public debt." A third reading of the bill was ordered on 1 Dec. and it became law on 14 Dec. (ibid., p. 78; Hening, *Statutes*, XII, 452–54). George Mason seems to have been a principal sponsor of the sinking fund bill. "I shall use my best Endeavours," he wrote Washington on 27 Nov. 1787, "to prevent the Rect. of public Securities of any kind in Taxes (as the only effectual Means of digging up Speculation by the Roots) and appropriating a good Fund for purchasing them up at the Market Price" (Rutland, *Papers of George Mason*, III, 1021).

[6] See Jones to JM, 7 June 1787 and n. 2. Stuart meant that much of the revenue previously applied to the Continental treasury would be diverted to the sinking fund for the purpose of buying public securities. The revenue act of 1786 had appropriated half the slave tax, most of the land tax, and all specie collected from "An act imposing new taxes" to meet the requisition of Congress (Hening, *Statutes*, XII, 324–25). The revenue act of 1787, however, omitted from the Continental fund the half tax on slaves and the land tax (except for $150,000). This

act appropriated the entire slave tax to the payment of interest on military certificates. That part of the land tax formerly appropriated to Congress now became "a fund for the support of civil government" (ibid., XII, 425–28). Any surplus revenue or unappropriated money in the public treasury, instead of being sent to the Continental treasury, was henceforth assigned to the sinking fund. The duty of six shillings per hogshead on tobacco exported, formerly levied to meet the special requisition of Congress of 21 Oct. 1786, was also to be applied "in aid of the sinking fund" (ibid., XII, 452–54).

⁷The resolutions of 25 Oct. 1787 calling for a convention failed to provide for the pay of delegates. When the House sought to remedy this oversight on 30 Nov., opponents of the Constitution seized the opportunity for registering their dissent by pushing through resolutions providing for the pay of deputies to another federal convention (if one were called) and providing for the expenses in case the Virginia convention "should deem it necessary to hold any communications with any of the sister states or the conventions thereof" (*JHDV*, Oct. 1787, pp. 15, 77; Hening, *Statutes*, XII, 462–63).

⁸If Thomas Mathews wrote to JM, his letter has not been found. Mathews had represented Norfolk borough in the House of Delegates since 1781 and was its delegate to the convention of 1788 (Swem and Williams, *Register*, p. 406).

From James Monroe

RICHMOND Decr. 6th. 1787.

DEAR SIR

I have had hopes of being able to give you something from the proceedings of the Assembly of an interesting nature which might also be agreeable. But perhaps yr. wishes in this respect may not even yet be gratified. The resolutions respecting the Constitution you have long since receiv'd. In those you find no provision for the pay or priviledges of the members of the Convention. These especially the former were thought the subject matter for an act & were seperated from them. A few days since resolutions were brought in by Mr. Hopkins¹ & supported by Messrs. Henry & Mason for this purpose & providing funds for defraying the expence of deputies to attend other convention or Conventions of the States, if this Convention shod. think the measure expedient, wh. were adopted by the house by a majority of abt. 15. The bill is not yet brought in. The B. debt business hath also been another subject of curious managment. Resolutions of absolute repeal pass'd the committee first by a great majority. Without any apparent necessity Messrs. Mason & Nicholas who advocated them agreed to a clause of suspension untill the other states shod. pass similar laws of repeal. When the bill was under discussion yesterday Nicholas who had been most active & zealous in the business chang'd his former ground in every instance and acceded to the proposition of Mr. Henry wh. suspended its effect untill G.B. shall have complied. Owning himself convinc'd by the arguments that had been us'd, this Gentn. appears to have abandon'd the prospect of instalments wh. he brought forward early in the session. That of district or circuit courts seems also to be despair'd of by those who are desirous of amending this branch of our system. A bill of Mr. Henry's for prohibiting the importation of foreign distill'd spirits & other purposes, is among the orders of the day & will most probably be thrown out. It appears difficult to organize the affrs. of this & perhaps of any one State in a tolerable manner & it is doubtful, if it were done whether it cod. be executed or whether the people wod. not have it repeal'd the next Assembly. The ct. of chy. break up tomorrow. The chancelor[2] is yet present but in a low state of health. I doubt whether I shall stay untill the end of the session, Mrs. M. & her sister are with me. What is new with you. I think the cloud wh. hath hung over us for sometime past is not yet dispell'd or likely soon to be. Sincerely I am dr Sir yr. friend & servant

JAS. MONROE

Since the above the house went in committee on a bill for amending the cty ct. law. It terminated in 2. resolutions, 1. that the administration of justice shod. be made more equal & expeditious 2. that under executns. property sold so low as to require some legislative provision for preventing it. Afterwards in the house a proposition for establishing district courts was agreed to; the alternative of extendg the term of the genl. ct. was rejected by a great majority.[3] The plan of instalmt. will be brot. forward, and that of altering the executn. law so as to prevent property being sold but for ¾ its value. The former is the favorite of Mr. N. the latter of Mr. Henry. It is not improbable but that the district bill may fail if incumber'd with either, cod. either get a decided majority in preference to the other, yet it is possible that their division upon this point may lessen the weight of opposition to the district bill & promote its adoption.

RC (DLC). Addressed by Monroe and franked.

[1] Samuel Hopkins, Jr. (1753–1819), of Mecklenburg County. In 1797 he moved to Kentucky, where the town of Hopkinsville was named for him. He served in the Thirteenth Congress. See Hopkins, *Hopkins Families of Virginia*, pp. 14–17.

[2] Edmund Pendleton.

[3] After the debate in the Committee of the Whole on 6 Dec., the House adopted resolutions calling for bills to reform the execution law, to establish district courts, and to reform the county courts. These bills passed both houses early in January (*JHDV*, Oct. 1787, p. 85; Hening, *Statutes*, XII, 457–62, 467–74, 532–58).

From Benjamin Hawkins

Letter not found.

ca. 6 December 1787, Tarborough. Mentioned in Hawkins to JM, 14 Feb. 1788. Reports the time set for the election and meeting of the North Carolina ratifying convention.

To George Washington

NEW YORK Decr. 7. 1787

DEAR SIR

My last inclosed a continuation of the Fœderalist to number 14. inclusive. I now add the numbers which have succeeded.

No authentic information has yet arrived concerning the posture of Europe. Reports, with some less doubtful symtoms, countenance the suspicions of war.

I understand that the Constitution will certainly be adopted in Connecticut; the returns of the deputies being now known, and a very great majority found to be its declared and firm friends. There will be more opposition in Massachussetts, but its friends there continue to be very sanguine of victory. N Hampshire, as far as I can learn, may be set down, on the right list. I remain Dear Sir, with the highest respect and the most unfeigned attachment Your Obedient humble servant

Js. MADISON JR

RC (PHi); Tr (DLC). Enclosures not found.

From Henry Lee

STRATFORD Decr. 7t. 87

DEAR MADISON

Having a few moments only to devote, you must be satisfied with a very laconic letr. Such is my distance from the line of posts, that to use it, I must avail myself of accidental conveyances, which are often like the present, sudden. It is with real Grief I inform you that by a late vote of the assembly of Virga. on a collateral question, they have manifested hostility to the new constitution. Henry whose art is equal to his talents for declamation, conducted this business & gained a majority on the vote of sixteen.

We are told by Gentlemen from Richmond, that the whole district south of James river are in the opposition. In this corner the people are warmly attached to the new system, but we are small in size, being only four or five countys.

I saw Genl. Washington on my return, he continues firm as a rock. The Pages are all zealous abettors of the constitution so is R Wormely & F. Lightfoote Lee. Both of these Gentlemen are candidates for the convention. The last is an important acquisition & breaks the influence of the stratford Lees. It becomes you to return in time to secure your election. If possible let me see you. I have offered myself for Westmoreland, but such is the number who contend for this distinction, it is not probable that I may succeed.[1] God bless you—

HENRY LEE

RC (DLC). Docketed by JM.

[1] The "stratford Lees" were the progeny of Thomas and Hannah Lee of Stratford Hall. They included the brothers Francis Lightfoot, Richard Henry, and Arthur. Francis Lightfoot Lee was evidently a candidate for the convention from Richmond County but was defeated. Ralph Wormeley, Jr., was elected from Middlesex County, as was Henry Lee from Westmoreland County. The latter came into possession of Stratford Hall through his wife and cousin Matilda, a Stratford Lee (Lee, *Lee Chronicle*, pp. 70–78, 85; Swem and Williams, *Register*, p. 244).

From George Washington

MOUNT VERNON Decr. 7th. 1787.

MY DEAR SIR,

Since my last to you, I have been favored with your letters of the 28th. of Octr: & 18th. of Novr. With the last came 7 numbers of the Fœderalist under the signature of Publius. For these I thank you. They are forwarded to a Gentleman in Richmond for re-publication. The doing of which, in this State, will, I am persuaded, have a good effect; as there are certainly characters in it who are no friends to a general government—perhaps I might go further, & add, who would have no great objection to the introduction of anarchy & confusion.

The sollicitude, to know what the several State Legislatures would do with the Constitution, is now transferred to the several Conventions thereof; the decisions of which being more interesting & conclusive, is consequently more anxiously expected than the other. What Pensylvania & Delaware have done, or will do, must soon be known. Other Conventions[1] are treading closely on their heels—but what the three Southern

States have done, or in what light the New Constitution is viewed by them, I have not been able to learn. North Carolina it is said (by some Accts. from Richmond) will be governed in a great measure by the conduct of Virga. The pride of South Carolina will not, I conceive, suffer this influence to operate in her Councils; and the disturbances in Georgia will, or at least ought to shew the people of it, the propriety of a strict Union,[2] and the necessity there is for a general government.

If these, with the States Eastward and Northward of us, should accede to the proposed plan, I think the Citizens of this State will have no cause to bless the opponents of it here, if they should carry their point.

A Paragraph in the Baltimore Paper has announced a change in the Sentiments of Mr. Jay on this subject; and adds, that from being an admirer of it, he is become a bitter enemy.[3] This relation, without knowing Mr. Jays opinion, I discredit, from a conviction that he would consider the matter well before he would pass Judgment,[4] and having done so, would not change his opinion, *almost* in the same breath. I am anxious however to know, on what ground this report originates, especially the indelicacy of the expresn.

It would have given me great pleasure to have complied with your request in behalf of your foreign Acquaintance. At *present* I am unable to do it. The Survey of the Country between the Eastern and Western Waters is not yet reported by the Commissioners, tho' promised to be made very shortly—the Survey being compleated. No draught that can convey an adequate idea of the Work, on this river, has been yet taken. Much of the labour, except at the great falls, has been bestowed in the bed of the River; in a removal of Rocks, and deepning the Water. At the great falls, the labour has indeed been great. The Water there (a sufficiency I mean) is taken into a Canal about 200 yards above the Cataract, & conveyed by a level cut (thro' a solid rock in some places, and much stone every where) more than a mile to the lock seats; five in number; by means of which, when compleated, the craft will be let into the River below the falls (which together amount to 76 feet). At the Seneca falls, Six miles above the great Falls, a channel which has been formed by the River when inundated, is under improvement for the Navigation. The same, *in part*, at Shanondah. At the lower falls, where nothing has yet been done, a level cut and locks are proposed. These constitute the principal difficulties & will [be] the great expence of this undertaking;[5] The parts of the river between requiring loose stones only to be removed, in order to deepen the Water where it is too shallow in dry seasons. With very great esteem & regard I am, My dear Sir Yr. Most Obedt. & Affece Ser

GO: WASHINGTON

PS. Since writing the foregoing, I have received a letter from a member of our Assembly at Richmond, dated the 4th. instt. giving the following information.[6]

"I am sorry to inform you that the Constitution has lost ground so considerably that it is doubtful whether it has any longer a majority in its favor. From a vote which took place the other day this would appear certain, tho' I cannot think it so decisive as the enemies to it consider it. It marks however the inconsistency of some of its opponants. At the time the Resolutions calling a Convention were entered into Colo. M——n sided with the friends to the Constitution, and opposed any hint being given, expressive of the sentiments of the House as to amendments. But as it was unfortunately omitted at that time to make provision for the subsistence of the Convention, it became necessary to pass some resolutions for that purpose; among these is one providing for any expence which may attend an attempt to make amendments. As M—— had on the former occasion declared that it would be improper to make any discovery of the sentiments of the House on the subject, and that we had no right to suggest any thing to a body paramount to us, his advocating such a resolution was matter of astonishment. It is true he declared it was not declaratory of our opinion; but the contrary must be very obvious. As I have heard many declare themselves friends to the Constitution since the vote, I do not consider it as altogether decisive of the opinion of the House with respect to it."

"In a debating society here, which meets once a week, this subject has been canvassed at two successive meetings, and is to be finally decided on tomorrow evening. As the whole Assembly almost has attended on these occasions, their opinion will then be pretty well ascertained.[7] And as the opinion on this occasion will have much influence, some of Colo. Innis's friends have obtained a promise from him to enter the lists.

"I am informed both by Genl. Wilkinson (who is just arrived from New Orleans by way of No. Carolina) and Mr Ross, that North Carolina is almost unanimous for adopting it. The latter received a letter from a member of that Assembly now sitting."

"The Bill respecting British debts has passed our house, but with such a clause as I think makes it worse than a rejection."

The letter of which I enclose you a printed Copy, from Colo R H. Lee to the Govr. has been circulated with great industry in manuscript, four weeks before it went to press, and is said to have had a bad influence.[8] The enemies to the Constitution leave no stone unturned to encrease the opposition to it. Yr. &ct

G: W.

RC (MA); FC (DLC: Washington Papers). FC in a clerk's hand. RC docketed by JM. Minor variations between the RC and the FC have not been noted. Enclosure not found.

¹The FC has here, "to the Northward and Eastward of them."

²The FC reads, "the propriety of being United."

³The Baltimore *Md. Journal* of 30 Nov. 1787 carried a brief item announcing that John Jay now believed the Constitution to be "as deep and wicked a conspiracy as has been ever invented in the darkest ages against the liberties of a free people." The piece originally appeared in the 24 Nov. 1787 issue of the Philadelphia *Independent Gazetteer*, published by Antifederalist Eleazer Oswald. In his reply of 20 Dec., JM called the piece "an arrant forgery" and referred Washington to a Philadelphia paper containing Jay's denial of a conversion to Antifederalism. See the extract of a letter from Jay to John Vaughan, 1 Dec. 1787, in the *Pa. Packet* of 7 Dec. 1787.

⁴The FC from here to the end of the paragraph reads, "It is very unlikely therefore that a man of his knowledge and foresight should turn on both sides of a question in so short a space. I am anxious however to know the foundation (if any) for this."

⁵The FC reads, "These constitute the principal part of the work to compleat the navigation."

⁶Washington's correspondent was doubtless David Stuart. His letter of 4 Dec. 1787 has not been found, but was acknowledged by Washington on 11 Dec. (Fitzpatrick, *Writings of Washington*, XXIX, 335).

⁷The *Pa. Gazette* of 2 Jan. 1788 reported: "In the Political Society lately instituted at Richmond, in Virginia, the new fœderal constitution was the subject of a public debate. After three evenings spent in discussing it, the *Yeas* in favour of it were 128, the *Nays* were only 15. The members of this society consist of the principal characters in Virginia. The principal Speaker against the government was Patrick Henry, Esq;—the principal speaker in favour of it was Mr. Nicholas. It is expected there will be the same majority in favour of the government in the State Convention." See also Coxe to JM, 28 Dec. 1787, and Washington to JM, 10 Jan. 1788.

⁸Richard Henry Lee to Edmund Randolph, 16 Oct. 1787, Ballagh, *Letters of Richard Henry Lee*, II, 450–55. A broadside copy of the letter has not been located. The letter was among the essays on the Constitution included in a pamphlet published in Richmond by Augustine Davis (Burnley to JM, 15 Dec. 1787, n. 2). Contemporary printings of this letter included a postscript in which Lee offered a series of amendments to the proposed Constitution. See *American Museum*, II (1787), 553–58. Ballagh omitted the postscript.

The Federalist Number 18

[7 December 1787]

Among the confederacies of antiquity, the most considerable was that of the Grecian republics associated under the Amphyctionic council. From the best accounts transmitted of this celebrated institution, it bore a very instructive analogy to the present confederation of the American states.

The members retained the character of independent and sovereign states, and had equal votes in the federal council. This council had a general authority to propose and resolve whatever it judged necessary for the common welfare of Greece—to declare and carry on war—to decide in the last resort all controversies between the members—to fine the aggressing party—to employ the whole force of the confederacy against the disobedient—to admit new members. The Amphyctions were the guardians of religion, and of the immense riches belonging to the temple of Delphos, where they had the right of jurisdiction in controversies between the inhabitants and those who came to consult the oracle. As a further provision for the efficacy of the federal powers, they took an oath mutually to defend and protect the united cities, to punish the violators of this oath, and to inflict vengeance on sacrilegious despoilers of the temple.

In theory and upon paper, this apparatus of powers, seems amply sufficient for all general purposes. In several material instances, they exceed the powers enumerated in the articles of confederation. The Amphyctions had in their hands the superstition of the times, one of the principal engines by which government was then maintained; they had a declared authority to use coertion against refractory cities, and were bound by oath to exert this authority on the necessary occasions.

Very different nevertheless was the experiment from the theory. The powers, like those of the present congress, were administered by deputies appointed wholly by the cities in their political capacities; and exercised over them in the same capacities. Hence the weakness, the disorders, and finally the destruction of the confederacy. The more powerful members, instead of being kept in awe and subordination, tyrannized successively over all the rest. Athens, as we learn from Demosthenes, was the arbiter of Greece seventy-three years. The Lacedemonians next governed it twenty-nine years; at a subsequent period, after the battle of Leuctra, the Thebans had their turn of domination.[1]

It happened but too often, according to Plutarch, that the deputies of the strongest cities, awed and corrupted those of the weaker, and that judgment went in favor of the most powerful party.[2]

Even in the midst of defensive and dangerous wars with Persia and Macedon, the members never acted in concert, and were more or fewer of them, eternally the dupes, or the hirelings of the common enemy. The intervals of foreign war, were filled up by domestic vicissitudes, convulsions and carnage.

After the conclusion of the war with Xerxes, it appears that the Lacedemonians required that a number of the cities should be turned out of the confederacy for the unfaithful part they had acted. The Athenians finding that the Lacedemonians would lose fewer partizans by such a measure than themselves, and would become masters of the public deliberations, vigorously opposed and defeated the attempt. This piece of history proves at once the inefficiency of the union; the ambition and jealousy of its most powerful members, and the dependent and degraded condition of the rest. The smaller members, though entitled by the theory of their system, to revolve in equal pride and majesty around the common center, had become in fact satellites of the orbs of primary magnitude.

Had the Greeks, says the Abbé Milot, been as wise as they were courageous, they would have been admonished by experience of the necessity of a closer union, and would have availed themselves of the peace which followed their success against the Persian arms, to establish such a reformation. Instead of this obvious policy, Athens and Sparta, inflated with the victories and the glory they had acquired, became first rivals, and then enemies; and did each other infinitely more mischief, than they had suffered from Xerxes.[3] Their mutual jealousies, fears, hatreds and injuries, ended in the celebrated Peloponnesian war; which itself ended in the ruin and slavery of the Athenians who had begun it.

As a weak government, when not at war, is ever agitated by internal dissentions; so these never fail to bring on fresh calamities from abroad. The Phocians having ploughed up some consecrated ground belonging to the temple of Apollo, the Amphyctionic council, according to the superstition of the age, imposed a fine on the sacrilegious offenders. The Phocians, being abetted by Athens and Sparta, refused to submit to the decree. The Thebans, with others of the cities, undertook to maintain the authority of the Amphyctions, and to avenge the violated god. The latter being the weaker party, invited the assistance of Philip of Macedon, who had secretly fostered the contest. Philip gladly seized the opportunity of executing the designs he had long planned against the liberties of Greece. By his intrigues and bribes he won over to his interests the popular leaders of several cities; by their influence and votes, gained admission into the Amphyctionic council; and by his arts and his arms, made himself master of the confederacy.

Such were the consequences of the fallacious principle, on which this interesting establishment was founded. Had Greece, says a judicious observer on her fate, been united by a stricter confederation, and persevered in her union, she would never have worn the chains of Macedon; and might have proved a barrier to the vast projects of Rome.[4]

The Achæan league, as it is called, was another society of Grecian republics, which supplies us with valuable instruction.

The union here was far more intimate, and its organization much wiser, than in the preceding instance. It will accordingly appear, that though not exempt from a similar catastrophe, it by no means equally deserved it.

The cities composing this league, retained their municipal jurisdiction, appointed their own officers, and enjoyed a perfect equality. The senate in which they were represented, had the sole and exclusive right of peace and war—of sending and receiving ambassadors—of entering into treaties and alliances—of appointing a chief magistrate or pretor, as he was called, who commanded their armies; and who with the advice and consent of ten of the senators, not only administered the government in the recess of the senate, but had a great share in its deliberation, when assembled. According to the primitive constitution, there were two pretors associated in the administration, but on trial, a single one was preferred.

It appears that the cities had all the same laws and customs, the same weights and measures, and the same money. But how far this effect proceeded from the authority of the federal council, is left in uncertainty. It is said only, that the cities were in a manner compelled to receive the same laws and usages. When Lacedemon was brought into the league by Philopœmen, it was attended with an abolition of the institutions and laws of Lycurgus, and an adoption of those of the Achæans. The Amphyctionic confederacies, of which she had been a member, left her in the full exercise of her government and her legislation. This circumstance alone proves a very material difference in the genius of the two systems.

It is much to be regretted that such imperfect monuments remain of this curious political fabric. Could its interior structure and regular operation be ascertained, it is probable that more light would be thrown by it on the science of federal government, than by any of the like experiments with which we are acquainted.

One important fact seems to be witnessed by all the historians who take notice of Achæan affairs. It is, that as well after the renovation of the league by Aratus, as before its dissolution by the arts of Macedon, there was infinitely more of moderation and justice in the administration of its government, and less of violence and sedition in the people, than were to be found in any of the cities exercising *singly* all the prerogatives of sovereignty. The abbé Mably in his observations on Greece, says that the popular government, which was so tempestuous elsewhere, caused no disorders in the members of the Achæan republic, *because it was there tempered by the general authority and laws of the confederacy.*[5]

We are not to conclude too hastily, however, that faction did not in a certain degree agitate the particular cities; much less, that a due subordination and harmony reigned in the general system. The contrary is sufficiently displayed in the vicissitudes and fate of the republic.

Whilst the Amphyctionic confederacy remained, that of the Achæans, which comprehended the less important cities only, made little figure on the theatre of Greece. When the former became a victim to Macedon, the latter was spared by the policy of Philip and Alexander. Under the successors of these princes, however, a different policy prevailed. The arts of division were practised among the Achæans; each city was seduced into a separate interest; the union was dissolved. Some of the cities fell under the tyranny of Macedonian garrisons; others under that of usurpers springing out of their own confusions. Shame and oppression ere long awakened their love of liberty. A few cities re-united. Their example was followed by others, as opportunities were found of cutting off their tyrants. The league soon embraced almost the whole Peloponnesus. Macedon saw its progress; but was hindered by internal dissentions from stopping it. All Greece caught the enthusiasm, and seemed ready to unite in one confederacy, when the jealousy and envy in Sparta and Athens, of the rising glory of the Achæans, threw a fatal damp on the enterprize. The dread of the Macedonian power induced the league to court the alliance of the kings of Egypt and Syria; who, as successors of Alexander were rivals of the king of Macedon. This policy was defeated by Cleomenes, king of Sparta, who was led by his ambition to make an unprovoked attack on his neighbours the Achæans; and who as an enemy to Macedon, had interest enough with the Egyptian and Syrian princes, to effect a breach of their engagements with the league. The Achæans were now reduced to the dilemma of submitting to Cleomenes, or of supplicating the aid of Macedon, its former oppressor. The latter expedient was adopted. The contest of the Greeks always afforded a pleasing opportunity to that powerful neighbour, of intermeddling in their affairs. A Macedonian army quickly appeared: Cleomenes was vanquished. The Achæans soon experienced, as often happens, that a victorious and powerful ally, is but another name for a master. All that their most abject compliances could obtain from him was a toleration of the exercise of their laws. Philip, who was now on the throne of Macedon, soon provoked, by his tyrannies, fresh combinations among the Greeks. The Achæans, though weakened by internal dissentions, and by the revolt of Messene one of its members, being joined by the Etolians and Athenians, erected the standard of opposition. Finding themselves, though thus supported unequal to the undertaking, they once more had recourse to the dangerous expedient of introducing the succour of foreign arms. The Romans to whom the invitation was made, eagerly embraced it. Philip was conquered: Macedon subdued. A new crisis ensued to the league. Dissentions broke out among its members. These the Romans fostered. Callicrates and other popular leaders, became mercenary instruments for inveigling their countrymen. The more effectually to nourish discord and disorder, the Romans had, to the astonishment of those who confided in their sincerity, already proclaimed universal liberty* throughout Greece. With the same insidious views, they now seduced the members from the league, by representing to their pride, the

*This was but another name more specious for the independence of the members on the federal head.

violation it committed on their sovereignty. By these arts, this union, the last hope of Greece, the last hope of antient liberty, was torn into pieces; and such imbecility and distraction introduced, that the arms of Rome found little difficulty in compleating the ruin which their arts had commenced. The Achæans were cut to pieces; and Achaia loaded with chains, under which it is groaning at this hour.

I have thought it not superfluous to give the outlines of this important portion of history; both because it teaches more than one lesson; and because, as a supplement to the outlines of the Achæan constitution, it emphatically illustrates the tendency of federal bodies, rather to anarchy among the members than to tyranny in the head.

PUBLIUS.

McLean, I, 107–14. JM wrote the following undated note in Richard Rush's copy of *The Federalist* (see Madison's Authorship of *The Federalist*, 22 Nov. 1787–1 Mar. 1788) at the bottom of the pages on which No. 18 is printed: "A. H. had drawn up something on the subjects of this (No. 18) and the two next Nos. (19 & 20). On finding that J. M. was engaged in them with larger materials, and with a view to a more precise delineation, he put what he had written into the hands of J. M. It is possible, tho' not recollected that something in the draught may have been incorporated into the numbers as printed. But it was certainly not of a nature or amount to affect the impression left on the mind of J. M. from whose pen the papers went to the Press, that they were of the class written by him. As the historical materials of A. H. as far as they went, were doubtless similar, or the same with those provided by J. M. and as a like application of them probably occurred to both, an impression might be left on the mind of A. H. that the nos. in question were written jointly. These remarks are made, as well to account for a statement to that effect if made by A. H., as in justice to J. M, who always regarding them in a different light had so stated them to an enquiring friend long before it was known or supposed that a different impression existed anywhere. J. M." George Bancroft printed this note, without disclosing its source, in his *History of the Formation of the Constitution of the United States of America* (6th ed.; 2 vols.; New York, 1903), II, 336–37 n. JM wrote a briefer explanation in the 1799 copy of *The Federalist* (Tiebout ed.) that he sent to Jacob Gideon in 1818 (now in the Rare Book Division, Library of Congress): "The subject of this and the two following numbers happened to be taken up by both Mr. H. and Mr. M. What had been prepared by Mr. H. who had entered more briefly into the subject, was left with Mr. M, on its appearing that the latter was engaged in it, with larger materials, & with a view to a more precise delineation; and from the pen of the latter the several papers went to the Press." This note appears at the bottom of the page where No. 18 begins, and Gideon printed it as a footnote to No. 18 in his 1818 edition of *The Federalist*. Another copy of the note, in JM's hand, is filed with JM's copy of his letter to Gideon of 28 Jan. 1818 (DLC). For the "larger materials" referred to by JM, see his Notes on Ancient and Modern Confederacies (*PJM*, IX, 4–22).

[1]JM was referring to Demosthenes' Third Philippic (Demosthenes, *Olynthiacs, Philippics, Leptines, Etc.*, Loeb Classical Library [1930; London, 1970 reprint], p. 237).

[2]This sentence was taken from Notes on Ancient and Modern Confederacies, where JM referred to "Plutarch's Themistocles" (*PJM*, IX, 6). See *Plutarch's Lives* (3d ed.; 6 vols.; London, 1778), I, 280–325.

[3]Claude-François-Xavier Millot, *Élémens d'histoire générale . . .* (9 vols.; Paris, 1772–73). For the passage cited by JM, see *Elements of General History. Translated from the French of the Abbé Millot. Part First. Ancient History* (2 vols.; Worcester, Mass., 1789; Evans 21965), I, 205–6. JM may have used the English edition (5 vols.; London, 1778–79).

[4]JM took this information from Notes on Ancient and Modern Confederacies, where he cited *Code de l'Humanité* (*PJM*, IX, 6–7).
[5]Gabriel Bonnot de Mably, *Observations sur l'histoire de la Grèce* ... (Geneva, 1766). See *Collection Complète des Oeuvres de l'Abbé de Mably* (15 vols.; Paris, 1794–95), IV, 209–10: "Cette démocratie, toujours si orageuse dans le reste de la Grèce, ne causa aucun désordre dans l'Achaie, soit parce que les lois étoient établies sur de sages proportions, et qu'en donnant aux magistrats assez d'autorité pour se faire obéir, on ne leur en avoit pas assez laissé pour en pouvoir abuser; soit parce que les Achéens, toujours exposés aux injures des Etoliens leurs voisins, n'avoient pas le loisir de s'occuper de querelles domestiques, et que le conseil général de leur association apportoit un soin extrême à les prèvenir ou à les étouffer dans leur naissance."

The Federalist Number 19

[8 December 1787]

The examples of antient confederacies, cited in my last paper, have not exhausted the source of experimental instruction on this subject. There are existing institutions, founded on a similar principle, which merit particular consideration. The first which presents itself is the Germanic body.

In the early ages of christianity Germany was occupied by seven distinct nations, who had no common chief. The Franks, one of the number, having conquered the Gauls, established the kingdom which has taken its name from them. In the ninth century, Charlemagne, its warlike monarch, carried his victorious arms in every direction; and Germany became a part of his vast dominions. On the dismemberment, which took place under his sons, this part was erected into a separate and independent empire. Charlemagne and his immediate descendants possessed the reality, as well as the ensigns and dignity of imperial power. But the principal vassals, whose fiefs had become hereditary, and who composed the national diets which Charlemagne had not abolished, gradually threw off the yoke, and advanced to sovereign jurisdiction and independence. The force of imperial sovereignty was insufficient to restrain such powerful dependents; or to preserve the unity and tranquility of the empire. The most furious private wars, accompanied with every species of calamity, were carried on between the different princes and states. The imperial authority, unable to maintain the public order, declined by degrees, till it was almost extinct in the anarchy, which agitated the long interval between the death of the last emperor of the Suabian, and the accession of the first emperor of the Austrian lines. In the eleventh century, the emperors enjoyed full sovereignty: In the fifteenth they had little more than the symbols and decorations of power.

Out of this feudal system, which has itself many of the important features of a confederacy, has grown the federal system, which constitutes the Germanic empire. Its powers are vested in a diet representing the component members of the confederacy; in the emperor who is the executive magistrate, with a negative on the decrees of the diet; and in the imperial chamber and aulic council, two judiciary tribunals having supreme jurisdiction in controversies which concern the empire, or which happen among its members.

The diet possesses the general power of legislating for the empire—of making war and peace—contracting alliances—assessing quotas of troops and money—constructing fortresses—regulating coin—admitting new members—and subjecting disobedient members to the ban of the empire, by which the party is degraded from his sovereign rights, and his possessions forfeited. The members of the confederacy are expressly restricted from entering into compacts, prejudicial to the empire, from imposing tolls and duties on their mutual intercourse, without the consent of the emperor and diet; from altering the value of money; from doing injustice to one another; or from affording assistance or retreat to disturbers of the public peace. And the ban is denounced against such as shall violate any of these restrictions. The members of the diet, as such, are subject in all cases to be judged by the emperor and diet, and in their private capacities, by the aulic council and imperial chamber.

The prerogatives of the emperor are numerous. The most important of them are, his exclusive right to make propositions to the diet—to negative its resolutions—to name ambassadors—to confer dignities and titles—to fill vacant electorates—to found universities—to grant privileges not injurious to the states of the empire—to receive and apply the public revenues—and generally to watch over the public safety. In certain cases, the electors form a council to him. In quality of emperor he possesses no territory within the empire; nor receives any revenue for his support. But his revenue and dominions, in other qualities, constitute him one of the most powerful princes in Europe.

From such a parade of constitutional powers, in the representatives and head of this confederacy, the natural supposition would be, that it must form an exception to the general character which belongs to its kindred systems. Nothing would be farther from the reality. The fundamental principle, on which it rests, that the empire is a community of sovereigns; that the diet is a representation of sovereigns; and that the laws are addressed to sovereigns; render the empire a nerveless body; incapable of regulating its own members; insecure against external dangers; and agitated with unceasing fermentations in its own bowels.

The history of Germany is a history of wars between the emperor and the princes and states; of wars among the princes and states themselves; of the licentiousness of the strong, and the oppression of the weak; of foreign intrusions, and foreign intrigues; of requisitions of men and money, disregarded, or partially complied with; of attempts to enforce them, altogether abortive, or attended with slaughter and desolation, involving the innocent with the guilty; of general imbecility, confusion and misery.

In the sixteenth century, the emperor with one part of the empire on his side, was seen engaged against the other princes and states. In one of the conflicts, the emperor himself was put to flight, and very near being made prisoner by the elector of Saxony. The late king of Prussia was more than once pitted against his imperial sovereign; and commonly proved an overmatch for him. Controversies and wars among the members themselves have been so common, that the German annals are crowded with the bloody pages which describe them. Previous to the peace of Westphalia, Germany was desolated by a war of thirty years, in which the emperor, with one half of the empire was on one side; and Sweden with the other half on the opposite side. Peace was at length negotiated and dictated by foreign powers; and the articles of it, to which foreign powers are parties, made a fundamental part of the Germanic constitution.

If the nation happens, on any emergency, to be more united by the necessity of self defence; its situation is still deplorable. Military preparations must be preceded by so many tedious discussions, arising from the jealousies, pride, separate views, and clashing pretensions, of sovereign bodies; that before the diet can settle the arrangements, the enemy are in the field; and before the federal troops are ready to take it, are retiring into winter quarters.

The small body of national troops which has been judged necessary in time of peace, is defectively kept up, badly paid, infected with local prejudices, and supported by irregular and disproportionate contributions to the treasury.

The impossibility of maintaining order, and dispensing justice among these sovereign subjects, produced the experiment of dividing the empire into nine or ten circles or districts; of giving them an interior organization; and of charging them with the military execution of the laws against delinquent and contumacious members. This experiment has only served to demonstrate more fully, the radical vice of the constitution. Each circle is the miniature picture of the deformities of this political monster. They either fail to execute their commissions, or they do it with all the devastation and carnage of civil war. Sometimes whole circles are defaulters, and then they increase the mischief which they were instituted to remedy.

We may form some judgment of this scheme of military coertion, from a sample given by Thuanus.[1] In Donawerth, a free and imperial city, of the circle of Suabia, the abbè de St. Croix enjoyed certain immunities which had been reserved to him. In the exercise of these, on some public occasion, outrages were committed on him, by the people of the city. The consequence was, that the city was put under the ban of the empire; and the duke of Bavaria, though director of another circle, obtained an appointment to enforce it. He soon appeared before the city, with a corps of ten thousand troops and finding it a fit occasion, as he had secretly intended from the beginning, to revive an antiquated claim, on the pretext that his ancestors had suffered the place to be dismembered from his territory*; he took possession of it, in his own name; disarmed and punished the inhabitants, and re-annexed the city to his domains.

It may be asked perhaps what has so long kept this disjointed machine from falling entirely to pieces? The answer is obvious. The weakness of most of the members, who are unwilling to expose themselves to the mercy of foreign powers; the weakness of most of the principal members, compared with the formidable powers all around them; the vast weight and influence which the emperor derives from his separate and hereditary dominions; and the interest he feels in preserving a system, with which his family pride is connected, and which constitutes him the first prince in Europe; these causes support a feeble and precarious union; whilst the repellent quality, incident to the nature of sovereignty, and which time continually strengthens, prevents any reform whatever, founded on a proper consolidation. Nor is it to be imagined, if this obstacle could be surmounted, that the neighbouring powers would suffer a revolution to take place, which would give to the empire the force and pre-eminence to which it is entitled. Foreign nations have long considered themselves as interested in the changes made by events in this constitution; and have, on various occasions, betrayed their policy of perpetuating its anarchy and weakness.

If more direct examples were wanting, Poland as a government over local sovereigns, might not improperly be taken notice of. Nor could any proof more striking, be given of the calamities flowing from such institutions. Equally unfit for self government, and self defence, it has long been at the mercy of its powerful neighbours; who have lately had the mercy to disburden it of one third of its people and territories.

The connection among the Swiss cantons scarcely amounts to a confed-

---

*Pfeffel, Nouvel abreg. chronol. de l'hist. &c. d'Allemagne, says the pretext was to indemnify himself for the expence of the expedition.[2]

eracy; though it is sometimes cited as an instance of the stability of such institutions.

They have no common treasury—no common troops even in war—no common coin—no common judicatory, nor any other common mark of sovereignty.

They are kept together by the peculiarity of their topographical position, by their individual weakness and insignificancy; by the fear of powerful neighbours, to one of which they were formerly subject; by the few sources of contention among a people of such simple and homogeneous manners; by their joint interest in their dependent possessions; by the mutual aid they stand in need of, for suppressing insurrections and rebellions; an aid expressly stipulated, and often required and afforded; and by the necessity of some regular and permanent provision for accommodating disputes among the cantons. The provision is, that the parties at variance shall each chuse four judges out of the neutral cantons who in case of disagreement, chuse an umpire. This tribunal, under an oath of impartiality, pronounces definitive sentence; which all the cantons are bound to enforce. The competency of this regulation may be estimated, by a clause in their treaty of 1683, with Victor Amadeus of Savoy; in which he obliges himself to interpose as mediator in disputes between the cantons; and to employ force, if necessary, against the contumacious party.

As far as the peculiarity of their case will admit of comparison with that of the United States; it serves to confirm the principle intended to be established. Whatever efficacy the union may have had in ordinary cases, it appears that the moment a cause of difference sprang up, capable of trying its strength, it failed. The controversies on the subject of religion, which in three instances have kindled violent and bloody contests, may be said in fact to have severed the league. The Protestant and Catholic cantons have since had their separate diets; where all the most important concerns are adjusted, and which have left the general diet little other business than to take care of the common bailages.

That separation had another consequence which merits attention. It produced opposite alliances with foreign powers; of Bern as the head of the Protestant association, with the United Provinces; and of Luzerne, as the head of the Catholic association, with France.

PUBLIUS.

McLean, I, 114–20.

[1]"Thuanus" was Jacques-Auguste de Thou, author of the massive *Historiarum sui temporis* (5 vols.; Paris, 1604–8). For the incident referred to by JM, see the French translation, *Histoire Universelle de Jacques-Auguste de Thou* . . . (11 vols.; The Hague, 1740), X, 195–97.

[2]Christian Friedrich Pfeffel von Kriegelstein, *Nouvel Abrégé chronologique de l'Histoire et du*

Droit Public d'Allemagne ... (2 vols.; Paris, 1776). Using this edition, Cooke cites volume II, 235–36, for the passage referred to by JM (*The Federalist* [Cooke ed.], p. 619 n.).

To André Limozin

Letter not found.

8 December 1787. Acknowledged in Limozin to JM, 26 Jan. 1788. Forwarded by Jefferson to Limozin on 22 Jan. 1788 (Boyd, *Papers of Jefferson*, XII, 528). Encloses bill of lading for the box of fruit trees, two barrels of apples, and two barrels of cranberries sent to Jefferson.

To Philip Mazzei

Letter not found.

8 December 1787. Acknowledged in Mazzei to JM, 4 Feb. 1788. Encourages Mazzei's hopes for some immediate remittance in his complicated financial dealings with Dohrman.

To Thomas Jefferson

New York. Decr. 9th. 1787.

Dear Sir

Your favour of the 17th. of Sepr. with sundry other letters and Packets, came duly by the last packet. Such of them as were addressed to others, were duly forwarded. The three Boxes, marked IM, G.W. and AD, it appears were never shipped from Havre.[1] Whenever they arrive your commands with regard to the two last shall be attended to, as well as those relating to some of the contents of the first. I have not been able to get any satisfactory account of Willm. S. Browne. Alderman Broom tells me that he professed to receive the money from him, for the use of Mr. Burke. I shall not lose sight of the subject, and will give you the earliest information of the result of my enquiries. The annexed list of trees will shew you that I have ventured to substitute half a dozen sorts of apples in place of the pippins alone, and to add 8 other sorts of American trees, including 20 of the Sugar maple. They were obtained from a Mr. Prince in the neighbourhood of this City, who deals largely in this way, and is considered as a man of worth. I learn from him that he has executed various commissions from Europe & the West Indies, as well as places less distant;

the upper and lower Country, and in the Northern neck, are as far as I can gather, much disposed to adopt the new Constitution. The middle Country, and the South side of James River are principally in the opposition to it. As yet a large majority of the people are under the first description. As yet also are a majority of the Assembly. What change may be produced by the united influence & exertions of Mr. Henry, Mr. Mason, & the Governor with some pretty able auxiliaries, is uncertain. My information leads me to suppose there must be three parties in Virginia. The first for adopting without attempting Amendments. This includes Genl. W—— and the other deputies, who signed the Constitution, Mr. Pendleton—(Mr. Marshal I believe)—Mr. Nicholas—Mr. Corbin, Mr. Zachy. Johnson, Col. Innis, (Mr. B. Randolph as I understand) Mr. Harvey Mr. Gabl. Jones, Docr. Jones—&c &c. At the head of the 2d. party which urges amendments are the Govr. & Mr. Mason. These do not object to the substance of the Governt. but contend for a few additional Guards in favor of the Rights of the States and of the people. I am not able to enumerate the characters which fall in with their ideas, as distinguished from those of a third Class, at the head of which is Mr. Henry. This class concurs at present with the patrons of Amendments, but will probably contend for such as strike at the essence of the System, and must lead to an adherence to the principle of the existing Confederation, which most thinking men are convinced is a visionary one, or to a partition of the Union into several Confederacies. Mr. Harrison the late Govr. is with Mr. Henry. So are a number of others. The General & Admiralty Courts with most of the Bar, oppose the Constitution, but on what particular grounds I am unable to say. Genl. Nelson, Mr. Jno. page, Col. Bland, &c. are also opponents, but on what principle and to what extent, I am equally at a loss to say. In general I must note, that I speak with respect to many of these names, from information that may not be accurate, and merely as I should do in a free and confidential conversation with you. I have not yet heard mr. Wythe's sentiments on the subject. Docr. McClurg the other absent deputy, is a very strenuous defender of the New Government. Mr. Henry is the great adversary who will render the event precarious. He is I find with his usual address, working up every possible interest, into a spirit of opposition. It is worthy of remark that whilst in Virga. and some of the other States in the middle & Southern Districts of the Union,[2] the men of intelligence, patriotism, property, and independent circumstances, are thus divided; all of this description, with a few exceptions, in the Eastern States, & most of the Middle States, are zealously attached to the proposed Constitution. In N. England, the men of letters, the principal Off[i]cers of Govt. the Judges & Lawyers, the Clergy, and men of property, furnish only here and there an adversary. It is not less worthy of remark that in Virginia where the mass of the people have been so much accustomed to be guided by their rulers on all new and intricate questions, they should on the present which certainly surpasses the judgment of the greater part of them, not only go before, but contrary to, their most popular leaders. And the phenomenon is the more wonderful, as a popular ground is taken by all the adversaries to the new Constitution. Perhaps the solution in both these cases, would not be very difficult; but it would lead to observations too diffusive; and to you unnecessary. I will barely observe that the case in Virga. seems to prove that the body of sober & steady people, even of the lower order, are tired of the vicicitudes, injustice and follies which have so much characterised public measures, and are impatient for some change which promises stability & repose. The proceedings of the present assembly are more likely to cherish than remove this disposition. I find Mr. Henry has carried a Resolution for *prohibiting* the importation of Rum, brandy, and other ardent spirits; and if I am not misinformed all manufactured leather, hats and sundry other articles are included in the *prohibition*. [3] Enormous duties at least are likely to take place on the last & many other articles. A project of this sort without the concurrence of the other States, is little short of madness. With such concurrence, it is not practicable without resorting to expedients equally noxious to liberty and œconomy. The consequences of the experiment in a single State, as unprepared for manufactures as Virginia may easily be preconceived. The Revised Code will not be resumed. Mr. Henry is an inveterate adversary to it. Col. Mason made a regular and powerful attack on the Port Bill; but was left in a very small minority. I found at the last Session that that regulation was not to be shaken; though it certainly owes its success less to its principal merits, than to collateral & casual considerations. The popular ideas are that by favoring the collection of duties on imports it saves the solid property from direct taxes; and that it injures G. Britain by lessening the advantage she has over other Nations, in the trade of Virginia.

We have no certain information from the three Southern States concerning the temper relative to the New Government. It is in general favorable according to the vague accounts we have. Opposition however will be made in each. Mr. Wiley Jones, and Governour Caswell have been named as Opponents in N. Carolina.

So few particulars have come to hand concerning the State of things in Georgia that I have nothing to add on that subject, to the contents of my last, by Commodore Jones.

We have two or three States only yet met for Congs. As many more can be called in when their attendance will make a quorum. It continues to be problematical, whether the interregnum will not be spun out through the winter.

We remain in great uncertainty here with regard to a war in Europe. Reports and suspicions are strongly on the side of one. Such an event may be considered in various relations to this Country. It is pretty certain I think that if the present lax State of our General Government should continue, we shall not only lose certain capital advantages which might be drawn from it; but be in danger of being plunged into difficulties which may have a very serious effect on our future fortunes. I remain Dear Sir with the most sincere esteem & Affection, Your Obedt. servt.[4]

PS. I have delivered your message to Mr. Thomson & settled the pecuniary matter with him.

The letters which you put under the same cover, with the seals of one joining the superscription of the contiguous letter, come when the weather has been warm, in such a State that it is often difficult to separate them without tearing out the superscription. A bit of paper between the adjoining letters over the seal would prevent this inconveniency.

[Enclosure]

No.					
1.– 6	New Town Spitzenburg apples				
2.–20.	New Town Pippins	do.			
3 – 6.	Esopus Spitzenburg	do.		50 trees at 2/-	£5. 0- 0
4 – 6.	Jersey Greening	do.			
5 – 6	R. Island Greening	do.			
6 – 6.	Everlasting	do.			

7.–10.	American Plumbs	1/6	15.
8 – 8.	live Oaks	9d	6.
9 –20.	Sugar Maples	2/	2.
10 –10.	Candle berry-Myrtles	9d	7- 6
11 – 6.	Standing American Honey-Suckles	1/6	9.
12.– 6.	Three thorned Accacia	1/6	9
13 – 6.	Rhododendrons	2/	12
14 – 6.	Dogwood Trees	1/6	9
	Box & Matts		5- 6

Dollar at 8 Shillgs.   £10.13

RC and enclosure (DLC). Unsigned; see n. 4 below. JM failed to enclose the catalogue of Prince's nursery that he mentioned (Jefferson to JM, 6 Feb. 1788).

¹See Limozin to JM, 10 Jan. 1788 and n. 2.
²JM interlined "of the Union" at some later time.
³See Dawson to JM, ca. 10 Nov. 1787 and n. 5.
⁴JM began his signature here, but did not complete it; "Js" is faintly visible, apparently having been erased.

To Horatio Gates

NEW YORK Decr. 11. 1787.

DEAR SIR

Your favour of the 26 Ult: was duly handed to me by Majr. Drumgole. However important the object of his errand may have been, it has not been possible to take any step with regard to it. No authority equal to the business exists in the recess of Congress; and the Authority of Congress has been out of existence for some time, and if we are to judge from the present aspect of things, will continue so for some time longer.

There seem to be pretty strong symtoms of approaching war on the other side of the Atlantic. Its flames are actually kindled between the Turks and Russians. If the English & French do not follow the example, the forbearance will be more the effect of inability than of disinclination. The fate of the Dutch Patriots is not yet decided here by any authentic communications, but every report and probability is ominous to their cause. A general war in Europe will open a new scene to this Country: a scene which might be contemplated with pleasure if our humanity could forget the calamities in which it must involve others; and if we were in a condition to maintain the rights and pursue the advantages of Neutrality. I am Dear Sir with the greatest respect and esteem your Obedt. & humble servt

JS. MADISON JR.

RC (NHi). Addressed by JM, and "Favoured by Majr. Drumgole." Docketed by Gates.

From George Lee Turberville

RICHMOND CITY Decr. 11th. 1787.

DEAR SIR

Will you excuse an abrupt tresspass upon your leizure which has its rise from a desire to promote the welfare of Virginia & the Union a cause that has so long been the object of your pursuits—& that has already received so many beneficial supports from your attention—& still expects to receive so much future aid from your Counsel, Assiduity & patriotism?

Tis not sir to draw from you—your opinions—but merely to be informed of some parts of the Plan of Government proposed by the convention at Philadelphia—which appear obscure to a Reader that I have ventured to interrupt you, seeing that it is impossible to receive any information in the circle here—but what manifestly bears the Stamp of faction—rancour—or intemperance.

Upon a question of Such importance (on which perhaps it may be my lot to have a Vote) you will therefore excuse me for endeavoring to understand the subject as well as possible to the end that I may be enabled to form cooly & deliberately such an opinion of it as my best abilities—aided by extreme attention—& all the information I can obtain—will admit. Without further apology therefore I will proceed to mention such parts of the plan as appear obscure to me—always premising that it is not my wish to draw from you your own opinions, but only the reasonings thereon—& the objects thereof that weighed with the convention.

The principal objection that the opponents bring forward against this Constitution, is the total want of a Bill of Rights. This they build upon as an essential—and altho' I am satisfied that an enumeration of those priviledges which are retained—wou'd have left floating in uncertainty a number of non enumerated contingent powers and priviledges—either in the powers granted or in those retained—thereby indisputably trenching upon the powers of the states—& of the Citizens—insomuch as those not specially retained might by just implication have been consider'd as surrender'd. Still it wou'd very much assist me in my determination upon this subject if the sense of the Convention and their opinion upon it cou'd be open'd to me.

Another objection (and that I profess appears very weighty with me) is the want of a Council of State to assist the President. To detail to you the various reasons that lead to this opinion is useless. You have seen them in all the publications almost that pretend to analyze this System—most particularly in Colo. Masons. We have heard from *private persons* that a system of government was engrossed which had an Executive council—and that the priviledge of importing slaves (another great evil) was not mention'd in it—but that a Coalition took place between the members of the small States & those of the southern States & they barter'd the Council for the Priviledge—and the present plan thus defective—owes it origin to this Junction. If this was the case it takes greatly off from the confidence that I ever conceived to be due to this Convention. Such conduct wou'd appear rather like the attempt of a party to carry an interested measure in a state legislature than the production of the United Wisdom—Virtue—& Uprightness of America called together to deliberate upon a form of Government that will affect themselves & their latest Posterity.

The operation of the Judiciary is a matter so far beyond the reach of most of our fellow Citizens that we are bounden to receive—& not to originate our opinions upon this branch of the Federal government. Lawyers alone conceive themselves masters of this subject & they hold it forth to us *danger* & *distress* as the inevitable result of the new system—& that this will proceed from the immense power of the general Judiciary which will pervade the states from one extremity to the other & will finally absorb & destroy the state Court[s.] But to me their power seem's very fairly defined by the clauses that constitute them—& the mention of Juries, in criminal cases—seeming therefor by implication in civil cases not to be allowed is the only objection *I* have to this Branch.

Why shou'd the United States in Congress Assembled be enabled to fix on the places of choosing the Representatives?

Why shou'd the Laws of the Union operate agt. & supercede the state Constitutions?

Wou'd not an uniform duty—impost—or excise of £5. pr. hhd onTobo. exported—throughout the United States—operate upon the Tobo. States alone? & have not the U.S. the power of levying this impost?

Why shou'd the states be prevented from raising a Revenue by Duties or Taxes on their own Exports? Are the states not bound down to direct Taxation for the support of their police & government?

Why was not that truely republican mode of forcing the Rulers or Sovereigns of the States to mix after stated Periods with the people again observed as is the case with the present members of Congress—Governors of this state &c &c?

For what Reason—or to an[s]wer what republican Veiw is it, that the way is left open for the importation of Negro slaves for twenty one Yrs.?

May not the powers of the Congress from the clause which enables them to pass all Laws necessary to carry this system into effect—& that clause also which declares their Laws to be paramount to the Constitutions of the states—be so operated upon as to annihilate the State Governments?

If the Laws of the United States are to be superior to the Laws & Constitutions of the several States, why was not a Bill of Rights affixed to this Constitution by which the Liberties of individuals might have been secured against the abuse of Fœderal Power?

If Treaties are to be the Laws of the Land and to supercede all laws and Constitutions of the States—why is the Ratification of them left to the senate & President—and not to the house of Representatives also?

These queries if satisfactorily answer'd will defeat all the attempts of the opposition—many of them I can readily answer to satisfy myself—but I still doubt whether my fondness for the new government may not make me as improper a Judge in its favor, as the rage of the opposition renders those who are under its influence inadequate to decide even agt. it.

You will I hope my good sir excuse this scrawl which is scarcely legible it has been written by peice meals—& as I cou'd snatch an opportunity from the hurry of business—& from the noise & clamour of the disputants at the house in which I lodge. The Mail is just going out and I have not time to add the detail of State politics—but as I have written on the subject of the federal Constitution—I will Just detain you for a moment on the present Situation of it in this state.

The people in the Country generally for it—the doctrine of amendments exploded by them—the Assembly I fear agt. it—Mr. Henry—Mr. Harrison—Mr. Smith—All the Cabells & Colo. Mason—agt., or at least favorer's of the Amendatory system—& notwithstanding our Resolutions of the 25th. of October I fear we shall still pass some measure that may have an influence unwarrantable & derogatory. Mr. Henry has declared his intention (and perhaps this day may see his plan effectuated) of bringing in a bill for the purpose of promoting a second Convention at Philadelphia to consider amendments—& that the Speakers of the two houses shou'd form a Committee of Correspondence to communicate with our sister States on that Subject. You know the force of this wonderful mans oratory upon a Virginia house of Delegates—& I am sure will with me lament that that force shou'd be ever erroneously or injudiciously directed.

Much I hope sir that we shall have the assistance of your Counsel in the Convention. My best regards to Mr. Carrington—Mr. Griffin & Mr. Brown if they have arrived—& beleive me dear sir to remain with regard & respect Yr. Most Affectionate humble servant

GEORGE LEE TURBERVILLE[1]

RC (NN). Docketed by JM. The bracketed "s" in "Courts" is obscured in the right-hand margin of the Ms.

[1]George Lee Turberville (1760–1798) of Epping, Richmond County, was educated in England, rose to the rank of major in the Continental army during the war, and served in the House of Delegates from 1785 to 1789 (Lee, *Lee Chronicle*, pp. 208–10; Swem and Williams, *Register*, p. 439; *VMHB*, XXVIII [1920], 368–69).

Virginia Delegates to Edmund Randolph

New York Decr. 11. 1787

Sir,

We have been honoured with your Excellencies favor of the 24th. Ult. together with its enclosures.

Congress have not yet Assembled nor have we an early prospect of a sufficient number of States upon the floor for business. In the recess of that body, there is no authority in existence for making the appointment you request with respect to the Cherokee and other tribes of Indians in the Western parts of Virginia & North Carolina. The Indian Ordinance provides for no more than one Superintendant, for all the southern Indians. To this Office Doctor White was appointed by Congress in October 1786, and he has lately resigned. How far Congress may be induced to make a separate or subordinate appointment for the Indians in your Excellencies Contemplation, we cannot Undertake to say. To us the idea appears a good & reasonable one, and We Will submit it to the consideration of Congress as soon as there are Nine States present.[1] Some time must elapse before any Step at all can be taken with respect to the southern Indians, other than what were provided for late in the last session of Congress. A few days before the end of the federal year some Resolutions were passed, for appropriating Six thousand dollars for holding Treaties with the Southern Indians; & North Carolina, So. Carolina, & Georgia, are requested to appoint, each, a Commissioner, who are to hold the Treaties.[2] How far these States will act upon these resolutions we cannot undertake to say, having heard nothing from them.

In this State of things it must remain with your Excellency to determine what it may be necessary for the Government of Virginia to do. We cannot however encourage any proceedure under an expectation that Congress will recognize the expence, nor have we reason to think, that should the appointment suggested by your Excellency be approved of, Major Drumgole would be the Man elected. Colo. Martin who long acted in this business under the Authority of Virga. & whose communications have eventually reached Congress would probably be prefered. Indian Agents necessarily have the exercise of powers which Congress will not confer on any but Characters tolerably well known.

Doctor White is now here[3] and we have conversed with him upon the subject of his late department. He says the State of Indian Affairs in Georgia has been such as to engage his whole time and attention while in Office; this occasioned him to neglect the business as it respected those under your Excellencies consideration, and of course he had no ground of Correspondence with the Government of Virginia.[4]

We do not undertake to decide upon the fitness of this Gentleman for the appointment he held, but in justice to him we beg leave to observe that the Sentiments of the Georgians who alone have known him in the execution of his duty, may very possibly be formed upon views intirely opposite to those which would found a wise & just Conduct in the Superintendant of Indian affairs. Had these people conformed to his advice and Agency, it is probable they would have avoided the bloody War in which they are now involved in consequence of their own violations of the Treaties held by the Commissioners of the United States with the Indians. We have the Honor to be, with the greatest respect your Excellencies Most Obt. Servts.

Js. Madison Jr
Ed. Carrington
J: Brown
C: Griffin

RC (Vi). Addressed, franked, and written by Carrington, except for the signatures of the other delegates. Docketed by a clerk.

[1]Governor Randolph had complained the previous spring that White was neglecting Virginia's Indian problems (*PJM*, IX, 366, 367 n. 3). The Cherokee also believed that White was ignoring them and sought to obtain the separate appointment of Alexander Dromgoole as superintendent for their nation (Gates to JM, 26 Nov. 1787 and n. 2).

[2]See *JCC*, XXXIII, 707–9.

[3]James White was a delegate from North Carolina.

[4]Arthur Campbell wrote to Governor Randolph on 20 Nov. 1787: "That there is an urgent necessity, for some regular authority to step forward, and manage the Indian affairs in the Southern department, differently from what it has been for some time past, need not be argued; every man of common understanding in the Western Country, wonders at, and laments the neglect." This letter, now among the Madison Papers (DLC), may have been an enclosure in Randolph's missing letter of 24 Nov. 1787 to the Virginia delegates. When he learned of White's resignation, Campbell himself became a candidate for the Indian superintendency of the Southern Department (Stuart to JM, 14 Jan. 1788 and n. 4).

The Federalist Number 20

[11 December 1787]

The United Netherlands are a confederacy of republics, or rather of aristocracies, of a very remarkable texture; yet confirming all the lessons derived from those which we have already reviewed.

The union is composed of seven co-equal and sovereign states, and each state or province is a composition of equal and independent cities. In all important cases not only the provinces, but the cities must be unanimous.

The sovereignty of the union is represented by the states general, consisting usually of about fifty deputies appointed by the provinces. They hold their seats, some for life, some for six, three and one years. From two provinces they continue in appointment during pleasure.

The states general have authority to enter into treaties and alliances—to make war and peace—to raise armies and equip fleets—to ascertain quotas and demand contributions. In all these cases however, unanimity and the sanction of their constituents are requisite. They have authority to appoint and receive ambassadors—to execute treaties and alliances already formed—to provide for the collection of duties on imports and exports—to regulate the mint, with a saving to the provincial rights—to govern as sovereigns the dependent territories. The provinces are restrained, unless with the general consent, from entering into foreign treaties—from establishing imposts injurious to others, or charging their neighbours with higher duties than their own subjects. A council of state, a chamber of accounts, with five colleges of admiralty, aid and fortify the federal administration.

The executive magistrate of the union is the stadtholder, who is now a hereditary prince. His principal weight and influence in the republic are derived from his independent title; from his great patrimonial estates; from his family connections with some of the chief potentates of Europe; and more than all, perhaps, from his being stadtholder in the several provinces, as well as for the union, in which provincial quality, he has the appointment of town magistrates under certain regulations, executes provincial decrees, presides when he pleases in the provincial tribunals; and has throughout the power of pardon.

As stadtholder of the union, he has however considerable prerogatives.

In his political capacity he has authority to settle disputes between the provinces, when other methods fail—to assist at the deliberations of the states general, and at their particular conferences—to give audiences to foreign ambassadors, and to keep agents for his particular affairs at foreign courts.

In his military capacity, he commands the federal troops—provides for garrisons, and in general regulates military affairs—disposes of all appointments from colonels to ensigns, and of the governments and posts of fortified towns.

In his marine capacity, he is admiral general, and superintends and directs every thing relative to naval forces, and other naval affairs—presides in the admiralties in person or by proxy—appoints lieutenant admirals and other officers—and establishes councils of war, whose sentences are not executed till he approves them.

His revenue, exclusive of his private income, amounts to 300,000 florins. The standing army which he commands consists of about 40,000 men.

Such is the nature of the celebrated Belgic confederacy, as delineated on parchment. What are the characters which practice has stampt upon it? Imbecility in the government; discord among the provinces; foreign influence and indignities; a precarious existence in peace, and peculiar calamities from war.

It was long ago remarked by Grotius, that nothing but the hatred of his countrymen to the house of Austria, kept them from being ruined by the vices of their constitution.[1]

The union of Utrecht, says another respectable writer, reposes an authority in the states general seemingly sufficient to secure harmony, but the jealousy in each province renders the practice very different from the theory.[2]

The same instrument says another, obliges each province to levy certain contributions; but this article never could and probably never will be executed; because the inland provinces who have little commerce cannot pay an equal quota.[3]

In matters of contribution, it is the practice to wave the articles of the constitution. The danger of delay obliges the consenting provinces to furnish their quotas, without waiting for the others; and then to obtain reimbursement from the others, by deputations, which are frequent, or otherwise as they can. The great wealth and influence of the province of Holland, enable her to effect both these purposes.

It has more than once happened that the deficiencies have been ultimately to be collected at the point of the bayonet; a thing practicable, though dreadful, in a confederacy, where one of the members exceeds in force all the rest; and where several of them are too small to meditate resistance: But utterly impracticable in one composed of members, several of which are equal to each other in strength and resources, and equal singly to a vigorous and persevering defence.

Foreign ministers, says Sir William Temple, who was himself a foreign minister, elude matters taken *ad referendum*, by tampering with the provinces and cities.[4] In 1726, the treaty of Hanover was delayed by these means a whole year. Instances of a like nature are numerous and notorious.

In critical emergencies, the states general are often compelled to overleap their constitutional bounds. In 1688, they concluded a treaty of themselves at the risk of their heads. The treaty of Westphalia in 1648, by which their independence was formally and finally recognized, was concluded without the consent of Zealand. Even as recently as the last treaty of peace with Great-Britain, the constitutional principle of unanimity was departed from. A weak constitution must necessarily terminate in dissolution, for want of proper powers, or the usurpation of powers requisite for the public safety. Whether the usurpation, when once begun, will stop at the salutary point, or go forward to the dangerous extreme, must depend on the contingencies of the moment. Tyranny has perhaps oftener grown out of the assumptions of power, called for, on pressing exigencies, by a defective constitution, than out of the full exercise of the largest constitutional authorities.

Notwithstanding the calamities produced by the stadtholdership, it has been supposed, that without his influence in the individual provinces, the causes of anarchy manifest in the confederacy, would long ago have dissolved it. "Under such a government," says the abbé Mably, "the union could never have subsisted, if the provinces had not a spring within themselves, capable of quickening their tardiness, and compelling them to the same way of thinking. This spring is the stadtholder."[5] It is remarked by Sir William Temple, "that in the intermissions of the stadtholdership, Holland by her riches and her authority which drew the others into a sort of dependence, supplied the place."[6]

These are not the only circumstances which have controuled the tendency to anarchy and dissolution. The surrounding powers impose an absolute necessity of union to a certain degree, at the same time, that they nourish by their intrigues, the constitutional vices, which keep the republic in some degree always at their mercy.

The true patriots have long bewailed the fatal tendency of these vices and have made no less than four regular experiments, by *extraordinary assemblies*, convened for the special purpose, to apply a remedy: As many times, has their laudable zeal found it impossible to *unite the public councils* in reforming the known, the acknowledged, the fatal evils of the existing constitution. Let us pause my fellow citizens, for one moment, over this melancholy and monitory lesson of history; and with the tear that drops for the calamities brought on mankind by their adverse opinions and selfish passions; let our gratitude mingle an ejaculation to Heaven, for the propitious concord which has distinguished the consultations for our political happiness.

A design was also conceived of establishing a general tax to be administered by the federal authority. This also had its adversaries and failed.

This unhappy people seem to be now suffering from popular convulsions, from dissentions among the states and from the actual invasion of foreign arms, the crisis of their destiny. All nations have their eyes fixed on the awful spectacle. The first wish prompted by humanity is, that this severe trial may issue in such a revolution of their government, as will establish their union, and render it the parent of tranquility, freedom and happiness: The next, that the asylum under which, we trust, the enjoyment of these blessings, will speedily be secured in this country, may receive and console them for the catastrophe of their own.

I make no apology for having dwelt so long on the contemplation of these federal precedents. Experience is the oracle of truth; and where its responses are unequivocal, they ought to be conclusive and sacred. The important truth, which it unequivocally pronounces in the present case, is, that a sovereignty over sovereigns, a government over governments, a legislation for communities, as contradistinguished from individuals; as it is a solecism in theory; so in practice, it is subversive of the order and ends of civil polity, by substituting *violence* in place of *law*, or the destructive *coertion* of the *sword*, in place of the mild and salutary *coertion* of the *magistracy*.

PUBLIUS.

McLean, I, 121–26.

[1] This sentence was taken from Notes on Ancient and Modern Confederacies, where JM identified his source as "Mably. Etude d'Hist." (*PJM*, IX, 17). The cited work is Gabriel Bonnot de Mably, *De l'étude de l'histoire* . . . (Paris, 1778). For the remark attributed to Grotius, see *Collection Complète des Oeuvres de l'Abbé de Mably*, XII, 205.

[2] This reference is to Felice, *Code de l'Humanité*. See Notes on Ancient and Modern Confederacies (*PJM*, IX, 16).

[3] The work alluded to is Onslow Burrish, *Batavia Illustrata* . . . (2 vols.; London, 1728). See *PJM*, IX, 17.

[4] Sir William Temple, *Observations upon the United Provinces of the Netherlands* (7th ed.; London, 1705), pp. 115–17. In Notes on Ancient and Modern Confederacies, JM cited "Temple p. 116," which would indicate that he used this edition or one with the same pagination (*PJM*, IX, 17).

[5] JM actually was using his own statement in Notes on Ancient and Modern Confederacies, which paraphrased these remarks by Mably: "Avec un pareil gouvernement, jamais l'union n'auroit subsisté, si en effet les provinces n'avoient eu en elles-mêmes un ressort capable de hater leur lenteur, et de ramener à la même manière de penser. . . . Ce ressort c'est le stathouderat" (*PJM*, IX, 17; *Collection Complète des Oeuvres de l'Abbé de Mably*, XII, 199–200).

[6] Again JM was using his own statement in Notes on Ancient and Modern Confederacies, which paraphrased these remarks by Temple: "However, these Defects were for near Twenty Years supply'd in some measure, and this Frame supported by the great Authority and Riches of the Province of *Holland*, which drew a sort of Dependance from the other Six" (*PJM*, IX, 17; *Observations upon the United Provinces* [7th ed.], p. 135).

From Samuel S. Smith

PRINCETON Decr. 12th. 1787.

SIR,

Mr. Jno. Fitch is about to make application to Congress for some assistance to complete his steam-boat.[1] It is a proof of so much native
ingenuity, that I could wish to see him encouraged on that footing alone, if
the finances of the continent were in a situation to be liberal to the inventors of ingenious arts. But from the report of the most capable judges, his
boat may be rendered so useful to the internal navigation of the United-
States, that I hope Congress will not esteem his application unreasonable,
even under the present embarrassment of their finances. I am perfectly
aware of their good disposition towards the arts, & of their capacity of
judging of Mr Fitch's mechanical merit, if they had the works before
them. As this is not the case, I hope that such certificates as he is able to
produce, will render Congress secure from the imputation of misapplying
the public property, by enabling Mr. Fitch to complete his scheme. His
perseverance as well as his ingenuity is meritorious. If my opinion should
have the least weight, in this affair, with you or with any member of
Congress, I shall feel myself happy in rendering him this service. I am,
Sir, Yr. Mo. obdt. hble. servt.

SAML S SMITH

RC (DLC). Docketed by JM.
[1]See Fitch to JM, 10 Feb. 1788 and n. 2.

To Archibald Stuart

N. YORK Decr. 14th. 1787.

DEAR SIR

I was yesterday favored with yours of the 2d. inst: and am particularly
obliged by the accuracy and fulness of its communications. The mutability of the Legislature on great points has been too frequently exemplified
within my own observation, for any fresh instance of it to produce much
surprize. The only surprize I feel at the last Steps taken with regard to the
New Constitution, is that it does not strike the well meaning adversaries
themselves with the necessity of some anchor for the fluctuations which
threaten shipwreck to our liberty. I am persuaded that the scheme of
amendments is pursued by some of its patrons at least, with the most
patriotic & virtuous intentions. But I am equally persuaded that it is
pregnant with consequences which they fail to bring into view. The vote

of Virga. on that subject, will either dismember the Union, or reduce her to a dilemma as mortifying to her pride, as it will be injurious to her foresight. I verily believe that if the patrons of this scheme, were to enter into an explicit & particular communication with each other, they wd find themselves as much at variance in detail as they are agreed in the general plan of amendments. Or if they could agree at all it would be only on a few points of very little substance, and which would not comprehend the objections of most weight in other States. It is impossible indeed to trace the progress and tendency of this fond experiment without perceiving difficulty and danger in every Stage of it.

We have received neither confirmation nor contradiction of the Reports concerning war between G.B. and France. The Dutch are prostrate before the prussian arms. The follies and misfortunes on the other side of the Atlantic ought to be lessons of wisdom to this side. I fear we shall not derive from them the profit of any sort, which they are calculated to afford us.

We have no Congs as yet; nor any increase of the materials for one. If one were formed, it would only perhaps make the nakedness of the federal situation more conspicuous. The contributions to the Treasury are every where failing. Massts. I am told has lately taken some resolution which effectually diverts the stream to some of her internal purposes.

I perceive by the Newspapers that Delaware has decided unanimously in favor of the new Constitution. Penna. has not yet decided. No delay however will diminish the great majority which are on the affirmative Side. The Convention of New Jersey, is meeting or actually met. The vote there will be nearly if not quite unanimous. That of Connecticut will succeed, and will pretty certainly make four ninths of the requisite number. The same cause which has instituted & countenanced the opposition in Virga. excites it in Massts. In one respect there is a remarkable difference. In Virginia we see men equally respectable in every point of character & marshalled in opposition to each other. In Massts. almost all the intelligent & considerable people are on the side of the new Government. The Governor & the late Govr. though rivals & enemies, the Judges and the Bar—the men of letters—the Clergy and all the other learned professions, with that part of the Society which has the greatest interest in Good Government, are with but few exceptions in favor of the plan as it stands. The weight of this description of friends, seems to countenance the assurance which that side professes, of success. I am Dear Sir Yr. friend & servt

Js. Madison Jr

I think I have recd. the letter which you suppose had miscarried.[1]

RC (CSmH).
¹See Stuart to JM, 2 Dec. 1787 and n. 2.

To George Washington

NEW YORK Decr. 14. 1787.

DEAR SIR

Along with this are inclosed a few of the latest gazettes containing the additional papers in favor of the federal Constitution.

I find by letters from Richmond that the proceedings of the Assembly, are as usual, rapidly degenerating with the progress of the Session: and particularly that the force opposed to the Act of the Convention has gained the ascendance. There is still nevertheless a hope left that different characters and a different spirit may prevail in their successors who are to make the final decision. In one point of view the present Assembly may perhaps be regarded as pleading most powerfully the cause of the new Government, for it is impossible for stronger proofs to be found than in their conduct, of the necessity of some such anchor against the fluctuations which threaten shipwreck to our liberty. I am Dear [Sir] with the most sincere & perfect Esteem, Your Affecte & Obedt. humble servt.

Js. MADISON JR

RC (PHi); Tr (DLC). RC docketed by Washington. Enclosures not found.

From Hardin Burnley

RICHMOND Decr. the 15th. 1787

DR. SIR

The Assembly have proceeded with so much tardiness that notwithstanding the length of time we have been convened our Journals furnish but little which would merit your attention. We have been more engaged in rejecting than in adopting the various political projects which have been proposed. The instalment plan was at first received with much seeming approbation. But ever since its first introduction its decline has been gradual & its death has at length become certain.

The scheme at present proposed to be substituted in its place is to this effect. When an execution is levied the property must be sold if it will command three fourths of its value, if not the Debtor will be suffered to replevy his property on giving bond & security for the Debt & Costs payable in twelve Months, if neither of these take place the property is to be sold at twelve months credit; in either of which Cases the bonds so taken will have the force of Judgments on which no appeal or replevy will be allowed.[1] A Bill for the establishment of district Courts is now before the house. These two bills are intended as a kind of barter between the Creditor & Debtor & are to be so mutually dependant on each other that the fate of the one will determine that of the other. A Collection of pieces on the federal Constitution is just published by Davis[2] one of which I should have inclosed you but am informed that Colo. Barbour has already done it. Another Collection is now on foot by Mr. Dixon.[3] This I shall bring to Orange with me & shall be submitted to your perusal. It is [at] present expected that one half the tax on young Negroes & white tytheables will be taken off.[4] Nothing will be done by this assembly which will injure the credit of public securities. With the highest esteem for yourself & family I remain Dr. Sir yr. Most Obt. Servt.

HARDIN BURNLEY

RC (DLC). Docketed by JM.

[1] See "An act directing the mode of proceeding under certain executions" (Hening, *Statutes,* XII, 457–62). As Joseph Jones pointed out, the "principal object" of the bill was to appoint and authorize commissioners (instead of the county sheriff) to determine whether a debtor's property could be sold for three-fourths its value to satisfy claims (Jones to JM, 18 Dec. 1787). If the property could not be sold at such a price, the debtor was allowed to recover his property for twelve months (instead of three), when the claim again became due.

[2] Augustine Davis (d. 1825) was publisher of the *Va. Independent Chronicle.* The collection of pieces was undoubtedly *Various Extracts on the Fœderal Government* (Stuart to JM, 9 Nov. 1787 and n. 2). Included in the pamphlet, which attempted to balance opposing views, were the letters of "An American Citizen" (Tench Coxe), the first two numbers of "The Centinel" (Samuel Bryan), James Wilson's speech to the citizens of Philadelphia, Richard Henry Lee's letter to Edmund Randolph of 16 Oct. 1787, Elbridge Gerry's objections to the Constitution, and Benjamin Franklin's last speech at the Federal Convention.

[3] John Dixon (1741–1791) was printer for the commonwealth. His collection is not listed in Evans's *American Bibliography.*

[4] The revenue act of 1 Jan. 1788 repealed entirely the "very burthensome" poll taxes on white tithables—free males above the age of twenty-one—and on slaves under the age of sixteen. At the same time, however, the act provided for a future tax of ten shillings on slaves above the age of twelve (Hening, *Statutes,* XII, 431).

From Lawrence Taliaferro

ROSE HILL Decemr: the 16th 1787

DEAR SIR,

I recd: your vary Frendly Letter from New york sumtime ago & Am Much Oblige to you for the Information you gave Me of My Nephu John Taliaferro at Princetown.[1] I am sorry to inform you that the Federal Sistum is rufly Handeld by sum vary Able Men in this State tho. we have

328

sum vary good & Able Men that are Frends to that & thear Cuntary & Wish it to be Adopted as spedily as Posable. I am inform'd that that Exilent good Man Genl: Washington has Offer'd himself for the Spring convention & it is the sincere Wish & desier of Myself & a Grate Many others that you will Also represent the Peopel of this County in the Spring Convention & we Earnestly Beg that you will be hear sum time before the Elextion for even those that are Oppos'd to the Federal Sistum wish to have an Opportunity of conversing with you on it. I dare say you will be gratly suppd: to hear that it is report'd that you Are Opos'd to the Sistum & I was told the other day that you ware Actually writing a Pece against it. I am a vary pore Penman & dont wish to take up two Much of you time in reding a Long Letter or I could give you a grat many More Instances of the Rancor of the Enemes to Peac & Good Goverment & will only repet our ernest desier that you will be hear a Week or two before the Elextion by which Menes I make n[o] doubt but the Citicens of this state wi[ll] be prevented from being led into an Err[or] by a few Men that seme vary ernest in doing it. Am Dr Sir with the Gratest Esteme your Most Obt: Huml: Set

LAWE: TALIAFERRO

RC (DLC). Docketed by JM. Bracketed letters indicate a torn portion of the Ms.

[1]JM most likely stopped at Princeton during his trip to Philadelphia in November. He returned to New York on 17 Nov. (JM to Randolph, 18 Nov. 1787). John Taliaferro (1768–1852) of King George County served nine terms in the U.S. House of Representatives between 1801 and 1843 (*Biographical Directory of Congress* [1971 ed.], p. 1788).

From Joseph Jones

RICHMOND 18th. Decr. 1787.

DR SR.

Mr. Lambert has executed Col. Thompsons survey of James River excepting that part of it that comprehends the Canal—for a sketch of this part he depends on Mr. Harris[1] the Manager of the Work who has not yet been pleased to furnish it. I shall if the day is fair ride there Tomorow myself and prevail on Harris to give me a sketch of it that Mr. Lambert may compleat the business which I think he has executed exceeding well. Col. R. Goode had promised me to endeavour to procure as many wild crab-tree scions as you wrote for but having heard nothing from him since I made the request, Anthony has gone over to try what he can do about them. I fear if they shall be procured an opportunity will not offer that can convey them by the time you proposed.

The Legislature have proceeded so slowly in the public business, and have even now concluded so few things of consequence that they are scarce worth mentioning. The Delegates will pass the district bill, and it is probable the Senate will do the same but of this there is some doubt—this measure would not have succeeded but for its being accompanied with another bill called a bill for amending the Execution law, which it is said is calculated to give some relief to Debtors, without any direct interference with private contracts. The principal object of this bill is to appoint Comrs. to act on oath to determine, instead of the Sheriff, whether the property offered to sale under executions goes at three forths the value. If they think it does not, the sale may be postponed on bond and security being given to pay in twelve month—which, at the end of the Term, shall be carryed in to a Judt. on motion and no further delay obtained if the money is not punctually paid. It is proposed these bills shall go together and commence the first of June next.[2] The revenue bills is to be considered by a Committee this day. A short law has passed making some appropriations for a sinking fund the produce to be applied by the Executive to purchasing public securities carrying int. The revenue bill at present makes further provision for this fund but how it will terminate depends on the pleasure of the two Houses. A new naval office bill is before a Committee, but not yet reported.[3] We are told you mean to come in and give us your assistance in the Convention. I hope you will do so. Publius is variously ascribed to M—d—n, H—lt—n, J—y. It is certainly among the first publications on the subject of the N. Constitution of Government. What has been done by the [states] on the business and when do their Conventions assemble. I am Dr Sr

RC (DLC). Addressed by Jones and docketed by JM. Signature clipped. Word in brackets partly obscured by a tear in the Ms.

[1] James Harris (d. 1794) was manager of the James River Company (*Va. Gazette, and General Advertiser*, 18 Feb. 1794).

[2] The execution law as finally adopted by the assembly contained no clause suspending its operation until 1 June 1788, but the act establishing district courts was not to take effect until 1 July 1788 (Hening, *Statutes*, XII, 558). Following a remonstrance of the superior court judges against the district court act, a special session of the legislature of June 1788 further suspended the act until 1 Jan. 1789. The act was subsequently repealed by a new district court law passed at the October 1788 session (ibid., XII, 644, 730–63; Mays, *Edmund Pendleton*, II, 273–74).

[3] The bill "to amend the several acts of Assembly concerning naval officers and the collection of Duties" became law on 7 Jan. 1788 (Hening, *Statutes*, XII, 438–52).

To Thomas Jefferson

Dear Sir

The packet has been detained here since the date of the letter which you will receive along with this, by some preparations suggested by an apprehension of war. The delay is very unfavorable to the trees on board for you.

Mr. *de la Forest* the *consul here called on me a* few days ago and *told me he had information* that the *farmers general &*[1] *Mr.* Morris having found their *contract mutually advantageous* are *evading* the *resolutions of the committee* by *tacit arrangements for its continuance.*[2] He observed that the object of the *farmers was singly profit* that of the *government twofold revenue & commerce.* It was consequently the wish of the *latter* to render the *monopoly as little hurtful* to the *trade with America as possible.* He suggested as an *expedient that farmers should be* required *to divide* the *contract*[3] *among six or seven houses French & American* who should be *required to ship annually* to *America a* reasonable proportion *of goods.* This he supposed would produce some *competition* in the *purchases here* and would introduce a *competition also* with *British goods here.* The latter *condition he said* could not be well required of, or executed by a *single contractor.* And the *government could not abolish the farm.* These ideas were *meant for you.*

Since the date of my other letter, The Convention of Delaware have unanimously adopted the new Constitution. That of Pennsylvania has adopted it by a Majority of 46 agst. 23. That of New Jersey is sitting and will adopt pretty unanimously. These are all the Conventions that have met. I hear from North Carolina that the Assembly there is well disposed. Mr. Henry, Mr. Mason, R. H. Lee, and the Governour, continue by their influence to strengthen the opposition in Virginia. The Assembly there is engaged in several mad freaks. Among others a bill has been agreed to in the House of Delegates *prohibiting*,[4] the importation of Rum, *brandy*, and all other spirits not distilled from some American production. All brewed liquors under the same description, with Beef, Tallow-candles, cheese &c. are included in the prohibition. In order to enforce this despotic measure the most despotic means are resorted to. If any person be found after the commencement of the Act, in the use or *possession* of any of the prohibited articles, tho' acquired previous to the law, he is to lose them, and pay a heavy fine. This is the form in which the bill was agreed to by a large majority in the House of Delegates. It is a child of Mr. Henry, & said to be his favorite one. They first voted by a *majority of 30.* that all legal obstructions to the Treaty of peace, should cease in Virginia as soon as laws complying with it should have passed in all the other States. This was the result of four days debate with the most violent opposition from Mr. Henry. A few days afterwards He renewed his efforts, and got a vote, *by a majority of 50*, that Virginia would not comply until G.B. shall have complied.[5]

The States seem to be either wholly omitting to provide for the federal Treasury; or to be withdrawing the scanty appropriations made to it. The latter course has been taken by Massachussetts, Virginia and Delaware.[6] The Treasury Board seem to be in despair of maintaining the shadow of Government much longer. Without money, the Offices must be shut up, and the handful of troops on the frontier disbanded, which will probably bring on an Indian war, and make an impression to our disadvantage on the British Garrisons within our limits.

A letter from Mr. Archd. Stuart dated Richd. Decr. 2d. has the following paragraph "Yesterday a Boat with sixteen men, was brought down the Canal from Westham to its termination which is within one mile & an half of Richmond."

I subjoin an extract from a letter from Genl. Washington dated Decr. 7th. which contains the best information I can give you as to the progress of the works on the Potowmack.

"The survey of the Country between the Eastern & Western waters is not yet reported by the Commissioners, though promised to be made very shortly, the survey being compleated. No draught that can convey an adequate idea of the work on this river has been yet taken. Much of the labour, except at the great falls, has been bestowed in the bed of the river, in a removal of rocks, and deepening the water. At the great falls the labour has indeed been great. The water there (a sufficiency I mean) is taken into a Canal about two hundred yards above the Cateract, & conveyed by a level cut (through a solid rock in some places, and much Stone every where) more than a mile to the lock Seats, five in number by means of which when compleated, the craft will be let into the River below the falls (wch. together amounts to seventy six feet). At the Seneca falls, six miles above the great falls, a channel which has been formed by the river when inundated is under improvement for navigation. The same, *in part*, at Shanandoah. At the lower falls, where nothing has yet been done, a level cut and locks are proposed. These constitute the principal difficulties and will be the great expence of this undertaking. The parts of the river between requiring loose stones only to be removed in order to deepen the water where it is too shallow in dry seasons."

The triennial purge administered to the Council in Virga. has removed

from their seats Samson Matthews—and Mr. Selden. Col. Wm. Heth and
Majr. Jos: Egglestone supply their places.[7] I remain Dr. Sir Yrs. Affectly.

Js. MADISON JR.

RC (DLC). Docketed by Jefferson. Italicized words, unless otherwise noted, are those
encoded by JM using the code Jefferson sent him 11 May 1785. Jefferson decoded the
ciphered paragraph interlinearly.

[1] Throughout the ciphered paragraph JM used the symbol for "a" where "&" was intended.
Jefferson made the corrections in his interlinear decoding.

[2] The "committee" was the "American Committee," a group of French officials investigating Franco-American trade. Formed in early 1786, the committee opposed the tobacco
monopoly of the Farmers General and sought to abolish its contract with Robert Morris. The
"resolutions" evidently referred to the decision of the committee in May 1786 that the Morris
contract should not be renewed at the end of 1787 (Price, *France and the Chesapeake*, II,
761–69).

[3] Miscoded as *contratu*, but corrected by Jefferson in his interlinear decoding.

[4] This and subsequent italicized words are underscored in the Ms.

[5] See Stuart to JM, 2 Dec. 1787 and n. 3.

[6] See Stuart to JM, 2 Dec. 1787 and n. 6.

[7] See Dawson to JM, ca. 10 Nov. 1787 and n. 6. According to the Virginia Constitution
two council members were to "be removed by joint ballot of both Houses of Assembly at the
end of every three years"—hence the "triennial purge" (Hening, *Statutes*, IX, 116).

To George Washington

NEW YORK Decr. 20. 1787.

DEAR SIR

I was favoured on Saturday with your letter of the 7th. instant, along
with which was covered the printed letter of Col. R. H. Lee to the
Governour. It does not appear to me to be a very formidable attack on the
new Constitution; unless it should derive an influence from the names of
the correspondents, which its intrinsic merits do not entitle it to. He is
certainly not perfectly accurate in the statement of all his facts; and I
should infer from the tenor of the objections in Virginia that his plan of an
Executive would hardly be viewed as an amendment of that of the Convention. It is a little singular that three of the most distinguished Advocates for amendments; and who expect to unite the thirteen States in their
project, appear to be pointedly at variance with each other on one of the
capital articles of the System. Col. Lee proposes that the President should
chuse a Council of Eleven and with their advice have the absolute appointment of all Officers. Col: Mason's proposition is that a Council of six
should be appointed by the Congress. What degree of power he would
confide to it I do not know. The idea of the Governour is that there should

be a plurality of co-equal heads, distinguished probably by other peculiarities in the organization. It is pretty certain that some others who make a common cause with them in the general attempt to bring about alterations differ still more from them, than they do from each other; and that they themselves differ as much on some other great points as on the Constitution of the Executive.

You did not judge amiss of Mr Jay. The paragraph affirming a change in His opinion of the plan of the Convention, was an arrant forgery. He has contradicted it in a letter to Mr. J. Vaughan which has been printed in the Philadelphia Gazettes. Tricks of this sort are not uncommon with the Enemies of the new Constitution. Col. Mason's objections were as I am told published in Boston mutilated of that which pointed at the regulation of Commerce.[1] Docr. Franklin's concluding speech which you will meet with in one of the papers herewith inclosed, is both mutilated & adulterated so as to change both the form & the spirit of it.[2]

I am extremely obliged by the notice you take of my request concerning the Potowmack. I must insist that you will not consider it as an object of any further attention.

The Philada. papers will have informed you of the result of the Convention of that State. N. Jersey is now in Convention, & has probably by this time adopted the Constitution. Genl. Irvine of the Pena. Delegation who is just arrived here, and who conversed with some of the members at Trenton tells me that great unanimity reigns in the Convention.

Connecticut it is pretty certain will decide also in the Affirmative by a large majority. So it is presumed will N. Hampshire; though her Convention will be a little later than could be wished. There are not enough of the returns in Massts. known for a final judgment of the probable event in that State. As far as the returns are known they are extremely favorable; but as they are cheifly from the maritime parts of the State, they are a precarious index of the public sentiment. I have good reason to believe that if you are in correspondence with any Gentlemen in that quarter, and a proper occasion offered for an explicit communication of your good wishes for the plan, so as barely to warrant an explicit assertion of the fact, that it would be attended with valuable effects. I barely drop the idea. The circumstances on which the propriety of it depends, are best known to, as they will be best judged of by yourself. The information from N. Carolina gave me great pleasure. We hear nothing from the States South of it. With the most perfect esteem & regard I am Dear Sir Your Affecte. friend & Obedt. servt.

Js. Madison Jr

RC (DLC: Washington Papers). Docketed by Washington. Enclosures not found.

[1] Mason strongly objected to the provision in the Constitution requiring only a simple majority in Congress to pass laws regulating commerce. This criticism was not included in the copy of Mason's "Objections" published in the Boston *Mass. Centinel* of 21 Nov. 1787 and the Boston *Independent Chronicle* of 22 Nov. 1787. According to Paul L. Ford, it was omitted in all the copies sent to newspapers north of Maryland (*Essays on the Constitution*, p. 162 n.). Oliver Ellsworth noted the omission and used it as the basis for a sharp attack on Mason in his "Landholder" essays (ibid., pp. 161–62, 172–73). See also JM to Washington, 26 Dec. 1787 and n. 1.

[2] JM evidently referred to the commentary on Franklin's concluding speech at the Federal Convention by "Z," an Antifederalist, in the 17 Dec. 1787 issue of the *N.Y. Journal* (taken from the Boston *Independent Chronicle* of 6 Dec. 1787). "Z" quoted only those parts of the speech expressing doubts about the Constitution, making Franklin appear as a lukewarm Federalist at best.

From Thomas Jefferson

Paris Dec. 20. 1787.

Dear Sir

My last to you was of Oct. 8. by the Count de Moustier. Yours of July 18. Sep. 6. & Oct. 24. have been successively received, yesterday, the day before & three or four days before that. I have only had time to read the letters, the printed papers communicated with them, however interesting, being obliged to lie over till I finish my dispatches for the packet, which dispatches must go from hence the day after tomorrow. I have much to thank you for. First and most for the cyphered paragraph respecting myself. These little informations are very material towards forming my own decisions. I would be glad even to know when any individual member thinks I have gone wrong in any instance. If I know myself it would not excite ill blood in me, while it would assist to guide my conduct, perhaps to justify it, and to keep me to my duty, alert. I must thank you too for the information in Thos. Burke's case, tho' you will have found by a subsequent letter that I have asked of you a further investigation of that matter. It is to gratify the lady who is at the head of the Convent wherein my daughters are, & who, by her attachment & attention to them, lays me under great obligations. I shall hope therefore still to receive from you the result of the further enquiries my second letter had asked. The parcel of rice which you informed me had miscarried accompanied my letter to the Delegates of S. Carolina. Mr. Bourgoin was to be the bearer of both and both were delivered together into the hands of his relation here who introduced him to me, and who at a subsequent moment undertook to convey them to Mr. Bourgoin. This person was an engraver

335

particularly recommended to Dr. Franklin & mr. Hopkinson.[1] Perhaps he may have mislaid the little parcel of rice among his baggage. I am much pleased that the sale of Western lands is so succesful. I hope they will absorb all the Certificates of our Domestic debt speedily in the first place, and that then offered for cash they will do the same by our foreign one.

The season admitting only of operations in the Cabinet, and these being in a great measure secret, I have little to fill a letter. I will therefore make up the deficiency by adding a few words on the Constitution proposed by our Convention. I like much the general idea of framing a government which should go on of itself peaceably, without needing continual recurrence to the state legislatures. I like the organization of the government into Legislative, Judiciary & Executive. I like the power given the Legislature to levy taxes, and for that reason solely approve of the greater house being chosen by the people directly. For tho' I think a house chosen by them will be very illy qualified to legislate for the Union, for foreign nations &c. yet this evil does not weigh against the good of preserving inviolate the fundamental principle that the people are not to be taxed but by representatives chosen immediately by themselves. I am captivated by the compromise of the opposite claims of the great & little states, of the latter to equal, and the former to proportional influence. I am much pleased too with the substitution of the method of voting by persons, instead of that of voting by states: and I like the negative given to the Executive with a third of either house, though I should have liked it better had the Judiciary been associated for that purpose, or invested with a similar and separate power. There are other good things of less moment. I will now add what I do not like. First the omission of a bill of rights providing clearly & without the aid of sophisms for freedom of religion, freedom of the press, protection against standing armies, restriction against monopolies, the eternal & unremitting force of the habeas corpus laws, and trials by jury in all matters of fact triable by the laws of the land & not by the law of Nations. To say, as mr. Wilson does, that a bill of rights was not necessary because all is reserved in the case of the general government which is not given, while in the particular ones all is given which is not reserved, might do for the Audience to whom it was addressed, but is surely a gratis dictum, opposed by strong inferences from the body of the instrument, as well as from the omission of the clause of our present confederation which had declared that in express terms.[2] It was a hard conclusion to say because there has been no uniformity among the states as to the cases triable by jury, because some have been so incautious as to abandon this mode of trial, therefore the more prudent states shall be reduced to the same level of calamity. It would have been much more just & wise to have concluded the other way that as most of the states had judiciously preserved this palladium, those who had wandered should be brought back to it, and to have established general right instead of general wrong. Let me add that a bill of rights is what the people are entitled to against every government on earth, general or particular, & what no just government should refuse or rest on inference.[3] The second feature I dislike, and greatly dislike, is the abandonment in every instance of the necessity of rotation in office, and most particularly in the case of the President. Experience concurs with reason in concluding that the first magistrate will always be re-elected if the constitution permits it. He is then an officer for life. This once observed it becomes of so much consequence to certain nations to have a friend or a foe at the head of our affairs that they will interfere with money & with arms. A Galloman or an Angloman will be supported by the nation he befriends. If once elected, and at a second or third election outvoted by one or two votes, he will pretend false votes, foul play, hold possession of the reins of government, be supported by the states voting for him, especially if they are the central ones lying in a compact body themselves & separating their opponents: and they will be aided by one nation of Europe, while the majority are aided by another. The election of a President of America some years hence will be much more interesting to certain nations of Europe than ever the election of a king of Poland was. Reflect on all the instances in history antient & modern, of elective monarchies, and say if they do not give foundation for my fears. The Roman emperors, the popes, while they were of any importance, the German emperors till they became hereditary in practice, the kings of Poland, the Deys of the Ottoman dependancies. It may be said that if elections are to be attended with these disorders, the seldomer they are renewed the better. But experience shews that the only way to prevent disorder is to render them uninteresting by frequent changes. An incapacity to be elected a second time would have been the only effectual preventative. The power of removing him every fourth year by the vote of the people is a power which will not be exercised. The king of Poland is removeable every day by the Diet, yet he is never removed. Smaller objections are the Appeal in fact as well as law, and the binding all persons Legislative Executive & Judiciary by oath to maintain that constitution. I do not pretend to decide what would be the best method of procuring the establishment of the manifold good things in this constitution, and of getting rid of the bad. Whether by adopting it in hopes of future amendment, or, after it has been duly weighed & canvassed by the people, after seeing the parts they generally dislike, & those they generally approve, to say to them 'We see now what you wish. Send together your deputies again, let them frame a constitution for you omitting what you have condemned, & establishing the powers you approve. Even these will be a great addition to the energy of your government.' At all events I hope you will not be discouraged from other trials, if the present one should fail of it's full effect. I have thus told you freely what I like & dislike: merely as a matter of curiosity, for I know your own judgment has been formed on all these points after having heard every thing which could be urged on them. I own I am not a friend to a very energetic government. It is always oppressive. The late rebellion in Massachusets has given more alarm than I think it should have done. Calculate that one rebellion in 13 states in the course of 11 years, is but one for each state in a century & a half. No country should be so long without one. Nor will any degree of power in the hands of government prevent insurrections. France, with all it's despotism, and two or three hundred thousand men always in arms has had three insurrections in the three years I have been here in every one of which greater numbers were engaged than in Massachusets & a great deal more blood was spilt. In Turkey, which Montesquieu supposes more despotic, insurrections are the events of every day. In England, where the hand of power is lighter than here, but heavier than with us they happen every half dozen years. Compare again the ferocious depredations of their insurgents with the order, the moderation & the almost self extinguishment of ours. After all, it is my principle that the will of the Majority should always prevail. If they approve the proposed Convention[4] in all it's parts, I shall concur in it chearfully, in hopes that they will amend it whenever they shall find it work wrong. I think our governments will remain virtuous for many centuries; as long as they are chiefly agricultural; and this will be as long as there shall be vacant lands in any part of America. When they get piled upon one another in large cities, as in Europe, they will become corrupt as in Europe. Above all things I hope the education of the common people will be attended to; convinced that on their good sense we may rely with the most security for the preservation of a due degree of liberty. I have tired you by this time with my disquisitions & will therefore only add assurances of the sincerety of those sentiments of esteem & attachment with which I am Dear Sir your affectionate friend & servant

TH: JEFFERSON

P.S. The instability of our laws is really an immense evil. I think it would be well to provide in our constitutions that there shall always be a twelve-month between the ingrossing a bill & passing it: that it should then be offered to it's passage without changing a word: and that if circumstances should be thought to require a speedier passage, it should take two thirds of both houses instead of a bare majority.

RC (DLC); FC (DLC: Jefferson Papers). Jefferson enclosed a copy of an extract of this letter, with numerous changes, in his letter to Uriah Forrest, 31 Dec. 1787 (Boyd, *Papers of Jefferson*, XII, 442–43 n., 475–79).

[1]François-Joseph Bourgoin, a French miniaturist, "skilled in drawing and engraving." In the fall of 1787 he left Paris for America where he hoped to establish himself—in particular, in Philadelphia (Jefferson to Francis Hopkinson, 18 Sept. 1787, Boyd, *Papers of Jefferson*, XII, 140; George C. Groce and David H. Wallace, *The New-York Historical Society's Dictionary of Artists in America, 1564–1860* [New Haven, 1957], p. 69; E. Bénézit, *Dictionnaire critique et documentaire des Peintres, Sculpteurs, Dessinateurs et Graveurs* [new ed.; 8 vols.; n.p., France, 1955], II, 74).

[2]Jefferson had undoubtedly seen a newspaper report of James Wilson's speech of 6 Oct. 1787 attacking critics of the proposed Constitution. The "Audience to whom it was addressed" was a sympathetic crowd at the State House in Philadelphia (*Pa. Gazette*, 17 Oct. 1787; reprinted in McMaster and Stone, *Pennsylvania and the Federal Constitution*, I, 143–49). The "clause of our present confederation" was Art. II of the Articles of Confederation: "Each state retains its sovereignty, freedom and independence, and every power, jurisdiction and right, which is not by this confederation expressly delegated to the United States in Congress assembled."

[3]This often-quoted sentence was interlined.

[4]Jefferson's slip of the pen—he meant "Constitution."

From Henry Lee

[ca. 20 December 1787]

My DEAR SIR

I am so far on my return from a visit to Richmond. On my route I spent a day with Judge Pendleton. He continues amidst the strange change of opinion on the worth of the fœderal Government, unalterable. This firmness does not belong to all the bench, for it was declared as indubitable, that the Cheif Justice had abandoned his first sentiments on this subject. I wished to have given you a particular explanation of the politics in this country—but my absence from home has been longer than I intended & the approach of a snow storm renders it prudent to delay as little as possible. Three sets of men are to be found on the question of Government. One opposed to any system, was it even sent from heaven which tends to confirm the union of the states. Henry is leader of this band. Another who would accept the new constitution from conviction of its own excellence, or any fœderal system, sooner than risk the dissolution of the confederacy, & a third who dislike the proposed Government, wish it amended, but if this is not practicable, would adopt it sooner than jeopardize the Union.

Mason may be considered as the head of this set.

From such a discordance in opinion, I beleive if the friends to the Govt. in the state convention should manage wisely, & if nine states should have ratified it before Virga. assembles that we may count on the dominion as an accepting state. Your county is divided like many others in their sentiments. Barber & Burnley are warmly opposed, & may perhaps consider it their duty to prevent your election. This you ought to apprehend & ought without respect to delicacy or any other motive stop in its progress.

Then return soon among them & use your endeavors to secure your election. If you think you may fail in orange several countys in Kentucky would on application by letr. elect you. Deliver my enclosed letr if you please. Adieu

Henry Lee.

RC (DLC). Docketed by JM, "Decr. 1787."

To Philip Mazzei

Letter not found.

20 December 1787. Acknowledged in Mazzei to JM, 4 Feb. 1788. Leads Mazzei to conclude that he has no hope of relief in the Dohrman business until a federal government is established in America.

From Philip Mazzei

Parigi, 21. Dicembre 1787.

Carmo: Amico,

Mi perviene la stimma: vostra dei 5. del passato mentre ò appena tempo da rispondere, non per trascuratezza del Comr: Jones o di Mr. Jefferson, ma a motivo di circostanze locali, &c. Riguardo all'affare di Mr. Dorhman, ò gran piacere di non essermi ingannato nel buon concetto che ne avevo formato; ma egli non sarà mai scusabile d'avermi assicurato su quel che sapeva dovere almen dubitare, dopo averlo io candidamente informato della mia trista situazione, e dell'irreparabil danno che mi avrebbe apportato un contrattempo. Nè l'ottenere adesso rigorosa giustizia, nè i suoi sforzi generosi a mio favore possono indennizzarmi. Io però non ò diritto di chiedere, nè chiedo più di quel che le leggi dichiarano. Da questo non posso astenermi senza essere ingiusto verso i miei creditori. Il denaro sarà preferibile ai certificati del Congresso, ma la sbrigazione è di tanta importanza, che dovendo aspettare per ottenerlo preferirei i certificati subito, purchè fossero valutati al prezzo corrente e messi in testa dei Sigri:

Nicholas e Jacob Vanstaphorst, conforme vi scrissi già. Potete dunque ricevere denaro, o certificati, o porzione dell'uno e degli altri, conforme giudicherete più sbrigativo e più conveniente al mio interesse. Quanto alle cambiali (ricevendo denaro) vi prego di prenderle per quella piazza d'Europa, ove il cambio sarà più vantaggioso, o piuttosto meno svantaggioso per me. Soprattutto vi raccomando la sicurezza. Io dovrò continovare a pagare il cambio e ricambio, del debito che avrei dovuto pagare col denaro della cambiale di Dorhman, fino alla scadenza delle future cambiali che avrete la bontà di rimettermi. Troppo ci vorrebbe a dirvi quel che ò sofferto, e la vostra sensibilità non me lo permette. Vo' dirvi un solo aneddoto, che non direi qui *neppure a Jefferson*. Il legno da bruciare, come forse saprete, qui è carissimo. La mia miseria è tale, che fino agli 11. Novembre fui senza fuoco. Ciò à probabilmente contribuito a produrmi qualche infermità corporale, della quale tuttavia mi risento. Il principal motivo, per cui vi informo di questa particolarità, è la sparanza che vogliate degnarvi di ragguagliarne Mr. Edmond Randolph, per tentar di risvegliare la sua compassione verso di me.

Quanto al mio libro, le vostre riflessioni mi paiono tutte savie e prudenti, sicchè mi regolarò a norma delle medesime. Vedo che non avete ricevuto tutti i foglj stampati chi vi ò mandato, ma poco importa, poichè tra 15 giorni circa potrò spedirvi tutta l'opera divisa in 4 parti, e legata in 3. volumi. Nel supplemento, di cui si stampa ora l'ultimo foglio, vedrete le mie osservazioni sulla proposta costituzion federativa, le quali spero che non vi dispiaceranno, quantunque non siamo *unisoni* in tutto. Il tempo è breve e la mano non mi regge; addio. Continovatemi la vostra cara amicizia, e credetemi invariabilmente, e di vero cuore, vostro sincero Amico

FILIPPO MAZZEI.

P.S. Vi prego di spedir l'inclusa in modo che vada sicura al suo destino.

CONDENSED TRANSLATION

Mazzei has not had time to reply to JM's letter of 5 November because of local circumstances. In settling his affair with Dohrman, Mazzei prefers money to congressional certificates, but a quick settlement is so important that he directs JM to accept money, certificates, or both—whichever JM thinks best serves Mazzei's interests. Mazzei's financial plight is so desperate, and kindling wood so expensive, that he could not afford to light a fire until 11 November—a fact probably contributing to his present illness. He wants JM to tell Randolph this to arouse his compassion. JM's reflections on Mazzei's book seem wise and prudent. Within fifteen days Mazzei will be able to forward the entire work bound in three volumes. The supplement will contain his observations on the proposed American Constitution.

RC (DLC).

From William Short

Dear Sir

I am at present to acknowlege the reciept of your favor dated Oct. 24. If you consider yourself obliged to thank me for having procured you the acquaintance of M. de Crevecoeur; his friends here, of which he has a great number, are equally thankful to me on the occasion. They consider, & with great reason, that it would have been impossible to render him a more agreeable service. Allow me at the same time Sir to express to you my gratitude for the real information contained in your letter. It made us more master of the subjects, to which the convention has given rise, than any thing we had seen or heard till then. Since that, your letter to Mr. Jefferson by Commodore Jones has arrived. On the statement which you gave me Sir, of the advocates & opponents to the new Constitution in Virginia, it seems impossible that it should pass in that State. Should it have the same fate in Rhode-Island, N. York & Maryland, we shall see the ill consequences of a clause which alarmed me from the beginning; I mean the adoption of the new constitution by nine States. The dissenting States being thus dispersed seem to have the quality only of separating the assenting States without the power of uniting themselves. I think the adoption by nine & the refusal by four of the States is the worst possible situation to which the new plan can give birth; & it seems probable that that will be the situation. Would it not have been better to have fixed on the number eleven or twelve instead of nine? In that case the plan would have been either refused altogether or adopted by such a commanding majority as would almost necessarily have brought in the others in the end. There is one thing however which may be opposed to all the arguments that may be adduced in opposition to the new plan; & that is that the members who composed the convention must have had a fuller & better view of the ground & must have considered it more attentively than those who object to it. They must have seen certainly a variety of difficulties which their debates must have presented in full view & which are hidden perhaps from the most penetrating observation under other circumstances. Particularly to us at this distance, I am sure it is impossible to form a proper opinion on the subject. There is only one reflexion wch. occurs to me in which I have any confidence of being right: & that is that the Members of the convention would not have proposed so desperate a remedy if the evil had not appeared to them equally desperate. I am afraid the case will not be mended by the Patient's refusing to take the violent dose prescribed.

You form a very proper idea of the little weight which the opinions of the learned in Europe on the result of the convention, deserve. I have only seen as yet such of that character as are in Paris, where they are so much occupied with their own affairs, as scarcely to have had time to have read the new plan, much less to have considered it attentively. In Europe however they are almost uniformly for strengthening the hands of Congress or the federal head. In this they are probably right; but they are right on wrong ground—there are many who have no idea of their being a governmental force existing any where but in Congress: you cannot put into their heads their being actually an efficient government in each of the States. They know only Congress as the Governors & the rest of the United States as the governed. When therefore they have read the act which forms the Congress, they determine that there is not power enough delegated by the governed & determine that the quantum ought to be increased—they leave out of the account altogether the governing force existing elsewhere. Still however their conclusion is right though the terms by which they get to it, are wrong. The fact is Sir, that they are inconcievably ignorant of whatever relates to the practice of free government, although they have many of them made valuable researches in the theory of it. Such of the English politicians as are here exult much at seeing that the American governments begin to consider themselves under the necessity of approximating toward the *British constitution.*

War or peace for the ensuing spring poses a problem impossible as yet to solve. I believe it depends on the arrangement of the finances of this country: they are certainly ameliorating; but slowly. A loan of 120. millions of livres has been opened some time ago. No body can say whether it is filled—or goes on well—or goes on slowly. I have heard all the three propositions advanced & equally well supported in the space of twenty four hours. The 1st. of Jan. a situation of the finances is to be made public. Until then opinions on the subject must be suspended. You will have heard that the King came to Paris & took a seat in the Parliament in order to engage them to enregister the edict of annual loans for five years—that the Duke of Orleans & two members of the Parliament were exiled the day after for their boldness in opposing Majesty that day. The King has promised the States-general in 1791. at the latest. This will be a revolution completely operated in the government in this country. Should it effect a permanent constitution this country will unquestionably be the richest & most powerful in the world in twenty years. I hope Congress will be pleased with the Count de Moustier. He is so good a man & so well disposed that it can hardly be otherwise. I am glad they have not renewed a commission for the court of London. Yet as that court thinks of sending out a minister to New-York, I fear that step will make Congress change their system. It would do them however no honor in Europe or any where else I think if they did. Their present Servants at London however are very worthy & deserving men notwithstanding the error into which one has fallen of having written a book, & the misfortune of the other in its being addressed to him.[1] Adieu my dear Sir & be assured that no body can be more attached to your happiness than your ob

W SHORT

RC (DLC). Addressed by Short. Docketed by JM.

[1] As originally published, John Adams's *Defence of the Constitutions of Government* was in the form of a series of letters addressed to William Stephens Smith, secretary to the American legation at London.

From Andrew Shepherd

ORANGE 22th. December 1787

DR. SIR

With pleasure not long since I heard of your welfare of which I sincerely wish a continuance, from your last,[1] it has been intimated to your freinds in this County, that it will be agreeable to you to represent them in the Convention, which I think in my own opinion will meet with a general approbation, but as there is no guarding against artfull persons from injecting their poison into the unwarie, I would beg leave to recommend your presence as soon as you conveniently could; I have not as yet heard of any other Candidate but your freind Majr. Moore, Jnr. J. G. prepares himself for the Assbly, and am pretty certain that youl. both meet with his influence.[2] I think at present there are but few in this County agt. the new Constitution, it has lately in Richdn. been much opposed, but since I have been informed that its gaining freinds. Our Old Senator Capt Walker stands forth in Culpepper, As do's Genl. Stevens.[3] I have not heared for certain of any other, however it is expected there will be as there are some very great oponents. Our Assembly are still setting, & the last Accotts. we have from there, that nothing very materiale was finally done. The Tax on White persons & Young Negro's is expected to be taken off, as it had passed the lower house, that the Certificate Tax was to be with drawn, & to be purchased up by the Executive as they could from the holders—an additionall duty expected to be laid on Spirits &ca.[4] I wish they may not go into extremes on that afair. As youl. no doubt be more fully informed of these circumstances from other correspondents, youl. please execuse

344

me from takeing up yr time, on so triffling an information. All freinds in their common situation, & wishing you a safe return to them I am with the Compliments of the approaching Season D Sir Your most affet & Hul Svt

ANDREW SHEPHERD[5]

RC (NN). Docketed by JM.

[1] Letter not found.

[2] James Gordon, Jr. (1759–1799), was elected to both the House of Delegates and the June convention. William Moore evidently dropped his candidacy for the convention in favor of JM and Gordon. Their opponents were Thomas Barbour and Charles Porter (Swem and Williams, *Register*, pp. 29, 244; James Madison, Sr., to JM, 30 Jan. 1788; Gordon to JM, 17 Feb. 1788).

[3] James Walker had represented the Senate district that included Orange, Culpeper, and Spotsylvania counties in 1777 and 1778. Edward Stevens (1745–1820) represented the same district in 1776 and from 1779 to 1790. Neither man was elected to the convention from Culpeper, where the successful candidates were French Strother and Joel Early (*PJM*, I, 148 n. 2; II, 68 n. 2; Swem and Williams, *Register*, pp. 243, 432, 441).

[4] See Stuart to JM, 21 Oct. 1787 and n. 3. Although the certificate tax was eliminated, the legislature laid an additional duty on imported goods payable in certificates as an alternative means of retiring them. In addition, the interest on the certificates collected in taxes and duties was appropriated to the sinking fund, to be employed by the governor and council in the direct purchase of certificates still outstanding.

[5] Andrew Shepherd, a justice of the peace and vestryman of St. Thomas's Parish, had been sheriff of Orange County since October 1786 (Scott, *History of Orange County*, p. 71; *JCSV*, III, 585).

To George Washington

NEW YORK Decr. 26. 1787.

DEAR SIR

I am just informed by a Delegate from New Hamshire that he has a letter from President Sullivan which tells him that the Legislature had unanimously agreed to call a convention as recommended, to meet in February. The second wednesday is the day if I have not mistaken it. We have no further information of much importance from Massachussetts. It appears that Cambridge the residence of Mr. Gerry has left him out of the choice for the Convention, and put in Mr. Dana formerly Minister of the U. States in Europe, and another Gentleman, both of them firmly opposed to Mr. Gerry's Politics. I observe too in a Massts. paper that the omission of Col. Mason's objection with regard to commerce, in the first publication of his Objections, has been supplied. This will more than undo the effect of the mutilated view of them.[1] New Jersey the Newspapers tell us has adopted the Constitution unanimously. Our European intelligence remains perfectly as it stood at the date of my last. With the most Affectionate esteem & attachment I am Dear [Sir], Your Obedient & very hble servt.

Js. Madison Jr.

RC (DLC: Washington Papers); Tr (DLC). RC docketed by Washington.

[1] The omitted paragraph was published in the Boston *Mass. Centinel* of 19 Dec. 1787, preceded by an extract of a letter to the printer from his New York correspondent. The correspondent explained that the copy of Mason's "Objections" he had sent to the paper earlier had been obtained "from a certain antifederal character, in this city—who, it since appears, like a true antifederalist, omitted one objection, which was the principal in Col. Mason's mind."

From Edmund Randolph

Richmond decr. 27. 1787.

My dear friend

Altho' many mails have passed since I wrote to you last, I am not without excuses of a satisfactory nature; which are too long and unimportant to you to hear in detail. Having shaken off the impediments to writing, I shall be hereafter punctual.

My letter is now inclosed to you.[1] What the general opinion is, I would not undertake to vouch because I stay much at home, and I find daily reason to distrust reports, which always receive a tincture from the wishes of the narrator. But I rather suspect, that the current sets violently against the new constitution. Nay I must be permitted to express a fear, lest true fœderalism should be pressed hard in the convention. General Wilkinson from Kentucke, who is now here, is not to be appeased in his violence against the constitution; and it is presumed that thro his means the vote of Kentucky will have the same direction. He is rivetted by Colo. Harry Lee, declaring to him, that the surrender of the Mississippi would probably be among the early acts of the new congress. Mr. Meriwether Smith moved yesterday for a circular letter from our to the other legislatures, intimating the likelihood of amendment here. But his motion was changed into an instruction to the executive to forward the late act.[2] Mr. Henry is implacable. Colo. Mason seems to rise beyond his first ground. He will be elected, it is said, for Stafford, and Colo. Mercer, it is also said, will be sent for by the people of that county for a similar purpose.[3] I need not assure you, that it would give me no pleasure to see my conduct in refusing to sign, sanctified, if it was to produce a hazard to the union; and if I know myself, I have no extreme ardor to acquire converts to my opinions. But I verily believe, that the only expedient which can save the fœderal government in any shape in Virginia, will be the adoption of some such plan, as mine.[4] However the high-toned friends to the constitution are still very sanguine, that the whole will run thro with ease.

A district bill has passed the delegates. It sticks with the Senate, who are employed in making amendments, to which the delegates will not agree. The fate of the bill is uncertain.

The prohibition of the importation of spirituous liquors is gone & indeed cannot be executed, even if it was to be enacted into a law.

A sinking fund has been established and the executive are to speculate with it in the purchase of public securities.

A heavy impost is laid in certificates on goods imported. The object of it was to detach from the fœderal government those, who might be allured by the revenue. Yrs mo. afftely

E. R.

RC (DLC). Docketed by JM. Enclosure not found.

[1]Randolph's published letter to the Speaker of the House of Delegates, 10 Oct. 1787, explaining his reasons for not signing the Constitution. See Randolph to JM, 23 [ca. 29] Oct. 1787 and n. 3. A copy of the letter in pamphlet form is in the Rare Book Division, Library of Congress. The letter was also printed in the *Va. Independent Chronicle* of 2 Jan. 1788 and the *Va. Gazette and Weekly Advertiser* of 3 and 10 Jan. 1788.

[2]"*Resolved*, That the Governor be desired to transmit to the Executive and Legislature of the respective States, a copy of the act passed at the present session, entitled 'an act, concerning the Convention to be held in June next,'" (*JHDV*, Oct. 1787, p. 119; Hening, *Statutes*, XII, 462–63).

[3]Mason was elected, but his Stafford colleague at the June convention was Andrew Buchanan, also an Antifederalist (Swem and Williams, *Register*, p. 244; Elliot, *Debates* [1836 ed.], III, 588, 590). John Francis Mercer had moved to Anne Arundel County in Maryland and opposed the Constitution in the Maryland ratifying convention (Rutland, *Papers of George Mason*, I, lxxix).

[4]During the closing days of the Philadelphia convention Randolph had proposed that the state conventions should be permitted to submit amendments "to a second General Convention, with full power to settle the Constitution finally" (Farrand, *Records*, II, 479, 561). He repeated this proposition, with some modifications, in his public letter on the Constitution (P. L. Ford, *Pamphlets on the Constitution*, p. 274).

From Tench Coxe

PHILADA. Decemr. 28th. 1787.

DEAR SIR

I trouble you once more with an Attempt of mine to explain a point connected wth. the new federal constitution. Finding from a conversation with Mr. Wilson & Dr. Rush that an Idea in Mr. R. H Lee's letter to your

Governor concerning the commercial powers of Congress was doing mischief in Virginia I devoted last Sunday to an investigation of it. I take the liberty of enclosing a couple of copies of it, under the signature of *an American*.[1] I shall take some pains to have it republished to the *Southward*, and wish it could be inserted in some of the country News papers of New York and New England, or that it might be put into the hands of some proper person in the Connecticut Convention to be made use of, if *occasion* should appear. I do not think it can answer any good purpose in their Seaports, tho from the decided approbation of the System along the Coast I do not think any thing is to be feared from its consequences among the Merchants there. It is likely you may have some earlier opty. than we for S. Carolina, or Georgia. I have pursued the advice of the proverb that *fair Words* go the furthest, for as I meant it principally for the *gentlemen* of Virga. and for Mr. Lee's friends I think it more likely to have a good effect from treating him with all the Respect they can claim for him. Col. Hamilton will be able to give you an Opinion on its usefulness in the interior parts of the State of new york, and will also be a good Judge of New England.

Our advices from Georgia recd. on Thursday are very agreeable. From them I should not be surprized at an Unanimous adoption there. The political Society of Richmond (whose respectability I know not) have approved of it after a formal discussion by a great Majority. I am very truely dear Sir, yr. mo. respectf. h. Servt

TENCH COXE

RC (DLC). Docketed by JM. Enclosures not found.

[1] Coxe's piece, signed "An American," was published in the Philadelphia *Independent Gazetteer* of 28 Dec. 1787, immediately preceded by Richard Henry Lee's letter of 16 Oct. 1787 to Edmund Randolph. It was also printed (unaccompanied by Lee's letter) in the *Pa. Gazette* of 16 Jan. 1788. Coxe sought to answer Lee's complaint that "in this congressional legislature a bare majority can enact commercial laws, so that the representatives of the seven northern states, as they will have a majority, can, by law, create the most oppressive monopolies upon the five southern states, whose circumstances and productions are essentially different from theirs, although not a single man of their voters are the representatives of, or amenable to, the people of the southern states" (Ballagh, *Letters of Richard Henry Lee*, II, 454). Disputing Lee's notion of a sectional division between the agrarian South and the commercial North, Coxe argued that agriculture was overwhelmingly predominant in all of the U.S., not in the South alone.

To Tench Coxe

NEW YORK Jany. 3d. 1788

DEAR SIR

I have been favored with yours of the 28 Ult: and thank you for the paper which it inclosed. Your arguments appear to me to place the subject to which they relate in its true light, and must be satisfactory to the writer himself whom they oppose, if he can suspend for a moment his preconceived opinions. But whether they should have any effect or not on him, they will unquestionably be of service in Virginia, and probably in the other Southern States. Col. Hamilton has read the paper with equal pleasure & approbation with myself. He seems to think that the Farmers of New York are in no danger of being infected with an improper jealousy of a sacrifice of their interests to a partiality for commerce or navigation. Connecticut is more likely perhaps to be awake to suspicions of that sort; and it will be well to counteract them every where by candid and judicious explanations. I propose to send a copy of yours to S. Carolina by the first conveyance; and to put another into the hands of some Gentleman who corresponds with Georgia if I can find one. I have no correspondent in that State.

I never till very lately received an answer from Virga. on the subject of your former observations in support of the fœdl Constitution. I find now that the three first letters were published at Richmond in a pamphlet with one or two other little pieces, and that they had a very valuable effect. The 4th. was circulated in the Newspapers, not having arrived in time to be put into the pamphlet.[1]

We have received no information of very late date or of a satisfactory nature from Europe. The London Head in the paper of this morning which I inclose, mentions a circumstance which leads to some new reflections on the situation of the Dutch.[2]

I have no intelligence from the States Eastward of this worth adding. The elections in Massts. must by this time authorize a pretty good estimate of the two parties with regard to the plan of the Convention, but I am not yet possessed of the conjectures on the subject. It seems that both Mr. Gerry who opposed the plan in Convention, and Mr. Dana who followed the example in Congs. are left out of the returns from their respective districts. Perhaps the enmity of the former may not only be embittered, but rendered more active and successful by this disappointment. On the floor of the Convention he could only have urged bad arguments, which might be answered & exposed by good ones. Without doors he will be able not only to urge them without opposition, but to insinuate that he could

349

say much more, had he not been deprived of a hearing by the machinations of those who were afraid of being confronted.[3]

The post from the South being not yet come in I can not give you any Richmond News. The last I received was a continuation of the evidences of an increasing opposition to the new Government. The Characters which head it account fully for the change of opinions. With very great esteem & regard I am Dr Sir, Yr Obedt. & very hble servt.

Js. Madison Jr

RC (DLC). Enclosure not found.

[1] The pamphlet that JM referred to was probably an early version of the collection entitled *Various Extracts on the Fœderal Government*. The later edition contained all four numbers of "An American Citizen" (Tench Coxe). See Stuart to JM, 9 Nov. 1787 and n. 2.

[2] The N.Y. *Daily Advertiser* of 3 Jan. 1788 carried an item from London, dated 23 Oct. 1787, reporting that King Frederick William II of Prussia had demanded payment for the expenses of Prussian troops then occupying Amsterdam.

[3] Although Gerry was not elected to the Massachusetts convention, he was invited to attend and answer questions concerning the Constitution (Samuel B. Harding, *The Contest over the Ratification of the Federal Constitution in the State of Massachusetts* [Cambridge, 1896], p. 62). See also King to JM, 16 and 20 Jan. 1788.

From Edmund Randolph

Richmond Jany. 3. 1788.

My dear friend

By this time the district-bill has passed, in nearly the same form with that of the last year, except that four additional judges are to be created. Mr. Jos: Jones, who is now absent, has thro' Colo. Monroe signified his wish to be regenerated a judge. He will succeed. It is conjectured that the other three will appear in St. G. Tucker, Grayson, and Prentis.[1]

The constitution is not even spoken of; not from a want of zeal in either party, but from downright weariness. No new conjectures have arisen. Mr. G. Morris is confident that the plan will run thro' safely. I question it, unless nine states should adopt it before June.

You must come in. Some people in Orange are opposed to your politicks. Your election to the convention is, I believe, sure; but I beg you not to hazard it by being absent at the time.

A terrible fire began here yesterday in the same quarter of the town, which fell a victim to the flames last year. But it was stopped with difficulty after the loss of four houses.[2]

The assembly will rise about the beginning of next week. Adieu yrs. mo. affetly.

Edm: Randolph

RC (NN: Emmet Collection). Addressed by Randolph and franked.

[1] Joseph Jones had served as a judge of the General Court in 1778 and 1779 (Brocken-brough, *Virginia Cases*, II, x). Contrary to Randolph's prediction, Jones, though nominated, was not elected to a judgeship. The four additional judges of the General Court chosen by the General Assembly on 4 Jan. 1788 were Joseph Prentis, St. George Tucker, Gabriel Jones, and Richard Parker (Stuart to JM, 14 Jan. 1788; *JHDV*, Oct. 1787, p. 134).

[2] "Yesterday afternoon about 4 o'clock, a fire broke out in the house occupied by Mrs. Gilbert (about 80 yards distant from the Assembly house, and 100 from Shockoe ware-houses) which was burnt to the ground; from the activity of some carpenters and others (who deserve great praise) in cutting down the adjacent buildings, to which the fire had, and was like to communicate; the flames were happily extinguished, although in the midst of a number of wooden buildings; there was but little loss sustained, excepting the house, and a few beds and furniture which were in a room where the fire broke out" (*Va. Gazette and Weekly Advertiser*, 3 Jan. 1788).

From Rufus King

Sunday 6. Jan. 88

Dr. Sir

I send you a copy of the confederation between the New England Colonies, together with a few Extracts from the Journals of the Commissioners.[1] As I hope to leave Town on Tuesday for Boston, I pray you to return me these papers Sometime Tomorrow. You are sensible that information from the southern States relative to the proposed Constitution will be of importance to us at Boston while engaged on that subject. This remark will apologize for the request which I take the liberty of making, that you wd. have the Goodness to inform me by Post of any thing interesting on that Subject, which you may obtain during my Absince, on [the other hand I will inform you of our hopes and fears. With great esteem]

RC (DLC); Tr (NHi). RC docketed by JM. Lower portion of the RC clipped. The words in brackets are written at the bottom of the RC in an unknown hand.

[1] In May 1643 representatives of the colonies of Massachusetts, Plymouth, Connecticut, and New Haven agreed on articles of union establishing the "United Colonies of New England." The government was composed of eight commissioners empowered to declare war and clothed with jurisdiction in matters of interstate quarrels, runaway servants, fugitives from justice, and Indian affairs. The commissioners met annually until 1664 and occasionally thereafter until the confederation was dissolved in 1684 (Henry S. Commager, ed., *Documents of American History* [7th ed.; 2 vols. in 1; New York, 1963], I, 26–28). The proceedings of the commissioners are printed in Nathaniel B. Shurtleff and David Pulsifer, eds., *Records of the Colony of New Plymouth in New England* (1855–61; 12 vols. in 6; New York, 1968 reprint), IX, 9 and passim; X, 3 and passim. Presumably JM wished to consult these materials in preparing his "Publius" essays.

To Edward Carrington

Letter not found.

7 January 1788. Acknowledged in Carrington to JM, 18 Jan. 1788. Reports foreign news, including "the Memorials of France & England."

From George Lee Turberville

RICHMOND CITY January 8th. 1788.

DEAR SIR

The Commissioners appointed to liquidate the claim of this state against the United States on Acct. of the Ceded Territory were by some very animated resolutions of our house yesterday stopped from further proceeding in the business untill a remonstrance had been presented to Congress. This will no doubt be officially transmitted to you in a few days. The construction of the Words, "all necessary and reasonable expences" is what has given rise to the interposition of the Legislature—it appearing to be the design of the Continental commissioner to take up the business de novo—to contest the propriety of the payments actually made by the State, & to refuse even the Bills with the Acceptance of our Governor, as vouchers for the sums expended. Not having been one of the Committee & being totally unacquainted with the business altogether, I was not a little astonished to hear the Clerk read a Resolution (which was after those agreed to by the house) declaring that no further payments shou'd be made to Congress untill they had given us the fullest indemnification for our expenditures for the Conquest of the Illinois Country. The person who introduced the Measure (Colo. Mason), the Critical situation of this state—and of the Continent—and the violent features of the first resolutions—& the absolutely antifederal tendency of the last, occasion'd me to oppose the last—& eventually it was stricken out. Much I fear—least those which have passed shou'd be productive of heat—but as they will pass through the hands of our Delegation I have no doubt but that they will be placed in such a light before Congress—as shall be most conducive to our Interests.[1]

A District-Court Bill has passed both houses—much like that which was before our house last year. Four additional Judges are appointed (Mesrs. Prentis—Gabriel Jones—St George Tucker & Richard Parker) and three Judges are to attend his District. This as a most important & beneficial Measure—I am sure will be pleasing to you—& I have therefore inserted it.

352

Upon the subject of the proposed plan (some communications touching which I have a great desire to receive from yr. hands) I can only say that it appears to be gaining ground. The Letter of the Governor, has been of great service in promoting the adoption of it—he convinced its Enemies of the necessity of a change, & has pointed out not a single objection to the new plan in which they will coincide with him.

Our house will rise to day. So that shou'd you find it convenien[t] to favor me with a Letter—you will be pleased to direct it to Richmond County Via Hobbs Hole. I will promise you to be punctual correspondent— altho it will not be in my power to render my Letters either as usefull—as agreeable or as instructiv[e] as yours will be.

Please sir to present me most affectionately to Colo. Carrington & Mr. Brown—& beleive me to remain With great Regard your most Obedt. humble servant

GEORGE LEE TURBERVILLE

RC (NN). Addressed by Turberville and franked. Docketed by JM. Enclosure not found. Brackets enclose letters obscured in right-hand margin of Ms.

[1] On the settlement of the accounts between Virginia and the U.S. concerning the cession of the Northwest Territory, see *PJM*, VIII, 343 n. 1; IX, 328, 329 n. 5. The initiative for legislative "interposition" in this matter had come from the state commissioner William Heth, who favored far greater compensation to Virginia for defending and maintaining the ceded territory than did the parsimonious John Pierce, the Continental commissioner. Although recognizing that many of the vouchers needed to support Virginia's claims were lost, destroyed, or in an otherwise chaotic state, Heth believed the commonwealth in equity should be reimbursed about £200,000. He was willing to accept anything above £150,000, however. The third commissioner, David Henley, whom Heth regarded "as a real honest man," would support a claim of "£120,000 perhaps, while the principles rigidly maintained by Mr. Pierce would have reduced it to £50,000." In this situation Heth decided that the legislature should be informed of the proceedings of the commissioners (Heth to Edmund Randolph, 21 Mar. 1788, *CVSP*, IV, 414–15). The House responded on 17 Dec. 1787 by appointing a committee, with Mason as chairman, to request a statement of the proceedings and make a report (*JHDV*, Oct. 1787, p. 105). For the report and resolutions submitted by Mason to the House on 7 Jan. 1788, see Rutland, *Papers of George Mason*, III, 1031–37. The report noted that Heth and Henley had agreed to the Mason committee's request to inspect the proceedings of the commissioners, but that Pierce had refused to "communicate any official information" before the completion of the final report. After examining the proceedings, "as laid before them by Mess'rs *Heth* and *Henley*," the committee concluded that "*Virginia*, unless the General Assembly shall interpose, will be denied a credit for a great part of the money she has actually and bona fide paid in acquiring and maintaining the [Northwest] territory." The House then adopted resolutions suspending further proceedings of the commissioners until the assembly's protest had been laid before Congress and instructing the state's delegates in Congress to urge that body "to take measures for doing justice to this state." Heth carried the report, resolutions, and other papers on the subject to the Virginia delegates, who submitted them to Congress on 3 Mar. (*JCSV*, IV, 209; JM to Randolph, 3 Mar. 1788; *JCC*, XXXIV, 77 n.1). On 5 May the committee considering Virginia's protest reported that the business was properly in the hands of the commissioners and should be settled by them without interference from Congress or Virginia (*JCC*, XXXIV, 134–35). This report reflected an earlier private understanding between Heth and the committee that

Virginia's Northwest claim should be negotiated by the commissioners, "for it would be a damn'd disagreeable piece of work to bring before Congress." From conversations with committee members Heth concluded that Pierce could be persuaded "to rescind his former opinions so far as to meet me on such terms as I should think myself Justifiable in closing with, or . . . resign his appointment" (Heth to Edmund Randolph, 9 Mar. 1788, *CVSP*, IV, 406). He accordingly requested and received authority from the Council of State to resume negotiations with the other commissioners (Heth to Edmund Randolph, 21 Mar. 1788, ibid., IV, 414–16; *JCSV*, IV, 226; Virginia Delegates to Heth, 20 Apr. 1788, Burnett, *Letters*, VIII, 723). On 15 May the commissioners awarded Virginia the generous sum of $500,000 in specie. The liberality of the award was perhaps owing in part to the absence of the indisposed Pierce during the final negotiations (James, *George Rogers Clark Papers, 1781–1784*, pp. 465–66). Congress, however, rejected Secretary Thomson's recommendation that the award be transmitted to the Board of Treasury office (*JCC*, XXXIV, 180–81). This action reflected the opposition of Northern delegates, who grumbled that Virginia's claim for compensation was too high a price for the cession of the Northwest Territory, but it apparently did not affect the validity of the award (Nicholas Gilman to John Sullivan, 22 Mar. 1788; Paine Wingate to Samuel Lane, 12 Apr. and 2 June 1788, Burnett, *Letters*, VIII, 709, 716, 745–46). When the final settlement of accounts between the states and the U.S. took place in 1793, Virginia's special Northwest claim, including interest, amounted to $740,000 (*CVSP*, VII, 55).

To Edmund Randolph

N. YORK Jany. 10. 1788.

MY DEAR FRIEND

I have put off writing from day to day for some time past, in expectation of being able to give you the news from the packet, which has been looked for every hour. Both the French & English have overstaid their usual time ten or 15 days, and are neither of them yet arrived. We remain wholly in the dark with regard to the posture of things in Europe.

I received two days ago your favor of Decr. 27. inclosing a copy of your letter to the Assembly. I have read it with attention, and I can add with pleasure, because the spirit of it does as much honor to your candour, as the general reasoning does to your abilities. Nor can I believe that in this quarter the opponents to the Constitution will find encouragement in it. You are already aware that your objections are not viewed in the same decisive light by me as they are by you. I must own that I differ still more from your opinion, that a prosecution of the experiment of a second Convention will be favorable even in Virginia to the object which I am sure you have at heart. It is to me apparent that had your duty led you to throw your influence into the opposite scale, that it would have given it a decided and unalterable preponderancy; and that Mr. Henry would either have suppressed his enmity, or been baffled in the policy which it has dictated. It appears also that the ground taken by the opponents in different quarters, forbids any hope of concord among them. Nothing can be farther from your views than the principles of different setts of men, who have carried on their opposition under the respectability of your name. In this State the party adverse to the Constitution, notoriously meditate either a dissolution of the Union, or protracting it by patching up the Articles of Confederation. In Connecticut & Massachussetts, the opposition proceeds from that part of the people who have a repugnancy in general to good government, to any substantial abridgment of State powers, and a part of whom in Massts. are known to aim at confusion, and are suspected of wishing a reversal of the Revolution. The Minority in Pennsylva. as far as they are governed by any other views than an habitual & factious opposition, to their rivals, are manifestly averse to some essential ingredients in a national Government. You are better acquainted with Mr. Henry's politics than I can be, but I have for some time considered him as driving at a Southern Confederacy and as not farther concurring in the plan of amendments than as he hopes to render it subservient to his real designs. Viewing the matter in this light, the inference with me is unavoidable that were a second trial to be made, the friends of a good constitution for the Union would not only find themselves not a little differing from each other as to the proper amendments; but perplexed & frustrated by men who had objects totally different. A second Convention would of course be formed under the influence, and composed in great measure of the members of opposition in the several States. But were the first difficulties overcome, and the Constitution re-edited with amendments, the event would still be infinitely precarious. Whatever respect may be due to the rights of private judgment, and no man feels more of it than I do, there can be no doubt that there are subjects to which the capacities of the bulk of mankind are unequal, and on which they must and will be governed by those with whom they happen to have acquaintance and confidence. The proposed Constitution is of this description. The great body of those who are both for & against it, must follow the judgment of others not their own. Had the Constitution been framed & recommended by an obscure individual, instead of a body possessing public respect & confidence, there can not be a doubt, that altho' it would have stood in the identical words, it would have commanded little attention from most of those who now admire its wisdom. Had yourself, Col. Mason, Col. R. H. L. Mr. Henry & a few others, seen the Constitution in the same light with those who subscribed it, I have no doubt that Virginia would have been as zealous & unanimous as she is now divided on the subject. I infer from these considerations that if a Government be ever adopted in America, it must result from a fortunate coincidence of leading opinions, and a general confidence of the people in those who may rec-

355

ommend it. The very attempt at a second Convention strikes at the confidence in the first; and the existence of a second by opposing influence to influence, would in a manner destroy an effectual confidence in either, and give a loose[1] to human opinions; which must be as various and irreconcileable concerning theories of Government, as doctrines of Religion; and give opportunities to designing men which it might be impossible to counteract.

The Connecticut Convention has probably come to a decision before this; but the event is not known here. It is understood that a great majority will adopt the Constitution. The accounts from Massts. vary extremely according to the channels through which they come. It is said that S. Adams who has hitherto been reserved, begins to make open declaration of his hostile views. His influence is not great, but this step argues an opinion that he can calculate on a considerable party. It is said here, and I believe on good ground that N. Carolina has postponed her Convention till July, in order to have the previous example of Virga. Should N. Carolina fall into Mr. H——y's politics which does not appear to me improbable, it will endanger the Union more than any other circumstance that could happen. My apprehensions of this danger increase every day. The multiplied inducements at this moment to the local sacrifices necessary to keep the States together, can never be expected to co-incide again, and they are counteracted by so many unpropitious circumstances, that their efficacy can with difficulty be confided in. I have no information from S. Carolina or Georgia, on which any certain opinion can be formed of the temper of those States. The prevailing idea has been that both of them would speedily & generally embrace the Constitution. It is impossible however that the example of Virga. & N. Carolina should not have an influence on their politics. I consider every thing therefore as problematical from Maryland Southward.

I am surprised that Col. H. Lee who is a well-wisher to the Constitution should have furnished Wilkinson with the alarm concerning the Mississippi, but the political connections of the latter in Pena. would account for his biass on the subject.

We have no Congress yet. The number of Sts on the Spot does not exceed five. It is probable that a quorum will now be soon made. A Delegate from N. Hampshire is expected which will make up a representation from that State. The termination of the Connecticut Convention will set her delegates at liberty. And the Meeting of the Assembly of this State, will fill the vacancy which has some time existed in her Delegation. I wish you every happiness, and am with the sincerest affection Yrs.

Js. MADISON JR

RC (DLC). Docketed by Randolph.

[1] Here JM surely intended, but failed to add, "rein."

From André Limozin

HAVRE DE GRACE 10 Janry 1788

MOST HONORED SIR

I have the honor to inclose you a large Bundle of Papers sent to my Care by his Excellency Thoms Jefferson Ambassador of the US at the Court of Versailles to be Forwarded to you. I comply with a very great pleasure with his Excellency's orders, Since it procures me the opportunity to assure you that I have the honor to be with the highest regard Most Honored Sir Your most obedt Hble Servt

ANDR LIMOZIN[1]

I have the honor to inclose you likewise Charles Jenkin's Bill of Lading for 3 Boxes Books sent to me by our said Mutuall worthy Friend Thoms Jefferson Esquire.[2]

RC and enclosure (DLC). Addressed by a clerk. Docketed by JM. For enclosure, see n. 2.

[1] Limozin was agent for the U.S. at Le Havre (Jefferson to Limozin, 17 Oct. 1787, Boyd, *Papers of Jefferson*, XII, 244).

[2] Jefferson wrote JM on 17 Sept. 1787 that the three boxes of books for JM, George Wythe, and Alexander Donald were to be forwarded "by the present packet." The shipment of books was delayed until 27 Jan. 1788, however, when the *Juno*, under Capt. Charles Jenkins, finally left Le Havre (Limozin to Jefferson, 1 Feb. 1788, Boyd, *Papers of Jefferson*, XII, 552). The enclosed bill of lading is dated 20 Dec. 1787. On the verso is Jenkins's receipt, dated New York, 11 Apr. 1788, to Richard Philips for payment of the freight. Jefferson also enclosed copies of the bill of lading in his letter to JM of 6 Feb. 1788.

From George Washington

MOUNT VERNON Jany. 10th. 1788.

MY DEAR SIR,

I stand indebted to you for your favors of the 20th. & 26th. Ult; and I believe for that of the 14th. also, & their enclosures.

It does not appear to me that there is any *certain* criterion in this State, by which a decided Judgment can be formed of the opinion which is entertained by the mass of its Citizens with respect to the New Constitution. My belief on this occasion is, that whenever the matter is brought to a final decision, that not only a majority, but a large one, will be found in its favor.

That the opposition should have gained strength, among the members of the Assembly in Richmond, admitting the fact, is not to be wondered at when it is considered that the powerful adversaries to the Constitution are all assembled at that place, acting conjunctly; with the promulgated sentiments of Col. R. H. L as auxiliary. It is said however, and I believe it may be depended upon, that the latter (tho' he may retain his sentiments) has with-drawn, or means to withdraw his opposition; because, as he has expressed himself, or as others have done it for him, he finds himself in bad Company; such as with M——r. Sm——th's[1] &ca &ca. His brother, Francis L. Lee on whose Judgment the family place much reliance, is decidedly in favor of the new form, under a conviction that it is the best that can be obtained, and because it promises energy—stability—and that security which is, or ought to be, the wish of every good Citizen of the Union.

How far the determination of the question before the debating club (of which I made mention in a former letter) may be considered as auspicious of the final decision in Convention, I shall not prognosticate; but in this Club, this question it seems, was determined by a very large majority in favor of the Constitution; but of all the arguments which may be used at this time, none will be so forcible, I expect, as that nine States have acceded to it. And if the unanimity, or majorities in those which are to follow, are as great as in those which have acted, the power of these arguments will be irrisistable.

The Governor has given his reasons to the Publick for withholding his signature to the Constitution. A copy of them I send you.[2]

Our Assembly has been long in Session—employed chiefly (according to my information) in rectifying the mistakes of the last, and committing others for emendations at the next. Yet, "who so wise as we are." We are held in painful suspence with respect to European Intelligence. Peace or War, by the last accts. are equally balanced a grain added to either scale will give it the preponderancy.[3]

I have no regular corrispondt. in Massachusetts; otherwise, as the occasional subject of a letter I should have had no objection to the communication of my sentiments on the proposed Government as they are unequivocal & decided. With the greatest esteem & regd I am My dear Sir Yr. Most Obedt. & Affe Ser

Go: WASHINGTON

PS. I have this mom't. been informed, that the Assembly of No Carolina have postponed the meeting of the Convention of that State until July. This seems evidently calculated to take the Tone from Virginia.

RC (MA); FC (DLC: Washington Papers). FC in a clerk's hand. Minor variations between the FC and the RC have not been noted. RC docketed by JM. Enclosure not found.

[1] Meriwether Smith.

[2] Randolph had sent JM a copy of his pamphlet on 27 Dec. 1787.

[3] In the FC this sentence reads: "War, or Peace, seems yet undecided altho' the first is loudly talked of."

The Federalist Number 37

[11 January 1788]

　In reviewing the defects of the existing confederation, and shewing that they cannot be supplied by a government of less energy than that before the public, several of the most important principles of the latter fell of course under consideration. But as the ultimate object of these papers is to determine clearly and fully the merits of this constitution, and the expediency of adopting it, our plan cannot be compleated without taking a more critical and thorough survey of the work of the convention; without examining it on all its sides; comparing it in all its parts, and calculating its probable effects. That this remaining task may be executed under impressions conducive to a just and fair result, some reflections must in this place be indulged, which candour previously suggests. It is a misfortune, inseparable from human affairs, that public measures are rarely investigated with that spirit of moderation which is essential to a just estimate of their real tendency to advance or obstruct the public good; and that this spirit is more apt to be diminished than promoted, by those occasions which require an unusual exercise of it. To those who have been led by experience to attend to this consideration, it could not appear surprising, that the act of the convention which recommends so many important changes and innovations, which may be viewed in so many lights and relations, and which touches the springs of so many passions and interests, should find or excite dispositions unfriendly both on one side, and on the other, to a fair discussion and accurate judgment of its merits. In some, it has been too evident from their own publications, that they have scanned the proposed constitution, not only with a predisposition to censure; but with a predetermination to condemn: As the language held by others betrays an opposite predetermination or bias, which must render their opinions also of little moment in the question. In placing however, these different characters on a level, with respect to the weight of their opinions, I wish not to insinuate that there may not be a material difference in the purity of their intentions. It is but just to remark in favor of the latter description, that as our situation is universally admitted to be peculiarly critical, and to require indispensably, that something should be done for our relief, the predetermined patron of what has been actually done, may have taken his bias from the weight of these considerations, as well as from considerations of a sinister nature. The predetermined adversary on the other hand, can have been governed by no venial motive whatever. The intentions of the first may be upright, as they may on the contrary be culpable. The views of the last cannot be upright, and must be culpable. But the truth is, that these papers are not addressed to persons falling under either of these characters. They solicit the attention of those only, who add to a sincere zeal for the happiness of their country, a temper favorable to a just estimate of the means of promoting it.

Persons of this character will proceed to an examination of the plan submitted by the convention, not only without a disposition to find or to magnify faults; but will see the propriety of reflecting that a faultless plan was not to be expected. Nor will they barely make allowances for the errors which may be chargeable on the fallibility to which the convention, as a body of men, were liable; but will keep in mind that they themselves also are but men, and ought not to assume an infallibility in rejudging the fallible opinions of others.

With equal readiness will it be perceived, that besides these inducements to candour, many allowances ought to be made for the difficulties inherent in the very nature of the undertaking referred to the convention.

The novelty of the undertaking immediately strikes us. It has been shewn in the course of these papers, that the existing confederation is founded on principles which are fallacious; that we must consequently change this first foundation, and with it, the superstructure resting upon it. It has been shewn, that the other confederacies which could be consulted as precedents, have been viciated by the same erroneous principles, and can therefore furnish no other light than that of beacons, which give warning of the course to be shunned, without pointing out that which ought to be pursued. The most that the convention could do in such a situation, was to avoid the errors suggested by the past experience of other countries, as well as of our own; and to provide a convenient mode of rectifying their own errors, as future experience may unfold them.

Among the difficulties[1] encountered by the convention, a very important one must have lain, in combining the requisite stability and energy in government with the inviolable attention due to liberty, and to the republican form. Without substantially accomplishing this part of their undertaking, they would have very imperfectly fulfilled the object of their appointment, or the expectation of the public: Yet, that it could not be easily accomplished, will be denied by no one, who is unwilling to betray his ignorance of the subject. Energy in government is essential to that security against external and internal danger, and to that prompt and salutary execution of the laws, which enter into the very definition of good government. Stability in government, is essential to national character, and to the advantages annexed to it, as well as to that repose and confidence in the minds of the people, which are among the chief blessings of civil society. An irregular and mutable legislation is not more an evil in itself, than it is odious to the people; and it may be pronounced with assurance, that the people of this country, enlightened as they are, with regard to the nature, and interested, as the great body of them are, in the effects of good government will never be satisfied, till some remedy be applied to the vicissitudes and uncertainties, which characterize the state administrations. On comparing, however these valuable ingredients with the vital principles of liberty, we must perceive at once, the difficulty of mingling them together in their due proportions. The genius of republican liberty, seems to demand on one side, not only, that all power should be derived from the people; but, that those entrusted with it should be kept in dependence on the people, by a short duration of their appointments; and, that, even during this short period, the trust should be placed not in a few, but in a number of hands. Stability, on the contrary, requires, that the hands, in which power is lodged, should continue for a length of time the same. A frequent change of men will result from a frequent return of electors, and a frequent change of measures, from a frequent change of men; whilst energy in government requires not only a certain duration of power, but the execution of it by a single hand. How far the convention may have succeeded in this part of their work, will better appear on a more accurate view of it. From the cursory view, here taken, it must clearly appear to have been an arduous part.

Not less arduous must have been the task of marking the proper line of partition, between the authority of the general, and that of the state governments. Every man will be sensible of this difficulty, in proportion as he has been accustomed to contemplate and discriminate objects, extensive and complicated in their nature. The faculties of the mind itself have never yet been distinguished and defined, with satisfactory precision, by all the efforts of the most acute and metaphysical philosophers. Sense, perception, judgment, desire, volition, memory, imagination, are found to be separated, by such delicate shades and minute gradations, that their boundaries have eluded the most subtle investigations, and remain a pregnant source of ingenious disquisition and controversy. The boundaries between the great kingdoms of nature, and still more, between the various provinces, and lesser portions, into which they are subdivided, afford another illustration of the same important truth. The most sagacious and laborious naturalists have never yet succeeded, in tracing with certainty, the line which separates the district of vegetable life from the neighbouring region of unorganized matter, or which marks the termination of the former and the commencement of the animal empire. A still greater obscurity lies in the distinctive characters, by which the objects in each of these great departments of nature have been arranged and assorted. When we pass from the works of nature, in which all the delineations are perfectly accurate, and appear to be otherwise only from the imperfection of the eye which surveys them, to the institutions of man, in which the obscurity arises as well from the object itself, as from the organ by which it is contemplated; we must perceive the necessity of moderating still farther our expectations and hopes from the efforts of human sagacity. Experience has instructed us that no skill in the science of government has yet been able to discriminate and define, with sufficient certainty, its three great provinces, the legislative, executive and judiciary; or even the privileges and powers of the different legislative branches. Questions daily occur in the course of practice, which prove the obscurity which reigns in these subjects, and which puzzles the greatest adepts in political science. The experience of ages, with the continued and combined labors of the most enlightened legislators and jurists, have been equally unsuccessful in delineating the several objects and limits of different codes of laws and different tribunals of justice. The precise extent of the common law, the statute law, the maritime law, the ecclesiastical law, the law of corporations and other local laws and customs, remain still to be clearly and finally established in Great Britain, where accuracy in such subjects has been more industriously pursued than in any other part of the world. The jurisdiction of her several courts, general and local, of law, of equity, of admiralty, &c. is not less a source of frequent and intricate discussions, sufficiently denoting the indeterminate limits by which they are respectively circumscribed. All new laws, though penned with the greatest technical skill, and passed on the fullest and most mature deliberation, are considered as more or less obscure and equivocal, until their meaning be liquidated and ascertained by a series of particular discussions and adjudications. Besides the obscurity arising from the complexity of objects, and the imperfection of the human faculties, the medium through which the conceptions of men are conveyed to each other, adds a fresh embarrassment. The use of words is to express ideas. Perspicuity therefore requires not only that the ideas should be distinctly formed, but that they should be expressed by words distinctly and exclusively appropriated to them. But no language is so copious as to supply words and phrases for every complex idea, or so correct as not to include many equivocally denoting different ideas. Hence it must happen, that however accurately objects may be discriminated in themselves, and however accurately the discrimination may be considered, the definition of them may be rendered inaccurate by the inaccuracy of the terms in which it is delivered. And this unavoidable inaccuracy must be greater or less, according to the complexity and novelty of the objects defined. When the Almighty himself condescends to address mankind in their own language, his meaning luminous as it must be, is rendered dim and doubtful, by the cloudy medium through which it is communicated. Here then are three sources of vague and incorrect definitions; indistinctness of the object, imperfection of the organ of conception, inadequateness of the vehicle of ideas. Any one of these must produce a certain degree of obscurity. The convention, in delineating the boundary between the federal and state jurisdictions, must have experienced the full effect of them all.

To the difficulties already mentioned, may be added the interfering pretensions of the larger and smaller states. We cannot err in supposing that the former would contend for a participation in the government, fully proportioned to their superior wealth and importance; and that the latter would not be less tenacious of the equality at present enjoyed by them. We may well suppose that neither side would entirely yield to the other, and consequently that the struggle could be terminated only by compromise. It is extremely probable also, that after the ratio of representation had been adjusted, this very compromise must have produced a fresh struggle between the same parties, to give such a turn to the organization of the government, and to the distribution of its powers, as would increase the importance of the branches, in forming which they had respectively obtained the greatest share of influence. There are features in the constitution which warrant each of these suppositions; and as far as either of them is well founded, it shews that the convention must have been compelled to sacrifice theoretical propriety to the force of extraneous considerations.

Nor could it have been the large and small states only which would marshal themselves in opposition to each other on various points. Other combinations, resulting from a difference of local position and policy, must have created additional difficulties. As every state may be divided into different districts, and its citizens into different classes, which give birth to contending interests and local jealousies; so the different parts of the United States are distinguished from each other, by a variety of circumstances, which produce a like effect on a larger scale. And although this variety of interests, for reasons sufficiently explained in a former paper, may have a salutary influence on the administration of the government when formed; yet every one must be sensible of the contrary influence which must have been experienced in the task of forming it.

Would it be wonderful if under the pressure of all these difficulties, the convention should have been forced into some deviations from that artificial structure and regular symmetry, which an abstract view of the subject might lead an ingenious theorist to bestow on a constitution planned in his closet or in his imagination? The real wonder is, that so many difficulties should have been surmounted; and surmounted with an unanimity almost as unprecedented as it must have been unexpected. It is impossible for any man of candor to reflect on this circumstance, without partaking of the astonishment. It is impossible for the man of pious reflection not to perceive in it, a finger of that Almighty Hand which has been so frequently and signally extended to our relief in the critical stages of the revolution. We had occasion in a former paper, to take notice of the repeated trials which have been unsuccessfully made in the United Netherlands, for reforming the baneful and notorious vices of their constitution. The history of almost all the great councils and consultations, held among mankind for reconciling their discordant opinions, assuaging their mutual jealousies, and adjusting their respective interests, is a history of factions, contentions and disappointments; and may be classed among the most dark and degrading pictures which display the infirmities and depravities of the human character. If, in a few scattered instances, a brighter aspect is presented, they serve only as exceptions to admonish us of the general truth; and by their lustre to darken the gloom of the adverse prospect to which they are contrasted. In revolving the causes from which these exceptions result, and applying them to the particular instance before us, we are necessarily led to two important conclusions. The first is, that the convention must have enjoyed in a very singular degree, an exemption from the pestilential influence of party animosities; the diseases most incident to deliberative bodies, and most apt to contaminate their proceedings. The second conclusion is, that all the deputations composing the convention, were either satisfactorily accommodated by the final act; or were induced to accede to it, by a deep conviction of the necessity of sacrificing private opinions and partial interests, to the public good, and by a despair of seeing this necessity diminished by delays or by new experiments.

PUBLIUS.

McLean, II, 1–9.

¹JM had employed the following classification of "difficulties" faced by the convention in his letter to Jefferson of 24 Oct. 1787.

The Federalist Number 38

[12 January 1788]

It is not a little remarkable that in every case reported by antient history, in which government has been established with deliberation and consent, the task of framing it has not been committed to an assembly of men; but has been performed by some individual citizen of pre-eminent wisdom and approved integrity. Minos, we learn, was the primitive founder of the government of Crete; as Zaleucus was of that of the Locrians. Theseus first, and after him Draco and Solon, instituted the government of Athens. Lycurgus was the lawgiver of Sparta. The foundation of the original government of Rome was laid by Romulus; and the work compleated by two of his elective successors, Numa, and Tullus Hostilius. On the abolition of royalty, the consular administration was substituted by Brutus, who stepped forward with a project for such a reform, which he alledged had been prepared by Servius Tullius, and to which his address obtained the assent and ratification of the senate and people. This remark is applicable to confederate governments also. Amphyction, we are told, was the author of that which bore his name. The Achæan league received its first birth from Achæus, and its second from Aratus. What degree of agency these reputed lawgivers might have in their respective establishments, or how far they might be cloathed with the legitimate authority of the people, cannot in every instance be ascertained. In some, however, the proceeding was strictly regular. Draco appears to have been entrusted by the people of Athens, with indefinite powers to reform its government and laws. And Solon, according to Plutarch, was in a manner compelled by the universal suffrage of his fellow citizens, to take upon him the sole and absolute power of new modelling the constitution. The proceedings under Lycurgus were less regular; but as far as the advocates for a regular reform could prevail, they all turned their eyes towards the single efforts of that celebrated patriot and sage, instead of seeking to bring about a revolution, by the intervention of a deliberative body of citizens. Whence could it have proceeded that a people, jealous as the Greeks were of their liberty, should so far abandon the rules of caution, as to place their destiny in the hands of a single citizen? Whence could it have proceeded that the Athenians, a people who would not suffer an army to be commanded by fewer than ten generals, and who required no other proof of danger to their liberties than the illustrious merit of a fellow citizen, should consider one illustrious citizen as a more eligible depositary of the fortunes of themselves and their posterity, than a select body of citizens, from whose common deliberations more wisdom, as well as more safety, might have been expected? These questions cannot be fully answered without supposing that the fears of discord and disunion among a number of counsellors, exceeded the apprehension of treachery or incapacity in a single individual. History informs us likewise of the difficulties with which these celebrated reformers had to contend; as well as of the expedients which they were obliged to employ, in order to carry their reforms into effect. Solon, who seems to have indulged a more temporising policy, confessed that he had not given to his countrymen the government best suited to their happiness, but most tolerable to their prejudices. And Lycurgus, more true to his object, was under the necessity of mixing a portion of violence with the authority of superstition; and of securing his final success, by a voluntary renunciation, first of his country, and then of his life. If these lessons teach us, on one hand, to admire the improvement made by America on the ancient mode of preparing and establishing regular plans of government; they serve not less on the other, to admonish us of the hazards and difficulties incident to such experiments, and of the great imprudence of unnecessarily multiplying them.

Is it an unreasonable conjecture that the errors which may be contained in the plan of the convention are such as have resulted rather from the defect of antecedent experience on this complicated and difficult subject, than from a want of accuracy or care in the investigation of it; and consequently such as will not be ascertained until an actual trial shall have pointed them out? This conjecture is rendered probable not only by many considerations of a general nature, but by the particular case of the articles of confederation. It is observable that among the numerous objections and amendments suggested by the several states, when these articles were submitted for their ratification, not one is found which alludes to the great and radical error, which on actual trial has discovered itself.[1] And if we except the observations which New-Jersey was led to make rather by her local situation than by her peculiar foresight, it may be questioned whether a single suggestion was of sufficient moment to justify a revision of the system.[2] There is abundant reason nevertheless to suppose that immaterial as these objections were, they would have been adhered to with a very dangerous inflexibility in some states, had not a zeal for their opinions and supposed interests, been stifled by the more powerful sentiment of self-preservation. One state, we may remember, persisted for several years in refusing her concurrence, although the enemy remained the whole period at our gates, or rather in the very bowels of our country. Nor was her pliancy in the end effected by a less motive than the fear of being chargeable with protracting the public calamities, and endangering the event of the contest.[3] Every candid reader will make the proper reflections on these important facts.

A patient who finds his disorder daily growing worse; and that an efficacious remedy can no longer be delayed without extreme danger; after coolly revolving his situation, and the characters of different physicians, selects and calls in such of them as he judges most capable of administering relief, and best entitled to his confidence. The physicians attend: The case of the patient is carefully examined: a consultation is held. They are unanimously agreed that the symptoms are critical, but that the case, with proper and timely relief, is so far from being desperate, that it may be made to issue in an improvement of his constitution. They are equally unanimous in prescribing the remedy by which this happy effect is to be produced. The prescription is no sooner made known however, than a number of persons interpose, and without denying the reality or danger of the disorder, assure the patient that the prescription will be poison to his constitution, and forbid him under pain of certain death to make use of it. Might not the patient reasonably demand before he ventured to follow this advice, that the authors of it should at least agree among themselves, on some other remedy to be substituted? And if he found them differing as much from one another, as from his first counsellors, would he not act prudently, in trying the experiment unanimously recommended by the latter, rather than in hearkening to those who could neither deny the necessity of a speedy remedy, nor agree in proposing one?

Such a patient, and in such a situation is America at this moment. She has been sensible of her malady. She has obtained a regular and unanimous advice from men of her own deliberate choice. And she is warned by others against following this advice, under pain of the most fatal consequences. Do the monitors deny the reality of her danger? No. Do they deny the necessity of some speedy and powerful remedy? No. Are they agreed, are any two of them agreed in their objections to the remedy proposed, or in the proper one to be substituted? Let them speak for themselves. This one tells us that the proposed constitution ought to be rejected, because it is not a confederation of the states, but a government over individuals. Another admits that it ought to be a government over individuals, to a certain extent, but by no means to the extent proposed.[4] A third does not object to the government over individuals or to the extent proposed, but to the want of a bill of rights. A fourth concurs in the absolute necessity of a bill of rights, but contends that it ought to be declaratory not of the personal rights of individuals, but of the rights reserved to the states in their political capacity. A fifth is of opinion that a bill of rights of any sort would be superfluous and misplaced, and that the plan would be unexceptionable, but for the fatal power of regulating the times and places of election. An objector in a large state exclaims loudly against the unreasonable equality of representation in the senate. An objector in a small state is equally loud against the dangerous inequality in the house of representatives. From this quarter we are alarmed with the amazing expence from the number of persons who are to administer the new government. From another quarter, and sometimes from the same quarter, on another occasion, the cry is, that the congress will be but the shadow of a representation,[5] and that the government would be far less objectionable, if the number and the expence were doubled. A patriot in a state that does not import or export, discerns insuperable objections against the power of direct taxation. The patriotic adversary in a state of great exports and imports, is not less dissatisfied that the whole burthen of taxes may be thrown on consumption. This politician discovers in the constitution a direct and irresistible tendency to monarchy. That is equally sure, it will end in aristocracy. Another is puzzled to say which of these shapes it will ultimately assume, but sees clearly it must be one or other of them.[6] Whilst a fourth is not wanting, who with no less confidence affirms that the constitution is so far from having a bias towards either of these dangers, that the weight on that side will not be sufficient to keep it upright and firm against its opposite propensities. With another class of adversaries to the constitution, the language is that the legislative, executive and judiciary departments are intermixed in such a manner as to contradict all the ideas of regular government, and all the requisite precautions in favour of liberty. Whilst this objection circulates in vague and general expressions, there are not a few who lend their sanction to it. Let each one come forward with his particular explanation and scarce any two are exactly agreed on the subject. In the eyes of one the junction of the senate with the president in the responsible function of appointing to offices, instead of vesting this executive power in the executive, alone, is the vicious part of the organisation. To another, the exclusion of the house of representatives, whose numbers alone could be a due security against corruption and partiality in the exercise of such a power, is equally obnoxious. With another, the admission of the president into any share of a power which must ever be a dangerous engine in the hands of the executive magistrate, is an unpardonable violation of the maxims of republican jealousy. No part of the arrangement according to some is more admissible[7] than the trial of impeachments by the senate, which is alternately a member both of the legislative and executive departments, when this power so evidently belonged to the judiciary department. We concur fully, reply others, in the objection to this part of the plan, but we can never agree that a reference of impeachments to the judiciary authority would be an amendment of the error. Our principal dislike to the organisation arises from the extensive powers already lodged in that department. Even among the zealous patrons of a council of state, the most irreconcilable variance is discovered concerning the mode in which it ought to be constituted. The demand of one gentleman is that the council should consist of a small number, to be appointed by the most numerous branch of the legislature. Another would prefer a larger number, and considers it as a fundamental condition that the appointment should be made by the president himself.[8]

As it can give no umbrage to the writers against the plan of the federal constitution, let us suppose that as they are the most zealous, so they are also the most sagacious of those who think the late convention were unequal to the task assigned them, and that a wiser and better plan might and ought to be substituted. Let us further suppose that their country should concur both in this favourable opinion of their merits, and in their unfavourable opinion of the convention; and should accordingly proceed to form them into a second convention, with full powers and for the express purpose of revising and remoulding the work of the first. Were the experiment to be seriously made, though it requires some effort to view it seriously even in fiction, I leave it to be decided by the sample of opinions just exhibited, whether with all their enmity to their predecessors, they would in any one point depart so widely from their example, as in the discord and ferment that would mark their own deliberations; and whether the constitution, now before the public, would not stand as fair a chance for immortality, as Lycurgus gave to that of Sparta, by making its change to depend on his own return from exile and death, if it were to be immediately adopted, and were to continue in force, not until a BETTER, but until ANOTHER should be agreed upon by this new assembly of lawgivers.

It is a matter both of wonder and regret, that those who raise so many objections against the new constitution, should never call to mind the defects of that which is to be exchanged for it. It is not necessary that the former should be perfect; it is sufficient that the latter is more imperfect. No man would refuse to give brass for silver or gold, because the latter had some alloy in it. No man would refuse to quit a shattered and tottering habitation, for a firm and commodious building, because the latter had not a porch to it; or because some of the rooms might be a little larger or smaller, or the ceiling a little higher or lower than his fancy would have planned them. But waving illustrations of this sort, is it not manifest that most of the capital objections urged against the new system, lie with tenfold weight against the existing confederation? Is an indefinite power to raise money dangerous in the hands of a federal government? The present congress can make requisitions to any amount they please; and the states are constitutionally bound to furnish them; they can emit bills of credit as long as they will pay for the paper; they can borrow both abroad and at home, as long as a shilling will be lent. Is an indefinite power to raise troops dangerous? The confederation gives to congress that power also; and they have already begun to make use of it. Is it improper and unsafe to intermix the different powers of government in the same body of men? Congress, a single body of men, are the sole depository of all the federal powers. Is it particularly dangerous to give the keys of the treasury, and the command of the army, into the same hands? The confederation places them both in the hands of congress. Is a bill of rights essential to liberty? The confederation has no bill of rights. Is it an objection against the new constitution, that it empowers the senate with the concurrence of the executive to make treaties which are to be the laws of the land? The existing congress, without any such controul, can make treaties which they themselves have declared, and most of the states have recognized, to be the supreme law of the land. Is the importation of slaves permitted by the new constitution for twenty years? By the old, it is permitted for ever.

I shall be told that however dangerous this mixture of powers may be in theory, it is rendered harmless by the dependence of congress on the states for the means of carrying them into practice: That however large the mass of powers may be, it is in fact a lifeless mass. Then say I in the first place, that the confederation is chargeable with the still greater folly of declaring certain powers in the federal government to be absolutely necessary, and at the same time rendering them absolutely nugatory: And in the next place, that if the union is to continue, and no better government be substituted, effective powers must either be granted to or assumed by the existing congress, in either of which events the contrast just stated will hold good. But this is not all. Out of this lifeless mass has already grown an excrescent power, which tends to realize all the dangers that can be apprehended from a defective construction of the supreme government of the union. It is now no longer a point of speculation and hope that the western territory is a mine of vast wealth to the United States; and although it is not of such a nature as to extricate them from their present distresses, or for some time to come, to yield any regular supplies for the public expences, yet must it hereafter be able under proper management both to effect a gradual discharge of the domestic debt, and to furnish for a certain period, liberal tributes to the federal treasury. A very large proportion of this fund has been already surrendered by individual states; and it may with reason be expected, that the remaining states will not persist in withholding similar proofs of their equity and generosity. We may calculate therefore that a rich and fertile country, of an area equal to the inhabited extent of the United States, will soon become a national stock. Congress have assumed the administration of this stock. They have begun to render it productive. Congress have undertaken to do more, they have proceeded to form new states; to erect temporary governments; to appoint officers for them; and to prescribe the conditions on which such states shall be admitted into the confederacy. All this has been done; and done without the least colour of constitutional authority. Yet no blame has been whispered; no alarm has been sounded. A GREAT and INDEPENDENT fund of revenue is passing into the hands of a SINGLE BODY of men, who can RAISE TROOPS to an INDEFINITE NUMBER, and appropriate money to their support for an INDEFINITE PERIOD OF TIME. And yet there are men who have not only been silent spectators of this prospect; but who are advocates for the system which exhibits it; and at the same time urge against the new system the objections which we have heard. Would they not act with more consistency in urging the establishment of the latter, as no less necessary to guard the union against the future powers and resources of a body constructed like the existing congress, than to save it from the dangers threatened by the present impotency of that assembly?

I mean not by any thing here said to throw censure on the measures which have been pursued by congress. I am sensible they could not have done otherwise. The public interest, the necessity of the case, imposed upon them the task of overleaping their constitutional limits. But is not the fact an alarming proof of the danger resulting from a government which does not possess regular powers commensurate to its objects? A dissolution or usurpation is the dreadful dilemma to which it is continually exposed.

PUBLIUS.

McLean, II, 10–19.

[1] For a discussion of the amendments proposed by the states to the Articles of Confederation, see Merrill Jensen, *The Articles of Confederation: An Interpretation of the Social-Constitutional History of the American Revolution, 1774–1781* (Madison, Wis., 1940), pp. 185–97.

[2] On 25 June 1778 Congress considered a series of objections to the proposed Articles of Confederation submitted by the New Jersey legislature. Among the recommendations contained in this "representation" was a proposal that "the sole and exclusive power of regulating

the trade of the United States with foreign nations, ought to be clearly vested in the Congress" (*JCC*, XI, 647–51).

[3]Maryland refused to ratify the Articles of Confederation until 1781 (Jensen, *Articles of Confederation*, pp. 201–5, 236–38).

[4]The "Federal Farmer" was one Antifederalist who conceded the necessity for some form of national government. See *Observations Leading to a Fair Examination of the System of Government Proposed by the Late Convention . . . in a Number of Letters from the Federal Farmer to the Republican* ([New York], 1787), in Kenyon, *The Antifederalists*, pp. 206–8. Authorship of this work has long been attributed to Richard Henry Lee, but Gordon S. Wood has persuasively argued that Lee was not the writer and suggests that the "Federal Farmer" was probably a New Yorker ("The Authorship of the *Letters from the Federal Farmer*," *WMQ*, 3d ser., XXXI [1974], 299–308).

[5]George Mason objected: "In the House of Representatives there is not the substance, but the shadow only of representation" (Kenyon, *The Antifederalists*, p. 192).

[6]See, for example, the remarks of "Centinel" (Samuel Bryan), George Mason, and "Cato" (ibid., pp. 8, 195, 306). The identity of "Cato" as Gov. George Clinton of New York has been questioned (Linda Grant De Pauw, *The Eleventh Pillar: New York State and the Federal Constitution* [Ithaca, N.Y., 1966], pp. 283–92).

[7]Should read "inadmissible," as in *The Federalist* (Cooke ed.), p. 245.

[8]JM referred to the proposals of George Mason and Richard Henry Lee (Kenyon, *The Antifederalists*, p. 193; *American Museum*, II [1787], 557). See also Washington to JM, 7 Dec. 1787 and n. 8; JM to Washington, 20 Dec. 1787.

To George Washington

N. York Jany. 14. 1788.

Dear Sir

The Daily Advertizer of this date contains several important articles of information, which need only be referred to.[1] I inclose it with a few other late papers. Neither French nor English packet is yet arrived; and the present weather would prevent their getting in if they should be on the Coast. I have heard nothing of Consequence from Massachussetts since my last. The accounts from New Hampshire continue to be as favorable as could be wished. From South Carolina we get no material information. A letter from Georgia, of the 25. of Decr. says that the Convention was getting together at Augusta and that every thing wore a fœderal complexion. N. Carolina it seems, has been so complaisant to Virginia as to postpone her Convention till July. We are still without a Congress. With perfect esteem & attachment I remain Dear Sir Your Obedt. humble servt.

Js. Madison Jr

RC (DLC: Washington Papers); Tr (DLC). RC docketed by Washington. Enclosures not found.

[1]Among the "articles of information" in the N.Y. *Daily Advertiser* of 14 Jan. 1788 were (1) the report by Robert Yates and John Lansing to Governor Clinton, dated 21 Dec. 1787, containing their objections to the Constitution; (2) news that France had withdrawn its

pledge to aid Holland, and that Great Britain and France had agreed to discontinue "all warlike preparations"; and (3) an announcement that the Connecticut convention had ratified the Constitution, 127 to 40.

From Henry Lee

STRATFORD. Jany 14t. 88

DEAR MADISON,

To aid Mr. Twining[1] I put my name on his bill & procured the endorsement of Mr. Constable[2] to authenticate it in N York. Mr. Twinings bill is not paid by the Postmaster General[3] who gave me his written assurance that it should be paid when due on condition that the contract was performed relating to the mail.[4] This letr. Mr. Constable has & you can see. I am called on for the money & without the assistance of my friends may loose the whole. Will you exert your self for me & if possible releive me, advise with Col. Hamilton who will I am sure heartily support me. Let me have your answer without loss of time. Yours truely

H: L

RC (DLC). Docketed by JM.

[1] Nathaniel Twining, a stagecoach proprietor and mail contractor. See n. 4.
[2] William Constable. See JM to Randolph, 7 Oct. 1787 and n. 3.
[3] Ebenezer Hazard.
[4] On Twining and his ambitious scheme to carry the southern mail, see Oliver W. Holmes, "Shall Stagecoaches Carry the Mail? A Debate of the Confederation Period," *WMQ*, 3d ser., XX (1963), 555–73; *JCC*, XXXIII, 508 n., 531–33, 536.

From Archibald Stuart

RICHMOND Jany. 14th 1788

DR SIR

The uncertainty of our final Decision on all publick questions has been the cause of My late silence. As the Session is now over I can venture to give you some information with certainty—for this purpose I inclose you two Acts with a Statement of Our private Debts. The Law concerning Executions is the Companion of the District Bill which passed by a Very Large Majority—four additional Genl. Court Judges are chosen for the purpose of alloting at least three Judges to each Circuit.[1] The Gent in nomination for this appointment were Jos. Prentis, St Geo Tucker, Gabl. Jones, Colo. Parker of Westmoreland, Jos: Jones of K George, Edmund Winstone, Lee Massy, Cut. Bullitt Daniel Fisher & Colo. Grayson, Cyrus

Griffin being Withdrawn Out of Whom the four first mentioned Were Elected. An Act has passed to subject the Lands of publick Debtors to discharge the Commonwealths Judgments, & to Authorize the removal of their property to any part of the State where the Executive shall Direct the Officer executing any process on such property.[2] Several alterations have taken place in the port-Bill in favor of American Vessels & relaxing the rigor of the Law which has been so loudly complained of. I fear we have made it worse & that every Departure from its first principles will be found ruinous.

The anti-constitutional Fever which raged here some time ago begins to abate & I am not without hopes that many patients will be restored to their senses. Mr. Page of Rosewell has become a Convert. Genl. Nelson begins to view the Govt with a More favorable eye & I am told St. G: Tucker has confessed his sins.

Publius is in general estimation, his greatness is acknowledged universally. Colo. Carrington has sent me his numbers as late down as the 24th. inclusive Which Dixon has been printing for some time past.[3] Should he leave New York I must rely upon Yourself & Mr. Brown to transmit the remainder of them as they shall appear. They May be Directed to Me or in my Absence to Mr. John Dixon—as I leave this place tomorrow not to return before the first of April.

Pray let nothing Divert you from Coming to the Convention. I am Dr Sir with respect & esteem Yr Very H sevt

ARCHD STUART

I had almost forgotten to express my Wish that a Superintendant of Indian Affairs may be appointed as soon As possible, I verily believe it would essentially serve some of Our suffering Western Brethren.

Colo. Arthur Campbell has spoken to me in such terms as convince me he would be pleased with the appointment & I own that I am far from thinking him disqualifyed for it, he has resided among the Indians to the Age of 7 his situation is favorable & he is a man of Considerable Abilities.[4] From &c

A: S:

RC (DLC). Addressed by Stuart and docketed by JM. Enclosures not found.

[1]See Hening, *Statutes*, XII, 457–62, 532–58.

[2]See "An act for the more speedy recovery of debts due to this commonwealth" (ibid., XII, 558–63). The lands of sheriffs, coroners, and other public collectors were to be sold only if their "goods and chattels" were insufficient to satisfy the debt. The act further provided that if the public debtor's property (i.e., goods and chattels) could not be sold in his county, it could be removed and sold in any adjacent county. Stuart inaccurately stated that such property could be removed "to any part of the State."

[3] John Dixon published the Richmond *Va. Gazette and Independent Chronicle.*

[4] Campbell had written Governor Randolph on 31 Dec. 1787 announcing his availability for the position of Indian superintendent for the Southern Department. His hopes were disappointed, however, for on 29 Feb. 1788 Congress elected Richard Winn to succeed James White in that post (*CVSP*, IV, 375; *JCC*, XXXIV, 72; Secretary of Congress to Richard Winn, 1 Mar. 1788, Burnett, *Letters*, VIII, 704).

From Tench Coxe

PHILADA. Jany 16th. 1788.

DEAR SIR

I have obtained from the Editor about sixty pages of the debates of our State Convention,[1] wch. I am anxious to get into the hands of Mr. King, for the use of the gentlemen in the Massachussets convention. Uncertain whether he is in New York or Boston I have taken the liberty of enclosing it to you with a request that you will as early as possible have it sent forward to him under a franked cover from yourself.

I observe the letters of Publius are to be printed by Subscription at New Yk. Shall I ask the favor of your delivering the enclosed bills to the printer, and requesting him to set me down for a copy. They are most valuable disquisitions of Government in its peculiar relations and connexions with this Country.

Enclosed is a little paper the republication of wch. may possibly be useful in New York.[2] I am, Sir, with very sincere esteem, your most respectf. h. Servt.

TENCH COXE

RC (DLC). Docketed by JM. Enclosures not found.

[1] The editor of *Debates of the Convention, of the State of Pennsylvania, on the Constitution, Proposed for the Government of the United States . . .* (Philadelphia, 1788) was Thomas Lloyd (1756–1827), who later reported the debates of the First Federal Congress. A Federalist sympathizer, Lloyd promised a full account of the debates in two volumes. The first volume contained only the speeches of Federalists James Wilson and Thomas McKean, however, and the second never appeared. These circumstances gave rise to charges that Lloyd had deliberately suppressed Antifederalist arguments (Marion Tinling, "Thomas Lloyd's Reports of the First Federal Congress," *WMQ*, 3d ser., XVIII [1961], 520–26).

[2] The enclosure may have been the essay of "Philanthropos," which appeared in the *Pa. Gazette* of 16 Jan. 1788 and was reprinted in the N.Y. *Daily Advertiser* of 23 Jan. 1788. "Philanthropos" compared the arguments of George Mason, Elbridge Gerry, and Edmund Randolph in order to show that they disagreed with one another in their opposition to the Constitution. JM mentioned this piece in his letter to Randolph of 27 Jan. 1788, but did not attribute its authorship to Coxe.

From Rufus King

BOSTON 16. Jany. 1788

DEAR SIR

We may have 360 members in our Convention, not more than 330 have yet taken their Seats. Immediately after the settlement of Elections the Convention resolved that they would consider and freely deliberate on each paragraph without taking a [question on any of them individually,] & that on the question whether they wd. ratify, each [member] shd. be at liberty [to disc]uss the plan at large. This Resolution seems to preclude the [idea] of Amendments; and hitherto the measure has not been suggested. I however do not from this Circumstance conclude that it may not hereafter occur. The Opponents of the Constitution moved that Mr. Gerry shd. be requested to take a seat in the Convention to answer such Enquiries as the Convention should make concerning Facts which happened in *the passing of the* Constitution; although this seems to be a very irregular proposal, yet considering the Jealousies which prevail with those who made it (who are certainly not the most enlightened part of the Convention) and the doubt of the issue had it been made a trial of strength, several Friends of the Constitution united with their Opponents and the resolution was agreed to, & Mr. Gerry has taken his Seat.[1]

Tomorrow we are told certain Enquiries are to be moved for by the Opposition, & that Mr. Gerry under the Idea of stating Facts is to state his reasons &c—this will be opposed and we shall on the division be able to form some Idea of our relative Strength.

From the Men who are in favor of the Constitution every reasonable explanation will be given, and arguments really new and in my Judgment most excellent have been & will be produced in its Support. But what will be its fate I confess I am unable to discern. No question ever classed the people of this State in a more extraordinary manner, or with more apparent Firmness. Farewel, your's &c

RUFUS KING

RC (DLC); Tr (NHi). RC docketed by JM. Brackets indicate words obscured by blotting in the RC and supplied by the editors from the Tr.

[1] For the circumstances related to Gerry's special status, see *Massachussetts Debates*, p. 100.

The Federalist Number 39

[16 January 1788]

The last paper having concluded the observations which were meant to introduce a candid survey of the plan of government reported by the convention, we now proceed to the execution of that part of our undertaking. The first question that offers itself is, whether the general form and aspect of the government be strictly republican? It is evident that no other form would be reconcileable with the genius of the people of America; with the fundamental principles of the revolution; or with that honorable determination, which animates every votary of freedom, to rest all our political experiments on the capacity of mankind for self-government. If the plan of the convention therefore be found to depart from the republican character, its advocates must abandon it as no longer defensible.

What then are the distinctive characters of the republican form? Were an answer to this question to be sought, not by recurring to principles, but in the application of the term by political writers, to the constitutions of different states, no satisfactory one would ever be found. Holland, in which no particle of the supreme authority is derived from the people, has passed almost universally under the denomination of a republic. The same title has been bestowed on Venice, where absolute power over the great body of the people, is exercised in the most absolute manner, by a small body of hereditary nobles. Poland, which is a mixture of aristocracy and of monarchy in their worst forms, has been dignified with the same appellation. The government of England, which has one republican branch only, combined with a hereditary aristocracy and monarchy, has with equal impropriety been frequently placed on the list of republics. These examples, which are nearly as dissimilar to each other as to a genuine republic, shew the extreme inaccuracy with which the term has been used in political disquisitions.

If we resort for a criterion, to the different principles on which different forms of government are established, we may define a republic to be, or at least may bestow that name on, a government which derives all its powers directly or indirectly from the great body of the people; and is administered by persons holding their offices during pleasure, for a limited period, or during good behaviour. It is *essential* to such a government, that it be derived from the great body of the society, not from an inconsiderable proportion, or a favored class of it; otherwise a handful of tyrannical nobles, exercising their oppressions by a delegation of their powers, might aspire to the rank of republicans, and claim for their government the honorable title of republic. It is *sufficient* for such a government, that the persons administering it be appointed, either directly or indirectly, by the people; and that they hold their appointments by either of the tenures just specified; otherwise every government in the United States, as well as every other popular government that has been or can be well organised or well executed, would be degraded from the republican character. According to the constitution of every state in the union, some or other of the officers of government are appointed indirectly only by the people. According to most of them the chief magistrate himself is so appointed. And according to one, this mode of appointment is extended to one of the co-ordinate branches of the legislature. According to all the constitutions also, the tenure of the highest offices is extended to a definite period, and in many instances, both within the legislative and executive departments, to a period of years. According to the provisions of most of the constitutions, again, as well as according to the most respectable and received opinions on the subject, the members of the judiciary department are to retain their offices by the firm tenure of good behaviour.

On comparing the constitution planned by the convention, with the standard here fixed, we perceive at once that it is in the most rigid sense conformable to it. The house of representatives, like that of one branch at least of all the state legislatures, is elected immediately by the great body of the people. The senate, like the present congress, and the senate of Maryland, derives its appointment indirectly from the people. The president is indirectly derived from the choice of the people, according to the example in most of the states. Even the judges, with all other officers of the union, will, as in the several states, be the choice, though a remote choice, of the people themselves. The duration of the appointments is equally conformable to the republican standard, and to the model of the state constitutions. The house of representatives is periodically elective as in all the states; and for the period of two years as in the state of South Carolina. The senate is elective for the period of six years; which is but one year more than the period of the senate of Maryland; and but two more than that of the senates of New-York and Virginia. The president is to continue in office for the period of four years; as in New-York and Delaware, the chief magistrate is elected for three years, and in South Carolina for two years. In the other states the election is annual. In several of the states however, no explicit provision is made for the impeachment of the chief magistrate. And in Delaware and Virginia, he is not impeachable till out of office. The president of the United States is impeachable at any time during his continuance in office. The tenure by which the judges are to

hold their places, is, as it unquestionably ought to be, that of good behaviour. The tenure of the ministerial offices generally will be a subject of
legal regulation, conformably to the reason of the case, and the example of
the state constitutions.

Could any further proof be required of the republican complexion of
this system, the most decisive one might be found in its absolute prohibition of titles of nobility, both under the federal and the state governments;
and in its express guarantee of the republican form to each of the latter.

But it was not sufficient, say the adversaries of the proposed constitution, for the convention to adhere to the republican form. They ought
with equal care, to have preserved the *federal* form, which regards the
union as a *confederacy* of sovereign states; instead of which, they have
framed a *national* government, which regards the union as a *consolidation* of
the states. And it is asked by what authority this bold and radical innovation was undertaken. The handle which has been made of this objection
requires, that it should be examined with some precision.

Without enquiring into the accuracy of the distinction on which the
objection is founded, it will be necessary to a just estimate of its force, first
to ascertain the real character of the government in question; secondly, to
enquire how far the convention were authorised to propose such a government; and thirdly, how far the duty they owed to their country, could
supply any defect of regular authority.

First. In order to ascertain the real character of the government it may
be considered in relation to the foundation on which it is to be established;
to the sources from which its ordinary powers are to be drawn; to the
operation of those powers; to the extent of them; and to the authority by
which future changes in the government are to be introduced.

On examining the first relation, it appears on one hand that the constitution is to be founded on the assent and ratification of the people of
America, given by deputies elected for the special purpose; but on the
other that this assent and ratification is to be given by the people, not as
individuals composing one entire nation; but as composing the distinct and
independent states to which they respectively belong. It is to be the assent
and ratification of the several states derived from the supreme authority in
each state, the authority of the people themselves. The act therefore establishing the constitution, will not be a *national* but a *federal* act.

That it will be a federal and not a national act, as these terms are
understood by the objectors, the act of the people as forming so many
independent states, not as forming one aggregate nation is obvious from

this single consideration, that it is to result neither from the decision of a *majority* of the people of the union, nor from that of a *majority* of the states. It must result from the *unanimous* assent of the several states that are parties to it, differing no other wise from their ordinary assent than in its being expressed, not by the legislative authority, but by that of the people themselves. Were the people regarded in this transaction as forming one nation, the will of the majority of the whole people of the United States, would bind the minority; in the same manner as the majority in each state must bind the minority; and the will of the majority must be determined either by a comparison of the individual votes; or by considering the will of the majority of the states, as evidence of the will of a majority of the people of the United States. Neither of these rules has been adopted. Each state in ratifying the constitution, is considered as a sovereign body independent of all others, and only to be bound by its own voluntary act. In this relation then the new constitution will, if established, be a *federal* and not a *national* constitution.

The next relation is to the sources from which the ordinary powers of government are to be derived. The house of representatives will derive its powers from the people of America, and the people will be represented in the same proportion, and on the same principle, as they are in the legislature of a particular state. So far the government is *national* not *federal*. The senate on the other hand will derive its powers from the states, as political and co-equal societies; and these will be represented on the principle of equality in the senate, as they now are in the existing congress. So far the government is *federal*, not *national*. The executive power will be derived from a very compound source. The immediate election of the president is to be made by the states in their political characters. The votes allotted to them, are in a compound ratio, which considers them partly as distinct and co-equal societies; partly as unequal members of the same society. The eventual election, again is to be made by that branch of the legislature which consists of the national representatives; but in this particular act, they are to be thrown into the form of individual delegations from so many distinct and co-equal bodies politic. From this aspect of the government, it appears to be of a mixed character, presenting at least as many *federal* as *national* features.

The difference between a federal and national government, as it relates to the *operation of the government*, is, by the adversaries of the plan of the convention, supposed to consist in this, that in the former, the powers operate on the political bodies composing the confederacy, in their political capacities; in the latter, on the individual citizens composing the nation, in their individual capacities. On trying the constitution by this criterion, it falls under the *national*, not the *federal* character; though perhaps not so compleatly as has been understood. In several cases, and particularly in the trial of controversies to which states may be parties, they must be viewed and proceeded against in their collective and political capacities only. But[1] the operation of the government on the people in their individual capacities, in its ordinary and most essential proceedings, will on the whole, in the sense of its opponents, designate it in this relation, a *national* government.

But if the government be national with regard to the *operation* of its powers, it changes its aspect again when we contemplate it in relation to the *extent* of its powers. The idea of a national government involves in it, not only an authority over the individual citizens, but an indefinite supremacy over all persons and things, so far as they are objects of lawful government. Among a people consolidated into one nation, this supremacy is compleatly vested in the national legislature. Among communities united for particular purposes, it is vested partly in the general, and partly in the municipal legislatures. In the former case, all local authorities are subordinate to the supreme; and may be controuled, directed, or abolished by it at pleasure. In the latter, the local or municipal authorities form distinct and independent portions of the supremacy, no more subject within their respective spheres to the general authority, than the general authority is subject to them within its own sphere. In this relation then, the proposed government cannot be deemed a *national* one; since its jurisdiction extends to certain enumerated objects only, and leaves to the several states a residuary and inviolable sovereignty over all other objects. It is true that in controversies relating to the boundary between the two jurisdictions, the tribunal which is ultimately to decide, is to be established under the general government. But this does not change the principle of the case. The decision is to be impartially made, according to the rules of the constitution; and all the usual and most effectual precautions are taken to secure this impartiality. Some such tribunal is clearly essential to prevent an appeal to the sword, and a dissolution of the compact; and that it ought to be established under the general, rather than under the local governments; or to speak more properly, that it could be safely established under the first alone, is a position not likely to be combated.

If we try the constitution by its last relation, to the authority by which amendments are to be made, we find it neither wholly *national*, nor wholly *federal.* Were it wholly national, the supreme and ultimate authority would reside in the *majority* of the people of the union; and this authority would be competent at all times, like that of a majority of every national society, to alter or abolish its established government. Were it wholly federal on the other hand, the concurrence of each state in the union would be essential to every alteration that would be binding on all. The mode provided by the plan of the convention, is not founded on either of these principles. In requiring more than a majority, and particularly, in computing the proportion by *states*, not by *citizens*, it departs from the *national*, and advances towards the *federal* character: In rendering the concurrence of less than the whole number of states sufficient, it loses again the *federal*, and partakes of the *national* character.

The proposed constitution therefore, even when tested by the rules laid down by its antagonists, is in strictness, neither a national nor a federal constitution; but a composition of both. In its foundation it is federal, not national; in the sources from which the ordinary powers of the government are drawn, it is partly federal, and partly national; in the operation of these powers, it is national, not federal; in the extent of them again, it is federal, not national; and finally, in the authoritative mode of introducing amendments, it is neither wholly federal, nor wholly national.

PUBLIUS.

McLean, II, 20–27.

[1] In place of "But," the newspaper version reads: "So far the national countenance of the Government on this side seems to be disfigured by a few federal features. But this blemish is perhaps unavoidable in any plan; and" (*The Federalist* [Cooke ed.], p. 255).

From Edward Carrington

RICHMOND Jan. 18. 1788

MY DEAR SIR,

I arrived here on Wednesday night last, and have as yet had but little opportunity to sound the people in any part of the Country upon the constitution. The leaders of the opposition appear generally to be preparing for a decent Submission—the language amongst them is, that amendments must be tried if there should, at the setting of the convention, be a prospect of carrying them down in a respectable number of States, but that should this appear improbable, the constitution must be adopted. I have seen but few of these Gentlemen but have good information as to most of their dispositions upon the subject. The Governors letter to the

Public, which you doubtless have before this seen, marks out this conduct, and I think that publication will be of great service. Mr. Henry, it is said, is determined to amend & leave the fate of the measure to depend on all the other States conforming to the Will of Virginia. His language is, that the other States cannot do without us, and therefore we can dictate to them what terms we please—should they be weak enough to stand out, we may alone enter into foreign alliances. The Value of our Staple is such that any Nation will be ready to treat with us separately. I have not heard of any who have shewn a disposition to go this length with him, except Mr. Bullet[1] whom I saw at Dumfries, and I think at the day of trial but few will be found so mad.

Mr. B. Randolph whose apprehensions from the Gigantic features in the constitution, appear to be as high as any whatever, is of opinion with the Governor. He thinks that should Nine States have adopted when the convention of Virginia meets, every idea of amendment ought to be abandoned, but that should there be a less number the attempt must be made, but with such caution as not to hazard intirely the fate of the measure. I am persuaded that this will become the prevailing sentiment amongst the Malcontents, and in that case there will be tolerable safety, because I see no prospect of more than Rhode Isld. N. York & North Carolina holding out—the latter, it is said, & I beleive with truth, have, out of respect for Virginia, defered her convention until after the time appointed for ours to set.

I shall go up the Country tomorrow and shall do myself the pleasure to write you more fully as soon as my information shall enable me to give you a more satisfactory account of the Public opinion.

I was last night favoured with yours of the 7th. Instant and thank you for it—the Memorials of France & England had not appeared when I left N. York. I am glad to see that our good Ally can still speak in a decided & manly tone.[2]

Inclosed is a copy of the Revenue Act passed at the last Assembly.[3] I am my dear Sir Your Affe. Hl Servt.

ED. CARRINGTON

P.S. Since writing the above I have procured a Copy of the Govrs. letter which is inclosed—be good enough to let our Freind at No. 73. King Street, have a sight of it with my compliments.

RC (DLC). Enclosures not found.

[1]Cuthbert Bullitt (1740–1791) represented Prince William County in the House of Delegates from 1776 to 1777 and again from 1785 to 1788. He was also one of that county's delegates to the convention of 1788 (Swem and Williams, *Register*, p. 353).

²Carrington evidently referred to the "Declaration" of England and "Counter Declaration" of France, dated 27 Oct. 1787, by which the two governments agreed to discontinue "all warlike preparations" (JM to Washington, 14 Jan. 1788, n. 1).
³See Hening, *Statutes*, XII, 412–32.

The Federalist Number 40

[18 January 1788]

The *second* point to be examined is, whether the convention were authorised to frame and propose this mixed constitution.

The powers of the convention ought in strictness to be determined by an inspection of the commissions given to the members by their respective constituents. As all of these however, had reference, either to the recommendation from the meeting at Annapolis in September, 1786, or to that from congress in February, 1787, it will be sufficient to recur to these particular acts.

The act from Annapolis recommends the "appointment of commissioners to take into consideration the situation of the United States, to devise *such further provisions* as shall appear to them necessary to render the constitution of the federal government *adequate to the exigencies of the union;* and to report such an act for that purpose, to the United States in congress assembled, as, when agreed to by them, and afterwards confirmed by the legislature of every state, will effectually provide for the same."

The recommendatory act of congress is in the words following: "Whereas there is provision in the articles of confederation and perpetual union, for making alterations therein, by the assent of a congress of the United States, and of the legislatures of the several states: And whereas experience hath evinced, that there are defects in the present confederation, as a mean to remedy which several of the states, and *particularly the state of New-York*, by express instructions to their delegates in congress, have suggested a convention for the purposes expressed in the following resolution; and such convention appearing to be the most probable mean of establishing in these states, *a firm national government.*"

"Resolved, That in the opinion of congress, it is expedient, that on the 2d Monday in May next, a convention of delegates, who shall have been appointed by the several states, be held at Philadelphia, for the sole and express purpose *of revising the articles of confederation*, and reporting to congress and the several legislatures, such *alterations and provisions therein*, as shall, when agreed to in congress, and confirmed by the states, render the federal constitution *adequate to the exigencies of government and the preservation of the union.*"

From these two acts it appears, 1st. that the object of the convention was to establish in these states, *a firm national government;* 2d. that this government was to be such as would be *adequate to the exigencies of government* and *the preservation of the union;* 3d. that these purposes were to be effected by *alterations and provisions in the articles of confederation,* as it is expressed in the act of congress, or by *such further provisions as should appear necessary,* as it stands in the recommendatory act from Annapolis; 4th. that the alterations and provisions were to be reported to congress, and to the states, in order to be agreed to by the former, and confirmed by the latter.

From a comparison and fair construction of these several modes of expression, is to be deduced the authority under which the convention acted. They were to frame a *national government,* adequate to the *exigencies of government* and *of the union,* and to reduce the articles of confederation into such form as to accomplish these purposes.

There are two rules of construction dictated by plain reason, as well as founded on legal axioms. The one is, that every part of the expression ought, if possible, to be allowed some meaning, and be made to conspire to some common end. The other is, that where the several parts cannot be made to coincide, the less important should give way to the more important part; the means should be sacrificed to the end, rather than the end to the means.

Suppose then that the expressions defining the authority of the convention, were irreconcileably at variance with each other; that a *national* and *adequate government* could not possibly, in the judgment of the convention, be effected by *alterations* and *provisions* in the *articles of confederation,* which part of the definition ought to have been embraced, and which rejected? Which was the more important, which the less important part? Which the end, which the means? Let the most scrupulous expositors of delegated powers; let the most inveterate objectors against those exercised by the convention, answer these questions. Let them declare, whether it was of most importance to the happiness of the people of America, that the articles of confederation should be disregarded, and an adequate government be provided, and the union preserved; or that an adequate government should be omitted, and the articles of confederation preserved. Let them declare, whether the preservation of these articles was the end for securing which a reform of the government was to be introduced as the means; or whether the establishment of a government, adequate to the national happiness, was the end at which these articles themselves originally aimed, and to which they ought, as insufficient means, to have been sacrificed.

But is it necessary to suppose that these expressions are absolutely irreconcileable to each other; that no *alterations* or *provisions* in the *articles of the confederation*, could possibly mould them into a national and adequate government; into such a government as has been proposed by the convention?

No stress it is presumed will in this case be laid on the *title*, a change of that could never be deemed an exercise of ungranted power. *Alterations* in the body of the instrument, are expressly authorised. *New provisions* therein are also expressly authorised. Here then is a power to change the title; to insert new articles; to alter old ones. Must it of necessity be admitted that this power is infringed, so long as a part of the old articles remain? Those who maintain the affirmative, ought at least to mark the boundary between authorised and usurped innovations, between that degree of change which lies within the compass of *alterations and further provisions;* and that which amounts to a *transmutation* of the government. Will it be said that the alterations ought not to have touched the substance of the confederation? The states would never have appointed a convention with so much solemnity, nor described its objects with so much latitude, if some *substantial* reform had not been in contemplation. Will it be said that the *fundamental principles* of the confederation were not within the purview of the convention, and ought not to have been varied? I ask what are these principles? Do they require that in the establishment of the constitution, the states should be regarded as distinct and independent sovereigns? They are so regarded by the constitution proposed. Do they require that the members of the government should derive their appointment from the legislatures, not from the people of the states? One branch of the new government is to be appointed by these legislatures; and under the confederation the delegates to congress *may all* be appointed immediately by the people, and in two states* are actually so appointed. Do they require that the powers of the government should act on the states, and not immediately on individuals? In some instances, as has been shewn, the powers of the new government will act on the states in their collective characters. In some instances also those of the existing government act immediately on individuals: In cases of capture, of piracy, of the post-office, of coins, weights and measures, of trade with the Indians, of claims under grants of land by different states, and above all, in the case of trials by courts-martial in the army and navy, by which death may be inflicted without the intervention of a jury, or even of a civil magistrate; in all these cases the powers of the confederation operate immediately on the persons and interests of individual citizens. Do these fundamental principles require particularly that no tax should be levied without the intermediate

*Connecticut and Rhode-Island.

agency of the states? The confederation itself authorises a direct tax to a certain extent on the post-office. The power of coinage has been so construed by congress, as to levy a tribute immediately from that source also. But pretermitting these instances, was it not an acknowledged object of the convention, and the universal expectation of the people, that the regulation of trade should be submitted to the general government in such a form as would render it an immediate source of general revenue? Had not congress repeatedly recommended this measure as not inconsistent with the fundamental principles of the confederation? Had not every state but one, had not New-York herself, so far complied with the plan of congress, as to recognize the *principle* of the innovation? Do these principles in fine require that the powers of the general government should be limited, and that beyond this limit, the states should be left in possession of their sovereignty and independence? We have seen that in the new government as in the old, the general powers are limited, and that the states, in all unenumerated cases, are left in the enjoyment of their sovereign and independent jurisdiction.

The truth is, that the great principles of the constitution proposed by the convention, may be considered less as absolutely new, than as the expansion of principles which are found in the articles of confederation. The misfortune under the latter system has been, that these principles are so feeble and confined as to justify all the charges of inefficiency which have been urged against it; and to require a degree of enlargement which gives to the new system, the aspect of an entire transformation of the old.

In one particular it is admitted that the convention have departed from the tenor of their commission. Instead of reporting a plan requiring the confirmation *of all the states*, they have reported a plan which is to be confirmed and may be carried into effect by *nine states only*. It is worthy of remark, that this objection, though the most plausible, has been the least urged in the publications which have swarmed against the convention. The forbearance can only have proceeded from an irresistible conviction of the absurdity of subjecting the fate of twelve states, to the perverseness or corruption of a thirteenth; from the example of inflexible opposition given by a *majority* of one sixtieth of the people of America, to a measure approved and called for by the voice of twelve states comprising fifty-nine sixtieths of the people; an example still fresh in the memory and indignation of every citizen who has felt for the wounded honor and prosperity of his country. As this objection therefore, has been in a manner waved by those who have criticised the powers of the convention, I dismiss it without further observation.

The *third* point to be enquired into is, how far considerations of duty arising out of the case itself, could have supplied any defect of regular authority.

In the preceding enquiries, the powers of the convention have been analyzed and tried with the same rigour, and by the same rules, as if they had been real and final powers, for the establishment of a constitution for the United States. We have seen, in what manner they have borne the trial, even on that supposition. It is time now to recollect, that the powers were merely advisory and recommendatory; that they were so meant by the states, and so understood by the convention; and that the latter have accordingly planned and proposed a constitution, which is to be of no more consequence than the paper on which it is written, unless it be stamped with the approbation of those to whom it is addressed. This reflection places the subject in a point of view altogether different, and will enable us to judge with propriety of the course taken by the convention.

Let us view the ground on which the convention stood. It may be collected from their proceedings, that they were deeply and unanimously impressed with the crisis which had led their country almost with one voice to make so singular and solemn an experiment, for correcting the errors of a system by which this crisis had been produced; that they were no less deeply and unanimously convinced, that such a reform as they have proposed, was absolutely necessary to effect the purposes of their appointment. It could not be unknown to them, that the hopes and expectations of the great body of citizens, throughout this great empire, were turned with the keenest anxiety, to the event of their deliberations. They had every reason to believe that the contrary sentiments agitated the minds and bosoms of every external and internal foe to the liberty and prosperity of the United States. They had seen in the origin and progress of the experiment, the alacrity with which the *proposition*, made by a single state (Virginia) towards a partial amendment of the confederation, had been attended to and promoted. They had seen the *liberty assumed* by a *very few* deputies, from a *very few* states, convened at Annapolis, of recommending a great and critical object, wholly foreign to their commission, not only justified by the public opinion, but actually carried into effect, by twelve out of the Thirteen States. They had seen in a variety of instances, assumptions by congress not only of recommendatory, but of operative powers, warranted in the public estimation, by occasions and objects infinitely less urgent than those by which their conduct was to be governed. They must have reflected, that in all great changes of established governments, forms ought to give way to substance; that a rigid adherence in such cases to the former, would render nominal and nugatory, the transcendent and precious right of the people to "abolish or alter their governments as to them shall seem most likely to effect their safety and happiness"*; since it is impossible for the people spontaneously and universally, to move in concert towards their object; and it is therefore essential, that such changes be instituted by some *informal and unauthorised propositions*, made by some patriotic and respectable citizen or number of citizens. They must have recollected that it was by this irregular and assumed privilege of proposing to the people plans for their safety and happiness, that the states were first united against the danger with which they were threatened by their antient government; that committees and congresses were formed for concentrating their efforts, and defending their rights; and that *conventions* were *elected* in *the several states*, for establishing the constitutions under which they are now governed; nor could it have been forgotten that no little ill-timed scruples, no zeal for adhering to ordinary forms were any where seen, except in those who wished to indulge under these masks, their secret enmity to the substance contended for. They must have borne in mind, that as the plan to be framed and proposed, was to be submitted to *the people themselves*, the disapprobation of this supreme authority would destroy it for ever; its approbation blot out all antecedent errors and irregularities. It might even have occurred to them, that where a disposition to cavil prevailed, their neglect to execute the degree of power vested in them, and still more their recommendation of any measure whatever not warranted by their commission, would not less excite animadversion, than a recommendation at once of a measure fully commensurate to the national exigencies.

Had the convention under all these impressions, and in the midst of all these considerations, instead of exercising a manly confidence in their country, by whose confidence they had been so peculiarly distinguished, and of pointing out a system capable in their judgment of securing its happiness, taken the cold and sullen resolution of disappointing its ardent hopes of sacrificing substance to forms, of committing the dearest interests of their country to the uncertainties of delay, and the hazard of events; let me ask the man, who can raise his mind to one elevated conception; who can awaken in his bosom, one patriotic emotion, what judgment ought to have been pronounced by the impartial world, by the friends of mankind, by every virtuous citizen, on the conduct and character of this assembly, or if there be a man whose propensity to condemn, is susceptible of no controul, let me then ask what sentence he has in reserve for the twelve states who *usurped the power of* sending deputies to the convention, a body utterly unknown to their constitutions; for congress, who recommended

*Declaration of Independence.

the appointment of this body, equally unknown to the confederation; and for the state of New-York in particular, who first urged, and then complied with this unauthorised interposition.

But that the objectors may be disarmed of every pretext, it shall be granted for a moment, that the convention were neither authorised by their commission, nor justified by circumstances, in proposing a constitution for their country: Does it follow that the constitution ought for that reason alone to be rejected? If according to the noble precept, it be lawful to accept good advice even from an enemy, shall we set the ignoble example of refusing such advice even when it is offered by our friends? The prudent enquiry in all cases, ought surely to be not so much *from whom* the advice comes, as whether the advice be *good*.

The sum of what has been here advanced and proved, is that the charge against the convention of exceeding their powers, except in one instance little urged by the objectors, has no foundation to support it; that if they had exceeded their powers, they were not only warranted but required, as the confidential servants of their country, by the circumstances in which they were placed, to exercise the liberty which they assumed, and that finally, if they had violated both their powers, and their obligations in proposing a constitution, this ought nevertheless to be embraced, if it be calculated to accomplish the views and happiness of the people of America. How far this character is due to the constitution, is the subject under investigation.

PUBLIUS.

McLean, II, 28–37.

The Federalist Number 41

[19 January 1788]

The constitution proposed by the convention may be considered under two general points of view. The FIRST relates to the sum or quantity of power which it vests in the government, including the restraints imposed on the states. The SECOND, to the particular structure of the government, and the distribution of this power, among its several branches.

Under the first view of the subject two important questions arise; 1. Whether any part of the powers transferred to the general government be unnecessary or improper? 2. Whether the entire mass of them be dangerous to the portion of jurisdiction left in the several states?

Is the aggregate power of the general government greater than ought to have been vested in it? This is the first question.

It cannot have escaped those who have attended with candour to the arguments employed against the extensive powers of the government, that the authors of them have very little considered how far these powers were necessary means of attaining a necessary end. They have chosen rather to dwell on the inconveniences which must be unavoidably blended with all political advantages; and on the possible abuses which must be incident to every power or trust of which a beneficial use can be made. This method of handling the subject cannot impose on the good sense of the people of America. It may display the subtlety of the writer; it may open a boundless field for rhetoric and declamation; it may inflame the passions of the unthinking, and may confirm the prejudices of the misthinking. But cool and candid people will at once reflect, that the purest of human blessings must have a portion of alloy in them; that the choice must always be made, if not of the lesser evil, at least of the GREATER, not the PERFECT good; and that in every political institution, a power to advance the public happiness involves a discretion which may be misapplied and abused. They will see therefore that in all cases, where power is to be conferred, the point first to be decided is whether such a power be necessary to the public good; as the next will be, in case of an affirmative decision, to guard as effectually as possible against a perversion of the power to the public detriment.

That we may form a correct judgment on this subject, it will be proper to review the several powers conferred on the government of the union; and that this may be the more conveniently done, they may be reduced into different classes as they relate to the following different objects; 1. Security against foreign danger; 2. Regulation of the intercourse with foreign nations; 3. Maintenance of harmony and proper intercourse among the states; 4. Certain miscellaneous objects of general utility; 5. Restraint of the states from certain injurious acts; 6. Provisions for giving due efficacy to all these powers.

The powers falling within the first class, are those of declaring war, and granting letters of marque; of providing armies and fleets; of regulating and calling forth the militia; of levying and borrowing money.

Security against foreign danger is one of the primitive objects of civil society. It is an avowed and essential object of the American union. The powers requisite for attaining it, must be effectually confided to the federal councils.

Is the power of declaring war necessary? No man will answer this question in the negative. It would be superfluous therefore to enter into a proof of the affirmative. The existing confederation establishes this power in the most ample form.

Is the power of raising armies, and equipping fleets necessary? This is involved in the foregoing power. It is involved in the power of self-defence.

But was it necessary to give an INDEFINITE POWER of raising TROOPS, as well as providing fleets; and of maintaining both in PEACE, as well as in WAR?

The answer to these questions has been too far anticipated, in another place, to admit an extensive discussion of them in this place. The answer indeed seems to be so obvious and conclusive as scarcely to justify such a discussion in any place. With what colour of propriety could the force necessary for defence, be limited by those who cannot limit the force of offence? If a federal constitution could chain the ambition, or set bounds to the exertions of all other nations, then indeed might it prudently chain the discretion of its own government, and set bounds to the exertions for its own safety.

How could a readiness for war in time of peace be safely prohibited, unless we could prohibit in like manner the preparations and establishments of every hostile nation? The means of security can only be regulated by the means and the danger of attack. They will in fact be ever determined by these rules, and by no others. It is in vain to oppose constitutional barriers to the impulse of self-preservation. It is worse than in vain; because it plants in the constitution itself necessary usurpations of power, every precedent of which is a germ of unnecessary and multiplied repetitions. If one nation maintains constantly a disciplined army ready for the service of ambition or revenge, it obliges the most pacific nations, who may be within the reach of its enterprizes, to take corresponding precautions. The fifteenth century was the unhappy epoch of military establishments in time of peace. They were introduced by Charles VII. of France. All Europe has followed, or been forced into the example. Had the example not been followed by other nations, all Europe must long ago have worn the chains of a universal monarch. Were every nation except France now to disband its peace establishment, the same event might follow. The veteran legions of Rome were an overmatch for the undisciplined valour of all other nations, and rendered her mistress of the world.

Not less true is it, that the liberties of Rome proved the final victim to her military triumphs, and that the liberties of Europe, as far as they ever existed, have, with few exceptions been the price of her military establishments. A standing force therefore is a dangerous, at the same time that it may be a necessary provision. On the smallest scale it has its inconveniences. On an extensive scale, its consequences may be fatal. On any scale, it is an object of laudable circumspection and precaution. A wise nation will combine all these considerations; and whilst it does not rashly preclude itself from any resource which may become essential to its safety, will exert all its prudence in diminishing both the necessity and the danger of resorting to one which may be inauspicious to its liberties.

The clearest marks of this prudence are stamped on the proposed constitution. The union itself which it cements and secures, destroys every pretext for a military establishment which could be dangerous. America, united with a handful of troops, or without a single soldier, exhibits a more forbidding posture to foreign ambition, than America disunited, with an hundred thousand veterans ready for combat. It was remarked on a former occasion, that the want of this pretext had saved the liberties of one nation in Europe. Being rendered by her insular situation and her maritime resources, impregnable to the armies of her neighbours, the rulers of Great-Britain have never been able, by real or artificial dangers, to cheat the public into an extensive peace establishment. The distance of the United States from the powerful nations of the world, gives them the same happy security. A dangerous establishment can never be necessary or plausible, so long as they continue a united people. But let it never for a moment be forgotten, that they are indebted for this advantage to their union alone. The moment of its dissolution will be the date of a new order of things. The fears of the weaker or the ambition of the stronger states or confederacies, will set the same example in the new, as Charles VII. did in the old world. The example will be followed here from the same motives which produced universal imitation there. Instead of deriving from our situation the precious advantage which Great-Britain has derived from hers, the face of America will be but a copy of that of the continent of Europe. It will present liberty every where crushed between standing armies and perpetual taxes. The fortunes of disunited America will be even more disastrous than those of Europe. The sources of evil in the latter are confined to her own limits. No superior powers of another quarter of the globe intrigue among her rival nations, inflame their mutual animosities, and render them the instruments of foreign ambition, jealousy and revenge. In America, the miseries springing from her internal jealousies, contentions and wars, would form a part only of her lot. A plentiful addition of evils would have their source in that relation in which Europe stands to this quarter of the earth, and which no other quarter of the earth bears to Europe. This picture of the consequences of disunion cannot be too highly coloured, or too often exhibited. Every man who loves peace, every man who loves his country, every man who loves liberty, ought to have it ever before his eyes, that he may cherish in his heart a due attachment to the union of America, and be able to set a due value on the means of preserving it.

Next to the effectual establishment of the union, the best possible precaution against danger from standing armies, is a limitation of the term for which revenue may be appropriated to their support. This precaution the constitution has prudently added. I will not repeat here the observations, which I flatter myself have placed this subject in a just and satisfactory light. But it may not be improper to take notice of an argument against this part of the constitution, which has been drawn from the policy and practice of Great-Britain. It is said that the continuance of an army in that kingdom, requires an annual vote of the legislature; whereas the American constitution has lengthened this critical period to two years. This is the form in which the comparison is usually stated to the public: But is it a just form? Is it a fair comparison? Does the British constitution restrain the parliamentary discretion to one year? Does the American impose on the congress appropriations for two years? On the contrary, it cannot be unknown to the authors of the fallacy themselves, that the British constitution fixes no limit whatever to the discretion of the legislature, and that the American ties down the legislature to two years, as the longest admissible term.

Had the argument from the British example been truly stated, it would have stood thus: The term for which supplies may be appropriated to the army establishment, though unlimited by the British constitution, has nevertheless in practice been limited by parliamentary discretion, to a single year. Now if in Great-Britain, where the house of commons is elected for seven years; where so great a proportion of the members are elected by so small a proportion of the people; where the electors are so corrupted by the representatives, and the representatives so corrupted by the crown, the representative body can possess a power to make appropriations to the army for an indefinite term, without desiring, or without daring, to extend the term beyond a single year; ought not suspicion herself to blush in pretending that the representatives of the United States, elected FREELY, by the WHOLE BODY of the people, every SECOND YEAR, cannot be safely entrusted with a discretion over such appropriations, expressly limited to the short period of TWO YEARS?

A bad cause seldom fails to betray itself. Of this truth, the management of the opposition to the federal government is an unvaried exemplification. But among all the blunders which have been committed, none is more striking than the attempt to enlist on that side, the prudent jealousy entertained by the people, of standing armies. The attempt has awakened fully the public attention to that important subject; and has led to investigations which must terminate in a thorough and universal conviction, not only that the constitution has provided the most effectual guards against danger from that quarter, but that nothing short of a constitution fully adequate to the national defence, and the preservation of the union, can save

America from as many standing armies as it may be split into states or confederacies; and from such a progressive augmentation of these establishments in each, as will render them as burdensome to the properties and ominous to the liberties of the people; as any establishment that can become necessary, under a united and efficient government, must be tolerable to the former, and safe to the latter.

The palpable necessity of the power to provide and maintain a navy has protected that part of the constitution against a spirit of censure, which has spared few other parts. It must indeed be numbered among the greatest blessings of America, that as her union will be the only source of her maritime strength, so this will be a principal source of her security against danger from abroad. In this respect our situation bears another likeness to the insular advantage of Great-Britain. The batteries most capable of repelling foreign enterprizes on our safety, are happily such as can never be turned by a perfidious government against our liberties.

The inhabitants of the Atlantic frontier are all of them deeply interested in this provision for naval protection, and if they have hitherto been suffered to sleep quietly in their beds; if their property has remained safe against the predatory spirit of licentious adventurers; if their maritime towns have not yet been compelled to ransom themselves from the terrors of a conflagration, by yielding to the exactions of daring and sudden invaders, these instances of good fortune are not to be ascribed to the capacity of the existing government for the protection of those from whom it claims allegiance, but to causes that are fugitive and fallacious. If we except perhaps Virginia and Maryland, which are peculiarly vulnerable on their eastern frontiers, no part of the union ought to feel more anxiety on this subject than New-York. Her sea coast is extensive. The very important district of the state is an Island. The state itself is penetrated by a large navigable river for more than fifty leagues. The great emporium of its commerce, the great reservoir of its wealth, lies every moment at the mercy of events, and may almost be regarded as a hostage, for ignominious compliances with the dictates of a foreign enemy, or even with the rapacious demands of pirates and barbarians. Should a war be the result of the precarious situation of European affairs, and all the unruly passions attending it, be let loose on the ocean, our escape from insults and depredations, not only on that element but every part of the other bordering on it, will be truly miraculous. In the present condition of America, the states more immediately exposed to these calamities, have nothing to hope from the phantom of a general government which now exists; and if their single resources were equal to the task of fortifying themselves against the danger, the object to be protected would be almost consumed by the means of protecting them.

The power of regulating and calling forth the militia has been already sufficiently vindicated and explained.

The power of levying and borrowing money, being the sinew of that which is to be exerted in the national defence, is properly thrown into the same class with it. This power also has been examined already with much attention, and has I trust been clearly shewn to be necessary both in the extent and form given to it by the constitution. I will address one additional reflection only to those who contend that the power ought to have been restrained to external taxation, by which they mean taxes on articles imported from other countries.[1] It cannot be doubted that this will always be a valuable source of revenue, that for a considerable time, it must be a principal source, that at this moment it is an essential one. But we may form very mistaken ideas on this subject, if we do not call to mind in our calculations, that the extent of revenue drawn from foreign commerce, must vary with the variations both in the extent and the kind of imports, and that these variations do not correspond with the progress of population, which must be the general measure of the public wants. As long as agriculture continues the sole field of labour, the importation of manufactures must increase as the consumers multiply. As soon as domestic manufactures are begun by the hands not called for by agriculture, the imported manufactures will decrease as the numbers of people increase. In a more remote stage, the imports may consist in considerable part of raw materials which will be wrought into articles for exportation, and will therefore require rather the encouragement of bounties, than to be loaded with discouraging duties. A system of government, meant for duration ought to contemplate these revolutions, and be able to accommodate itself to them.

Some who have not denied the necessity of the power of taxation, have grounded a very fierce attack against the constitution on the language in which it is defined. It has been urged and echoed, that the power "to lay and collect taxes, duties, imposts and excises, to pay the debts, and provide for the common defence and general welfare of the United States," amounts to an unlimited commission to exercise every power which may be alledged to be necessary for the common defence or general welfare.[2] No stronger proof could be given of the distress under which these writers labour for objections, than their stooping to such a misconstruction.

Had no other enumeration or definition of the powers of the congress been found in the constitution, than the general expressions just cited, the authors of the objection might have had some colour for it; though it would have been difficult to find a reason for so awkward a form of describing an authority to legislate in all possible cases. A power to destroy the freedom of the press, the trial by jury or even to regulate the course of descents, or the forms of conveyances, must be very singularly expressed by the terms "to raise money for the general welfare."

But what colour can the objection have, when a specification of the objects alluded to by these general terms, immediately follows; and is not even separated by a longer pause than a semicolon. If the different parts of the same instrument ought to be so expounded as to give meaning to every part which will bear it; shall one part of the same sentence be excluded altogether from a share in the meaning; and shall the more doubtful and indefinite terms be retained in their full extent and the clear and precise expressions, be denied any signification whatsoever? For what purpose could the enumeration of particular powers be inserted, if these and all others were meant to be included in the preceding general power? Nothing is more natural or common than first to use a general phrase, and then to explain and qualify it by a recital of particulars. But the idea of an enumeration of particulars, which neither explain nor qualify the general meaning, and can have no other effect than to confound and mislead, is an absurdity which as we are reduced to the dilemma of charging either on the authors of the objection, or on the authors of the constitution, we must take the liberty of supposing, had not its origin with the latter.

The objection here is the more extraordinary, as it appears, that the language used by the convention is a copy from the articles of confederation. The objects of the union among the states as described in article 3d, are, "their common defence, security of their liberties, and mutual and general welfare." The terms of article 8th, are still more identical. "All charges of war, and all other expences, that shall be incurred for the common defence or general welfare, and allowed by the United States in congress shall be defrayed out of a common treasury, &c." A similar language again occurs in article 9. Construe either of these articles by the rules which would justify the construction put on the new constitution, and they vest in the existing Congress a power to legislate in all cases whatsoever. But what would have been thought of that assembly, if attaching themselves to these general expressions, and disregarding the specifications, which ascertain and limit their import, they had exercised an unlimited power of providing for the common defence and general welfare? I appeal to the objectors themselves, whether they would in that case have employed the same reasoning in justification of congress, as they now make use of against the convention. How difficult it is for error to escape its own condemnation.

PUBLIUS.

McLean, II, 37–48.

[1]See the remarks of "Brutus" and the "Federal Farmer" (Borden, *The Antifederalist Papers*, pp. 59–60, 85–86, 96–97).

[2] A point made by, among others, "Centinel" (Samuel Bryan) and "Brutus" (McMaster and Stone, *Pennsylvania and the Federal Constitution*, II, 610–11; Kenyon, *The Antifederalists*, pp. 330–31).

To Edmund Randolph

N. York Jany. 20. 1788

MY DEAR FRIEND

I have received your favor of the 3 inst. By a letter from Mr. Turberville of later date I have the mortification to find that our friend Mr. Jones has not succeeded in his wish to be translated from the Executive to the Judiciary Department. I had supposed that he stood on ground that could not fail him in a case of that sort; and am wholly at a loss to account for the disappointment.

The Count de Moustier arrived a few days ago as successor to the Chevr. de la Luzerne. He had so long a passage that I do not know whether the dispatches brought by him, contain much that is new. It seems that although the affairs of Holland are put into a pacific train, those of the Russians & Turks may yet produce a general broil in Europe. The Prussian Troops are to be withdrawn & the fate of the Dutch regulated by negociation.

The intelligence from Massachts. begins to be rather ominous to the Constitution. The Interest opposed to it is reinforced by all connected with the late insurrection, and by the province of Mayne which apprehends difficulties under the new System in obtaining a separate Government greater than may be otherwise experienced. Judging from the present state of the intelligence as I have it, the probabil[it]y is that the voice of that State will be in the negative. The Legislature of this State is much divided at present. The House of Assembly are said to be friendly to the merits of the Constitution. The Senate, at least a majority of those actually assembled, are opposed even to the calling a Convention. The decision of Massts. in either way, will decide the voice of this State. The minority of Penna. are extremely restless under their defeat, will endeavor at all events if they can get an assembly to their wish to undermine what has been done there, and will it is presumed be emboldened by a negative from Massts. to give a more direct & violent form to their attack. The accounts from Georgia are favorable to the Constitution. So they are also from S. Carolina, as far as they extend.

If I am not misinformed as to the arrival of some members of Congress in Town, a quorum is at length made up. Your's affectly.

Js. MADISON JR.

RC (DLC). Docketed by Randolph. Misdated 20 July 1788 in Stan. V. Henkels Catalogue No. 694 (1892).

To George Washington

N. York Jany. 20. 1788.

Dear Sir

The Count de Moustier arrived here a few days ago as Successor to the Chevr. de la Luzerne. His passage has been so tedious that I am not sure that the despatches from Mr. Jefferson make any considerable addition to former intelligence. I have not yet seen them, but am told that this is the case. In general it appears that the affairs of Holland are put into pacific train. The Prussian troops are to be withdrawn, and the event settled by negociations. But it is still possible that the war between the Russians & Turks may spread a general flame throughout Europe.

The intelligence from Massachussetts begins to be very ominous to the Constitution. The antifederal party is reinforced by the insurgents, and by the province of Mayne which apprehends greater obstacles to her scheme of a separate Government, from the new system than may be otherwise experienced. And according to the prospect at the date of the latest letters, there was very great reason to fear that the voice of that State would be in the negative. The operation of such an event on this State may easily be foreseen. Its Legislature is now sitting and is much divided. A majority of the Assembly are said to be friendly to the merits of the Constitution. A Majority of the Senators actually convened are opposed to a submission of it to a Convention. The arrival of the absent members will render the voice of that branch uncertain on the point of a Convention. The decision of Massachussetts either way will involve the result in this State. The minority in Penna. is very restless under their defeat. If they can get an Assembly to their wish they will endeavor to undermine what has been done there. If backed by Massts. they will probably be emboldened to make some more rash experiment. The information from Georgia continues to be favorable. The little we get from S. Carolina is of the same complexion.

If I am not misinformed as to the arrival of some members for Congress, a quorum is at length made up. With the most perfect esteem & attachment I remain Dear Sir Your Obedt. humble servant

Js. Madison Jr

RC (DLC: Washington Papers); Tr (DLC). RC docketed by Washington.

Account with the Commonwealth of Virginia

[20 January 1788]

1787. The Commonwealth of Virginia to James Madison Junr. Debr.

To attendance as a member of Congress from Octr.
20 to Jany. 20. being 92 days at 6 dollars per day } £165..12

Credit.

By surplus advanced by the hands of Govenr. Randolph £14.

Balance   £151..12

E. Exd.   Js. Madison Jr

Ms (Vi). In JM's hand. Docketed on cover: "Warrt issd. 27 Nov. '87 for attendance from 20 Octo. 87 to 20 Jany. '88."

From Rufus King

Boston 20 Jan 1788.

Dear Sir

Our convention proceeds slowly. An apprehension that the liberties of the people are in danger, and a distrust of men of property or Education have a more powerful Effect upon the minds of our Opponents than any specific Objections against the constitution. If the Opposition was grounded on any precise Points, I am persuaded that it might be weakened if not entirely overcome. But every Attempt to remove their fixed and violent Jealousy seems hitherto to operate as a confirmation of that baneful passion. The Opponents affirm to each other that they have an unalterable majority on their side; the Friends doubt the strength of their Adversaries but are not entirely confident of their own.

An Event has taken place relative to Mr. Gerry, which without great Caution may throw us into Confusion; I informed you by the last post on what Terms Mr. G. took a seat in the Convention. Yesterday in the Course of debate on the construction of the Senate, Mr. G. *unasked* informed the Convention that he had some Information to give the Convention on the Subject then in discussion.[1] Mr. Dana and a number of the most respectable Members, remarked upon the Impropriety of Mr. G——'s conduct. Mr. G. rose with a view to justify himself; he was immediately prevented by a number of Objectors; this brought on an irregular Conversation whether Mr. G. shd. be heard. The Hour of Adjournment arrived and the President adjourned the House. Mr. Gerry immediately charged Mr. Dana with a design of injuring his Reputation by partial Information, & preventing his having an Opportunity to communicate important Truths to the Convention; this charge drew a warm reply from Mr. Dana, the Members collected about them, took sides as they were for or against the Constitution, and we were in Danger of the utmost Confusion. However the Gentlemen separated—and I suppose Tomorrow Morning will renew the discussion before the Convention.[2]

I shall be better able to conjecture the final Issue by next Post. With real Esteem & Regard I am &c

R. KING

RC (DLC); Tr (NHi). RC docketed by JM.

[1]On 18 Jan. Gerry had been requested to answer the following question in writing: "Why, in the last requisition of Congress, the portion required of this State was thirteen times as much as of Georgia, and yet we have but eight representatives in the general government, and Georgia has three?" After Gerry submitted his answer the following morning, the convention proceeded to debate the section of the Constitution providing for equal representation in the Senate. It was during this debate that Gerry attempted to address the convention (enclosure, Benjamin Lincoln to Washington, 20 Jan. 1788, *Documentary History of the Constitution*, IV, 451–53).

[2]Gerry did not return to the convention, but his letter of 21 Jan. 1788, accompanied by a statement of the proceedings of the Federal Convention concerning representation in the Senate, was laid before the Massachusetts delegates on 22 Jan. (*Massachusetts Debates*, pp. 65–66, 175–76). The letter and statement, together with an account of this episode from the Boston *Mass. Centinel* of 2 Feb. 1788, are printed in *Massachusetts Debates*, pp. 65–75 n. 18.

To Tench Coxe

Letter not found.

20 January 1788. Mentioned in Coxe to JM, 23 and 27 Jan. 1788. Reports unfavorable prospects for the Constitution in Massachusetts.

From Joseph Jones

SPRING HILL 21st Janry. 1788.

DR. SR.

I beg your pardon for omiting to write to you the last two or three weeks. I have been little in Richmond during that period and of late have been confined by an attack of the Rhumatism, which, though very painfull for two or three days, has now left me. I mean, nothing unforeseen preventing, to visit Richmond next week. Before I came away Col. Goode had sent me a good many slips of the wild crab tree but not one scion—

these I knew wod. not answer your purpose and threw them away. He informed me there was not a scion to be got. Mr. Seldon could not discover any of the Trees at his place. The scion I suspect is not easily procured unless from Trees that can be found under inclosure. The season being now past for sending them to N. York in time for planting could they be procured, you must desire your friend to have patience untill next fall, by which time I doubt not to be able to gratify him. I think I have seen several of them near where Col. Carter resides. The tree at Col. Goodes bears the largest apple for a wild crab I ever saw. The Servant brought me one of them with the slips as large as a hens egg, and of very agreeable scent. The Map of James River was compleated when I left Richmond except the trace of the canal which being a material part of it more on account of the notes of reference that[1] any difficulty in laying it down I declined receiving it from Mr. Lambert untill these were added. Mr. Harris the manager of the work altho' he had promised me to furnish them had not then complied with his promise. Lambert promised me if he did not soon do it he would ride up to his House near the Canal and obtain his sketch and notes. Would you have the map forwarded to new york by some safe ha[n]d that offers or retain it here untill you come in in march which I hear you intend doing. It will be too large for a letter by Post.

The Assembly have passed the district plan into a law—much changed I am told from the former plan. Not having seen the law I can speak only from information. There are eighteen districts—four additional Judges of the genl. Court—the genl. Court Judges ride the upper districts three to a circuit. The Chancellors and Admiralty Judges take the six lower districts. Chancery, admiralty, and appeal Courts as heretofore. District Courts take cognizance of no demands under 30£. Civil process commences 1st Janry. next the criminal I am informed some time in the fall. The Judges have 20/ each a day, & 5d ℔ mile during their Journeys I think in addition to former allowance, so it stood in the bill and is so I presume in the law.[2] The lawyers fees 15/ & 30 the same as the County Courts.[3] The revenue law which is also the appropriation law is calculated to lessen all it may the State debt, I mean the internal debt. The certificate Tax is taken off and an additional duty on certain enumerated articles & 3 ℔ Cent on other goods payable in certificates is the present plan for sinking them. Yr. friend & Servt

JOS: JONES.

RC (DLC). Addressed by Jones and postmarked, "FREDS BURG, Jan 24." Docketed by JM.

[1] Jones meant to write "than."

[2] The bill as finally passed provided no additional compensation for the judges. In their "remonstrance" of 12 May 1788 the judges claimed that by increasing their duties without a

corresponding increase in their pay the act was "an attack upon the independency of the Judges" (Mays, *Papers of Edmund Pendleton*, II, 507). The assembly relented somewhat at its next session by granting a travel allowance of six pence per mile (Hening, *Statutes*, XII, 768–69).

³See ibid., XII, 547. The fee was thirty shillings or 240 pounds of tobacco "in real, personal, or mixed actions" involving land titles or boundaries, and fifteen shillings or 120 pounds of tobacco in all other causes.

The Federalist Number 42

[22 January 1788]

The *second* class of powers lodged in the general government, consists of those which regulate the intercourse with foreign nations, to wit, to make treaties; to send and receive ambassadors, other public ministers and consuls; to define and punish piracies and felonies committed on the high seas, and offences against the law of nations; to regulate foreign commerce, including a power to prohibit after the year 1808, the importation of slaves, and to lay an intermediate duty of ten dollars per head, as a discouragement to such importations.

This class of powers forms an obvious and essential branch of the federal administration. If we are to be one nation in any respect, it clearly ought to be in respect to other nations.

The powers to make treaties and to send and receive ambassadors, speak their own propriety. Both of them are comprised in the articles of confederation; with this difference only, that the former is disembarrassed by the plan of the convention of an exception, under which treaties might be substantially frustrated by regulations of the states; and that a power of appointing and receiving "other public ministers and consuls," is expressly and very properly added to the former provision concerning ambassadors. The term ambassador, if taken strictly, as seems to be required by the second of the articles of confederation, comprehends the highest grade only of public ministers; and excludes the grades which the United States will be most likely to prefer where foreign embassies may be necessary. And under no latitude of construction will the term comprehend consuls. Yet it has been found expedient, and has been the practice of congress to employ the inferior grades of public ministers; and to send and receive consuls. It is true that where treaties of commerce stipulate for the mutual appointment of consuls, whose functions are connected with commerce, the admission of foreign consuls may fall within the power of making commercial treaties; and that where no such treaties exist, the mission of American consuls into foreign countries, may *perhaps* be covered under the authority given by the 9th article of the confederation, to appoint all such civil officers as may be necessary for managing the general affairs of the United States. But the admission of consuls into the United States, where no previous treaty has stipulated it, seems to have been no where provided for. A supply of the omission is one of the lesser instances in which the convention have improved on the model before them. But the most minute provisions become important when they tend to obviate the necessity or the pretext for gradual and unobserved usurpations of power. A list of the cases in which congress have been betrayed, or forced by the defects of the confederation into violations of their chartered authorities, would not a little suprise those who have paid no attention to the subject; and would be no inconsiderable argument in favor of the new constitution, which seems to have provided no less studiously for the lesser, than the more obvious and striking defects of the old.

The power to define and punish piracies and felonies committed on the high seas, and offences against the law of nations, belongs with equal propriety to the general government; and is a still greater improvement on the articles of confederation.

These articles contain no provision for the case of offences against the law of nations; and consequently leave it in the power of any indiscreet member to embroil the confederacy with foreign nations.

The provision of the federal articles on the subject of piracies and felonies, extends no farther than to the establishment of courts for the trial of these offences. The definition of piracies might perhaps, without inconveniency, be left to the law of nations; though a legislative definition of them is found in most municipal codes. A definition of felonies on the high seas is evidently requisite. Felony is a term of loose signification even in the common law of England; and of various import in the statute law of that kingdom. But neither the common, nor the statute law of that or of any other nation, ought to be a standard for the proceedings of this, unless previously made its own by legislative adoption. The meaning of the term as defined in the codes of the several states, would be as impracticable as the former would be a dishonorable and illegitimate guide. It is not precisely the same in any two of the states; and varies in each with every revision of its criminal laws. For the sake of certainty and uniformity therefore, the power of defining felonies in this case, was in every respect necessary and proper.

The regulation of foreign commerce, having fallen within several views which have been taken of this subject, has been too fully discussed to need additional proofs here of its being properly submitted to the federal administration.

It were doubtless to be wished that the power of prohibiting the importation of slaves, had not been postponed until the year 1808, or rather that it had been suffered to have immediate operation. But it is not difficult to account either for this restriction on the general government, or for the manner in which the whole clause is expressed. It ought to be considered as a great point gained in favor of humanity, that a period of twenty years may terminate for ever within these states, a traffic which has so long and so loudly upbraided the barbarism of modern policy; that within that period it will receive a considerable discouragement from the federal government, and may be totally abolished by a concurrence of the few states which continue the unnatural traffic, in the prohibitory example which has been given by so great a majority of the union. Happy would it be for the unfortunate Africans, if an equal prospect lay before them, of being redeemed from the oppressions of their European brethren!

Attempts have been made to pervert this clause into an objection against the constitution, by representing it on one side as a criminal toleration of an illicit practice, and on another, as calculated to prevent voluntary and beneficial emigrations from Europe to America. I mention these misconstructions, not with a view to give them an answer, for they deserve none; but as specimens of the manner and spirit in which some have thought fit to conduct their opposition to the proposed government.

The powers included in the *third* class, are those which provide for the harmony and proper intercourse among the states.

Under this head might be included the particular restraints imposed on the authority of the states, and certain powers of the judicial department; but the former are reserved for a distinct class, and the latter will be particularly examined when we arrive at the structure and organization of the government. I shall confine myself to a cursory review of the remaining powers comprehended under this third description, to wit, to regulate commerce among the several states and the Indian tribes; to coin money, regulate the value thereof and of foreign coin; to provide for the punishment of counterfeiting the current coin and securities of the United States; to fix the standard of weights and measures; to establish an uniform rule of naturalization, and uniform laws of bankruptcy; to prescribe the manner in which the public acts, records and judicial proceedings of each state shall be proved, and the effect they shall have in other states, and to establish post-offices and post-roads.

The defect of power in the existing confederacy, to regulate the commerce between its several members, is in the number of those which have been clearly pointed out by experience. To the proofs and remarks which former papers have brought into view on this subject, it may be added, that without this supplemental provision, the great and essential power of regulating foreign commerce, would have been incomplete, and ineffectual. A very material object of this power was the relief of the states which import and export through other states, from the improper contributions levied on them by the latter. Were these at liberty to regulate the trade between state and state, it must be foreseen that ways would be found out, to load the articles of import and export, during the passage through their jurisdiction, with duties which would fall on the makers of the latter, and the consumers of the former: We may be assured by past experience, that such a practice would be introduced by future contrivances; and both by that and a common knowledge of human affairs, that it would nourish unceasing animosities, and not improbably terminate in serious interruptions of the public tranquility. To those who do not view the question through the medium of passion or of interest, the desire of the commercial states to collect in any form, an indirect revenue from their uncommercial neighbours, must appear not less impolitic than it is unfair; since it would stimulate the injured party, by resentment as well as interest, to resort to less convenient channels for their foreign trade. But the mild voice of reason, pleading the cause of an enlarged and permanent interest, is but too often drowned before public bodies as well as individuals, by the clamours of an impatient avidity for immediate and immoderate gain.

The necessity of a superintending authority over the reciprocal trade of confederated states has been illustrated by other examples as well as our own. In Switzerland, where the union is so very slight, each canton is obliged to allow to merchandizes, a passage through its jurisdiction into other cantons, without an augmentation of the tolls. In Germany, it is a law of the empire, that the princes and states shall not lay tolls or customs on bridges, rivers, or passages, without the consent of the emperor and diet; though it appears from a quotation in an antecedent paper, that the practice in this as in many other instances in that confederacy, has not followed the law, and has produced there the mischiefs which have been foreseen here. Among the restraints imposed by the union of the Netherlands, on its members, one is, that they shall not establish imposts disadvantageous to their neighbours, without the general permission.

The regulation of commerce with the Indian tribes is very properly unfettered from two limitations in the articles of confederation, which render the provision obscure and contradictory. The power is there restrained to Indians, not members of any of the states, and is not to violate or infringe the legislative right of any state within its own limits. What description of Indians are to be deemed members of a state, is not yet settled; and has been a question of frequent perplexity and contention in the federal councils. And how the trade with Indians, though not members of a state, yet residing within its legislative jurisdiction, can be regulated by an external authority, without so far intruding on the internal rights of legislation, is absolutely incomprehensible. This is not the only case in which the articles of confederation have inconsiderately endeavoured to accomplish impossibilities; to reconcile a partial sovereignty in the union, with complete sovereignty in the states; to subvert a mathematical axiom, by taking away a part, and letting the whole remain.

All that need be remarked on the power to coin money, regulate the value thereof, and of foreign coin, is that by providing for this last case, the constitution has supplied a material omission in the articles of confederation. The authority of the existing congress is restrained to the regulation of coin *struck* by their own authority, or that of the respective states. It must be seen at once, that the proposed uniformity in the *value* of the current coin might be destroyed by subjecting that of foreign coin to the different regulations of the different states.

The punishment of counterfeiting the public securities as well as of the current coin, is submitted of course to that authority, which is to secure the value of both.

The regulation of weights and measures is transferred from the articles of confederation, and is founded on like considerations with the preceding power of regulating coin.

The dissimilarity in the rules of naturalization, has long been remarked as a fault in our system, and as laying a foundation for intricate and delicate questions. In the 4th article of the confederation, it is declared "that the *free inhabitants* of each of these states, paupers, vagabonds, and fugitives from justice excepted, shall be entitled to all privileges and immunities of *free citizens*, in the several states, and *the people* of each state, shall in every other, enjoy all the privileges of trade and commerce, &c." There is a confusion of language here, which is remarkable. Why the terms *free inhabitants*, are used in one part of the article; *free citizens* in another, and *people* in another, or what was meant by superadding "to all privileges and immunities of free citizens,"—"all the privileges of trade and commerce," cannot easily be determined. It seems to be a construction scarcely avoidable, however that those who come under the denomination of *free inhabitants* of a state, although not citizens of such state, are entitled in every other state to all the privileges of *free citizens* of the latter; that is, to greater privileges than they may be entitled to in their own state; so that it may be in the power of a particular state, or rather every state is laid under a necessity, not only to confer the rights of citizenship in other states upon any whom it may admit to such rights within itself; but upon any whom it may allow to become inhabitants within its jurisdiction. But were an exposition of the term "inhabitants" to be admitted, which would confine the stipulated privileges to citizens alone, the difficulty is diminished only, not removed. The very improper power would still be retained by each state, of naturalizing aliens in every other state. In one state residence for a short term confers all the rights of citizenship. In another qualifications of greater importance are required. An alien therefore legally incapacitated for certain rights in the latter, may by previous residence only in the former elude his incapacity; and thus the law of one state, be preposterously rendered paramount to the law of another within the jurisdiction of the other. We owe it to mere casualty, that very serious embarrassments on this subject have been hitherto escaped. By the laws of several states, certain descriptions of aliens who had rendered themselves obnoxious, were laid under interdicts inconsistent, not only with the rights of citizenship, but with the privileges of residence. What would have been the consequence, if such persons, by residence or otherwise, had acquired the character of citizens under the laws of another state, and then asserted their rights as such, both to residence and citizenship within the state proscribing them? Whatever the legal consequences might have been, other consequences would probably have resulted of too serious a nature, not to be provided against. The new constitution has accordingly with great propriety made provision against them, and all others proceeding from the defect of the confederation, on this head by authorising the general government to establish an uniform rule of naturalization throughout the United States.

The power of establishing uniform laws of bankruptcy, is so intimately connected with the regulation of commerce, and will prevent so many frauds where the parties or their property may lie or be removed into different states, that the expediency of it seems not likely to be drawn into question.

The power of prescribing by general laws the manner in which the public acts, records and judicial proceedings of each state shall be proved, and the effect they shall have in other states, is an evident and valuable improvement on the clause relating to this subject in the articles of confederation. The meaning of the latter is extremely indeterminate; and can be of little importance under any interpretation which it will bear. The power here established, may be rendered a very convenient instrument of justice, and be particularly beneficial on the borders of contiguous states, where the effects liable to justice, may be suddenly and secretly translated in any stage of the process, within a foreign jurisdiction.

The power of establishing post-roads, must in every view be a harmless power; and may perhaps, by judicious management, become productive of great public conveniency. Nothing which tends to facilitate the intercourse between the states, can be deemed unworthy of the public care.

PUBLIUS.

McLean, II, 48–57.

To Rufus King

N. YORK Jany. 23 [1788]—½ after 8 OC.

DEAR SIR

I have this instant recd. your favr. of the 16. and have but a few moments to thank you for it. I have also just recd. a letter from Genl. Washington. It contains nothing very material or new. The Genl. thinks that although there is an uncertainty in the case, the final decision will prove that a large majority in Virga. are in favor of the Constitution. If nine States should precede it seems now to be admitted on all hands that Virga. will accede. Every post confirms the opinion that the Constn. is regaining its lost ground. It is impossible to express how much depends on the result of the deliberations of your Body. The arrival of the French Minister here must have got to Boston through the Gazettes. He has been too long on the way to add much to former intelligence. It seems still possible that war may take place; though the embers are stifled for the moment. A Congs. was made for the first time on Monday, & Mr. C. Griffin has been placed in the chair. Adieu. Yrs. sincerely

JS. MADISON JR

RC (NHi). Addressed and franked by JM. Docketed by King.

From Tench Coxe

PHILADA Jany 23d. 1788.

DEAR SIR

I am truely sorry that appearances are not more promising in Massachussets than I learn from your letter of 20th instant. The pamphlet may be of signal service as things unhappily are so circumstanced & I rejoice in having sent it. I hope the movements of the tradesmen will have an influence on a principal Character.[1] The peculiar situation of Maine is unfortunate. The greatest difficulty will arise, I fear, from circumstances wch. like this have Nothing to connect them with the constitution as matters of government.

I believe there is a real Change working in Virginia. Mr. Contee of Maryland,[2] now at New York, mentioned some Circumstances with regard to Mr. R. H. Lee that may be worth your possessing yourself of for the information of Mr. King. I am unacquainted with Mr. Contee but I am told he spoke of several things which promise a Change of Conduct, tho perhaps not of Opinion on the part of Mr. Lee. I am informed also that Col. Grierson[3] has written in these terms "that the game is up for George has been undoing all that they have done.["] The person who mentioned this to Me told Me he had seen the letter. Connecticut I hope will have influence every where especially in New York & Massachussets.

I observe Consolidation is the great Object of Apprehension in New York. The same thing, the benefits of State sovereignty, is the difficulty in my opinion most generally prevailing. It does all the Mischief in Pennsylvania. I have therefore thought a few well-tempered papers on this point might be useful & have commenced them under the signature of the freeman in this days Gazettee, of wch. I send you a copy.[4] It is incorrectly printed & hastily written for at this time I happen to be very much engaged. I wish I had time and more talents for the duty. I trust however some good may happen from them & little harm. Should they be of any use in New York or Massachussets it may be well to republish them there. I am with great truth, Sir, your most respectf. h. Servant

TENCH COXE

I add a second copy of the freeman, one of wch. perhaps it may be useful to send for republication to Mr. King.

RC (DLC). Docketed by JM. Enclosure not found.

[1]The *Pa. Packet* of 22 Jan. 1788 reported the proceedings of the "tradesmen" of Boston, who had met at the Green Dragon Tavern on 7 Jan. 1788 and passed resolutions in support of the Constitution as their state convention began its deliberations. The "principal Character" was Samuel Adams (John C. Miller, *Sam Adams: Pioneer in Propaganda* [Boston, 1936], pp. 378–79).

[2]Benjamin Contee, elected as a delegate to Congress on 4 Jan. 1788, took his seat on 23 Jan. (Burnett, *Letters*, VIII, lxxxvi).

[3]Coxe apparently meant William Grayson.

[4]The three numbers of "A Freeman," addressed "To the Minority of the Convention of Pennsylvania," were published in the *Pa. Gazette* of 23 Jan., 30 Jan., and 6 Feb. 1788.

From Rufus King

BOSTON 23. Jan. 1788

DEAR SIR

Our prospects are gloomy, but hope is not entirely extinguished. Gerry has not returned to the Convention, & I think will not again be invited. We are now thinking of amendments to be submitted not as a condition of our assent & Ratification; but as the opinion of the Convention subjoined to their Ratification. This scheme may gain a few members, but the issue is doubtful. Farewel

R KING

RC (DLC); Tr (NHi). RC docketed by JM.

The Federalist Number 43

[23 January 1788]

The *fourth* class comprises the following miscellaneous powers:

1. A power to "promote the progress of science and useful arts, by securing for a limited time, to authors and inventors, the exclusive right to their respective writings and discoveries."

The utility of this power will scarcely be questioned. The copy right of authors has been solemnly adjudged in Great Britain, to be a right at common law. The right to useful inventions, seems with equal reason to belong to the inventors. The public good fully coincides in both cases, with the claims of individuals. The states cannot separately make effectual provision for either of the cases, and most of them have anticipated the decision of this point, by laws passed at the instance of congress.

2. "To exercise exclusive legislation in all cases whatsoever, over such district (not exceeding ten miles square) as may by cession of particular states, and the acceptance of congress, become the seat of the government of the United States; and to exercise like authority over all places purchased by the consent of the legislature of the states, in which the same shall be, for the erection of forts, magazines, arsenals, dock yards, and other needful buildings."

The indispensable necessity of compleat authority at the seat of government, carries its own evidence with it. It is a power exercised by every legislature of the union, I might say of the world, by virtue of its general supremacy. Without it, not only the public authority might be insulted and its proceedings be interrupted, with impunity; but a dependence of the members of the general government on the state, comprehending the seat of the government for protection in the exercise of their duty, might bring on the national councils an imputation of awe or influence, equally dishonorable to the government, and dissatisfactory to the other members of the confederacy. This consideration has the more weight as the gradual accumulation of public improvements at the stationary residence of the government, would be both too great a public pledge to be left in the hands of a single state; and would create so many obstacles to a removal of the government, as still further to abridge its necessary independence. The extent of this federal district is sufficiently circumscribed to satisfy every jealousy of an opposite nature. And as it is to be appropriated to this use with the consent of the state ceding it; as the state will no doubt provide in the compact for the rights, and the consent of the citizens inhabiting it; as the inhabitants will find sufficient inducements of interest to become willing parties to the cession; as they will have had their voice in the election of the government which is to exercise authority over them; as a municipal legislature for local purposes, derived from their own suffrages, will of course be allowed them; and as the authority of the legislature of the state, and of the inhabitants of the ceded part of it, to concur in the cession, will be derived from the whole people of the state, in their adoption of the constitution, every imaginable objection seems to be obviated.[1]

The necessity of a like authority over forts, magazines, &c. established by the general government is not less evident. The public money expended on such places, and the public property deposited in them, require that they should be exempt from the authority of the particular state. Nor would it be proper for the places on which the security of the entire union may depend, to be in any degree dependent on a particular member of it. All objections and scruples are here also obviated by requiring the concurrence of the states concerned, in every such establishment.

3. "To declare the punishment of treason, but no attainder of treason shall work corruption of blood, or forfeiture, except during the life of the person attainted."

As treason may be committed against the United States, the authority of the United States ought to be enabled to punish it; but as new fangled and artificial treasons, have been the great engines, by which violent factions, the natural offspring of free governments, have usually wreaked their alternate malignity on each other, the convention have with great judgment opposed a barrier to this peculiar danger, by inserting a constitutional definition of the crime, fixing the proof necessary for conviction of it, and restraining the congress, even in punishing it, from extending the consequences of guilt beyond the person of its author.

4. "To admit new states into the union; but no new state shall be formed or erected within the jurisdiction of any other state; nor any state be formed by the junction of two or more states, or parts of states, without the consent of the legislatures of the states concerned, as well as of the congress."

In the articles of confederation no provision is found on this important subject. Canada was to be admitted of right on her joining in the measures of the United States; and the other *colonies*, by which were evidently meant, the other British colonies, at the discretion of nine states. The eventual establishment of *new states*, seems to have been overlooked by the compilers of that instrument. We have seen the inconvenience of this omission, and the assumption of power into which congress have been led by it. With great propriety therefore has the new system supplied the defect. The general precaution that no new states shall be formed without the concurrence of the federal authority and that of the states concerned, is consonant to the principles which ought to govern such transactions. The particular precaution against the erection of new states, by the partition of a state without its consent, quiets the jealousy of the larger states; as that of the smaller is quieted by a like precaution against a junction of states without their consent.

5. "To dispose of and make all needful rules and regulations respecting the territory or other property belonging to the United States, with a proviso that nothing in the constitution shall be so construed as to prejudice any claims of the United States, or of any particular state."

This is a power of very great importance, and required by considerations similar to those which shew the propriety of the former. The proviso annexed is proper in itself, and was probably rendered absolutely necessary, by jealousies and questions concerning the western territory, sufficiently known to the public.

6. "To guarantee to every state in the union a republican form of government; to protect each of them against invasion; and on application of the legislature, or of the executive (when the legislature cannot be convened) against domestic violence."

In a confederacy founded on republican principles, and composed of republican members, the superintending government ought clearly to possess authority to defend the system against aristocratic or monarchical innovations. The more intimate the nature of such a union may be, the greater interest have the members in the political institutions of each other; and the greater right to insist that the forms of government under which the compact was entered into, should be *substantially* maintained. But a right implies a remedy; and where else could the remedy be deposited, than where it is deposited by the constitution? Governments of dissimilar principles and forms, have been found less adapted to a federal coalition of any sort, than those of a kindred nature. "As the confederate republic of Germany," says Montesquieu, "consists of free cities and petty states, subject to different princes, experience shews us that it is more imperfect than that of Holland and Switzerland." "Greece was undone," he adds, "as soon as the king of Macedon obtained a seat among the Amphyctions."[2] In the latter case, no doubt, the disproportionate force, as well as the monarchical form of the new confederate, had its share of influence on the events. It may possibly be asked what need there could be of such a precaution, and whether it may not become a pretext for alterations in the state governments, without the concurrence of the states themselves. These questions admit of ready answers. If the interposition of the general government should not be needed, the provision for such an event will be a harmless superfluity only in the constitution. But who can say what experiments may be produced by the caprice of particular states, by the ambition of enterprizing leaders, or by the intrigues and influence of foreign powers? To the second question it may be answered, that if the general government should interpose by virtue of this constitutional authority, it will be of course bound to pursue the authority. But the authority extends no farther than to a *guaranty* of a republican form of government, which supposes a pre-existing government of the form which is to be guaranteed. As long therefore as the existing republican forms are continued by the states, they are guaranteed by the federal constitution. Whenever the states may chuse to substitute other republican forms, they have a right to do so, and to claim the federal guaranty for the latter. The only restriction imposed on them is, that they shall not exchange republican for anti-republican constitutions; a restriction which it is presumed will hardly be considered as a grievance.

A protection against invasion is due from every society to the parts composing it. The latitude of the expression here used, seems to secure each state not only against foreign hostility, but against ambitious or vindictive enterprizes of its more powerful neighbours. The history both of antient and modern confederacies, proves that the weaker members of the union ought not to be insensible to the policy of this article.

Protection against domestic violence is added with equal propriety. It has been remarked that even among the Swiss cantons, which properly speaking are not under one government, provision is made for this object; and the history of that league informs us, that mutual aid is frequently claimed and afforded; and as well by the most democratic, as the other cantons. A recent and well known event among ourselves, has warned us to be prepared for emergencies of a like nature.

At first view it might seem not to square with the republican theory, to suppose either that a majority have not the right, or that a minority will have the force to subvert a government; and consequently that the federal interposition can never be required but when it would be improper. But theoretic reasoning in this, as in most other cases, must be qualified by the lessons of practice. Why may not illicit combinations for purposes of violence be formed as well by a majority of a state, especially a small state, as by a majority of a county or a district of the same state; and if the authority of the state ought in the latter case to protect the local magistracy, ought not the federal authority in the former to support the state authority? Besides, there are certain parts of the state constitutions which are so interwoven with the federal constitution, that a violent blow cannot be given to the one without communicating the wound to the other. Insurrections in a state will rarely induce a federal interposition, unless the number concerned in them, bear some proportion to the friends of government. It will be much better that the violence in such cases should be repressed by the superintending power, than that the majority should be left to maintain their cause by a bloody and obstinate contest. The existence of a right to interpose will generally prevent the necessity of exerting it.

Is it true that force and right are necessarily on the same side in republican governments? May not the minor party possess such a superiority of pecuniary resources, of military talents and experience, or of secret succours from foreign powers, as will render it superior also in an appeal to the sword? May not a more compact and advantageous position turn the scale on the same side against a superior number so situated as to be less capable of a prompt and collected exertion of its strength? Nothing can be more chimerical than to imagine that in a trial of actual force, victory may be calculated by the rules which prevail in a census of the inhabitants, or which determine the event of an election! May it not happen in fine that the minority of *citizens* may become a majority of *persons*, by the accession of alien residents, of a casual concourse of adventurers, or of those whom the constitution of the state has not admitted to the rights of suffrage? I take no notice of an unhappy species of population abounding in some of the states, who during the calm of regular government are sunk below the level of men; but who in the tempestuous scenes of civil violence may emerge into the human character, and give a superiority of strength to any party with which they may associate themselves.[3]

In cases where it may be doubtful on which side justice lies, what better umpires could be desired by two violent factions, flying to arms and tearing a state to pieces, than the representatives of confederate states not heated by the local flame? To the impartiality of judges they would unite the affection of friends. Happy would it be if such a remedy for its infirmities, could be enjoyed by all free governments; if a project equally effectual could be established for the universal peace of mankind.

Should it be asked what is to be the redress for an insurrection pervading all the states, and comprizing a superiority of the entire force, though not a constitutional right; the answer must be, that such a case, as it would be without the compass of human remedies, so it is fortunately not within the compass of human probability; and that it is a sufficient recommendation of the federal constitution, that it diminishes the risk of a calamity, for which no possible constitution can provide a cure.

Among the advantages of a confederate republic enumerated by Montesquieu, an important one is, "that should a popular insurrection happen in one of the states, the others are able to quell it. Should abuses creep into one part, they are reformed by those that remain sound."[4]

7. "To consider all debts contracted and engagements entered into, before the adoption of this constitution, as being no less valid against the United States under this constitution, than under the confederation."

This can only be considered as a declaratory proposition; and may have been inserted, among other reasons, for the satisfaction of the foreign creditors of the United States, who cannot be strangers to the pretended doctrine that a change in the political form of civil society, has the magical effect of dissolving its moral obligations.

Among the lesser criticisms which have been exercised on the constitution, it has been remarked that the validity of engagements ought to have been asserted in favor of the United States, as well as against them; and in the spirit which usually characterises little critics, the omission has been transformed and magnified into a plot against the national rights. The authors of this discovery may be told, what few others need be informed of, that as engagements are in their nature reciprocal, an assertion of their validity on one side necessarily involves a validity on the other side; and that as the article is merely declaratory, the establishment of the principle in one case is sufficient for every case. They may be further told that every constitution must limit its precautions to dangers that are not altogether imaginary; and that no real danger can exist that the government would *dare*, with or even without this constitutional declaration before it, to remit the debts justly due to the public, on the pretext here condemned.

8. "To provide for amendments to be ratified by three-fourths of the states, under two exceptions only."

That useful alterations will be suggested by experience, could not but be foreseen. It was requisite therefore that a mode for introducing them should be provided. The mode preferred by the convention seems to be stamped with every mark of propriety. It guards equally against that extreme facility which would render the constitution too mutable; and that extreme difficulty which might perpetuate its discovered faults. It moreover equally enables the general and the state governments to originate the amendment of errors as they may be pointed out by the experience on one side or on the other. The exception in favor of the equality of suffrage in the senate was probably meant as a palladium to the residuary sovereignty of the states, implied and secured by that principle of representation in one branch of the legislature; and was probably insisted on by the states particularly attached to that equality. The other exception must have been admitted on the same considerations which produced the privilege defended by it.

9. "The ratification of the conventions of nine states shall be sufficient for the establishment of this constitution between the states ratifying the same."

This article speaks for itself. The express authority of the people alone could give due validity to the constitution. To have required the unanimous ratification of the thirteen states, would have subjected the essential interests of the whole to the caprice or corruption of a single member. It would have marked a want of foresight in the convention, which our own experience would have rendered inexcuseable.

Two questions of a very delicate nature present themselves on this occasion. 1. On what principle the confederation, which stands in the solemn form of a compact among the states, can be superceded without the unanimous consent of the parties to it? 2. What relation is to subsist between the nine or more states ratifying the constitution, and the remaining few who do not become parties to it.

The first question is answered at once by recurring to the absolute necessity of the case; to the great principle of self preservation; to the transcendent law of nature and of nature's God, which declares that the safety and happiness of society, are the objects at which all political institutions aim, and to which all such institutions must be sacrificed. *Perhaps* also an answer may be found without searching beyond the principles of the compact itself. It has been heretofore noted among the defects of the confederation, that in many of the states, it had received no higher sanction than a mere legislative ratification. The principle of reciprocality seems to require, that its obligation on the other states should be reduced to the same standard. A compact between independent sovereigns, founded on acts of legislative authority, can pretend to no higher validity

417

than a league or treaty between the parties. It is an established doctrine on the subject of treaties that all the articles are mutually conditions of each other; that a breach of any one article is a breach of the whole treaty; and that a breach committed by either of the parties absolves the others; and authorises them, if they please, to pronounce the compact violated and void. Should it unhappily be necessary to appeal to these delicate truths for a justification for dispensing with the consent of particular states to a dissolution of the federal pact, will not the complaining parties find it a difficult task to answer the *multiplied* and *important* infractions with which they may be confronted? The time has been when it was incumbent on us all to veil the ideas which this paragraph exhibits. The scene is now changed and with it, the part which the same motives dictate.

The second question is not less delicate; and the flattering prospect of its being merely hypothetical, forbids an over-curious discussion of it. It is one of those cases which must be left to provide for itself. In general it may be observed, that although no political relation can subsist between the assenting and dissenting states, yet the moral relations will remain uncancelled. The claims of justice, both on one side and on the other, will be in force, and must be fulfilled; the rights of humanity must in all cases be duly and mutually respected; whilst considerations of a common interest, and above all the remembrance of the endearing scenes which are past, and the anticipation of a speedy triumph over the obstacles to re-union, will, it is hoped, not urge in vain *moderation* on one side, and *prudence* on the other.

PUBLIUS.

McLean, II, 57–68.

[1]This reasoning did not convince Mason, Grayson, and Henry, who denounced this feature of the Constitution at the Virginia ratifying convention. That convention approved a proposed amendment stipulating that the powers granted to Congress "over the federal town and its adjacent district . . . shall extend only to such regulations as respect the police and good government thereof" (David Robertson, *Debates and Other Proceedings of the Convention of Virginia* [2d ed.; Richmond, 1805], pp. 306–14, 474).
[2]Montesquieu, *The Spirit of the Laws*, bk. IX, chap. II (trans. Thomas Nugent and ed. Franz Neumann [2 vols. in 1; New York, 1949], I, 128).
[3]This paragraph was derived from Vices of the Political System (*PJM*, IX, 350–51).
[4]Montesquieu, *The Spirit of the Laws*, bk. IX, chap. I ([Neumann ed.], I, 127).

From Eliza House Trist

Letter not found.

23 January 1788. Acknowledged in JM to Mrs. Trist, 27 Jan. 1788. Comments favorably on Luther Martin's *Genuine Information.*

To George Washington

DEAR SIR

I have been favoured since my last with yours of the 10th. inst: with a copy of the Governours letter to the Assembly. I do not know what impression the latter may make in Virginia. It is generally understood here that the arguments contained in it in favor of the Constitution are much stronger than the objections which prevented his assent. His arguments are forceable in all places, and with all persons. His objections are connected with his particular way of thinking on the subject, in which many of the Adversaries to the Constitution do not concur.

The information from Boston by the mail on the evening before last, has not removed our suspence. The following is an extract of a letter from Mr. King dated on the 16th. inst.

"We may have 360 members in our Convention. Not more than 330 have yet taken their seats. Immediately after the settlement of Elections, the Convention resolved that they would consider and freely deliberate on each paragraph without taking a question on any of them individually, & that on the question whether they would ratify, each member should be at liberty to discuss the plan at large. This Resolution seems to preclude the idea of amendments; and hitherto the measure has not been suggested. I however do not from this circumstance conclude that it may not hereafter occur. The opponents of the Constitution moved that Mr. Gerry should be requested to take a seat in the Convention to answer such enquiries as the Convention should make concerning facts which happened in the *passing of the* Constitution. Although this seems to be a very irregular proposal, yet considering the jealousies which prevail with those who made it (who are certainly not the most enlightened part of the Convention) and the doubt of the issue had it been made a trial of strength, several friends of the Constitution united with the opponents and the Resolution was agreed to and Mr. Gerry has taken his seat. Tomorrow we are told certain enquiries are to be moved for by the opposition, and that Mr. Gerry under the idea of stating facts is to state his reasons &c.—this will be opposed and we shall on the division be able to form some idea of our relative strength. From the men who are in favour of the Constitution every reasonable explanation will be given, and arguments really new and in my judgment most excellent have been and will be produced in its support. But what will be its fate, I confess I am unable to discern. No question ever classed the people of this State in a more extraordinary manner, or with more apparent firmness."

A Congress of seven States was made up on Monday. Mr. C. Griffin has been placed in the chair. This is the only step yet taken. I remain with the highest respect & attachmt Yrs affety.

Js MADISON JR

RC (DLC: Washington Papers); Tr (DLC). RC docketed by Washington.

The Federalist Number 44

[25 January 1788]

A *Fifth* class of provisions in favor of the federal authority, consists of the following restrictions on the authority of the several states.[1]

1. "No state shall enter into any treaty, alliance or confederation, grant letters of marque and reprisal, coin money, emit bills of credit, make any thing but gold and silver a legal tender in payment of debts; pass any bill of attainder, *ex post facto* law, or law impairing the obligation of contracts, or grant any title of nobility."

The prohibition against treaties, alliances and confederations, makes a part of the existing articles of union; and for reasons which need no explanation, is copied into the new constitution. The prohibition of letters of marque is another part of the old system, but is somewhat extended in the new. According to the former, letters of marque could be granted by the states, after a declaration of war. According to the latter, these licences must be obtained as well during war as previous to its declaration, from the government of the United States. This alteration is fully justified by the advantage of uniformity in all points which relate to foreign powers; and of immediate responsibility to the nation in all those, for whose conduct the nation itself is to be responsible.

The right of coining money, which is here taken from the states, was left in their hands by the confederation as a concurrent right with that of congress, under an exception in favor of the exclusive right of congress to regulate the alloy and value. In this instance also the new provision is an improvement on the old. Whilst the alloy and value depended on the general authority, a right of coinage in the particular states could have no other effect than to multiply expensive mints, and diversify the forms and weights of the circulating pieces. The latter inconveniency defeats one purpose for which the power was originally submitted to the federal head. And as far as the former might prevent an inconvenient remittance of gold and silver to the central mint for recoinage, the end can be as well attained by local mints established under the general authority.

The extension of the prohibition to bills of credit must give pleasure to every citizen in proportion to his love of justice, and his knowledge of the true springs of public prosperity. The loss which America has sustained since the peace, from the pestilent effects of paper money, on the necessary confidence between man and man; on the necessary confidence in the public councils; on the industry and morals of the people, and on the character of republican government, constitutes an enormous debt against the states chargeable with this unadvised measure, which must long remain unsatisfied; or rather an accumulation of guilt, which can be expiated no otherwise than by a voluntary sacrifice on the altar of justice, of the power which has been the instrument of it. In addition to these persuasive considerations, it may be observed that the same reasons which shew the necessity of denying to the states the power of regulating coin, prove with equal force that they ought not to be at liberty to substitute a paper medium in the place of coin. Had every state a right to regulate the value of its coin, there might be as many different currencies as states; and thus the intercourse among them would be impeded; retrospective alterations in its value might be made, and thus the citizens of other states be injured, and animosities be kindled among the states themselves. The subjects of foreign powers might suffer from the same cause, and hence the union be discredited and embroiled by the indiscretion of a single member. No one of these mischiefs is less incident to a power in the states to emit paper money, than to coin gold or silver. The power to make any thing but gold and silver a tender in payment of debts, is withdrawn from the states, on the same principle with that of striking of paper currency.

Bills of attainder, *ex post facto* laws, and laws impairing the obligation of contracts, are contrary to the first principles of the social compact, and to every principle of sound legislation. The two former are expressly prohibited by the declarations prefixed to some of the state constitutions, and all of them are prohibited by the spirit and scope of these fundamental charters. Our own experience has taught us nevertheless, that additional fences against these dangers ought not to be omitted. Very properly therefore have the convention added this constitutional bulwark in favor of personal security and private rights; and I am much deceived if they have not in so doing as faithfully consulted the genuine sentiments, as the undoubted interests of their constituents. The sober people of America are weary of the fluctuating policy which has directed the public councils. They have seen with regret and with indignation, that sudden changes and legislative interferences in cases affecting personal rights, become jobs in the hands of enterprizing and influential speculators; and snares to the more industrious and less informed part of the community. They have seen too, that one legislative interference is but the first link of a long chain of repetitions; every subsequent interference being naturally produced by the effects of the preceding. They very rightly infer, therefore, that some thorough reform is wanting which will banish speculations on public measures, inspire a general prudence and industry, and give a regular course to the business of society. The prohibition with respect to titles of nobility, is copied from the articles of confederation and needs no comment.

2. "No state shall, without the consent of the congress, lay any imposts or duties on imports or exports, except what may be absolutely necessary for executing its inspection laws, and the neat produce of all duties and imposts laid by any state on imports or exports, shall be for the use of the treasury of the United States; and all such laws shall be subject to the revision and controul of the congress. No state shall, without the consent of congress, lay any duty on tonnage, keep troops or ships of war in time of peace; enter into any agreement or compact with another state, or with a foreign power, or engage in war, unless actually invaded, or in such imminent danger as will not admit of delay."

The restraint on the power of the states over imports and exports is enforced by all the arguments which prove the necessity of submitting the regulation of trade to the federal councils. It is needless therefore to remark further on this head, than that the manner in which the restraint is qualified, seems well calculated at once to secure to the states a reasonable discretion in providing for the conveniency of their imports and exports, and to the United States a reasonable check against the abuse of this discretion. The remaining particulars of this clause, fall within reasonings which are either so obvious, or have been so fully developed, that they may be passed over without remark.

The sixth and last class consists of the several powers and provisions by which efficacy is given to all the rest.

1. "Of these the first is the power to make all laws which shall be necessary and proper for carrying into execution the foregoing powers, and all other powers vested by this constitution in the government of the United States."

Few parts of the constitution have been assailed with more intemperance than this; yet on a fair investigation of it, as has been elsewhere shewn, no part can appear more completely invulnerable.[2] Without the *substance* of this power, the whole constitution would be a dead letter. Those who object to the article therefore as a part of the constitution, can only mean that the *form* of the provision is improper. But have they considered whether a better form could have been substituted?

There are four other possible methods which the convention might have taken on this subject. They might have copied the second article of the existing confederation which would have prohibited the exercise of any power not *expressly* delegated; they might have attempted a positive enumeration of the powers comprehended under the general terms "necessary and proper"; they might have attempted a negative enumeration of them, by specifying the powers excepted from the general definition: They might have been altogether silent on the subject; leaving these necessary and proper powers, to construction and inference.

Had the convention taken the first method of adopting the second article of confederation; it is evident that the new congress would be continually exposed as their predecessors have been, to the alternative of construing the term *"expressly"* with so much rigour as to disarm the government of all real authority whatever, or with so much latitude as to destroy altogether the force of the restriction. It would be easy to shew if it were necessary, that no important power, delegated by the articles of confederation, has been or can be executed by congress, without recurring more or less to the doctrine of *construction* or *implication.* As the powers delegated under the new system are more extensive, the government which is to administer it would find itself still more distressed with the alternative of betraying the public interest by doing nothing; or of violating the constitution by exercising powers indispensably necessary and proper; but at the same time, not *expressly* granted.

Had the convention attempted a positive enumeration of the powers necessary and proper for carrying their other powers into effect; the attempt would have involved a compleat digest of laws on every subject to which the constitution relates; accommodated too not only to the existing state of things, but to all the possible changes which futurity may produce: For in every new application of a general power, the *particular powers*, which are the means of attaining the *object* of the general power, must always necessarily vary with that object; and be often properly varied whilst the object remains the same.

Had they attempted to enumerate the particular powers or means, not necessary or proper for carrying the general powers into execution, the task would have been no less chimerical; and would have been liable to this further objection; that every defect in the enumeration, would have been equivalent to a positive grant of authority. If to avoid this consequence they had attempted a partial enumeration of the exceptions and described the residue by the general terms, *not necessary or proper:* It must have happened that the enumeration would comprehend a few of the excepted powers only; that these would be such as would be least likely to be assumed or tolerated because the enumeration would of course select such as would be least necessary or proper, and that the unnecessary and improper powers included in the residuum, would be less forcibly excepted, than if no partial enumeration had been made.

Had the constitution been silent on this head, there can be no doubt that all the particular powers, requisite as means of executing the general powers, would have resulted to the government, by unavoidable implication. No axiom is more clearly established in law, or in reason, than that wherever the end is required, the means are authorised; wherever a general power to do a thing is given, every particular power necessary for doing it, is included. Had this last method therefore been pursued by the convention, every objection now urged against their plan, would remain in all its plausibility; and the real inconveniency would be incurred, of not removing a pretext which may be seized on critical occasions for drawing into question the essential powers of the union.

If it be asked, what is to be the consequence, in case the congress shall misconstrue this part of the constitution, and exercise powers not warranted by its true meaning? I answer the same as if they should misconstrue or enlarge any other power vested in them, as if the general power had been reduced to particulars, and any one of these were to be violated; the same in short, as if the state legislatures should violate their respective constitutional authorities. In the first instance, the success of the usurpation will depend on the executive and judiciary departments, which are to expound and give effect to the legislative acts; and in the last resort, a remedy must be obtained from the people, who can by the election of more faithful representatives, annul the acts of the usurpers. The truth is, that this ultimate redress may be more confided in against unconstitutional acts of the federal than of the state legislatures, for this plain reason, that as every such act of the former, will be an invasion of the rights of the latter, these will be ever ready to mark the innovation, to sound the alarm to the people, and to exert their local influence in effecting a change of federal representatives. There being no such intermediate body between the state legislatures and the people, interested in watching the conduct of the former, violations of the state constitution are more likely to remain unnoticed and unredressed.[3]

2. "This constitution and the laws of the United States which shall be made in pursuance thereof, and all treaties made, or which shall be made, under the authority of the United States, shall be the supreme law of the land, and the judges in every state shall be bound thereby, any thing in the constitution or laws of any state to the contrary notwithstanding."

The indiscreet zeal of the adversaries to the constitution, has betrayed them into an attack on this part of it also, without which it would have been evidently and radically defective. To be fully sensible of this we need only suppose for a moment, that the supremacy of the state constitutions had been left compleat by a saving clause in their favor.

In the first place, as these constitutions invest the state legislatures with absolute sovereignty, in all cases not excepted by the existing articles of confederation, all the authorities contained in the proposed constitution, so far as they exceed those enumerated in the confederation, would have been annulled, and the new congress would have been reduced to the same impotent condition with their predecessors.

In the next place, as the constitutions of some of the states do not even expressly and fully recognize the existing powers of the confederacy, an express saving of the supremacy of the former, would in such states have brought into question, every power contained in the proposed constitution.

In the third place, as the constitutions of the states differ much from each other, it might happen that a treaty or national law of great and equal importance to the states, would interfere with some and not with other constitutions, and would consequently be valid in some of the states at the same time that it would have no effect in others.

In fine, the world would have seen for the first time, a system of government founded on an inversion of the fundamental principles of all government; it would have seen the authority of the whole society every where subordinate to the authority of the parts; it would have seen a monster in which the head was under the direction of the members.

3. "The senators and representatives, and the members of the several state legislatures; and all executive and judicial officers, both of the United States, and the several states shall be bound by oath or affirmation, to support this constitution."

It has been asked, why it was thought necessary, that the state magistracy should be bound to support the federal constitution, and unnecessary that a like oath should be imposed on the officers of the United States in favour of the state constitutions?

Several reasons might be assigned for the distinctions. I content myself with one which is obvious and conclusive. The members of the federal government will have no agency in carrying the state constitutions into effect. The members and officers of the state governments, on the contrary, will have an essential agency in giving effect to the federal constitution. The election of the president and senate, will depend in all cases, on the legislatures of the several states. And the election of the house of representatives, will equally depend on the same authority in the first instance; and will probably, for ever be conducted by the officers and according to the laws of the states.

4. Among the provisions for giving efficacy to the federal powers, might be added, those which belong to the executive and judiciary departments: But as these are reserved for particular examination in another place, I pass them over in this.

We have now reviewed in detail all the articles composing the sum or quantity of power delegated by the proposed constitution to the federal government; and are brought to this undeniable conclusion, that no part of the power is unnecessary or improper for accomplishing the necessary objects of the union. The question therefore, whether this amount of power shall be granted or not, resolves itself into another question, whether or not a government commensurate to the exigencies of the union, shall be established; or in other words, whether the union itself shall be preserved.

PUBLIUS.

McLean, II, 68–77.

[1] Privately JM worried that the specific prohibitions on the states would be an inadequate substitute for a general negative on state laws: "Injustice may be effected by such an infinitude of legislative expedients, that where the disposition exists it can only be controuled by some provision which reaches all cases whatsoever. The partial provision made, supposes the disposition which will evade it" (JM to Jefferson, 24 Oct. 1787).

[2] Antifederalists argued that the "necessary and proper" clause, along with the "national supremacy" clause, would destroy the state governments. Indeed, "Centinel" (Samuel Bryan) claimed that the former "alone would be amply sufficient to carry the coup de grace to the state governments, to swallow them up in the grand vortex of general empire" (McMaster and Stone, *Pennsylvania and the Federal Constitution*, II, 610–11). See also the remarks of "Brutus" in Borden, *The Antifederalist Papers*, pp. 44–45, 84–85.

[3] Although several statements made by JM at the Federal Convention and in *The Federalist* No. 39 seem to imply his acceptance of judicial review, the foregoing remarks suggest the contrary, or at least that he had no clear notion of that doctrine at this time (Edward S. Corwin, *Court over Constitution: A Study of Judicial Review as an Instrument of Popular Government* [Princeton, 1938], pp. 31–33, 44–45, 47–50, 60–61).

To Joseph Jones

Letter not found.

25 January 1788. Acknowledged in Jones to JM, 14 Feb. 1788. Reports proceedings of the Massachusetts convention.

From André Limozin

MOST HONORED SIR

Mr Thoms Jefferson Ambassadr of the US at the Court of Versailles forwarded me the Letter your Excellency was so Kind as to honor me with the 8th Ulto, inclosing me Captain Fournier's Bill of Lading for

>2 Barrlls apples.
>2 dto   cranberries
> which were deliverd. in the most pityfull Condition, the fruit being intirely rotten

>1 Box containing Fruit trees which I have forwarded to Mr Jefferson in a good order.[2]

The Kind Contents of your Excellencys Letter for which I shall be at all times Sincerely gratefull intitle me to take the Freedom to inclose you Copy of a Letter I address by the same conveyance as this to his Excy: Dr B Franklin containing my petition to Congress for a certain recompense or indemnity for my disbursements pains troubles & expences I have been at & which are related in my said Letter.[3] I am in good hopes that Dr Franklin will not forget the promises he made me in my house to mentionn to Congress every particulars on that matter; therefore I dont doubt but he will Not refuse to lay my petition under the Consideration of Congress.

Give me leave to beg of your Excellency to render me the Service to favor me with your warm protection in that Circumstance, I am sensible that if all the Americans who have been here, could be Consulted every one would give their voice in the behalf of my petitions & that they would beg in my favor the most authentick instances of acknowledgement & gratitude however I submitt every thing to your Excellency's Consideration, & Since your Excellency is so Kind as to return me so many thanks for the trifling troubles I have been at in complying the orders of my most worthy & Honored friend Mr Thomas Jefferson for whatever they might concern your Excellency, I can't form the least doubt but my behavior in this Circumstance will likewise meet with your Excellency's approbation. I have the honor to be with the highest regard Your Excellency's Most obedient & very humble Servant,

ANDRE LIMOZIN

RC (DLC). For the cover to this letter and the enclosure (PCC), see n. 3.

[1]Limozin apparently first wrote "21st" and then changed the date.

[2]See JM to Jefferson, 9 Dec. 1787; Limozin to Jefferson, 24 Jan. 1788 (Boyd, *Papers of Jefferson*, XII, 533).

[3]Limozin sought compensation for his expenses in aiding American prisoners who had come to Le Havre from England after the war. JM forwarded his copy of Limozin's petition

to Franklin on 20 Apr. 1788. JM's covering letter to Franklin is the first of a group of papers relating to Limozin's claim (PCC) that appear in the following sequence: JM to Franklin, 20 Apr. 1788; Limozin to John Jay, 26 Jan. 1788 (similar to Limozin's letter to JM of the same date); copy of Limozin's letter to Franklin, 26 Jan. 1788 (apparently the copy forwarded by JM); cover to Limozin's letter to JM "pr the Juno Chs. Jenkins Mastr.," 26 Jan. 1788. Franklin evidently enclosed these papers in his letter to Jay of 27 June 1788 (*Diplomatic Correspondence of the U.S.*, I, 422).

The Federalist Number 45

[26 January 1788]

Having shewn that no one of the powers transferred to the federal government is unnecessary or improper, the next question to be considered is whether the whole mass of them will be dangerous to the portion of authority left in the several states.

The adversaries to the plan of the convention instead of considering in the first place what degree of power was absolutely necessary for the purposes of the federal government, have exhausted themselves in a secondary enquiry into the possible consequences of the proposed degree of power, to the governments of the particular states. But if the union, as has been shewn, be essential, to the security of the people of America against foreign danger; if it be essential to their security against contentions and wars among the different states; if it be essential to guard them against those violent and oppressive factions which imbitter the blessings of liberty, and against those military establishments which must gradually poison its very fountain; if, in a word the union be essential to the happiness of the people of America, is it not preposterous, to urge as an objection to a government without which the objects of the union cannot be attained, that such a government may derogate from the importance of the governments of the individual states? Was then the American revolution effected, was the American confederacy formed, was the precious blood of thousands spilt, and the hard earned substance of millions lavished, not that the people of America should enjoy peace, liberty, and safety; but that the governments of the individual states, that particular municipal establishments might enjoy a certain extent of power, and be arrayed with certain dignities and attributes of sovereignty? We have heard of the impious doctrine in the old world that the people were made for kings, not kings for the people. Is the same doctrine to be revived in the new, in another shape, that the solid happiness of the people is to be sacrificed to the views of political institutions of a different form? It is too early for politicians to presume on our forgetting that the public good, the real welfare of the great body of the people is the supreme object to be pursued; and that no form of government whatever, has any other value, than as it may be fitted for the attainment of this object. Were the plan of the convention adverse to the public happiness, my voice would be, reject the plan. Were the union itself inconsistent with the public happiness, it would be, abolish the union. In like manner as far as the sovereignty of the states cannot be reconciled to the happiness of the people; the voice of every good citizen must be, let the former be sacrificed to the latter. How far the sacrifice is necessary, has been shewn. How far the unsacrificed residue will be endangered, is the question before us.

Several important considerations have been touched in the course of these papers, which discountenance the supposition that the operation of the federal government will by degrees prove fatal to the state governments. The more I revolve the subject the more fully I am persuaded that the balance is much more likely to be disturbed by the preponderancy of the last than of the first scale.

We have seen in all the examples of antient and modern confederacies, the strongest tendency continually betraying itself in the members to despoil the general government of its authorities, with a very ineffectual capacity in the latter to defend itself against the encroachments. Although in most of these examples, the system has been so dissimilar from that under consideration, as greatly to weaken any inference concerning the latter from the fate of the former; yet as the states will retain under the proposed constitution a very extensive portion of active sovereignty, the inference ought not to be wholly disregarded. In the Achæan league, it is probable that the federal head had a degree and species of power, which gave it a considerable likeness to the government framed by the convention. The Lycian confederacy, as far as its principles and form are transmitted, must have borne a still greater analogy to it. Yet history does not inform us that either of them ever degenerated or tended to degenerate into one consolidated government. On the contrary, we know that the ruin of one of them proceeded from the incapacity of the federal authority to prevent the dissentions, and finally the disunion of the subordinate authorities. These cases are the more worthy of our attention, as the external causes by which the component parts were pressed together, were much more numerous and powerful than in our case; and consequently, less powerful ligaments within, would be sufficient to bind the members to the head, and to each other.

In the feudal system we have seen a similar propensity exemplified. Notwithstanding the want of proper sympathy in every instance between the local sovereigns and the people, and the sympathy in some instances between the general sovereign and the latter; it usually happened that the local sovereigns prevailed in the rivalship for encroachments. Had no external dangers enforced internal harmony and subordination; and particularly had the local sovereigns possessed the affections of the people, the great kingdoms in Europe, would at this time consist of as many independent princes as there were formerly feudatory barons.

The state governments will have the advantage of the federal government, whether we compare them in respect to the immediate dependence of the one on the other; to the weight of personal influence which each side will possess; to the powers respectively vested in them; to the predilection and probable support of the people; to the disposition and faculty of resisting and frustrating the measures of each other.

The state governments may be regarded as constituent and essential parts of the federal government; whilst the latter is no wise essential to the operation or organisation of the former. Without the intervention of the state legislatures, the president of the United States cannot be elected at all. They must in all cases have a great share in his appointment, and will perhaps in most cases of themselves determine it.[1] The senate will be elected absolutely and exclusively by the state legislatures. Even the house of representatives, though drawn immediately from the people, will be chosen very much under the influence of that class of men, whose influence over the people obtains for themselves an election into the state legislatures. Thus each of the principal branches of the federal government will owe its existence more or less to the favor of the state governments, and must consequently feel a dependence, which is much more likely to beget a disposition too obsequious, than too overbearing towards them. On the other side, the component parts of the state governments will in no instance be indebted for their appointment to the direct agency of the federal government, and very little if at all, to the local influence of its members.

The number of individuals employed under the constitution of the United States, will be much smaller, than the number employed under the particular states. There will consequently be less of personal influence on the side of the former, than of the latter. The members of the legislative, executive and judiciary departments of thirteen and more states; the justices of peace, officers of militia, ministerial officers of justice, with all the county corporation and town officers, for three millions and more of people, intermixed and having particular acquaintance with every class and circle of people, must exceed beyond all proportion, both in number and influence, those of every description who will be employed in the administration of the federal system. Compare the members of the three great departments, of the Thirteen States, excluding from the judiciary department the justices of peace, with the members of the corresponding departments of the single government of the union; compare the militia officers of three millions of people, with the military and marine officers of any establishment which is within the compass of probability, or I may add, of possibility, and in this view alone, we may pronounce the advantage of the states to be decisive. If the federal government is to have collectors of revenue, the state governments will have theirs also. And as those of the former will be principally on the sea-coast, and not very numerous; whilst those of the latter will be spread over the face of the country, and will be very numerous, the advantage in this view also lies on the same side. It is true that the confederacy is to possess, and may exercise, the power of collecting internal as well as external taxes throughout the states: But it is probable that this power will not be resorted to, except for supplemental purposes of revenue; that an option will then be given to the states to supply their quotas by previous collections of their own; and that the eventual collection under the immediate authority of the union, will generally be made by the officers, and according to the rules, appointed by the several states. Indeed it is extremely probable that in other instances, particularly in the organization of the judicial power, the officers of the states will be cloathed with the correspondent authority of the union. Should it happen however that separate collectors of internal revenue should be appointed under the federal government, the influence of the whole number would not be a comparison with that of the multitude of state-officers in the opposite scale. Within every district, to which a federal collector would be allotted, there would not be less than thirty or forty or even more officers of different descriptions and many of them persons of character and weight, whose influence would lie on the side of the state.

The powers delegated by the proposed constitution to the federal government, are few and defined. Those which are to remain in the state governments are numerous and indefinite. The former will be exercised principally on external objects, as war, peace, negociation, and foreign commerce; with which last the power of taxation will for the most part be connected. The powers reserved to the several states will extend to all the objects, which, in the ordinary course of affairs, concern the lives, liberties and properties of the people; and the internal order, improvement and prosperity of the state.

The operations of the federal government will be most extensive and important in times of war and danger; those of the state governments, in times of peace and security. As the former periods will probably bear a small proportion to the latter, the state governments will here enjoy another advantage over the federal government. The more adequate indeed the federal powers may be rendered to the national defence, the less frequent will be those scenes of danger which might favour their ascendancy over the governments of the particular states.

If the new constitution be examined with accuracy and candour, it will be found that the change which it proposes, consists much less in the addition of NEW POWERS to the union, than in the invigoration of its ORIGINAL POWERS. The regulation of commerce, it is true, is a new power; but that seems to be an addition which few oppose, and from which no apprehensions are entertained. The powers relating to war and peace, armies and fleets, treaties and finance, with the other more considerable powers, are all vested in the existing congress by the articles of confederation. The proposed change does not enlarge these powers; it only substitutes a more effectual mode of administering them. The change relating to taxation, may be regarded as the most important: and yet the present congress have as compleat authority to REQUIRE of the states indefinite supplies of money for the common defence and general welfare, as the future congress will have to require them of individual citizens; and the latter will be no more bound than the states themselves have been, to pay the quotas respectively taxed on them. Had the states complied punctually with the articles of confederation, or could their compliance have been enforced by as peaceable means as may be used with success towards single persons, our past experience is very far from countenancing an opinion that the state governments would have lost their constitutional powers, and have gradually undergone an entire consolidation. To maintain that such an event would have ensued, would be to say at once, that the existence of the state governments is incompatible with any system whatever that accomplishes the essential purposes of the union.

PUBLIUS.

McLean, II, 77–83.

[1]The Constitution stipulates that each state legislature shall direct the manner by which the presidential electors are appointed, and as JM hinted, six of the eligible eleven legislatures chose some or all of their states' electors in Washington's first election (U.S. Bureau of the Census, *Historical Statistics of the United States, Colonial Times to 1957* [Washington, 1960], p. 681).

To Edmund Randolph

N. York. Jany. 27. 1788.

MY DEAR FRIEND

A Congress was made for the first time on monday last and our friend C. Griffin placed in the chair. There was no competition in the case which you will wonder at as Virginia has so lately supplied a president.[1] N. Jersey did not like it I believe very well, but acquiesed.

I postponed writing by the last mail, in hopes of being able by this to acquaint you with the probable result of the Convention of Massts. It appears however that the prospect continues too equivocal to justify a conjecture on the subject. The representations vary somewhat but they all tend to excite rather than diminish anxiety. Mr. Gerry had been introduced to a seat for the purpose of stating facts. On the arrival of the discussion at the article concerning the Senate, he signified without being called on, that He had important information to communicate on that subject. Mr. Dana & several others remarked on the impropriety of Mr. G——y's Conduct. G—— rose to justify. Others opposed it as irregular. A warm conversation arose & continued till the adjournment; after which a still warmer one took place between Gerry & Dana. The members gathered around them, took sides as they were for or against the Constitution, and strong symtoms of Confusion appeared. At length however they separated. It was expected that the subject would be renewed in the Convention the next morning. This was the State of things when the post came off.

In one of the papers enclosed you will find your letter to the Assembly reviewed by some critic of this place. I can form no guess who he is.[2] I have seen another attack grounded on a comparative view of your Objections Col. Mason's & Mr. Gerry's. This was from Philadelphia.[3] I have not the paper or I would add it. With the sincerest affection & attachment I remain my dear Sir Yrs.

Js. MADISON JR

RC (DLC). Enclosures not found.

[1]Richard Henry Lee had served as president of Congress in 1784–1785.
[2]See the essay of "Americanus," No. VII, in the N.Y. *Daily Advertiser* of 21 Jan. 1788.
[3]See Coxe to JM, 16 Jan. 1788 and n. 2.

To Eliza House Trist

NEW YORK Jany. 27. 1788.

Yours of the 23d. instant by Mr. Jay has been delivered to me; but I have not yet been to thank him for it. I have had a cold which made me extremely hoarse, but did not otherw[ise] affect me much. At present I am clear even of that inconvenience. I hope this will find you equally recovered from your indisposition. I have not made a trial of my french with the Marchioness[1] yet, thou[gh] I have seen her twice; nor shall I venture to do so. She s[peaks lit]tle of our language, and in that a sort of conversati[on ...] up. Mr. Jefferson speaks of her as goodness itself; and [...] fully repay him. She is extremely plain in her dress a[nd man]ners, and cannot fail when she becomes more familiar with our languag[e] to be agreeable to every body. Her person is very small; but [her] features are or perhaps have been pretty. We have had a [Con]gress since monday last. The Newspapers will have pro[claimed] Mr. C. Griffin as President. Your friend Col. Wadsworth [is a mem]ber and has been here about a week. I have not yet se[en] L. M.——s publication of which you give so flattering an account.[2] It is impossible I think that he can be a very formidable [ad]versary to the Constitution; though he will certainly be a very noisy one. I had a letter a few days ago from Mr. Randolph.[3] He w[as well] and said nothing as to Mrs. Randolph's being otherwise. I expected another letter by the mail of Saturday but it is not yet arrived. As yet the new plan of Riders is less punctual than the Stages were.[4] I do not find however that any of my letters miscarry altogether. Should it be the fate of this the loss will not be very great to you. Adieu

Js MADISON JR.

Mr. Duane is at present attending at Poughkeepsy as a member [of th]e Legislature.

RC (Owned by Dr. Frederick M. Dearborn, New York, N.Y., 1959). Addressed by JM. Where possible, words or letters missing owing to the deteriorated right margin of the Ms are supplied from conjecture by the editors and appear within brackets.

[1]Madame de Bréhan (Jefferson to JM, 8 Oct. 1787).

[2]Luther Martin's address to the Maryland legislature, 29 Nov. 1787, published as *The Genuine Information, Delivered to the Legislature of the State of Maryland, Relative to the Proceedings of the General Convention, Held at Philadelphia, in 1787* ... (Philadelphia, 1788). It is reprinted in Farrand, *Records*, III, 172–232.

[3]JM was possibly referring to a letter from Edmund Randolph of a later date than 3 Jan. 1788. If so, the letter has not been found.

[4]On 15 Oct. 1787 Congress had adopted a resolution authorizing the postmaster general "to contract for the transportation of the mail for the year 1788 by stage carriages or horses as

he may judge most expedient and beneficial" (*JCC*, XXXIII, 684). See Henry Lee to JM, 14 Jan. 1788 and n. 4.

From Tench Coxe

PHILADA. Jany. 27th. 1788

DEAR SIR

From your letter with respect to the Convention at B. I have been anxious to procure the Remr. of Mr. Lloyd's debates to send to Mr. King. There were some pages more struck off, which I have obtained and cover them to you with a letter to be forwarded as before. I beg your pardon for the trouble I give & the freedom I have used.

I find our Opposition were possessed of the temper of the Western & Eastern Members of the Massachussets Convention very minutely when I recd. your letter. That evening a person much Opposed to the Constitution said Massachussets would reject it. I fancy Mr. G. & Mr. S. A. keep up a minute & regular correspondence.

There will be a good many unfavorable petitions, it is said, from our Western Counties; but the Assembly will certainly dismiss them by a Majority of two thirds. I apprehend a warm, unpleasant Session. They meet in about three Weeks. I am, dear Sir, with great truth your most respectf. h. Servt.

TENCH COXE

RC (DLC). Docketed by JM.

From Nathaniel Gorham

CHARLES TOWN Jany. 27h. 1788

MY DEAR SIR

Never was there an Assembly in this State in possession of greater ability & information than the present Convention—yet I am in doubt whether they will approve the Constitution. There is unhappily three parties opposed to it. First all Men who are in favour of paper money and tender Laws—those are more or less in every part of the State. Secondly all the late Insurgents and their abettors; & in the three great Western Counties they are very numerous—we have 18. or 20. who were actually in Shases Army now in the Convention. Thirdly a great majority of the members from the Province of Main—many of them & their Constituents are only squatters upon other Peoples Land, & they are afraid of being brought to account. They allso think though erroniously that their favorite plan of being a seperate State will be defeated. Ad[d] to those the honest doubting people—and they make a most powerfull host. The Leaders of this party are a Mr Wedgery Mr Thompson & Mr Nason from the Provi[n]ce of Main—& a Doctor Taylor from the County of Worcester & Mr Bishop from neighbourhood of Rhode Island. You need only to ask our Delegates their characters to judge of the opposition. To manage the cause against them are the present & Late Governor, 3 Judges of the supreme Court—15 Members of the Senate 20 from among the most respectable of the Clergy—10 or 12 of the first characters at the Bar—Judges of Probate High Sheriffs of Counties & many other respectable people Merchants &ca.—Generals Heath Lincoln Brooks & others of the late Army. With all this ability in support of the cause—I am pretty well satisfied we shall loose the question, unless we can take of[f] some of the opposition by amendments. I do not mean those to be made the condition of the ratification—but recommendatory only. Upon this plan I flatter myself we may possibly get a majority of 12 or 15—& not more. You need not mention my name as your informant. Belive me to be sincrly Yours

N GORHAM

RC (DLC: Rives Collection, Madison Papers). Docketed by JM.

From Rufus King

BOSTON 27 Jan. 88

DR. SIR,

I hope your information will be confirmed; that the Tide is again turning in favor of the Constitution in Virginia. We make but slow progress in our Convention, the Friends of the Constitution who in addition to their own weight, are respectable as they represent a very large proportion of the Good Sense and Property of this State, have the Task not only of answering, but also of stating and bringing forward, the Objections of their Opponents. The Opposition complain that the Lawyers, Judges, Clergymen, Merchants and men of Education are all in Favor of the constitution; & that for this reason they appear to be able to make the worst, appear the better cause. But say they if we had men of this Description on our Side we should alarm the People with the Imperfections of the Constitution, & be able to refute the Defence set up in its favor. Notwithstanding the superiority of Talents in favor of the constitution, yet the same infatuation, which prevailed not many months since in several Counties of this State, and which emboldened them to take arms agt. the Government seems to have an uncontroulable authority over a numerous part of our Convention. Their Objections are not directed against any part of the constitution, but their Opposition seems to arise from an Opinion, that is immoveable, that some injury is plotted against them, that the System is the production of the Rich, and ambitious; that *they* discern its operation, and that the consequence will be, the establishment of two Orders in the Society, one comprehending the Opulent & Great, the other the poor and illiterate.

The extraordinary union in favor of the Constitution in this State, of the wealthy and sensible part of it, is a confirmation of their Opinion; and every Exertion hitherto made to eradicate it has been in vain.

We have avoided every Question which would have shewn the division of the House, of consequence we are not positive of the numbers on each side, by the last calculation we made on our side, we were doubtful whether we exceeded them or they us in Numbers. They however say that they have a majority of Eight or Twelve agt. us. We by no means dispair.

RC (DLC); Tr (NHi). RC docketed by JM. Lower portion of the last page of the RC, including the complimentary close and signature, has been clipped.

To George Washington

NEW YORK Jany. 28. 1788

DEAR SIR

The information which I have by the Eastern mail rather increases than removes the anxiety produced by the last. I give it to you as I have recd. it in the words of Mr. King.

BOSTON 20. Jany. 88

"Our Convention proceeds slowly. An apprehension that the liberties of the people are in danger, and a distrust of men of property or education have a more powerful effect upon the minds of our opponents than any specific objections against the Constitution. If the opposition was grounded on any precise points, I am persuaded that it might be weakened, if not entirely overcome. But every attempt to remove their fixed and violent jealousy seems hitherto to operate as a confirmation of that baneful passion. The opponents affirm to each other that they have an unalterable majority on their side. The friends doubt the strength of their

437

adversaries but are not entirely confident of their own. An event has taken place relative to Mr. Gerry, which without great caution may throw us into confusion. I informed you by the last post on what terms Mr. Gerry took a Seat in the Convention. Yesterday in the course of debate on the Construction of the Senate, Mr. G. *unasked*, informed the Convention that he had some information to give the Convention on the subject then under discussion. Mr. Dana and a number of the most respectable members, remarked upon the impropriety of Mr. G——s conduct. Mr. G. rose with a view to justify himself. He was immediately prevented by a number of objectors. This brought on an irregular conversation whether Mr. G. should be heard. The Hour of adjournment arrived and the President adjourned the House. Mr. Gerry immediately charged Mr. Dana with a design of injuring his reputation by partial information, and preventing his having an opportunity to communicate important truths to the Convention. This charge drew a warm reply from Mr. Dana. The members collected about them, took sides as they were for or against the Constitution, and we were in danger of the utmost confusion. However the gentlemen separated, and I suppose tomorrow morning will renew the discussion before the Convention. I shall be better able to conjecture the final issue by next post."

There are other letters of the same date from other gentlemen on the spot which exhibit rather a more favorable prospect. Some of them I am told are even flattering. Accounts will always vary in such cases, because they must be founded on different opportunities of remarking the general complexion; where they take no tincture from the opinions or temper of the writer. I remain Dear Sir with the Most perfect esteem & attachment Your Obedt. servt.

Js. MADISON JR.

RC (DLC: Washington Papers); Tr (DLC).

The Federalist Number 46

[29 January 1788]

Resuming the subject of the last paper I proceed to enquire whether the federal government or the state governments will have the advantage with regard to the predilection and support of the people. Notwithstanding the different modes in which they are appointed, we must consider both of them, as substantially dependent on the great body of the citizens of the

United States. I assume this position here as it respects the first, reserving the proofs for another place. The federal and state governments are in fact but different agents and trustees of the people, instituted with different powers, and designated for different purposes. The adversaries of the constitution seem to have lost sight of the people altogether in their reasonings on this subject; and to have viewed these different establishments, not only as mutual rivals and enemies, but as uncontrouled by any common superior in their efforts to usurp the authorities of each other. These gentlemen must here be reminded of their error. They must be told that the ultimate authority, wherever the derivative may be found, resides in the people alone; and that it will not depend merely on the comparative ambition or address of the different governments, whether either, or which of them, will be able to enlarge its sphere of jurisdiction at the expence of the other. Truth no less than decency requires, that the event in every case should be supposed to depend on the sentiments and sanction of their common constituents.

Many considerations, besides those suggested on a former occasion, seem to place it beyond doubt, that the first and most natural attachment of the people will be to the governments of their respective states. Into the administration of these, a greater number of individuals will expect to rise. From the gift of these, a greater number of offices and emoluments will flow. By the superintending care of these, all the more domestic and personal interests of the people will be regulated and provided for. With the affairs of these, the people will be more familiarly and minutely conversant. And with the members of these, will a greater proportion of the people have the ties of personal acquaintance and friendship, and of family and party attachments; on the side of these, therefore, the popular bias may well be expected most strongly to incline.

Experience speaks the same language in this case. The federal administration, though hitherto very defective, in comparison with what may be hoped under a better system, had during the war, and particularly, whilst the independent fund of paper emissions was in credit, an activity and importance as great as it can well have, in any future circumstances whatever. It was engaged too in a course of measures, which had for their object, the protection of every thing that was dear, and the acquisition of every thing that could be desirable to the people at large. It was nevertheless, invariably found, after the transient enthusiasm for the early congresses was over, that the attention and attachment of the people were turned anew to their own particular governments; that the federal council was at no time the idol of popular favor; and that opposition to proposed enlargements of its powers and importance, was the side usually taken by the men who wished to build their political consequence on the prepossessions of their fellow citizens.

If therefore, as has been elsewhere remarked, the people should in future become more partial to the federal than to the state governments, the change can only result from such manifest and irresistible proofs of a better administration, as will overcome all their antecedent propensities. And in that case, the people ought not surely to be precluded from giving most of their confidence where they may discover it to be most due: But even in that case, the state governments could have little to apprehend, because it is only within a certain sphere, that the federal power can, in the nature of things, be advantageously administered.

The remaining points on which I proposed to compare the federal and state governments, are the disposition, and the faculty they may respectively possess, to resist and frustrate the measures of each other.

It has been already proved, that the members of the federal will be more dependent on the members of the state governments, than the latter will be on the former. It has appeared also, that the prepossessions of the people on whom both will depend, will be more on the side of the state governments, than of the federal government. So far as the disposition of each, towards the other, may be influenced by these causes, the state governments must clearly have the advantage. But in a distinct and very important point of view, the advantage will lie on the same side. The prepossessions which the members themselves will carry into the federal government, will generally be favorable to the states; whilst it will rarely happen, that the members of the state governments will carry into the public councils, a bias in favor of the general government. A local spirit will infallibly prevail much more in the members of the congress, than a national spirit will prevail in the legislatures of the particular states. Every one knows that a great proportion of the errors committed by the state legislatures proceeds from the disposition of the members to sacrifice the comprehensive and permanent interests of the state, to the particular and separate views of the counties or districts in which they reside. And if they do not sufficiently enlarge their policy to embrace the collective welfare of their particular state, how can it be imagined, that they will make the aggregate prosperity of the union, and the dignity and respectability of its government, the objects of their affections and consultations? For the same reason, that the members of the state legislatures will be unlikely to attach themselves sufficiently to national objects, the members of the federal legislature will be likely to attach themselves too much to local objects. The states will be to the latter, what counties and towns are to the former. Measures will too often be decided according to their probable effect, not on the national prosperity and happiness, but on the prejudices, interests and pursuits of the governments and people of the individual states. What is the spirit that has in general characterized the proceedings of congress? A perusal of their journals as well as the candid acknowledgments of such as have had a seat in that assembly, will inform us, that the members have but too frequently displayed the character, rather of partizans of their respective states, than of impartial guardians of a common interest; that where, on one occasion, improper sacrifices have been made of local considerations to the aggrandizement of the federal government; the great interests of the nation have suffered on an hundred, from an undue attention to the local prejudices, interests and views of the particular states. I mean not by these reflections to insinuate, that the new federal government will not embrace a more enlarged plan of policy than the existing government may have pursued, much less that its views will be as confined as those of the state legislatures; but only that it will partake sufficiently of the spirit of both, to be disinclined to invade the rights of the individual states, or the prerogatives of their governments.[1] The motives on the part of the state governments, to augment their prerogatives by defalcations from the federal government, will be over-ruled by no reciprocal predispositions in the members.

Were it admitted however that the federal government may feel an equal disposition with the state governments to extend its power beyond the due limits, the latter would still have the advantage in the means of defeating such encroachments. If an act of a particular state, though unfriendly to the national government, be generally popular in that state, and should not too grossly violate the oaths of the state officers, it is executed immediately, and of course, by means on the spot, and depending on the state alone. The opposition of the federal government, or the interposition of federal officers, would but inflame the zeal of all parties on the side of the state, and the evil could not be prevented or repaired, if at all, without the employment of means which must always be resorted to with reluctance and difficulty. On the other hand, should an unwarrantable measure of the federal government be unpopular in particular states, which would seldom fail to be the case, or even a warrantable measure be so, which may sometimes be the case, the means of opposition to it are powerful and at hand. The disquietude of the people, their repugnance and perhaps refusal to co-operate with the officers of the union, the frowns of the executive magistracy of the state, the embarrassments created by legislative devices, which would often be added on such occasions, would oppose in any state difficulties not to be despised; would form in a large state very serious impediments, and where the sentiments of several adjoining states happened to be in unison, would present obstructions which the federal government would hardly be willing to encounter.

But ambitious encroachments of the federal government, on the authority of the state governments, would not excite the opposition of a single state or of a few states only. They would be signals of general alarm. Every government would espouse the common cause. A correspondence would be opened. Plans of resistance would be concerted. One spirit would animate and conduct the whole. The same combination in short would result from an apprehension of the federal, as was produced by the dread of a foreign yoke; and unless the projected innovations should be voluntarily renounced, the same appeal to a trial of force would be made in the one case, as was made in the other. But what degree of madness could ever drive the federal government to such an extremity? In the contest with Great-Britain, one part of the empire was employed against the other. The more numerous part invaded the rights of the less numerous part. The attempt was unjust and unwise; but it was not in speculation absolutely chimerical. But what would be the contest in the case we are supposing? Who would be the parties? A few representatives of the people would be opposed to the people themselves; or rather one set of representatives would be contending against thirteen sets of representatives, with the whole body of their common constituents on the side of the latter.[2]

The only refuge left for those who prophecy the downfall of the state governments, is the visionary supposition that the federal government may previously accumulate a military force for the projects of ambition. The reasonings contained in these papers must have been employed to little purpose indeed, if it could be necessary now to disprove the reality of this danger. That the people and the states should for a sufficient period of time elect an uninterrupted succession of men ready to betray both; that the traitors should throughout this period, uniformly and systematically pursue some fixed plan for the extension of the military establishment; that the governments and the people of the states should silently and patiently behold the gathering storm, and continue to supply the materials, until it should be prepared to burst on their own heads, must appear to every one more like the incoherent dreams of a delirious jealousy, or the misjudged exaggerations of a counterfeit zeal, than like the sober apprehensions of genuine patriotism. Extravagant as the supposition is, let it however be made. Let a regular army, fully equal to the resources of the country be formed; and let it be entirely at the devotion of the federal government; still it would not be going too far to say, that the state governments with the people on their side would be able to repel the danger. The highest number to which, according to the best computation, a standing army can be carried in any country, does not exceed one hundredth part of the whole number of souls; or one twenty-fifth part of the number able to bear arms. This proportion would not yield in the United States an army of more than twenty-five or thirty thousand men. To these would be opposed a militia amounting to near half a million of citizens with arms in their hands, officered by men chosen from among themselves, fighting for their common liberties, and united and conducted by governments possessing their affections and confidence. It may well be doubted whether a militia thus circumstanced could ever be conquered by such a proportion of regular troops. Those who are best acquainted with the late successful resistance of this country against the British arms will be most inclined to deny the possibility of it. Besides the advantage of being armed, which the Americans possess over the people of almost every other nation, the existence of subordinate governments to which the people are attached, and by which the militia officers are appointed, forms a barrier against the enterprizes of ambition, more insurmountable than any which a simple government of any form can admit of. Notwithstanding the military establishments in the several kingdoms of Europe, which are carried as far as the public resources will bear, the governments are afraid to trust the people with arms. And it is not certain that with this aid alone, they would not be able to shake off their yokes. But were the people to possess the additional advantages of local governments chosen by themselves, who could collect the national will, and direct the national force, and of officers appointed out of the militia, by these governments and attached both to them and to the militia, it may be affirmed with the greatest assurance that the throne of every tyranny in Europe would be speedily overturned, in spite of the legions which surround it. Let us not insult the free and gallant citizens of America with the suspicion that they would be less able to defend the rights of which they would be in actual possession, than the debased subjects of arbitrary power would be to rescue theirs from the hands of their oppressors. Let us rather no longer insult them with the supposition, that they can ever reduce themselves to the necessity of making the experiment, by a blind and tame submission to the long train of insidious measures, which must precede and produce it.

The argument under the present head may be put into a very concise form, which appears altogether conclusive. Either the mode in which the federal government is to be constructed will render it sufficiently dependent on the people, or it will not. On the first supposition, it will be restrained by that dependence from forming schemes obnoxious to their constituents. On the other supposition it will not possess the confidence of

time for the preceding mail. What goes by name of consolidation in Pena. is I suspect at the bottom of the opposition to the New Govt. almost every where; and I am glad to find you engaged in developing the subject. I inclose some papers in which it has been taken up here, that if any hints are contained in them, they may be pursued in your enquiry.[1]

There is certainly a favorable change taking place in Virga. on the subject of the Constitution. Several converts of influence have been named to me. I had heard also that Col. R. H. Lee was relaxing in his opposition, if not in his opinions. The authority from which I have it is such as almost to overcome the improbability of the thing.[2]

Our anxiety for the event in Masts. was not relieved by the last mail. No decisive index had appeared of the relative force of parties. Some letters are flattering, others discouraging, and others again totally skeptical. My hopes & apprehensions are pretty nearly balanced by the sum of the probabilities on each side, tho' with rather a prepondenancy on the favorable side. With great esteem I am Dr Sir Yr. Obed hble servt.

Js. Madison Jr.

RC (DLC). Enclosure not found.

[1] In his reply to JM of 6 Feb. 1788, Coxe identified the enclosed papers as *The Federalist*, Nos. 44 and 45 (Nos. 45 and 46 in the McLean edition).
[2] See Washington to JM, 10 Jan. 1788.

From Rufus King

Boston 30. Jan 1788. Wednesday

Dear Sir,

This day for the first our President Mr. Hancock took his Seat in convention, and we shall probably terminate our business on Saturday or Tuesday next. I cannot predict the issue, but our Hopes are increasing—if Mr. Hancock does not disappoint our present Expectations our wishes will be gratified. But his character is not entirely free from a portion of caprice—this however is confidential. Farewel. Your's &c

Rufus King

RC (DLC); Tr (NHi). RC docketed by JM.

From James Madison, Sr.

Jany. 30. 1788.

[. . .]

I have defered writing to you till I saw our Delegates after their return from the Assembly, that I might more fully inform you of their sentiments of the proposed constitution. I have only seen Majr. Burnley at Court on Monday last, but did not hear him say any thing about it; He disapproves of it, but says very little about it, probably, as he does not intend to offer his service for the convention, he may hurt his interest in the election for Delegates to the Assembly, for which he intends to offer, if he opposes the adoption of the new Constitution too warmly.[1] Col. Barbour I have not seen, he was not at Court; probably was preparing for his Mothers funeral, who was to be intered the day after. He is much opposed to it, and is a candidate for the Convention. I believe there were but few that disapproved of it at first, in this County: but several being at Richmond with their Tobo. at the time the Assembly was sitting, & hearing the many objections made to it, altered their opinions, & have influ[en]ced some others who are no better acquainted with the necessity of adopting it than they themselves: And the pieces published against it, have had their intended effect with some others.

The Baptists are now generally opposed to it, as it is said; Col. Barbour has been down on Pamunky amongst them, & on his return, I hear, publickly declared himself a candidate, I suppose, on the encouragement he met with from the Antifederalists. I do not know at present any other Candidates but yourself & Mr. Gordon, who is a warm friend to the Constitution, & I believe no others that are for it will offer. I think you had better come in as early in March as you can: many of your friends wish it; there are some who suspends their opinion till they see you, & wish for an explanation, others wish you not to come, & will endeavor to shut you out of the Convention, the better to carry their point. Mr. R H. L.s Letter to the G——r. is much approved of by some, & as much ridiculed by others:[2] and so is the reasoning & representation of the minority of the Pennsylvania Convention.

The inclosed was brot. from Kentuckey by Mr. Thos. Jones; I guess it is from Mr. Wallace.[3]

The specimen you sent me from Mr. House of his method of reducing the gross Hundred, I have been acquainted with long since; before either you or he had existence; but the Acct. of Sales he sent did not agree with the rule, which I suppose was from some mistake in the calculations; I believe I gave you his Acct. to have it corrected; He also omitted to enter one of the Hhds. I should be glad of a seperate Acct. of my 30. Hhds Tobo. & of Frankey's 2 markt FM. if he can render it:[4] And of some money for it, if you have not made use of it all, for the prospect of my getting any for the Bonds you left with me is not very promising at present.

I shall be glad to receive a letter from you as soon as you receive this, & to know when we may expect you & how you expect to get from Fredg home, if you come there in the Stage. Corn is very scarce among us, & of course very dear; and the hard weather we have had for 5 or 6 weeks past, I am apprehensive will make it very difficult for many persons to shift till the summer grain is ripe.

Our family are as well as usual; Your bror. Am.s Wife[5] is very unwell, & has been for a month at least past. Dr Gilmer[6] left her Yesterday to go to Mrs. McDonald[7] at Mr. Isaac Hite's her Fathers; he had stayed with your sister, 5 or 6 days constantly; She is better, but not recovered. Your Sister Nelly was well a few days ago; as our family & friends are as usual. I am Your Afft. Father

JAMES MADISON

P.S. When Majr. James Coleman was here in Orange two Years ago, I gave him Continental Loan Office Certificates for 1500 Dollars, granted in N. Carolina to Col. George Baylor, & dated the 17 of May 1778, to get liquidated; he is now here & has brought them back, & says, that upon application for a settlement, he is referred to Congress, where there is a person appointed to settle them: I wish you to enquire into it, and inform me what step will be proper for me to take: I purpose to send them by you if they are to be settled at the Northward.[8]

RC (DLC). Addressed by James Madison, Sr., and docketed by JM. Salutation missing owing to a tear in the Ms. On the verso is William Moore to JM, 31 Jan. 1788.

[1] Hardin Burnley retained his seat in the House of Delegates (Swem and Williams, *Register*, p. 29).

[2] See Washington to JM, 7 Dec. 1787 and n. 8.

[3] Caleb Wallace to JM, 12 Nov. 1787.

[4] See JM to Ambrose Madison, 8 Nov. 1787. "FM" was JM's brother Francis Madison (*PJM*, III, 208 n. 3).

[5] Mrs. Ambrose Madison was the former Mary Wills Lee (Madison Family Tree, *PJM*, I, between 212 and 213, n. 6).

[6] George Gilmer, Jr. (1743–1795), eminent physician and friend of Jefferson. After studying medicine at the University of Edinburgh, Gilmer practiced in Williamsburg and later moved to Albemarle County (Blanton, *Medicine in Virginia in the Eighteenth Century*, pp. 316–17, 389; Richard Beale Davis, *Francis Walker Gilmer: Life and Learning in Jefferson's Virginia* [Richmond, 1939], pp. 5–6).

[7] Mrs. Mary McDonald (d. 1789), widow of Dr. John McDonald of Winchester (Winchester *Va. Centinel*, 7 Jan. 1789).

[8]JM evidently took the certificates with him on his return to Congress in the summer of 1788. After inquiring into the matter, JM informed his father on 6 Sept. 1788 that the certificates would have to "go to N. Carolina for settlement" (Madison, *Writings* [Hunt ed.], V, 251, 259–60).

The Federalist Number 47

[30 January 1788]

Having reviewed the general form of the proposed government, and the general mass of power allotted to it; I proceed to examine the particular structure of this government, and the distribution of this mass of power among its constituent parts.

One of the principal objections inculcated by the more respectable adversaries to the constitution, is its supposed violation of the political maxim, that the legislative, executive and judiciary departments ought to be separate and distinct. In the structure of the federal government, no regaiu, it is said, seems to have been paid to this essential precaution in favor of liberty. The several departments of power are distributed and blended in such a manner, as at once to destroy all symmetry and beauty of form; and to expose some of the essential parts of the edifice to the danger of being crushed by the disproportionate weight of other parts.[1]

No political truth is certainly of greater intrinsic value or is stamped with the authority of more enlightened patrons of liberty, than that on which the objection is founded. The accumulation of all powers legislative, executive and judiciary in the same hands, whether of one, a few or many, and whether hereditary, self appointed, or elective, may justly be pronounced the very definition of tyranny. Were the federal constitution therefore, really chargeable with this accumulation of power or with a mixture of powers, having a dangerous tendency to such an accumulation, no further arguments would be necessary to inspire a universal reprobation of the system. I persuade myself however, that it will be made apparent to every one, that the charge cannot be supported, and that the maxim on which it relies, has been totally misconceived and misapplied. In order to form correct ideas on this important subject, it will be proper to investigate the sense, in which the preservation of liberty requires, that the three great departments of power should be separate and distinct.

The oracle who is always consulted and cited on this subject, is the celebrated Montesquieu. If he be not the author of this invaluable precept in the science of politics, he has the merit at least of displaying and recommending it most effectually to the attention of mankind. Let us endeavour in the first place to ascertain his meaning on this point.

The British constitution was to Montesquieu, what Homer has been to the didactic writers on epic poetry. As the latter have considered the work of the immortal bard, as the perfect model from which the principles and rules of the epic art were to be drawn, and by which all similar works were to be judged; so this great political critic appears to have viewed the constitution of England as the standard, or to use his own expression, as the mirror of political liberty; and to have delivered in the form of elementary truths, the several characteristic principles of that particular system. That we may be sure then not to mistake his meaning in this case, let us recur to the source from which the maxim was drawn.

On the slightest view of the British constitution we must perceive, that the legislative, executive, and judiciary departments are by no means totally separate and distinct from each other. The executive magistrate forms an integral part of the legislative authority. He alone has the prerogative of making treaties with foreign sovereigns, which when made, have, under certain limitations, the force of legislative acts. All the members of the judiciary department are appointed by him; can be removed by him on the address of the two houses of parliament, and form, when he pleases to consult them, one of his constitutional councils. One branch of the legislative department forms also, a great constitutional council to the executive chief; as on another hand, it is the sole depositary of judicial power in cases of impeachment, and is invested with the supreme appellate jurisdiction, in all other cases. The judges again are so far connected with the legislative department, as often to attend and participate in its deliberations, though not admitted to a legislative vote.

From these facts by which Montesquieu was guided it may clearly be inferred, that in saying, "there can be no liberty where the legislative and executive powers are united in the same person, or body of magistrates," or, "if the power of judging be not separated from the legislative and executive powers," he did not mean that these departments ought to have no *partial agency* in, or no *control* over the acts of each other.[2] His meaning, as his own words import, and still more conclusively as illustrated by the example in his eye, can amount to no more than this, that where the *whole* power of one department is exercised by the same hands which possess the *whole* power of another department, the fundamental principles of a free constitution, are subverted. This would not have been the case[3] in the constitution examined by him, if the king who is the sole executive magistrate, had possessed also the complete legislative power, or the supreme administration of justice; or if the entire legislative body, had possessed the supreme judiciary, or the supreme executive authority. This however is not among the vices of that constitution. The magistrate in whom the whole executive power resides cannot of himself make a law, though he can put a negative on every law, nor administer justice in person, though he has the appointment of those who do administer it. The judges can exercise no executive prerogative, though they are shoots from the executive stock, nor any legislative function, though they may be advised with by the legislative councils. The entire legislature, can perform no judiciary act; though by the joint act of two of its branches, the judges may be removed from their offices; and though one of its branches is possessed of the judicial power in the last resort. The entire legislature again can exercise no executive prerogative, though one of its branches* constitutes the supreme executive magistracy; and another, on the impeachment of a third, can try and condemn all the subordinate officers in the executive department.

The reasons on which Montesquieu grounds his maxim are a further demonstration of his meaning. "When the legislative and executive powers are united in the same person or body," says he, "there can be no liberty, because apprehensions may arise lest *the same* monarch or senate should *enact* tyrannical laws, to *execute* them in a tyrannical manner." Again "Were the power of judging joined with the legislative, the life and liberty of the subject would be exposed to arbitrary control, for *the judge* would then be *the legislator*. Were it joined to the executive power, *the judge* might behave with all the violence of *an oppressor*."[4] Some of these reasons are more fully explained in other passages; but briefly stated as they are here, they sufficiently establish the meaning which we have put on this celebrated maxim of this celebrated author.[5]

If we look into the constitutions of the several states, we find that notwithstanding the emphatical, and in some instances, the unqualified terms in which this axiom has been laid down, there is not a single instance in which the several departments of power have been kept absolutely separate and distinct. New-Hampshire, whose constitution was the last formed, seems to have been fully aware of the impossibility and inexpediency of avoiding any mixture whatever of these departments; and has qualified the doctrine by declaring "that the legislative, executive and judiciary powers ought to be kept as separate from, and independent of each other *as the nature of a free government will admit; or as is consistent with that chain of connection, that binds the whole fabric of the constitution in one indissoluble bond of unity and amity*." Her constitution accordingly mixes

*The King.

these departments in several respects. The senate, which is a branch of the legislative department, is also a judicial tribunal for the trial of impeachments. The president who is the head of the executive department, is the presiding member also of the senate; and besides an equal vote in all cases, has a casting vote in case of a tie. The executive head is himself eventually elective every year by the legislative department; and his council is every year chosen by and from the members of the same department. Several of the officers of state are also appointed by the legislature. And the members of the judiciary department are appointed by the executive department.

The constitution of Massachusetts has observed a sufficient though less pointed caution in expressing this fundamental article of liberty. It declares, "that the legislative department shall never exercise the executive and judicial powers, or either of them: The executive shall never exercise the legislative and judicial powers, or either of them: The judicial shall never exercise the legislative and executive powers, or either of them." This declaration corresponds precisely with the doctrine of Montesquieu, as it has been explained, and is not in a single point violated by the plan of the convention. It goes no farther than to prohibit any one of the entire departments from exercising the powers of another department. In the very constitution to which it is prefixed, a partial mixture of powers has been admitted. The executive magistrate has a qualified negative on the legislative body; and the senate, which is a part of the legislature, is a court of impeachment for members both of the executive and judiciary departments. The members of the judiciary department again are appointable by the executive department, and removeable by the same authority, on the address of the two legislative branches. Lastly, a number of the officers of government are annually appointed by the legislative department. As the appointment to offices, particularly executive offices, is in its nature an executive function, the compilers of the constitution have in this last point at least, violated the rule established by themselves.

I pass over the constitutions of Rhode-Island and Connecticut, because they were formed prior to the revolution; and even before the principle under examination had become an object of political attention.

The constitution of New-York contains no declaration on this subject; but appears very clearly to have been framed with an eye to the danger of improperly blending the different departments. It gives nevertheless to the executive magistrate a partial controul over the legislative department; and what is more, gives a like controul to the judiciary department, and even blends the executive and judiciary departments in the exercise of this controul. In its council of appointment, members of the legislative are associated with the executive authority in the appointment of officers both executive and judiciary. And its court for the trial of impeachments and correction of errors, is to consist of one branch of the legislature and the principal members of the judiciary department.

The constitution of New-Jersey has blended the different powers of government more than any of the preceding. The governor, who is the executive magistrate, is appointed by the legislature; is chancellor and ordinary or surrogate of the state; is a member of the supreme court of appeals, and president with a casting vote, of one of the legislative branches. The same legislative branch acts again as executive council of the governor, and with him constitutes the court of appeals. The members of the judiciary department are appointed by the legislative department, and removeable by one branch of it, on the impeachment of the other.

According to the constitution of Pennsylvania, the president, who is head of the executive department, is annually elected by a vote in which the legislative department predominates. In conjunction with an executive council, he appoints the members of the judiciary department, and forms a court of impeachments for trial of all officers, judiciary as well as executive. The judges of the supreme court, and justices of the peace, seem also to be removeable by the legislature; and the executive power of pardoning in certain cases to be referred to the same department. The members of the executive council are made EX OFFICIO justices of peace throughout the state.

In Delaware, the chief executive magistrate is annually elected by the legislative department. The speakers of the two legislative branches are vice-presidents in the executive department. The executive chief, with six others, appointed three by each of the legislative branches, constitute the supreme court of appeals: He is joined with the legislative department in the appointment of the other judges. Throughout the states it appears that the members of the legislature may at the same time be justices of the peace. In this state, the members of one branch of it are EX OFFICIO justices of the peace; as are also the members of the executive council. The principal officers of the executive department are appointed by the legislative; and one branch of the latter forms a court of impeachments. All officers may be removed on address of the legislature.

Maryland has adopted the maxim in the most unqualified terms; declaring that the legislative, executive and judicial powers of government, ought to be forever separate and distinct from each other. Her constitution, notwithstanding makes the executive magistrate appointable by the legislative department; and the members of the judiciary, by the executive department.

The language of Virginia is still more pointed on this subject. Her constitution declares, "that the legislative, executive and judiciary departments, shall be separate and distinct; so that neither exercise the powers properly belonging to the other; nor shall any person exercise the powers of more than one of them at the same time; except that the justices of county courts shall be eligible to either house of assembly." Yet we find not only this express exception, with respect to the members of the inferior courts; but that the chief magistrate with his executive council are appointable by the legislature; that two members of the latter are triennially displaced at the pleasure of the legislature; and that all the principal officers,[6] both executive and judiciary, are filled by the same department. The executive prerogative of pardoning, also is in one case vested in the legislative department.

The constitution of North-Carolina, which declares, "that the legislative, executive and supreme judicial powers of government, ought to be forever separate and distinct from each other," refers at the same time to the legislative department, the appointment not only of the executive chief, but all the principal officers within both that and the judiciary department.

In South-Carolina, the constitution makes the executive magistracy eligible by the legislative department. It gives to the latter also the appointment of the members of the judiciary department, including even justices of the peace and sheriffs; and the appointment of officers in the executive department, down to captains in the army and navy of the state.

In the constitution of Georgia, where it is declared, "that the legislative, executive and judiciary departments shall be separate and distinct, so that neither exercise the powers properly belonging to the other," we find that the executive department is to be filled by appointments of the legislature; and the executive prerogative of pardoning, to be finally exercised by the same authority. Even justices of the peace are to be appointed by the legislature.

In citing these cases in which the legislative, executive and judiciary departments have not been kept totally separate and distinct, I wish not to be regarded as an advocate for the particular organizations of the several state governments. I am fully aware that among the many excellent principles which they exemplify, they carry strong marks of the haste, and still stronger of the inexperience, under which they were framed. It is but too obvious that in some instances, the fundamental principle under consideration has been violated by too great a mixture, and even an actual consolidation of the different powers; and that in no instance has a competent provision been made for maintaining in practice the separation delineated on paper. What I have wished to evince is, that the charge brought against the proposed constitution, of violating a sacred maxim of free government, is warranted neither by the real meaning annexed to that maxim by its author; nor by the sense in which it has hitherto been understood in America. This interesting subject will be resumed in the ensuing paper.

PUBLIUS.

McLean, II, 92–101.

[1]See Kenyon, *The Antifederalists*, pp. lxxvi–lxxx.
[2]Montesquieu, *The Spirit of the Laws*, bk. XI, chap. VI ([Neumann ed.], I, 151–52). JM may have been translating from a French edition of the work, for his quotations vary slightly from the standard English translation by Thomas Nugent.
[3]Should read: "This would have been the case," as in *The Federalist* (Cooke ed.), p. 326.
[4]Montesquieu, *The Spirit of the Laws*, bk. XI, chap. VI ([Neumann ed.], I, 151–52). Italics supplied by JM.
[5]A modern scholar supports JM's contention that Montesquieu was not a proponent of the "pure doctrine" of the separation of powers (M. J. C. Vile, *Constitutionalism and the Separation of Powers* [Oxford, 1967], pp. 93–97).
[6]Should read "offices," as in *The Federalist* (Cooke ed.), p. 330.

From William Moore

ORANGE 31st. Jany 1788

DEAR SIR,

From the foregoing information of your Father of the Fluctuating Sentiments of the Freeholders of this County on the Constitution proposed by the Convention at Philidelphia and the Arts of some Men in this County to mislead the People whose Interest you know are repugnant to a Govermt. that will Administer Justice, safety, protection, and true Liberty to the Good and Virtuous Citizens of America and as you well know the disadvantage of being absent at Elections to those who offer themselves to serve the Public I must therefore intreat and conjure you nay commd. you, if it was in my Power, to be here in February or the first of March Next if you do, I think your Election will be certain, (if not I believe from reports you[1] it will be uncertain) and you will in that case be able to silence the disaffected and give that assistance to the Constitution that your knowledge of it and the Necess[i]ty of such Establishment to the well being and the future Pro[s]perity of America. However Sir be assured that the Friends of the Constitution will promote your Interest at any rate. But let me repeat it again, as a Lover of your Country, pray dont disappoint the wishes of your Friends and many others who are wavering on the Constitution that are anxiously waiting for an Explanation from you in

454

short they want your Sentiments from your own mouth which they say will convin[c]e them of the necessity of adobpting it. I am my Dr Sir, yours Affectionately

WM. MOORE

P.S. I repeat again come—

RC (DLC). Written on the verso of James Madison, Sr., to JM, 30 Jan. 1788.

¹At this point Moore struck out "will be left out" and substituted "it will be uncertain." He forgot to strike out "you."

To George Washington

N. YORK Feby. 1. 1788

DEAR SIR

The Eastern Mail which arrived yesterday brought me a letter from Mr. King, of which a copy follows. "Our prospects are gloomy, but hope is not entirely extinguished. Gerry has not returned to the Convention, and I think will not again be invited. We are now thinking of Amendments to be submitted not as a condition of our assent & ratification, but as the Opinion of the Convention subjoined to their ratification. This scheme may gain a few members but the issue is doubtful."

In this case as in the last Mr. King's information is accompanied with letters from other persons on the spot which dwell more on the favorable side of the prospect. His anxiety on the subject may give a greater activity to his fears than to his hopes; and he would naturally lean to the cautious side. These circumstances encourage me to put as favorable a construction on his letter as it will bear.

A vessel is arrived here from Charlestown which brings letters that speak with confidence of an adoption of the fœdl Government in that State; and make it very probable that Georgia had actually adopted it. Some letters on the subject from N. Carolina speak a very equivocal language as to the prospect there.

The French Packet arrived yesterday. As she has been out since early in November little news can be expected by her. I have not yet got my letters if there be any for me and I have heard the contents of no others. I remain Dr Sir with the utmost respect & attachment Yr. Affete. servt.

Js. MADISON JR

RC (DLC: Washington Papers); Tr (DLC). RC docketed by Washington.

The Federalist Number 48

[1 February 1788]

It was shewn in the last paper, that the political apothegm there examined, does not require that the legislative, executive and judiciary departments should be wholly unconnected with each other. I shall undertake in the next place, to shew that unless these departments be so far connected and blended, as to give to each a constitutional controul over the others, the degree of separation which the maxim requires as essential to a free government, can never in practice be duly maintained.

It is agreed on all sides, that the powers properly belonging to one of the departments, ought not to be directly and compleatly administered by either of the other departments. It is equally evident, that neither of them ought to possess directly or indirectly, an over-ruling influence over the others in the administration of their respective powers. It will not be denied that power is of an encroaching nature, and that it ought to be effectually restrained from passing the limits, assigned to it. After discriminating therefore in theory, the several classes of power, as they may in their nature be legislative, executive or judiciary; the next and most difficult task, is to provide some practical security for each against the invasion of the others. What this security ought to be, is the great problem to be solved.

Will it be sufficient to mark with precision the boundaries of these departments in the constitution of the government, and to trust to these parchment barriers against the encroaching spirit of power? This is the security which appears to have been principally relied on by the compilers of most of the American constitutions. But experience assures us that the efficacy of the provision has been greatly over-rated; and that some more adequate defence is indispensably necessary for the more feeble, against the more powerful members of the government. The legislative department is every where extending the sphere of its activity, and drawing all power into its impetuous vortex.[1]

The founders of our republics have so much merit for the wisdom which they have displayed, that no task can be less pleasing than that of pointing out the errors into which they have fallen. A respect for truth however obliges us to remark, that they seem never for a moment to have turned their eyes from the danger to liberty from the overgrown and all-grasping prerogative of an hereditary magistrate, supported and fortified by an hereditary branch of the legislative authority. They seem never to have recollected the danger from legislative usurpations, which by assembling all power in the same hands, must lead to the same tyranny as is threatened by executive usurpations.

In a government, where numerous and extensive prerogatives are placed in the hands of a hereditary monarch, the executive department is very justly regarded as the source of danger, and watched with all the jealousy which a zeal for liberty ought to inspire. In a democracy, where a multitude of people exercise in person the legislative functions, and are continually exposed by their incapacity for regular deliberation and concerted measures, to the ambitious intrigues of their executive magistrates, tyranny may well be apprehended on some favourable emergency, to start up in the same quarter. But in a representative republic, where the executive magistracy is carefully limited both in the extent and the duration of its power; and where the legislative power is exercised by an assembly, which is inspired by a supposed influence over the people with an intrepid confidence in its own strength; which is sufficiently numerous to feel all the passions which actuate a multitude; yet not so numerous as to be incapable of pursuing the objects of its passions, by means which reason prescribes; it is against the enterprising ambition of this department, that the people ought to indulge all their jealousy and exhaust all their precautions.

The legislative department derives a superiority in our governments from other circumstances. Its constitutional powers being at once more extensive and less susceptible of precise limits, it can with the greater facility, mask under complicated and indirect measures, the encroachments which it makes, on the co-ordinate departments. It is not unfrequently a question of real nicety in legislative bodies, whether the operation of a particular measure, will, or will not extend beyond the legislative sphere. On the other side, the executive power being restrained within a narrower compass, and being more simple in its nature; and the judiciary being described by land marks, still less uncertain, projects of usurpation by either of these departments, would immediately betray and defeat themselves. Nor is this all: As the legislative department alone has access to the pockets of the people, and has in some constitutions full discretion, and in all, a prevailing influence over the pecuniary rewards of those who fill the other departments, a dependence is thus created in the latter, which gives still greater facility to encroachments of the former.

I have appealed to our own experience for the truth of what I advance on this subject. Were it necessary to verify this experience by particular proofs, they might be multiplied without end.[2] I might collect vouchers in abundance from the records and archives of every state in the union. But as a more concise and at the same time, equally satisfactory evidence I will refer to the example of two states, attested by two unexceptionable authorities.

The first example is that of Virginia, a state which, as we have seen, has expressly declared in its constitution, that the three great departments ought not to be intermixed. The authority in support of it is Mr. Jefferson, who, besides his other advantages for remarking the operation of the government, was himself the chief magistrate of it. In order to convey fully the ideas with which his experience had impressed him on this subject, it will be necessary to quote a passage of some length from his very interesting "Notes on the state of Virginia." (p. 195) "All the powers of government, legislative, executive and judiciary, result to the legislative body. The concentrating these in the same hands is precisely the definition of despotic government. It will be no alleviation that these powers will be exercised by a plurality of hands, and not by a single one. One hundred and seventy-three despots would surely be as oppressive as one. Let those who doubt it turn their eyes on the republic of Venice. As little will it avail us that they are chosen by ourselves. An *elective despotism* was not the government we fought for; but one which should not only be founded on free principles, but in which the powers of government should be so divided and balanced among several bodies of magistracy, as that no one could transcend their legal limits, without being effectually checked and restrained by the others. For this reason, that convention which passed the ordinance of government laid its foundation on this basis, that the legislative, executive and judiciary departments, should be separate and distinct, so that no person should exercise the powers of more than one of them at the same time. *But no barrier was provided between these several powers.* The judiciary and executive members were left dependent on the legislative for their subsistence in office, and some of them for their continuance in it. If therefore the legislature assumes executive and judiciary powers, no opposition is likely to be made; nor if made can be effectual; because in that case, they may put their proceeding into the form of an act of assembly, which will render them obligatory on the other branches. They have accordingly *in many* instances *decided rights* which should have been left to *judiciary controversy;* and *the direction of the executive, during the whole time of their session, is becoming habitual and familiar.*"[3]

The other state which I shall have for an example, is Pennsylvania; and the other authority the council of censors which assembled in the years 1783 and 1784. A part of the duty of this body, as marked out by the constitution, was "to enquire whether the constitution had been preserved inviolate in every part; and whether the legislative and executive branches of government had performed their duty as guardians of the people, or assumed to themselves, or exercised other or greater powers than they are entitled to by the constitution." In the execution of this trust, the council were necessarily led to a comparison, of both the legislative and executive proceedings, with the constitutional powers of these departments; and from the facts enumerated, and to the truth of most of which, both sides in the council subscribed, it appears that the constitution had been flagrantly violated by the legislature in a variety of important instances.

A great number of laws had been passed violating without any apparent necessity, the rule requiring that all bills of a publick nature shall be previously printed for the consideration of the people; although this is one of the precautions chiefly relied on by the constitution, against improper acts of the legislature.

The constitutional trial by jury had been violated; and powers assumed, which had not been delegated by the constitution.

Executive powers had been usurped.

The salaries of the judges, which the constitution expressly requires to be fixed, had been occasionally varied; and cases belonging to the judiciary department, frequently drawn within legislative cognizance and determination.

Those who wish to see the several particulars falling under each of these heads, may consult the journals of the council which are in print. Some of them, it will be found may be imputable to peculiar circumstances connected with the war: But the greater part of them may be considered as the spontaneous shoots of an ill-constituted government.[4]

It appears also, that the executive department had not been innocent of frequent breaches of the constitution. There are three observations however, which ought to be made on this head. *First.* A great proportion of the instances, were either immediately produced by the necessities of the war, or recommended by Congress or the commander in chief. *Second.* In most of the other instances, they conformed either to the declared or the known sentiments of the legislative department. *Third.* The executive department of Pennsylvania is distinguished from that of the other states, by the number of members composing it. In this respect it has as much affinity to a legislative assembly, as to an executive council. And being at once exempt from the restraint of an individual responsibility for the acts of the body, and deriving confidence from mutual example and joint influence; unauthorised measures would of course be more freely hazarded, than where the executive department is administered by a single hand or by a few hands.

The conclusion which I am warranted in drawing from these observations is, that a mere demarkation on parchment of the constitutional limits of the several departments, is not a sufficient guard against those encroachments which lead to a tyrannical concentration of all the powers of government in the same hands.

PUBLIUS.

McLean, II, 101–7.

[1] The encroaching nature of legislative power was the theme of JM's third speech of 17 July and his first speech of 21 July 1787 at the Federal Convention, where he also spoke of the legislature as a "vortex."

[2] Here the newspaper version has the following sentence, omitted in the McLean edition: "I might find a witness in every citizen who has shared in, or been attentive to, the course of public administrations" (*The Federalist* [Cooke ed.], p. 334).

[3] *Notes on Virginia* (Peden ed.), p. 120. JM quoted from pages 195–96 of the London edition of 1787. Except for the phrase, *"elective despotism,"* the italics were supplied by JM.

[4] JM's information was based on the report of a committee of the Council of Censors appointed to consider alleged violations of the state constitution. This report was printed in the *Journal of the Council of Censors . . .* (Philadelphia, 1783[–1784]; Evans 18093), pp. 134–42, and published separately as *The Constitution of . . . Pennsylvania . . . To Which is Added, A Report of the Committee Appointed to Enquire, "Whether the Constitution has been Preserved Inviolate . . ."* (Philadelphia, 1784; Evans 18680). For a summary of the council's proceedings, see Lewis H. Meader, "The Council of Censors," *Pa. Mag. Hist. and Biog.*, XXII (1898), 287–95. The minutes of the first of two sessions are printed in condensed form in *Pa. Archives*, 3d ser., X (1896), 787–809.

The Federalist Number 49

[2 February 1788]

The author of the "Notes on the state of Virginia," quoted in the last paper, has subjoined to that valuable work, the draught of a constitution which had been prepared in order to be laid before a convention expected to be called in 1783, by the legislature, for the establishment of a constitution for that commonwealth. The plan, like every thing from the same pen, marks a turn of thinking original, comprehensive and accurate; and is the more worthy of attention, as it equally displays a fervent attachment to republican government, and an enlightened view of the dangerous propensities against which it ought to be guarded. One of the precautions which he proposes, and on which he appears ultimately to rely as a palladium to the weaker departments of power, against the invasions of the stronger, is perhaps altogether his own, and as it immediately relates to the subject of our present enquiry, ought not to be overlooked.

His proposition is, "that whenever any two of the three branches of government shall concur in opinion, each by the voices of two thirds of their whole number, that a convention is necessary for altering the constitution or *correcting breaches of it*, a convention shall be called for the purpose."[1]

As the people are the only legitimate fountain of power, and it is from them that the constitutional charter, under which the several branches of government hold their power, is derived; it seems strictly consonant to the republican theory, to recur to the same original authority, not only whenever it may be necessary to enlarge, diminish, or new-model the powers of government; but also whenever any one of the departments may commit encroachments on the chartered authorities of the others. The several departments being perfectly co-ordinate by the terms of their common commission, neither of them, it is evident, can pretend to an exclusive or superior right of settling the boundaries between their respective powers; and how are the encroachments of the stronger to be prevented, or the wrongs of the weaker to be redressed, without an appeal to the people themselves; who, as the grantors of the commission, can alone declare its true meaning and enforce its observance?

There is certainly great force in this reasoning, and it must be allowed to prove, that a constitutional road to the decision of the people, ought to be marked out, and kept open, for certain great and extraordinary occasions. But there appear to be insuperable objections against the proposed recurrence to the people, as a provision in all cases for keeping the several departments of power within their constitutional limits.[2]

In the first place, the provision does not reach the case of a combination of two of the departments against a third. If the legislative authority, which possesses so many means of operating on the motives of the other departments, should be able to gain to its interest either of the others, or even one third of its members, the remaining department could derive no advantage from this remedial provision. I do not dwell however, on this objection, because it may be thought to lie rather against the modification of the principle, than against the principle itself.

In the next place, it may be considered as an objection inherent in the principle, that as every appeal to the people would carry an implication of some defect in the government, frequent appeals would in great measure deprive the government of that veneration which time bestows on every thing, and without which perhaps the wisest and freest governments would not possess the requisite stability. If it be true that all governments rest on opinion, it is no less true that the strength of opinion in each individual, and its practical influence on his conduct, depend much on the number which he supposes to have entertained the same opinion. The reason of man, like man himself, is timid and cautious, when left alone; and acquires firmness and confidence, in proportion to the number with which it is associated. When the examples, which fortify opinion, are *antient* as well as *numerous*, they are known to have a double effect. In a nation of philosophers, this consideration ought to be disregarded. A reverence for the laws, would be sufficiently inculcated by the voice of an enlightened reason. But a nation of philosophers is as little to be expected as the philosophical race of kings wished for by Plato. And in every other nation, the most rational government will not find it a superfluous advantage to have the prejudices of the community on its side.

The danger of disturbing the public tranquility by interesting too strongly the public passions, is a still more serious objection against a frequent reference of constitutional questions, to the decision of the whole society. Notwithstanding the success which has attended the revisions of our established forms of government, and which does so much honor to the virtue and intelligence of the people of America, it must be confessed, that the experiments are of too ticklish a nature to be unnecessarily multiplied. We are to recollect that all the existing constitutions were formed in the midst of a danger which repressed the passions most unfriendly to order and concord; of an enthusiastic confidence of the people in their patriotic leaders, which stifled the ordinary diversity of opinions on great national questions; of a universal ardor for new and opposite forms, produced by a universal resentment and indignation against the antient government; and whilst no spirit of party, connected with the changes to be made, or the abuses to be reformed, could mingle its leaven in the operation. The future situations in which we must expect to be usually placed, do not present any equivalent security against the danger which is apprehended.

But the greatest objection of all is that the decisions which would probably result from such appeals, would not answer the purpose of maintaining the constitutional equilibrium of the government. We have seen that the tendency of republican governments is to an aggrandizement of the legislative, at the expence of the other departments. The appeals to the people therefore, would usually be made by the executive and judiciary departments. But whether made by one side or the other, would each side enjoy equal advantages on the trial? Let us view their different situations. The members of the executive and judiciary departments, are few in number, and can be personally known to a small part only of the people. The latter by the mode of their appointment, as well as by the nature and permanency of it, are too far removed from the people to share much in their prepossessions. The former are generally the objects of jealousy: and their administration is always liable to be discoloured and rendered unpopular. The members of the legislative department, on the other hand, are numerous. They are distributed and dwell among the people at large.

Their connections of blood, of friendship and of acquaintance, embrace a great proportion of the most influential part of the society. The nature of their public trust implies a personal influence among the people, and that they are more immediately the confidential guardians of the rights and liberties of the people. With these advantages, it can hardly be supposed that the adverse party would have an equal chance for a favorable issue.[3]

But the legislative party would not only be able to plead their cause most successfully with the people: They would probably be constituted themselves the judges. The same influence which had gained them an election into the legislature, would gain them a seat in the convention. If this should not be the case with all, it would probably be the case with many, and pretty certainly with those leading characters, on whom every thing depends in such bodies. The convention in short would be composed chiefly of men, who had been, who actually were, or who expected to be, members of the department whose conduct was arraigned. They would consequently be parties to the very question to be decided by them.

It might however sometimes happen, that appeals would be made under circumstances less adverse to the executive and judiciary departments. The usurpations of the legislature might be so flagrant and so sudden, as to admit of no specious colouring. A strong party among themselves might take side with the other branches. The executive power might be in the hands of a peculiar favorite of the people. In such a posture of things, the public decision might be less swayed by prepossessions in favor of the legislative party. But still it could never be expected to turn on the true merits of the question. It would inevitably be connected with the spirit of pre-existing parties, or of parties springing out of the question itself. It would be connected with persons of distinguished character and extensive influence in the community. It would be pronounced by the very men who had been agents in, or opponents of the measures, to which the decision would relate. The *passions* therefore not the *reason*, of the public, would sit in judgment. But it is the reason of the public alone that ought to controul and regulate the government. The passions ought to be controuled and regulated by the government.

We found in the last paper that mere declarations in the written constitution, are not sufficient to restrain the several departments within their legal limits. It appears in this that occasional appeals to the people would be neither a proper nor an effectual provision, for that purpose. How far the provisions of a different nature contained in the plan above quoted, might be adequate, I do not examine. Some of them are unquestionably founded on sound political principles, and all of them are framed with singular ingenuity and precision.

PUBLIUS.

McLean, II, 107–12.

[1] JM condensed Jefferson's wording and supplied the italics (see *Notes on Virginia* [Peden ed.], p. 221).

[2] In his letter to Caleb Wallace of 23 Aug. 1785, JM had commented on Jefferson's proposition, but did not criticize it (*PJM*, VIII, 355).

[3] At the convention JM had supported a combination of the executive and judiciary in a council of revision, observing that "it was much more to be apprehended that notwithstanding this co-operation of the two departments, the Legislative would still be an overmatch for them" (first speech of 21 July 1787).

To George Washington

N. YORK Feby 3d. 1788.

DEAR SIR

Another mail has arrived from Boston without terminating the conflict between our hopes and fears. I have a letter from Mr. King of the 27. which after dilating somewhat on the ideas in his former letters, concludes with the following paragraph. "We have avoided every question which would have shewn the division of the House. Of consequence we are not positive of the numbers on each side. By the last calculation we made on our side, we were doubtful whether we exceeded them or they us in numbers. They however say that they have a majority of eight or twelve against us. We by no means despair." Another letter of the same date from another member[1] gives the following picture. "Never was there an Assembly in this State in possession of greater ability & information than the present Convention. Yet I am in doubt whether they will approve the Constitution. There are unhappily three parties opposed to it. 1. All men who are in favour of paper money & tender laws; those are more or less in every part of the State. 2. All the late insurgents & their abettors. In the three great western Counties they are very numerous. We have in the Convention 18 or 20. who were actually in Shay's Army. 3. A great majority of the members from the Province of Main. Many of them & their Constituents are only squatters upon other people's land, and they are afraid of being brought to account. They also think though erroneously that their favorite plan, of being a separate State will be defeated. Add to these the honest doubting people, and they make a powerful host. The leaders of this Party are a Mr. Wedgery Mr Thomson, & Mr Nason from the province of Main—A Docr. Taylor from the County of Worster & Mr. Bishop from the neighbourhood of R. Island. To manage the cause agst. them are the present and late Govr. 3 Judges of the supreme Court—15 members of the Senate—20 from among the most respectable of the Clergy, 10 or 12 of the first characters at the bar, Judges of probate,

High Sheriffs of Counties & many other respectable people Merchants
&c—Genls. Heath Lincoln, Brooks & others of the late army. With all
this ability in support of the cause, I am pretty well satisfied we shall lose
the question, unless we can take off some of the opposition by amendments. I do not mean such as are to be made conditions of the ratification,
but recommendatory only. Upon this plan I flatter myself we may possibly get a majority of 12 or 15. if not more."

The Legislature of this State has voted a Convention on June 17. I
remain Yrs. most respectfully & Affecly.

Js Madison Jr

RC (DLC: Washington Papers). Docketed by Washington.
[1] Nathaniel Gorham.

From Rufus King

Boston. Sunday 3d. Feb. 1788

Dear Sir

I inclose a newspaper of yesterday containing the propositions communicated by Mr. Hancock to the Convention, on Thursday last.[1] Mr.
Adams[2] who contrary to his own Sentiments has been hitherto silent in
convention, has given his public & explicit approbation of Mr. Hancock's
propositions.

We flatter ourselves that the weight of these two characters will insure
our success, but the Event is not absolutely certain. Yesterday a committee
was appointed on the motion of a doubtful Character to consider the
propositions submitted by Mr. Hancock, and to report Tomorrow Afternoon. We have a Majority of Fedaralists on this Committee and flatter
ourselves the result will be favorable. I have not Time to add except that I
am with Esteem &c yours &c.

R King

PS. We shall probably decide on Thursday or Friday next, when our
numbers will amount to about 363. Gerry has kept at Cambridge & Our
Opponents say nothing of his reinvitation.[3]

RC (DLC); Tr (NHi). RC addressed by King and franked. RC docketed by JM and
directed by him on the verso of the cover to "Col. Hamilton." See n. 3 below. Enclosure
forwarded to Washington on 11 Feb. 1788.

[1] The enclosed paper was the Boston *Mass. Centinel* of 2 Feb. 1788. On 31 Jan., Hancock
had submitted a series of amendments to the Constitution, proposing that the convention
recommend adoption of them as part of its agreement to ratify the Constitution (*Massachusetts*

Debates, pp. 79–81, 224–25). Hancock's conciliatory scheme was evidently the result of a political bargain. In return for his influence in favor of the Constitution, the Massachusetts Federalists promised full support for Hancock in the next gubernatorial election and even held out to him the prospect of the vice-presidency or presidency under the new federal government (Harding, *Contest over Ratification of the Constitution in Massachusetts*, pp. 82–87).
²JM placed an asterisk here and wrote in the left margin, "*Saml. Adams."
³Below the postscript JM wrote, probably to Alexander Hamilton, the following note: "Read the above immediately & send it back by the Bear[er] who will wait for it. I shall be glad of the Newspaper in about an Hour & an half."

From Philip Mazzei

PARIGI, 4. Febbraio 1788.

CARMO: AMICO,

Il mio libro è finalmente stampato, ma il breve tempo non à permesso di far legare il numero d'esemplari che ò destinato di raccomandare alla vostra amicizia per farmegli esitare. Mr. Jefferson essendo di parere che la novità può fàrne spacciare un piccol numero anche non legati, mi prendo la libertà di spedirvene una cassa cuciti, 64 in numero, 57 dei quali per vendersi, e 7 da distribuirsi come segue, cioè 2 per Edmond Randolph a cui scrivo di mandarne uno a Mr. de Rieux,¹ 1. per il Bellini,² 1. per Mr. Wythe, 1. per Mr. Blair, 1. per Mr. Oster, e 1 che spero mi farete la grazia d'accettare voi stesso. Se fosse possibile, sarebbe bene di mandare ad ognuno la sua lettera qui inclusa insieme coi libri. Quella di Mr. Wythe bisognerebbe mandarla per persona sicura, perchè contiene un sigillo che costa parecchie ghinee. Il libro in quarto, in cui questa e le altre lettere sono incluse, appartiene a Edmond Randolph, a cui lo manda l'Autore.

Mr. Jefferson crede che del mio libro se ne possano facilmente spacciare 25 in Boston, 50 in New-York, 50 in Filadelfia, 25 in Virginia, e 25 in Charlestoun; sicchè per il bastimento corriero, che deve partire il 25 di marzo, ve ne manderò altri 100 legati. Perdonate l'incomodo, caro Amico, sul principio che la necessità non à legge.

Mi son pervenute le 2. grate vostre degli 8 e 20 xbre., nella prima delle quali mi davi la speranza di qualche pronta rimessa, che mi togliete nella seconda. Vi rendo grazie d'aver terminato l'affare con Dohrman, come pure della maniera delicata con cui l'avete concluso. In luogo vostro avrei fatto lo stesso. Il rigor di giustizia in certi casi à un'apparenza di crudeltà, che l'anime delicate aborriscono. Le medesime riflessioni le confermerò a bocca a Mr. Dohrman; e dopo d'avergli fatto sentire quanto grato io vi sia del non avergli voi proposto un saldo di conti (al prezzo corrente de'suoi effetti) gli farò vedere, e lo convincerò, che tal condotta non sarebbe stata tanto crudele, quanto fù la sua verso di me, in tempo ch'io l'informai pienamente delle mie dure circostanze, e ch'ei *sapeva* che la sua cambiale non sarebbe stata pagata.

Nella mia precedente dei 21. xbre. v'informai della mia estrema povertà, e del mal fisico che me n'era risultato, oltre il morale che sempre è per me il maggiore. Dall'ultima vostra dei 20 xbre. vedo chiaramente, che non ò luogo di sperare alcun sollievo fino a tanto che il nostro governo federativo sia bene stabilito. Gli altri miei affari in Virginia soffrono per l'istessa causa, benchè non tanto direttamente. Io sono nell'estrama [*sic*] povertà, e non posso aver'ombra di speranza se non segue il detto stabilimento. Voi non ignorate che bramerei di servire in Europa la mia cara patria adottiva, perchè son persuaso che potrei esserle realmente utile, e che i miei amici d'America ne risentirebbero gran consolazione. È chiaro che anche questa remota speranza non può effettuarsi nella presente incerta situazione. Qualunque sia il nuovo sistema, le sue cattive conseguenze devon tardare più che non durerà la mia vita, ed io non ò, nè sono per aver figlj. Ma i posteri, caro e degno Amico mio, sono i figlj miei! Non posso mettere a competenza il mio solo interesse privato con quello di tanti milioni! Come avete voi potuto convenire nella proposta Costituzione di varj articoli, che preparano fulmini sterminatori alla povera libertà? Vi siete voi figurato Washington immortale? Vi siete voi lusingato che potrà esservi sempre un'egual successore? E quando vi fosse, come potrebbe ovviare agl'inconvenienti terribili, che nasceranno dalla cabala dell'Aristocrazia, colla quale l'avete circondato? Spero che non siate infettato della malattia, pur troppo epidemica, della bilancia e dei contrappesi in materia di governo. Livingston à ragione; dovendo ricorrere a un meccanismo, il girarrosto è più analogo senza paragone; o per meglio dire, la chimerica bilancia non lo è niente affatto.[3] Mr. Jefferson spera, che 9. Stati adotteranno la proposta Costituzione, che ciò basterà per metter la cosa in moto, che gli altri pubblicheranno i giusti motivi del loro scisma, e che i 9. per loro proprio vantaggio converranno cogli scismatici per fare le prudenti e necessarie modificazioni.

Se le mie osservazione, al fine del supplemento, vi paiono atte a produrre qualche buono effetto, vi prego di tradurle e farle inserire nelle nostre gazzette.[4] Addio, amico caro, scrivetemi presto, e consolatemi, chè ne ò gran bisogno. Tutto vostro

FILIPPO MAZZEI

CONDENSED TRANSLATION

Mazzei's book is finally printed. He is sending JM sixty-four sewn copies and will send another hundred on the mail vessel scheduled to depart 25 March. Mazzei has received JM's letters of 8 and 20 December, the first of which gave him hope of some immediate remittance and the second of which removed that hope. He thanks JM for concerning himself with the Dohrman business. He is in extreme poverty and sees no hope of relief until a federal government is well established in America. He reminds JM of his offer to serve his adopted country in Europe. Mazzei criticizes the new Constitution as tending toward the destruction of humble liberty. He asks if JM has imagined Washington to be immortal, and whether JM has deluded himself into thinking that there could ever be a successor to equal Washington. Even if there were, how could the terrible difficulties be avoided which would arise from the intrigues of the aristocracy who would surround him? He hopes that JM is not infected by the disease of balance and counterbalance in the governmental structure. Jefferson hopes that nine states will adopt the Constitution but favors some modifications. If JM thinks the observations at the end of the supplement to his book might be of value, Mazzei requests that he translate them and insert them in the newspapers.

RC and enclosure (DLC). For enclosure, see n. 4 below.

[1] Justin Pierre Plumard de Rieux (1756–1824), a native of France, married in 1780 Margarita Martin, whose mother subsequently became Mazzei's wife. He settled in Albemarle County in 1784 and lived in Virginia for the rest of his life (Boyd, *Papers of Jefferson*, VI, 555 n.; *WMQ*, 1st ser., XVII [1908–9], 20).

[2] Charles Bellini, a Tuscan who had come to Virginia in 1774 and four years later was appointed a professor at the College of William and Mary (*PJM*, I, 297 n. 11).

[3] Mazzei was evidently referring to the pamphlet by a "Farmer of New-Jersey," *Observations on Government, Including Some Animadversions on Mr. Adams's Defence of the Constitutions . . . and on Mr. De Lolme's Constitution of England* (New York, 1787). Contemporaries attributed the authorship to Gov. William Livingston of New Jersey, but the "farmer" in fact was John Stevens, later famous as an inventor (Palmer, *Age of the Democratic Revolution*, I, 279–81).

[4] Enclosed in this letter was a Ms of seven pages, written in French but not in Mazzei's hand. It is printed in Garlick, *Philip Mazzei*, pp. 117–20. After revision, it became the introduction to Mazzei's book (ibid., p. 120 n. 56).

From George Washington

MOUNT VERNON Feby. 5th. 1788.

MY DEAR SIR,

I am indebted to you for several of your favors, and thank you for their enclosures. The rumours of War between France and England have subsided; and the poor Patriots of Holland, it seems, are left to fight their own Battles or negotiate—in neither case with any great prospect of Advantage. They must have been deceived, or their conduct has been divided, precip[it]ant, & weak. The former, with some blunders, have, I conceive, been the causes of their misfortunes.[1]

I am sorry to find by yours, and other accts. from Massachusetts, that the decision of its Convention (at the time of their dates) remained problematical. A rejection of the New form by that State will envigorate the opposition, not only in New York, but in all those which are to follow; at the same time that it will afford materials for the Minority in such as have adopted it, to blow the Trumpet of discord more loudly. The acceptance by a *bare* majority, tho' preferable to rejection, is also to be depricated.

It is scarcely possible to form any decided opinion of the *general* sentiment of the people of this State, on this important subject. Many have asked me with anxious sollicitude, if you did not mean to get into the Convention; conceiving it of indispensable necessity. Colo. Mason, who returned home only yesterday, has offered himself, I am told, for the County of Stafford; and his friends add, he can be elected not only there, but for Prince William & Fauquier also. The truth of this I know not. I rarely go from home, and my visitors who for the most part are travellers and strangers, have not the best information.

At the time you suggested for my consideration, the expediency of a communication of my sentiments on the proposed Constitution, to any corrispondent I might have in Massachusetts, it did not occur to me that Genl Lincoln & myself frequently interchanged letters—much less did I expect that a hasty, and indigested extract of one which I had written— intermixed with a variety of other matter to Colo. Chas. Carter, in answer to a letter I had received from him respecting Wolf dogs—Wolves— Sheep—experiments in Farming &ca &ca. &ca.[2]—was then in the press, and would bring these sentiments to public view by means of the extensive circulation I find that extract has had. Altho' I never have concealed, and am perfectly regardless who becomes acquainted with my sentiments on the proposed Constitution, yet nevertheless, as no care had been taken to dress the ideas, nor any reasons assigned in support of my opinion, I felt myself hurt by the publication; and informed my friend the Colonel of it. In answer, he has fully exculpated himself from the *intention*, but his zeal in the cause prompted him to distributt copies, under a prohibition (which was disregarded) that they should not go to the press. As you have seen the rude, or crude extract (as you may please to term it), I will add no more on the subject.[3]

Perceiving that the Fœderalist, under the signature of Publius, is about to be re-published, I would thank you for forwarding to me three or four Copies; one of which to be neatly bound, and inform me of the cost.

Altho' we have not had many, or deep Snows since the commencement of them, yet we have had a very severe Winter; and if the cold of this day is proportionably keen with you, a warm room, & a good fire will be found no bad, or uncomfortable antidote to it.[4] With sentiments of perfect esteem and friendship I am, Dear Sir Yr. Affecte. & Obedt Servt

Go: Washington

RC (MA); FC (DLC: Washington Papers). RC docketed by JM. FC in a clerk's hand. Minor variations between the FC and the RC have not been noted.

¹In the FC the preceding sentences read: "They must have been much deceived, or their conduct has been weak and precipitate, and absurd. The former however I believe is the truth."

²In place of "&ca &ca. &ca." the FC has "and the lord k[n]ows what else."

³On this incident see Freeman, *Washington*, VI, 129–30. The extract submitted for publication was the last paragraph of Washington's letter to Carter of 14 Dec. 1787 (Fitzpatrick, *Writings of Washington*, XXIX, 339–40). It was first printed in the Fredericksburg *Va. Herald*, probably on 27 Dec. 1787, but no copy of that issue has been found. Among the other newspapers that printed the extract were the Baltimore *Md. Journal* of 1 Jan. 1788 and the *Pa. Gazette* of 16 Jan. 1788. Although Freeman (*Washington*, VI, 130 n. 82) noted that the newspaper version of the letter varied "perceptibly" from the text printed in Fitzpatrick, the variations in fact are insignificant. Fitzpatrick printed the letter as copied into Washington's letterbook by a clerk. The text in the newspapers was obviously taken from Carter's copy, which has not been found.

⁴In the FC this sentence reads: "Altho' we have not had many, or deep snows yet we have since the commencemt. of it, had a very severe winter; and if this day, with you, is as much keener than we now feel it, as the difference of lattitude ought to make it you will feel a comfortable fire no bad antidote against cold fingers and Toes."

The Federalist Number 50

[5 February 1788]

It may be contended perhaps, that instead of *occasional* appeals to the people, which are liable to the objections urged against them, *periodical* appeals are the proper and adequate means of *preventing and correcting infractions of the constitution.*

It will be attended to, that in the examination of these expedients, I confine myself to their aptitude for *enforcing* the constitution by keeping the several departments of power within their due bounds, without particularly considering them, as provisions for *altering* the constitution itself. In the first view, appeals to the people at fixed periods, appear to be nearly as ineligible, as appeals on particular occasions as they emerge. If the periods be separated by short intervals, the measures to be reviewed and rectified, will have been of recent date, and will be connected with all the circumstances which tend to viciate and pervert the result of occasional revisions. If the periods be distant from each other, the same remark will be applicable to all recent measures, and in proportion as the remoteness of the others may favor a dispassionate review of them, this advantage is inseparable from inconveniences which seem to counterbalance it. In the first place, a distant prospect of public censure would be a very feeble restraint on power from those excesses, to which it might be urged by the force of present motives. Is it to be imagined, that a legislative assembly, consisting of a hundred or two hundred members, eagerly bent on some favorite object, and breaking through the restraints of the constitution in pursuit of it, would be arrested in their career, by considerations drawn from a censorial revision of their conduct at the future distance of ten, fifteen or twenty years? In the next place, the abuses would often have completed their mischievous effects, before the remedial provision would be applied. And in the last place, where this might not be the case, they would be of long standing, would have taken deep root, and would not easily be extirpated.

The scheme of revising the constitution in order to correct recent breaches of it, as well as for other purposes, has been actually tried in one of the states. One of the objects of the council of censors, which met in Pennsylvania, in 1783 and 1784, was, as we have seen, to enquire "whether the constitution had been violated, and whether the legislative and executive departments had encroached on each other." This important and novel experiment in politics, merits in several points of view, very particular attention. In some of them it may perhaps as a single experiment, made under circumstances somewhat peculiar, be thought to be not absolutely conclusive. But as applied to the case under consideration, it involves some facts which I venture to remark, as a complete and satisfactory illustration of the reasoning which I have employed.

First. It appears from the names of the gentlemen who composed the council, that some at least of its most active and leading members, had also been active and leading characters in the parties which pre-existed in the state.

Second. It appears that the same active and leading members of the council, had been active and influential members of the legislative and executive branches, within the period to be reviewed; and even patrons or opponents of the very measures to be thus brought to the test of the constitution. Two of the members had been vice-presidents of the state, and several others, members of the executive council within the seven preceding years. One of them had been speaker, and a number of others distinguished members of the legislative assembly, within the same period.

Third. Every page of their proceedings witnesses the effect of all these circumstances on the temper of their deliberations. Throughout the continuance of the council, it was split into two fixed and violent parties. The fact is acknowledged and lamented by themselves. Had this not been the case, the face of their proceedings exhibit a proof equally satisfactory. In all questions, however unimportant in themselves, or unconnected with each other, the same names stand invariably contrasted on the opposite columns. Every unbiassed observer, may infer without danger of mistake, and at the same time, without meaning to reflect on either party, or any individuals of either party, that unfortunately *passion*, not *reason*, must have presided over their decisions. When men exercise their reason coolly and freely, on a variety of distinct questions, they inevitably fall into different opinions on some of them. When they are governed by a common passion, their opinions, if they are so to be called, will be the same.

Fourth. It is at least problematical, whether the decisions of this body do not, in several instances, misconstrue the limits prescribed for the legislative and executive departments, instead of reducing and limiting them within their constitutional places.

Fifth. I have never understood that the decisions of the council on constitutional questions, whether rightly or erroneously formed, have had any effect in varying the practice founded on legislative constructions. It even appears, if I mistake not, that in one instance, the cotemporary legislature denied the constructions of the council, and actually prevailed in the contest.

This censorial body, therefore, proves at the same time, by its researches, the existence of the disease; and by its example, the inefficacy of the remedy.[1]

This conclusion cannot be invalidated by alledging that the state in which the experiment was made, was at that crisis, and had been for a long time before, violently heated and distracted by the rage of party. Is it to be presumed, that at any future septennial epoch, the same state will be free from parties? Is it to be presumed that any other state, at the same or any other given period, will be exempt from them? Such an event ought to be neither presumed nor desired; because an extinction of parties necessarily implies either a universal alarm for the public safety, or an absolute extinction of liberty.

Were the precaution taken of excluding from the assemblies elected by the people to revise the preceding administration of the government, all persons who should have been concerned in the government within the given period, the difficulties would not be obviated. The important task would probably devolve on men, who with inferior capacities, would in other respects be little better qualified. Although they might not have been personally concerned in the administration, and therefore not immediately agents in the measures to be examined; they would probably have been involved in the parties connected with these measures, and have been elected under their auspices.

PUBLIUS.

not receive them till after I shall have sealed my letter. They are well chosen, as to the species, for this country. I wish there had been some willow oaks (Quercus Phellos Linnaei) among them, either the plants or acorns, as that tree is much desired here, & absolutely unknown. As the red-birds & opossums are not to be had at New York, I will release you from the trouble of procuring them elesewhere. This trouble, with the incertainty of their coming safe, is more than the importance of the object will justify. You omitted to inclose Prince's catalogue of plants which your letter mentions to have been inclosed. I send herewith two small boxes, one addressed to mr. Drayton to the care of the S. Carola. delegates, with a letter. Will you be so good as to ask those gentlemen to forward the letter & box without delay. The box contains cork acorns, & Sulla, which should arrive at their destination as quick as possible. The other box is addressed to you, & contains, cork acorns, Sulla, and peas. The two first articles to be forwarded to Monticello to Colo. Nicholas Lewis, taking thereout what proportion of them you please for yourself. The peas are brought me from the South of France and are said to be valuable. Considering the season of the year I think it would be best to sow them at New York, and to send the produce on next winter to such persons as you please in Virginia, in order to try whether they are any of them better than what we already have. The Sulla is a species of St. foin which comes from Malta, and is proof against any degree of drought. I have raised it in my garden here, and find it a luxuriant & precious plant. I inclose you the bills of lading for the three boxes of books which ought to have gone last fall, but are only lately gone by the Juno capt Jenkins.[1] Your pedometer is done, & I now wait only for some trusty passenger to take charge of it. I hope there will be one in the March packet. It cost 300. livres. Your watch you will have received by the Ct. de Moustier. With respect to the Mercures de France always forwarded to you for Bannister, I must beg you never to let them go so as to subject him to postage for them.

I am glad to hear that the new constitution is received with favor. I sincerely wish that the 9 first conventions may receive, & the 4. last reject it. The former will secure it finally; while the latter will oblige them to offer a declaration of rights in order to complete the union. We shall thus have all it's good, and cure it's principal defect. You will of course be so good as to continue to mark to me it's progress. I will thank you also for as exact a state as you can procure me of the impression made on the sum of our domestic debt by the sale of lands, & by federal & state exertions in any other manner. I have not yet heard whether the law passed in Virginia for *prohibiting the importation of brandies.*[2] *If it did the late arret here for encouraging our commerce will be repealed.*[3] *The minister will be glad of such a*

474

pretext to pacify the opposition. I do not see that there are at present any strong symptoms of rupture among the Western powers of Europe. Domestic effervescence & the want of money shackle all the movements of this court. Their prevailing sentiments are total distrust of.England, disgust towards the k. of Prussia, jealousy of the two empires, & I presume I may add a willingness to restore the affairs of the Dutch patriots, if it can be done without war.

I will beg the favor of you to send me a copy of the American philosophical transactions, both the 1st. & 2d. volumes, by the first packet and to accept assurances of the sincere esteem with which I am dear Sir your affectionate friend & servant

TH: JEFFERSON

P.S. Among the copies of my Notes to be sent to S. Carolina, be so good as to forward one for mr. Kinlock whom I think I omitted to name in the list.

RC (DLC); FC (DLC: Jefferson Papers). Italicized words are those encoded by Jefferson using the code he sent JM 11 May 1785. RC is decoded interlinearly in an unknown hand, probably that of an early editor. FC includes Jefferson's text *en clair* of the coded passage. Enclosure not found, but see n. 1 below.

[1]For another copy of the enclosed bill of lading, see Limozin to JM, 10 Jan. 1788 and n. 2.
[2]See Dawson to JM, ca. 10 Nov. 1787 and n. 5.
[3]For the English text of the arrêt, dated 29 Dec. 1787, see Boyd, *Papers of Jefferson*, XII, 468–71.

From Rufus King

BOSTON 6 Feb. 1788

MY DEAR SIR

I have the satisfaction to inform you that on the final Question of assinting to & ratifying the constitution our convention divided, and 187. were in the affirmative & 168 in the negative: the majority although small is extremely respectable, and the minority are in good Temper; they have the magnanimity to declare that they will devote their Lives & property to support the Government, and I have no Doubt but the ratification will be very cordially and universally approved through our State. N. Hampshire will undoubtedly decide in favor of the Constitution—their convention met Today. God bless you. Your's &c.

R KING

RC (DLC); Tr (NHi). RC docketed by JM.

The Federalist Number 51

[6 February 1788]

To what expedient then shall we finally resort for maintaining in practice the necessary partition of power among the several departments, as laid down in the constitution? The only answer that can be given is, that as all these exterior provisions are found to be inadequate, the defect must be supplied, by so contriving the interior structure of the government, as that its several constituent parts may, by their mutual relations, be the means of keeping each other in their proper places. Without presuming to undertake a full developement of this important idea, I will hazard a few general observations, which may perhaps place it in a clearer light, and enable us to form a more correct judgment of the principles and structure of the government planned by the convention.

In order to lay a due foundation for that separate and distinct exercise of the different powers of government, which to a certain extent, is admitted on all hands to be essential to the preservation of liberty, it is evident that each department should have a will of its own; and consequently should be so constituted that the members of each should have as little agency as possible in the appointment of the members of the others. Were this principle rigorously adhered to, it would require that all the appointments for the supreme executive, legislative and judiciary magistracies should be drawn from the same fountain of authority, the people, through channels, having no communication whatever with one another. Perhaps such a plan of constructing the several departments would be less difficult in practice than it may in contemplation appear. Some difficulties however, and some additional expence, would attend the execution of it. Some deviations therefore from the principle must be admitted. In the constitution of the judiciary department in particular, it might be inexpedient to insist rigorously on the principle; first, because peculiar qualifications being essential in the members, the primary consideration ought to be to select that mode of choice, which best secures these qualifications; secondly, because the permanent tenure by which the appointments are held in that department, must soon destroy all sense of dependence on the authority conferring them.

It is equally evident that the members of each department should be as little dependent as possible on those of the others, for the emoluments annexed to their offices. Were the executive magistrate, or the judges, not independent of the legislature in this particular, their independence in every other, would be merely nominal.

But the great security against a gradual concentration of the several powers in the same department, consists in giving to those who administer each department, the necessary constitutional means, and personal motives, to resist encroachments of the others. The provision for defence must in this, as in all other cases, be made commensurate to the danger of attack. Ambition must be made to counteract ambition. The interest of the man must be connected with the constitutional rights of the place. It may be a reflection on human nature, that such devices should be necessary to control the abuses of government. But what is government itself but the greatest of all reflections on human nature? If men were angels, no government would be necessary. If angels were to govern men, neither external nor internal controls on government would be necessary. In framing a government which is to be administered by men over men, the great difficulty lies in this: You must first enable the government to control the governed; and in the next place, oblige it to control itself. A dependence on the people is no doubt the primary control on the government; but experience has taught mankind the necessity of auxiliary precautions.

This policy of supplying by opposite and rival interests, the defect of better motives, might be traced through the whole system of human affairs, private as well as public.[1] We see it particularly displayed in all the subordinate distributions of power; where the constant aim is to divide and arrange the several offices in such a manner as that each may be a check on the other; that the private interest of every individual, may be a centinel over the public rights. These inventions of prudence cannot be less requisite in the distribution of the supreme powers of the state.

But it is not possible to give to each department an equal power of self-defence. In republican government the legislative authority necessarily predominates. The remedy for this inconveniency is, to divide the legislature into different branches; and to render them by different modes of election, and different principles of action, as little connected with each other, as the nature of their common functions, and their common dependence on the society, will admit. It may even be necessary to guard against dangerous encroachments by still further precautions. As the weight of the legislative authority requires that it should be thus divided, the weakness of the executive may require, on the other hand, that it should be fortified. An absolute negative, on the legislature, appears at first view to be the natural defence with which the executive magistrate should be armed. But perhaps it would be neither altogether safe, nor alone sufficient. On ordinary occasions, it might not be exerted with the requisite firmness; and on extraordinary occasions, it might be perfidiously abused. May not this defect of an absolute negative be supplied by some qualified connection between this weaker department, and the weaker branch of the stronger department, by which the latter may be led to support the constitutional rights of the former, without being too much detached from the rights of its own department?

If the principles on which these observations are founded be just, as I persuade myself they are, and they be applied as a criterion to the several state constitutions, and to the federal constitution, it will be found, that if the latter does not perfectly correspond with them, the former are infinitely less able to bear such a test.[2]

There are moreover two considerations particularly applicable to the federal system of America, which place that system in a very interesting point of view.

First. In a single republic, all the power surrendered by the people, is submitted to the administration of a single government; and the usurpations are guarded against by a division of the government into distinct and separate departments. In the compound republic of America, the power surrendered by the people, is first divided between two distinct governments, and then the portion allotted to each, subdivided among distinct and separate departments. Hence a double security arises to the rights of the people. The different governments will control each other; at the same time that each will be controled by itself.

Second. It is of great importance in a republic, not only to guard the society against the oppression of its rulers; but to guard one part of the society against the injustice of the other part. Different interests necessarily exist in different classes of citizens. If a majority be united by a common interest, the rights of the minority will be insecure. There are but two methods of providing against this evil: The one by creating a will in the community independent of the majority, that is, of the society itself; the other by comprehending in the society so many separate descriptions of citizens, as will render an unjust combination of a majority of the whole very improbable, if not impracticable. The first method prevails in all governments possessing an hereditary or self-appointed authority. This at best is but a precarious security; because a power independent of the society may as well espouse the unjust views of the major, as the rightful interests of the minor party, and may possibly be turned against both parties. The second method will be exemplified in the federal republic of the United States. Whilst all authority in it will be derived from, and dependent on the society, the society itself will be broken into so many parts, interests and classes of citizens, that the rights of individuals or of the minority, will be in little danger from interested combinations of the majority. In a free government, the security for civil rights must be the

478

same as that for religious rights. It consists in the one case in the multiplicity of interests, and in the other, in the multiplicity of sects. The degree of
security in both cases will depend on the number of interests and sects;
and this may be presumed to depend on the extent of country and number
of people comprehended under the same government. This view of the
subject must particularly recommend a proper federal system to all the
sincere and considerate friends of republican government: Since it shews
that in exact proportion as the territory of the union may be formed into
more circumscribed confederacies or states, oppressive combinations of a
majority will be facilitated, the best security under the republican form,
for the rights of every class of citizens, will be diminished; and consequently, the stability and independence of some member of the government, the only other security must be proportionally increased. Justice is
the end of government. It is the end of civil society. It ever has been, and
ever will be pursued, until it be obtained, or until liberty be lost in the
pursuit. In a society under the forms of which the stronger faction can
readily unite and oppress the weaker, anarchy may as truly be said to
reign, as in a state of nature where the weaker individual is not secured
against the violence of the stronger: And as in the latter state even the
stronger individuals are prompted by the uncertainty of their condition, to
submit to a government which may protect the weak as well as themselves:
So in the former state, will the more powerful factions or parties be
gradually induced by a like motive, to wish for a government which will
protect all parties, the weaker as well as the more powerful. It can be little
doubted, that if the state of Rhode-Island was separated from the confederacy, and left to itself, the insecurity of rights under the popular form of
government within such narrow limits, would be displayed by such reiterated oppressions of factious majorities, that some power altogether independent of the people would soon be called for by the voice of the very
factions whose misrule had proved the necessity of it. In the extended
republic of the United States, and among the great variety of interests,
parties and sects which it embraces, a coalition of a majority of the whole
society could seldom take place upon any other principles than those of
justice and the general good: Whilst there being thus less danger to a
minor from the will of the major party, there must be less pretext also, to
provide for the security of the former, by introducing into the government
a will not dependent on the latter; or in other words, a will independent of
the society itself. It is no less certain than it is important, notwithstanding
the contrary opinions which have been entertained, that the larger the
society, provided it lie within a practicable sphere, the more duly capable
it will be of self government. And happily for the *republican cause*, the

which is connected with the US. I mean the revenue act & the resolutions respecting the cession. In the former as much was advancd to the US. as cod. be obtain'd. In the latter more moderation was observ'd than at first appearances promis'd. It was perhaps brot. forward to serve other purposes, (I mean in the extent to wh. the Chairman advocated it) but it was put in its present form without debate & by his own consent, perhaps to avoid it. The rectitude of the measure depends on the want of it in some of the Comrs. Unless the objection agnst, at least one, is good, it cannot be defended. But you have the whole of the proceedings before you.[1]

This new Constitution still engages the minds of people with some zeal among the partizans on either side. It is impossible to say which preponderates. The northern part of the State is more generally for it than the southern. In this county (except in the town) they are agnst. it I believe universally. I have however this from report only, having not been from home. My late Colleague[2] is decidedly so. Mr. Page is for it & forms an exception to the above. It is said here that Georgia has adopted it, N.H.[3] also. The object in the postponment of the meeting of our Convention to so late a day was to furnish an evidence of the disposition of the other States to that body when it shod. be assembled. If they or many of them were agnst. it our State might mediate between contending parties & lead the way to an union more palitable to all. If all were for it let the knowledge of that circumstance have its weight in their deliberations. This I believe was the principle on wh. that measure was adopted, at least those whose sentiments I knew express'd it to be theirs. We expect you in soon & shall be happy to see you here. Sincerely I am yr. fnd. & servt.

JAS. MONROE

RC (DLC).

[1]See Turberville to JM, 8 Jan. 1788 and n. 1.
[2]John Dawson of Spotsylvania County.
[3]At a later time someone expanded the abbreviation to read "New Hampshire." In fact, New Hampshire did not ratify the Constitution until 21 June 1788.

To George Washington

NEW YORK Feby. 8—88

DEAR SIR

The prospect in Massts. seems to brighten, if I view in the true light the following representation of it. "This day, (Jany. 30) for the first our President Mr. Handcock took his seat in Convention, and we shall probably terminate our business on saturday or tuesday next. I can not predict the issue, but our hopes are increasing. If Mr. Hancock does not disappoint our present expectations, our wishes will be gratified."[1] Several reflections are suggested by this paragraph which countenance a favorable inference from it. I hope from the rapid advance towards a conclusion of the business, that even the project of recommendatory alterations has been dispensed with.

The form of the ratification of Georgia is contained in one of the papers herewith inclosed.[2] Every information from S. Carolina continues to be favorable. I have seen a letter from N. Carolina of pretty late date which admits that a very formidable opposition exists, but leans towards a fœderal result in that State. As far as I can discover, the state of the question in N Carolina, is pretty analagous to that in Virginia. The body of the people are better disposed than some of a superior order. The Resolutions of New York for calling a Convention, appear by the paper to have passed by a majority of two only in the House of Assembly. I am told this proceeded in some degree from an injudicious form in which the business was conducted; and which threw some of the fœderalists into the opposition.[3]

I am just informed by a gentleman who has seen another letter from Boston of the same date with mine, that the plan of recommendatory alterations has not been abandoned, but that they will be put into a harmless form, and will be the means of saving the Constitution from all risk in Massts. With the highest respect & attachment I remain Dear Sir, Your Affe hble servt.

Js. Madison Jr.

RC (DLC: Washington Papers); Tr (DLC). RC docketed by Washington. Enclosures not found.

[1] Rufus King to JM, 30 Jan. 1788.
[2] N.Y. *Daily Advertiser*, 5 Feb. 1788.
[3] The vote of the New York House of Assembly on resolutions for calling a convention to consider the proposed Constitution was reported in the *N.Y. Journal* of 7 Feb. 1788. See also De Pauw, *The Eleventh Pillar*, pp. 87–89.

The Federalist Number 52

[8 February 1788]

From the more general enquiries pursued in the four last papers, I pass on to a more particular examination of the several parts of the government. I shall begin with the house of representatives.

The first view to be taken of this part of the government, relates to the qualifications of the electors and the elected. Those of the former are to be the same with those of the electors of the most numerous branch of the state legislatures. The definition of the right of suffrage is very justly regarded as a fundamental article of republican government. It was incumbent on the convention, therefore, to define and establish this right in the constitution. To have left it open for the occasional regulation of the congress, would have been improper for the reason just mentioned. To have submitted it to the legislative discretion of the states, would have been improper for the same reason; and for the additional reason, that it would have rendered too dependent on the state governments, that branch of the federal government, which ought to be dependent on the people alone. To have reduced the different qualifications in the different states to one uniform rule, would probably have been as dissatisfactory to some of the states, as it would have been difficult to the convention. The provision made by the convention appears therefore, to be the best that lay within their option. It must be satisfactory to every state; because it is conformable to the standard already established, or which may be established by the state itself. It will be safe to the United States; because, being fixed by the state constitutions, it is not alterable by the state governments, and it cannot be feared that the people of the states will alter this part of their constitutions, in such a manner as to abridge the rights secured to them by the federal constitution.

The qualifications of the elected being less carefully and properly defined by the state constitutions, and being at the same time more susceptible of uniformity, have been very properly considered and regulated by the convention. A representative of the United States must be of the age of twenty-five years; must have been seven years a citizen of the United States; must at the time of his election, be an inhabitant of the state he is to represent, and during the time of his service must be in no office under the United States. Under these reasonable limitations, the door of this part of the federal government is open to merit of every description, whether native or adoptive, whether young or old, and without regard to poverty or wealth, or to any particular profession of religious faith.

The term for which the representatives are to be elected, falls under a second view which may be taken of this branch. In order to decide on the propriety of this article, two questions must be considered; first, whether biennial elections will, in this case, be safe; secondly, whether they be necessary or useful.

First. As it is essential to liberty, that the government in general should have a common interest with the people; so it is particularly essential that the branch of it under consideration should have an immediate dependence on, and an intimate sympathy with the people. Frequent elections are unquestionably the only policy by which this dependence and sympathy can be effectually secured. But what particular degree of frequency may be absolutely necessary for the purpose, does not appear to be susceptible of any precise calculation: And must depend on a variety of circumstances with which it may be connected. Let us consult experience, the guide that ought always to be followed, whenever it can be found.

The scheme of representation, as a substitute for a meeting of the citizens in person, being at most but very imperfectly known to antient polity; it is in more modern times only, that we are to expect instructive examples. And even here, in order to avoid a research too vague and diffusive, it will be proper to confine ourselves to the few examples which are best known, and which bear the greatest analogy to our particular case. The first to which this character ought to be applied, is the house of commons in Great-Britain. The history of this branch of the English constitution, anterior to the date of Magna Charta, is too obscure to yield instruction. The very existence of it has been made a question among political antiquaries. The earliest records of subsequent date prove, that parliaments were to *sit* only, every year; not that they were to be *elected* every year. And even these annual sessions were left so much at the discretion of the monarch, that under various pretexts, very long and dangerous intermissions were often contrived by royal ambition. To remedy this grievance, it was provided by a statute in the reign of Charles IId. that the intermissions, should not be protracted beyond a period of three years. On the accession of William IIId, when a revolution took place in the government, the subject was still more seriously resumed, and it was declared to be among the fundamental rights of the people, that parliaments ought to be held *frequently*. By another statute which passed a few years later in the same reign, the term "frequently" which had alluded to the triennial period settled in the time of Charles IId. is reduced to a precise meaning, it being expressly enacted that a new parliament shall be called within three years after the determination of the former. The last change from three to seven years is well known to have been introduced pretty early in the present century, under an alarm for the Hanoverian succession. From these facts it appears, that the greatest frequency of elections which has been deemed necessary in that kingdom, for binding the representatives to their constituents, does not exceed a triennial return of them. And if we may argue from the degree of liberty retained even under septennial elections, and all the other vicious ingredients in the parliamentary constitution, we cannot doubt that a reduction of the period from seven to three years, with the other necessary reforms, would so far extend the influence of the people over their representatives as to satisfy us, that biennial elections under the federal system, cannot possibly be dangerous to the requisite dependence of the house of representatives on their constituents.

Elections in Ireland, till of late, were regulated entirely by the discretion of the crown, and were seldom repeated except on the accession of a new prince, or some other contingent event. The parliament which commenced with George IId. was continued throughout his whole reign, a period of about thirty-five years. The only dependence of the representatives on the people, consisted in the right of the latter to supply occasional vacancies, by the election of new members, and in the chance of some event which might produce a general new election. The ability also of the Irish parliament to maintain the rights of their constituents, so far as the disposition might exist, was extremely shackled by the control of the crown over the subjects of their deliberation. Of late these shackles, if I mistake not, have been broken; and octennial parliaments have besides been established.[1] What effect may be produced by this partial reform, must be left to further experience. The example of Ireland, from this view of it, can throw but little light on the subject. As far as we can draw any conclusion from it, it must be, that if the people of that country have been able, under all these disadvantages, to retain any liberty whatever, the advantage of biennial elections would secure to them every degree of liberty which might depend on a due connection between their representatives and themselves.

Let us bring our enquiries nearer home. The example of these states when British colonies, claims particular attention; at the same time that it is so well known, as to require little to be said on it. The principle of representation, in one branch of the legislature at least, was established in all of them. But the periods of election were different. They varied from one to seven years. Have we any reason to infer from the spirit and conduct of the representatives of the people, prior to the revolution, that biennial elections would have been dangerous to the public liberties? The spirit which every where displayed itself at the commencement of the struggle; and which vanquished the obstacles to independence, is the best of proofs that a sufficient portion of liberty had been every where enjoyed to inspire both a sense of its worth, and a zeal for its proper enlargement. This remark holds good as well with regard to the then colonies, whose elections were least frequent, as to those whose elections were most frequent. Virginia was the colony which stood first in resisting the parliamentary usurpations of Great-Britain; it was the first also in espousing by public act, the resolution of independence. In Virginia, nevertheless, if I have not been misinformed, elections under the former government were septennial.[2] This particular example is brought into view, not as a proof of any peculiar merit, for the priority in those instances, was probably accidental; and still less of any advantage in *septennial* elections, for when compared with a greater frequency they are inadmissible; but merely as a proof, and I conceive it to be a very substantial proof, that the liberties of the people can be in no danger from *biennial* elections.

The conclusion resulting from these examples will be not a little strengthened by recollecting three circumstances. The first is, that the federal legislature will possess a part only of that supreme legislative authority which is vested completely in the British parliament, and which, with a few exceptions, was exercised by the colonial assemblies and the Irish legislature. It is a received and well founded maxim, that, where no other circumstances affect the case, the greater the power is, the shorter ought to be its duration; and conversely, the smaller the power, the more safely may its duration be protracted. In the second place, it has, on another occasion, been shewn that the federal legislature will not only be restrained by its dependence on the people, as other legislative bodies are; but that it will be moreover watched and controled by the several collateral legislatures, which other legislative bodies are not. And in the third place, no comparison can be made between the means that will be possessed by the more permanent branches of the federal government for seducing, if they should be disposed to seduce, the house of representatives from their duty to the people; and the means of influence over the popular branch, possessed by the other branches of the governments above cited. With less power therefore to abuse, the federal representatives can be less tempted on one side, and will be doubly watched on the other.

PUBLIUS.

McLean, II, 122–28.

[1] The "shackles" on the Irish Parliament had been removed with repeal of Poynings' Act in 1782. The 1494 act had "provided that no Parliament should be held in Ireland without the sanction of the King and Council, who should also be able to disallow statutes passed by the Irish Parliament" (Norman Wilding and Philip Laundy, *An Encyclopaedia of Parliament* [London, 1958], pp. 294–96).

[2] The basic election law of colonial Virginia during the eighteenth century was the act of 1705, which contained no requirement for septennial elections (Hening, *Statutes*, III, 236–46). In 1762 the General Assembly passed a new act requiring meetings of the assembly at least once every three years and limiting the duration of the assembly to seven years. This act apparently did not become law, for the home government seems to have withheld approval (ibid., VII, 517–30; Charles S. Sydnor, *Gentlemen Freeholders: Political Practices in Washington's*

Virginia [Chapel Hill, 1952], p. 147; Lucille B. Griffith, *The Virginia House of Burgesses,*
1750–1774 [rev. ed.; University, Ala., 1970], pp. 48–51).

From the Reverend James Madison

WILLIAMSBG Feby. 9. 1788.

I should, my dear Friend, have acknowledged the Favr of your last,
long before this, had my Answer been as little delayed, as the Satisfaction
reced. from it, was sincere: but as I always write to you, rather to get your
Observations upon political Subjects, than for the Sake of communicating
my own, I have been unwilling to impose that Burthen too frequently
upon you. Your Answer, tended greatly to satisfy some of my Doubts—
whilst those valuable Papers (the Federalist) wch. are generally attributed
to you, have well nigh worked a Conversion. Whoever may be the Author
of them, they are certainly well written, as far at least as I have seen them,
& well calculated to promote the great Object in View. They must be read
with much Pleasure & Advantage by every one who wishes to examine the
Subject with Candour.

But I fear, a Question of some Importance still remains, even admitting
that the Govt. proposed, would, if adopted & *conformed* to, be productive
of the Advantages expected. Is it, in reality practicable? You will say,
Nothing but Experience can solve such a Question; and that, if it be the
best, it should at all Events be tried—I agree with you—But we may still
reflect upon the Consequences which will probably attend the Adoption
of it. It's Execution, or it's Operation requires Sacrifices, wch. I suspect
our State Legislatures, & that of Virga. in particular, will never be willing
to make. For when has the Legislature of this State failed, evincing, as the
Oppy. presented itself, Principles directly the reverse of those wch. the
proposed Govt. requires. It's Conduct, during the last Session, with Respect to the Treaty, (notwithstanding the plain & sensible Address from
Congress upon that Subject, & notwithstanding the Impropriety of an
Interference must occur, one wd think, to every Man of Common Sense, I
do not say to those the least versed in the Laws of Nations) too plainly
shews a Degree of antifederal Spirit, wch. will not easily be assimilated to
the new Govt. Other Instances of the same Nature might easily be given
as Proofs of the real Existence of this Spirit. The Love of Power is too
great, the supposed Importance of an independent Legislator is too flattering to most, to admit of the least voluntary Diminution. Nor is it improbable, but that the same Spirit exists in most of the other States, because it

487

originates from Principles common to Amns.—Viz—the highest Idea of the independent Sovereignty of their own States—& at the same Time, the Desire of enjoying all the Advantages of Govt. at the least possible Expence to Natural Liberty. Whether the new Govt. can, in it's Operation, controul suffly. this Spirit, you are the best Judge. But that no Govt. can be durable wch. is not perfectly conformable to the Genius of the People, unless it be supported by Force, is plain, and whether this under Consideration will not meet with such Opposition from the Reaction or Jealousy of the State Legislatures, & from the Parties it will have to struggle with, in its very Infancy—as to render it impracticable, or of short Duration—is perhaps a Problem not unworthy of the Attention of a Philosopher. The Imperium in imperio will be the fruitful Source of a thousand jarring Principles, wch. will make the new Machine, notwithstanding all the Oil you can give it, to go heavily along.

Whether Virga. will adopt the Plan, if she be not in some Measure compelled by the previous Adoption of the other States, is considered as questionable, especially unless there be tack'd to it, some Clause of Amendment. How the Majority may be—is hard or impossible to determine. The opposite Parties however, greatly to their Credit, have hitherto observed the Line of candid Discussion. None of those acrimonious Principles have yet appeared wch. generally agitate a People, when Questions of such Importance create Divisions. It is hoped by all, that you will be in the Convention. The Atty Gen.[1] will represent this Town.

We did not receive the Packet you were so kind as to forward till about a Fortnight past—but it came at last, safe thro' the Hands of the Govr. Be pleased to remember me [to] Mr Griffin & Lady—& beleive me to be, my dear Col. Yr. truely Affe Friend

J MADISON

RC (DLC). Docketed by JM.
[1]James Innes.

The Federalist Number 53

[9 February 1788]

I shall here perhaps be reminded of a current observation, "that where annual elections end, tyranny begins." If it be true, as has often been remarked, that sayings which become proverbial, are generally founded in reason, it is not less true that when once established, they are often applied to cases to which the reason of them does not extend. I need not look for a proof beyond the case before us. What is the reason on which this proverbial observation is founded? No man will subject himself to the ridicule of pretending that any natural connection subsists between the sun or the seasons, and the period within which human virtue can bear the temptations of power. Happily for mankind, liberty is not in this respect confined to any single point of time; but lies within extremes, which afford sufficient latitude for all the variations which may be required by the various situations and circumstances of civil society. The election of magistrates might be, if it were found expedient, as in some instances it actually has been, daily, weekly, or monthly, as well as annual; and if circumstances may require a deviation from the rule on one side, why not also on the other side? Turning our attention to the periods established among ourselves, for the election of the most numerous branches of the state legislatures, we find them by no means coinciding any more in this instance, than in the elections of other civil magistrates. In Connecticut and Rhode-Island, the periods are half-yearly. In the other states, South-Carolina excepted, they are annual. In South-Carolina, they are biennial; as is proposed in the federal government. Here is a difference, as four to one, between the longest and the shortest periods; and yet it would be not easy to shew that Connecticut or Rhode-Island is better governed, or enjoys a greater share of rational liberty than South-Carolina; or that either the one or the other of these states are distinguished in these respects, and by these causes, from the states whose elections are different from both.

In searching for the grounds of this doctrine, I can discover but one, and that is wholly inapplicable to our case. The important distinction so well understood in America between a constitution established by the people, and unalterable by the government; and a law established by the government, and alterable by the government, seems to have been little understood and less observed in any other country. Wherever the supreme power of legislation has resided, has been supposed to reside also, a full power to change the form of the government. Even in Great Britain, where the principles of political and civil liberty have been most discussed, and where we hear most of the rights of the constitution, it is maintained that the authority of the parliament is transcendent and uncontrolable, as well with regard to the constitution, as the ordinary objects of legislative provision. They have accordingly, in several instances, actually changed, by legislative acts, some of the most fundamental articles of the government. They have in particular, on several occasions, changed the period of election; and on the last occasion, not only introduced septennial, in place of triennial elections; but by the same act continued themselves in place four years beyond the term for which they were elected by the people. An attention to these dangerous practices has produced a very natural alarm in the votaries of free government, of which frequency of elections is the corner stone; and has led them to seek for some security to liberty against the danger to which it is exposed. Where no constitution paramount to the government, either existed or could be obtained, no constitutional security similar to that established in the United States, was to be attempted. Some other security therefore was to be sought for; and what better security would the case admit, than that of selecting and appealing to some simple and familiar portion of time, as a standard for measuring the danger of innovations, for fixing the national sentiment, and for uniting the patriotic exertions. The most simple and familiar portion of time, applicable to the subject, was that of a year; and hence the doctrine has been inculcated by a laudable zeal to erect some barrier against the gradual innovations of an unlimited government, that the advance towards tyranny was to be calculated by the distance of departure from the fixed point of annual elections. But what necessity can there be of applying this expedient to a government, limited as the federal government will be, by the authority of a paramount constitution? Or who will pretend that the liberties of the people of America will not be more secure under biennial elections, unalterably fixed by such a constitution, than those of any other nation would be, where elections were annual or even more frequent, but subject to alterations by the ordinary power of the government?

The second question stated is, whether biennial elections be necessary or useful? The propriety of answering this question in the affirmative will appear from several very obvious considerations.

No man can be a competent legislator who does not add to an upright intention and a sound judgment, a certain degree of knowledge of the subjects on which he is to legislate. A part of this knowledge may be acquired by means of information which lie within the compass of men in private as well as public stations. Another part can only be attained, or at least thoroughly attained, by actual experience in the station which requires the use of it. The period of service ought therefore in all such cases to bear some proportion to the extent of practical knowledge, requisite to the due performance of the service. The period of legislative service established in most of the states for the more numerous branch is, as we have seen, one year. The question then may be put into this simple form; does the period of two years bear no greater proportion to the knowledge requisite for federal legislation, than one year does to the knowledge requisite for state legislation? The very statement of the question in this form, suggests the answer that ought to be given to it.

In a single state, the requisite knowledge relates to the existing laws which are uniform throughout the state, and with which all the citizens are more or less conversant; and to the general affairs of the state, which lie within a small compass, are not very diversified and occupy much of the attention and conversation of every class of people. The great theatre of the United States presents a very different scene. The laws are so far from being uniform, that they vary in every state; whilst the public affairs of the union are spread throughout a very extensive region, and are extremely diversified by the local affairs connected with them, and can with difficulty be correctly learnt in any other place, than in the central councils, to which a knowledge of them will be brought by the representatives of every part of the empire. Yet some knowledge of the affairs, and even of the laws of all the states, ought to be possessed by the members from each of the states. How can foreign trade be properly regulated by uniform laws, without some acquaintance with the commerce, the ports, the usages, and the regulations of the different states? How can the trade between the different states be duly regulated without some knowledge of their relative situations in these and other points? How can taxes be judiciously imposed, and effectually collected, if they be not accommodated to the different laws and local circumstances relating to these objects in the different states? How can uniform regulations for the militia be duly provided without a similar knowledge of some internal circumstances by which the states are distinguished from each other? These are the principal objects of federal legislation, and suggest most forceably, the extensive information which the representatives ought to acquire. The other inferior objects will require a proportional degree of information with regard to them.

It is true that all these difficulties will by degrees be very much diminished. The most laborious task will be the proper inauguration of the government, and the primeval formation of a federal code. Improvements on the first draught will every year become both easier and fewer. Past transactions of the government will be a ready and accurate source of information to new members. The affairs of the union will become more and more objects of curiosity and conversation among the citizens at large. And the increased intercourse among those of different states will contribute not a little to diffuse a mutual knowledge of their affairs, as this again will contribute to a general assimilation of their manners and laws. But with all these abatements the business of federal legislation must continue so far to exceed both in novelty and difficulty the legislative business of a single state, as to justify the longer period of service assigned to those who are to transact it.

A branch of knowledge which belongs to the acquirements of a federal representative, and which has not been mentioned, is that of foreign affairs. In regulating our own commerce, he ought to be not only acquainted with the treaties between the United States and other nations, but also with the commercial policy and laws of other nations. He ought not be altogether ignorant of the law of nations, for that as far as it is a proper object of municipal legislation is submitted to the federal government. And although the house of representatives is not immediately to participate in foreign negociations and arrangements, yet from the necessary connection between the several branches of public affairs, those particular branches will frequently deserve attention in the ordinary course of legislation, and will sometimes demand particular legislative sanction and cooperation. Some portion of this knowledge may no doubt be acquired in a man's closet; but some of it also can only be derived from the public sources of information; and all of it will be acquired to best effect by a practical attention to the subject during the period of actual service in the legislature.

There are other considerations of less importance perhaps, but which are not unworthy of notice. The distance which many of the representatives will be obliged to travel, and the arrangements rendered necessary by that circumstance, might be much more serious objections with fit men to this service if limited to a single year, than if extended to two years. No argument can be drawn on this subject from the case of the delegates to the existing congress. They are elected annually it is true; but their re-election is considered by the legislative assemblies almost as a matter of course. The election of the representatives by the people would not be governed by the same principle.

A few of the members, as happens in all such assemblies, will possess superior talents; will, by frequent re-elections, become members of long standing; will be thoroughly masters of the public business, and perhaps not unwilling to avail themselves of those advantages. The greater the proportion of new members, and the less the information of the bulk of the members, the more apt will they be to fall into the snares that may be laid for them. This remark is no less applicable to the relation which will subsist between the house of representatives and the senate.

It is an inconvenience mingled with the advantages of our frequent elections, even in single states, where they are large and hold but one legislative session in the year, that spurious elections cannot be investigated and annulled in time for the decision to have its due effect. If a return can be obtained, no matter by what unlawful means, the irregular member, who takes his seat of course, is sure of holding it a sufficient time to answer his purposes. Hence a very pernicious encouragement is given to the use of unlawful means for obtaining irregular returns. Were elections for the federal legislature to be annual, this practice might become a very serious abuse; particularly in the more distant states. Each house is, as it necessarily must be, the judge of the elections, qualifications and returns of its members, and whatever improvements may be suggested by experience for simplifying and accelerating the process in disputed cases, so great a portion of a year would unavoidably elapse, before an illegitimate member could be dispossessed of his seat, that the prospect of such an event would be little check to unfair and illicit means of obtaining a seat.

All these considerations taken together warrant us in affirming that biennial elections will be as useful to the affairs of the public, as we have seen that they will be safe to the liberties of the people.

PUBLIUS.

McLean, II, 128–35.

From Edward Carrington

MANCHESTER Feby. 10th: 1788

MY DEAR SIR,

Since my last from Richmond I have made a circuit, through Cumberland, Powhatan & Chesterfield, and taking Petersburg in my way arrived here last ev'ning. The state of the ice is such as renders the passage of the River unsafe. A Canoe with difficulty makes its way through the Falls and by that means my letters from the post Office have today got to me. Amongst them I am favoured with yours of the 11th. 15th. & 25 Ult.[1] inclosing sundry papers & letters for which be pleased to accept my most grateful thanks.

My Route has been pretty much within the Neighbourhood of Mr. Henry, and I find his politics to have been so industriously propagated, that the people are much disposed to be his blind followers. As an evidence of it the demagogues in the opposition suppose that their popularity is increased in proportion to the loudness of their clamours, whilst the Freinds to the constitution thinks it prudent to suppress their opinions, or at least to advance them with Caution. Without consulting the extent of my influence, or the dangers of facing the Torrent, I have thought it my

493

duty to make an unequivocal declaration of my sentiments, and if my efforts can work a change in even a single man, you may rely upon that change being made. My drift will be, principally, to turn the elections upon Men of discernment and to bring about instructions upon the point of preserving the Union, which must, at a certain stage, separate the members from Mr. Henry. I can not find that he has even once specified the amendments he would have in the project, it is therefore fairly to be concluded, that his views are a dismemberment of the Union, & I do verily believe this to be the case. I have seen Mr. Ronald—his opinions are extremely mysterious, his objections are made in terms that would be taken for absolute in all events, yet he is alarmed at the probable extent of Mr. Henries views, & professes a dertermination to do nothing which may even endanger the Union.[2] Judge Fleming is a Candidate for Powhatan, and is earnestly for amendments, but assures me he thinks the Union ought in no degree to be hazarded. He is one of the Characters whom I am for trusting in the convention.[3] The danger there, is from weak Men, whatever may be the professions of such, before they assemble, there is no accounting for the effects which Mr. Henries address and Rhetoric may have upon them afterwards. In Chesterfield Tucker & Baker are Candidates, and both against the constitution.[4] The former is for going equal lengths with Mr. H—— but with different views. He is unfortunately one of those who overrate the importance of Virga. and think she may dictate to the whole union. It happens that some of the most popular Men in the County are against both these Gentlemen in opinion & will oppose their election unless they alter their sentiments. From the more southern Counties I have as yet received no satisfactory information. Of this however I am pretty certain, that the doctrine of amendments has taken such strong ground, that the direct adoption of the Constitution cannot be well expected should less than Nine States have adopted when our Convention comes to set. Ideas of the necessity of preserving the Union are however so prevailent, that I think Mr. H—— will be able [to] draw but a small proportion of a discerning convention in opposition to that Number.

Your intelligence from Massachusetts is truly alarming because she is one of the Nine whose adoption can be counted upon by June. Indeed she is so important that even against Nine she & Virga. would be able, if not to prevent the effects of the Government altogether, to hold it in suspence longer than the State of our affairs can well admit of. I am anxcious to know the result in Massachusetts for on her every thing seems to depend. As to N. York her uniform opposition to every federal interest, for several years, gives us every reason to expect her dissent even to the calling a Convention. The letter of her dissenting deputies is perfectly in conformity with the views of their Mission.[5] Should reason and Common sense have fair play in our Convention the dissentions amongst the opponents in different quarters must operate as the strongest arguments that can be brought in support of the project which has received the unanimous vote of a large & respectable Assembly.

I have lately seen a Gentleman who removed from my Neighbourhood to N. Carolina and is intelligent. He came directly from the Assembly. He says the postponement of the convention in that State by no means indicates a disposition to follow the politics of Virga. On the contrary there is a decided opinion in favor of the Constitution. As an evidence of it, Willy Jones an opponent declines going into the Convention seeing that his opposition will be unavailing, and Allan Jones who is of the contrary party is to be a Member. Davie—Williamson—& Johnson,[6] all for the Constitution.

I shall do myself the pleasure to communicate to you from time to time the intelligence which events shall afford, and will thank you for such as may arise in your quarter. Be good enough to Present me in the most affectionate terms to the President and your other Worthy Colleague— also to Irvine & Reade, & beleive me to be with great sincerity Yr. Frd. &c.

ED. CARRINGTON

RC (DLC).

[1] Letters not found.

[2] William Ronald represented Powhatan County at the convention of 1788, where he voted in favor of ratification of the Constitution (Grigsby, *Virginia Convention of 1788*, I, 345 n. 263; II, 365).

[3] Judge William Fleming of the General Court was an unsuccessful candidate for the convention. The other delegate from Powhatan was Thomas Turpin, Jr. (ibid., II, 365). Judge Fleming should not be confused with Col. William Fleming of Botetourt County, who was elected to serve in the convention of 1788 (ibid., II, 54 n. 41).

[4] St. George Tucker and Jerman Baker were also unsuccessful candidates. Chesterfield County was represented by David Patteson and Stephen Pankey, Jr. (ibid., II, 364).

[5] The letter from Robert Yates and John Lansing to Governor Clinton, dated 21 Dec. 1787, was first published in the N.Y. *Daily Advertiser* of 14 Jan. 1788 (reprinted in Farrand, *Records*, III, 244–47).

[6] Samuel Johnston.

From Daniel Carroll

ROCK CREEK NEAR GEORGE TOWN feby 10th. 88

DEAR SIR

On my Brother's returning from N York he inform'd me, that you had left that City for Pha, in yr. way to Virga. I was at Annapolis, and had just then wrote you the proceedings in Assembly respecting the federal Constitution. Not knowing how to forward it to you with safety, must account for my Silence, untill this moment when I am inform'd by a Letter from my Brother, that you are in N. York; Indeed it is cheifly to account for this Silence, that I take up my pen. My situation, and the severity of the weather, have secluded me allmost from the World, since my return from Annapolis. It is therefore not in my power to give you any information to be depended on; I can only say with some degree of proba-bility, that the plan of the Antifedls. in this State, does not extend so far, as to obtain a rejection of the propos'd Constitun: by our Convention on its meeting; their force will probably be exerted to adjourn untill the Conven-tion of Virginia has decided. Was I to venture an opinion on this occasion, it is that they will not succeed. If New York Assembly appoint a Conven-tion, and Massachusetts have adopted the Constitution there will be less doubt. Some of the publications of the Antifederalists give strong proofs of a great degree of depravity prevailing, & Some things in a few of the federal publications respecting the Conduct of Individuals, had in my opinion better have been omitted.

Alltho' you cannot at present expect any material information from me respecting this State, I will not omit giving it when in my power. The time approaches when the parties will muster their forces. I hear nothing to be depended on respecting NC. SC. & Ga. You can afford me the most certain intelligence, & I beg it of you, not only as to the probable issue, but when their Conventions are to meet. It will allways give me much pleasure to hear from yself that you are well, & to find that you remember, Dear Sr. yr. afftn Hble. Servt &ca

DANL. CARROLL

PS. I tryd to make out something by our Chypher—but cannot—can you set me a few words, with [. . .]?

RC (DLC). Docketed by JM. Part of the last line of the postscript is cut off, thus making a few words illegible.

From John Fitch

New York the 10 February 1788

HONOURED SIR

My situation at present is tremendously allarming, it would be much less so, if I knew that I should sicken and die, than for me to return and inform the Company[1] I must be dependant on them for my sustinance, so

Vile a way of living, I heartily dispise. And was I under no obligations to any one, I would not solicit Courts for favours, was my claims ever so just, did I think it would be granted with reluctance. I would retire to the Wild forrests of Kentuckey, where My whole attention should be taken up in hoeing Corn & Tobacko, and where I could bid defiance to the blind unguided frowns of forturne, and if I ever came into public life again, it should be by the solicittations of others and not my own seeking.

When I heared of that report of Mr. Rumsey's, knowing that he could not merit the reward in his way, it induced me to undertake it; which was the principle stimilas I had at that time, as I was persuaded it was not offered to him as being a favourite Citizen.[2]

I do not wish it but on honourable terms, and altho I am conscious I have merited it, yet am willing to be laid under any reasonable restrictions. The following one I propose Viz—If I cannot make a Boat of fifty tons burthen, that two men shall be able to Navigate from the Rapids of Ohio to Fort Pitt, than and in such case I shall be obliged to pay the sum stipulated for Lands sold adjoining, or forfiet Said Lands. I really am Sir no more than a man, and it is as dificult for me to effect imposibilities as for another, and cannot compleat what I have begun without supplies. I have since I began been Idle more than six months waiting for the Casting of a Cylinder, and now am in doubts whether I can get it cast in america or not, and should I have to send to Europe for it, probable it would not arrive before August, when we should hardly be able to compleat our works next fall, which would be so discouraging to the Company it is hardly probable they would support me was I to request it.

Such delays has an inconceivable tendency to disharten more than we are aware of.

As to myselfe, I know that I have fortitude sufficient to dispise all the ill natured things that can be said, but the task of keeping twenty of the most delicate Characters in Countinence, will be too much for me with my other imbarrassments, espessially when so many feels themselves interested in preventing its coming to perfection, and no one more than good wishes to have it perfected. It is reasonable to suppose that the clammour will be much against it. And it is imposible to bring the World to reason on it; any more than what they hear from others. And where interest takes on one side, and nothing more than good wishes on the other, it is easily determinaed what the people at large will be. I do not wish Congress to give me because I am poor, but because the honour and interest of our Nation loudly calls for it. The Stigma of having it promoted by forign Nations, I pray Heaven may never be charged to the act. of the Country that gave me birth. And as to their interest, no man on Earth that will reason fairly, but must allow that two men can take a Boat of one hundred tons burthen up the Mississippi, which needs no commentation upon it, as it reduces them waters nearly equal to tide Water. And was the prayor of my Petition granted, I could build a Furnace and execute my own Castings myself, and whatever grants I have, shall be faithfully laid out for them purposes. Sir, you may have some faint Ideas of the situation of my mind, and can form a judgment whether a person so situated is altogether fit for so great an undertaking, as one who can give his whole thoughts and study to it. But Sir, should you not think it to be for the honour and interest of our Empire to grant my prayor, you may give it every opposition without the least offence.

But should you think my prayor reasonable and patronise my claim I should think I was in duty Bound ever to subscribe myselfe Your most Devoted much obliged and Very Humble Servant

JOHN FITCH

NB If there should be any securities required as to the application of the money arising from Sd. grant I can produce such as shall be satisfactory.

RC (DLC). Addressed by Fitch.

[1]Fitch had formed a company at Philadelphia in April 1786 to obtain financial support for his steamboat experiments (Westcott, *Life of John Fitch*, p. 152).

[2]Fitch had learned the previous October that James Rumsey was claiming to be the true inventor of the steamboat (ibid., p. 194; *PJM*, VIII, 131–33). On 24 Jan. 1788 Fitch submitted a petition to Congress requesting a special grant for inventing the steamboat. A committee reported favorably on 5 Mar., recommending that Fitch be granted land in the Northwest Territory. Congress took no action on the report, however, apparently because Fitch did not wish to risk a vote before the whole Congress (*JCC*, XXXIV, 26, 80–81, 626; Westcott, *Life of John Fitch*, pp. 199–204).

To George Washington

N. YORK Feby 11. 88.

DEAR SIR

The Newspaper inclosed with the letter which follows, comprises the information brought me by the mail of yesterday.[1]

BOSTON Feby. 3d.

"I inclose a Newspaper containing the propositions communicated by Mr. Hancock to the Convention, on thursday last. Mr. Adams who contrary to his own sentiments has been hitherto silent in Convention, has given his public and explicit approbation of Mr. Hancocks propositions. We flatter ourselves that the weight of these two characters will ensure our success; but the event is not absolutely certain. Yesterday a Committee was

the people of each state. The establishment of the same rule for the apportionment of taxes, will probably be as little contested; though the rule itself in this case, is by no means founded on the same principle. In the former case, the rule is understood to refer to the personal rights of the people, with which it has a natural and universal connection. In the latter, it has reference to the proportion of wealth, of which it is in no case a precise measure, and in ordinary cases, a very unfit one. But notwithstanding the imperfection of the rule as applied to the relative wealth and contributions of the states, it is evidently the least exceptionable among the practicable rules; and had too recently obtained the general sanction of America, not to have found a ready preference with the convention.

All this is admitted, it will perhaps be said: But does it follow from an admission of numbers for the measure of representation, or of slaves combined with free citizens, as a ratio of taxation, that slaves ought to be included in the numerical rule of representation? Slaves are considered as property, not as persons. They ought therefore to be comprehended in estimates of taxation which are founded on property, and to be excluded from representation which is regulated by a census of persons. This is the objection, as I understand it, stated in its full force. I shall be equally candid in stating the reasoning which may be offered on the opposite side.

We subscribe to the doctrine, might one of our southern brethren observe, that representation relates more immediately to persons, and taxation more immediately to property, and we join in the application of this distinction to the case of our slaves. But we must deny the fact that slaves are considered merely as property, and in no respect whatever as persons. The true state of the case is, that they partake of both these qualities; being considered by our laws, in some respects, as persons, and in other respects, as property. In being compelled to labor not for himself, but for a master; in being vendible by one master to another master; and in being subject at all times to be restrained in his liberty, and chastised in his body, by the capricious will of another, the slave may appear to be degraded from the human rank, and classed with those irrational animals, which fall under the legal denomination of property. In being protected on the other hand in his life and in his limbs, against the violence of all others, even the master of his labour and his liberty; and in being punishable himself for all violence committed against others; the slave is no less evidently regarded by the law as a member of the society; not as a part of the irrational creation; as a moral person, not as a mere article of property. The federal constitution therefore, decides with great propriety on the case of our slaves, when it views them in the mixt character of persons and of property. This is in fact their true character. It is the character bestowed on them by the laws under which they live; and it will not be denied that these are the proper criterion; because it is only under the pretext that the laws have transformed the negroes into subjects of property, that a place is disputed them in the computation of numbers; and it is admitted that if the laws were to restore the rights which have been taken away, the negroes could no longer be refused an equal share of representation with the other inhabitants.

This question may be placed in another light. It is agreed on all sides, that numbers are the best scale of wealth and taxation, as they are the only proper scale of representation. Would the Convention have been impartial or consistent, if they had rejected the slaves from the list of inhabitants when the shares of representation were to be calculated; and inserted them on the lists when the tariff of contributions was to be adjusted? Could it be reasonably expected that the southern states would concur in a system which considered their slaves in some degree as men, when burdens were to be imposed, but refused to consider them in the same light when advantages were to be conferred? Might not some surprize also be expressed that those who reproach the southern states with the barbarous policy of considering as property, a part of their human brethren, should themselves contend that the government to which all the states are to be parties, ought to consider this unfortunate race more compleatly in the unnatural light of property, than the very laws of which they complain?

It may be replied perhaps that slaves are not included in the estimate of representatives in any of the states possessing them. They neither vote themselves, nor increase the votes of their masters. Upon what principle then ought they to be taken into the federal estimate of representation? In rejecting them altogether, the constitution would in this respect, have followed the very laws which have been appealed to, as the proper guide.

This objection is repelled by a single observation. It is a fundamental principle of the proposed constitution, that as the aggregate number of representatives allotted to the several states is to be determined by a federal rule founded on the aggregate number of inhabitants, so the right of choosing this allotted number in each state is to be exercised by such part of the inhabitants, as the state itself may designate. The qualifications on which the right of suffrage depend, are not perhaps the same in any two states. In some of the states the difference is very material. In every state a certain proportion of inhabitants are deprived of this right by the constitution of the state, who will be included in the census by which the federal constitution apportions the representatives. In this point of view, the southern states might retort the complaint, by insisting, that the principle laid down by the convention required that no regard should be had to the policy of particular states towards their own inhabitants; and consequently, that the slaves as inhabitants should have been admitted into the census according to their full number, in like manner with other inhabitants, who by the policy of other states, are not admitted to all the rights of citizens. A rigorous adherence however, to this principle, is waved by those who would be gainers by it. All that they ask is, that equal moderation be shewn on the other side. Let the case of the slaves be considered, as it is in truth a peculiar one. Let the compromising expedient of the constitution be mutually adopted, which regards them as inhabitants, but as debased by servitude below the equal level of free inhabitants, which regards the *slave* as divested of two fifths of the *man*.

After all, may not another ground be taken on which this article of the constitution will admit of a still more ready defence? We have hitherto proceeded on the idea that representation related to persons only, and not at all to property. But is it a just idea? Government is instituted no less for protection of the property, than of the persons of individuals. The one as well as the other, therefore, may be considered as represented by those who are charged with the government. Upon this principle it is, that in several of the states, and particularly in the state of New-York, one branch of the government is intended more especially to be the guardian of property, and is accordingly elected by that part of the society which is most interested in this object of government.[1] In the federal constitution this policy does not prevail. The rights of property are committed into the same hands with the personal rights. Some attention ought therefore to be paid to property in the choice of those hands.

For another reason the votes allowed in the federal legislature to the people of each state, ought to bear some proportion to the comparative wealth of the states. States have not, like individuals, an influence over each other arising from superior advantages of fortune. If the law allows an opulent citizen but a single vote in the choice of his representative, the respect and consequence which he derives from his fortunate situation, very frequently guide the votes of others to the objects of his choice; and through this imperceptible channel the rights of property are conveyed into the public representation. A state possesses no such influence over other states. It is not probable that the richest state in the confederacy will ever influence the choice of a single representative in any other state. Nor will the representatives of the larger and richer states, possess any other advantage in the federal legislature over the representatives of other states, than what may result from their superior number alone; as far therefore as their superior wealth and weight may justly entitle them to any advantage, it ought to be secured to them by a superior share of representation. The new constitution is in this respect materially different from the existing confederation, as well as from that of the United Netherlands, and other similar confederacies. In each of the latter, the efficacy of the federal resolutions depends on the subsequent and voluntary resolutions of the states composing the union. Hence the states, though possessing an equal vote in the public councils, have an unequal influence, corresponding with the unequal importance of these subsequent and voluntary resolutions. Under the proposed constitution, the federal acts will take effect without the necessary intervention of the individual states. They will depend merely on the majority of votes in the federal legislature, and consequently each vote, whether proceeding from a larger or smaller state, or a state more or less wealthy or powerful, will have an equal weight and efficacy; in the same manner as the votes individually given in a state legislature, by the representatives of unequal counties or other districts, have each a precise equality of value and effect; or if there be any difference in the case, it proceeds from the difference in the personal character of the individual representative, rather than from any regard to the extent of the district from which he comes.

Such is the reasoning which an advocate for the southern interests might employ on this subject: And although it may appear to be a little strained in some points, yet on the whole, I must confess, that it fully reconciles me to the scale of representation, which the convention have established.

In one respect the establishment of a common measure for representation and taxation will have a very salutary effect. As the accuracy of the census to be obtained by the congress, will necessarily depend in a considerable degree on the disposition, if not the co-operation of the states, it is of great importance that the states should feel as little bias as possible to swell or to reduce the amount of their numbers. Were their share of representation alone to be governed by this rule, they would have an interest in exaggerating their inhabitants. Were the rule to decide their share of taxation alone, a contrary temptation would prevail. By extending the rule to both objects, the states will have opposite interests, which will control and balance each other; and produce the requisite impartiality.

PUBLIUS.

McLean, II, 135–41.

[1]The 1777 New York Constitution provided that only freeholders owning property worth "one hundred pounds, over and above all debts charged thereon," could vote for senators (Thorpe, *Federal and State Constitutions*, V, 2631).

The Federalist Number 55

[13 February 1788]

The number of which the house of representatives is to consist, forms another, and a very interesting point of view under which this branch of the federal legislature may be contemplated. Scarce any article indeed in the whole constitution seems to be rendered more worthy of attention, by the weight of character and the apparent force of argument, with which it has been assailed. The charges exhibited against it are, first, that so small a number of representatives will be an unsafe depositary of the public interests; secondly that they will not possess a proper knowledge of the local circumstances of their numerous constituents; thirdly, that they will be taken from that class of citizens which will sympathize least with the feelings of the mass of the people, and be most likely to aim at a permanent elevation of the few on the depression of the many; fourthly, that defective as the number will be in the first instance, it will be more and more disproportionate, by the increase of the people, and the obstacles which will prevent a correspondent increase of the representatives.[1]

In general it may be remarked on this subject, that no political problem is less susceptible of a precise solution, than that which relates to the number most convenient for a representative legislature; nor is there any point on which the policy of the several states is more at variance; whether we compare their legislative assemblies directly with each other, or consider the proportions which they respectively bear to the number of their constituents. Passing over the difference between the smallest and largest states, as Delaware, whose most numerous branch consists of twenty-one representatives, and Massachusetts, where it amounts to between three and four hundred; a very considerable difference is observable among states nearly equal in population. The number of representatives in Pennsylvania is not more than one fifth of that in the state last mentioned. New-York, whose population is to that of South-Carolina as six to five, has little more than one third of the number of representatives. As great a disparity prevails between the states of Georgia and Delaware, or Rhode-Island. In Pennsylvania the representatives do not bear a greater proportion to their constituents than of one for every four or five thousand. In Rhode-Island, they bear a proportion of at least one for every thousand. And according to the constitution of Georgia, the proportion may be carried to one for every ten electors; and must unavoidably far exceed the proportion in any of the other states.[2]

Another general remark to be made is, that the ratio between the representatives and the people, ought not to be the same where the latter are very numerous, as where they are very few. Were the representatives in Virginia to be regulated by the standard in Rhode-Island, they would at this time amount to between four and five hundred; and twenty or thirty years hence, to a thousand. On the other hand, the ratio of Pennsylvania, if applied to the state of Delaware, would reduce the representative assembly of the latter to seven or eight members. Nothing can be more fallacious than to found our political calculations on arithmetical principles. Sixty or seventy men, may be more properly trusted with a given degree of power than six or seven. But it does not follow, that six or seven hundred would be proportionally a better depositary. And if we carry on the supposition to six or seven thousand, the whole reasoning ought to be reversed. The truth is, that in all cases a certain number at least seems to be necessary to secure the benefits of free consultation and discussion, and to guard against too easy a combination for improper purposes: As on the other hand, the number ought at most to be kept within a certain limit, in order to avoid the confusion and intemperance of a multitude. In all very numerous assemblies, of whatever characters composed, passion never fails to wrest the sceptre from reason. Had every Athenian citizen been a Socrates, every Athenian assembly would still have been a mob.

It is necessary also to recollect here the observations which were applied to the case of biennial elections. For the same reason that the limited powers of the congress and the control of the state legislatures, justify less frequent elections than the public safety might otherwise require; the members of the congress need be less numerous than if they possessed the whole power of legislation, and were under no other than the ordinary restraints of other legislative bodies.

With these general ideas in our minds, let us weigh the objections which have been stated against the number of members proposed for the house of representatives. It is said in the first place, that so small a number cannot be safely trusted with so much power.

The number of which this branch of the legislature is to consist at the outset of the government, will be sixty-five. Within three years a census is to be taken, when the number may be augmented to one for every thirty thousand inhabitants; and within every successive period of ten years, the census is to be renewed, and augmentations may continue to be made under the above limitation. It will not be thought an extravagant conjecture, that the first census will, at the rate of one for every thirty thousand, raise the number of representatives to at least one hundred. Estimating the negroes in the proportion of three-fifths, it can scarcely be doubted that the population of the United States will by that time, if it does not already, amount to three millions. At the expiration of twenty-five years, according to the computed rate of increase, the number of representatives will amount to two hundred; and of fifty years to four hundred. This is a number which I presume will put an end to all fears arising from the smallness of the body. I take for granted here what I shall in answering the fourth objection hereafter shew, that the number of representatives will be augmented from time to time in the manner provided by the constitution. On a contrary supposition, I should admit the objection to have very great weight indeed.

The true question to be decided then is, whether the smallness of the number as a temporary regulation, be dangerous to the public liberty: Whether sixty-five members for a few years, and a hundred or two hundred for a few more, be a safe depositary for a limited and well guarded power of legislating for the United States? I must own that I could not give a negative answer to this question, without first obliterating every impression which I have received with regard to the present genius of the people of America, the spirit which actuates the state legislatures, and the principles which are incorporated with the political character of every class of citizens. I am unable to conceive that the people of America in their present temper, or under any circumstances which can speedily happen, will chuse, and every second year repeat the choice of sixty-five or an hundred men, who would be disposed to form and pursue a scheme of tyranny or treachery. I am unable to conceive that the state legislatures which must feel so many motives to watch, and which possess so many means of counteracting the federal legislature, would fail either to detect or to defeat a conspiracy of the latter against the liberties of their common constituents. I am equally unable to conceive that there are at this time, or can be in any short time, in the United States, any sixty-five or an hundred men capable of recommending themselves to the choice of the people at large, who would either desire or dare within the short space of two years, to betray the solemn trust committed to them. What change of circumstances time and a fuller population of our country may produce, requires a prophetic spirit to declare, which makes no part of my pretensions. But judging from the circumstances now before us, and from the probable state of them within a moderate period of time, I must pronounce that the liberties of America cannot be unsafe in the number of hands proposed by the federal constitution.[3]

From what quarter can the danger proceed? Are we afraid of foreign gold? If foreign gold could so easily corrupt our federal rulers, and enable them to ensnare and betray their constituents, how has it happened that we are at this time a free and independent nation? The congress which conducted us through the revolution were a less numerous body than their successors will be; they were not chosen by nor responsible to their fellow citizens at large; though appointed from year to year, and recallable at pleasure, they were generally continued for three years; and prior to the ratification of the federal articles, for a still longer term; they held their consultations always under the veil of secrecy; they had the sole transaction of our affairs with foreign nations; through the whole course of the war, they had the fate of their country more in their hands, than it is to be hoped will ever be the case with our future representatives; and from the greatness of the prize at stake and the eagerness of the party which lost it, it may well be supposed, that the use of other means than force would not have been scrupled: Yet we know by happy experience that the public trust was not betrayed; nor has the purity of our public councils in this particular ever suffered even from the whispers of calumny.

Is the danger apprehended from the other branches of the federal government? But where are the means to be found by the president or the senate, or both? Their emoluments of office it is to be presumed will not, and without a previous corruption of the house of representatives cannot, more than suffice for very different purposes: Their private fortunes, as they must all be American citizens, cannot possibly be sources of danger. The only means then which they can possess, will be in the dispensation of appointments. Is it here that suspicion rests her charge? Sometimes we are told that this fund of corruption is to be exhausted by the president in subduing the virtue of the senate. Now the fidelity of the other house is to be the victim. The improbability of such a mercenary and perfidious combination of the several members of government standing on as different foundations as republican principles will well admit, and at the same time accountable to the society over which they are placed, ought alone to quiet this apprehension. But fortunately the constitution has provided a still further safeguard. The members of the congress are rendered ineligible to any civil offices that may be created or of which the emoluments may be increased, during the term of their election. No offices therefore can be dealt out to the existing members, but such as may become vacant by ordinary casualties; and to suppose that these would be sufficient to purchase the guardians of the people, selected by the people themselves, is to renounce every rule by which events ought to be calculated, and to substitute an indiscriminate and unbounded jealousy, with which all reasoning must be vain. The sincere friends of liberty who give themselves up to the extravagancies of this passion are not aware of the injury they do their own cause. As there is a degree of depravity in mankind which requires a certain degree of circumspection and distrust:

So there are other qualities in human nature, which justify a certain portion of esteem and confidence. Republican government presupposes the existence of these qualities in a higher degree than any other form. Were the pictures which have been drawn by the political jealousy of some among us, faithful likenesses of the human character, the inference would be that there is not sufficient virtue among men for self-government; and that nothing less than the chains of despotism can restrain them from destroying and devouring one another.

PUBLIUS.

McLean, II, 141–47.

[1] Antifederalists frequently pointed to the small number of representatives in denouncing the Constitution as undemocratic (Kenyon, *The Antifederalists*, pp. li–lvi). See, for example, "Centinel" (Samuel Bryan), the "Federal Farmer," and "Brutus" (ibid., pp. 12, 216–17; *Massachusetts Debates*, pp. 388–91, 392–96).

[2] JM referred to the article of the Georgia Constitution of 1777 stipulating that "at their first institution each county shall have one member, provided the inhabitants of the said county shall have ten electors." As soon as a county had 100 or more electors, it could send ten representatives to the legislature (Thorpe, *Federal and State Constitutions*, II, 778–79).

[3] On 10 July JM had moved to double the number of representatives, observing that "a *majority* of a Quorum of 65 members, was too small a number to represent the whole inhabitants of the U. States."

From Benjamin Hawkins

WARRENTON[1] 14th Feby. 1788.

DEAR SIR,

A neighbour of mine who is a Wheelwright called last sunday to see me; he told me he had been reading for some days past the New-Constitution, and Richard Henry Lee's letter,[2] and he wished me to answer him some questions. They were the following literally

Is Mr. Lee thought to be a great man?

Is he not a proud passionate man?

Was he one of the Convention?

Could it be from Ignorance or design that he declares Virginia has but a thirteenth vote in the election of a president. For I who am illiterate saw at the first reading he was rong?

Is he fond of popularity?

Is he an enemy to General Washington and Docr. Franklin?

I informed you from Tarborough, of the time appointed for the election, and enacting of our Convention. I believe the Constitution is daily gaining friends, as far as I have been able to know, it is certain, that the honest part of the community whether merchants or planters, are for it.

People in debt, and of dishonesty and cunning in their transactions are against it, this will apply universally to those of this class who have been members of the legislature. If you or our friend Mr. Jefferson should publish any thing upon it, I wish you would send it to me, this you can readily do by the Post to Petersburg. Addresse to me in Warrenton via Petersburg. Adieu & god bless you!

B: H:

RC (DLC). Docketed by JM.

[1] Hawkins wrote from Warrenton, North Carolina, located near the Virginia-North Carolina border.

[2] See Washington to JM, 7 Dec. 1787 and n. 8.

From Joseph Jones

RICHMOND 14th: Febry. 1788

DR. SR.

From Fredericksburg I informed you of the issue of my endeavours to procure the Crab tree scyons. On my return to Richmond I found the chart of James River in the state it was when I left that place. Mr. Lambert says after waiting sometime in expectation of hearing from Harris respecting the canal he at length finding he did not call on him rode to his House but was disappointed in meeting with him. The trace of the canal is noted on the Map but some descriptive notes are wanting to make it more compleat, these I am in hopes I shall obtain Tomorow from Mr. Harris who I have just seen and he promises me they shall be left out at his house in the morning shod. business occasion his absence when I call. Col. Heth being soon to set out for N-York I shall, if it is ready, as I expect it will, confide the conveyance and delivery of it to him.[1]

Your two last favors I have received that of the 25th. since my arrival here and am much obliged to you for the communications they contain.[2] S. Adams's silence as to the N. plan of Government, if not calculated to secure him a seat in the Convention, proceeded very probably from his desire of discovering the temper of the people in General before he took a decided part. This with the admission of Gerry to a seat in the Convention when not a member and the great number that compose the Body are unfavourable circumstances, and authorise a conjecture that the new system will not be adopted by Massts. Should that State give it a negative and not proceed to offer some amendments and propose another convention, I fear it will produce disagreeable consequences, as it will not only confirm N. York in her opposition but will contribute greatly to strengthen the opposition in the States that are yet to consider the measure. If nine States assent before Virga. meets in convention her course I think will be to adopt the plan, protesting or declaring her disapprobation of those parts she does not approve or if not agreed to by nine she will in that case propose amendments and another general Convention. H——y will I think use all his influence to reject at all events, but am satisfied those who are for it as it stands, and those who wish some alterations in it before its adoption if circumstances authorise the attempt, will be greatly the majority. What change may be produced shod. Mass. reject cannot well be foreseen; I think however in that event Virga. will propose amendments, and another Convention, and I trust such will be the conduct of Mass. rather than hazard the loss of the System, and the mischevous consequences that may result from disagreement and delay. I congratulate my friend Griffin on his being placed in the Chair to whom Be pleased to present my best wishes. R——d——h R. H. L. M——n, have been assailed in our papers. The inclosed will if you have not seen them exhibit some specimens, and serve to amuse you.[3] Yr. aff: Servt.

Jos: Jones.

RC (DLC). Docketed by JM. Enclosures not found.

[1]William Heth, one of the commissioners appointed to settle the accounts between Virginia and the U.S. (Turberville to JM, 8 Jan. 1788, n. 1; *JCSV*, IV, 209).

[2]Neither letter has been found.

[3]Jones probably enclosed four numbers of the Richmond *Va. Independent Chronicle* containing the following essays: "Valerius" on Richard Henry Lee (23 Jan. 1788), "Civis Rusticus" on Mason (30 Jan. 1788), "Philanthropos" (Tench Coxe?) on Mason, Gerry, and Randolph (6 Feb. 1788), and "A Plain Dealer" (Spencer Roane) on Randolph (13 Feb. 1788).

To George Washington

N. York Feby. 15. [1788]

Dear Sir

    I have at length the pleasure to inclose you the favorable result of the Convention at Boston.[1] The amendments are a blemish, but are in the least Offensive form. The minority also is very disagreeably large, but the temper of it is some atonement. I am assured by Mr. King[2] that the leaders of it as well as the members of it in general are in good humour; and will countenance no irregular opposition there or elsewhere. The Convention of N Hampshire is now sitting. There seems to be no question that the issue there will add a *seventh* pillar, as the phrase now is, to the fœderal Temple. With the greatest respect & attachmt I am Dr. Sir Yrs.

Js. Madison Jr

RC (Universiteitsbibliotheek, Amsterdam); Tr (DLC). Enclosure not found.

[1] The form of ratification of the Constitution by the convention of Massachusetts appeared in the N.Y. *Daily Advertiser* on 11 Feb. 1788.
[2] Rufus King had returned to New York two days earlier (N.Y. *Daily Advertiser*, 14 Feb. 1788).

From Tench Coxe

PHILADA. Feb. 15th. 1788

DEAR SIR

If you thought it worth attention to publish N. 1. of the Pennsylvanian perhaps No. 2, enclosed may also be properly inserted in the same paper. The first was in Hall & Sellers's of 6th. sent before.

I wish to believe the accot. of the 11th from New York informing of the Adoption by Massachussets on 5th instant—but we wait for the Numbers, the form, the more perfect Certainty. To Morrow I trust will bring it.

Will you take the trouble of mentioning to the hon. Mr. Contee from Maryland that Judge Hanson sent me a large pacquet of Pamphlets for him which I sent on yesterday.[1] Mr. Hanson writes me there is no doubt in Maryland, and tho [he] considers the Opposition in Virga. as very powerful, he says he is well grounded in assuring me of its final Success there.

I am gratified by the Unanimity of Georgia, and by the unanimous Vote of thanks by the Senate of S. Carolina.

I have two letters from gentlemen of very opposite characters, and very differently situated in London, who assure me, one that the Constitution is approved by all the warmest friends of America in England, the other that [it] is in his opinion & all he has conversed with most likely to retrieve the lost Reputation of this Country. Those things are of little really consequence, opposite letters & opinions would have been used to its prejudice here. I shall therefore furnish some extracts to our printers.[2]

I am very troublesome to you, but I can never be so again because I believe Nothing will ever happen again that will furnish so great an Apology. I am with sincere Esteem, Sir, yr. mo. respectf. Servt.

TENCH COXE

RC (DLC). Docketed by JM. Enclosure not found. This letter is printed in *Documentary History of the Constitution*, IV, 522–23, under date of 25 Feb. 1788. Coxe originally wrote "25," but corrected himself by writing "1" over the "2." Internal evidence in the letter conclusively establishes 15 Feb. as the correct date.

[1] "Judge Hanson"—Alexander Contee Hanson—was Benjamin Contee's nephew. The

pamphlets forwarded by Coxe may have been copies of Hanson's *Remarks on the Proposed Plan of a Federal Government* . . . (Annapolis, [1788]). The pamphlet, signed "Aristides" and dated 1 Jan. 1788, is reprinted in P. L. Ford, *Pamphlets on the Constitution*, pp. 217–57.

[2]See "Extract of a letter from an American gentleman in London, dated November 14, 1787" in the *Pa. Gazette* of 20 Feb. 1788.

The Federalist Number 56

[16 February 1788]

The *second* charge against the house of representatives is, that it will be too small to possess a due knowledge of the interests of its constituents.

As this objection evidently proceeds from a comparison of the proposed number of representatives, with the great extent of the United States, the number of their inhabitants, and the diversity of their interests, without taking into view at the same time the circumstances which will distinguish the congress from other legislative bodies, the best answer that can be given to it, will be a brief explanation of these peculiarities.

It is a sound and important principle, that the representative ought to be acquainted with the interests and circumstances of his constituents. But this principle can extend no farther than to those circumstances and interests to which the authority and care of the representative relate. An ignorance of a variety of minute and particular objects, which do not lie within the compass of legislation, is consistent with every attribute necessary to a due performance of the legislative trust. In determining the extent of information required in the exercise of a particular authority, recourse then must be had to the objects within the purview of that authority.

What are to be the objects of federal legislation? Those which are of most importance, and which seem most to require local knowledge, are commerce, taxation and the militia.

A proper regulation of commerce requires much information, as has been elsewhere remarked; but as far as this information relates to the laws and local situation of each individual state, a very few representatives would be very sufficient vehicles of it to the federal councils.

Taxation will consist in great measure, of duties which will be involved in the regulation of commerce. So far the preceding remark is applicable to this object. As far as it may consist of internal collections, a more diffusive knowledge of the circumstances of the state may be necessary. But will not this also be possessed in sufficient degree by a very few intelligent men, diffusively elected within the state. Divide the largest state into ten or twelve districts, and it will be found that there will be no peculiar local interest in either, which will not be within the knowledge of the representative of the district. Besides this source of information, the laws of the state framed by representatives from every part of it, will be almost of themselves a sufficient guide. In every state there have been made, and must continue to be made, regulations on this subject, which will in many cases leave little more to be done by the federal legislature, than to review the different laws, and reduce them into one general act. A skilful individual in his closet, with all the local codes before him, might compile a law on some subjects of taxation for the whole union, without any aid from oral information; and it may be expected, that whenever internal taxes may be necessary, and particularly in cases requiring uniformity throughout the states, the more simple objects will be preferred. To be fully sensible of the facility which will be given to this branch of federal legislation, by the assistance of the state codes, we need only suppose for a moment, that this or any other state were divided into a number of parts, each having and exercising within itself a power of local legislation. Is it not evident that a degree of local information and preparatory labour would be found in the several volumes of their proceedings, which would very much shorten the labours of the general legislature, and render a much smaller number of members sufficient for it? The federal councils will derive great advantage from another circumstance. The representatives of each state will not only bring with them a considerable knowledge of its laws, and a local knowledge of their respective districts; but will probably in all cases have been members, and may even at the very time be members of the state legislature, where all the local information and interests of the state are assembled, and from whence they may easily be conveyed by a very few hands into the legislature of the United States.

With regard to the regulation of the militia, there are scarcely any circumstances in reference to which local knowledge can be said to be necessary. The general face of the country, whether mountainous or level, most fit for the operations of infantry or cavalry, is almost the only consideration of this nature that can occur. The art of war teaches general principles of organization, movement and discipline, which apply universally.[1]

The attentive reader will discern that the reasoning here used to prove the sufficiency of a moderate number of representatives, does not in any respect contradict what was urged on another occasion with regard to the extensive information which the representatives ought to possess, and the time that might be necessary for acquiring it. This information, so far as it may relate to local objects, is rendered necessary and difficult, not by a difference of laws and local circumstances within a single state, but of those among different states. Taking each state by itself, its laws are the same, and its interests but little diversified. A few men therefore will possess all the knowledge requisite for a proper representation of them. Were the interests and affairs of each individual state, perfectly simple and uniform, a knowledge of them in one part would involve a knowledge of them in every other, and the whole state might be competently represented, by a single member taken from any part of it. On a comparison of the different states together, we find a great dissimilarity in their laws, and in many other circumstances connected with the objects of federal legislation, with all of which the federal representatives ought to have some acquaintance. Whilst a few representatives therefore from each state may bring with them a due knowledge of their own state, every representative will have much information to acquire concerning all the other states. The changes of time, as was formerly remarked, on the comparative situation of the different states, will have an assimilating effect. The effect of time on the internal affairs of the states taken singly, will be just the contrary. At present some of the states are little more than a society of husbandmen. Few of them have made much progress in those branches of industry, which give a variety and complexity to the affairs of a nation. These however will in all of them be the fruits of a more advanced population; and will require on the part of each state a fuller representation. The foresight of the convention has accordingly taken care that the progress of population may be accompanied with a proper increase of the representative branch of the government.

The experience of Great Britain which presents to mankind so many political lessons, both of the monitory and exemplary kind, and which has been frequently consulted in the course of these enquiries, corroborates the result of the reflections which we have just made. The number of inhabitants in the two kingdoms of England and Scotland, cannot be stated at less than eight millions. The representatives of these eight millions in the house of commons, amount to five hundred fifty eight. Of this number one ninth are elected by three hundred and sixty four persons, and one half by five thousand seven hundred and twenty three persons.* It cannot be supposed that the half thus elected, and who do not even reside among the people at large, can add any thing either to the security of the people against the government, or to the knowledge of their circumstances and interests, in the legislative councils. On the contrary it is notorious that they are more frequently the representatives and instruments of the executive magistrate, than the guardians and advocates of the

*Burgh's Political Disquisitions.[2]

popular rights. They might therefore with great propriety be considered as something more than a mere deduction from the real representatives of the nation. We will however consider them, in this light alone, and will not extend the deduction, to a considerable number of others, who do not reside among their constituents, are very faintly connected with them, and have very little particular knowledge of their affairs. With all these concessions two hundred and seventy nine persons only will be the depositary of the safety, interest and happiness of eight millions; that is to say; there will be one representative only to maintain the rights and explain the situation *of twenty-eight thousand six hundred and seventy* constituents, in an assembly exposed to the whole force of executive influence, and extending its authority to every object of legislation within a nation whose affairs are in the highest degree diversified and complicated.[3] Yet it is very certain not only that a valuable portion of freedom has been preserved under all these circumstances, but that the defects in the British code are chargeable in a very small proportion, on the ignorance of the legislature concerning the circumstances of the people. Allowing to this case the weight which is due to it; and comparing it with that of the house of representatives as above explained, it seems to give the fullest assurance that a representative for every *thirty thousand inhabitants* will render the latter both a safe and competent guardian of the interests which will be confided to it.

PUBLIUS.

McLean, II, 147–52.

[1]The newspaper version of this paragraph reads: "The observations made on the subject of taxation apply with greater force to the case of the militia. For however different the rules of discipline may be in different states; They are the same throughout each particular state; and depend on circumstances which can differ but little in different parts of the same state" (*The Federalist* [Cooke ed.], pp. 380–81).
[2]Burgh, *Political Disquisitions*, I, 45–48.
[3]In his third letter, "Brutus" divided eight million by 558 and arrived at a proportion of one member of Parliament for every 14,000 inhabitants (*Massachusetts Debates*, pp. 390–91). JM argued that the true representation was at least twice that proportion.

From James Gordon, Jr.

February 17th. 1788

DEAR SIR
    Being favd. by Colo. Monroe with a sight of your letter of the 27 January[1] and finding no mention therein of your being in our county in a short time, [I] take the Liberty as yr. Friend to solicit your attendance at march Orange court. I am induced to make such a request as I believe it

will give the county in general great satisfaction to hear your sentiments on the new Constitution. Your Friends are very solicitous for your appointment in the convention to meet in June next. I trust were it not practicable for you to attend your election will be secured, but your being present would not admit a doubt. Colo. Thomas Barbour, Mr. Charles Porter & myself enter the list with you the two former gentlemen are exceedingly averse to the adoption of the constitution in this state and being acquainted with them you will readily determine, no means in their power will be wanting to procure a seat in convention. The sentiments of the people of Orange are much dividid the best men in my judgement are for the constitution but several of those who have much weight with the people are opposed, Parson Bledsoe & Leeland[2] with Colo. Z. Burnley.[3] Upon the whole sir I think it is incumbent on you with out delay, to repair to this state; as the loss of the constitution in this state may involve consequences the most alarming to every citizen of America. I am Dr Sir yr. Most Obt Sr

JAS GORDON JUN

RC (DLC). Docketed by JM.

[1] JM's letter to James Monroe of 27 Jan. 1788 has not been found.

[2] Aaron Bledsoe (ca. 1730–1809) was a Baptist minister who preached at "North Fork of Pamunkey," about eight miles southeast of Orange (John T. Bledsoe, *The Bledsoe Family* [Pine Bluff, Ark., 1973], pp. 63, 128; Semple, *History of the Rise and Progress of the Baptists in Virginia* [rev. ed., 1894], pp. 219–20). John Leland (1754–1841), the leader of the Virginia Baptists, was born in Massachusetts and moved to Culpeper County in 1777. The next year he moved to Orange and remained there until he returned to New England in 1791. In 1788 Leland baptized 300 converts—"more than I have ever baptized in any other year" (*The Writings of the Late Elder John Leland* . . . [New York, 1845], pp. 9, 19, 27, 29, 49–50). For an account of Leland's career, see L. H. Butterfield, "Elder John Leland, Jeffersonian Itinerant," *Proceedings of the American Antiquarian Society*, n.s., LXII (1952), 155–242.

[3] Zachariah Burnley (*PJM*, I, 148 n. 2; VIII, 273 n. 1).

From Joseph Jones

RICHMOND 17th. Febry 1788.

DR. SR.

Col. Heth came to Town and proceeded on his journey sooner than I expected and before I had an opportunity of seeing Mr. Harris. After calling upon him and geting the survey of the Canal I found little information could be collected from it and inserted on the map. I have therefore sent what Mr. Lambert had executed by Col. Henley[1] who I understand means to go on Tomorow and has promised to deliver it safe to you. Some notes respecting the canal obtained from Mr. Harris's information I send inclosed. They may be usefull if any thing beyond the labour of Mr. Lambert is intended.

We anxiously wait for the decision of the Masstts: convention—turn as it may the deliberations of the States yet to meet will be greatly affected by what shall be determined by that Body. Davis's next paper will I expect contain another publication under the signature of Cassius agt. R H. L.[2] You shall have it if printed. The *plain dealer* is suspected from the manuscript to come from essex R——ne.[3] Pray do not fail to keep me informed from time to time of the proceedings of the States in the important business of the new government as they shall come to your knowledge. Yr. friend & Servt

Jos: Jones.

PS. I am well informed Col. Pendleton and Col. James Taylor will come from Caroline.[4] H——y is preaching to the people in some of the Southern Counties.

RC (DLC). Docketed by JM. Enclosure not found.

[1]David Henley, one of the commissioners appointed to settle the accounts between Virginia and the U.S. (Turberville to JM, 8 Jan. 1788, n. 1).

[2]Three letters of "Cassius" addressed to Richard Henry Lee were printed in the Richmond *Va. Independent Chronicle* on 2, 9, and 23 Apr. 1788. No earlier publication under that signature has been found. This "Cassius" should not be confused with the northern "Cassius" (James Sullivan), whose essays appeared in the Boston *Mass. Gazette* between September and December 1787 (reprinted in P. L. Ford, *Essays on the Constitution*, pp. 5–48).

[3]That is, Spencer Roane of Essex County, son-in-law of Patrick Henry. The essay of "Plain Dealer," a critique of Edmund Randolph's letter on the Constitution, appeared in the Richmond *Va. Independent Chronicle* of 13 Feb. 1788 (reprinted in P. L. Ford, *Essays on the Constitution*, pp. 389–92). See also Randolph to JM, 29 Feb. 1788.

[4]Edmund Pendleton and James Taylor were elected delegates to the convention from Caroline County (Grigsby, *Virginia Convention of 1788*, II, 362).

From John Dawson

Frdksburg. Feby 18. 1788.

Dear sir

It is now several months since I was honord with a letter from you. During the recess of Congress, while your attention was not closely confind to public business, and while the situation of the Union must have furnishd you with daily information which woud have been interesting to you, I flatterd myself you woud not have neglected your friend.

The approaching elections are the subject of general conversation in this state at this time, and uncommon exertions are made by all parties to have elected those persons whose sentiments agree with their own. In Orange I am inform'd there are three candadates, besides yourself, and that the election is very doubtful, as two of the Gentlemen, Barber and Porter, have declard their opposition to the proposd Goverment. I must therefore join your other friends and intreat your attendance at the election. Mr. Mason will *probably* be returnd for Stafford, as the people have signd a petition and sent it to him, requesting his services. He is however warmly opposd by Colo Carter and Mr. Fitzhugh.[1] There is scarce a doubt but Mr. Randolph will be elected in Henrico, altho "the plain Dealer" thinks he ought not to be, as you will observe by the enclosd paper.[2] Mr. Jones offers for King George.[3] His election is doubtful. In this county the candadates are Genl. Spotswood, Mr. Page Mr. Monroe and my self. It is impossible to say who will be elected. The contest will probably be between the three last mentiond.[4]

Never perhaps was a state more divided than Virginia is on the new Constitution. Its fate appears to hang in a great measure on the decision of Massachusetts bay. Shoud the convention of that state adjourn without doing any thing decisive, or shoud amendments be proposd, I think, Virginia will go hand in hand with her. Shoud *she* adopt, I cannot say what will be done. But shoud *nine states* agree to it in toto, I apprehend there will be a decided majority in this state for accepting it. Whatever the event may be I sincerely pray that my countrymen may act with moderation, altho I very much doubt it, and that they may weigh the subject with that coolness and impartiality, which its importance requires. With much respect and esteem, I am, dear sir Your Friend & hm: Sert.

                                                              J DAWSON

RC (DLC). Enclosure not found.

[1]George Mason and Andrew Buchanan defeated Charles Carter and William Fitzhugh in the Stafford election (Swem and Williams, *Register*, p. 244).
[2]See Jones to JM, 17 Feb. 1788 and n. 3.
[3]Joseph Jones was an unsuccessful candidate.
[4]The Spotsylvania freeholders chose Monroe and Dawson over Alexander Spotswood and Mann Page (Swem and Williams, *Register*, p. 244).

To Thomas Jefferson

                                              NEW YORK Feby. 19. 1788
DEAR SIR

By the Count de Moustier I received your favour of the 8th. of October. I recd. by his hands also the watch which you have been so good as to provide for me, and for which I beg you to accept my particular thanks.

During the short trial I have made, she goes with great exactness. Since the arrival of the Count de Moustier, I have recd. also by the Packet Mr. Calonne's publication[1] for myself, and a number of the Mercure's for Mr. Banister. The bearer was a Mr. Stuart. I had a conveyance to Mr. Banister a few days after the Mercure's came to hand.

The Public here continues to be much agitated by the proposed fœderal Constitution and to be attentive to little else. At the date of my last Delaware Pennsylvania and New Jersey had adopted it. It has been since adopted by Connecticut, Georgia, and Massachussetts. In the first the minority consisted of 40 against 127. In Georgia the adoption was unanimous. In Massachussetts the conflict was tedious and the event extremely doubtful. On the final question the vote stood 187 against 168; a majority of 19 only being in favor of the Constitution. The prevailing party comprized however all the men of abilities, of property, and of influence. In the opposite multitude there was not a single character capable of uniting their wills or directing their measures. It was made up partly of deputies from the province of Maine who apprehended difficulties from the New Government to their scheme of separation, partly of men who had espoused the disaffection of Shay's; and partly of ignorant and jealous men, who had been taught or had fancied that the Convention at Philada. had entered into a conspiracy against the liberties of the people at large, in order to erect an aristocracy for the rich the *well-born*, and the men of Education. They had no plan whatever. They looked no farther than to put a negative on the Constitution and return home. The amendments as recommended by the Convention, were as I am well informed not so much calculated for the minority in the Convention, on whom they had little effect, as for the people of the State. You will find the amendments in the Newspapers which are sent from the office of foreign Affairs. It appears from a variety of circumstances that disappointment had produced no asperity in the minority, and that they will probably not only acquiesce in the event, but endeavour to reconcile their constituents to it. This was the public declaration of several who were called the leaders of the party. The minority of Connecticut behaved with equal moderation. That of Pennsylvania has been extremely intemperate and continues to use a very bold and menacing language. Had the decision in Massachussetts been adverse to the Constitution, it is not improbable that some very violent measures would have followed in that State. The cause of the inflamation however is much more in their State factions, than in the system proposed by the Convention. New Hampshire is now deliberating on the Constitution. It is generally understood that an adoption is a matter of certainty. South Carolina & Maryland have fixed on April or May for their Conventions. The former it is currently said will be one of the ratifying States. Mr. Chace and a few others will raise a considerable opposition in the latter. But the weight of personal influence is on the side of the Constitution, and the present expectation is that the opposition will be outnumbered by a great majority. This State is much divided in its sentiment. Its Convention is to be held in June. The decision of Massts. will give the turn in favor of the Constitution unless an idea should prevail or the fact should appear, that the voice of the State is opposed to the result of its Convention. North Carolina has put off her Convention till July.[2] The State is much divided it is said. The temper of Virginia, as far as I can learn, has undergone but little change of late. At first there was an enthusiasm for the Constitution. The tide next took a sudden and strong turn in the opposite direction. The influence and exertions of Mr. Henry, and Col. Mason and some others will account for this. Subsequent information again represented the Constitution as regaining in some degree its lost ground. The people at large have been uniformly said to be more friendly to the Constitution than the Assembly. But it is probable that the dispersion of the latter will have a considerable influence on the opinions of the former. The previous adoption of nine States must have a very persuasive effect on the minds of the opposition, though I am told that a very bold language is held by Mr. H——y and some of his partizans. Great stress is laid on the self-sufficiency of that State; and the prospect of external props is alluded to.

Congress have done no business of consequence yet, nor is it probable that much more of any sort will precede the event of the great question before the public.

The Assembly of Virginia have passed the district Bill of which I formerly gave you an account. There are 18 districts, with 4 new Judges, Mr. Gabl Jones, Richd. Parker, St. George Tucker and Jos. Prentis. They have reduced much the taxes, and provided some indulgences for debtors. The question of British debts underwent great vicicitudes. It was after long discussion resolvd. by a majority of 30 agst. the utmost exertions of Mr. Henry that they sd. be paid as soon as the other States sd. have complied with the treaty. A few days afterwards he carried his point by a majority of 50 that G.B. should first comply. Adieu Yrs. Affety.

Js. Madison Jr

P.S. Mr. St. John[3] has given me a very interisting description of a System of Nature lately published at Paris—will you add it for me. The Boxes which were to have come for myself G. W. & A. D. &c have not yet arrived.

RC (DLC).

[1]Calonne had been dismissed from the office of controller general of finance in April 1787. His "publication" may have been *Requête au Roi. Adressée à Sa Majesté, par M. de Calonne, Ministre d'État* (London, 1787). See Jefferson to Madame de Corny, 19 Oct. 1787, Boyd, *Papers of Jefferson*, XII, 246–47.
[2]At a later time JM placed an asterisk here and wrote at the bottom of the page: "*see letter from Col: Davie to J. M." JM evidently referred to the letter of William R. Davie to him, dated 10 June 1789, discussing the prospect for ratification of the Constitution by North Carolina (DLC). This is the only extant letter from Davie to JM.
[3]Michel-Guillaume St. Jean de Crèvecoeur.

The Federalist Number 57

[19 February 1788]

The *third* charge against the house of representatives is, that it will be taken from that class of citizens which will have least sympathy with the mass of the people, and be most likely to aim at an ambitious sacrifice of the many to the aggrandizement of the few.

Of all the objections which have been framed against the federal constitution, this is perhaps the most extraordinary. Whilst the objection itself is levelled against a pretended oligarchy, the principle of it strikes at the very root of republican government.

The aim of every political constitution is, or ought to be, first, to obtain for rulers men who possess most wisdom to discern, and most virtue to pursue the common good of the society; and in the next place, to take the most effectual precautions for keeping them virtuous, whilst they continue to hold their public trust. The elective mode of obtaining rulers is the characteristic policy of republican government. The means relied on in this form of government for preventing their degeneracy, are numerous and various. The most effectual one is such a limitation of the term of appointments, as will maintain a proper responsibility to the people.

Let me now ask what circumstance there is in the constitution of the house of representatives, that violates the principles of republican government; or favors the elevation of the few on the ruins of the many? Let me ask whether every circumstance is not, on the contrary, strictly conformable to these principles; and scrupulously impartial to the rights and pretensions of every class and description of citizens?

Who are to be the electors of the federal representatives? Not the rich more than the poor; not the learned more than the ignorant; not the haughty heirs of distinguished names, more than the humble sons of obscure and unpropitious fortune. The electors are to be the great body of the people of the United States. They are to be the same who exercise the right in every state of electing the correspondent branch of the legislature of the state.

Who are to be the objects of popular choice? Every citizen whose merit may recommend him to the esteem and confidence of his country. No qualification of wealth, of birth, of religious faith, or of civil profession, is permitted to fetter the judgment or disappoint the inclination of the people.

If we consider the situation of the men on whom the free suffrages of their fellow citizens may confer the representative trust, we shall find it involving every security which can be devised or desired for their fidelity to their constituents.

In the first place, as they will have been distinguished by the preference of their fellow citizens, we are to presume, that in general, they will be somewhat distinguished also, by those qualities which entitle them to it, and which promise a sincere and scrupulous regard to the nature of their engagements.

In the second place, they will enter into the public service under circumstances which cannot fail to produce a temporary affection at least to their constituents. There is in every breast a sensibility to marks of honour, of favour, of esteem, and of confidence, which, apart from all considerations of interest, is some pledge for grateful and benevolent returns. Ingratitude is a common topic of declamation against human nature; and it must be confessed, that instances of it are but too frequent and flagrant both in public and in private life. But the universal and extreme indignation which it inspires, is itself a proof of the energy and prevalence of the contrary sentiment.

In the third place, those ties which bind the representative to his constituents are strengthened by motives of a more selfish nature. His pride and vanity attach him to a form of government which favors his pretensions, and gives him a share in its honors and distinctions. Whatever hopes or projects might be entertained by a few aspiring characters, it must generally happen that a great proportion of the men deriving their advancement from their influence with the people, would have more to hope from a preservation of the favor, than from innovations in the government subversive of the authority of the people.

All these securities however would be found very insufficient without the restraint of frequent elections. Hence, in the fourth place, the house of representatives is so constituted as to support in the members an habitual recollection of their dependence on the people. Before the sentiments impressed on their minds by the mode of their elevation, can be effaced by the exercise of power, they will be compelled to anticipate the moment when their power is to cease, when their exercise of it is to be reviewed, and when they must descend to the level from which they were raised; there forever to remain, unless a faithful discharge of their trust shall have established their title to a renewal of it.

I will add as a fifth circumstance in the situation of the house of representatives, restraining them from oppressive measures, that they can make no law which will not have its full operation on themselves and their friends, as well as on the great mass of the society. This has always been deemed one of the strongest bonds by which human policy can connect the rulers and the people together. It creates between them that communion of interest and sympathy of sentiments of which few governments have furnished examples; but without which every government degenerates into tyranny. If it be asked what is to restrain the house of representatives from making legal discriminations in favor of themselves and a particular class of the society? I answer, the genius of the whole system, the nature of just and constitutional laws, and above all the vigilant and manly spirit which actuates the people of America, a spirit which nourishes freedom, and in return is nourished by it.

If this spirit shall ever be so far debased as to tolerate a law not obligatory on the legislature as well as on the people, the people will be prepared to tolerate any thing but liberty.

Such will be the relation between the house of representatives and their constituents. Duty, gratitude, interest, ambition itself, are the cords by which they will be bound to fidelity and sympathy with the great mass of the people. It is possible that these may all be insufficient to control the caprice and wickedness of men. But are they not all that government will admit, and that human prudence can devise? Are they not the genuine and the characteristic means by which republican government provides for the liberty and happiness of the people? Are they not the identical means on which every state government in the union, relies for the attainment of these important ends? What then are we to understand by the objection which this paper has combated? What are we to say to the men who profess the most flaming zeal for republican government, yet boldly impeach the fundamental principle of it; who pretend to be champions for the right and the capacity of the people to chuse their own rulers, yet maintain that they will prefer those only who will immediately and infallibly betray the trust committed to them?

Were the objection to be read by one who had not seen the mode prescribed by the constitution for the choice of representatives, he could suppose nothing less than that some unreasonable qualification of property was annexed to the right of suffrage; or that the right of eligibility was limited to persons of particular families or fortunes; or at least that the mode prescribed by the state constitutions was in some respect or other very grossly departed from. We have seen how far such a supposition would err as to the two first points. Nor would it in fact be less erroneous as to the last. The only difference discoverable between the two cases is, that each representative of the United States will be elected by five or six thousand citizens; whilst in the individual states the election of a representative is left to about as many hundred. Will it be pretended that this difference is sufficient to justify an attachment to the state governments and an abhorrence to the federal government? If this be the point on which the objection turns, it deserves to be examined.

Is it supported by *reason*? This cannot be said, without maintaining that five or six thousand citizens are less capable of chusing a fit representative, or more liable to be corrupted by an unfit one, than five or six hundred. Reason, on the contrary assures us, that as in so great a number, a fit representative would be most likely to be found, so the choice would be less likely to be diverted from him, by the intrigues of the ambitious, or the bribes of the rich.

Is the *consequence* from this doctrine admissible? If we say that five or six hundred citizens are as many as can jointly exercise their right of suffrage, must we not deprive the people of the immediate choice of their public servants in every instance where the administration of the government does not require as many of them as will amount to one for that number of citizens?

Is the doctrine warranted by *facts*? It was shewn in the last paper, that the real representation in the British house of commons very little exceeds the proportion of one for every thirty thousand inhabitants. Besides a variety of powerful causes, not existing here and which favor in that country, the pretensions of rank and wealth, no person is eligible as a representative of a county, unless he possess real estate of the clear value of six hundred pounds sterling per year; nor of a city or borough, unless he possess a like estate of half that annual value. To this qualification on the part of the county representatives, is added another on the part of the county electors, which restrains the right of suffrage to persons having a freehold estate of the annual value of more than twenty pounds sterling, according to the present rate of money. Notwithstanding these unfavourable circumstances, and notwithstanding some very unequal laws in the British code, it cannot be said that the representatives of the nation have elevated the few on the ruins of the many.

But we need not resort to foreign experience on this subject. Our own is explicit and decisive. The districts in New-Hampshire in which the senators are chosen immediately by the people, are nearly as large as will be necessary for her representatives in the congress. Those of Massachusetts are larger than will be necessary for that purpose. And those of New-York still more so. In the last state the members of assembly, for the cities and counties of New-York and Albany, are elected by very nearly as many voters as will be entitled to a representative in the congress, calculating on the number of sixty-five representatives only. It makes no difference that in these senatorial districts and counties, a number of representatives are voted for by each elector at the same time. If the same electors, at the same time, are capable of choosing four or five representatives, they cannot be incapable of choosing one. Pennsylvania is an additional example. Some of her counties which elect her state representatives, are almost as large as her districts will be by which her federal representatives will be elected. The city of Philadelphia is supposed to contain between fifty and sixty thousand souls. It will therefore form nearly two districts for the choice of federal representatives. It forms however but one county, in which every elector votes for each of its representatives in the state legislature. And what may appear to be still more directly to our purpose, the whole city actually elects a *single member* for the executive council. This is the case in all the other counties of the state.

Are not these facts the most satisfactory proofs of the fallacy which has been employed against the branch of the federal government under consideration? Has it appeared on trial that the senators of New-Hampshire, Massachusetts and New-York; or the executive council of Pennsylvania; or the members of the assembly in the two last states, have betrayed any peculiar disposition to sacrifice the many to the few; or are in any respect less worthy of their places than the representatives and magistrates appointed in other states, by very small divisions of the people?

But there are cases of a stronger complexion than any which I have yet quoted. One branch of the legislature of Connecticut is so constituted that each member of it is elected by the whole state. So is the governor of that state, of Massachusetts, and of this state, and the president of New Hampshire. I leave every man to decide whether the result of any one of these experiments can be said to countenance a suspicion that a diffusive mode of chusing representatives of the people tends to elevate traitors, and to undermine the public liberty.

PUBLIUS.

McLean, II, 153–59.

To Thomas Jefferson

Dear Sir

I have this moment received an answer to a letter written to Mr. W. S. Browne on the subject of Mr. Burke's affairs. The answer is written by direction of Mrs. Brown and informs me that her husband is absent on a voyage to the West Indies and is not expected back till April; that when "he arrives he no doubt will be ready to deliver the effects on proper application. The amount of effects I can say nothing to, but they have been stored ever since with care. The cash I believe is the same as you mention. As to tendering any thing but the hard cash you need be under no apprehension. His character is well established in this town (Providence R. Island) and he despises the man that would offer paper when he had received cash." This is all the information I have to give on the subject.

By letters just received from Virginia I find that I shall be under the necessity of setting out in 8 or 10 days for Virginia. I mention this circumstance that it may explain the cause if I should not write by the next conveyance. Yrs. Affey.

Js. Madison Jr

RC (DLC). Docketed by Jefferson.

To George Washington

New York Feby 20. 1788

Dear Sir

I am just favored with yours of the 7th.[1] inst: and will attend to your wishes as to the political essays in the press.

I have given notice to my friends in Orange that the County may command my services in the Convention if it pleases. I can say with great truth however that in this overture I sacrifice every private inclination to considerations not of a selfish nature. I foresee that the undertaking will involve me in very laborious and irksome discussions; that public opposition to several very respectable characters whose esteem and friendship I greatly prize may unintentionally endanger the subsisting connection; and that disagreeable misconstructions, of which samples have been already given, may be the fruit of those exertions which fidelity will impose. But I have made up my determination on the subject; and if I am informed that my presence at the election in the County be indispensable, shall submit to that condition also; though it is my particular wish to decline it, as well to avoid apparent solicitude on the occasion; as a journey of such length at a very unpleasant season.

I had seen the extract of your letter to Col. Carter, and had supposed from the place where it first made its appearance that its publication was the effect of the zeal of a correspondent. I cannot but think on the whole that it may have been of service, notwithstanding the scandalous misinterpretations of it which have been attempted. As it has evidently the air of a paragraph to a familiar friend, the omission of an argumentative support of the opinion given will appear to no candid reader unnatural or improper.

We have no late information from Europe, except through the English papers, which represent the affairs of France as in the most ticklish state. The facts have every appearance of authenticity, and we wait with great impatience for the packet which is daily expected. It can be little doubted that the patriots have been abandoned; whether from impotency in France, misconduct in them, or from what other cause is not altogether clear. The french apologists are visibly embarrassed by the dilemma of submitting to the appearance of either weakness or the want of faith. They seem generally to alledge that their engagements being with the Republic, the Nation could not oppose the regular Authority of the Country by supporting a single province, or perhaps a party in it only. The validity of this excuse will depend much on the real connection between France and the patriots, and the assurances given as an encouragement to the latter. From the British King's speech it would seem that France had avowed her purpose of supporting her Dutch friends;[2] though it is *possible*, her menaces to England might be carried farther than her real promises to the patriots. All these circumstances however must have galled the pride of France, and I have little doubt that a war will prove it as soon as her condition will admit of it; perhaps she may be the sooner forced into it on account of her being in a contrary situation.

I hear nothing yet from the Convention of N. Hampshire. I remain yours most: respectfully & Affectly.

Js. MADISON JR

RC (DLC: Washington Papers); Tr (DLC). RC docketed by Washington.

[1] JM should have written "5th."
[2] George III's speech, delivered to Parliament on 27 Nov. 1787, was printed in the N.Y. *Daily Advertiser* of 13 Feb. 1788.

The Federalist Number 58

[20 February 1788]

The remaining charge against the house of representatives which I am to examine, is grounded on a supposition that the number of members will not be augmented from time to time, as the progress of population may demand.

It has been admitted that this objection, if well supported, would have great weight. The following observations will shew that like most other objections against the constitution, it can only proceed from a partial view of the subject; or from a jealousy which discolours and disfigures every object which is beheld.

1. Those who urge the objection seem not to have recollected that the federal constitution will not suffer by a comparison with the state constitutions, in the security provided for a gradual augmentation of the number of representatives. The number which is to prevail in the first instance is declared to be temporary. Its duration is limited to the short term of three years.

Within every successive term of ten years, a census of inhabitants is to be repeated. The unequivocal objects of these regulations are, first, to re-adjust from time to time the apportionment of representatives to the number of inhabitants; under the single exception that each state shall have one representative at least: Secondly, to augment the number of representatives at the same periods; under the sole limitation, that the whole number shall not exceed one for every thirty thousand inhabitants. If we review the constitutions of the several states, we shall find that some of them contain no determinate regulations on this subject; that others correspond pretty much on this point with the federal constitution; and that the most effectual security in any of them is resolvable into a mere directory provision.

2. As far as experience has taken place on this subject, a gradual increase of representatives under the state constitutions, has at least kept pace with that of the constituents; and it appears that the former have been as ready to concur in such measures, as the latter have been to call for them.

3. There is a peculiarity in the federal constitution which ensures a watchful attention in a majority both of the people and of their representatives, to a constitutional augmentation of the latter. The peculiarity lies in this, that one branch of the legislature is a representation of citizens; the other of the states: In the former, consequently the larger states will have

most weight; in the latter, the advantage will be in favor of the smaller states. From this circumstance it may with certainty be inferred, that the larger states will be strenuous advocates for increasing the number and weight of that part of the legislature in which their influence predominates. And it so happens that four only of the largest, will have a majority of the whole votes in the house of representatives. Should the representatives or people therefore of the smaller states oppose at any time a reasonable addition of members, a coalition of a very few states will be sufficient to overrule the opposition; a coalition, which notwithstanding the rivalship and local prejudices which might prevent it on ordinary occasions, would not fail to take place, when not merely prompted by common interest but justified by equity and the principles of the constitution.

It may be alledged, perhaps, that the senate would be prompted by like motives to an adverse coalition; and as their concurrence would be indispensable, the just and constitutional views of the other branch might be defeated. This is the difficulty which has probably created the most serious apprehensions in the jealous friends of a numerous representation. Fortunately it is among the difficulties which, existing only in appearance, vanish on a close and accurate inspection. The following reflections will, if I mistake not, be admitted to be conclusive and satisfactory on this point.

Notwithstanding the equal authority which will subsist between the two houses on all legislative subjects, except the originating of money bills, it cannot be doubted that the house composed of the greater number of members, when supported by the more powerful states, and speaking the known and determined sense of a majority of the people, will have no small advantage in a question depending on the comparative firmness of the two houses.

This advantage must be increased by the consciousness felt by the same side, of being supported in its demands, by right, by reason, and by the constitution; and the consciousness on the opposite side, of contending against the force of all these solemn considerations.

It is farther to be considered that in the gradation between the smallest and largest states, there are several which, though most likely in general to arrange themselves among the former, are too little removed in extent and population from the latter, to second an opposition to their just and legitimate pretensions. Hence it is by no means certain that a majority of votes, even in the senate, would be unfriendly to proper augmentations in the number of representatives.

It will not be looking too far to add, that the senators from all the new states may be gained over to the just views of the house of representatives, by an expedient too obvious to be overlooked. As these states will for a great length of time advance in population with peculiar rapidity, they will be interested in frequent re-apportionments of the representatives to the number of inhabitants. The large states therefore, who will prevail in the house of representatives, will have nothing to do, but to make re-apportionments and augmentations mutually conditions of each other; and the senators from all the most growing states will be bound to contend for the latter, by the interest which their states will feel in the former.

These considerations seem to afford ample security on this subject; and ought alone to satisfy all the doubts and fears which have been indulged with regard to it. Admitting however, that they should all be insufficient to subdue the unjust policy of the smaller states, or their predominant influence in the councils of the senate; a constitutional and infallible resource still remains with the larger states, by which they will be able at all times to accomplish their just purposes. The house of representatives can not only refuse, but they alone can propose the supplies requisite for the support of government. They in a word hold the purse; that powerful instrument by which we behold in the history of the British constitution, an infant and humble representation of the people, gradually enlarging the sphere of its activity and importance, and finally reducing, as far as it seems to have wished, all the overgrown prerogatives of the other branches of the government. This power over the purse, may in fact be regarded as the most compleat and effectual weapon with which any constitution can arm the immediate representatives of the people, for obtaining a redress of every grievance, and for carrying into effect every just and salutary measure.

But will not the house of representatives be as much interested as the senate in maintaining the government in its proper functions, and will they not therefore be unwilling to stake its existence or its reputation on the pliancy of the senate? Or if such a trial of firmness between the two branches were hazarded, would not the one be as likely first to yield as the other? These questions will create no difficulty with those who reflect, that in all cases the smaller the number and the more permanent and conspicuous the station of men in power, the stronger must be the interest which they will individually feel in whatever concerns the government. Those who represent the dignity of their country in the eyes of other nations, will be particularly sensible to every prospect of public danger or of a dishonorable stagnation in public affairs. To those causes we are to ascribe the continual triumph of the British house of commons over the other branches of the government, whenever the engine of a money bill has been employed. An absolute inflexibility on the side of the latter, although it could not have failed to involve every department of the state in the general confusion, has neither been apprehended nor experienced. The utmost degree of firmness that can be displayed by the federal senate or president will not be more than equal to a resistance in which they will be supported by constitutional and patriotic principles.

In this review of the constitution of the house of representatives, I have passed over the circumstance of economy, which in the present state of affairs might have had some effect in lessening the temporary number of representatives; and a disregard of which would probably have been as rich a theme of declamation against the constitution as has been furnished by the smallness of the number proposed. I omit also any remarks on the difficulty which might be found, under present circumstances, in engaging in the federal service, a large number of such characters as the people will probably elect. One observation however, I must be permitted to add on this subject, as claiming in my judgment a very serious attention. It is, that in all legislative assemblies, the greater the number composing them may be, the fewer will be the men who will in fact direct their proceedings. In the first place, the more numerous any assembly may be, of whatever characters composed, the greater is known to be the ascendancy of passion over reason. In the next place, the larger the number, the greater will be the proportion of members of limited information and of weak capacities. Now it is precisely on characters of this description that the eloquence and address of the few are known to act with all their force. In the antient republics, where the whole body of the people assembled in person, a single orator, or an artful statesman, was generally seen to rule with as compleat a sway, as if a sceptre had been placed in his single hands. On the same principle the more multitudinous a representative assembly may be rendered, the more it will partake of the infirmities incident to collective meetings of the people. Ignorance will be the dupe of cunning; and passion the slave of sophistry and declamation. The people can never err more than in supposing that by multiplying their representatives beyond a certain limit, they strengthen the barrier against the government of a few. Experience will forever admonish them that on the contrary, *after securing a sufficient number for the purposes of safety, of local information, and of diffusive sympathy with the whole society*, they will counteract their own views by every addition to their representatives. The countenance of the government may become more democratic; but the soul that animates it will be more oligarchic. The machine will be enlarged, but the fewer, and often the more secret, will be the springs by which its motions are directed.

As connected with the objection against the number of representatives, may properly be here noticed, that which has been suggested against the number made competent for legislative business. It has been said that more than a majority ought to have been required for a quorum, and in particular cases, if not in all, more than a majority of a quorum for a decision. That some advantages might have resulted from such a precaution, cannot be denied. It might have been an additional shield to some particular interests, and another obstacle generally to hasty and partial measures. But these considerations are outweighed by the inconveniencies in the opposite scale. In all cases where justice or the general good might require new laws to be passed, or active measures to be pursued, the fundamental principle of free government would be reversed. It would be no longer the majority that would rule; the power would be transferred to the minority. Were the defensive privilege limited to particular cases, an interested minority might take advantage of it to screen themselves from equitable sacrifices to the general weal, or in particular emergencies to extort unreasonable indulgences. Lastly, it would facilitate and foster the baneful practice of secessions; a practice which has shewn itself even in states where a majority only is required; a practice subversive of all the principles of order and regular government; a practice which leads more directly to public convulsions, and the ruin of popular governments, than any other which has yet been displayed among us.

PUBLIUS.

McLean, II, 160–66.

To Edmund Pendleton

NEW YORK Feby. 21. 88

DEAR SIR

The receipt of your favor of the 29th Ult: which did not come to hand till a few days ago was rendered particularly agreeable to me by the prospect it gives of a thorough reestablishment of your health. I indulge the reflection and the hope that it denotes a remaining energy in the Constitution, which will long defend it against the gradual waste of time.

Your representation of the politics of the State coincides with the information from every other quarter. Great fluctuations and divisions of opinion, naturally result in Virginia from the causes which you describe; but they are not the less ominous on that account. I have for some time been persuaded that the question on which the proposed Constitution must turn, is the simple one whether the Union shall or shall not be continued. There is in my opinion no middle ground to be taken. The opposition

with some has disunion assuredly for its object; and with all for its real
tendency. Events have demonstrated that no coalition can ever take place
in favor of a new Plan among the adversaries to the proposed one. The
grounds of objection among the non-signing members of the Convention,
are by no means the same. The disapproving members who were absent
but who have since published their objections differ irreconcileably from
each of them. The writers against the Constitution are as little agreed with
one another; and the principles which have been disclosed by the several
minorities where the Constitution has not been unanimously adopted, are
as heterogeneous as can be imagined. That of Massachussetts, as far as I
can learn was averse to any Government that deserved the name, and it is
certain looked no farther than to reject the Constitution in toto and return
home in triumph. Out of the vast number which composed it there was
scarce a man of respectability, and not a single one capable of leading the
formidable band.[1] The men of Abilities, of property, of character, with
every judge, lawyer of eminence, and the Clergy of all Sects, were with
scarc[e] an exception deserving notice, as unanimous in that State as the
same description of characters are divided and opposed to one another in
Virginia. This contrast does not arise from circumstances of local interest,
but from causes which will in my opinion produce much regret hereafter
in the Opponents in Virginia, if they should succeed in their opposition.
N. Hampshire is now in Convention. It is expected that the result will be
in favor of the Constitution. R. Island takes no notice of the matter. N.
York is much divided. The weight of Abilities and of property is on the
side of the Constitution. She must go with the Eastern States let the
direction be what it may. By a vessel just from Charlestown we understand that opposition will be made there. Mr. Lowndis[2] is the leader of it.

A *British* packet brings a picture of affairs in France which indicates
some approaching events in that Kingdom which may almost amount to a
revolution in the form of its Government. The authority is in itself suspicious; but it coincides with a variety of proofs that the spirit of-liberty
has made a progress which must lead to some remarkable conclusion of the
scene. The Dutch patriots seem to have been the victims partly of their
own folly, and partly of something amiss in their friends. The present
state of that Confederacy is or ought to be a very emphatic lesson to the U.
States. The want of Union and a capable Government is the source of all
their calamities; and particularly of that dependence on foreign powers,
which is as dishonorable to their Character as it is destructive of their
tranquility. I remain Dr Sir Yours very Affely.

Js. MADISON JR.

RC (DLC). Docketed by Pendleton.

[1] At a later time someone, probably William C. Rives, placed parentheses around this sentence, which is omitted in the Rives edition of JM's writings (*Letters* [Cong. ed.], I, 381).
[2] Rawlins Lowndes.

From John Fitch

NEW YORK the 25 February 1788

HONOURED SIR

I beg leave to make you acquainted with a late proposition I made to the Committee of Congress,[1] which was founded on the following Certificate, by a Gentleman inhabitant of the Natchies—A Coppy.

The most common custom of Navigating up the River Mississippi from the City of New Orleans to the Illinois are as followeth Viz—

They commonly employ one man to every ton on Board, their wages for the trip about one hundred dollars each, their provisions and a pint of Taffy pr day found them, dureing their passage thether—John Woods.[2]

Propositions &c—I suppose each man with his Baggage and Oar to Weigh 200 lbs., I suppose provisions and liquor for 30 men 100 days at 3 lb. pr man pr. day to be 9,000 lb., in all 15,000. Taffy for 100 days at ½ a dollar pr Gallon is 187½ Dollars, provisions for 100 days at ⅛ of a dollar pr day is 375 Dollars, wages 3,000 dollars in all is 3562½ dollars. Therefore propose that I am restricted to make and navigate a Boat from New Orleans to the Illinois of 60 tons burthen for 3562½ dollars, or in other words I say, I will build a Boat with the Engine and all compleat every trip, and transport the goods at half the price they now cost, or pay for said Lands, and give indisputable security for the performance. (How the Committee will report I do not know, but if they can look upon me to be serious, and these to be facts, I should fain hope they would not Treat it with Contempt.)[3] At the same time I have prayed them to make certain stipulations to a Boat on the Delaware, which with other matters will here be too tedious, and shall be happy if I have not already exceeded the bounds of modesty, and may once more be permitted to subscribe myself your most Devoted and Very Humble Servant

JOHN FITCH

RC (DLC). Addressed by Fitch. Docketed by JM.

[1] See Fitch to JM, 11 Feb. 1788 and n. 2.
[2] According to the endorsement on Fitch's petition, John Woods's certificate was one of the documents turned over to the committee considering the petition (*JCC*, XXXIV, 26 and n. 4; PCC).
[3] See Fitch to JM, 10 Feb. 1788 and n. 2.

From André Limozin

HAVRE DE GRACE 27th february 1788.

MOST HONORED SIR

I took the Freedom to trouble your Excellency yesterday & begd to procure the Forwarding of Sundry inclosed.[1]

I have the honor to remitt you a Bill of Lading of Captn Rolland of the Kings Packet No 3 for two Cases which Mr Jefferson Ambassor. of the US of America at the Court of Versailles our mutuall worthy Friend hath desired me to forward to your Excellency. I hope they will be deliverd in as good order as I have Shipped them. I have already payd the freight for them.[2] I have the Honor to be with the very highest regard Your Excellency's Most obedient & very Humble Servant

ANDRE LIMOZIN

RC and enclosure (DLC).

[1] Letter not found.

[2] See Jefferson to JM, 6 Feb. 1788; Jefferson to Limozin, 14 Feb. 1788 (Boyd, *Papers of Jefferson*, XII, 591). The enclosed bill of lading, printed in French with the blanks filled in, is dated 26 Feb. 1788.

The Federalist Number 62

[27 February 1788]

Having examined the constitution of the house of representatives, and answered such of the objections against it as seemed to merit notice, I enter next on the examination of the senate. The heads into which this member of the government may be considered, are—I. the qualifications of senators—II. the appointment of them by the state legislatures—III. the equality of representation in the senate—IV. the number of senators, and the term for which they are to be elected—V. the powers vested in the senate.

I. The qualifications proposed for senators, as distinguished from those of representatives, consist in a more advanced age, and a longer period of citizenship. A senator must be thirty years of age at least; as a representative, must be twenty-five. And the former must have been a citizen nine years; as seven years are required for the latter. The propriety of these distinctions is explained by the nature of the senatorial trust; which requiring greater extent of information and stability of character, requires at the same time that the senator should have reached a period of life most likely

535

to supply these advantages; and which participating immediately in transactions with foreign nations, ought to be exercised by none who are not thoroughly weaned from the prepossessions and habits incident to foreign birth and education. The term of nine years appears to be a prudent mediocrity between a total exclusion of adopted citizens, whose merit and talents may claim a share in the public confidence; and an indiscriminate and hasty admission of them, which might create a channel for foreign influence on the national councils.

II. It is equally unnecessary to dilate on the appointment of senators by the state legislatures. Among the various modes which might have been devised for constituting this branch of the government, that which has been proposed by the convention is probably the most congenial with the public opinion. It is recommended by the double advantage of favoring a select appointment, and of giving to the state governments such an agency in the formation of the federal government, as must secure the authority of the former, and may form a convenient link between the two systems.

III. The equality of representation in the senate is another point, which, being evidently the result of compromise between the opposite pretensions of the large and the small states, does not call for much discussion. If indeed it be right that among a people thoroughly incorporated into one nation, every district ought to have a *proportional* share in the government; and that among independent and sovereign states bound together by a simple league, the parties however unequal in size, ought to have an *equal* share in the common councils, it does not appear to be without some reason, that in a compound republic partaking both of the national and federal character, the government ought to be founded on a mixture of the principles of proportional and equal representation. But it is superfluous to try by the standard of theory, a part of the constitution which is allowed on all hands to be the result not of theory, but "of a spirit of amity, and that mutual deference and concession which the peculiarity of our political situation rendered indispensable."[1] A common government, with powers equal to its objects, is called for by the voice, and still more loudly by the political situation of America. A government founded on principles more consonant to the wishes of the larger states, is not likely to be obtained from the smaller states. The only option then for the former lies between the proposed government and a government still more objectionable. Under this alternative the advice of prudence must be, to embrace the lesser evil; and instead of indulging a fruitless anticipation of the possible mischiefs which may ensue, to contemplate rather the advantageous consequences which may qualify the sacrifice.

In this spirit it may be remarked, that the equal vote allowed to each state, is at once a constitutional recognition of the portion of sovereignty remaining in the individual states, and an instrument for preserving that residuary sovereignty. So far the equality ought to be no less acceptable to the large than to the small states; since they are not less solicitous to guard by every possible expedient against an improper consolidation of the states into one simple republic.

Another advantage accruing from this ingredient in the constitution of the senate, is the additional impediment it must prove against improper acts of legislation. No law or resolution can now be passed without the concurrence first of a majority of the people, and then of a majority of the states. It must be acknowledged that this complicated check on legislation may in some instances be injurious as well as beneficial; and that the peculiar defence which it involves in favor of the smaller states would be more rational, if any interests common to them, and distinct from those of the other states, would otherwise be exposed to peculiar danger. But as the larger states will always be able by their power over the supplies, to defeat unreasonable exertions of this prerogative of the lesser states; and as the facility and excess of law making seem to be the diseases to which our governments are most liable, it is not impossible that this part of the constitution may be more convenient in practice than it appears to many in contemplation.

IV. The number of senators and the duration of their appointment come next to be considered. In order to form an accurate judgment on both these points, it will be proper to enquire into the purposes which are to be answered by a senate; and in order to ascertain these it will be necessary to review the inconveniencies which a republic must suffer from the want of such an institution.

First. It is a misfortune incident to republican government, though in a less degree than to other governments, that those who administer it, may forget their obligations to their constituents, and prove unfaithful to their important trust. In this point of view, a senate, as a second branch of the legislative assembly, distinct from, and dividing the power with, a first, must be in all cases a salutary check on the government. It doubles the security to the people, by requiring the concurrence of two distinct bodies in schemes of usurpation or perfidy, where the ambition or corruption of one, would otherwise be sufficient. This is a precaution founded on such clear principles, and now so well understood in the United States, that it would be more than superfluous to enlarge on it. I will barely remark that as the improbability of sinister combinations will be in proportion to the dissimilarity in the genius of the two bodies; it must be politic to distinguish them from each other by every circumstance which will consist with a due harmony in all proper measures, and with the genuine principles of republican government.

Second. The necessity of a senate is not less indicated by the propensity of all single and numerous assemblies, to yield to the impulse of sudden and violent passions, and to be seduced by factious leaders into intemperate and pernicious resolutions. Examples on this subject might be cited without number; and from proceedings within the United States, as well as from the history of other nations. But a position that will not be contradicted need not be proved. All that need be remarked is that a body which is to correct this infirmity ought itself be free from it, and consequently ought to be less numerous. It ought moreover to possess great firmness, and consequently ought to hold its authority by a tenure of considerable duration.

Third. Another defect to be supplied by a senate lies in a want of due acquaintance with the objects and principles of legislation. It is not possible that an assembly of men called for the most part from pursuits of a private nature, continued in appointment for a short time, and led by no permanent motive to devote the intervals of public occupation to a study of the laws, the affairs and the comprehensive interests of their country, should, if left wholly to themselves, escape a variety of important errors in the exercise of their legislative trust. It may be affirmed, on the best grounds, that no small share of the present embarrassments of America is to be charged on the blunders of our governments; and that these have proceeded from the heads rather than the hearts of most of the authors of them. What indeed are all the repealing, explaining and amending laws, which fill and disgrace our voluminous codes, but so many monuments of deficient wisdom; so many impeachments exhibited by each succeeding, against each preceding session; so many admonitions to the people of the value of those aids which may be expected from a well constituted senate?

A good government implies two things; first, fidelity to the object of government, which is the happiness of the people; secondly, a knowledge of the means by which that object can be best attained. Some governments are deficient in both these qualities: Most governments are deficient in the first. I scruple not to assert that in the American governments, too little attention has been paid to the last. The federal constitution avoids this error; and what merits particular notice, it provides for the last in a mode which increases the security for the first.

Fourth. The mutability in the public councils, arising from a rapid succession of new members, however qualified they may be, points out in the strongest manner, the necessity of some stable institution in the government. Every new election in the states, is found to change one half of the representatives. From this change of men must proceed a change of opinions; and from a change of opinions, a change of measures. But a continual change even of good measures is inconsistent with every rule of prudence, and every prospect of success. The remark is verified in private life, and becomes more just as well as more important, in national transactions.

To trace the mischievous effects of a mutable government would fill a volume. I will hint a few only, each of which will be perceived to be a source of innumerable others.

In the first place it forfeits the respect and confidence of other nations, and all the advantages connected with national character. An individual who is observed to be inconstant to his plans, or perhaps to carry on his affairs without any plan at all, is marked at once by all prudent people, as a speedy victim to his own unsteadiness and folly. His more friendly neighbours may pity him; but all will decline to connect their fortunes with his; and not a few will seize the opportunity of making their fortunes out of his. One nation is to another what one individual is to another; with this melancholy distinction perhaps, that the former with fewer of the benevolent emotions than the latter, are under fewer restraints also from taking undue advantage of the indiscretions of each other. Every nation consequently, whose affairs betray a want of wisdom and stability, may calculate on every loss which can be sustained from the more systematic policy of its wiser neighbours. But the best instruction on this subject is unhappily conveyed to America by the example of her own situation. She finds that she is held in no respect by her friends; that she is the derision of her enemies; and that she is a prey to every nation which has an interest in speculating on her fluctuating councils and embarrassed affairs.

The internal effects of a mutable policy are still more calamitous. It poisons the blessings of liberty itself. It will be of little avail to the people that the laws are made by men of their own choice, if the laws be so voluminous that they cannot be read, or so incoherent that they cannot be understood; if they be repealed or revised before they are promulged, or undergo such incessant changes that no man who knows what the law is to-day can guess what it will be to-morrow. Law is defined to be a rule of action; but how can that be a rule, which is little known and less fixed?

Another effect of public instability is the unreasonable advantage it gives to the sagacious, the enterprising and the moneyed few, over the industrious and uninformed mass of the people. Every new regulation concerning commerce or revenue; or in any manner affecting the value of the different species of property, presents a new harvest to those who watch the change and can trace its consequences; a harvest reared not by themselves but by the toils and cares of the great body of their fellow citizens. This is a state of things in which it may be said with some truth that laws are made for the *few* not for the *many.*

In another point of view great injury results from an unstable government. The want of confidence in the public councils damps every useful undertaking; the success and profit of which may depend on a continuance of existing arrangements. What prudent merchant will hazard his fortunes in any new branch of commerce, when he knows not but that his plans may be rendered unlawful before they can be executed? What farmer or manufacturer will lay himself out for the encouragement given to any particular cultivation or establishment, when he can have no assurance that his preparatory labours and advances will not render him a victim to an inconstant government? In a word, no great improvement or laudable enterprise can go forward, which requires the auspices of a steady system of national policy.

But the most deplorable effect of all is that diminution of attachment and reverence which steals into the hearts of the people, towards a political system which betrays so many marks of infirmity, and disappoints so many of their flattering hopes. No government any more than an individual will long be respected, without being truly respectable, nor be truly respectable without possessing a certain portion of order and stability.

PUBLIUS.

McLean, II, 184–91. Parts of this essay were derived from Vices of the Political System (*PJM*, IX, 348–57). See also JM's first speech of 26 June 1787 at the Federal Convention (Bourne, "The Authorship of *The Federalist*," in *Essays in Historical Criticism* [1967 reprint], pp. 137–41).

[1] The quotation is from Washington's letter to the president of Congress, 17 Sept. 1787, enclosing the Constitution (Farrand, *Records*, II, 667).

From Joseph Spencer

ORANGE COUNTY Febry. 28th 1788

D SIR

The Federal Constitution, has it Enimyes in Orange as well as in other parts, Col. Thos. Barber offers as a Candedit for our March Election, he is as grate an Enimy to it as he posabley can be, & if not as grate as any it has, as grate as his abiliteys will alow him to be, which if our County men admired his Politickes no more then I do, the Constitution would have but Little to fear from that Quarter, but his unwared Labours Riding his

Carquits & the Instrements he makes use of to Obtain his Election, mis-represents things in such Horred carrecters that the weker clas of the people are much predegessed agains it by which meens he has many which as yet, appears grately in favour of him, amoungs his Friends appears, in a General way the Baptus's, the Prechers of that Society are much alarm'd fearing Religious liberty is not Sufficiently secur'd thay pretend to other objections but that I think is the principle objection, could that be Re-moved by sum one Caperble of the Task I think thay would become friends to it, that body of people has become Very formible in pint of Elections, as I can think of no Gentln. of my Acquaintance so Suitible to the task as your Self I have taken the liberty to Request it of you, Several of your Conections in Orange Joines me in oppinion, thinking it would Answer a Valuable purpus for I am Cartain that pople Relye much on your integerity & Candure, Mr. Leeland & Mr. Bledsoe and Sanders[1] are the most publick men of that Society in Orange, therefore as Mr. Leeland Lyes in your Way home from Fredricksburg to Orange would advise you'l call on him & Spend a few Howers in his Company, in Clos'd youl Receive his Objections which was Sent by me to, Barber, a Coppy I tooke,[2] this copy was first Design'd for Capt Walker,[3] but as I hoped youl be in this state in a few days thought proper to Send it to you, by which means youl be made Acquainted with their objections & have time to Consider them should you think it an Object worth yr. Attention, my fears are that Except you & yr. friends do Exerte yr. Selves Very much youl not obtain yr. Election in Orange Such are the predegeses of the people for in short there is nothing so Vile, but what the Constitution is Charged with, hope to See you in Orange in a few days[4] I am with the Gratest Respect yr. most obedt h Sarve

JOSEPH SPENCER[5]

RC and enclosure (DLC). After his signature Spencer added the date of 26 Feb. 1788, but the editors have accepted the date given by Spencer at the beginning of the letter. Addressed by Spencer "to the care of Mr. F Murey [Maury] in Fredricksburg." Docketed by JM, "Feby. 26. 1788." For enclosure, see n. 2 below.

[1] Nathaniel Saunders (d. 1808), one of the first Baptist preachers in Orange County (Sem-ple, *History of the Rise and Progress of the Baptists in Virginia* [rev. ed., 1894], pp. 234–35).

[2] At the end of the enclosure Spencer wrote, "Revd. John Leeland's Objections to the Federal Constitution Sent to Col. Thos. Barber by his Request, a Coppy taken by Jos. Spencer, entended for the Consideration of Capt Jas. Walker Culpeper." It is printed in *Documentary History of the Constitution*, IV, 526–29, and in Butterfield, "Elder John Leland," *Proceedings of the American Antiquarian Society*, n.s., LXII (1952), 187–88. Leland believed the new plan of government was insufficiently republican and was particularly critical of the omission of a bill of rights and a specific guarantee of religious liberty. On 7 Mar. 1788 the Virginia Baptist General Committee discussed the Constitution and agreed unanimously that it did not make "sufficient provision for the secure enjoyment of religious liberty" (Semple, *History of the Rise and Progress of the Baptists in Virginia* [rev. ed., 1894], p. 102).

[3]James Walker, a candidate for the convention in Culpeper County (Andrew Shepherd to JM, 22 Dec. 1787 and n. 3).

[4]JM left New York on 3 or 4 Mar., stopped at Mount Vernon on 18 Mar., and resumed his homeward journey two days later, taking the stage to Fredericksburg. He arrived in Orange on 23 Mar. (Fitzpatrick, *Washington Diaries*, III, 313; Vi: Francis Taylor Diary). Although accounts of JM's famous meeting with Leland are fanciful, the tradition is strong that such a meeting did in fact occur, probably on 22 Mar. According to this tradition JM persuaded Leland to change his mind on the Constitution and thereby gained Baptist support on election day. The election took place on 24 Mar. with the following results recorded by Francis Taylor: JM 202, Gordon 187, Barbour 56, and Porter 34 (Butterfield, "Elder John Leland," *Proceedings of the American Antiquarian Society*, n.s., LXII [1952], 188–92).

[5]The writer's identity is uncertain. A Joseph Spencer (d. 1829) organized a company of Orange County militiamen at the outbreak of the Revolution, was commissioned a captain in the Continental line on 8 May 1776, and resigned his commission on 14 Nov. 1777 (*JCSV*, I, 62; II, 454; Heitman, *Historical Register Continental*, p. 511). Perhaps this was the Joseph Spencer who as a dissenting minister was jailed for preaching in Orange County in 1773 (see Lewis Peyton Little, *Imprisoned Preachers and Religious Liberty in Virginia* [Lynchburg, Va., 1938], pp. 380–83).

From Edmund Randolph

RICHMOND Feby 29. 1788.

MY DEAR FRIEND

The decision of Massts., had it been adverse to the constn, wd. have damned it here. But as it is, it fixes the event, if N. York, N. Hamp. and Maryland should follow the example. This must be understood with this restriction; that altho' 9 states will *force* Va. by their assent to come in, there is reason to believe that no intelligence of that sort can reach us before our convention meets; as So. Carolina will sit on the 12th. of may only. I received a letter last night from Mr. P. H——y, mentioning his having resumed the practice of the law, and his determination to oppose the constn. even if only ½ a state should oppose.[1] The baptist interest and the Counties on the So. Side of Jas. river from Isle of Wight, upwards, are highly incensed by H——y's opinions, and public speeches, whensoever occasion has presented. As to the temper on the North side, I cannot clearly discern it. But upon a review made by Mr. Marshall of their comparative strength, he seems to think, that the question will be very nice. The election of Henrico commences on Monday. The persons proposed are Dr. Foushee,[2] Marshall and myself. Nothing but a small degree of favor, acquired by me, independently of the constitution, could send me; my politicks not being sufficiently strenuous against the constn. Marshall is in danger; but F. is not popular enough on other scores to be elected, altho he is perfectly a Henryite.[3]

But to return to Massts—what a paltry snare? Some of the amts. are inadmissible, others pointed against the Negro states, and others milk & water. The first is among the rocks on which the old confn. has split; the 2d. is aimed against the So. Ss—the 3d. provides vs.[4] no real danger; the first part of the 4th. is as the 3d. and moreover destroys an essential idea of a national govt.; the 5th. tho' a new and juster theory now prevails, ought to be left to the occasional wisdom of congress; the 6th. sounds an unnecessary alarm; the 7th. strikes not at all the most exceptionable points of the jurisdiction; the 8th. I conceive is not true in supposing even at common law a trial of fact to be best *on all occasions* by a jury; and the 9th. can have been designed only to make out a number of amts. equal to the no. of states, who may give birth to the govt. In short H——k. proposes them not in the form of objections, but *to remove fears*, and I do not conceive that Massts. may be yet said to be fairly inlisted; altho' to me it is satisfactory, since the men of talents and property are in its favor, vs. the Shayites, and the gentlemen of bad fame, with whom we recusants have been classed.

A writer, calling himself Plain dealer, who is bitter in principle vs. the constn. has attacked me in the paper. I suspect the author to be Mr. Spencer Roane, and the importunities of some to me in public and private are designed to throw me unequivocally and without condition into the opposition.[5]

But pray answer me, what is to become of our debit for the old contl. money? Shall we not be obliged to compensate the Indiana company for our legislative violence?[6] Does not the exception as to a religious test imply, that the congress by the general words had power over religion? I expect a coalition between the high and low fœderalists. Nothing less can save the fœderal govt.

RC (DLC). Unsigned. Docketed by JM.

[1] The letter from Patrick Henry to Randolph has not been found.

[2] A physician and first mayor of the city of Richmond, William Foushee (1749–1824) later served in the House of Delegates and on the Council of State (Blanton, *Medicine in Virginia in the Eighteenth Century*, pp. 327–28).

[3] Randolph was easily elected with 373 votes, but the contest for the second seat was close. John Marshall was chosen, receiving 198 votes to Foushee's 187 (*Va. Independent Chronicle*, 5 Mar. 1788).

[4] Versus, i.e., against.

[5] See Jones to JM, 17 Feb. 1788 and n. 3.

[6] In 1768 the Indiana Company had purchased a large tract of land in present-day West Virginia from the Iroquois confederacy, and the deed was subsequently confirmed by the Treaty of Fort Stanwix in the same year. Virginia disputed the grant to the Indiana Company because this territory fell within the boundaries of the colony as defined in the charter of 1609 and reaffirmed in the state constitution of 1776. In 1779 the Virginia Assembly declared that the Indiana Company deed was "utterly void" and passed an act invalidating all unauthorized purchases from Indians of lands within the state's boundaries (*PJM*, II, 178 nn. 1, 2; Lewis, *Indiana Company*, pp. 199–222). The company then turned to Congress to seek

confirmation of its title, but was again unsuccessful (ibid., pp. 225–65). Randolph was well acquainted with this matter, having advocated the company's claim before the Virginia House of Delegates in 1779 (Randolph to Governor of Virginia [Henry Lee], 24 June 1793, *CVSP*, VI, 411). Concern over a revival of the Indiana claim was also expressed by George Mason in his speech of 19 June 1788 to the Virginia ratifying convention (Rutland, *Papers of George Mason*, III, 1108–9). Such concern was well founded, for representatives of the company soon began a new series of attempts to gain compensation, first through the state legislature and then through the federal Supreme Court. Despite several favorable rulings from the Supreme Court, however, the company failed to recover its losses. The final blow came in 1798 with the passage of the eleventh amendment, which stripped the Supreme Court of jurisdiction in cases "commenced or prosecuted against one of the United States by Citizens of another State, or by Citizens or Subjects of any Foreign State" (Lewis, *Indiana Company*, pp. 275–93).

The Federalist Number 63

[1 March 1788]

A fifth desideratum illustrating the utility of a senate, is the want of a due sense of national character. Without a select and stable member of the government, the esteem of foreign powers will not only be forfeited by an unenlightened and variable policy, proceeding from the causes already mentioned; but the national councils will not possess that sensibility to the opinion of the world, which is perhaps not less necessary in order to merit, than it is to obtain, its respect and confidence.

An attention to the judgment of other nations is important to every government for two reasons: The one is, that independently of the merits of any particular plan or measure, it is desirable on various accounts, that it should appear to other nations as the offspring of a wise and honorable policy: The second is, that in doubtful cases, particularly where the national councils may be warped by some strong passion, or momentary interest, the presumed or known opinion of the impartial world, may be the best guide that can be followed. What has not America lost by her want of character with foreign nations? And how many errors and follies would she not have avoided, if the justice and propriety of her measures had in every instance been previously tried by the light in which they would probably appear to the unbiassed part of mankind.

Yet however requisite a sense of national character may be, it is evident that it can never be sufficiently possessed by a numerous and changeable body. It can only be found in a number so small, that a sensible degree of the praise and blame of public measures may be the portion of each individual; or in an assembly so durably invested with public trust, that the pride and consequence of its members may be sensibly incorporated with the reputation and prosperity of the community. The half-yearly representatives of Rhode-Island, would probably have been little affected in their deliberations on the iniquitous measures of that state, by arguments drawn from the light in which such measures would be viewed by foreign nations, or even by the sister states; whilst it can scarcely be doubted, that if the concurrence of a select and stable body had been necessary, a regard to national character alone, would have prevented the calamities under which that misguided people is now labouring.

I add as a *sixth* defect, the want in some important cases of a due responsibility in the government to the people, arising from that frequency of elections, which in other cases produces this responsibility. The remark will perhaps appear not only new but paradoxical. It must nevertheless be acknowledged, when explained, to be as undeniable as it is important.

Responsibility in order to be reasonable must be limited to objects within the power of the responsible party; and in order to be effectual, must relate to operations of that power, of which a ready and proper judgment can be formed by the constituents. The objects of government may be divided into two general classes; the one depending on measures which have singly an immediate and sensible operation; the other depending on a succession of well chosen and well connected measures, which have a gradual and perhaps unobserved operation. The importance of the latter description to the collective and permanent welfare of every country needs no explanation. And yet it is evident, that an assembly elected for so short a term as to be unable to provide more than one or two links in a chain of measures, on which the general welfare may essentially depend, ought not to be answerable for the final result, any more than a steward or tenant, engaged for one year, could be justly made to answer for places or improvements, which could not be accomplished in less than half a dozen years. Nor is it possible for the people to estimate the *share* of influence which their annual assemblies may respectively have on events resulting from the mixed transactions of several years. It is sufficiently difficult, at any rate, to preserve a personal responsibility in the members of a *numerous* body, for such acts of the body as have an immediate, detached and palpable operation on its constituents.

The proper remedy for this defect must be an additional body in the legislative department, which having sufficient permanency to provide for such objects as require a continued attention, and a train of measures, may be justly and effectually answerable for the attainment of those objects.

Thus far I have considered the circumstances which point out the necessity of a well constructed senate, only as they relate to the representatives of the people. To a people as little blinded by prejudice, or corrupted by flattery, as those whom I address, I shall not scruple to add, that such an institution may be sometimes necessary, as a defence to the people against their own temporary errors and delusions. As the cool and deliberate sense of the community ought in all governments, and actually will in all free governments ultimately prevail over the views of its rulers; so there are particular moments in public affairs, when the people stimulated by some irregular passion, or some illicit advantage, or misled by the artful misrepresentations of interested men, may call for measures which they themselves will afterwards be the most ready to lament and condemn. In these critical moments, how salutary will be the interference of some temperate and respectable body of citizens, in order to check the misguided career, and to suspend the blow meditated by the people against themselves, until reason, justice and truth, can regain their authority over the public mind? What bitter anguish would not the people of Athens have often escaped, if their government had contained so provident a safeguard against the tyranny of their own passions? Popular liberty might then have escaped the indelible reproach of decreeing to the same citizens, the hemlock on one day, and statues on the next.

It may be suggested that a people spread over an extensive region, cannot like the crouded inhabitants of a small district, be subject to the infection of violent passions; or to the danger of combining in the pursuit of unjust measures. I am far from denying that this is a distinction of peculiar importance. I have on the contrary endeavoured in a former paper to shew that it is one of the principal recommendations of a confederated republic. At the same time this advantage ought not to be considered as superseding the use of auxiliary precautions. It may even be remarked that the same extended situation which will exempt the people of America from some of the dangers incident to lesser republics, will expose them to the inconveniency of remaining for a longer time, under the influence of those misrepresentations which the combined industry of interested men may succeed in distributing among them.

It adds no small weight to all these considerations, to recollect, that history informs us of no long lived republic which had not a senate. Sparta, Rome and Carthage are in fact the only states to whom that character can be applied. In each of the two first there was a senate for life. The constitution of the senate in the last, is less known. Circumstantial evidence makes it probable that it was not different in this particular from the two others. It is at least certain that it had some quality or other which rendered it an anchor against popular fluctuations; and that a smaller council drawn out of the senate was appointed not only for life, but filled up vacancies itself. These examples, though as unfit for the imitation as they are repugnant to the genius of America, are notwithstanding, when compared with the fugitive and turbulent existence of other antient republics, very instructive proofs of the necessity of some institution that will blend stability with liberty. I am not unaware of the circumstances which distinguish the American from other popular governments, as well antient as modern; and which render extreme circumspection necessary in reasoning from the one case to the other. But after allowing due weight to this consideration, it may still be maintained that there are many points of similitude which render these examples not unworthy of our attention. Many of the defects as we have seen, which can only be supplied by a senatorial institution, are common to a numerous assembly frequently elected by the people, and to the people themselves. There are others peculiar to the former, which require the controul of such an institution. The people can never wilfully betray their own interests: but they may possibly be betrayed by the representatives of the people; and the danger will be evidently greater where the whole legislative trust is lodged in the hands of one body of men, than where the concurrence of separate and dissimilar bodies is required in every public act.

The difference most relied on between the American and other republics, consists in the principle of representation, which is the pivot on which the former move, and which is supposed to have been unknown to the latter, or at least to the antient part of them. The use which has been made of this difference, in reasonings contained in former papers, will have shewn that I am disposed neither to deny its existence nor to undervalue its importance. I feel the less restraint therefore in observing that the position concerning the ignorance of the antient governments on the subject of representation is by no means precisely true in the latitude commonly given to it. Without entering into a disquisition which here would be misplaced, I will refer to a few known facts in support of what I advance.

In the most pure democracies of Greece, many of the executive functions were performed not by the people themselves, but by officers elected by the people, and *representing* the people in their *executive* capacity.

Prior to the reform of Solon, Athens was governed by nine archons, annually *elected by the people at large*. The degree of power delegated to them seems to be left in great obscurity. Subsequent to that period, we find an assembly first of four and afterwards of six hundred members, annually *elected by the people*; and *partially* representing them in their *legislative* capacity, since they were not only associated with the people in the function of making laws; but had the exclusive right of originating legislative propositions to the people. The senate of Carthage also, whatever might be its power or the duration of its appointment, appears to have been elective by the suffrages of the people. Similar instances might be traced in most if not all the popular governments of antiquity.

Lastly in Sparta, we meet with the Ephori, and in Rome with the tribunes; two bodies, small indeed in number, but annually *elected by the whole body of the people*, and considered as the *representatives* of the people, almost in their *plenipotentiary* capacity. The Cosmi of Crete were also annually *elected by the people*: and have been considered by some authors as an institution analogous to those of Sparta and Rome, with this difference only, that in the election of that representative body the right of suffrage was communicated to a part only of the people.

From these facts, to which many others might be added, it is clear that the principle of representation was neither unknown to the ancients, nor wholly overlooked in their political constitutions. The true distinction between these and the American governments lies *in the total exclusion of the people in their collective capacity* from any share in the *latter*, and not in the *total exclusion of representatives of the people*, from the administration of the *former*. The distinction however thus qualified must be admitted to leave a most advantageous superiority in favour of the United States. But to ensure to this advantage its full effect, we must be careful not to separate it from the other advantage, of an extensive territory. For it cannot be believed that any form of representative government, could have succeeded within the narrow limits occupied by the democracies of Greece.

In answer to all these arguments, suggested by reason, illustrated by examples, and enforced by our own experience, the jealous adversary of the constitution will probably content himself with repeating, that a senate appointed not immediately by the people, and for the term of six years, must gradually acquire a dangerous pre-eminence in the government, and finally transform it into a tyrannical aristocracy.

To this general answer the general reply ought to be sufficient; that liberty may be endangered by the abuses of liberty, as well as by the abuses of power; that there are numerous instances of the former as well as of the latter; and that the former rather than the latter is apparently most to be apprehended by the United States. But a more particular reply may be given.

Before such a revolution can be effected, the senate, it is to be observed, must in the first place corrupt itself; must next corrupt the state legislatures, must then corrupt the house of representatives, and must finally corrupt the people at large. It is evident that the senate must be first corrupted, before it can attempt an establishment of tyranny. Without corrupting the legislatures, it cannot prosecute the attempt, because the periodical change of members would otherwise regenerate the whole body. Without exerting the means of corruption with equal success on the house of representatives, the opposition of that co-equal branch of the government would inevitably defeat the attempt; and without corrupting the people themselves, a succession of new representatives would speedily restore all things to their pristine order. Is there any man who can seriously persuade himself that the proposed senate can, by any possible means within the compass of human address, arrive at the object of a lawless ambition, through all these obstructions?

If reason condemns the suspicion, the same sentence is pronounced by experience. The constitution of Maryland furnishes the most apposite example. The senate of that state is elected, as the federal senate will be, indirectly by the people; and for a term less by one year only, than the federal senate. It is distinguished also by the remarkable prerogative of filling up its own vacancies within the term of its appointment; and at the same time, is not under the control of any such rotation, as is provided for the federal senate. There are some other lesser distinctions, which would expose the former to colorable objections that do not lie against the latter. If the federal senate therefore really contained the danger which has been so loudly proclaimed, some symptoms at least of a like danger ought by this time to have been betrayed by the senate of Maryland; but no such symptoms have appeared. On the contrary the jealousies at first entertained by men of the same description with those who view with terror the correspondent part of the federal constitution, have been gradually extinguished by the progress of the experiment; and the Maryland constitution is daily deriving from the salutary operations of this part of it, a reputation in which it will probably not be rivalled by that of any state in the union.

But if any thing could silence the jealousies on this subject, it ought to be the British example. The senate there, instead of being elected for a term of six years, and of being unconfined to particular families or fortunes, is an hereditary assembly of opulent nobles. The house of representatives, instead of being elected for two years, and by the whole body of the people, is elected for seven years; and in very great proportion, by a very small proportion of the people. Here unquestionably ought to be seen in full display, the aristocratic usurpations and tyranny, which are at some future period to be exemplified in the United States. Unfortunately however for the antifederal argument, the British history informs us, that this hereditary assembly has not even been able to defend itself against the continual encroachments of the house of representatives; and that it no sooner lost the support of the monarch, than it was actually crushed by the weight of the popular branch.

As far as antiquity can instruct us on this subject, its examples support the reasoning which we have employed. In Sparta the Ephori, the annual representatives of the people, were found an overmatch for the senate for life, continually gained on its authority, and finally drew all power into their own hands. The tribunes of Rome, who were the representatives of the people, prevailed, it is well known, in almost every contest with the senate for life, and in the end gained the most complete triumph over it. This fact is the more remarkable, as unanimity was required in every act of the tribunes, even after their number was augmented to ten. It proves the irresistible force possessed by that branch of a free government, which has the people on its side. To these examples might be added that of Carthage, whose senate, according to the testimony of Polybius, instead of drawing all power into its vortex, had at the commencement of the second punic war, lost almost the whole of its original portion.

Besides the conclusive evidence resulting from this assemblage of facts, that the federal senate will never be able to transform itself, by gradual usurpations, into an independent and aristocratic body; we are warranted in believing that if such a revolution should ever happen from causes which the foresight of man cannot guard against, the house of representatives with the people on their side will at all times be able to bring back the constitution to its primitive form and principles. Against the force of the immediate representatives of the people, nothing will be able to maintain even the constitutional authority of the senate, but such a display of enlightened policy, and attachment to the public good, as will divide with that branch of the legislature, the affections and support of the entire body of the people themselves.

PUBLIUS.

McLean, II, 191–201. Much of the material in this paper was derived from JM's earlier memorandums, Vices of the Political System (*PJM*, IX, 348–57) and Additional Memorandums on Ancient and Modern Confederacies, ante 30 Nov. 1787 (Bourne, "The Authorship of *The Federalist*," in *Essays in Historical Criticism* [1967 reprint], pp. 141–44).

To George Lee Turberville

Letter not found.

1 March 1788. Acknowledged in Turberville to JM, 16 Apr. 1788 (NN). Replies to Turberville's queries concerning the Constitution put forward in his letter to JM of 11 Dec. 1787. Includes in his reply "powerfull reasons that may be urged agt. the adoption of a Bill of Rights."

From Moustier

À Newyork le 2. Mars 1788

Monsieur

Rien ne me dedommagera certainement de l'agrement que je vais perdre par votre depart. Quand on s'attache aux personnes il est necessaire de pouvoir communiquer avec Elles. C'est avec peine que je mêle des regrets aux assurances de l'estime et de l'affection que vous m'avez inspirées. Je sens egalement combien je perds du coté de l'utilité que j'aurois pû retirer de vos lumieres et de vos conseils, qui m'auroient été d'autant plus necessaires que j'entrevois ici plus de difficultés que je m'y etois attendu. Je me suis flatté que vous auriez la complaisance de me seconder neanmoins, autant que l'eloignement peut le permettre, dans la recherche des moyens de remplir le but que je me propose de concilier les interets reciproques. La France a toujours temoigné son empressement à faire les avancer. Pour rendre ce Système durable il faut qu'Elle puisse en recueillir des fruits. C'est servir la patrie de la part d'un Americain que de montrer que les demandes de ses compatriotes peuvent s'accorder avec les interets de la France. C'est dans cette persuasion, Monsieur, que je prends la liberté de vous adresser quelques questions. Si je n'avois craint d'etre indiscret, je les aurois un peu plus etendues. Ce que vous voudriez bien ajouter au delà des objets auxquels je me suis borné, ne ferois qu'augmenter ma reconnoissance. Je vous prie d'en etre bien convaincu ainsi que du très sincere et parfait attachement avec lequel j'ai l'honneur d'etre, Monsieur, Votre très humble et très obeissant Serviteur

Le Cte. de Moustier

[Enclosure]

Questions, dont M. le Cte. de Moustier prie Monsieur Madison de vouloir bien lui addresser la solution, quand ses occupations le lui permettront.[1]

1.

Quelle est l'opinion des habitans les plus instruits dela Virginie sur le Contrat dela Ferme avec M. Rob. Morris et quel est le systeme qu'ils voudroient y substituer?

2.

Ne pourrions nous pas fournir à très bon marché le gros lainage pour l'habillement des negres?

3.

Quels sont en general les objets de Commerce, dont il pourroit être interessant d'encourager l'importation soit en France, soit aux Antilles.

4.

Quelles sont d'un autre coté les marchandises du Royaume ou des Isles, dont les Virginiens paroissent avoir le plus grand besoin?

5.

Est-il vraisemblable que les eaux de vie de France fassent tomber entierement le Rum des Isles?*

6.

Se sert-on beaucoup du sel de France pour les Salaisons et que faut-il faire pour en rendre l'usage plus commun?

7.

La Virginie commence-t-elle à exporter elle même ses denrées et quelle est la proportion de sa navigation avec celle des autres nations pour le transport des tabacs et autres articles.

8.

Comme les Americains desirent beaucoup d'obtenir de nouvelles faveurs dans nos Antilles, que pourroient-ils proposer pour faciliter un arrangement de cette nature sans trop prejudicier aux avantages que la France ne cesse de tirer de ses Colonies?

*A quoi peut se monter la consommation annuelle des Vins de France en Virginie?[2]

CONDENSED TRANSLATION

Moustier regrets JM's departure. He appreciates JM's support of his investigation of the reciprocal trade interests of France and the United States and requests that JM answer questions concerning the opinion of Virginians on the tobacco contract between the Farmers General and Robert Morris; the products of Virginia and of France and her West Indian colonies that could be traded to mutual advantage; the consumption of French wines and salt in Virginia; the extent to which Virginia products are transported in ships registered in Virginia; and the kind of trade arrangement that JM thinks should exist between the United States and the French West Indies.

RC and enclosure (DLC). Enclosure in a different hand. Enclosure docketed by JM.

[1] Moustier enclosed the same questions in a letter to Washington, which JM delivered when he stopped at Mount Vernon on his way home (Washington to Moustier, 26 Mar. and 17 Aug. 1788, Fitzpatrick, *Writings of Washington*, XXIX, 446–49; XXX, 43–47). JM's reply to Moustier's queries, dated 30 Oct. 1788, is printed in Madison, *Writings* (Hunt ed.), V, 281–84. JM based his reply largely on information supplied by Thomas Pleasants, Jr. See Pleasants to JM, and enclosure, 25 July 1788 (DLC). On the efforts to promote trade between France and the U.S. during the 1780s, see John F. Stover, "French-American Trade during the Confederation, 1781–1789," *N.C. Historical Review*, XXXV (1958), 399–414.

[2] This note was written in the left margin.

From George Washington

MY DEAR SIR,

The decision of Massachusetts, notwithstanding its concomitants, is a severe stroke to the opponents of the proposed Constitution in this State; and with the favorable determinations of the States which have gone before, and such as are likely to follow after, will have a powerful operation on the Minds of Men who are not actuated more by disappointment, passion and resentment, than they are by moderation, prudence & candor. Of the first description however, it is to be lamented that there are so many—and among them, *some* who would hazard *every* thing rather than their opposition should fail, or the sagacity of their prognostications should be impeached by an issue contrary to their predictions.

The determination you have come to, will give pleasure to your friends. From those in your own County you will learn with more certainty than from me, the expediency of your attending the Election in it. With *some*, to have differed in sentiment, is to have passed the Rubicon of their friendship, altho' you should go no further. With others (for the honor of humanity) I hope there is more liberallity; but the consciousness of having discharged that duty which we owe to our Country, is superior to all other considerations, and will place smaller matters in a secondary point of view.

His Most Ch——n M——y speaks, & acts in a style not very pleasing to republican ears, or to Republican forms; nor do I think this language is altogether so to the temper of his own Subjects at *this* day. Liberty, when it begins to take root, is a plant of rapid growth. The checks he endeavors to give it, however warrantable by ancient usage, will, more than probably, kindle a flame which may not easily be extinguished; tho' for a while it may be smothered by the Armies at his command, & the Nobility in his interest. When the people are oppressed with Taxes, & have cause to suspect that there has been a misapplication of their money, the language of despotizm is but illy brooked. This, & the mortification which the pride of the Nation has sustained in the Affairs of Holland (if one may judge from appearances) may be productive of events which prudence will not mention.

To-morrow, the Elections for delegates to the Convention of this State commences—and as they will tread close on the heels of each other this month becomes interesting and important. With the most friend[l]y sentiments, and affectionate regards, I am, My dear Sir Your Obedient

GO: WASHINGTON

RC (NN); FC (DLC: Washington Papers). RC docketed by JM. FC in a clerk's hand. Minor variations between the FC and the RC have not been noted.

To Edmund Pendleton

N. York Mar. 3. 88.

Dear Sir

The Convention of N. Hampshire have disappointed much the general expectation. Instead of adopting the Constitution they have adjourned without any final decision until June; this expedient being found necessary to prevent a rejection. It seems that a majority of 3 or 4 members would have voted in the negative, but in this majority were a number who had been proselyted by the discussions, but were bound by positive instructions. These concurred with the federalists in the adjournment, and carried it by a majority of 57 agst. 47. It is not much doubted that in the event N. Hampshire will be among the adopting States. But the influence of this check will be very considerable in this State (N. York) and in several others. I have enquired whether June was preferred for the 2d. meeting, from any reference to Virga. or N. York, and am informed that it was merely an accommodation to the intermediate annual elections & Courts.

I am just setting out for Virga. and shall not write again from this place. I wish you every happiness & am Dr Sir Yr Affe friend

Js. Madison Jr

RC (DLC). Docketed by Pendleton.

To Edmund Randolph

N. York Mar. 3. 88.

My dear friend

The Convention of N. Hampshire have disappointed the general expectation. They have not rejected the Constitution, but they have adjourned without adopting it. It was found that on a final question there would be a majority of 3 or 4 in the negative but in this number were included some who with instructions from their Towns against the Constitution, had been proselyted by the discussions. These concurring with the fœderalists in the adjournment, carried it by 57 agst. 47. if I am rightly informed as to the numbers. The second meeting is not to be till the last week in June. I have enquired from the Gentlemen from that quarter what particularly recommended so late a day, supposing it might refer to the times fixed by N.Y. & Virga. They tell me it was governed by the intermediate annual elections and Courts. If the opposition in that State be such as they are described it is not probable that they pursue any sort of plan, more than that of Massts. This event whatever causes may have produced it, or whatever consequences it may have in N.H. is no small check to the progress of the business. The opposition here which is unquestionably hostile to every thing beyond the *fœderal* principle, will take new spirits. The event in Massts. had almost extinguished their hopes. That in Pena. will probably be equally encouraged.

Col. Heth arrived a day or two ago with the proceedings of the Commissrs.[1] They will be laid before Congs. to day. I have been detained from setting out for Virga. by this circumstance having fixed on yesterday for the purpose. I shall probably get away tomorrow, and possibly this afternoon. Yrs. Affey.

Js. Madison Jr

RC (DLC). Docketed by Randolph.

[1]See Turberville to JM, 8 Jan. 1788 and n. 1.

To George Washington

N. York. March 3d. 1788

Dear Sir

The Convention of N. Hampshire has afforded a very disagreeable subject of communication. It has not rejected the Constitution; but it has failed to adopt it. Contrary to all the calculations that had been made it appeared on the meeting of the members that a majority of 3 or four was adverse to the object before them, and that on a final question on the merits, the decision would be in the negative. In this critical state of things, the fœderalists thought it best to attempt an adjournment, and having proselyted some of the members who were positively instructed agst. the Constitution, the attempt succeeded by a majority of 57 agst. 47. if my information as to the numbers be correct. It seems to be fully expected that some of the instructed members will prevail on their towns to unfetter them and that in the event N. Hampshire will [be] among the adopting States. The mischief elsewhere will in the mean time be of a serious nature. The second meeting is to be in June. This circumstance will probably be construed in Virga. as making cotemporary arrangements with her. It is explained to me however as having reference merely

555

INDEX

Davis, Augustine, 328 and **n. 2**, 517
Dawson, John (*see* VII, 199 n. 17), 481 and
n. 2, 518 n. 4; letters to JM, 47, 100,
131–32, 173–74, 198, 247–48, 517–18
Delaware, 28, 59, 61 n. 10, 88, 89 n. 1, 93,
93–94 n. 1, 151, 332, 504; attitude toward Constitution, 221, 311; ratifies
Constitution, 326, 331; state constitution, 378, 452
Delaware River, 99
Democracy: defined by JM, 267, 285
Denmark, 275–76, 277
Derby, Elias Hasket, 150, 151 n. 1
Detroit, 114, and n. 3, 119, 250
Dickinson, John, 23, 28, 39, 40
Dickinson, Philemon, 61 n. 10
Dixon, John, 328 and **n. 3**, 374, 375 n. 3
Dodds, Captain, 84, 85 n. 4
Dohrman, Arnold Henry (*see* II, 34 n. 4),
36; Mazzei's claim on, 30, 31 n. 6, 70,
71, 106, 136–37, 138, 165, 340–41,
466, 468
Donald, Alexander, 169
Drayton, William, 474
Dromgoole, Alexander, 271, 272–73 and
n. 2, 315, 319, 320 n. 1
Duane, James, 434
Duer, William (*see* IX, 135 n. 4), 254 and
n. 3, 259
Dumas, Charles Guillaume Frédéric (*see* V,
136 n. 16), 65, 67 n. 3, 164

Early, Joel, 345 n. 3
Eggleston, Joseph, 248, 249 n. 6, 292, 333
Ellsworth, Oliver, 335 n. 1; at Federal Convention, 28, 70, 78, 88, 89, 102 n. 3,
112, 115, 143 n. 2
Eppes, John Wayles: copies JM's Debates,
7, 8
Europe: balance of powers in, 81, 82–83
n. 1, 257–58; opinion of U.S. Constitution, 343; influence of, in American
politics feared, 115–16; standing armies
in, 87, 87–88 n. 3, 392–94; threat of
war in, reported, 122, 133, 162, 244,
252–53, 257–58, 284, 289, 314, 315,
326, 398, 399
Executive, federal: role in revisionary power,
16, 25 and n. 1, 35–36, 36 n. 1, 109,
109–10; *see also* President
Executives, state: JM's opinion of, 104

Factions; *see* Republican government, factions in

Fairfax County, Va., 190, 191 n. 5, 198,
215
Federal Convention, 31, 105, 107; and assumption of state debts, 234 and n. 2;
attendance at, 10, 11–12, 28–29, 43,
51, 146; authority of, 55, 61 n. 11,
384–90; adopts compromise on representation, 4, 5, 215, 363, 536–37; difficulties faced by, 360–64; goals of,
207–8; journal of, 8, 14, 15; large-small
state conflict at, 3, 4, 42, 55, 59–61,
61–62 n. 11, 80–82, 82–83 n. 1, 86,
87–88 n. 3, 92–93, 93–94 n. 1, 100–
102, 215, 363; JM at, 3–6; JM's Notes
on Debates at, 6–10; motives of, 388–
90; report of, acted on by Congress, 172
and n. 2, 179–81; debates representation, 3, 4, 18–19, 39, 40 n. 1, 79–82,
82–83 n. 1, 86–87, 87–88 n. 3, 88–89,
89 n. 1, 89–90, 91 n. 3, 91, 92 n. 2,
92–93, 93–94 n. 1, 96 and n. 1, 97,
100–102; results of, reported by JM,
163–64, 207–15; secrecy rule, 29, 43,
51, 52; split in Va. delegation to, 135
and n. 2, 167
Federal district, 411–12, 418 n. 1
"Federal Farmer," 367, 372 n. 4, 397 n. 1,
508 n. 1
Federal government: powers of, analyzed,
390–97, 403–9, 411–18, 420–26; ability
of state governments to resist, 440–44;
compared with state governments, 430–
32, 438–44; division of power with state
governments, 209–14, 286, 361–63; encroachments by state governments on,
57–58, 61–63 n. 11, 67–68, 68–69 n. 2;
see also Congress, federal; House of
Representatives; Senate
Federalism, 55, 61–62 n. 11, 67–68, 68–69
n. 2, 210–11, 379–82, 430–32, 438–44;
and republican government, 478–80
Federalist, The, 205, 220 nn. 6, 9, 10, 11,
245, 246 n. 1, 273–74, 375, 445 and
n. 1, 469, 487; authorship of, 254 and
n. 3, 259–63, 290, 304 n., 330, 487;
JM forwards copies, 254, 283–84, 290,
295, 296, 445 and n. 1, 473 and n. 2;
influence in Va., 374
Federalists: in Mass., 326, 436, 436–37,
533; in Va., 312–13, 339; *see also* attitude toward Constitution *under state
entries*
Few, William, 29
Findley, William, 176

The Papers of James Madison

DESIGNED BY JOHN B. GOETZ
COMPOSED BY THE UNIVERSITY OF CHICAGO PRESS
IN JANSON WITH DISPLAY LINES IN
JANSON AND CASLON OLD STYLE
PRINTED BY NORTH CENTRAL PUBLISHING COMPANY
ON WARREN'S LIBRARY TEXT
BOUND BY NORTH CENTRAL PUBLISHING COMPANY
IN COLUMBIA BAYSIDE LINEN